Microsoft® Office 2013

2013 IN PRACTICE

powerpoint

COMPLETE

Pat Graves

EASTERN ILLINOIS UNIVERSITY

Randy Nordell

AMERICAN RIVER COLLEGE

McGraw
Hill
Education

Microsoft® Office 2013

2013 IN PRACTICE

powerpoint

COMPLETE

Graves
Nordell

MICROSOFT OFFICE PowerPoint 2013 Complete: IN PRACTICE
Published by McGraw-Hill/Irwin, a business unit of The McGraw-Hill Companies, Inc., 1221 Avenue of the Americas, New York, NY, 10020. Copyright © 2014 by The McGraw-Hill Companies, Inc. All rights reserved. Printed in the United States of America. No part of this publication may be reproduced or distributed in any form or by any means, or stored in a database or retrieval system, without the prior written consent of The McGraw-Hill Companies, Inc., including, but not limited to, in any network or other electronic storage or transmission, or broadcast for distance learning.

Some ancillaries, including electronic and print components, may not be available to customers outside the United States.

This book is printed on acid-free paper.

1 2 3 4 5 6 7 8 9 0 QVS/QVS 1 0 9 8 7 6 5 4 3

ISBN   978-0-07-748693-8
MHID   0-07-748693-5

Senior Vice President, Products & Markets: *Kurt L. Strand*
Vice President, Content Production & Technology Services: *Kimberly Meriwether David*
Director: *Scott Davidson*
Senior Brand Manager: *Wyatt Morris*
Executive Director of Development: *Ann Torbert*
Development Editor II: *Alan Palmer*
Freelance Development Editor: *Erin Mulligan*
Digital Development Editor II: *Kevin White*
Senior Marketing Manager: *Tiffany Russell*
Lead Project Manager: *Rick Hecker*
Buyer II: *Debra R. Sylvester*
Designer: *Jana Singer*
Interior Designer: *Jesi Lazar*
Cover Image: *Corbis Images*
Content Licensing Specialist: *Joanne Mennemeier*
Manager, Digital Production: *Janean A. Utley*
Media Project Manager: *Cathy L. Tepper*
Typeface: *11/13.2 Adobe Caslon Pro*
Compositor: *Laserwords Private Limited*
Printer: *Quad/Graphics*

Library of Congress Cataloging-in-Publication Data

Graves, Pat R.
    Microsoft Office PowerPoint 2013 complete: in practice / Pat Graves, Eastern Illinois University.
       pages cm
    Includes index.
    ISBN 978-0-07-748693-8 (acid-free paper)—ISBN 0-07-748693-5 (acid-free paper)
    1. Microsoft PowerPoint (Computer file) 2. Presentation graphics software. I. Title.
    P93.53.M534G73 2014
    005.5'8—dc23

                                                                    2013025269

The Internet addresses listed in the text were accurate at the time of publication. The inclusion of a website does not indicate an endorsement by the authors or McGraw-Hill, and McGraw-Hill does not guarantee the accuracy of the information presented at these sites.

www.mhhe.com

dedication

To Brent. Thank you for the many ways you have helped me while I have been working on this book. Your love and support mean so much to me. I also appreciate my friends who shared their expertise and provided content for projects.

—Pat Graves

To Kelly. Thank you for your love, support, and encouragement during the seemingly endless hours of writing and editing throughout this project. Your feedback on the content and proofreading were immensely valuable. I could not have done this without you! I'm looking forward to a summer with you without deadlines.

—Randy Nordell

brief contents

contents

about the authors

PAT GRAVES, Ed.D.

Pat Graves is a Professor Emeritus at Eastern Illinois University in Charleston, Illinois. She began her career as a high school teacher. After receiving her doctorate in Education from Memphis State University (now the University of Memphis), she taught in the Eastern Illinois University School of Business for 20 years. Pat has been an author of PowerPoint textbooks for McGraw-Hill Higher Education since 2002 and has authored textbooks about Microsoft Office 2003, 2007, and 2010. When not writing, she travels, spends time with family and friends, enjoys the music city of Nashville, and appreciates the peacefulness of the Tennessee mountains.

RANDY NORDELL, Ed.D.

Randy Nordell is a Professor of Business Technology at American River College in Sacramento, California. He has been an educator for over 20 years and has taught at the high school, community college, and university levels. He holds a bachelor's degree in Business Administration from California State University, Stanislaus; a single subject teaching credential from Fresno State University; a master's degree in Education from Fresno Pacific University; and a doctorate in Education from Argosy University. Randy is the author of *Microsoft Office 2013: In Practice* and *Microsoft Outlook 2010*, and he speaks regularly at conferences on the integration of technology into the curriculum. When he is not teaching, he enjoys spending time with his family, cycling, skiing, swimming, and enjoying the California weather and terrain.

preface

What We're About

We wrote *Microsoft Office PowerPoint 2013 Complete: In Practice* to meet the diverse needs of both students and instructors. Our approach focuses on presenting Office topics in a logical and structured manner, teaching concepts in a way that reinforces learning with practice projects that are transferable, relevant, and engaging. Our pedagogy and content are based on the following beliefs.

Students Need to Learn and Practice Transferable Skills

Students must be able to transfer the concepts and skills learned in the text to a variety of projects, not simply follow steps in a textbook. Our material goes beyond the instruction of many texts. In our content, students practice the concepts in a variety of current and relevant projects *and* are able to transfer skills and concepts learned to different projects in the real world. To further increase the transferability of skills learned, this text is integrated with SIMnet so students also practice skills and complete projects in an online environment.

Your Curriculum Drives the Content

The curriculum in the classroom should drive the content of the text, not the other way around. This book is designed to allow instructors and students to cover all the material they need to in order to meet the curriculum requirements of their courses no matter how the courses are structured. *Microsoft Office PowerPoint 2013 Complete: In Practice* teaches the marketable skills that are key to student success. McGraw-Hill's Custom Publishing site, **Create**, can further tailor the content material to meet the unique educational needs of any school.

Integrated with Technology

Our text provides a fresh and new approach to an Office applications course. Topics integrate seamlessly with SIMnet with 1:1 content to help students practice and master concepts and skills using SIMnet's interactive learning philosophy. Projects in SIMnet allow students to practice their skills and receive immediate feedback. This integration with SIMnet meets the diverse needs of students and accommodates individual learning styles. Additional textbook resources found on the text's Online Learning Center (**www.mhhe.com/office2013inpractice**) integrate with the learning management systems that are widely used in many online and onsite courses.

Reference Text

In addition to providing students with an abundance of real-life examples and practice projects, we designed this text to be used as a Microsoft Office 2013 reference source. The core material, uncluttered with exercises, focuses on real-world use and application. Our text provides clear step-by-step instructions on how readers can apply the various features available in Microsoft Office in a variety of contexts. At the same time, users have access to a variety of both online (SIMnet) and textbook practice projects to reinforce skills and concepts.

Textbook Learning Approach

Microsoft Office PowerPoint 2013 Complete: In Practice uses the *T.I.P.* approach:

- **T**opic
- **I**nstruction
- **P**ractice

Topics

- Each PowerPoint section begins with foundational skills and builds to more complex topics as the text progresses.
- Topics are logically sequenced and grouped.
- Student Learning Outcomes (SLOs) are thoroughly integrated with and mapped to chapter content, projects, end-of-chapter review, and test banks.
- Reports are available within SIMnet for displaying how students have met these Student Learning Outcomes.

Instruction (How To)

- How To guided instructions about chapter topics provide transferable and adaptable instructions.
- Because How To instructions are not locked into single projects, this textbook functions as a reference text, not just a point-and-click textbook.
- Chapter content is aligned 1:1 with SIMnet.

Practice (Pause & Practice and End-of-Chapter Projects)

- Within each chapter, integrated Pause & Practice projects (three to five per chapter) reinforce learning and provide hands-on guided practice.
- In addition to Pause & Practice projects, each chapter has 10 comprehensive and practical practice projects: Guided Projects (three per chapter), Independent Projects (three per chapter), Improve It Project (one per chapter), and Challenge Projects (three per chapter). Additional projects can also be found on **www.mhhe.com/office2013inpractice**.
- Pause & Practice and end-of-chapter projects are complete content-rich projects, not small examples lacking context.
- Select auto-graded projects are available in SIMnet.

Chapter Features

All chapters follow a consistent theme and instructional methodology. Below is an example of chapter structure.

Main headings are organized according to the *Student Learning Outcomes (SLOs)*.

SLO 1.1 **Creating, Opening, and Saving Presentations**

In this section, you explore how to start and view a PowerPoint presentation and to save sentation in different formats. It is important to save a presentation before closing it so access it again if necessary. If you close the presentation before saving it, your content

CHAPTER 1

Creating and Editing Presentations

CHAPTER OVERVIEW

Microsoft PowerPoint is the leading presentation software. Whether you need to create a quick display or a very polished presentation with dazzling graphics, creative animation effects, and video, PowerPoint has all the tools you need. You can use PowerPoint for slide shows with computer projection equipment in meeting rooms, for self-running presentations viewed by individuals, or for presentations shown on the web. This chapter covers the basics of starting and editing a PowerPoint presentation.

STUDENT LEARNING OUTCOMES (SLOs)

After completing this chapter, you will be able to:

SLO 1.1 Create, open, and save a presentation (p. P1-3).

SLO 1.2 Develop presentation content by adding slides, choosing layouts, moving and resizing placeholders, editing text, and reusing slides from another presentation (p. P1-14).

SLO 1.3 Rearrange presentation content by moving, copying and pasting, duplicating, and deleting slides (p. P1-22).

SLO 1.4 Use the *Slide Master* to change theme colors and fonts (p. P1-26).

SLO 1.5 Use headers and footers to add identifying information (p. P1-29).

SLO 1.6 Insert, resize, and align a picture from a file (p. P1-33).

SLO 1.7 Apply and modify transition effects to add visual interest (p. P1-35).

SLO 1.8 Preview a presentation and print slides, handouts, and outlines (p. P1-37).

SLO 1.9 Change presentation properties (p. P1-39).

CASE STUDY

A list of Student Learning Outcomes begins each chapter. All chapter content, examples, and practice projects are organized according to the chapter SLOs.

POWERPOINT

and resizing placeholders, editing text, and reusing slides from another presentation (p. P1-14).

SLO 1.3 Rearrange presentation content by moving, copying and pasting, duplicating, and deleting slides (p. P1-22).

SLO 1.4 Use the *Slide Master* to change theme colors and fonts (p. P1-26).

SLO 1.5 Use headers and footers to add identifying information (p. P1-29).

SLO 1.6 Insert, resize, and align a picture from a file (p. P1-33).

SLO 1.7 Apply and modify transition effects to add visual interest (p. P1-35).

SLO 1.8 Preview a presentation and print slides, handouts, and outlines (p. P1-37).

SLO 1.9 Change presentation properties (p. P1-39).

CASE STUDY

Hamilton Civic Center (HCC) is a nonprofit community fitness center with an indoor pool, sauna, indoor track, exercise room, racquetball courts, and meeting rooms. HCC partners with the local hospital to bring doctors and nurses in to provide classes on a variety of health and wellness issues for adults. It also works with local schools to support their academic programs and sponsors events for children, including a summer day care program.

For the Pause & Practice projects in this chapter, you create and modify a presentation about training for an upcoming marathon that is being promoted to members by the Civic Center.

The *Case Study* for each chapter is a scenario that establishes the theme for the entire chapter. Chapter content, examples, figures, Pause & Practice projects, SIMnet skills, and projects throughout the chapter are closely related to this case study content. The three to five Pause & Practice projects in each chapter build upon each other and address key case study themes.

How To instructions enhance transferability of skills with concise steps and screen shots.

HOW TO: Create a Presentation When First Opening PowerPoint

1. Open PowerPoint and you will automatically see the *Backstage* view (Figure 1-1).
2. Click the **Blank Presentation** theme to go directly to your first slide.

Or

3. Click a **Theme** to open a dialog box (Figure 1-2).
4. Click the arrow buttons below the slide to see how colors are applied to different layouts.

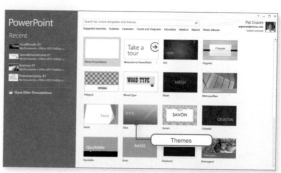

1-1 PowerPoint *Backstage* view

How To instructions are easy-to-follow, concise steps. Screen shots and other figures fully illustrate How To topics.

Students can complete hands-on exercises either in the Office application or in SIMnet.

Pause & Practice 1-1: Create a presentation and develop text content.

Pause & Practice 1-2: Impose consistency to a presentation's design.

Pause & Practice 1-3: Add interest with pictures and apply transitions. Print supplements.

Pause & Practice projects, which each cover two to three of the student learning outcomes in the chapter, provide students with the opportunity to review and practice skills and concepts. Every chapter contains three to five Pause & Practice projects.

▶ MORE INFO

Your computer must be connected to the Internet to download themes and templates.

More Info provides readers with additional information about chapter content.

Another Way notations teach alternative methods of accomplishing the same task or feature such as keyboard shortcuts.

▶ **ANOTHER WAY**
Ctrl+F12 opens the *Open* dialog box.

Marginal notations present additional information and alternative methods.

End-of-Chapter Projects

Ten learning projects at the end of each chapter provide additional reinforcement and practice for students. Many of these projects are available in SIMnet for completion and automatic grading.

- *Guided Projects (three per chapter):* Guided Projects provide guided step-by-step instructions to apply Office features, skills, and concepts from the chapter. Screen shots guide students through the more challenging tasks. End-of-project screen shots provide a visual of the completed project.
- *Independent Projects (three per chapter):* Independent Projects provide students further opportunities to practice and apply skills, instructing them what to do, but not how to do it. These projects allow students to apply previously learned content in a different context.
- *Improve It Project (one per chapter):* In these projects, students apply their knowledge and skills to enhance and improve an existing presentation. Improve It projects are open-ended and allow students to use their critical thinking and creativity to produce attractive professional presentations.
- *Challenge Projects (three per chapter):* Challenge Projects encourage creativity and critical thinking by integrating Office concepts and features into relevant and engaging projects.

Appendix

- *Office 2013 Shortcuts:* Appendix A covers the shortcuts available in Microsoft Office and within each of the specific Office applications. Information is in table format for easy access and reference.

Online Learning Center: www.mhhe.com/office2013inpractice

Students and instructors can find the following resources at the Online Learning Center, **www.mhhe.com/ office2013inpractice**

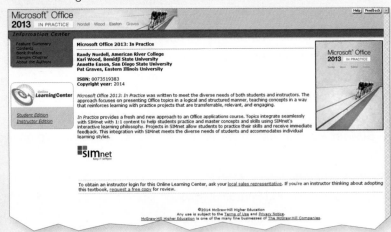

Student Resources

- **Data Files:** Files contain start files for all Pause & Practice, Integration, and end-of-chapter projects.
- **SIMnet Resources:** Resources provide getting started and informational handouts for instructors and students.
- **Check for Understanding:** A combination of multiple choice, fill-in, matching, and short answer questions are available online to assist students in their review of the skills and concepts covered in the chapter.

Integration Projects

- **Integrating Applications:** Projects provide students with the opportunity to learn, practice, and transfer skills using multiple Office applications.
- **Integrating Skills:** Projects provide students with a comprehensive and integrated review of all the topics covered in each application (Word, Excel, Access, and PowerPoint). Available in individual application texts.

Appendices

- **SIMnet User Guide:** Appendix B introduces students to the SIMnet user interface; content demonstrates how to use SIMnet to complete lessons and projects, take quizzes, and search for specific topics as well as how to create practice exercises.
- **Office 2013 for Mac Users:** Appendix C presents instructions for Mac users on how to partition their computer drive to use the PC version of Microsoft Office 2013.
- **Business Document Formats:** Appendix D is a guide to regularly used business document formatting and includes numerous examples and detailed instructions.

Instructor Resources

- **Instructor's Manual:** An Instructor's Manual provides teaching tips and lecture notes aligned with the PowerPoint presentations for each chapter. The Manual also includes the solutions for online **Check for Understanding** questions.
- **Test Bank:** The extensive test bank integrates with learning management systems (LMSs) such as Blackboard, WebCT, Desire2Learn, and Moodle.
- **PowerPoint Presentations:** PowerPoint presentations for each chapter can be used in onsite course formats for lectures or can be uploaded to LMSs.
- **SIMnet Resources:** These resources provide getting started and informational handouts for instructors.
- **Solution Files:** Files contain solutions for all Pause & Practice, Integration, Check for Understanding, and End-of-Chapter projects.

acknowledgments

REVIEWERS

We would like to thank the following instructors, whose invaluable insights shaped the development of this series.

Frank Abnet
Baker College
Sven Aelterman
Troy University
Nisheeth Agrawal
Calhoun Community College
Jack Alanen
California State University
Doug Albert
Finger Lakes Community College
Lancie Anthony Alfonso
College of Charleston
Farha Ali
Lander University
Beverly Amer
Northern Arizona University
Penny Amici
Harrisburg Area Community College
Leon Amstutz
Taylor University
Chris Anderson
North Central Michigan College
Wilma Andrews
Virginia Commonwealth University
Mazhar Anik
Owens Community College
M. Hashem Anwari
Nova Community College
Ralph Argiento
Guilford Technical Community College
Karen M. Arlien
Bismarck State College
Gary Armstrong
Shippensburg University
Tom Ashby
Oklahoma City Community College
Laura Atkins
James Madison University
William Ayen
University of Colorado
Abida Awan
Savannah State University
Ijaz Awan
Savannah State University
Tahir Aziz
J. Sargeant Reynolds Community College
Mark Bagley
Northwestern Oklahoma State University
Greg Ballinger
Miami Dade College
David Barnes
Penn State Altoona
Emily Battaglia
United Education Institute
Terry Beachy
Garrett College
Michael Beard
Lamar University—Beaumont
Anita Beecroft
Kwantlen Polytechnic University
Julia Bell
Walters State Community College
Paula Bell
Lock Haven University of Pennsylvania
David Benjamin
Pace University
Shantanu Bhagoji
Monroe College
Sai Bhatia
Riverside City College
Cindy Hauki Blair
West Hills College
Scott Blanchard
Rockford Career College
Ann Blackman
Parkland College
Jessica Blackwelder
Wilmington University
James Boardman
Alfred State College
John Bodden
Trident Technical College
Gary Bond
New Mexico State University
Abigail Bornstein
City College of San Francisco
Gina Bowers
Harrisburg Area Community College

Craig Bradley
Shawnee Community College
Gerlinde Brady
Cabrillo College
Gerald Braun
Xavier University
Janet Bringhurst
Utah State University
Brenda Britt
Fayetteville Technical Community College
Annie Brown
Hawaii Community College
Judith Brown
University of Memphis
Menka Brown
Piedmont Technical College
Shawn Brown
Kentucky Community & Technical College
Sylvia Brown
Midland College
Cliff Brozo
Monroe College
Barbara Buckner
Lee University
Sheryl Starkey Bulloch
Columbia Southern University
Rebecca Bullough
College of Sequoias
Kate Burkes
Northwest Arkansas Community College
Sharon Buss
Hawkeye Community College
Angela Butler
Mississippi Gulf Coast Community College
Lynn Byrd
Delta State University
Carolyn Calicutt
Saint Louis Community College
Anthony Cameron
Fayetteville Technical Community College
Eric Cameron
Passaic County Community College
Michael Carrington
Nova Community College
Debby Carter
Los Angeles Pierce College
Cesar Augustus Casas
St. Thomas Aquinas College
Sharon Casseday
Weatherford College
Mary Ann Cassidy
Westchester Community College
Terri Castillo
New Mexico Military Institute
Diane Caudill
Kentucky Community & Technical College
Emre Celebi
Louisiana State University
Jim Chaffee
The University of Iowa Tippie College of Business
Jayalaxmi Chakravarthy
Monroe Community College
Bob Chambers
Endicott College
Debra Chapman
University of South Alabama
Marg Chauvin
Palm Beach Community College
Stephen Cheskiewicz
Keystone College
Mark Choman
Luzerne County Community College
Kungwen Chu
Purdue University
Carin Chuang
Purdue University—North Central
Tina Cipriano
Gateway Technical College
Angela Clark
University of South Alabama
James Clark
University of Tennessee
Steve Clements
Eastern Oregon University
Sandra Cobb
Kaplan University
Paulette Comet
Community College of Baltimore County

Marc Condos
American River College
Ronald Conway
Bowling Green State University
Margaret Cooksey
Tallahassee Community College
Lennie Cooper
Miami Dade College—North
Michael Copper
Palm Beach State College—Lake Worth
Terri Cossey
University of Arkansas
Shannon Cotnam
Pitt Community College
Missie Cotton
North Central Missouri College
Charles Cowell
Tyler Junior College
Elaine Crable
Xavier University
Grace Credico
Lethbridge Community College
Doug Cross
Clackamas Community College
Kelli Cross
Harrisburg Area Community College
Geoffrey Crosslin
Kalamazoo Valley Community College
Christy Culver
Marion Technical College
Urska Cvek
Louisiana State University
Penny Cypert
Tarrant County College
Janet Czarnecki
Brown Mackie College
Don Danner
San Francisco State University
Michael Danos
Central Virginia Community College
Louise Darcy
Texas A&M University
Tamara Dawson
Southern Nazarene University
JD Davis
Southwestern College
Elaine Day
Johnson & Wales University
Jennifer Day
Sinclair Community College
Ralph De Arazoza
Miami Dade College
Lucy Decaro
College of Sequoias
Chuck Decker
College of the Desert
Corey DeLaplain
Keiser University East Campus
Edward Delean
Nova Community College Alexandria
Darren Denenberg
University of Nevada—Las Vegas
Joy DePover
Minneapolis Community & Technical College
Charles DeSassure
Tarrant County Community College
John Detmer
Del Mar College
Michael Discello
Pittsburgh Technical College
Sallie Dodson
Radford University
Veronica Dooly
Asheville-Buncombe Technical Community College
Gretchen Douglas
State University of New York College—Cortland
Debra Duke
Cleveland State University
Michael Dumdei
Texarkana College
Michael Dunklebarger
Alamance Community College
Maureen Dunn
Penn State University
Robert Dusek
Nova Community College
Barbara Edington
St. Francis College
Margaret Edmunds
Mount Allison University
Annette Edwards
Tennessee Technology Center
Sue Ehrfurth
Aims Community College

Donna Ehrhart
Genesee Community College
Roland Eichelberger
Baylor University
Issam El-Achkar
Hudson County Community College
Glenda Elser
New Mexico State University
Emanuel Emanouilidis
Kean University
Bernice Eng
Brookdale Community College
Joanne Eskola
Brookdale Community College
Mohammed Eyadat
California State University—Dominguez Hills
Nancy Jo Evans
Indiana University—Purdue University Indianapolis
Phil Feinberg
Palomar College
Deb Fells
Mesa Community College
Patrick Fenton
West Valley College
Jean Finley
Asheville-Buncombe Technical Community College
George Fiori
Tri-County Technical College Pendleton
Richard Flores
Citrus College
Kent Foster
Winthrop University
Penny Foster
Anne Arundel Community College
Brian Fox
Santa Fe College
Deborah Franklin
Bryant & Stratton College
Judith Fredrickson
Truckee Meadows Community College
Dan Frise
East Los Angeles College
Michael Fujita
Leeward Community College
Susan Fuschetto
Cerritos College
Janos Fustos
Metropolitan State College—Denver
Samuel Gabay
Zarem Golde Ort Technical Institute
Brian Gall
Berks Technical Institute
Lois Galloway
Danville Community College
Saiid Ganjalizadeh
The Catholic University of America
Lynnette Garetz
Heald College Corporate Office
Kurt Garner
Pitt Community College
Randolph Garvin
Tyler Junior College
Deborah Gaspard
Southeast Community College
Marilyn Gastineau
University of Louisiana
Bob Gehling
Auburn University—Montgomery
Amy Giddens
Central Alabama Community College
Tim Gill
Tyler Junior College
Sheila Gionfriddo
Luzerne County Community College
Mostafa Golbaba
Langston University Tulsa
Kemit Grafton
Oklahoma State University—Oklahoma City
Deb Gross
Ohio State University
Judy Grotefendt
Kilgore College
Debra Giblin
Mitchell Technical Institute
Robin Greene
Walla Walla Community College
Nancy Gromen
Eastern Oregon University
Lewis Hall
Riverside City College
Linnea Hall
Northwest Mississippi Community College
Kevin Halvorson
Ridgewater College

Peggy Hammer
Chemeketa Community College
Patti Hammerle
Indiana University—Purdue University Indianapolis
Dr. Bill Hammerschlag
Brookhaven College
Danielle Hammoud
West Coast University Corporate Office
John Haney
Snead State Community College
Ashley Harrier
Hillsborough Community College
Ranida Harris
Indiana University Southeast
Dorothy Harman
Tarrant County College
Marie Hartlein
Montgomery County Community College
Shohreh Hashemi
University of Houston Downtown
Michael Haugrud
Minnesota State University
Rebecca Hayes
American River College
Terri Helfand
Chaffey College
Julie Heithecker
College of Southern Idaho
Gerry Hensel
University of Central Florida—Orlando
Cindy Herbert
Metropolitan Community College
Jenny Herron
Paris Junior College
Marilyn Hibbert
Salt Lake Community College
Will Hilliker
Monroe County Community College
Ray Hinds
Florida College
Rachel Hinton
Broome Community College
Emily Holliday
Campbell University
Mary-Carole Hollingsworth
Georgia Perimeter College
Terri Holly
Indian River State College
Timothy Holston
Mississippi Valley State University
David Hood
East Central College
Kim Hopkins
Weatherford College
Wayne Horn
Pensacola Junior College
Christine Hovey
Lincoln Land Community College
Derrick Huang
Florida Atlantic University
Susan Hudgins
East Central University
Jeff Huff
Missouri State University—West Plains
Debbie Huffman
North Central Texas College
Michelle Hulett
Missouri State University
Laura Hunt
Tulsa Community College
Bobbie Hyndman
Amarillo College
Jennifer Ivey
Central Carolina Community College
Bill Jaber
Lee University
Sherry Jacob
Jefferson Community College
Yelena Jaffe
Suffolk University
Rhoda James
Citrus Community College
Ted Janicki
Mount Olive College
Jon Jasperson
Texas A&M University
Denise Jefferson
Pitt Community College
John Jemison
Dallas Baptist University
Joe Jernigan
Tarrant County College—NE
Mary Johnson
Mt. San Antonio College
Mary Johnson
Lone Star College
Linda Johnsonius
Murray State University
Robert Johnston
Heald College
Irene Joos
La Roche College
Yih-Yaw Jou
University of Houston—Downtown

Jan Kamholtz
Bryant & Stratton College
Valerie Kasay
Georgia Southern University
James Kasum
University of Wisconsin
Nancy Keane
NHTI Concord Community College
Michael Keele
Three Rivers Community College
Debby Keen
University of Kentucky
Judith Keenan
Salve Regina University
Jan Kehm
Spartanburg Community College
Rick Kendrick
Antonelli College
Annette Kerwin
College of DuPage
Manzurul Khan
College of the Mainland
Julia Khan-Nomee
Pace University
Karen Kidder
Tri-State Business Institute
Hak Joon Kim
Southern Connecticut State University
James Kirby
Community College of Rhode Island
Chuck Kise
Brevard Community College
Paul Koester
Tarrant County College
Kurt Kominek
Northeast State Tech Community College
Diane Kosharek
Madison Area Technical College
Carolyn Kuehne
Utah Valley University
Ruth Kurlandsky
Cazenovia College
John Kurnik
Saint Petersburg College
Lana LaBruyere
Mineral Area College
Anita Laird
Schoolcraft College
Charles Lake
Faulkner State Community College
Marjean Lake
LDS Business College
Kin Lam
Medgar Evers College
Jeanette Landin
Empire College
Richard Lanigan
Centura College Online
Nanette Lareau
University of Arkansas Community College Morrilton
David Lee Largent
Ball State University
Linda Lannuzzo
LaGuardia Community College
Robert La Rocca
Keiser University
Dawn D. Laux
Purdue University
Deborah Layton
Eastern Oklahoma State College
Art Lee
Lord Fairfax Community College
Ingyu Lee
Troy University
Kevin Lee
Guilford Technical Community College
Leesa Lee
Western Wyoming College
Thomas Lee
University of Pennsylvania
Jamie Lemley
City College of San Francisco
Linda Lemley
Pensacola State College
Diane Lending
James Madison University
Sherry Lenhart
Terra Community College
Julie Lewis
Baker College—Flint
Sue Lewis
Tarleton State University
Jane Liefert
Middlesex Community College
Renee Lightner
Florida State College
Nancy Lilly
Central Alabama Community College
Mary Locke
Greenville Technical College
Maurie Lockley
University of North Carolina
Haibing Lu
San Diego Mesa College

Frank Lucente
Westmoreland County Community College
Clem Lundie
San Jose City College
Alicia Lundstrom
Drake College of Business
Linda Lynam
Central Missouri State University
Lynne Lyon
Durham Technical Community College
Matthew Macarty
University of New Hampshire
Sherri Mack
Butler County Community College
Heather Madden
Delaware Technical Community College
Susan Mahon
Collin College Plano
Nicki Maines
Mesa Community College
Lynn Mancini
Delaware Technical Community College
Amelia Maretka
Wharton County Junior College
Suzanne Marks
Bellevue Community College
Juan Marquez
Mesa Community College
Carlos Martinez
California State University—Dominguez Hills
Santiago Martinez
Fast Train College
Lindalee Massoud
Mott Community College
Joan Mast
John Wood Community College
Deborah Mathews
J. Sargeant Reynolds Community College
Becky McAfee
Hillsborough Community College
Roberta Mcclure
Lee College
Martha McCreery
Rend Lake College
Sue McCrory
Missouri State University
Brian Mcdaniel
Palo Alto College
Rosie Mcghee
Baton Rouge Community College
Jacob McGinnis
Park University
Mike Mcguire
Triton College
Bruce McLaren
Indiana State University
Bill McMillan
Madonna University
David Mcnair
Mount Wachusett Community College
Gloria Mcteer
Ozarks Technical Community College
Dawn Medlin
Appalachian State University
Peter Meggison
Massasoit Community College
Barbara Meguro
University of Hawaii
Linda Mehlinger
Morgan State University
Gabriele Meiselwitz
Towson University
Joni Meisner
Portland Community College
Dixie Mercer
Kirkwood Community College
Donna Meyer
Antelope Valley College
Mike Michaelson
Palomar College
Michael Mick
Purdue University
Debby Midkiff
Huntington Jr. College of Business
Jenna Miley
Bainbridge College
Dave Miller
Monroe County Community College
Pam Milstead
Bossier Parish Community College
Shayan Mirabi
American Intercontinental University
Johnette Moody
Arkansas Tech University
Christine Moore
College of Charleston
Carmen Morrison
North Central State College
Gary Mosley
Southern Wesleyan University
Tamar Mosley
Meridian Community College
Ed Mulhern
Southwestern College

Carol Mull
Greenville Technical College
Melissa Munoz
Dorsey Business School
Marianne Murphy
North Carolina Central University
Karen Musick
Indiana University—Purdue University Indianapolis
Warner Myntti
Ferris State University
Brent Nabors
Reedley College
Shirley Nagg
Everest Institute
Anozie Nebolisa
Shaw University
Barbara Neequaye
Central Piedmont Community College
Patrick Nedry
Monroe County Community College
Melissa Nemeth
Indiana University—Purdue University Indianapolis
Eloise Newsome
Northern Virginia Community College
Yu-Pa Ng
San Antonio College
Fidelis Ngang
Houston Community College
Doreen Nicholls
Mohawk Valley Community College
Brenda Nickel
Moraine Park Technical College
Brenda Nielsen
Mesa Community College
Phil Nielson
Salt Lake Community College
Suzanne Nordhaus
Lee College
Ronald Norman
Grossmont College
Karen Nunam
Northeast State Technical Community College
Mitchell Ober
Tulsa Community College
Teri Odegard
Edmonds Community College
Michael Brian Ogawa
University of Hawaii
Lois Ann O'Neal
Rogers State University
Stephanie Oprandi
Stark State College of Technology
Marianne Ostrowksky
Luzerne County Community College
Shelley Ota
Leeward Community College
Youcef Oubraham
Hudson County Community College
Paul Overstreet
University of South Alabama
John Panzica
Community College of Rhode Island
Donald Paquet
Community College of Rhode Island
Lucy Parker
California State University—Northridge
Patricia Partyka
Schoolcraft College
James Gordon Patterson
Paradise Valley Community College
Laurie Patterson
University of North Carolina
Joanne Patti
Community College of Philadelphia
Kevin Pauli
University of Nebraska
Kendall Payne
Coffeyville Community College
Deb Peairs
Clark State Community College
Charlene Perez
South Plains College
Lisa Perez
San Joaquin Delta College
Diane Perreault
Tusculum College
Michael Picerno
Baker College
Janet Pickard
Chattanooga State Technical Community College
Walter Pistone
Palomar College
Jeremy Pittman
Coahoma Community College
Morris Pondfield
Towson University
James Powers
University of Southern Indiana
Kathleen Proietti
Northern Essex Community College
Ram Raghuraman
Joliet Junior College
Patricia Rahmlow
Montgomery County Community College

Robert Renda
Fulton Montgomery Community College

Margaret Reynolds
Mississippi Valley State University

David Richwine
Indian River State College—Central

Terry Rigsby
Hill College

Laura Ringer
Piedmont Technical College

Gwen Rodgers
Southern Nazarene University

Stefan Robila
Montclair State University

Terry Rooker
Germanna Community College

Seyed Roosta
Albany State University

Sandra Roy
Mississippi Gulf Coast Community College—Gautier

Antoon Rufi
Ecpi College of Technology

Wendy Rader
Greenville Technical College

Harold Ramcharan
Shaw University

James Reneau
Shawnee State University

Robert Robertson
Southern Utah University

Cathy Rogers
Laramie County Community College

Harry Reif
James Madison University

Shaunda Roach
Oakwood University

Ruth Robbins
University of Houston—Downtown

Randy Rose
Pensacola State College

Kathy Ruggieri
Lansdale School of Business

Cynthia Rumney
Middle Georgia Technical College

Paige Rutner
Georgia Southern University

Candice Ryder
Colorado State University

Russell Sabadosa
Manchester Community College

Gloria Sabatelli
Butler County Community College

Glenn Sagers
Illinois State University

Phyllis Salsedo
Scottsdale Community College

Dolly Samson
Hawaii Pacific University

Yashu Sanghvi
Cape Fear Community College

Ramona Santamaria
Buffalo State College

Diane Santurri
Johnson & Wales University

Kellie Sartor
Lee College

Allyson Saunders
Weber State University

Theresa Savarese
San Diego City College

Cem Saydam
University of North Carolina

Jill Schaumloeffel
Garrett College

William Schlick
Schoolcraft College

Rory Schlueter
Glendale College

Art Schneider
Portland Community College

Helen Schneider

University of Findlay

Cheryl Schroeder-Thomas
Towson University

Paul Schwager
East Carolina University

Kay Scow
North Hennepin Community College

Karen Sarratt Scott
University of Texas—Arlington

Michael Scroggins
Missouri State University

Janet Sebesy
Cuyahoga Community College Western

Vicky Seehusen
Metropolitan State College Denver

Paul Seibert
North Greenville University

Pat Serrano
Scottsdale Community College

Patricia Sessions
Chemeketa Community College

Judy Settle
Central Georgia Technical College

Vivek Shah
Texas State University

Abul Sheikh
Abraham Baldwin Agricultural College

Lal Shimpi
Saint Augustine's College

Lana Shryock
Monroe County Community College

Joanne Shurbert
NHTI Concord Community College

Sheila Sicilia
Onondaga Community College

Pam Silvers
Asheville-Buncombe Technical Community College

Eithel Simpson
Southwestern Oklahoma State University

Beth Sindt
Hawkeye Community College

Mary Jo Slater
College of Beaver County

Diane Smith
Henry Ford College

Kristi Smith
Allegany College of Maryland

Nadine Smith
Keiser University

Thomas Michael Smith
Austin Community College

Anita Soliz
Palo Alto College

Don Southwell
Delta College

Mimi Spain
Southern Maine Community College

Sri' V. Sridharan
Clemson University

Diane Stark
Phoenix College

Jason Steagall
Bryant & Stratton College

Linda Stoudemayer
Lamar Institute of Technology

Nate Stout
University of Oklahoma

Lynne Stuhr
Trident Technical College

Song Su
East Los Angeles College

Bala Subramanian
Kean University

Liang Sui
Daytona State College

Denise Sullivan
Westchester Community College

Frank Sun
Lamar University

Beverly Swisshelm
Cumberland University

Cheryl Sypniewski
Macomb Community College

Martin Schedlbauer
Suffolk University

Lo-An Tabar-Gaul
Mesa Community College

Kathleen Tamerlano
Cuyahoga Community College

Margaret Taylor
College of Southern Nevada

Sandra Thomas
Troy University

Joyce Thompson
Lehigh Carbon Community College

Jay Tidwell
Blue Ridge Community and Technical College

Astrid Todd
Guilford Technical Community College

Byron Todd
Tallahassee Community College

Kim Tollett
Eastern Oklahoma State College

Joe Torok
Bryant & Stratton College

Tom Trevethan
Ecpi College of Technology

David Trimble
Park University

Charulata Trivedi
Quinsigamond Community College

Alicia Tyson-Sherwood
Post University

Angela Unruh
Central Washington University

Patricia Vacca
El Camino College

Sue van Boven
Paradise Valley Community College

Scott Van Selow
Edison College—Fort Myers

Linda Kavanaugh Varga
Robert Morris University

Kathleen Villarreal
Apollo University of Phoenix

Asteria Villegas
Monroe Community College

Michelle Vlaich-Lee
Greenville Technical College

Carol Walden
Mississippi Delta Community College

Dennis Walpole
University of South Florida

Merrill Warkentin
Mississippi State University

Jerry Waxman
The City University of New York, Queens College

Sharon Wavle
Tompkins Cortland Community College

Rebecca Webb
Northwest Arkansas Community College

Sandy Weber
Gateway Technical College

Robin Weitz
Ocean County College

Karen Welch
Tennessee Technology Center

Marcia Welch
Highline Community College

Lynne Weldon
Aiken Tech College

Jerry Wendling
Iowa Western Community College

Bradley West
Sinclair Community College

Stu Westin
University of Rhode Island

Billie Jo Whary
McCann School of Business & Technology

Charles Whealton
Delaware Technical Community College

Melinda White

Seminole State College

Reginald White
Black Hawk College

Lissa Whyte-Morazan
Brookline College

Sophia Wilberscheid
Indian River State College

Casey Wilhelm
North Idaho College

Amy Williams
Abraham Baldwin Agricultural College

Jackie Williams
University of North Alabama

Melanie Williamson
Bluegrass Community & Technical College

Jan Wilms
Union University

Rhonda Wilson
Connors State College

Diana Wolfe
Oklahoma State University—Oklahoma City

Veryl Wolfe
Clarion University of Pennsylvania

Paula Worthington
Northern Virginia Community College

Dezhi Wu
Southern Utah University

Judy Wynekoop
Florida Gulf Coast University

Kevin Wyzkiewicz
Delta College

Catherine Yager
Pima Community College

Paul Yaroslaski
Dodge City Community College

Annette Yauney
Herkimer County Community College

Yuqiu You
Morehead State University

Bahram Zartoshty
California State University—Northridge

Suzann Zeger
William Rainey Harper College

Steven Zeltmann
University of Central Arkansas

Cherie Zieleniewski
University of Cincinnati—Batavia

Mary Ann Zlotow
College of DuPage

Laurie Zouharis
Suffolk College

Matthew Zullo
Wake Technical Community College

TECHNICAL EDITORS

Chris Anderson
North Central Michigan College

Susan Fuschetto
Cerritos College

Vicky Seehusen
Metropolitan State College Denver

Amie Mayhall
Olney Central College

Julia Bell
Walters State Community College

Argie Nichols
University of Arkansas, Fort Smith

Russell English
San Diego Mesa College

Karen May
Blinn College, Bryan

Beverly Swisshelm
Cumberland University

Thank you to the wonderful team at McGraw-Hill for your confidence in us and support on this first edition. Paul, Alan, Erin, Wyatt, Tiffany, Rick, and Julianna, we thoroughly enjoy working with you all! Thank you also to Debbie Hinkle, Michael-Brian Ogawa, Laurie Zouharis, Amie Mayhall, Sarah Clifford, Jeanne Reed, Lyn Belisle, and all of the reviewers and technical editors for your expertise and invaluable insight, which helped shape this book.

— Pat, Randy

Windows 8 and Office 2013 Overview

CHAPTER OVERVIEW

Microsoft Office 2013 and Windows 8 introduce many new features including cloud storage for your files, Office file sharing, and enhanced online content. The integration of Office 2013 and Windows 8 means that files are more portable and accessible than ever when you use *SkyDrive*, Microsoft's free online cloud storage. The new user interface on Office 2013 and Windows 8 allows you to work on tablet computers and smart phones in a working environment that resembles that of your desktop or laptop computer.

STUDENT LEARNING OUTCOMES (SLOs)

After completing this chapter, you will be able to:

SLO 1.1 Use the basic features of Windows 8 and Microsoft Office 2013 products (p. O1-2).

SLO 1.2 Create, save, close, and open Office files (p. O1-12).

SLO 1.3 Print, share, and customize Office files (p. O1-20).

SLO 1.4 Use the *Ribbon*, tabs, groups, dialog boxes, task panes, galleries, and the *Quick Access* toolbar (p. O1-23).

SLO 1.5 Use context menus, mini toolbars, and keyboard shortcuts in Office applications (p. O1-27).

SLO 1.6 Customize the view and display size in Office applications and work with multiple Office files (p. O1-31).

SLO 1.7 Organize and customize Office files and Windows folders (p. O1-34).

CASE STUDY

American River Cycling Club (ARCC) is a community cycling club that promotes fitness. ARCC members include recreational cyclists who enjoy the exercise and camaraderie and competitive cyclists who compete in road, mountain, and cyclocross races throughout the cycling season.

In the Pause & Practice projects, you incorporate many of the topics covered in the chapter to create, save, customize, and share Office 2013 files.

Pause & Practice 1-1: Log into Windows using your Microsoft account, customize the Windows *Start* page, open Office files, create a new file, open and rename an existing file, and share a file.

Pause & Practice 1-2: Modify an existing document, add document properties, customize the *Quick Access* toolbar, export a file as a PDF file, and share a document by sending a link.

Pause & Practice 1-3: Modify the working environment in Office and organize files and folders.

O1-1

Using Windows 8 and Office 2013

Windows 8 is the *operating system* that makes your computer function and controls the working environment. The Office 2013 software provides you with common application programs such as Word, Excel, Access, and PowerPoint. These applications give you the ability to work with word processing documents, spreadsheets, presentations, and databases in your personal and business projects. Although the Windows 8 operating system and the Office software products work together, they have different functions on your computer.

Windows 8

The operating system on your computer makes all of the other software programs, including Office 2013, function. *Windows 8* has a new user interface—the new *Start page*—where you can select and open a program. Alternatively you can go to the *Windows desktop*, which has the familiar look of previous versions of Windows. You also have the option with Windows 8 to log in to your computer using a Windows account that synchronizes your Windows, Office, and *SkyDrive* cloud storage between computers.

Microsoft Account

In Windows 8 and Office 2013, your files and account settings are portable. In other words, your Office settings and files can travel with you and be accessed from different computers. You are not restricted to a single computer. When you create a free *Microsoft account* (Live, Hotmail, MSN, Messenger, or other Microsoft service account), you are given a free email account, a *SkyDrive* account, and access to Office Web Apps. If you do not yet have a Microsoft account, you can create one at www.live.com (Figure 1-1).

1-1 **Create a Microsoft account**

> **MORE INFO**
>
> You will use your Microsoft account for projects in this text.

When you sign in to your computer using Windows 8, you can log in with your Microsoft username and password. Windows uses this information to transfer your Office 2013 settings to the computer you are using and connects you to your *SkyDrive* folder.

Start Page

After logging in to Windows 8 using your Microsoft account (see *Pause & Practice: Office 1-1,* Step 1 on page O1-17), you are taken to the *Start page* (Figure 1-2), which is new to Windows 8. The *Start* page displays different *apps* (applications) as tiles (large and small buttons). Click an app tile to launch a program or task.

Windows 8 uses the term *apps* generically to refer to applications and programs. Apps include the Windows 8 Weather app, Microsoft Excel program, Control Panel, Google Chrome, or File Explorer.

When you start using Windows 8, you can customize your *Start* page. Include the apps you most regularly use, remove the apps you don't want displayed on the *Start* page, and rearrange apps tiles to your preference.

1-2 Windows *Start* page

HOW TO: Customize the Start Page

1. To move an app tile, click and drag the app tile to a new location on the *Start* page. The other app tiles shuffle to accommodate the placement of the app tile.
2. To remove an app tile from the *Start* page, right-click the app tile you want to remove to select it and display your options, and then select **Unpin from Start** (Figure 1-3).
   - When an app tile is selected, a check mark appears in the upper right corner.
   - The app tile is removed from the *Start* page, but the program or task is not removed from your computer.
   - Your options differ depending on the app tile you select.
   - You can right-click multiple app tiles, one after the other, to select and apply an option to all of them.
3. To add an app tile to the *Start* page, right-click a blank area of the *Start* page and click **All Apps** at the bottom right (Figure 1-4).
4. Right-click the app you want to add to select it and click **Pin to Start** (Figure 1-5).
5. To resize an app tile, right-click the app tile to select it and click **Larger** or **Smaller**.
   - All options do not apply to all apps.
6. To uninstall an app, right-click the app you want to uninstall to select it and click **Uninstall**.
   - Unlike the unpin option, this option uninstalls the program from your computer, not just your *Start* page.

1-3 App options

1-4 Display all apps

1-5 Pin selected app to *Start* page

Windows 8 Navigation Options

You can access the Windows 8 options and navigate quickly to other areas from the *Start* page, the Windows desktop, or anywhere on your computer. The **Windows 8 navigation area** and options appear on the right side of your computer monitor when you place your pointer on the small horizontal line at the bottom right corner (Figure 1-6). The following list describes the different options available from the navigation area:

- **Search:** Displays all of the apps available on your computer and opens a search area at the right of your screen.
- **Share:** Displays options for sharing selected apps with other users.
- **Start:** Displays the *Start* page.
- **Devices:** Displays the devices available on your computer.
- **Settings:** Displays options for customizing computer settings; displays power options (Figure 1-7).

▶ **ANOTHER WAY**

Click the bottom left corner of your computer screen to toggle between the *Start* page and the desktop.

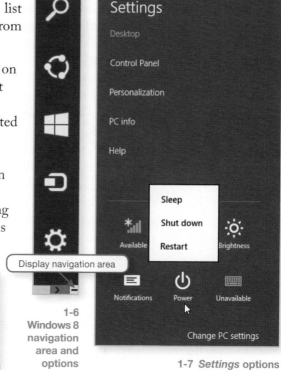

1-6
Windows 8
navigation
area and
options

1-7 *Settings* options

Desktop and Taskbar

The **Windows desktop** is the working area of Windows and is similar to previous versions of Windows. Click the **Desktop** app tile on the *Start* page to go to the desktop (Figure 1-8). When you install a program on your computer, typically a shortcut to the program is added to the desktop. When you open a program from the *Start* page, such as Microsoft Word, the desktop displays and the program opens.

The *Taskbar* displays at the bottom of the desktop. You can open programs and folders from the *Taskbar* by clicking on an icon on the *Taskbar* (Figure 1-9). You can pin programs and other Windows items, such as the Control Panel or File Explorer, to the *Taskbar*.

1-8 Windows *Desktop* tile on the *Start* page

1-9 *Taskbar* at the bottom of the desktop

HOW TO: Pin a Program to the Taskbar

....

1. Go to the *Start* page if it is not already displayed.
   - Put your pointer in the bottom right corner of your computer monitor and select **Start** in the navigation area.
   - If you are on the desktop, you can also click the **Start page** icon that appears when you place your pointer in the bottom left corner of your monitor.

2. Right-click a program or Windows item to select it (Figure 1-10).

   - A check appears in the upper right of a selected item.
   - Options display at the bottom of the *Start* page.

3. Click **Pin to taskbar**.

> **MORE INFO**
>
> You can drag items on the *Taskbar* to rearrange them.

1-10 Pin selected item to the *Taskbar*

File Explorer

The **File Explorer** is a window that opens on your desktop where you can browse for files stored on your computer (Figure 1-11). This window displays the libraries and folders on your computer on the left. When you select a library or folder on the left, the contents of the selection are displayed on the right. Double-click a file or folder on the right to open it.

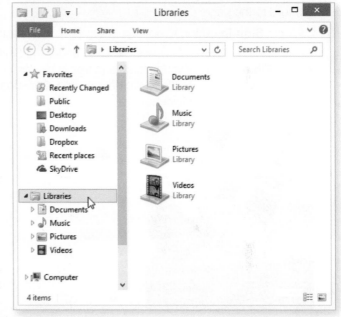

1-11 *File Explorer* window

SkyDrive

SkyDrive is a cloud storage area where you can store files in a private and secure online location that you can access from any computer. With cloud storage you don't have to be tied to one computer, and you don't have to carry your files with you on a portable storage device. When you store your files on *SkyDrive*, the files are actually saved on both your computer and on the cloud. *SkyDrive* synchronizes your files so when you change a file it is automatically updated on the *SkyDrive* cloud.

With Windows 8, the *SkyDrive folder* is one of your storage location folder options, similar to your *Documents* or *Pictures* folders (Figure 1-12). You can

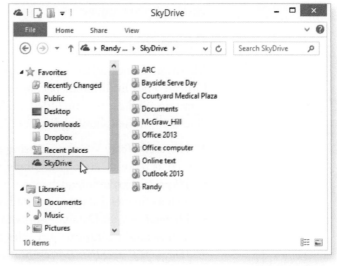

1-12 *SkyDrive* folder

save, open, and edit your *SkyDrive* files from a Windows folder. Your *SkyDrive* folder looks and functions similar to other Windows folders.

In addition to the *SkyDrive* folder on your computer, you can also access your *SkyDrive* files online using an Internet browser such as Internet Explorer, Google Chrome, or Mozilla Firefox. When you access *SkyDrive* online using a web browser, you can upload files, create folders, move and copy files and folders, and create Office files using Office Web Apps (see *Office Web Apps* later in this section).

HOW TO: Use SkyDrive Online

1. Open an Internet browser Window and navigate to the *SkyDrive* website (www.skydrive.com), which takes you to the *SkyDrive* sign in page (Figure 1-13).
   - You can use any Internet browser to access *SkyDrive* (e.g., Internet Explorer, Google Chrome, Mozilla Firefox).
2. Type in your Microsoft account email address and password.
   - If you are on your own computer, check the **Keep me signed in** box to stay signed in to *SkyDrive* when you return to the page.
3. Click the **Sign In** button to go to your *SkyDrive* web page.
   - The different areas of *SkyDrive* are listed under the *SkyDrive* heading on the left (Figure 1-14).
   - Click **Files** to display your folders and files in the folder area.
   - At the top of the page, there are buttons and drop-down menus that list the different actions you can perform on selected files and folders.

1-13 Log in to *SkyDrive* online

1-14 *SkyDrive* online

Office 2013

Microsoft Office 2013 is a suite of personal and business software applications. Microsoft Office comes in different packages and the applications included in each package vary. The common applications included in Microsoft Office and the primary purpose of each are described in the following list:

- ***Microsoft Word:*** Word processing software used to create, format, and edit documents such as reports, letters, brochures, and resumes.
- ***Microsoft Excel:*** Spreadsheet software used to perform calculations on numerical data such as financial statements, budgets, and expense reports.
- ***Microsoft Access:*** Database software used to store, organize, compile, and report information such as product information, sales data, client information, and employee records.
- ***Microsoft PowerPoint:*** Presentation software used to graphically present information in slides such as a presentation on a new product or sales trends.

- *Microsoft Outlook:* Email and personal management software used to create and send email and create and store calendar items, contacts, and tasks.
- *Microsoft OneNote:* Note-taking software used to take and organize notes, which can be shared with other Office applications.
- *Microsoft Publisher:* Desktop publishing software used to create professional-looking documents containing text, pictures, and graphics such as catalogs, brochures, and flyers.

Office Web Apps

Office Web Apps is free online software from Microsoft that works in conjunction with your online *SkyDrive* account (Figure 1-15). With Office Web Apps, you can work with Office files online, even on computers that do not have Office 2013 installed. This is a useful option when you use a computer at a computer lab or use a friend's computer that does not have Office 2013 installed.

1-15 Office Web Apps

You can access Office Web Apps from your *SkyDrive* web page and create and edit Word documents, Excel workbooks, PowerPoint presentations, and One-Note notebooks. Office Web Apps is a scaled-down version of Office 2013 and not as robust in terms of features, but you can use it to create, edit, print, share, and insert comments on files. If you need more advanced features, you can open Office Web Apps files in Office 2013.

In *SkyDrive*, you can share files with others. When you share files or folders with others, you establish the access they have to the items you share. You can choose whether other users can only view files or view and edit files. To share a file or folder in your *SkyDrive*, send an email with a link to the shared items or generate a hyperlink that gives access to the shared files to others.

HOW TO: Share an Office Web Apps File

1. Log in to your *SkyDrive* account.
2. Click an Office file to open the file in Office Web Apps.
3. In read-only mode, click the **Share** button above the file. A sharing window opens with different options (Figure 1-16).
   - You can also click the **File** tab and select **Share** on the left.

1-16 Share an Office Web Apps file

4. To send an email, click **Send email**, type the recipient's email address, and type a brief message.
   - Enter a space after typing an email address to add another recipient.
   - Alternatively, you can click **Get a link** to generate a link to send to recipients.
5. Check the **Recipients can edit** box if you want the recipient to be able to edit the file.
   - Deselect this check box if you want recipients to only view the file.
   - You can also require recipients to sign in to *SkyDrive* in order to view or edit the file by checking the **Require everyone who accesses this to sign in** box.
6. Click the **Send** button.
   - Recipients receive an email containing a link to the shared file or folder.
   - A window may open, prompting you to enter a displayed code to prevent unauthorized sharing. Enter the displayed code to return to the sharing window and click **Send**.
7. Click the **X** in the upper right corner or the browser window to exit *SkyDrive*.

Office Web Apps let you synchronously (i.e., at the same time) or asynchronously (i.e., not at the same time) collaborate on an Office file with others who have access to the shared file. If two or more users are working on the same file in Office Web Apps, collaboration information is displayed at the bottom of the Office Web Apps window (Figure 1-17). You are alerted to available updates and told how many people are editing the file.

1-17 Collaboration information displayed in the *Status* bar

Click **Updates Available** in the *Status* bar to apply updates to your file. Click **People Editing** to view the names of users who are currently editing the file.

> **MORE INFO**
>
> The *Status* bar is displayed at the bottom of the application window and is available on all Office applications.

Open an Office Application

When using Windows 8, you click an app tile to open an Office application. If your *Start* page has the Office applications displayed, you can click the **Word 2013**, **Excel 2013**, **Access 2013**, or **PowerPoint 2013** tile to launch the application (Figure 1-18).

If the Office application apps are not on the *Start* page, you can search for the app.

1-18 Launch an Office 2013 application

HOW TO: Search for an App

1. Put your pointer at the bottom right corner of your computer screen to display the Windows 8 navigation options.
2. Click **Search** to display all apps and the *Search* pane on the right (Figure 1-19).
3. Type the name of the application to open (e.g., Access). Windows displays the apps matching the search text.
4. Click the app to launch it.
   - Alternatively, you can click a blank area away from the *Search* pane to close the *Search* pane, scroll through the available apps on your computer, and click an app to launch it.

1-19 Search for an app

> **MORE INFO**
>
> Add commonly used apps to your Windows *Start* page to save you time.

Office Start Page

In addition to the new *Start* page in Windows 8, most of the Office applications (except Outlook and OneNote) have a new **Start page** that displays when you launch the application (Figure 1-20). From this *Start* page, you can create a new blank file (e.g., a Word document, an Excel workbook, an Access database, or a PowerPoint presentation), create a file from an online template, search for an online template, open a recently used file, or open another file. These options vary depending on the Office application.

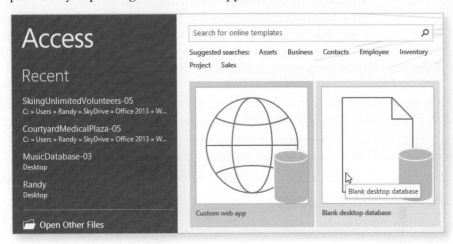

1-20 Access *Start* page

Press the **Esc** key to exit the *Start* page and enter the program. In Access, you have to open an existing database or create a new one to enter the program.

Backstage View

Office 2013 incorporates the **Backstage view** into all Office applications. Click the **File** tab on the *Ribbon* to open the *Backstage* view (Figure 1-21). *Backstage* options vary depending on the Office application. The following list describes some of the common tasks you can perform from the *Backstage* view:

1-21 *Backstage* view in Excel

- **Info:** Displays document properties and other protection, inspection, and version options.
- **New:** Creates a new blank file or a new file from a template or theme.
- **Open:** Opens an existing file from a designated location or a recently opened file.
- **Save:** Saves a file. If the file has not been named, the *Save As* dialog box opens when you select this option.
- **Save As:** Opens the *Save As* dialog box.
- **Print:** Prints a file, displays a preview of the file, or displays print options.
- **Share:** Invites people to share a file or email a file.

- *Export:* Creates a PDF file from a file or saves as a different file type.
- *Close:* Closes an open file.
- *Account:* Displays your Microsoft account information.
- *Options:* Opens the *[Application] Options* dialog box (e.g., Excel Options).

Office 2013 Help

In each of the Office applications, a help feature is available where you can search for a topic and view help information related to that topic. Using the *[Application] Help* dialog box (e.g., *Access Help*), type in key words for your search. Links to online help resources display in the dialog box.

HOW TO: Use Office Help

1. Click the **Help** button (question mark) in the upper right corner of the Office application window (Figure 1-22). The *[Application] Help* dialog box opens (Figure 1-23).

1-22 *Help* button

2. In the *Search* text box, type in key words for your search and press **Enter** or click the **Search** button. A list of related articles appears in the dialog box (Figure 1-24).

- You can also click one of the links in the *Popular searches* and *Basics and beyond* areas to view related help articles.

1-23 *Access Help* dialog box

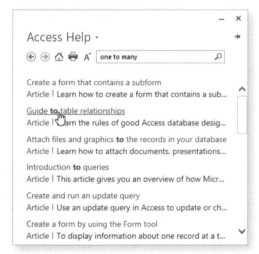

1-24 Related articles displayed in the dialog box

3. Click a link to display the article in the dialog box.

- You can use the *Back*, *Forward*, or *Home* buttons to navigate in the *Help* dialog box.
- Scroll down to the bottom of the list of articles to use the *Next* and *Previous* buttons to view more articles.

4. Click the **X** in the upper right corner to close the *Help* dialog box.

> **ANOTHER WAY**
> **F1** opens the *Help* dialog box.

Mouse and Pointers

If you are using Office on a desktop or laptop computer, use your mouse (or touch pad) to navigate around files, click tabs and buttons, select text and objects, move text and objects, and resize objects. The following table lists mouse and pointer terminology used in Office.

Mouse and Pointer Terminology

Term	Description
Pointer	When you move your mouse, the pointer moves on your screen. There are a variety of pointers that are used in different contexts in Office applications. The following pointers are available in most of the Office applications (the appearance of these pointers varies depending on the application and the context used): • *Selection pointer:* Select text or an object. • *Move pointer:* Move text or an object. • *Copy pointer:* Copy text or an object. • *Resize pointer:* Resize objects or table column or row. • *Crosshair:* Draw a shape.
Insertion point	The vertical flashing line where text is inserted in a file or text box. Click the left mouse button to position the insertion point.
Click	Click the left mouse button. Used to select an object or button or to place the insertion point in the selected location.
Double-click	Click the left mouse button twice. Used to select text.
Right-click	Click the right mouse button. Used to display the context menu and the mini toolbar.
Scroll	Use the scroll wheel on the mouse to scroll up and down through your file. You can also use the horizontal or vertical scroll bars at the bottom and right of an Office file window to move around in a file.

Office 2013 on a Tablet

The new user interface in Windows 8 and Office 2013 is designed to facilitate use of Windows and the Office applications on a tablet computer or smart phone. With tablets and smart phones, you use a touch screen rather than using a mouse, so the process of selecting text and objects and navigating around a file is different from when you select and navigate on a desktop or laptop computer. The following table lists some of the gestures used when working on a tablet or smart phone (some of these gestures vary depending on the application used and the context).

Tablet Gestures

Gesture	Used To	How To
Tap	Make a selection or place the insertion point. Double tap to edit text in an object or cell.	
Pinch	Zoom in or resize an object.	
Stretch	Zoom out or resize an object.	
Slide	Move an object or selected text.	
Swipe	Select text or multiple objects.	

Creating, Saving, Closing, and Opening Files

Creating, saving, and opening files is primarily done from the *Start* page or *Backstage* view. These areas provide you with many options and a central location to perform these tasks. You can also use shortcut commands to create, save, and open files.

Create a New File

When you create a new file in an Office application, you can create a new blank file or a new file based on a template (in PowerPoint, you can also create a presentation based on a theme). On the *Start* page, click **Blank [file type]** to create a new blank file in the application you are using (in Word, you begin with a blank document; in Excel, a blank workbook; in Access, a blank desktop database; and in PowerPoint, a blank presentation). From the *Backstage* view, the new file options are available in the *New* area.

HOW TO: Create a New File from the Start Page

1. Open the Office application you want to use. The *Start* page displays when the application opens.
2. From the *Start* page, click **Blank [file type]** or select a template or theme to use for your new blank file. A new file opens in the application you are using.
   - The new file is given a generic file name (e.g., *Document1*, *Book1*, or *Presentation1*). You can name and save this file later.
   - When creating a new Access database, you are prompted to name the new file when you create it.
   - Some templates and themes (in PowerPoint only) are displayed on the *Start* page, but you can search for other online templates and themes using the *Search* text box at the top of the *Start* page.

>
> **MORE INFO**
> **Esc** closes the *Start* page and takes you into the Office application (except in Access).

If you have been using an application already and want to create a new file, you create it from the *Backstage* view.

HOW TO: Create a New File from the Backstage View

1. Click the **File** tab to display the *Backstage* view.
2. Select **New** on the left to display the *New* area (Figure 1-25).
3. Click **Blank [file type]** or select a template or theme to use in your new blank file. A new file opens in the application.
   - The new file is given a generic file name (e.g., *Document1*, *Book1*, or *Presentation1*). You can name and save this file later.
   - When you are creating a new Access database, you are prompted to name the new file when you create it.
   - Some templates and themes (in PowerPoint only) are displayed on the *Start* page, but you can search for other online templates and themes using the *Search* text box at the top of the *Start* page.

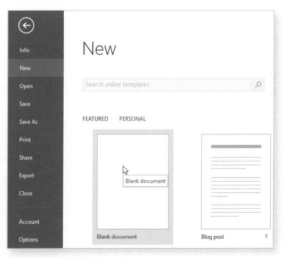

1-25 *New* area in Word

▶ ANOTHER WAY

Ctrl+N opens a new file from within an Office application. In Access, **Ctrl+N** opens the *New* area in the *Backstage* view.

Save a File

In Access, you name a file as you create it, but in Word, Excel, and PowerPoint, you name a file after you have created it. When you save a file, you type a name for the file and select the location where the file is saved.

HOW TO: Save a File

1. Click the **File** tab to display the *Backstage* view.
2. Select **Save** or **Save As** on the left to display the *Save As* area (Figure 1-26).
   - If the file has not already been saved, clicking *Save* or *Save As* takes you to the *Save As* area on the *Backstage* view.
3. Select a place to save your file in the *Places* area.
4. On the right, click a folder in the *Recent Folders* area or click the **Browse** button to open the *Save As* dialog box (Figure 1-27).
5. In the *Folder* list on the left, select a location to save the file.
6. In the *File name* area, type a name for the file.
7. In the *Save as type*, select the file type to save.
   - By default, Office selects the file type, but you can change the file type in this area.
8. Click **Save** to close the dialog box and save the file.

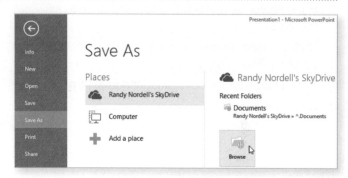

1-26 *Save As* area in PowerPoint

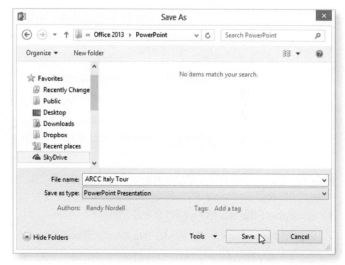

1-27 *Save As* dialog box

▶ ANOTHER WAY

Ctrl+S opens the *Save As* area on the *Backstage* view when a file does not have a name. If a file has already been named, **Ctrl+S** saves the file without opening the *Backstage* view.

Create a Folder

When saving files, it is a good idea to create folders to organize your files. Organizing your files in folders makes it easier to find your files and saves you time when you are searching for a specific file (see *SLO 1.7: Organizing and Customizing Folders and Files* for more information on this topic). When you save an Office file, you can also create a folder in which to store that file.

HOW TO: Create a Folder

1. Click the **File** tab to display the *Backstage* view.
2. Select **Save As** on the left to display the *Save As* area.
3. Select a place to save your file in the *Places* area.
4. On the right, click a folder in the *Recent Folders* area or the **Browse** button to open the *Save As* dialog box.
5. In the *Folder* list at the left, select a location to save the file.
6. Click the **New Folder** button to create a new folder (Figure 1-28).
7. Type a name for the new folder and press **Enter**.

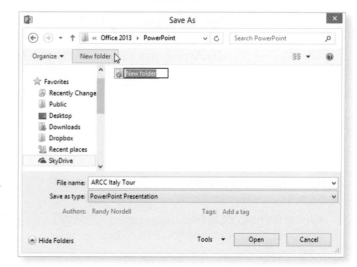

1-28 Create a new folder

> ### ANOTHER WAY
> **F12** opens the *Save As* dialog box (except in Access).

Save As a Different File Name

After you have saved a file, you can save it again with a different file name. If you do this, you have preserved the original file and you can continue to revise the second file for a different purpose. For example, you might want to save a different version of a file with a different file name.

HOW TO: Save As a Different File Name

1. Click the **File** tab to display the *Backstage* view.
2. Select **Save As** on the left to display the *Save As* area.
3. Select the location where you want to save your file in the *Places* area.
4. On the right, click a folder in the *Recent Folders* area or the **Browse** button to open the *Save As* dialog box.
5. In the *Folder* list on the left, select a location to save the file.
6. In the *File name* area, type a name for the file.
7. Click **Save** to close the dialog box and save the file.

Office 2013 File Types

When you save an Office file, by default Office saves the file in the most recent file format for that application. You also have the option of saving files in older versions of the Office application you are using. For example, you can save a Word document as an older version to share with or send to someone who uses an older version of Word. Each file has an extension at the end of the file name that determines the file type. The *file name extension* is automatically added to a file when you save it.

The following table lists some of the common file types used in the different Office applications.

Office File Types

File Type	Extension
Word Document	.docx
Word Template	.dotx
Word 97-2003 Document	.doc
Rich Text Format	.rtf
Excel Workbook	.xlsx
Excel Template	.xltx
Excel 97-2003 Workbook	.xls
Comma Separated Values (CSV)	.csv
Access Database	.accdb
Access Template	.accdt
Access Database (2000-2003 format)	.mdb
PowerPoint Presentation	.pptx
PowerPoint Template	.potx
PowerPoint 97-2003 Presentation	.ppt
Portable Document Format (PDF)	.pdf

Close a File

There are a few different methods you can use to close a file.

- Click the **File** tab and select **Close** on the left.
- Press **Ctrl+W**.
- Click the **X** in the upper right corner of the file window. This method closes the file and the program.

When you close a file, you are prompted to save the file if it has not been named or if changes were made after the file was last saved (Figure 1-29). Click **Save** to save and close the file or click **Don't Save** to close the file without saving. Click **Cancel** to return to the file.

1-29 Prompt to save a document before closing

Open an Existing File

You can open an existing file from the *Start* page when you open an Office application or you can open an existing file while you are working on another Office file.

HOW TO: Open a File from the Start Page

1. Open an Office application to display the *Start* page (Figure 1-30).
2. Select a file to open in the *Recent* area on the left.
   - If you select a file in the *Recent* area, the file must be located on the computer or an attached storage device in order to open. If the file has been renamed, moved, or on a storage device not connected to the computer, you received an error message.
3. Alternatively, click the **Open Other [file type]** (e.g., Documents, Workbooks, Files, or Presentations) link to open the *Open* area of the *Backstage* view (Figure 1-31).
4. Select a location in the *Places* area.
5. Select a folder in the *Recent Folders* area or click the **Browse** button to open the *Open* dialog box (Figure 1-32).
6. Select a location from the *Folder* list on the left.
7. Select the file to open and click the **Open** button.

1-30 Open a file from the *Start* page

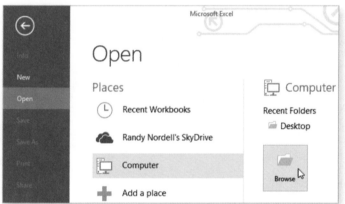

1-31 *Open* area in the *Backstage* view

1-32 *Open* dialog box

To open a file from within an Office application, click the **File** tab to open the *Backstage* view and select **Open** on the left to display the *Open* area. Follow steps 4–7 above to open a file.

You can also open a file from a Windows folder. When you double-click a file in a Windows folder, the file opens in the appropriate Office application. Windows recognizes the file name extension and launches the correct program.

> **ANOTHER WAY**
>
> **Ctrl+F12** opens the *Open* dialog box when you are in the working area of an Office application (except in Access).

For this project, you log in to Windows using your Microsoft account, customize the Windows *Start* page, create and save a PowerPoint presentation, create a folder, open and rename an Excel workbook, use *Help*, and share a file in *SkyDrive*.

Note to Students and Instructor:
Students: *For this project, you share an Office Web App file with your instructor. You also create a Microsoft account if you don't already have one.*
Instructor: *In order to complete this project, your students need your Microsoft email address. You can create a new Live or Hotmail account for projects in this chapter.*

File Needed: ***ARCC2015Budget-01.xlsx***
Completed Project File Names: ***[your initials] PP O1-1a.pptx*** and ***[your initials] PP O1-1b.xlsx***

1. Log in to Windows using your Microsoft account if you are not already logged in.
    a. If you are not logged in to Windows using your Microsoft account, you might need to log out or restart to display the log in page. When Windows opens, type in your Windows account username and password.
    b. If you have not yet created a Microsoft account, open a browser Window and go to www.live.com and click the **Sign up now** link. Enter the required information to create your free Windows account.

2. After logging in to Windows, customize the *Start* page to include Office 2013 apps. If these apps tiles are already on the *Start* page, skip steps 2a–e.
    a. Right-click a blank area of the *Start* page.
    b. Click **All apps** on the bottom right to display the *Apps* area of Windows.
    c. Locate and right-click **Word 2013** to select it (Figure 1-33).
    d. Click **Pin to Start** on the bottom left to add this app to the *Start* page.
    e. Repeat steps 2a–d to pin *Excel 2013*, *Access 2013*, and *PowerPoint 2013* to the *Start* page.

   1-33 Word 2013 selected

3. Return to the *Start* page and arrange apps.
    a. Place your pointer on the bottom right of your screen and select **Start** from the Windows navigation options.

> **ANOTHER WAY**
>
> Click the bottom left corner of your screen to return to the *Start* page.

   b. Drag the app tiles you added to the *Start* page to your preferred locations.

4. Create a PowerPoint presentation and save in a new folder.
    a. Click the **PowerPoint 2013** app tile on your *Start* page to open the application.
    b. On the PowerPoint *Start* page, click **Blank presentation** to create a new blank presentation (Figure 1-34). A new blank presentation opens.

1-34 Create a new blank PowerPoint presentation

c. Click in the **Click to add title** area and type American River Cycling Club.

d. Click the **File** tab to open the *Backstage* view and click **Save As** on the left to display the *Save As* area.

e. Click *[your name's]* **SkyDrive** in the *Places* area and click **Browse** to open the *Save As* dialog box (Figure 1-35).

f. Click the **New Folder** button to create a new folder in your *SkyDrive* folder.

g. Type American River Cycling Club and press **Enter**.

h. Double-click the folder you created to open it.

i. In the *File name* area, type [your initials] PP O1-1a (Figure 1-36).

j. Click **Save** to close the dialog box and save the presentation.

k. Click the **X** in the upper right corner of the window to close the file and PowerPoint.

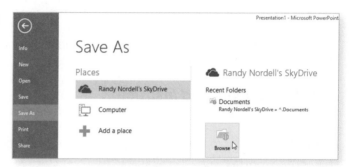

1-35 Save the file in *SkyDrive*

1-36 *Save As* dialog box

5. Open an Excel file and save as a different file name.

a. Return to the Windows *Start* page.

b. Click the **Excel 2013** app tile to open it.

c. From the Excel *Start* page, click the **Open Other Workbooks** link on the bottom left to display the *Open* area of the *Backstage* view.

d. Click **Computer** in the *Places* area and click **Browse** to open the *Open* dialog box (Figure 1-37).

e. Browse to your student data files and select the ***ARCC2015Budget-01*** file.

f. Click **Open** to open the workbook.

g. Press **F12** to open the *Save As* dialog box.

h. Click **SkyDrive** in the *Folder* list on the left.

i. Double-click the **American River Cycling Club** folder to open it.

j. In the *File name* area type [your initials] PP O1-1b.

k. Click **Save** to close the dialog box and save the workbook.

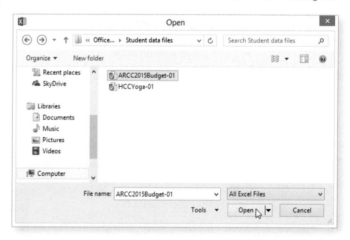

1-37 *Open* dialog box

6. Use *Excel Help* to find articles about selected topics.

a. Click the **Help** button in the upper right corner of the Excel window. The *Excel Help* dialog box opens.

b. Type pivot table in the *Search* text box and press **Enter**.

c. Click one of the displayed articles and quickly read about pivot tables.

d. Click the **Home** button to return to the home page of Excel help.

e. Type sum function in the *Search* text box and press **Enter**.

f. Click one of the displayed articles and quickly read about sum functions.

g. Click the **X** in the upper right corner to close the *Excel Help* dialog box.

h. Press **Ctrl+W** to close the Excel workbook.

i. Click the **X** in the upper right corner of the Excel window to close Excel.

7. Share an Office Web Apps file on *SkyDrive* with your instructor.

a. Return to the Windows *Start* page.

b. Open an Internet browser window and go to the *SkyDrive* (www.skydrive.com) sign-in page (Figure 1-38).

c. Type in your Microsoft account email address and password and click the **Sign In** button to go to your *SkyDrive* web page.

1-38 Log in to *SkyDrive* online

d. Click the navigation button on the upper left and select **SkyDrive** (if your *SkyDrive* is not already displayed) (Figure 1-39).

e. Click the **American River Cycling Club** folder to open it.

1-39 Go to your *SkyDrive*

f. Click the **PP O1-1b** Excel workbook to open it in Office Web Apps (Figure 1-40).

g. Click the **File** tab to open the *Backstage* view.

h. Click **Share** on the left and select **Share with People**. A sharing window opens with different options (Figure 1-41). Sharing requires the recipient to have a Microsoft account. Also, you might be directed to complete an online form for security purposes the first time you share a file.

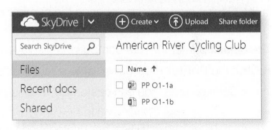

1-40 Open a file in Office Web Apps

i. Click **Send email**, type your instructor's email address, and type a brief message.

j. Check the **Recipients can edit** check box.

k. Click the **Share** button.

8. Select **[your name]** on the upper right of the *SkyDrive* window and select the **Sign out** from the *Account* drop-down list.

1-41 Share an Office Web App file

Printing, Sharing, and Customizing Files

On the *Backstage* view of any of the Office applications, you can print a file and customize how a file is printed. You can also export an Office file as a PDF file in most of the Office applications. In addition, you can add and customize document properties for an Office file and share a file in a variety of formats.

Print a File

You can print an Office file if you need a paper copy of it. The *Print* area on the *Backstage* view displays a preview of the open file and many print options. For example, you can choose which page or pages to print and change the margins of the file in the *Print* area. Some of the print settings vary depending on the Office application you are using and what you are printing.

HOW TO: Print a File

1. Open the file you want to print from a Windows folder or within an Office program.
2. Click the **File** tab to open the *Backstage* view.
3. Click **Print** on the left to display the *Print* area (Figure 1-42).
   - A preview of the file displays on the right. Click the **Show Margins** button to adjust margins or **Zoom to Page** button to change the view in the *Preview* area. The *Show Margins* button is only available in Word and Excel.
   - On the left a variety of options are listed in the *Settings* area.
   - The *Settings* options vary depending on the Office application you are using and what you are printing.
4. In the *Copies* area, you can change the number of copies to print.

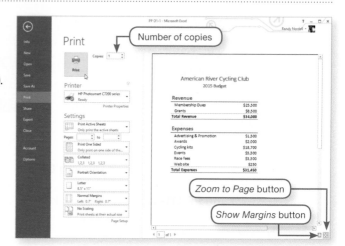

1-42 *Print* area on the *Backstage* view

5. The default printer for your computer is displayed in the *Printer* drop-down list.
   - Click the **Printer** drop-down list to select a different printer.
6. In the *Settings* area, you can customize what is printed and how it is printed.
   - In the *Pages* area (*Slides* area in PowerPoint), you can select a page or range of pages (slides) to print.
   - By default all pages (slides) are printed when you print a file.
7. Click the **Print** button to print your file.

> **ANOTHER WAY**
>
> **Ctrl+P** opens the *Print* area on the *Backstage* view.

Export as a PDF File

Portable document format, or **PDF**, is a specific file format that is often used to share files that are not to be changed or to post files on a web site. When you create a PDF file from an Office application file, you are actually exporting a static image of the original file, similar to taking a picture of the file.

The advantage of working with a PDF file is that the format of the file is retained no matter who opens the file. PDF files open in Adobe Reader, which is free software that is installed on most computers, or Adobe Acrobat, which is software users have to buy. Because a PDF file is a static image of a file, it is not easy for other people to edit your files. When you want people to be able to view a file but not make changes, PDF files are a good choice.

> **MORE INFO**
> Word 2013 allows you to open PDF files and edit the file as a Word document.

When you export an Office application file as a PDF file, Office creates a static image of your file and prompts you to save the file. The file is saved as a PDF file.

HOW TO: Export a File as a PDF File

1. Open the file you want to export to a PDF file.
2. Click the **File** tab and click **Export** to display the *Export* area on the Backstage view (Figure 1-43).
3. Select **Create PDF/XPS Document** and click the **Create PDF/XPS**. The *Publish as PDF or XPS* dialog box opens.
4. Select a location to save the file.
5. In the *File name* area, type a name for the file.
6. Click **Publish** to close the dialog box and save the PDF file.
   - A PDF version of your file may open. You can view the file and then close it.

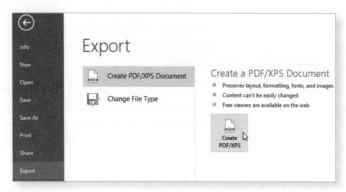

1-43 Export a file as a PDF file

Document Properties

Document properties are hidden codes in a file that contain identifying information about that file. Each piece of document property information is called a *field*. You can view and modify document properties in the *Info* area of the *Backstage* view.

Some document properties fields are automatically generated when you work on a file, such as *Size*, *Total Editing Time*, *Created*, and *Last Modified*. But you can modify other document properties fields, such as *Title*, *Comments*, *Subject*, *Company*, and *Author*. You can use document property fields in different ways such as inserting the *Company* field in a document footer.

HOW TO: View and Modify Document Properties

1. Click the **File** tab and click **Info**. The document properties display on the right (Figure 1-44).
2. Click in the text box area of a field that can be edited (e.g., *Add a title* or *Add a tag*) and type your custom document property information.
3. Click the **Show All Properties** link at the bottom to display additional document properties.
   - When all properties are displayed, click **Show Fewer Properties** to display fewer properties.
   - This link toggles between *Show All Properties* and *Show Fewer Properties*.
4. Click the **File** tab to return to the file.

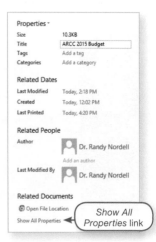

1-44 Document properties

Share a File

Windows 8 and Office 2013 have been developed to help you share and collaborate effectively. The *Share* area on the *Backstage* view provides different options for sharing files from within an Office application. When you save a file to your *SkyDrive*, Office gives you a variety of options to share your file (Figure 1-45). Your sharing options vary depending on the Office application you are using. The following list describes some common ways you can share files with others:

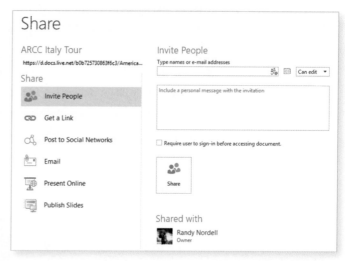

1-45 Share an Office file

- *Invite People* to view or edit your file.
- *Get a Link* to the online file that you can send to others or post online.
- *Post to Social Networks* such as LinkedIn or Facebook.
- *Email* the file as an attachment, link, or PDF file.

> **MORE INFO**
>
> There is not a *Sharing* area on the *Backstage* view in Access.

HOW TO: Share a File

1. Click the **File** tab and select **Share**.
   - If your file is not saved on *SkyDrive*, select **Invite People** and click **Save to Cloud** (Figure 1-46).
   - Save your file to your *SkyDrive* folder.
   - If your file is not saved to *SkyDrive*, you will not have all of the sharing options.

2. Select one of the *Share* options on the left. Additional information is displayed on the right (Figure 1-47).
   - In most of the *Share* options, you can set the permission level to **Can view** or **Can edit**, which controls what others can do with your file.
   - In order to post a file to a social network site, you must connect your social network site to your Microsoft account. Go to the *Account* area of the *Backstage* view to connect to social network sites.

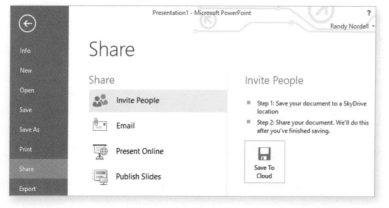

1-46 Save a file to the cloud before sharing

1-47 Share a file on a social network site

Program Options

Using the program options, you can make changes that apply globally to the Office program. For example, you can change the default save location to your *Sky-Drive* folder or you can turn off the *Start* page that opens when you open an Office application.

Click the **File** tab and select **Options** on the left to open the **[Program] Options** dialog box (e.g., Word Options, Excel Options, etc.) (Figure 1-48). Click one of the categories on the left to display the category options on the right. The categories and options vary depending on the Office application you are using.

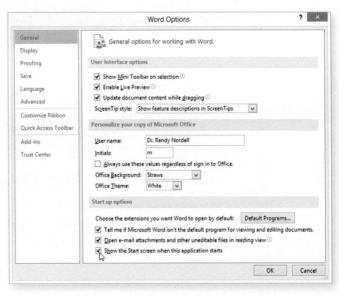

1-48 *Word Options* dialog box

Using the Ribbon, Tabs, and Quick Access Toolbar

You can use the *Ribbon*, tabs, groups, buttons, drop-down lists, dialog boxes, task panes, galleries, and the *Quick Access* toolbar to modify your Office files. This section describes the different tools you can use to customize your files.

The Ribbon, Tabs, and Groups

The **Ribbon**, which appears at the top of an Office file window, displays the many features available to use on your files. The *Ribbon* is a collection of **tabs**. On each tab are **groups** of features. The tabs and groups that are available on each Office application vary. Click a tab to display the groups and features available on that tab.

Some tabs are always displayed on the *Ribbon* (e.g., *File* tab and *Home* tab). Other tabs are **context-sensitive**, which means that they only appear on the *Ribbon* when a specific object is selected in your file. Figure 1-49 displays the context-sensitive *Table Tools Table* tab that displays in Access when you open a table.

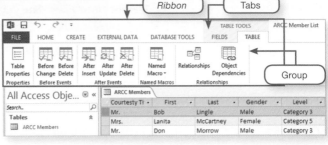

1-49 Context-sensitive *Table Tools Table* tab displayed

Ribbon Display Options

The *Ribbon* is by default displayed when an Office application is open, but you can customize how the *Ribbon* displays. The **Ribbon Display Options** button is in the upper right corner of an Office application window (Figure 1-50). Click the **Ribbon Display Options** button to select one of the three options.

1-50 *Ribbon Display Options*

- *Auto-Hide Ribbon:* Hides the *Ribbon.* Click at the top of the application to display the *Ribbon.*
- *Show Tabs: Ribbon* tabs display. Click a tab to open the *Ribbon* and display the tab.
- *Show Tabs and Commands:* Displays the *Ribbon* and tabs, which is the default setting in Office applications.

> **MORE INFO**
>
> **Ctrl+F1** collapses or expands the *Ribbon* to display only tabs.

Buttons, Drop-Down Lists, and Galleries

Groups on each of the tabs contain a variety of *buttons*, *drop-down lists*, and *galleries.* The following list describes each of these features and how they are used:

1-51 *Bold* button in the *Font* group on the *Home* tab

- *Button:* Applies a feature to selected text or object. Click a button to apply the feature (Figure 1-51).
- *Drop-Down List:* Displays the various options available for a feature. Some buttons are drop-down lists only, which means when you click one of these buttons the drop-down list of options appears (Figure 1-52). Other buttons are *split buttons,* which have both a button you click to apply a feature and an arrow you click to display a drop-down list of options (Figure 1-53).

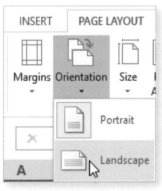

1-52 Drop-down list

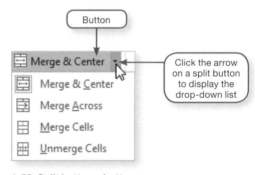

1-53 Split button—button and drop-down list

- *Gallery:* Displays a collection of option buttons. Click an option in a gallery to apply the feature. Figure 1-54 is the *Styles* gallery. You can click the **More** button to display the entire gallery of options or click the **Up** or **Down** arrow to display a different row of options.

1-54 *Styles* gallery in Word

Dialog Boxes, Task Panes, and Launchers

Not all of the features that are available in an Office application are displayed in the groups on the tabs. Additional options for some groups are displayed in a *dialog box* or *task pane*. A *launcher*, which is a small square in the bottom right of some groups, opens a dialog box or displays a task pane when you click it (see Figure 1-56).

1-55 *Datasheet Formatting* dialog box

- *Dialog box:* A new window that opens to display additional features. You can move a dialog box by clicking and dragging on the title bar, which is the top of the dialog box where the title is displayed. Figure 1-55 is the *Datasheet Formatting* dialog box that opens when you click the *Text Formatting* launcher in Access.
- *Task pane:* Opens on the left or right of the Office application window. Figure 1-56 is the *Clipboard* pane, which is available in all Office applications. Task panes are named according to their feature (e.g., *Clipboard* pane or *Navigation* pane). You can resize a task pane by clicking and dragging on its left or right border. Click the **X** in the upper right corner to close a task pane.

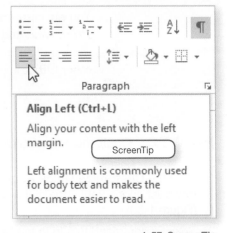

1-56 *Clipboard* pane

ScreenTips

ScreenTips display descriptive information about a button, drop-down list, launcher, or gallery selection in the groups on the *Ribbon*. When you put your pointer on an item on the *Ribbon*, a Screen-Tip displays information about the selection (Figure 1-57). The ScreenTip appears temporarily and displays the command name, keyboard shortcut (if available), and a description of the command.

1-57 *ScreenTip*

Radio Buttons, Check Boxes, and Text Boxes

Within dialog boxes and task panes there are a variety of features you can apply using radio buttons, check boxes, text boxes, drop-down lists, and other buttons. A *radio button* is a round button that you click to select one option from a list of options. A selected radio button has a solid dot inside the round button. When you see a *check box*, you can use it to select one or more options. A check appears in a check box you have selected. A *text box* is an area where you can type text.

A task pane or dialog box may also include drop-down lists or other buttons that open additional dialog boxes. Figure 1-58 shows the *Page Setup* dialog box in Excel, which includes a variety of radio buttons, check boxes, text boxes, drop-down lists, and other buttons that open additional dialog boxes.

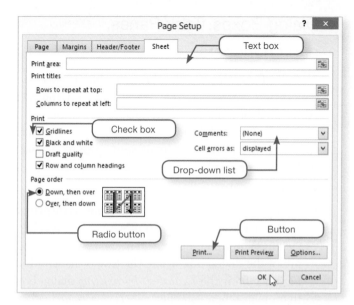

1-58 *Page Setup* dialog box in Excel

Quick Access Toolbar

The **Quick Access toolbar** is located above the *Ribbon* on the upper left of each Office application window. It contains buttons you can use to apply commonly used features such as *Save, Undo, Redo,* and *Open* (Figure 1-59). The *Undo* button is a split button. You can click the button to undo the last action performed or you can click the drop-down arrow to display and undo multiple previous actions.

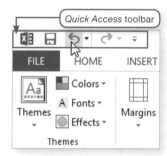

1-59 *Quick Access* toolbar

Customize the Quick Access Toolbar

You can customize the *Quick Access* toolbar to include features you regularly use, such as *Quick Print, New,* and *Spelling & Grammar.* The following steps show how to customize the *Quick Access* toolbar in Word. The customization process is similar for the *Quick Access* toolbar in the other Office applications.

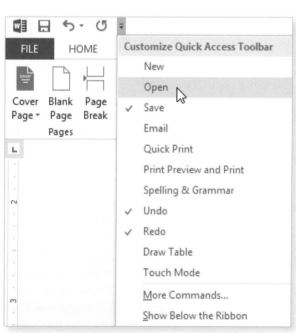

HOW TO: Customize the Quick Access Toolbar

1. Click the **Customize Quick Access Toolbar** drop-down list on the right edge of the *Quick Access* toolbar (Figure 1-60).

2. Select a command to add to the *Quick Access* toolbar. The command appears on the *Quick Access* toolbar.

   - Items on the *Customize Quick Access Toolbar* drop-down list with a check mark are displayed on the *Quick Access* toolbar.
   - Deselect a checked item to remove it from the *Quick Access* toolbar.

3. To add a command that is not listed on the *Customize Quick Access Toolbar,* click the **Customize Quick Access Toolbar** drop-down list and select **More Commands**.

1-60 Customize the *Quick Access* toolbar

The *Word Options* dialog box opens with the *Quick Access Toolbar* area displayed (Figure 1-61).

4. Click the **Customize Quick Access Toolbar** drop-down list on the right and select **For all documents** or the current document.

   • If you select *For all documents*, the change is made to the *Quick Access* toolbar for all documents you open in Word.
   • If you select the current document, the change is made to the *Quick Access* toolbar in that document only.

5. On the left, select the command you want to add.

   • If you can't find the command you're looking for, click the **Choose commands from** drop-down list and select **All Commands**.

6. Click the **Add** button and the command name appears in the list on the right.

7. Add other commands as desired.

8. To rearrange commands on the *Quick Access* toolbar, select the command to move and click the **Move Up** or **Move Down** button.

9. Click **OK** to close the *Word Options* dialog box.

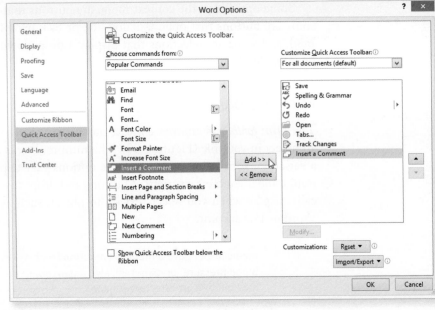

1-61 Customize the *Quick Access* toolbar in the *Word Options* dialog box

---

> **MORE INFO**
>
> To remove an item from the *Quick Access* toolbar, right-click an item and select **Remove from Quick Access Toolbar**.

Using a Context Menu, Mini Toolbar, and Keyboard Shortcuts

Most of the formatting and other features you will want to apply to text are available in groups on the different tabs. But many of these features are also available using content menus, mini toolbars, and keyboard shortcuts. You can use these tools to quickly apply formatting or other options to text or objects.

Context Menu

A ***context menu*** is displayed when you right-click text, a cell, or an object such as a picture, drawing object, chart, or *SmartArt* (Figure 1-62). The context menu is a vertical rectangle menu that lists a variety of options. These options are context-sensitive, which means they vary depending on what you right-click.

1-62 Context menu

Some options on the context menu are buttons that perform an action (e.g., *Cut* or *Copy*), some are buttons that open a dialog box or task pane (e.g., *Save as Picture* or *Size and Position*), and some are selections that display a drop-down list of selections (e.g., *Bring to Front* or *Wrap Text*).

Mini Toolbar

The **mini toolbar** is another context menu that displays when you right-click text, a cell, or an object in your file (Figure 1-63). The mini toolbar is a horizontal rectangle menu that lists a variety of formatting options. These options vary depending on what you right-click. The mini toolbar contains a variety of buttons and drop-down lists. Some mini toolbars automatically display when you select text or an object, such as when you select a row of a table in Word or PowerPoint.

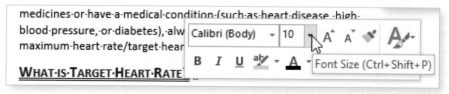

1-63 Mini toolbar

Keyboard Shortcuts

You can also use a **keyboard shortcut** to quickly apply formatting or perform actions. A keyboard shortcut is a keyboard key or combination of keyboard keys that you press at the same time. These can include the *Ctrl, Shift, Alt,* letter, number, and function keys (e.g., *F1* or *F7*). The following table lists some common Office keyboard shortcuts.

> **MORE INFO**
>
> See Appendix A for more Office 2013 keyboard shortcuts.

Common Office Keyboard Shortcuts

Keyboard Shortcut	Action or Displays	Keyboard Shortcut	Action or Displays
Ctrl+S	Save	Ctrl+Z	Undo
F12	*Save As* dialog box	Ctrl+Y	Redo or Repeat
Ctrl+O	*Open* area on the *Backstage* view	Ctrl+1	Single space
Shift+F12	*Open* dialog box	Ctrl+2	Double space
Ctrl+N	New blank file	Ctrl+L	Align left
Ctrl+P	*Print* area on the *Backstage* view	Ctrl+E	Align center
Ctrl+C	Copy	Ctrl+R	Align right
Ctrl+X	Cut	F1	*Help* dialog box
Ctrl+V	Paste	F7	*Spelling* pane
Ctrl+B	Bold	Ctrl+A	Select All
Ctrl+I	Italic	Ctrl+Home	Move to the beginning
Ctrl+U	Underline	Ctrl+End	Move to the end

For this project, you work with a document for the American River Cycling Club. You modify the existing document, add document properties, customize the *Quick Access* toolbar, export the document as a PDF file, and share a link to the document.

Note to Instructor:

Students: *For this project, you share an Office Web App file with your instructor.*
Instructor: *In order to complete this project, your students need your Microsoft email address. You can create a new Live or Hotmail account for projects in this chapter.*

File Needed: ***ARCCTraining-01.docx***
Completed Project File Names: ***[your initials] PP O1-2.docx*** and ***[your initials] PP O1-2.pdf***

1. Open Word 2013 and open the ***ARCCTraining-01*** file from your student data files.

2. Save this document as ***[your initials] PP O1-2*** in the *American River Cycling Club* folder in your *SkyDrive* folder.

3. Use a button, drop-down list, and dialog box to modify the document.
   a. Select the first heading, "**What is Maximum Heart Rate?**"
   b. Click the **Bold** button [*Home* tab, *Font* group].
   c. Click the **Underline** drop-down arrow and select **Double underline** (Figure 1-64).
   d. Click the **launcher** in the *Font* group [*Home* tab] to open the *Font* dialog box (Figure 1-65).
   e. In the *Size* area, select **12** from the list or type 12 in the text box.
   f. In the *Effects* area, click the **Small caps** check box to select it.
   g. Click **OK** to close the dialog box and apply the formatting changes.
   h. Select the next heading, "**What is Target Heart Rate?**"
   i. Repeat steps 3b–g to apply formatting to selected text.

4. Add document properties.
   a. Click the **File** tab to display the *Backstage* view.
   b. Select **Info** on the left. The document properties are displayed on the right.
   c. Click in the **Add a title** text box and type ARCC Training.
   d. Click the **Show All Properties** link near the bottom to display more document properties.
   e. Click in the **Specify the subject** text box and type Heart rate training.
   f. Click in the **Specify the company** text box and type American River Cycling Club.
   g. Click the **Show Fewer Properties** link to display fewer document properties.
   h. Click the **Back** arrow on the upper left to close the *Backstage* view and return to the document.

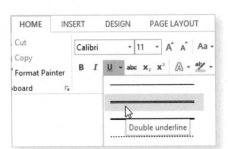

1-64 Apply *Double underline* to selected text

1-65 *Font* dialog box

5. Customize the *Quick Access* toolbar.
   a. Click the **Customize Quick Access Toolbar** drop-down arrow and select **Open** (Figure 1-66).
   b. Click the **Customize Quick Access Toolbar** drop-down arrow again and select **Spelling & Grammar**.
   c. Click the **Customize Quick Access Toolbar** drop-down arrow and select **More Commands**. The *Word Options* dialog box opens (Figure 1-67).
   d. Click the **Customize Quick Access Toolbar** drop-down list on the right and select **For all documents**.

1-66 *Customize Quick Access Toolbar* drop-down list

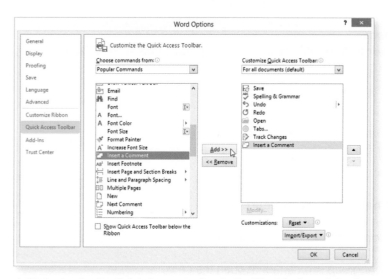

1-67 Customize the *Quick Access* toolbar in the *Word Options* dialog box

   e. In the list of commands at the left, click **Insert a Comment**.
   f. Click the **Add** button to add it to your *Quick Access* toolbar list on the right.
   g. Click **OK** to close the *Word Options* dialog box.
   h. Click the **Save** button on the *Quick Access* toolbar to save the document.

6. Export the file as a PDF file.
   a. Click the **File** tab to go to the *Backstage* view.
   b. Select **Export** on the left.
   c. Select **Create PDF/XPS Document** and click the **Create PDF/XPS** button. The *Publish as PDF or XPS* dialog box opens (Figure 1-68).
   d. Select the **American River Cycling Club** folder in your *SkyDrive* folder as the location to save the file.
   e. In the *File name* area, type [your initials] PP O1-2 if it is not already there.
   f. Deselect the **Open file after publishing** check box if it is checked.

1-68 *Publish as PDF or XPS* dialog box

g. Select the **Standard** (publishing online and printing) radio button.

h. Click **Publish** to close the dialog box and create a PDF version of your file.

7. Get a link to share a document with your instructor.

   a. Click the **File** tab to open the *Backstage* view.

   b. Select **Share** at the left. Your file is already saved to *SkyDrive* so all of the *Share* options are available.

   c. Select **Get a Sharing Link** on the left (Figure 1-69).

   d. In the *View Link* area, click the **Create Link** button. A link for the document is created and displayed on the right of the button.

   e. Select this link and press **Ctrl+C** to copy the link.

   f. Click the **Back** arrow to close the *Backstage* view and return to your document.

8. Save and close the document (Figure 1-70).

9. Email the sharing link to your instructor.

   a. Using your email account, create a new email to send to your instructor.

   b. Include an appropriate subject line and a brief message in the body.

   c. Press **Ctrl+V** to paste the link to your document in the body of the email.

   d. Send the email message.

1-69 *Get a Link* to share a file

1-70 PP O1-2 completed

Working with Files

When you work with Office files, there are a variety of views to display your file. You can change how a file is displayed, adjust the display size, work with multiple files, and arrange the windows to view multiple files. Because most people work with multiple files at the same time, Office makes it intuitive to move from one file to another or display multiple document windows at the same time.

File Views

Each of the different Office applications provides you with a variety of ways to view your document. In Word, Excel, and PowerPoint, the different views are available on the *View* tab

(Figure 1-71). You can also change views using the buttons on the right side of the *Status* bar at the bottom of the file window (Figure 1-72). In Access, the different views for each object are available in the *Views* group on the *Home* tab.

The following table lists the views that are available in each of the different Office applications.

1-71 *Workbook Views* group on the *View* tab in Excel

1-72 PowerPoint views on the *Status* bar

File Views

Office Application	Views	Office Application	Views
Word	Read Mode Print Layout Web Layout Outline Draft	**Access** *(Access views vary depending on active object)*	Layout View Design View Datasheet View Form View SQL View Report View Print Preview
Excel	Normal Page Break View Page Layout View Custom Views	**PowerPoint**	Normal Outline View Slide Sorter Notes Page Reading View Presenter View

Change Display Size

You can use the **Zoom feature** to increase or decrease the display size of your file. Using *Zoom* to change the display size does not change the actual size of text or objects in your file; it only changes the size of your display. For example, if you change the *Zoom* level to 120%, you increase the display of your file to 120% of its normal size (100%), but changing the display size does not affect the actual size of text and objects in your file. You could also decrease the *Zoom* level to 80% to display more of your file on the screen.

There are a few different ways you can increase or decrease the *Zoom* level on your file. Your *Zoom* options vary depending on the Office application you are using.

- **Zoom level on the Status bar** (Figure 1-73): Click the + or – buttons to increase or decrease *Zoom* level.

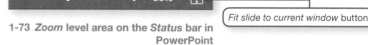

1-73 *Zoom* level area on the *Status* bar in PowerPoint

- **Zoom group on the View tab** (Figure 1-74): There are a variety of *Zoom* options in the *Zoom* group. These vary depending on application.

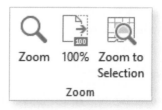

1-74 *Zoom* group in Excel

O1-32

- *Zoom dialog box* (Figure 1-75): Click the **Zoom** button in the *Zoom* group on *View* tab or click **Zoom level** on the *Status* bar to open the *Zoom* dialog box.

> **MORE INFO**
>
> The *Zoom* feature is only available in Access in *Print Preview* view when you are working with reports.

1-75 *Zoom* dialog box in Word

Manage Multiple Open Files and Windows

When you are working on multiple files in an Office application, each file is opened in a new window. You can *minimize* an open window to place the file on the Windows *Taskbar* (the bar at the bottom of the Windows desktop), *restore down* an open window so it does not fill the entire computer screen, or *maximize* a window so it fills the entire computer screen. The *Minimize, Restore Down/Maximize,* and *Close* buttons are in the upper right of a file window (Figure 1-76).

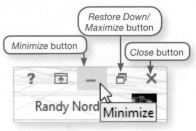

1-76 Window options buttons

> **MORE INFO**
>
> You can open only one Access file at a time. If you open another Access file, the first one closes.

- *Minimize:* Click the **Minimize** button to hide this window. When a document is minimized, it is not closed. It is collapsed so the window is not displayed on your screen. Click the application icon on the Windows *Taskbar* at the bottom to display thumbnails of open files. You can click an open file thumbnail to display the file (Figure 1-77).
- *Restore Down/Maximize:* Click the **Restore Down/Maximize** button to decrease the size of an open window or maximize the window to fill the entire screen. This button toggles between *Restore Down* and *Maximize*. When

1-77 Display open files on the Windows *Taskbar*

a window is restored down, you can change the size of a window by clicking and dragging on a border of the window. You can also move the window by clicking and dragging on the title bar at the top of the window.
- *Close:* Click the **Close** button to close the window. If there is only one open file, the Office application also closes when you click the *Close* button on the file.

You can switch between open files or arrange the open files to display more than one window at the same time. There are a few ways to do this.

- *Switch Windows button:* Click the **Switch Windows** button [*View* tab, *Window* group] (not available in Access) to display a drop-down list of open files. Click a file from the drop-down list to display the file.

- *Windows Taskbar:* Click an Office application icon on the Windows *Taskbar* to display the open files in that application. Click an open file to display it (see Figure 1-77).
- *Arrange All button:* Click the **Arrange All** button [*View* tab, *Window* group] to display all windows in an application. You can resize or move the open file windows.

Organizing and Customizing Folders and Files

The more you use your computer and create and use files, the more important it is to stay organized. You can do this by using folders to store related files, which makes it easier for you to find, edit, and share your files. For example, you can create a folder for the college you attend. Inside the college folder, you can create a folder for each of your courses. Inside each of the course folders you might create a folder for student data files, solution files, and group projects. Folders can store any type of files, and you are not limited to Office files.

Create a Folder

You can create folders inside of other folders. In *SLO 1.2: Creating, Saving, Closing, and Opening Files,* you learned how to create a new folder when saving an Office file in the *Save As* dialog box. You can also create a folder using a Windows folder.

HOW TO: Create a Windows Folder

1. Open a Windows folder.
   - From the Windows *Start* page, click **File Explorer**, **Computer**, or **Documents** to open a Windows window.
   - Your folders and computer locations are listed on the left.
2. Select the location where you want to create a new folder.
3. Click the **New folder** button on the top left of the window. A new folder is created in the folders area (Figure 1-78).
   - You can also click the **Home** tab and click the **New folder** button [*New* group].
4. Type the name of the new folder and press **Enter**.

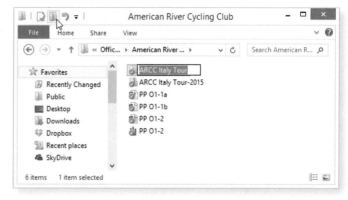

1-78 Create a new Windows folder

> **ANOTHER WAY**
>
> **Ctrl+Shift+N** creates a new folder in a Windows folder.

Move and Copy Files and Folders

You can move or copy files and folders using the *Move to* or *Copy to* buttons on the *Home* tab of a Windows folder. You can also use the move or copy keyboard shortcuts (**Ctrl+X, Ctrl+C, Ctrl+V**) or the drag and drop method. When you move a file or folder, you cut it from one location and paste it in another location. When you copy a file or folder, you create a copy of it and paste it in another location so the file or folder is in two or more locations. If there are files in a folder you move or copy, the files in the folder are moved or copied with the folder.

To move or copy multiple folders or files at the same time, press the **Ctrl** key and select multiple items to move or copy. Use the *Ctrl* key to select or deselect multiple non-adjacent files or folders. You can also use the *Shift* key to select a range of files or folders. Click the first file or folder in a range, press the **Shift** key, and select the last file or folder in the range to select all of the items in the range.

HOW TO: Move or Copy a File or Folder

1. In a Windows folder, select a file or folder to move or copy.
2. Click the **Home** tab to display the tab in the open window.
3. Click the **Move to** or **Copy to** button [*Organize* group] and select the location where you want to move or copy the file or folder (Figure 1-79).

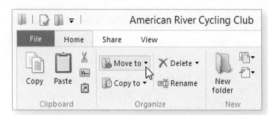

1-79 Move or copy a selected file or folder

- If the folder you want is not available, select **Choose location** to open the *Move Items* or *Copy Items* dialog box.
- To use the keyboard shortcuts, press **Ctrl+X** to cut the file or folder or **Ctrl+C** to copy the file or folder from its original location, go to the desired new location, and press **Ctrl+V** to paste it.
- To use the drag and drop method to move a file or folder, select the file or folder and drag and drop on the new location.
- To use the drag and drop method to copy a file or folder, press the **Ctrl** key, select the file or folder, and drag and drop on the new location.

> **ANOTHER WAY**
>
> Right-click a file or folder to display the context menu where you can select **Cut**, **Copy**, or **Paste**.

Rename Files and Folders

When you need to change the name of a file or folder, you can rename these in a Windows folder.

HOW TO: Rename a File or Folder

1. In a Windows folder, select the file or folder you want to rename.
2. Click the **Rename** button [*Home* tab, *Organize* group].
3. Type the new name of the file or folder and press **Enter**.

> **ANOTHER WAY**
>
> Select a file or folder to rename, press **F2**, type the new name, and press **Enter**. You can also right-click a file or folder and select **Rename** from the context menu.

Delete Files and Folders

You can also easily delete files and folders. When you delete a file or folder, it is moved from its current location to the ***Recycle Bin*** on your computer, which is the location where deleted items are stored. If a file or folder is in the *Recycle Bin,* you can restore this item to its original location or move it to a different location. You also have the option to permanently delete a file or folder; the item is deleted and not moved to the *Recycle Bin*. If an item is permanently deleted, you do not have the restore option.

There are several ways to delete a file or folder. To ensure that you don't delete anything by mistake, when you delete a file or folder, a confirmation dialog box opens, prompting you to confirm whether or not you want to delete the selected file or folder.

HOW TO: Delete Files and Folders

1. Select the file or folder you want to delete.
   - You can select multiple files and folders to delete at the same time.
2. Click the **Delete** drop-down arrow [*Home* tab, *Organize* group] to display the list of delete options (Figure 1-80).
3. Click **Recycle** or **Permanently delete**. A confirmation dialog box opens.
   - *Recycle* deletes the selected item(s) and moves them to the *Recycle Bin*.
   - *Permanently delete* deletes the item(s) from your computer.
   - The default action when you click the *Delete* button (not the drop-down arrow) is *Recycle*.
4. Click **Yes** to delete.

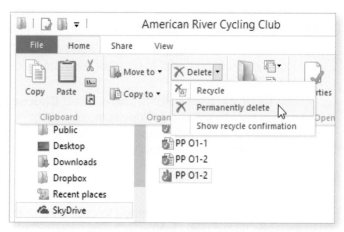

1-80 Delete selected files and folders

> **ANOTHER WAY**
>
> Press **Ctrl+D** or the **Delete** key on your keyboard to recycle selected item(s).
> Press **Shift+Delete** to permanently delete selected item(s).

Compressed and Zipped Folders

If you want to share multiple files or a folder of files with classmates, coworkers, friends, or family, you can *zip* the files into a *zipped folder* (also called a *compressed folder*). For example, you can't attach an entire folder to an email message, but you can attach a zipped folder to an email message. Compressing files and folders decreases their size. You can zip a group of selected files, a folder, or a combination of files and folders, and then share the zipped folder with others through email or in a cloud storage location such as *SkyDrive*.

HOW TO: Create a Zipped Folder

1. Select the file(s) and/or folder(s) you want to compress and send.
2. Click the **Zip** button [*Share* tab, *Send* group] (Figure 1-81). A zipped folder is created.
   - The name of the zipped folder is the name of the first item you selected to zip. You can rename this folder.
   - The icon for a zipped folder looks similar to the icon for a folder except it has a vertical zipper down the middle of the folder.

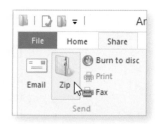

1-81 Create a zipped folder

> ### ANOTHER WAY
>
> Right-click a selected file(s) and/or folder(s), click **Send to**, and select **Compressed (zipped) folder**.

If you receive a zipped folder from someone via email, save the zipped folder and then you can *extract* its contents. Extracting a zipped folder creates a regular Window folder from the zipped folder.

HOW TO: Extract a Zipped Folder

1. After saving the zipped folder to a location on your computer, select the folder (Figure 1-82).
2. Click the **Extract all** button [*Compress Folder Tools Extract* tab]. The *Extract Compressed (Zipped) Folders* dialog box opens (Figure 1-83).
3. Click **Extract** to extract the folder.
   - Both the extracted folder and the zipped folder display in the folder where they are located.
   - If you check the **Show extracted files when complete** check box, the extracted folder will open after extracting.

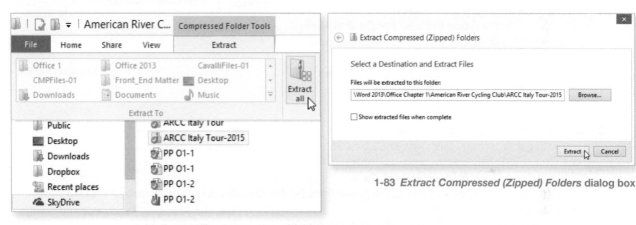

1-83 *Extract Compressed (Zipped) Folders* dialog box

1-82 Extract files from a zipped folder

PAUSE & PRACTICE: OFFICE 1-3

For this project, you copy and rename files in your *SkyDrive* folder on your computer, create a folder, move and copy files, create a zipped folder, and rename a zipped folder.

Files Needed: *[your initials] PP O1-1a.pptx*, *[your initials] PP O1-1b.xlsx*, and *[your initials] PP O1-2.docx*
Completed Project File Names: *[your initials] PP O1-3a.pptx*, *[your initials] PP O1-3b.xlsx*, *[your initials] PP O1-3c.docx*, and **ARCC Italy Tour-[current year]** (zipped folder)

1. Open your *SkyDrive* folder.
   a. From the Windows *Start* page, click the **File Explorer** or **Computer** tile to open a Windows folder. If these options are not available on the *Start* page, use *Search* to find and open the *File Explorer* or *Computer* window.

b. Click the **SkyDrive** folder on the left to display the folders in your *SkyDrive* folder.
   c. Double click the **American River Cycling Club** folder to open it.

2. Copy and rename files.
   a. Select the ***[your initials] PP O1-1a*** file (this is a PowerPoint file).
   b. Click the **Copy to** button [*Home* tab, *Organize* group] and select **Choose Location** to open the *Copy Items* dialog box (Figure 1-84).
   c. Select the **American River Cycling Club** folder in your *SkyDrive* folder and click **Copy**.
   d. Select the copy of the file (***[your initials] PP O1-1a – Copy***) and click the **Rename** button [*Home* tab, *Organize* group].
   e. Type [your initials] PP O1-3a and press **Enter**.
   f. Select the ***[your initials] PP O1-1b*** file (this is an Excel file).
   g. Press **Ctrl+C** to copy the file and then press **Ctrl+V** to paste a copy of the file.
   h. Rename this file [your initials] PP O1-3b.
   i. Right-click the ***[your initials] PP O1-2*** file (this is a Word file and the third one in the list) and select **Copy** from the context menu.
   j. Right-click a blank area of the open window and select **Paste** from the context menu.
   k. Rename this file [your initials] PP O1-3c.

1-84 Copy selected file

3. Create a new folder and move files.
   a. With the *American River Cycling Club* folder still open, click the **New folder** button on the upper left.
   b. Type ARCC Italy Tour and press **Enter**.
   c. Select the ***[your initials] PP O1-3a*** file.
   d. Hold down the **Ctrl** key, select the ***[your initials] PP O1-3b*** and ***[your initials] PP O1-3c*** files.
   e. Click the selected files and drag and drop on the *ARCC Italy Tour* folder (don't hold down the *Ctrl* key while dragging). The files are moved to the *ARCC Italy Tour* folder.
   f. Double-click the **ARCC Italy Tour** folder to open it and confirm the files are moved.
   g. Click the **Up** or **Back** arrow to return to the *American River Cycling Club* folder.

4. Create a zipped folder.
   a. Select the **ARCC Italy Tour** folder.
   b. Click the **Zip** button [*Share* tab, *Send* group]. A zipped (compressed) folder is created.
   c. Right-click the zipped folder and select **Rename** from the context menu.
   d. At the end of the folder name, type - (a hyphen), type the current year, and press **Enter** (Figure 1-85).

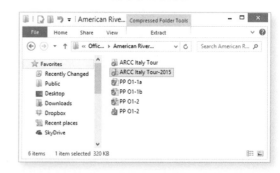

1-85 PP O1-3 completed

5. Email the zipped folder to your instructor.
   a. Using your email account, create a new email to send to your instructor.
   b. Include an appropriate subject line and a brief message in the body.
   c. Attach the ***ARCC Italy Tour-[current year]*** zipped folder to the email message.
   d. Send the email message.

Chapter Summary

1.1 Use the basic features of Windows 8 and Microsoft Office 2013 products (p. O1-2).

- **Windows 8** is the operating system on your computer.
- A **Microsoft account** is a free account you create. When you create a Microsoft account, you are given an email address, a **SkyDrive** account, and access to **Office Web Apps**.
- **SkyDrive** is the **cloud storage** area where you can store files in a private and secure online location.
- In Windows 8, the **SkyDrive folder** is one of your file storage location options.
- The **Start page** in Windows 8 is where you select what you want to do on your computer.
- The **Windows desktop** is the working area of Windows and the **Taskbar** is at the bottom of the desktop. You can pin applications to the *Taskbar*.
- The **File Explorer** is a window that displays libraries, files, and folders on your computer.
- You can access your *SkyDrive* folders and files using an Internet browser window.
- **Apps** are the applications or programs on your computer. App buttons are arranged in tiles on the Windows 8 *Start* page.
- You can customize the *Start* page to add, remove, or arrange apps.
- **Navigation options** display on the right side of your computer monitor when you put your pointer in the bottom right corner.
- **Office 2013** is application software that contains **Word**, **Excel**, **Access**, **PowerPoint**, **Outlook**, **OneNote**, and **Publisher**.
- **Office Web Apps** is free online software that works in conjunction with your online *SkyDrive* account.
- In *SkyDrive*, you can share Office files with others.
- When you open each of the Office applications, a **Start page** is displayed where you can open an existing file or create a new file.
- In the **Backstage view** in each of the Office applications, you can perform many common tasks such as saving, opening an existing file, creating a new file, printing, and sharing.
- **Office Help** contains searchable articles related to specific topics.

- Use the mouse (or touch pad) on your computer to navigate the pointer on your computer screen. Use the pointer or click buttons to select text or objects.
- When using Office 2013 on a tablet, use the touch screen to perform actions.

1.2 Create, save, close, and open Office files (p. O1-12).

- You can create a new Office file from the *Start* page or *Backstage* view of the Office application you are using.
- When you **save a file** for the first time, you give it a **file name**.
- You can create **folders** to organize saved files, and you can save a file as a different file name.
- A variety of different **file types** are used in each of the Office applications.
- You can close an Office file when you are finished working on it. If the file has not been saved or changes have been made to the file, you are prompted to save the file before closing.
- In each of the Office applications, you can open an existing file from the *Start* page or from the *Backstage* view.

1.3 Print, share, and customize Office files (p. O1-20).

- You can print a file in a variety of formats. The *Print* area on the *Backstage* view lists your print options and displays a preview of your file.
- You can export a file as a **PDF file** and save the PDF file to post to a web site or share with others.
- **Document properties** contain information about a file.
- You can **share** Office files in a variety of ways and allow others to view or edit shared files.
- **Program options** are available on the *Backstage* view. You can use the program options to make global changes to an Office application.

1.4 Use the Ribbon, tabs, groups, dialog boxes, task panes, galleries, and the Quick Access toolbar (p. O1-23).

- The **Ribbon** appears at the top of an Office window. It contains **tabs** and **groups** that allow you to access features you regularly use.

- The **Ribbon Display Options** provides different ways the *Ribbon* can be displayed in Office applications.
- Within groups on each tab are a variety of **buttons**, **drop-down lists**, and **galleries**.
- **Dialog boxes** contain additional features not always displayed on the *Ribbon*.
- Click the **launcher** in the bottom right corner of some groups to open a dialog box for that group.
- A **ScreenTip** displays information about commands on the *Ribbon*.
- Dialog boxes contain **radio buttons**, **check boxes**, **drop-down lists**, and **text boxes** you can use to apply features.
- The **Quick Access toolbar**, which contains buttons that allow you to perform commands, is displayed in all Office applications on the upper left.
- You can add or remove commands on the *Quick Access* toolbar.

1.5 Use context menus, mini toolbars, and keyboard shortcuts in Office applications (p. O1-27).

- A **context menu** displays when you right-click text or an object. The context menu contains different features depending on what you right-click.
- The **mini toolbar** is another context menu that displays formatting options.
- You can use **keyboard shortcuts** to apply features or commands.

1.6 Customize the view and display size in Office applications and work with multiple Office files (p. O1-31).

- In each of the Office applications, there are a variety of **views**.
- The **Zoom feature** changes the display size of your file.
- You can work with multiple Office files at the same time and switch between open files.

1.7 Organize and customize Office files and Windows folders (p. O1-34).

- **Folders** store and organize your files.
- You can create, move, or copy files and folders. Files stored in a folder are moved or copied with that folder.
- You can rename a file to change the file name.
- When you delete a file or folder, it is moved to the **Recycle Bin** on your computer by default. Alternatively, you can permanently delete files and folders.
- A **zipped (compressed) folder** makes it easier and faster to email or share multiple files. You can zip files and/or folders into a zipped folder.
- When you receive a zipped folder, you can **extract** the zipped folder to create a regular Windows folder and access its contents.

Check for Understanding

In the **Online Learning Center** for this text (www.mhhe.com/office2013inpractice), there are a variety of resources that can be used to review the concepts covered in this chapter.

The following Online Learning Resources are available in the Online Learning Center:

- Multiple choice questions
- Short answer questions
- Matching exercises

In these projects, you use your *SkyDrive* to store files. If you don't have a Microsoft account, see *SLO 1.1: Using Windows 8 and Office 2013* for information about obtaining a free personal Microsoft account.

Guided Project 1-1

For this project, you organize and edit files for Emma Cavalli at Placer Hills Real Estate. You extract a zipped folder, rename files, manage multiple documents, and apply formatting.
[Student Learning Outcomes 1.1, 1.2, 1.4, 1.5, 1.6, 1.7]

Files Needed: ***CavalliFiles-01*** (zipped folder)
Completed Project File Names: ***[your initials] Office 1-1a.docx***, ***[your initials] Office 1-1b.docx***, ***[your initials] Office 1-1c.xlsx***, and ***[your initials] Office 1-1d.pptx***

Skills Covered in This Project

- Copy and paste a zipped folder.
- Create a new folder in your *SkyDrive* folder.
- Extract a zipped folder.
- Move a file.
- Rename a file.
- Open a Word document.
- Switch between two open Word documents.

- Save a Word document with a different file name.
- Change display size.
- Use a mini toolbar, keyboard shortcut, context menu, and dialog box to apply formatting to selected text.
- Close a Word document.

1. Copy a zipped folder and create a new *SkyDrive* folder.
   a. From the Windows *Start* page, click **File Explorer** or **Computer** to open a Windows folder. If these options are not available on the *Start* page, use *Search* to find and open a Windows folder.
   b. Browse to the location on your computer where you store your student data files.
   c. Select the ***CavalliFiles-01*** zipped folder and press **Ctrl+C** to copy the folder.
   d. Select your **SkyDrive** folder at the left and click the **New folder** button to create a new folder.
   e. Type PHRE and press **Enter**.
   f. Press **Enter** again to open the *PHRE* folder.
   g. Press **Ctrl+V** to paste the copied ***CavalliFiles-01*** zipped folder in the *PHRE* folder.

2. Extract a zipped folder.
   a. Select the ***CavalliFiles-01*** zipped folder.
   b. Click the **Compressed Folder Tools Extract** tab and click the **Extract all** button. The *Extract Compressed (Zipped) Folders* dialog box opens.
   c. Deselect the **Show extracted files when complete** check box.
   d. Click the **Extract** button. The zipped folder is extracted and there are now two *CavalliFiles-01* folders. One folder is zipped and the other is a regular folder.
   e. Select the zipped ***CavalliFiles-01*** folder and press **Delete** to delete the zipped folder.

3. Move and rename files.
   a. With the *PHRE* folder still open, double-click the **CavalliFiles-01** folder to open it.
   b. Click the first file, press and hold the **Shift** key, and click the last file to select all four files.
   c. Press **Ctr+X** to cut the files from the current location.

d. Click the **Up** button to move up to the *PHRE* folder (Figure 1-86).
e. Press **Ctrl+V** to paste and move the files.
f. Select the ***Cavalli files-01*** folder and press **Delete** to delete the folder.
g. Select the ***CavalliPHRE-01*** file, click the **File** tab, and click the **Rename** button [*Organize* group].
h. Type [your initials] Office 1-1a and press **Enter**.
i. Right-click the ***FixedMortgageRates-01*** file and select the **Rename** from the context menu.
j. Type [your initials] Office 1-1b and press **Enter**.

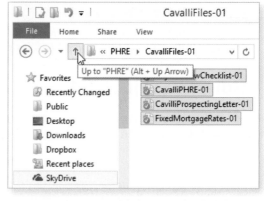

1-86 Go up to the *PHRE* folder

4. Open two Word documents and rename a Word document.
   a. Press the **Ctrl** key and click the ***BuyerEscrowChecklist-01*** and ***CavalliProspectingLetter-01*** files to select both files.
   b. Press the **Enter** key to open both files in Word.
   c. If the *BuyerEscrowChecklist-01* document is not displayed, click the **Switch Documents** button [*View* tab, *Window* group] and select ***BuyerEscrowChecklist-01***. You can also switch documents by selecting the document on the *Taskbar*.
   d. Click the **File** tab and select **Save As** at the left.
   e. Select **[your name's] SkyDrive** in the *Places* area and select the **PHRE** folder or click **Browse** and select the **PHRE** folder. The *Save As* dialog box opens.
   f. Type [your initials] Office 1-1c in the *File name* text box and click **Save**.
   g. Press **Ctrl+W** to close the document. The *Cavalli Prospecting Letter_01* remains open.

5. Change display size and edit and rename a Word document.
   a. Click the **Zoom In** or **Zoom Out** button at the bottom right of the document window to change the display size to 120% (Figure 1-87). This will vary depending on the current display size.

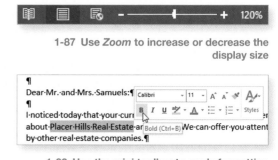

1-87 Use *Zoom* to increase or decrease the display size

   b. Select "**Placer Hills Real Estate**" in the first body paragraph of the letter and the mini toolbar is displayed (Figure 1-88).
   c. Click the **Bold** button on the mini toolbar to apply bold formatting to the selected text.

1-88 Use the mini toolbar to apply formatting

   d. Select the first sentence in the second body paragraph ("**I am also a Whitney Hills . . .** ") and press **Ctrl+I** to apply italic formatting to the selected sentence.
   e. Select the text that reads "**Emma Cavalli**," below "Best regards."
   f. Right-click the selected text and select **Font** from the context menu to open the *Font* dialog box.
   g. Check the **Small Caps** check box in the *Effects* area and click **OK** to close the *Font* dialog box.
   h. With "**Emma Cavalli**" still selected, click the **Bold** button [*Home* tab, *Font* group].
   i. Press **F12** to open the *Save As* dialog box.
   j. Type [your initials] Office 1-1d in the *File name* text box and click **Save**.
   k. Click the **X** in the upper right corner of the document window to close the document and close Word.

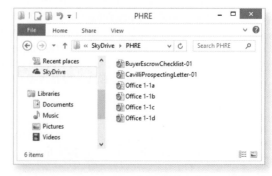

6. Your *PHRE* folder should contain the files shown in Figure 1-89.

1-89 Office 1-1 completed

Guided Project 1-2

For this project, you modify an Excel file for Hamilton Civic Center. You rename a file, add document properties, use *Help* to search a topic, share the file, and export a file as a PDF file.
[Student Learning Outcomes 1.1, 1.2, 1.3, 1.4]

Note to Students and Instructor:
Students: *For this project, you share an Office file with your instructor.*
Instructor: *In order to complete this project, your students need your Microsoft email address. You can create a new Live or Hotmail account for projects in this chapter.*

File Needed: ***HCCYoga-01.xlsx***
Completed Project File Names: ***[your initials] Office 1-2.xlsx*** and ***[your initials] Office 1-2.pdf***

Skills Covered in This Project

- Open Excel and an Excel workbook.
- Create a new *SkyDrive* folder.
- Save an Excel workbook with a different file name.
- Add document properties to a file.

- Use *Microsoft Excel Help* to search for a topic.
- Open a Word document.
- Share a file.
- Export a file as a PDF file.

1. Open Excel 2013 and open an Excel workbook.
   a. From the Windows *Start* page, click **Excel 2013** to open this application. If Excel 2013 is not available on the *Start* page, use *Search* to find and open it.
   b. From the Excel *Start* page, click **Open Other Workbooks** to display the *Open* area of the *Backstage* view.
   c. In the *Places* area, select where your student data files are stored and click the **Browse** button to open the *Open* dialog box.
   d. Browse to the location where your student data files are stored, select the ***HCCYoga-01*** file, and click **Open** to open the Excel workbook.

2. Save a file as a different file name in your *SkyDrive* folder.
   a. Click the **File** tab to open the *Backstage* view and select **Save As** at the left.
   b. In the *Places* area, select **[your name's] SkyDrive**.
   c. Click the **Browse** button to open the *Save As* dialog box.
   d. Select the **SkyDrive** folder on the left and click the **New folder** button to create a new folder.
   e. Type HCC and press **Enter**.
   f. Double-click the **HCC** folder to open it.
   g. In the *File name* area, type [your initials] Office 1-2 and click **Save** to close the dialog box and save the file.

3. Add document properties to the Excel workbook.
   a. Click the **File** button to open the *Backstage* view and select **Info** on the left. The document properties are displayed on the right.
   b. Put your insertion point in the *Title* text box ("Add a title") and type Yoga Classes.
   c. Click the **Show All Properties** link to display more properties.

d. Put your insertion point in the *Company* text box and type Hamilton Civic Center.
   e. Click the **back arrow** in the upper left of the *Backstage* window to return to the Excel workbook.

4. Use *Help* to learn about a topic.
   a. Click **Microsoft Excel Help** button (question mark) in the upper right corner of the Excel window or press **F1** to open the *Excel Help* dialog box.
   b. Put your insertion point in the *Search help* text box, type AutoSum, and press **Enter**.
   c. Click the first link and read about *AutoSum*.
   d. Click the **Back** button to return to the search list of articles and click the second link.
   e. Read about *AutoSum* and then click the **X** in the upper right corner to close the *Excel Help* dialog box.

5. Share an Excel workbook with your instructor.
   a. Click the **File** tab and select **Share** at the left.
   b. In the *Share* area, select **Invite People** (Figure 1-90).
   c. Type your instructor's email address in the *Type names or email addresses* area.
   d. In the drop-down list to the right of the email address, select **Can edit**.
   e. In the body, type a brief message.
   f. Click the **Share** button.
   g. Click the **Save** button to save and return to the workbook.

1-90 Invite people to share a file

6. Export the Excel workbook as a PDF file.
   a. Click the **File** button and select **Export** at the left.
   b. In the *Export* area, select **Create PDF/XPS Document** and click the **Create PDF/XPS** button. The *Publish as PDF or XPS* dialog box opens.
   c. Check the **Open file after publishing** check box. The publish location and file name are the same as the Excel file; don't change these.
   d. Click **Publish** to create and open the PDF file (Figure 1-91). The PDF file opens in an Internet browser window in *SkyDrive*.
   e. Close the Internet browser window.

7. Save and close the Excel file.
   a. Click the **Excel** icon on the Windows *Taskbar* to display the Excel file.
   b. Press **Ctrl+S** to save the file.
   c. Click the **X** in the upper right corner of the Excel window to close the file and Excel.

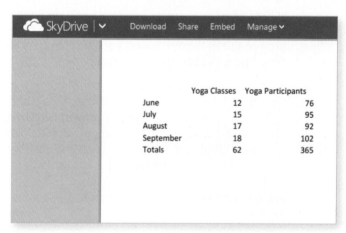

1-91 PDF file displayed in *SkyDrive*

Independent Project 1-3

For this project, you organize and edit files for Courtyard Medical Plaza. You extract a zipped folder, rename files, export a file as a PDF file, and share a file in *SkyDrive*.
[Student Learning Outcomes 1.1, 1.3, 1.6, 1.7]

Note to Students and Instructor:
Students: *For this project, you share an* Office Web App *file with your instructor.*
Instructor: *In order to complete this project, your students need your Microsoft email address.*
You can create a new Live or Hotmail account for projects in this chapter.

Files Needed: **CMPFiles-01** (zipped folder)
Completed Project File Names: **[your initials] Office 1-3a.pptx, [your initials] Office 1-3a-pdf.pdf,**
[your initials] Office 1-3b.accdb, [your initials] Office 1-3c.xlsx, and **[your initials] Office 1-3d.docx**

Skills Covered in This Project

- Copy and paste a zipped folder.
- Create a new folder in your *SkyDrive* folder.
- Extract a zipped folder.
- Move a file.
- Rename a file.
- Open a PowerPoint presentation.
- Export a file as a PDF file.
- Use *SkyDrive* to share a file.

1. Copy a zipped folder and create a new *SkyDrive* folder.
   a. Using a Windows folder, browse to locate the **CMPFiles-01** zipped folder in your student data files and copy the zipped folder.
   b. Go to your *SkyDrive* folder and create a new folder named Courtyard Medical Plaza within the *SkyDrive* folder.

2. Copy and extract the zipped folder and move files.
   a. Paste the zipped folder in the *Courtyard Medical Plaza* folder.
   b. Extract the zipped folder and then delete the zipped folder.
   c. Open the **CMPFiles-01** folder and move all of the files to the *Courtyard Medical Plaza* folder.
   d. Delete the **CMPFiles-01** folder.

3. Rename files in the *Courtyard Medical Plaza* folder.
   a. Rename the **CMPStayingActive-01** PowerPoint file to [your initials] Office 1-3a.
   b. Rename the **CourtyardMedicalPlaza-01** Access file to [your initials] Office 1-3b.
   c. Rename the **EstimatedCalories-01** Excel file to [your initials] Office 1-3c.
   d. Rename the **StayingActive-01** Word file to [your initials] Office 1-3d.

4. Export a PowerPoint file as a PDF file.
   a. From the *Courtyard Medical Plaza* folder, open the **[your initials] Office 1-3a** file. The file opens in PowerPoint.
   b. Export this file as a PDF file. Don't have the PDF file open after publishing.
   c. Save the file as [your initials] Office 1-3a-pdf and save in the *Courtyard Medical Plaza* folder.
   d. Close the PowerPoint file and exit PowerPoint.

5. Use *SkyDrive* to share a file with your instructor.
    a. Open an Internet browser window and log in to your *SkyDrive* (www. skydrive.com) using your Microsoft account.
    b. Go to your *SkyDrive* files and open the **Courtyard Medical Plaza** folder.
    c. Open the *[your initials] Office 1-3a* file in PowerPoint Web App.
    d. Share this file with your instructor.
    e. Send an email to share the file and include your instructor's email address and a brief message. Allow your instructor to edit the file.
    f. Sign out of *SkyDrive*.

6. Close the Windows folder containing the files for this project (Figure 1-92).

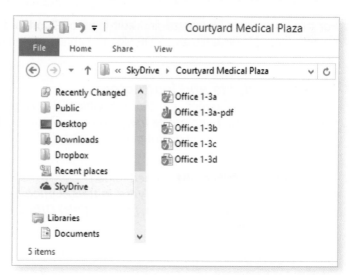

1-92 Office 1-3 completed

Independent Project 1-4

For this project, you modify a Word file for Life's Animal Shelter. You rename the document, add document properties, modify the document, share a link to the document, export a document as a PDF file, and create a zipped folder.
[Student Learning Outcomes 1.1, 1.2, 1.3, 1.4, 1.5, 1.6, 1.7]

Note to Students and Instructor:
Students: *For this project, you share an Office file with your instructor.*
Instructor: *In order to complete this project, your students need your Microsoft email address. You can create a new Live or Hotmail account for projects in this chapter.*

File Needed: ***LASSupportLetter-01.docx***
Completed Project File Names: *[your initials] Office 1-4.docx*, *[your initials] Office 1-4.pdf*, and *LAS files* (zipped folder)

Skills Covered in This Project

-   Open Excel and an Excel file.
-   Create a new *SkyDrive* folder.
-   Save a file with a different file name.
-   Apply formatting to selected text.
-   Add document properties to the file.

-   Use *Microsoft Excel Help* to search for a topic.
-   Open a Word document.
-   Share a file.
-   Export a file as a PDF file.

1. Open Word 2013 and open a Word document.
   a. From the Windows *Start* page, open Word 2013.
   b. From the Word *Start* page, open the ***LASSupportLetter-01*** document from your student data files.

2. Create a new folder and save the document with a different file name.
   a. Open the **Save As** dialog box and create a new folder named LAS in your *SkyDrive* folder.
   b. Save this document as [your initials] Office 1-4.

3. Apply formatting changes to the document using a dialog box, keyboard shortcut, and mini toolbar.
   a. Select "**To**" and use the **launcher** to open the *Font* dialog box.
   b. Apply **Bold** and **All caps** to the selected text.
   c. Repeat the formatting on the other three memo guide words: "**From**," "**Date**," and "**Subject**."
   d. Select "**Life's Animal Shelter**" in the first sentence of the first body paragraph and use the keyboard shortcut to apply **bold** formatting.
   e. Select the first sentence in the second body paragraph ("**Would you again consider** . . . ") and use the mini toolbar to apply **italic** formatting.

4. Add the following document properties to the document:
   Title: Support Letter
   Company: Life's Animal Shelter

5. Get a link to share this document with your instructor.
   a. Create and copy an **Edit Link** you can email to your instructor.
   b. Create a new email to send to your professor using the email you use for this course.
   c. Include an appropriate subject line and a brief message in the body.
   d. Paste the link in the body of the email message and send the message.

6. Use the keyboard shortcut to **save** the file before continuing.

7. Export this document as a PDF file.
   a. Save the file in the same location and use the same file name.
   b. Close the PDF file if it opens after publishing.

8. Save and close the Word file and exit Word (Figure 1-93).

9. Create a zipped folder.
   a. Using a Windows folder, open the **LAS** folder in your *SkyDrive* folder.
   b. Select the two files and create a zipped folder.
   c. Rename the zipped folder LAS files (Figure 1-94).

10. Close the open Windows folder.

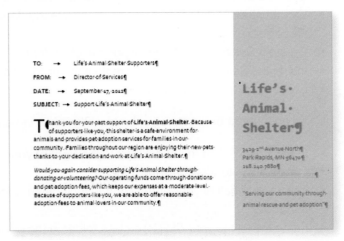

1-93 Office 1-4 completed

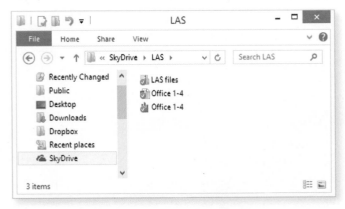

1-94 Office 1-4 completed

O1-47

Challenge Project 1-5

For this project, you create folders to organize your files for this class and use *SkyDrive* to share a link with your professor.
[Student Learning Outcomes 1.1, 1.7]

Note to Students and Instructor:

Students: *For this project, you share an Office file with your instructor.*
Instructor: *In order to complete this project, your students need your Microsoft email address. You can create a new Live or Hotmail account for projects in this chapter.*

File Needed: None
Completed Project File Name: Email link to shared folder to your instructor

Using a Windows folder, create *SkyDrive* folders to contain all of the files for this class. Organize your files and folders according to the following guidelines:

* Create a *SkyDrive* folder for this class.
* Create a *Student data files* folder inside the class folder.
* Extract student data files if you have not already done so. Make sure they are in the *Student data files* folder.
* Create a *Solution files* folder inside the class folder.
* Inside the *Solution files* folder, create a folder for each chapter.
* Create a folder to store miscellaneous class files such as the syllabus and other course handouts.

Using an Internet browser, log in to your *SkyDrive* and share your class folder with your instructor.

* In *SkyDrive*, select the check box to the right of your class folder and click the **Share** button.
* Create a link to *View only* the folder.
* Create an email to your professor and include an appropriate subject line and a brief message in the body.
* Paste the link to your *SkyDrive* class folder in the body of the email message and send the email.

Challenge Project 1-6

For this project, you save a file as a different file name, customize the *Quick Access* toolbar, share a file with your professor, and export a file as a PDF file.
[Student Learning Outcomes 1.1, 1.2, 1.3, 1.4]

Note to Students and Instructor:
Students: *For this project, you share an Office file with your instructor.*
Instructor: *In order to complete this project, your students need your Microsoft email address.
You can create a new Live or Hotmail account for projects in this chapter.*

File Needed: Use an existing Office file
Completed Project File Name: ***[your initials] Office 1-6***

Open an existing Word, Excel, or PowerPoint file. Save this file in a *SkyDrive* folder and name it ***[your initials] Office 1-6***. If you don't have any of these files, use one from your Pause & Practice projects or select a file from your student data files.

With your file open, perform the following actions:

- Customize the *Quick Access* toolbar to add command buttons. Add commands such as *New*, *Open*, *Quick Print*, and *Spelling* that you use regularly in the Office application.
- Share your file with your instructor. Use *Invite People* and include your instructor's email, an appropriate subject line, and a brief message in the body. Allow your instructor to edit the file.
- Export the document as a PDF file. Use the same file name and save it in the same *SkyDrive* folder as your open file.

Microsoft® Office
IN PRACTICE

powerpoint

Creating and Editing Presentations

POWERPOINT

CHAPTER OVERVIEW

Microsoft PowerPoint is the leading presentation software. Whether you need to create a quick display or a very polished presentation with dazzling graphics, creative animation effects, and video, PowerPoint has all the tools you need. You can use PowerPoint for slide shows with computer projection equipment in meeting rooms, for self-running presentations viewed by individuals, or for presentations shown on the web. This chapter covers the basics of starting and editing a PowerPoint presentation.

STUDENT LEARNING OUTCOMES (SLOs)

After completing this chapter, you will be able to:

SLO 1.1 Create, open, and save a presentation (p. P1-3).

SLO 1.2 Develop presentation content by adding slides, choosing layouts, moving and resizing placeholders, editing text, and reusing slides from another presentation (p. P1-14).

SLO 1.3 Rearrange presentation content by moving, copying and pasting, duplicating, and deleting slides (p. P1-22).

SLO 1.4 Use the *Slide Master* to change theme colors and fonts (p. P1-26).

SLO 1.5 Use headers and footers to add identifying information (p. P1-29).

SLO 1.6 Insert, resize, and align a picture from a file (p. P1-33).

SLO 1.7 Apply and modify transition effects to add visual interest (p. P1-35).

SLO 1.8 Preview a presentation and print slides, handouts, and outlines (p. P1-37).

SLO 1.9 Change presentation properties (p. P1-39).

CASE STUDY

Hamilton Civic Center (HCC) is a nonprofit community fitness center with an indoor pool, sauna, indoor track, exercise room, racquetball courts, and meeting rooms. HCC partners with the local hospital to bring doctors and nurses in to provide classes on a variety of health and wellness issues for adults. It also works with local schools to support their academic programs and sponsors events for children, including a summer day care program.

For the Pause & Practice projects in this chapter, you create and modify a presentation about training for an upcoming marathon that is being promoted to members by the Civic Center.

Pause & Practice 1-1: Create a presentation and develop text content.

Pause & Practice 1-2: Impose consistency to a presentation's design.

Pause & Practice 1-3: Add interest with pictures and apply transitions. Print supplements.

Creating, Opening, and Saving Presentations

In this section, you explore how to start and view a PowerPoint presentation and to save a presentation in different formats. It is important to save a presentation before closing it so you can access it again if necessary. If you close the presentation before saving it, your content is lost.

Create a Presentation

When PowerPoint first opens, you are presented with several ways to start a new presentation or open an existing presentation. Clickable images called *thumbnails* have a name below each one. If you prefer to work on text content only, click the **Blank Presentation** thumbnail to go directly to your first slide so you can begin developing content.

Other thumbnails represent built-in *Themes* that provide a unified look for all the slides in a presentation. One theme has a plain, dark background while most of them have a background design. When you click a theme, a dialog box opens where you can choose from different color combinations called *Variants.* Then you start developing content.

The following examples demonstrate ways to start a presentation.

HOW TO: Create a Presentation When First Opening PowerPoint

1. Open PowerPoint and you will automatically see the *Backstage* view (Figure 1-1).
2. Click the **Blank Presentation** theme to go directly to your first slide.

Or

3. Click a **Theme** to open a dialog box (Figure 1-2).
4. Click the arrow buttons below the slide to see h ow colors are applied to different layouts.

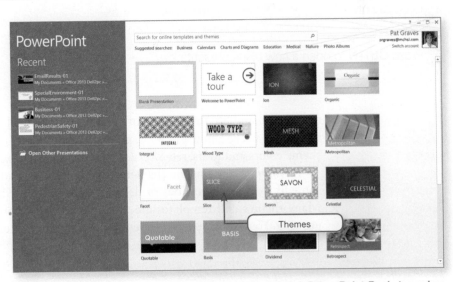

1-1 PowerPoint *Backstage* view

5. Select one of four *Variants* that provide different color combinations.

6. Click **Create**.

1-2 Theme *Variants*

When you create a new presentation, the PowerPoint title bar displays the generic name *Presentation1*. When you create additional new presentations, PowerPoint names them *Presentation2, Presentation3,* and so on, until you save the presentations and the new names appear in the title bar.

> **MORE INFO**
>
> When your content is complete, save your presentation (discussed on pages P1-10–P1-13) and then close it. Click the **File** tab, and then click **Close**. To close PowerPoint, click the **Close** button in the upper right corner of the title bar.

HOW TO: Create a New Presentation when PowerPoint is Open

1. Click the **File** tab to open the *Backstage* view.
2. Click the **New** button.
3. Select a *Theme* and *Variant*.
4. Click **Create**.

Or

5. Press **Ctrl+N** to open a new blank presentation.

Themes simplify the process of creating professional-looking presentations. They provide consistent background graphics, colors, and font settings. For more on selecting different theme colors and fonts, see *SLO 1.4: Working with Themes*.

A **template** contains the characteristics of a theme and usually provides sample content you can edit for your own slides or delete if you want only the background a template provides. Many themes and templates are available at Office.com and the online collection is ever-growing. You can save downloaded themes and templates so they are available for future use.

> **MORE INFO**
>
> Your computer must be connected to the Internet to download themes and templates.

HOW TO: Create a New Presentation from Online Templates and Themes

1. Click the **File** tab to open the *Backstage* view.

2. Click the **New** button. In the search box, type a keyword and click the **Start searching** button (Figure 1-3). Available templates and themes appear.

   - Filter your results by typing the word or before another search word and searching again.

Or

3. Click one of the *Suggested searches* for general topics, and available templates and themes will appear.

   - Filter your results by clicking one of the terms in the *Category* list on the right (Figure 1-4).
   - Filter your results by typing the word or before another search word and searching again.

4. Click a template thumbnail to open a dialog box to review other slides in addition to the title slide. Some templates include a description.

5. Click **Create**.

6. The presentation opens; it may contain sample content that you need to delete before adding your content.

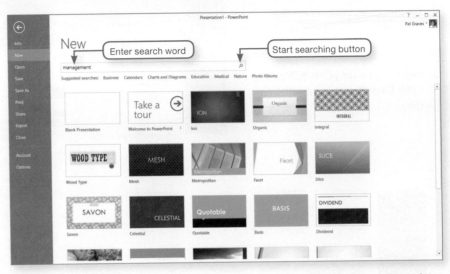

1-3 Search for online themes and templates

1-4 Search results for online themes and templates

You can use an existing presentation to start a new presentation. To do this, open a presentation file from a source such as your computer, USB drive, local network, cloud space such as SkyDrive, or an email attachment.

HOW TO: Open a Recent Presentation

1. With PowerPoint open, click the **File** tab to open the *Backstage* view.

2. Click the **Open** button.

3. Select **Recent Presentations** below the *Open* title.

4. Click a presentation on the right (Figure 1-5) to open it.

Or

5. Select your **SkyDrive**, then click **Browse** to locate the file (Figure 1-6).

1-5 Open a recent presentation

1-6 Open a presentation saved on your *SkyDrive*

> **MORE INFO**
>
> For instructions to set up a SkyDrive account, refer to *SLO 1.1 Using Windows 8 and Office 2013 in Office Chapter 1, Windows 8 and Office 2013 Overview.*

Or

6. Select **Computer** and then click **Browse** to locate the file on your computer or other place such as a USB drive or local network (Figure 1-7).

7. Select the file and click **Open**.

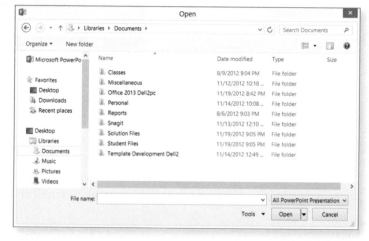

1-7 *Open* dialog box

> **ANOTHER WAY**
>
> **Ctrl+O** opens the *Backstage* view where you can open a presentation.

Views

PowerPoint provides different views to help you create slides, organize them, and display them in a slide show. When you start a new presentation, it opens in *Normal* view. The *Ribbon* is displayed across the top of the window and has nine tabs with commands organized in groups (Figure 1-8). Additional tabs, such as the *Drawing Tools Format* tab, open depending on what you are doing. Some tabs contain commands similar to those in Word, whereas other tabs display features that are unique to PowerPoint.

1-8 PowerPoint *Ribbon* with *Home* tab displayed

The area below the *Ribbon* is divided into two panes that display slide thumbnails on the left and a large area for working on individual slides. You can change views using commands on the *View* tab [*View* tab, *Presentation Views* group] (Figure 1-9) or the *View* buttons on the *Status bar* at the bottom of the window.

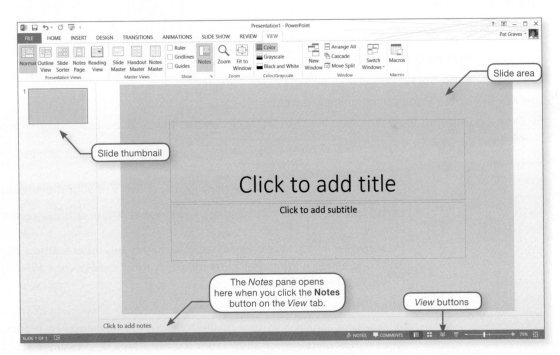

1-9 *Normal* view with *View* tab and *Notes* pane displayed

The five *Presentation Views* with commands on the *View* tab include the following:

- **Normal:** This is the default view where you enter the content of the slides and move between slides as you develop them. Click the *Normal* button or the *Notes* button to open a *Notes* pane below the slide to add speaker notes for individual slides.
- **Outline View:** This view expands the pane at the left of your slide area to show slide titles and bulleted text. Slide thumbnails are not displayed.

- **Slide Sorter:** This view displays slides as thumbnails so it is easy to reorganize slides and apply transition effects to control how the slides advance.
- **Notes Page:** This view displays each slide on a page with space below the slide where you can type speaker notes. You can also use the *Notes* pane below each slide to type speaker notes.
- **Reading View:** This view displays the slide show at full-screen or another window size controlled by the viewer. Navigation controls are in the *Status bar* at the bottom of the window.
- **Slide Master, Handout Master, and Notes Master:** These views are used to make changes that affect the whole presentation.

View Buttons are located on the *Status bar* to provide easy access regardless of which tab is currently open (Figure 1-10).

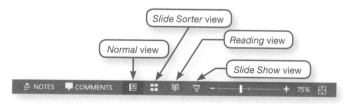

1-10 *View* buttons

HOW TO: Change Views

1. Click the **View** tab. Note that *Normal* is selected in the *Presentation Views* group.
2. Click the **Outline** button on the *View* tab.
3. Click the **Slide Sorter** button on the *View* tab or *Status bar*.
4. Click the **Notes Page** button on the *View* tab.
5. Click the **Reading View** button on the *View* tab or *Status bar*. To return to *Normal* view, click the **Normal** button on the *Status bar*.

Two more views are very important for the delivery of your presentation.

- **Slide Show view:** This view displays slides one at a time at full-screen size for audience viewing.
- **Presenter View:** This view displays speaker notes and other features that are helpful for delivering a presentation. For more on this feature, see *Presenter View* in *SLO 3.5: Controlling Display Options*.

While developing your presentation, test it in *Slide Show* view so you can see the content in the way your audience will see it, and rehearse your presentation before using it.

Start a presentation slide show from the beginning by pressing **F5**; start with the current slide by clicking the **Slide Show** button on the *Status bar*. You may also use buttons on the *Slide Show* tab (Figure 1-11).

1-11 *Slide Show* tab

HOW TO: Start a Presentation from the Slide Show Tab

1. Click the **Slide Show** tab.
2. Click the **From Beginning** button [*Start Slide Show* group] to display slides from the beginning, regardless of which slide is the current slide.
3. Click the **From Current Slide** button to display slides starting with the current slide.
4. To move through the slides, click the screen or press one of several keys on the keyboard: **spacebar**, **arrow keys**, **Enter**, **Page Down**, or **N**.

Adjust Pane Sizes in Normal View

You can adjust the pane size to help you better focus on one aspect of your presentation. For example, you can make slide thumbnails larger or increase the area for notes. In each case, the slide becomes a little smaller.

HOW TO: Adjust Pane Sizes

1. Point to the border line separating the slide thumbnails and the slide area until your pointer turns into a sizing pointer with two arrows (Figure 1-12).

2. Click and drag the pane border to the right to make the thumbnails larger and to the left to make the thumbnails smaller.

3. If the *Notes* pane is not open, click the **Notes** button [*View* tab, *Show* group].

4. With the sizing pointer, click and drag the pane border line between the *Slide* area and the *Notes* pane up to make the *Notes* pane larger or down to make it smaller.

5. With the sizing pointer, click and drag the *Notes* pane border line down to the bottom of the window or click the **Notes** button to remove this area.

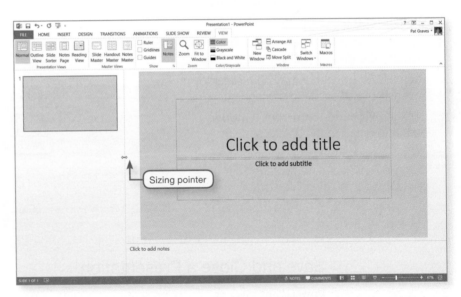

1-12 Slide thumbnail and *Notes* pane size is increased

Use Zoom

Use **Zoom** to increase the size of the slide on which you are working when you need to see detail. You can set a specific magnification level by using the *Zoom* dialog box or adjust the magnification by using the *Zoom* slider. You can use *Zoom* on the *Slide Sorter* view also.

HOW TO: Use the Zoom Dialog Box

1. Click the **Zoom** button [*View* tab, *Zoom* group].
2. Select a preset zoom percentage or enter a percentage number such as 200% (Figure 1-13).
3. Click **OK**. The slide size is increased and you can see only a portion of the slide
4. Click the **Fit slide to window** button [*View* tab, *Zoom* group] to return to the default setting so the entire slide is displayed.

1-13 *Zoom* dialog box

The *Zoom* controls are located on the right side of the *Status bar* and the current slide size percentage is shown. At 100%, the slider is in the center. Drag the slider or click the **Zoom** buttons to adjust the slide size.

HOW TO: Use the Zoom Controls

1. Click the **Zoom Out** button several times to decrease the view to 50% (Figure 1-14).
2. Drag the *Zoom* slider to the center.
3. Click the **Zoom In** button several times to increase the view to 150%.
4. Click the left or right of the *Zoom* slider to increase or decrease the percentage.
5. Click the **Fit slide to current window** button to return to the default setting.
6. Click the percentage to open the *Zoom* dialog box. Select a percentage and click **OK** to close the dialog box.

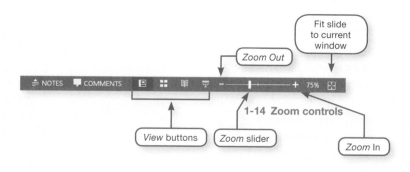

1-14 Zoom controls

Save and Close a Presentation

PowerPoint gives each new presentation a generic name, so you should name each presentation the first time you save it.

HOW TO: Save a Presentation

1. Click the **File** tab to open the *Backstage* view.
2. Click **Save** or **Save As** to display the *Save As* area (Figure 1-15).
3. Select the place where you want to save your presentation. You can save to your SkyDrive, computer, or other place such as a different web location.
4. Select a folder in the *Current Folder* or *Recent Folders* area or click the **Browse** button to open the *Save As* dialog box (Figure 1-16).

5. Browse to the folder on your computer or other place to save the file.
6. Type the file name in the *File name* area.
7. Click the **Save** button.

1-15 *Save As* area on the *Backstage* view

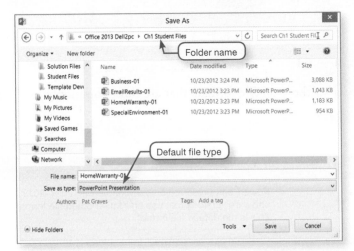

1-16 *Save As* dialog box

When saving for the first time, you can also click the **Save** button on the *Quick Access* toolbar, or press **Ctrl+S**, to open the *Save As* area on the *Backstage* view. As you make revisions to your presentation, simply clicking the **Save** button on the *Quick Access* toolbar will resave it with the same name in the same location.

If you want to create a second version of that file, then click the **File** tab and the **Save As** button to resave it with a different name in the same or different location. The original presentation is not affected by any changes you make to the second presentation.

> ### ANOTHER WAY
> Press **F12** to open the *Save As* dialog box.

You can save PowerPoint presentations in a variety of formats. By default, PowerPoint 2013 presentations are saved with the *.pptx* file extension. To change the type of presentation format, select the format of your choice from the *Save as type* area in the *Save As* dialog box (Figure 1-17).

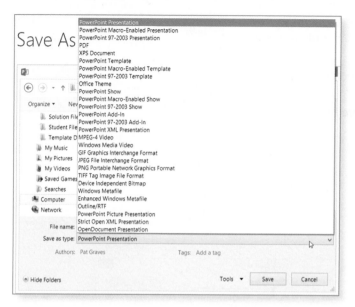

1-17 *Save As* file types

The following table lists some of the available formats that are most commonly used for PowerPoint.

Save Formats

Type of Presentation	File Extension	Uses of this Format
PowerPoint Presentation	.pptx	PowerPoint presentation compatible with 2007–2013 software versions that use an XML-enabled file format. This is the default file format.
PowerPoint 97-2003 Presentation	.ppt	PowerPoint presentation compatible with 1997–2003 software versions. Current software features are not supported.
PDF (Portable Document Format)	.pdf	Similar to pictures of slides, with each slide shown as a separate page. The file size may be smaller than the original presentation, so this format often works well for presentations distributed electronically.
PowerPoint Template	.potx	PowerPoint template that can be used to format future presentations.
Windows Media Video or MPEG-4 Video	.wmv or .mp4	PowerPoint presentation saved as a video that will play on many media players. Three resolution sizes are available, and all create large file sizes.
Outline/RTF	.rtf	A presentation text-only outline with a small file size for easy sharing.
PowerPoint Picture Presentation	.pptx	PowerPoint presentation that converts each slide into an image. It helps to reduce file size or create images for inclusion in other documents.
Open Document Presentation	.odp	PowerPoint presentation that can be opened in applications that use the *Open Document Presentation* format, such as Google.Docs or Open Office.org.

> **MORE INFO**
>
> Other file formats are used to save individual slides or images on slides. These graphic file formats include .jpg, .png, .tif, .bmp, .wmf, or .emf. These formats are explained on page P1-34.

When you are finished with a presentation, save your final version and then close the presentation. Click the **File** tab, and then click **Close**. To close PowerPoint, click the **Close** button in the upper right corner of the title bar.

Share and Export Options

From the *Backstage* view you have options for ***sharing*** (Figure 1-18) or ***exporting*** (Figure 1-19) your presentation using different file formats. Although these options take advantage of the distribution capabilities of Microsoft Office, not all classroom computer lab configurations permit access to shared online sites or network locations.

1-18 *Share* options

Share

- ***Invite People:*** Saves your presentation to a *SkyDrive* location so you can share it with people.
- ***Email:*** Sends your presentation as an attachment in the file type you choose.
- ***Present Online:*** Requires a Microsoft account so people can link to your slide show through a web browser.
- ***Publish Slides:*** Sends presentation files to a shared library or SharePoint site.

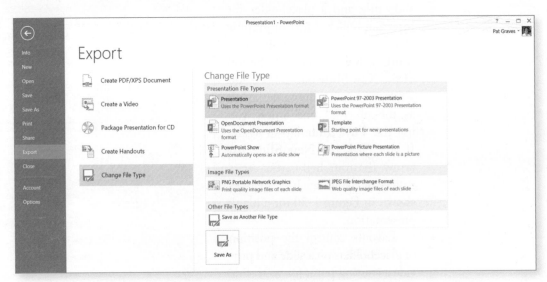

1-19 *Export* options

Export

- ***Create PDF/XPS Document:*** Preserves formatting and reduces file size for easier distribution.
- ***Create a Video:*** Saves your presentation as a video.
- ***Package Presentation for CD:*** Saves your presentation and all linked or embedded files.
- ***Create Handouts:*** Transfers slides and notes to a Word document that you can re-format.
- ***Change File Type:*** Saves your presentation or individual slides in different file formats.

Adding and Editing Presentation Text

As you begin developing presentation content, you will enter most text and objects such as pictures, tables, and charts using ***placeholders*** on slides in *Normal* view. By default, these placeholders have no fill color or border, but you may choose to emphasize them by adding color. You can resize placeholders as needed to fit text content. Usually, slide titles and subtitles contain a single line of text; body placeholders contain bulleted text.

When PowerPoint first opens or when you start a blank presentation, the first slide has a ***Title Slide*** layout with two placeholders: a presentation title and a subtitle. You can add text directly into these placeholders or you can type slide titles and bulleted text in *Outline* view. The font, font size, and alignment are preset, but you can change them as you develop your presentation.

As you write text, keep in mind that it should be brief, straight to the point, and easy to read.

Add Slides and Choose Layouts

After a title slide, PowerPoint automatically inserts a ***Title and Content*** layout when you click the **New Slide** button. This layout is the one used for developing most slides; it has a placeholder for the slide title and a placeholder for inserting bulleted text or graphic elements. From that point forward, each time you click the top of the **New Slide** button, you add a new slide with the same layout as the previous one unless you use the **Title Slide** layout again. If you click the **New Slide** list arrow (bottom half), you see a gallery of layouts such as the ones shown in Figure 1-20 for a blank presentation.

Layouts control the position of placeholders on a slide and provide a starting point for your slide designs. You can change layouts or

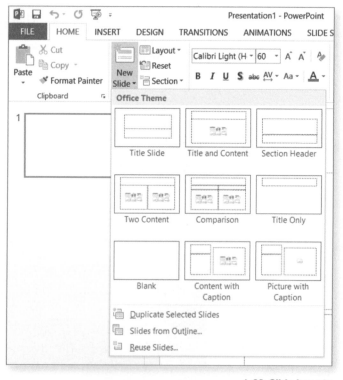

1-20 Slide layouts

customize each slide for the content you are developing. The available layouts vary based on the current theme. The most common layouts are described in the following table.

Slide Layouts

Layout Name	Layout Description
Title Slide	This layout is used for a presentation's opening slide. It contains a title and subtitle placeholder.
Title and Content	This slide layout makes up the body of a presentation. It contains a placeholder for the slide title and a larger placeholder for many different kinds of content.
Section Header	Similar to a title slide layout, it has a title and subtitle placeholder. Depending on the theme being used, it usually has a different appearance from the title slide. Slides with this layout can divide a lengthy presentation or introduce different topics or speakers.
Two Content	This layout has a slide title placeholder and two smaller content placeholders to display either two brief lists or a list and a graphic object, such as a picture or chart.
Comparison	This layout is similar to the *Two Content* layout, but it works better for comparing two lists because it provides a heading area above each content placeholder.
Title Only	Only one placeholder is provided for the title (usually at the top) of the slide.
Blank	This layout has no placeholders.
Content with Caption	This layout is similar to the *Two Content* layout, but one area is designated for the content, such as a table or chart, while the other area is meant for descriptive text.
Picture with Caption	This layout has a large area for a picture and another area for descriptive text.

HOW TO: Choose and Change Slide Layouts

1. Click the **New Slides** button [*Home* tab, *Slides* group] to insert a slide with the default layout after the current slide.
2. Click the **New Slides** list arrow [*Home* tab, *Slides* group], and select the layout you want from the *Office Theme Layout* gallery.
3. To change the layout of a selected slide, click **Layout** [*Home* tab, *Slides* group].
4. From the *Office Theme Layout* gallery, select the layout you want. Repeat this process to try another layout.
5. Click the **Undo** button to remove the layout change.

Enter Text in Placeholders

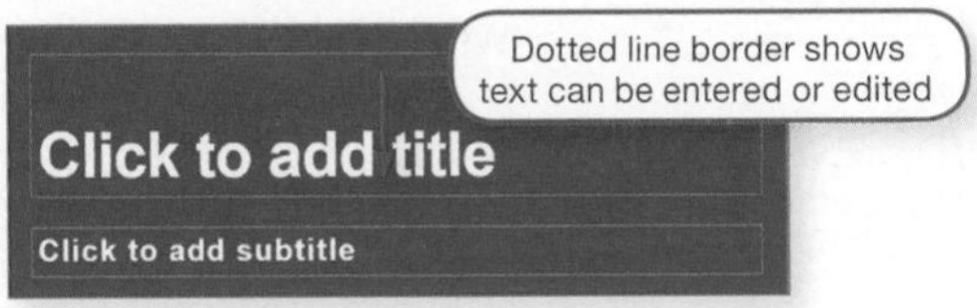

When you first see placeholders on slides, they appear as boxes with a thin border. When you click inside the placeholder, it becomes active with a blinking insertion point where you can type or edit text (Figure 1-21). Click the border to select the placeholder (Figure 1-22). In both cases, sizing handles that are small white squares appear on the corners and sides. A rotation handle that is a circular arrow appears at the top.

Dotted line border shows text can be entered or edited

Click to add title

Click to add subtitle

1-21 Edit text in a selected placeholder

Keep the wording of titles concise so the text does not become too small. Depending on the font that is used, title text for individual slides is usually 36–44 points. When using the *Title Slide* layout, the title text is usually 54–72 points.

In body placeholders, a bullet automatically appears when you type text and press **Enter**. Bullets help mark the beginning point, so people recognize items as separate. You can also add subpoints that are indented below a bulleted item. Be sure your list is very concise, usually no more than six items, and the text size is 20–28 points. Larger font sizes are very important if you are presenting in a large room so your audience can read slide text from a distance. However, if you are preparing a presentation to be viewed on a computer or online, you can use smaller font sizes.

Bulleted lists are appropriate when items require no particular order. If you need to show items in order, use a numbered list instead.

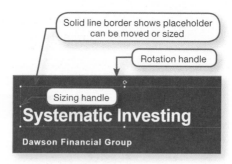

1-22 Selected placeholder to move or resize

HOW TO: Work with Lists

1. In the body placeholder, click after the first bullet and type the text.

2. Press **Enter** to type another bulleted item in the same position (the list level).

3. To indent a bulleted item to the right (Figure 1-23), press **Tab** or click the **Increase List Level** button [*Home* tab, *Paragraph* group] (Figure 1-24).

4. If you need to enter several text slides, click the **Outline View** button [*View* tab, *Presentation Views* group] to display all slide titles and bulleted text on the left of the window.

5. Use *Outline View* to move a bulleted item to the left to create a slide title.

   a. Position your insertion point before the text to move left (Figure 1-25).
   b. Press **Shift+Tab** or click the **Decrease List Level** button [*Home* tab, *Paragraph* group].
   c. Change text capitalization as needed for a title (Figure 1-26).

6. To switch to a numbered list, click the **Numbering** button [*Home* tab, *Paragraph* group].

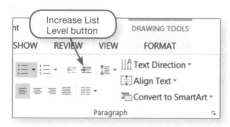

1-23 Bulleted list slide

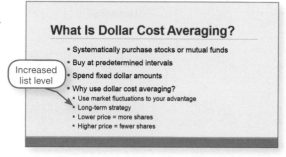

1-24 Paragraph group on the *Home* tab

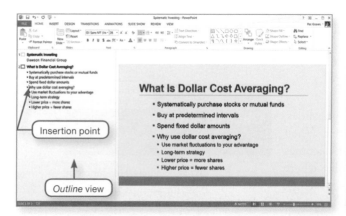

1-25 Slide with bulleted text before list level changes

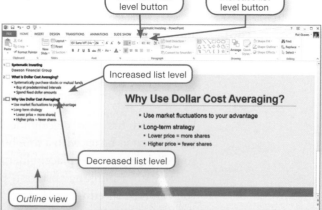

1-26 New slide created by decreasing the list level

PowerPoint 2013 Chapter 1 Creating and Editing Presentations

▶ MORE INFO

To move from the title to the body placeholder, press **Ctrl+Enter**. If you are in the last placeholder, press **Ctrl+Enter** to create a new slide.

Move, Align, and Resize Placeholders

To move a placeholder, point to the border so your pointer changes to a move arrow (with four points) and then drag the placeholder to its new position.

Align text within placeholders using the buttons on the *Home* tab in the *Paragraph* group.

- *Horizontal alignment:* **Left**, **Center**, **Right**, or **Justified** (rarely used on slides) buttons
- *Vertical alignment:* **Top**, **Middle**, or **Bottom** buttons

Align placeholders with one another or with the slide by clicking the **Align** button in the *Arrange* group on the *Drawing Tools Format* tab (Figure 1-27). Select from the following alignment options from the drop-down list:

- *Horizontal alignment:* **Left**, **Center**, **Right**
- *Vertical alignment:* **Top**, **Middle**, **Bottom**

1-27 Alignment options

To increase or decrease placeholder size, point to one of the corner or side *sizing* handles (Figure 1-28) until your pointer changes to a two-pointed arrow (Figure 1-29). Drag to resize. The corner sizing handles move diagonally to change both the horizontal and vertical dimensions at the same time.

Systematic Investing

1-28 Sizing handles on a placeholder

You can control the way placeholders and other objects are resized by pressing one of three keys as you drag:

- *Ctrl:* The placeholder size changes from a fixed center point.
- *Shift:* The height and width proportions are maintained as the size changes.
- *Ctrl+Shift:* The placeholder resizes from the center and remains in proportion.

1-29 Sizing pointers

Another way to precisely resize a placeholder is to enter the exact dimensions on the *Drawing Tools Format* tab.

All of these techniques for moving, aligning, and resizing also apply to pictures and other objects. If you make a change to a slide layout that you do not like, click the **Reset** button in the *Slides* group on the *Home* tab.

Edit Text

As you are writing text, you can cut, copy, or paste text. All of your font commands, such as bold, italic, underline, font, and font size are available in the *Font* group on the *Home* tab. Also, these text formatting options are available on the mini toolbar (Figure 1-30), which appears when text is selected. You can undo or redo actions using commands on the *Quick Access* toolbar.

1-30 Mini toolbar

Notice that your pointer changes when you are working with text. When you see a blinking insertion point, PowerPoint is waiting for you to type text. When you point to text, your pointer changes to a text selection tool so you can click and drag to select text.

> **ANOTHER WAY**
>
> **Ctrl+X** Cut
> **Ctrl+C** Copy
> **Ctrl+V** Paste
> **Ctrl+Z** Undo
> **Ctrl+Y** Redo

HOW TO: Delete Text

1. Press **Delete** to remove text to the right of the insertion point.
2. Press **Backspace** to remove text to the left of the insertion point.
3. Select text and press **Delete** to remove several words at one time.

Click outside a text placeholder to deselect it. Handles no longer appear.

Change Text Case

Text case refers to how text is capitalized. Sometimes text appears in a placeholder in uppercase (all capital) letters. Be careful when using uppercase letters, because text may not be as easy to read as text with initial caps (the first letter only is capitalized). People are more experienced at reading lowercase text and, therefore, can generally read that text faster. Also, uppercase words in email are thought to represent shouting, and this negative connotation might carry over to your presentation if you overuse capital letters. Use uppercase letters when you really want to emphasize selected words or brief phrases.

HOW TO: Change Case

1. Select the text to be changed.
2. Click the **Change Case** button [*Home* tab, *Font* group].
3. Choose from the options **Sentence case**, **lowercase**, **UPPERCASE**, **Capitalize Each Word**, or **tOGGLE cASE** (Figure 1-31).

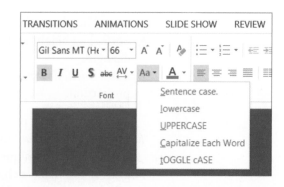

1-31 *Change Case* options

Change List Bullet Symbols

If a bullet that automatically appears seems inappropriate or if its color blends too much with the slide background, you can change the bullet symbol.

HOW TO: Change Bullet Symbols

1. Select the text where you want to change the bullet.
2. Click the **Bullets** button list arrow [*Home* tab, *Paragraph* group] and then select **Bullets and Numbering** to open the *Bullets and Numbering* dialog box.
3. Select one of the pre-defined bullets (Figure 1-32).
4. In the *Size* box, enter a different number to increase or decrease the bullet size.
5. Click the **Color** button to select a different bullet color.
6. Click the **Customize** button to open the *Symbol* dialog box (Figure 1-33), where you can select from many symbols displayed in several fonts.
7. After you select a symbol, click **OK** to add that symbol to the *Bullets and Numbering* dialog box.
8. Select the bullet and click **OK** to change the bullets on selected text.

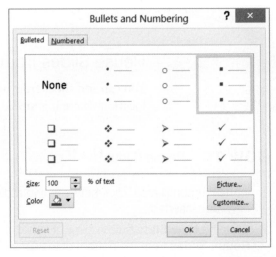

1-32 *Bullets and Numbering* dialog box

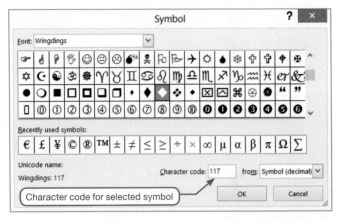

1-33 *Symbol* dialog box

The three **Wingdings** fonts have most of the available character bullets from the *Symbols* dialog box. You can also select picture bullets that are more decorative from the *Bullets and Numbering* dialog box.

The Format Painter

To copy formatting changes from text, shapes, or pictures and apply these changes to another selection, use the **Format Painter**. You can apply the changes on the same slide or on different slides.

HOW TO: Use the Format Painter

1. Select the text or other object with the format that you want to copy.
2. Click **Format Painter** [*Home* tab, *Clipboard* group] (Figure 1-34).

1-34 *Format Painter* button on the *Home* tab

3. Your pointer changes to a paintbrush.

4. Select the text or other object and click to apply the formatting.

5. If you want to apply the change to multiple selections, double-click the **Format Painter** button. Press **Esc** to stop formatting.

Reuse Slides from Another Presentation

You can add slides from another presentation without opening it as long as you can access the location where it is stored.

HOW TO: Reuse Slides

1. In the thumbnail area, click between two slides where you want the new slide inserted.

2. Click the **New Slide** button arrow [*Home* tab, *Slides* group] and select **Reuse Slides** from the bottom of the *Office Theme Layout* gallery.

3. In the *Reuse Slides* pane that automatically opens, click **Browse** and then click **Browse File** (Figure 1-35).

4. Find the location where your existing presentation file is saved and select the file name.

5. Click **Open**. The slides in this second presentation appear in the *Reuse Slides* pane (Figure 1-36).

6. Point to each of the slide thumbnails so you can read the slide titles.

7. Select the **Keep source formatting** checkbox at the bottom of the *Reuse Slides* pane if you want the inserted slides to retain their design from the original presentation.

8. Click the slides you want to reuse to duplicate them in your current presentation. By default, the reused slides will appear with the formatting of your current presentation.

9. Click the **Close** button at the top of the *Reuse Slides* pane.

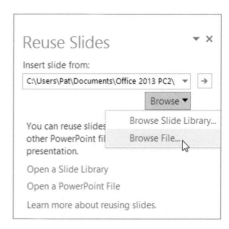

1-35 *Reuse Slides* task pane

1-36 Reuse slides

> ### MORE INFO
>
> When task panes open, they are docked on the right side of the PowerPoint window. If you have a wide computer screen and you are using PowerPoint in a window size that does not fill the screen, you can drag a task pane away from the window so your slide size becomes larger. Double-click the task pane to dock it on the right of the window again.

Check Spelling and Word Usage

PowerPoint's *AutoCorrect* feature fixes many simple errors as you are typing. You can customize *AutoCorrect* options. Even when using *AutoCorrect*, you still need to check for errors when your presentation is complete. If your audience sees mistakes when viewing your slide show, your credibility is undermined. After using PowerPoint's spelling feature, carefully read the content to find any words that may have been missed, such as names or words that might not be in the spelling dictionary.

HOW TO: Check Spelling

1. From any slide in your presentation, click the **Spelling** button [*Review* tab, *Proofing* group] (Figure 1-37).

2. From the *Spelling* pane that opens on the right (Figure 1-38), consider each word that is identified and whether or not the suggested spelling is correct.

3. Click the **Audio** button on the *Spelling* pane to hear the word pronounced.

1-37 Spelling button on the Review tab

4. Click the **Change** button to insert a suggested spelling; click the **Ignore** button if you want to skip the suggestion.

5. When the spell check is complete, click **OK**.

6. Click the **Close** button at the top of the *Spelling* pane.

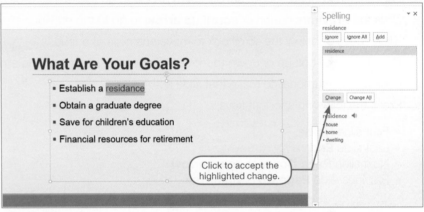

1-38 Spelling pane

If you want to replace an awkward word or one that is used too frequently, use PowerPoint's ***Thesaurus*** to find a more appropriate word.

HOW TO: Use the Thesaurus

1. Click in the word you want to change.

2. Click the **Thesaurus** button [*Review* tab, *Proofing* group]. Your word is selected and the *Thesaurus* pane opens (Figure 1-39).

3. Your selected word appears in the search box, and words with similar meanings appear below it.

4. Click a word from this list to see more options; click the **Back** arrow to return to the original list.

5. On a highlighted word in the list, click the **Down** arrow and choose **Insert** to replace the selected word.

6. Click the **Close** button at the top of the *Thesaurus* pane.

1-39 Thesaurus word choices

SLO 1.3

Rearranging Slides

When developing a presentation, you might need to move between slides as ideas occur to you or when you have new information to add. You can rearrange slides at any time. However, always carefully examine your sequence when all slides are complete. The final order must be logical to you and to your audience.

Move between Slides

In *Normal* view, you can move between slides by clicking the **Next** and **Previous** buttons, clicking scroll arrows, or dragging the scroll box on the right of the window. You can also click thumbnails or use keyboard shortcuts.

HOW TO: Move between Slides

1. Click the **Next** button or the **scroll down arrow** to go to the next slide (Figure 1-40).
2. Click the **Previous** button or **scroll up arrow** to go to the previous slide.
3. Click above or below the scroll box to move one slide at a time.
4. Drag the *Scroll* box up or down to move to a specific slide, using the slide indicator.
5. Click a slide thumbnail to make that slide active.
6. Press the following shortcut keys:

   - First slide **Home**
   - Last slide **End**
   - Next slide **Page Down** or **down arrow**
   - Previous slide **Page Up** or **up arrow**

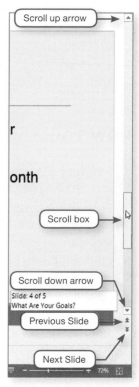

1-40 Move between slides

Copy, Paste, and Duplicate Slides

To reuse a slide's content or format, copy the thumbnail. The original slide remains in its position. Paste the copied slide where you need it and edit the text.

HOW TO: Copy and Paste Slides

1. Select the thumbnail of the slide to be copied (Figure 1-41).
2. Press **Ctrl+C** or click the **Copy** button [*Home* tab, *Clipboard* group] to copy the slide.
3. Move the insertion point to the place between slides where you want the copied slide to appear.
4. Press **Ctrl+V** or click the **Paste** button [*Home* tab, *Clipboard* group] to paste the slide.
5. You can also right-click a slide thumbnail and then select **Copy** or **Paste** from the shortcut menu.
6. On the new slide, edit the text with new content.

1-41 Copy and paste a selected slide

Duplicating slides is similar to *Copy* and *Paste*, except it requires only one step to make the second slide.

HOW TO: Duplicate Slides

1. Select the thumbnail of the slide to be duplicated.
2. Press **Ctrl+D** to duplicate the slide. The second slide is placed immediately after the original slide.
3. You can also right-click a slide thumbnail and select **Duplicate Slide** from the shortcut menu.

Select Multiple Slides

If you need to make the same changes to more than one slide, you can select more than one slide thumbnail.

HOW TO: Select Multiple Slides

1. To select multiple slides in order, select the first slide and then press **Shift** while you click the last slide (Figure 1-42).
2. To select multiple nonadjacent slides (not in order), select the first slide and then press **Ctrl** while you click each of the slides you need to select (Figure 1-43).

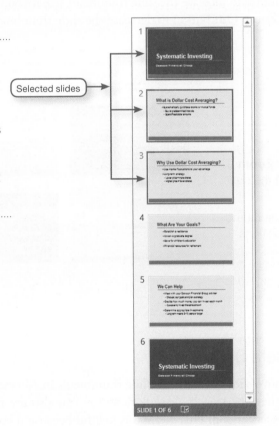

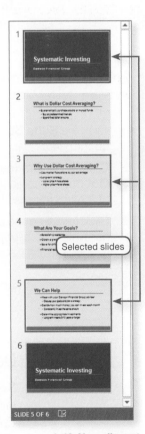

1-42 Adjacent slides selected

1-43 Nonadjacent slides selected

Rearrange Slide Order

You can rearrange slides at any time while developing a presentation. You can drag slide thumbnails up or down. On the *Outline* view, you can drag the slide icons. You can also cut slides and paste them into a different position. However, when your presentation has more slides than can be seen in the thumbnail pane, it is best to rearrange slides using *Slide Sorter* view (Figure 1-44).

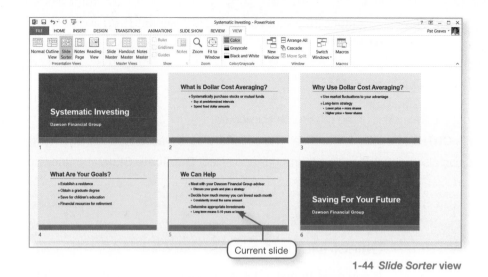

1-44 *Slide Sorter* view

The *Slide Sorter* view enables you to see your presentation as a whole. The thumbnails are arranged from left to right in rows. By default, they are shown at a 100% size. Click the **Zoom In** button to increase the slide thumbnail size if you need to see the slide content better; click the **Zoom Out** button to decrease the slide thumbnail size and see more slides at one time.

HOW TO: Rearrange Slides in Slide Sorter View

1. Click the **Slide Sorter** button on the *Status bar*.
2. Click the **Zoom In** or **Zoom Out** buttons to adjust the size of the thumbnails.
3. Click and drag the slide thumbnails into their new positions (Figure 1-45).

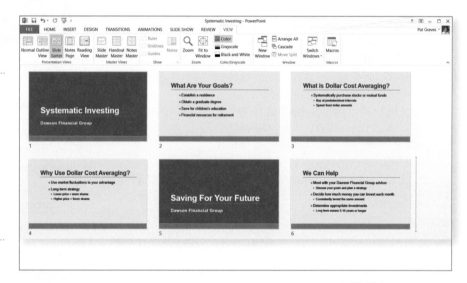

1-45 Slides rearranged

Delete Slides

Remove slides by deleting slide thumbnails in *Normal* view and *Slide Sorter* view or by deleting the slide icon in *Outline* view. You can also use the **Cut** button on the *Home* tab in the *Clipboard* group. This method is helpful because if you change your mind about the deletion later, you can paste the deleted slides back into the presentation from the *Clipboard*.

HOW TO: Delete Slides

1. Right-click the slide thumbnail (or the *Slide* icon in *Outline* view) and click **Delete Slide** from the shortcut menu.
2. Select the slide thumbnail (or the *Slide* icon in *Outline* view) and press **Delete**.
3. Select the slide thumbnail (or the *Slide* icon in *Outline* view) and click **Cut** [*Home* tab, *Clipboard* group].

In this project, you develop the text for a presentation about upcoming marathon events. At the Hamilton Civic Center, this presentation promotes event preparation for participants. You start with a blank presentation, add slides, reuse slides from another presentation, and make format changes.

File Needed: **MarathonInfo-01.pptx**
Completed Project File Name: **[your initials] PP P1-1.pptx**

1. Start a new presentation. Press **Ctrl+N**, or click the **File** tab, click **New**, and then click **Blank Presentation**.

2. Name and save the presentation.
   a. Press **F12** to open the *Save As* dialog box.
   b. Browse to the location where you want to save your files.
   c. Type [your initials PP P1-1] in the *File name* area (Figure 1-46).
   d. Be sure that the *Save as type* says "PowerPoint Presentation."
   e. Click **Save**. The *Save As* dialog box closes.

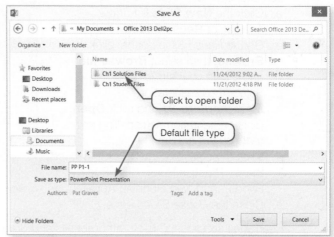

1-46 *Save As* dialog box

3. On slide 1, type the following text in the placeholders:

Title	Take the Right Steps
Subtitle	Train for a Marathon

4. Click the **New Slide** button [*Home* tab, *Slides* group] twice to add two new slides that automatically have the *Title and Content* layout. Type the following text in slides 2 and 3:

Slide 2 Title	What Is Your Goal?
Bulleted items	Run the second half faster
	Beat a time you've run before
	Or
	Finish the marathon
Slide 3 Title	Start Early to Be Ready
Bulleted items	Begin 5–16 weeks in advance
	Get a physical check up
	Prepare gear for running
	Join a training group
	Enjoy camaraderie
	Be accountable
	Run 3-4 times a week

5. Change slide 3 to a *Two Context* layout and adjust the text.
   a. Select slide 3 and click the **Layout** button [*Home* tab, *Slides* group]. Next, select the **Two Content** layout.
   b. Select the last four bulleted items on the left placeholder and press **Ctrl+X** to cut them.

c. Click in the right placeholder and press **Ctrl+V** to paste them.
d. If an extra bullet appears after the last text, delete it by pressing the Backspace key.
e. Select the middle two bulleted items on the right place-holder and press **Tab** or click the **Increase List Level** button [*Home* tab, *Paragraph* group] to format them as sub-points under the first-level item (Figure 1-47).

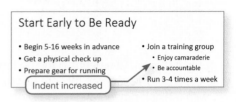

1-47 *Two Content* layout

6. Insert three slides from another presenta-tion after slide 3.
   a. Click the **New Slide** list arrow and select **Reuse Slides**.
   b. On the *Reuse Slides* pane, click **Browse;** then select **Browse file** and locate your student files.
   c. Select the presentation ***MarathonInfo-01*** and click **Open**. (This presentation has spelling errors that you will fix later.)
   d. Click three slides (Figure 1-48) to insert them: "Practice Runs," "Eat Energy Foods," and "Get Running Apparel."
   e. Close the *Reuse Slides* pane.

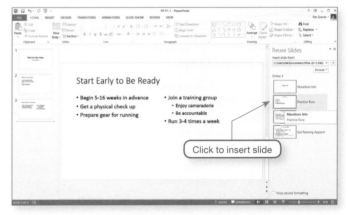

1-48 Reuse slides

7. Rearrange six slides. Click the thumbnails and drag them up or down so the six slides are in this order: "Take the Right Steps," "What is Your Goal?," "Start Early to Be Ready," "Get Running Apparel," "Eat Energy Foods," and "Practice Runs."

8. Insert a new slide.
   a. With slide 6 selected, click the **New Slide** list arrow and select the **Title Only** layout.
   b. In the title placeholder, type Look It UP! (Figure 1-49).
   c. Select the title text and change the font size to **72 pts**.
   d. Select this slide thumbnail and press **Ctrl+D** to duplicate it to create slide 8.

1-49 Placeholder text resized

9. Edit and duplicate slide 8.
   a. On slide 8, edit the title text and type Mark It DOWN!
   b. Select this slide thumbnail and press **Ctrl+D** to duplicate it to create slide 9.

10. On slide 9, edit the title text and type See You THERE!

11. Click the **Spelling** button [*Review* tab, *Proofing* group] and correct each of the spelling errors.

12. Save the presentation. You will continue to work on this presentation for *Pause & Practice PowerPoint 1-2* and *PowerPoint 1-3*.

SLO 1.4

Working with Themes

You can use the same themes for presentations, documents, and worksheets created in all Microsoft Office applications to create a cohesive look. In PowerPoint, the ***Slide Master*** stores information about slide backgrounds, layouts, and fonts for each theme. Changing the *Slide Master* can help you work more efficiently because the entire presentation is affected. In this section, you change theme colors and fonts. In Chapter 3 you create unique backgrounds.

When you start a new presentation and search online, you may find themes or templates that contain artwork or pictures that fit your topic perfectly. The file names you see below each thumbnail do not distinguish between themes and templates. Many of the presentations that appear in a search will have the PowerPoint default file extension (.pptx). Those saved as template files will have a different file extension (.potx). Depending on how your software is set up, you may not see these file extensions when you open files.

You can search through general categories or enter a specific search word to get more targeted results. Themes and templates are provided by Microsoft and other companies.

Your searches will provide results that include the following:

- **Theme:** A slide show with only background graphics and text treatments but no content. Different layouts control where slide objects are positioned. You can control design elements with the *Slide Master* to create custom designs.
- **Template:** A slide show with the characteristics of a theme but also with sample content on several slides. You can edit the content or remove individual slides you do not need to create your presentation. You can control design elements with the *Slide Master* to create custom designs.
- **Template, title slide only:** While the thumbnail may show a title slide, that slide might be the only content in the presentation. Other slides may be blank or have no related graphic background. The *Slide Master* has not been used.
- **Template, individual slide only:** Some thumbnails show only a single diagram or chart that can be revised for a new presentation. Usually, the *Slide Master* has not been used.
- **Different slide sizes:** Two slide sizes will appear. The thumbnails that have an almost square appearance are shown in a 4:3 aspect ratio, the ratio of width to height, which has been the standard for many years. The thumbnails in a wide-screen size are shown in a 16:9 aspect ratio, which is the newer size that reflects the shape of current computer screens.

People who see a lot of presentations become very familiar with the designs that appear in common software. So seeing a presentation with a contemporary looking design that truly fits the topic is refreshing. Caring enough to match your theme to your topic speaks volumes to people about your preparedness and competence. Consider carefully what you select so the design is suitable for your topic and for how your presentation will be used.

HOW TO: Apply a Theme to an Existing Presentation

1. Click the **Design** tab.
2. Click the **More** list arrow in the *Themes* gallery to see additional themes.
3. Point to a thumbnail to see a live preview of that theme on the current slide (Figure 1-50).
4. Click the thumbnail to apply the theme.

1-50 *Themes* gallery

▶ ANOTHER WAY

To apply two themes in one presentation, apply your first theme to all slides then select the slides that should be different. Right-click another theme and select **Apply to Selected Slides**. Be careful when using this option so that your content does not seem disjointed.

Use the Slide Master to Change Theme Colors

When you choose theme colors for your slide show, consider colors that are appropriate for your topic. Also consider where you will present. Because of room lighting, colors for a slide show projected on a large-screen are not as clear or vibrant as what you see on the computer screen directly in front of you. These differences can influence your color choices. Be sure your text is easy to read with a high contrast between the text and background colors (dark on light or light on dark).

Every presentation, even a blank one, begins with a set of colors that have been chosen to work well together. With each built-in theme, PowerPoint provides *Variants* on the *Design* tab that show different theme colors. Many more theme colors are available from the *Design* tab and from the *Slide Master* tab. Generally, the *Design* tab is best to use when you want to change only theme colors or theme fonts. You will use this technique in Chapter 3 when you customize theme colors and theme fonts.

It is best to use the *Slide Master* tab to change theme colors or theme fonts when you want to make additional changes to customize slide layouts or background graphics such as to add a company logo to all slides in a presentation.

HOW TO: Change Theme Colors

1. Click the **View** tab.
2. Click the **Slide Master** button [*Master Views* group] (Figure 1-51).
3. Click the **Colors** button [*Slide Master* tab, *Background* group] (Figure 1-52).
4. A list of theme colors appears and you see a live preview of those colors as you point to each one. The blank, Office theme will show a live preview only if the background colors have been changed.
5. Click a theme color name to apply it.
6. Select one or more Slide Master layouts on the left and click the **Background Styles** button [*Slide Master* tab, *Background* group] to change the background to light or dark variations.
7. Click the **Close Master View** button [*Slide Master* tab, *Close* group].

1-51 *Slide Master* button on the *View* tab

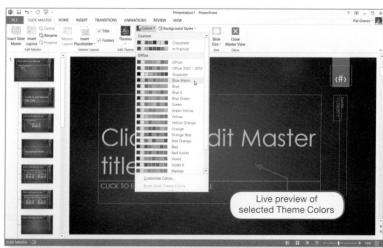

1-52 *Slide Master* tab and *Theme Colors*

The first two colors shown represent the background and text colors; the remaining six show accent colors. For more on customizing theme colors, see *SLO 3.1: Creating Custom Theme and Background Colors.*

Not all of the themes you find online permit color changes in the same way. It depends on how the background design was created originally.

Use the Slide Master to Change Theme Fonts

Select your fonts carefully. Some seem very traditional and serious; others appear more playful and flamboyant. Use fonts that are appropriate for your presentation topic.

Consider how legible the font is with the background color you are using. In some fonts, the letters appear very thin and are not easy to read unless you make the text bold. Also consider the issues related to where you present. The lighting and room size affect how readable the text is on a large screen and you must use large font sizes. If you design a presentation to be displayed for a single person on your notebook or tablet computer, you can use smaller font sizes.

Every presentation, even a blank one, begins with a pair of *Theme Fonts*. The heading font is used for slide titles and the body font is used for all other text. Sometimes the same font is used for both. You can view or change *Theme Fonts* from the *Design* tab or from the *Slide Master* tab.

HOW TO: Change Theme Fonts

1. Click the **View** tab.
2. Click the **Slide Master** button [*Master Views* group].
3. Click the **Fonts** button [*Slide Master* tab, *Background* group] (Figure 1-53).
4. A list of Theme Fonts appears and you see a live preview of Theme Fonts applied to placeholder text as you point to each pair.
5. Click a Theme Font pair to apply it.
6. Click the **Close Master View** button [*Slide Master* tab, *Close* group].

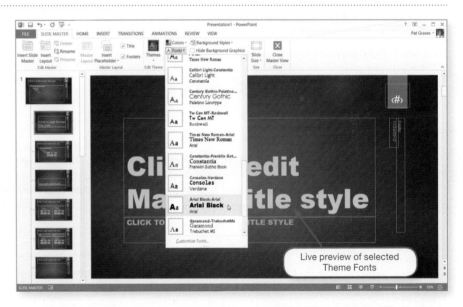

1-53 *Slide Master* tab and *Theme Fonts*

Inserting Headers and Footers

If you want to include identifying information on all slides of a presentation, use the ***Header & Footer*** command on the *Insert* tab (Figure 1-54). Footers are displayed on every slide with placeholders for the date and time, slide number, and footer text. These placeholders often appear across the bottom of the slide, but depending on the theme, they may appear in different places. You can choose to show footers on all slides or only on selected slides.

1-54 *Insert* tab

Create a Slide Footer

When you enter information using the *Header and Footer* dialog box, placeholders appear on the slides. You can move these placeholders if you wish.

HOW TO: Create a Slide Footer

1. Click the **Insert** tab.
2. Click the **Header & Footer** button [*Text* group].
3. In the *Header and Footer* dialog box, click the **Slide** tab (Figure 1-55).
4. Click the check boxes to select the following:
   a. **Date and time:** Choose between **Update automatically** to show the current date or **Fixed** to enter a specific date.
   b. **Slide number:** Each slide is numbered.
   c. **Footer:** Type text you want to appear on each slide.
5. Check the box for **Don't show on title slide** if you do not want footer information to appear on any slide created with the *Title Slide* layout.
6. Click the **Apply** button to apply the settings only to the current slide.
7. Click the **Apply to All** button to apply the settings to all slides.

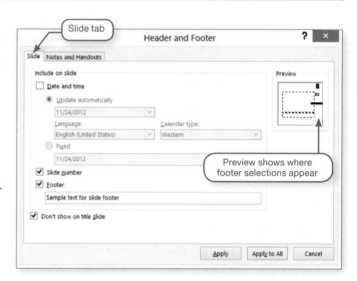

1-55 *Slide* tab on the *Header* and *Footer* dialog box

Create a Notes and Handouts Header

Because notes and handouts are usually printed documents, they can include header information that appears at the top of each page. Control all settings for notes and handouts in the same way you control slide footers.

HOW TO: Create a Notes and Handouts Header

1. Click the **Insert** tab.
2. Click the **Header & Footer** button [*Text* group].
3. In the *Header and Footer* dialog box, click the **Notes and Handouts** tab (Figure 1-56).
4. Click the check boxes to select the following:
   a. **Date and time:** Choose between **Update automatically** to show the current date or **Fixed** to enter a specific date.
   b. **Page number:** Each page is numbered.

1-56 *Notes and Handouts* tab in the *Header and Footer* dialog box

c. **Header:** Type text you want to appear on each page.

d. **Footer:** Type text you want to appear on each page.

5. Click the **Apply to All** button to apply your settings to all pages.

If you leave items blank in the *Header and Footer* dialog box, empty placeholders show on your slide, but no information appears in *Slide Show* view.

PAUSE & PRACTICE: POWERPOINT 1-2

For this project, you continue working on the presentation you created in *Pause & Practice*: *PowerPoint 1-1*. You apply a theme then change theme colors and fonts to revise two individual slides. Finally, you add a footer to your slides and add page numbering to the notes and handout pages.

File Needed: ***[your initials] PP P1-1.pptx***
Completed Project File Name: ***[your initials] PP P1-2.pptx***

1. Open and rename the presentation file.
   a. Click the **File** tab; then click the **Open** button.
   b. Locate the folder where your files are saved.
   c. Open the presentation file **[your initials] PP P1-1**.
   d. Click the **File** tab; then click **Save As** or press **F12**.
   e. Locate the folder where your files are saved.
   f. Save the presentation as **[your initials] PP P1-2**.

2. Apply a theme.
   a. Click the **Design** tab.
   b. Click the **More** button [*Themes* group] to open the *Themes* gallery (Figure 1-57).
   c. Click the **Facet** theme so it is applied to all slides.

3. Change the background style.
   a. Click the **View** tab.
   b. Click the **Slide Master** button.
   c. Scroll to the top of the slide master layouts and select the first layout (Facet Slide Master) so your color change is applied to all slides.
   d. Click the **Colors** button [*Slide Master* tab, *Background* group].
   e. Scroll down the list and select the **Aspect** theme.
   f. Click the **Background Styles** button [*Slide Master* tab, *Background* group].
   g. Select **Style 4**, which applies a solid black background (Figure 1-58).

1-57 *Themes* gallery

1-58 *Background Styles*

4. Change the fonts.
   a. Click the **Fonts** button [*Slide Master* tab, *Background* group].
   b. Scroll down the list and click the **TrebuchetMS** font pair (Figure 1-59).
   c. Click the **Close Master View** button [*Slide Master* tab].

5. On slide 1, modify the title and subtitle text.
   a. Select all of the title text and make these changes:
      • Apply **bold**, change to **left alignment**, and increase the font size to **60 pts**. [*Home* tab, *Font* group].
      • Click the **Arrange** button [*Home* tab, *Drawing* group], **Align**, and select **Align Top**.
      • Select the word **Right**. Click the **Change Case** button [*Home* tab, *Font* group] and select **UPPERCASE**.
      • Resize the placeholder on the right by dragging the horizontal sizing handle so the text fits on one line.
   b. Select the subtitle and make these changes:
      • Apply **bold**, change to **left alignment**, and increase the font size to **36 pts**. [*Home* tab, *Font* group].
      • Position the subtitle below the title.

6. On slide 2, change the bullet.
   a. Select the bulleted text and click the **Bullets** list arrow [*Home* tab, *Font* group].
   b. Select **Bullets and Numbering**.
   c. Change the *Size* to **100%** of text.
   d. Click the **Color** button and select **Red**, **Accent 2** (Figure 1-60).
   e. Click the **Customize** button to open the *Symbol* dialog box. Change the font (if necessary) to **Wingdings** (Figure 1-61)
   f. Scroll down and select the **solid square** (Character code 110) and click **OK**.
   g. Click **OK** again to close the *Bullets and Numbering* dialog box.
   h. Click to put your insertion point before the word "Or" on the third bulleted item.
   i. Press **Backspace** to remove the bullet from this item only. Make this text bold.

7. Add a slide footer.
   a. On slide 2, click the **Header & Footer** button [*Insert* tab, *Text* group] (Figure 1-62).
   b. On the *Slide* tab, select **Slide number** and **Footer**.
   c. In the *Footer* text box, type Take the Right Steps, Train for a Marathon.
   d. Select **Don't show on title slide**.

1-59 *Theme* font change

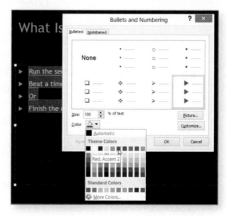

1-60 Change bullet size and color

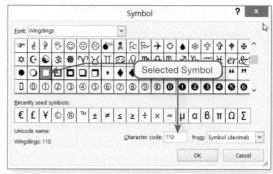

1-61 *Symbol* dialog box

e. Click the **Apply** button. The dialog box closes and the footer appears only on this slide.

f. Select the footer text and the page number. Increase the font size to **18 pts**.

8. Add page numbers for a handout.
   a. On slide 2, click the **Header & Footer** button [*Insert* tab, *Text* group].
   b. Click the **Notes and Handouts** tab.
   c. Select **Page number**.
   d. Click the **Apply to All** button and the dialog box closes.

9. Save the presentation.

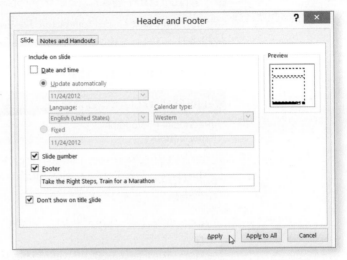

1-62 *Header and Footer* dialog box with changes

Working with a Picture from a File

There is an old adage, "A picture is worth a thousand words." That saying is still true today, because pictures bring a sense of realism to a presentation. Select pictures appropriate for your topic. Include pictures obtained from web sites only if you have the permission of the image owner to avoid copyright infringement. For academic purposes, you may include images if you reference their sources as you would any other research citation.

Insert a Picture

PowerPoint supports different graphic file types, so you can insert almost any digital image from a camera, or one created by scanning a document, into a slide show. To insert a picture, click the **Picture** button in the *Images* group on the *Insert* tab. Be aware that pictures can increase the file size of your presentation dramatically.

HOW TO: Insert a Picture

1. Click the **Insert** tab.
2. Click the **Pictures** button.
3. Select the drive and folder where your picture is saved.
4. Select the file you want to insert (Figure 1-63).
5. Click **Insert**.

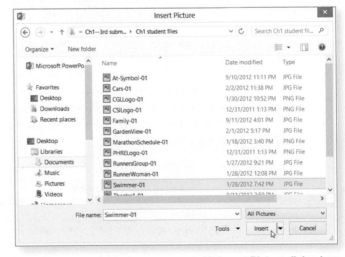

1-63 *Insert Picture* dialog box

ANOTHER WAY

Once you have located your picture file, insert the picture by double clicking the file name.

Graphic File Formats

Picture File Type	Extension	Uses of This Format
JPEG (Joint Photographic Experts Group)	.jpg	Designed for photographic images. Handles gradual color blending and complex graphics well. Produces a smaller file size than most other formats because of compression.
PNG (Portable Network Graphics)	.png	Handles photographic images and complex graphics well. Originally designed for web applications, this format works well for presentations also. Supports transparency so areas removed from the image appear blank on the slide.
GIF (Graphics Interchange Format)	.gif	Suited for line art and simple drawings, but not optimal for photographs because it only supports 256 colors. Used for simple animated graphics. Does not handle gradual color blending well. Supports transparency.
Windows Metafile and Enhanced Windows Metafile	.wmf and .emf	Used for many Windows illustrations available through searches using the Clip Art task pane.
Device Independent Bitmap	.bmp	Images usually display well in their original size, but if you increase size, the image will be distorted.
TIFF (Tagged Image File Format)	.tiff	Designed for print publications. Produces high-quality images with large file sizes. Supports transparency.

Resize a Picture

You can make a picture smaller and still retain its clarity, but some pictures cannot be made larger without becoming blurred or distorted.

To resize a picture, point to one of the corner or side sizing handles and drag it. The corner sizing handles move diagonally to change both horizontal and vertical dimensions at the same time.

You can precisely resize a picture by entering the exact dimensions on the *Picture Tools Format* tab that appears when a picture is selected. When changing the size of pictures, maintain the correct ratio between height and width to avoid distorting the image. The selected picture of the swimmer in Figure 1-64 is shown in the original size on the left. The pictures on the right were resized horizontally to be too wide and too narrow.

If you change the size incorrectly, restore the picture's original dimensions by clicking the **Reset Picture** button in the *Adjust* group on the *Picture Tools Format* tab (Figure 1-65).

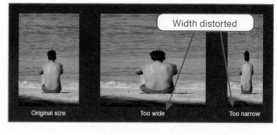

1-64 Resizing examples

1-65 *Picture Tools Format* tab

Align a Picture

As you place pictures and other graphic objects on slides, consider how they are aligned on the slide and how they align with other objects on the slide. Everything on the slide should align in some way. You can align pictures and other objects with each other or on the slide by clicking the *Align* button in the *Arrange* group on the *Picture Tools Format* tab and selecting the alignment from the drop-down list (Figure 1-66).

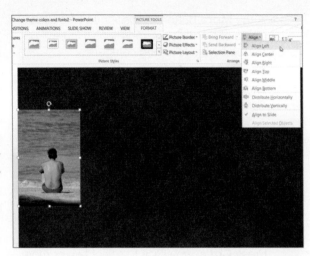

1-66 Left align on the slide

- **Horizontal alignment:** *Left, Center,* or *Right*
- **Vertical alignment:** *Top, Middle,* or *Bottom*

SLO 1.7 ## Applying Transitions

A *transition* is the visual effect of movement that occurs when one slide changes into another slide. Each transition effect in PowerPoint provides a different type of movement. You can find these in the *Transition to This Slide* gallery on the *Transitions* tab (Figure 1-67).

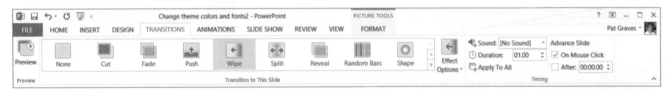

1-67 *Transitions* tab

Each slide can have only one transition. You can set transitions for one slide at a time in *Normal* view or apply the same transition to all slides. If you want to use different transitions, select thumbnails in *Normal* view or *Slide Sorter* view. Once a transition has been applied, an icon symbolizing movement appears with the slide thumbnails.

Although it is possible to apply different transitions on every slide in a presentation, it is neither practical nor advisable. People are very accustomed to PowerPoint use today and know that slides are going to change in some way. Random movements using many different transitions do not entertain an audience and may be distracting or even annoying. Control movement skillfully to reinforce your message. Some people prefer to use a "quiet" transition for most of a presentation (sort of like turning pages in a book or an e-reader). They apply a more "energetic" transition to key slides to grab attention or signal the beginning of a new topic. Use the *Slide Sorter* view to see more slides at once and decide which slides might benefit from a different movement.

In the *Timing* group, the **Advance Slide** options control whether slides advance **On Mouse Click** (the default) or after a specific number of seconds that you choose. Sound can also be associated with a transition.

HOW TO: Apply Transitions

1. Select the slide thumbnail where you want a transition to appear.
2. Click the **Transitions** tab.

3. Click the **More** button [*Transition to This Slide* group] to see additional transitions (Figure 1-68) organized by the following categories:
   a. *Subtle*
   b. *Exciting*
   c. *Dynamic Content*

4. Apply one transition to all slides in the presentation.
   a. Select a transition effect for the current slide.
   b. Be sure **On Mouse Click** is checked.
   c. Click the **Apply to All** button [*Timing* group]

5. Apply more than one transition.
   a. Click the **Slide Sorter** button on the *Status bar*.
   b. Press **Ctrl** as you click to select two or more slides that should have a different transition.
   c. Click a different transition effect and a live preview shows on the selected slides.
   d. Be sure **On Mouse Click** is checked (Figure 1-69).

6. Click the **Normal View** button on the *Status bar*.
   a. Select the first slide and click **Preview** [*Transitions* tab, *Preview* group] to test the movement.
   b. Click the **Next Slide** button and click **Preview** again for each slide.

7. Click the **Slide Show** tab.
   a. Click the **From Beginning** button to view the slide show from the first slide.
   b. Click to advance from slide to slide.

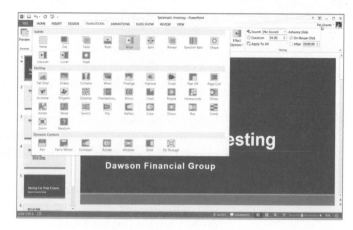

1-68 *Transitions* gallery

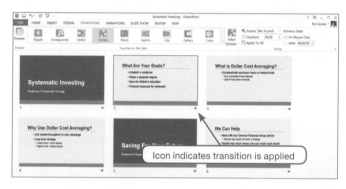

Icon indicates transition is applied

1-69 Change transitions on selected slides in *Slide Sorter* view

Duration, shown in seconds, controls how fast the slides change. Duration seconds vary based on the selected transition effect. Movement might be barely visible if the duration is fast; a slower duration of five or more seconds can make the movement much more noticeable. Enter a different number to change the duration and experiment to see what works best for your content.

Select Effect Options

Effect Options control the direction of transition movement and options vary based on the transition. Each transition can have only one effect option.

HOW TO: Select Effect Options

1. In *Slide Sorter* view, select the slide (or slides) with the same transition.
2. Click the **Transitions** tab.
3. Click the **Effect Options** button to see a drop-down list showing directional movements (Figure 1-70).
4. Select an option to apply it.
5. Repeat this process if you have more than one transition.

6. Click **Preview** to test the movement in *Normal View*.

7. Click the **Slide Show** tab.

8. Click the **From Beginning** button to view the slide show from the first slide.

9. Click to advance from slide to slide.

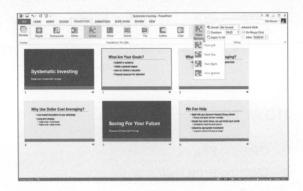

1-70 *Transition Effect* options

SLO 1.8

Exploring Print Options

You may want to proofread your presentation content on paper or review the slides with a colleague. Or you may want to prepare audience handouts or your own printed materials to use while you are giving the presentation. PowerPoint 2013 provides convenient ways to preview and print presentation slides, handouts, notes pages, or outlines.

Preview a Presentation

Before printing, check your slides to ensure everything looks as you intended. The *Backstage* view [*File* tab, *Print* button] displays each slide or handout page in your presentation as it will look when printed. Use the navigation controls at the bottom of the window to go through the slides or pages one at a time. You can also press **Page Up** or **Page Down**, or you can use the scroll bar on the right. Adjust slide sizes using the *Zoom* controls on the lower right.

The look of your slides in *Backstage* view is influenced by the selected printer. If you are using a color printer, the preview image is shown in color; if it prints in black and white, the preview image will be shown in *grayscale* (shades of black). In a work setting, you may have a small desktop printer for printing rough draft copies with black print and a network printer for printing more expensive, high-quality color pages. If you design slides in color and plan to print slides or handouts in grayscale, preview your slides to make sure that all text is readable. You may need to adjust some colors to get good results.

In *Backstage* view, select a printer from the available list of local and network printers. Print **Settings** are shown as buttons with the current setting displayed. Click the list arrow for a list of the following options:

- **Which Slides to Print:** Choose among *Print All Slides, Print Selection, Print Current Slide,* or *Custom Range* using slide numbers entered in the *Slides* box (e.g., slides 1-3 or slides 1-3, 5, 8).
- **What to Print:** Choose *Full Page Slides, Notes Pages, Outline,* or *Handouts.* You can print handouts with three to nine slides on a page using a horizontal or vertical arrangement on the page. You can also specify *Frame Slides, Scale to Fit Paper* (makes slides larger), or *High Quality.*
- **Print Side:** Choose between *Print One Side* or *Print Both Sides.* However, not all printers can print on both sides.
- **Print Order:** Choose between *Collated* and *Uncollated.* Usually slides print in order, but you may want to print multiple copies page by page.
- **Orientation:** Choose between *Landscape* and *Portrait.* By default, slides print in landscape orientation; notes and handouts print in portrait orientation. This option is not available if you are printing full-size slides.
- **Color Range:** Choose among *Color, Grayscale,* or *Pure Black and White.*

Below the print *Settings* in *Backstage* view, you can click the **Edit Header & Footer** link to open the *Header and Footer* dialog box and then enter or revise information.

Print a Slide

The default print settings print each slide on letter-size paper. Adjust settings as needed to print the current or selected slides.

HOW TO: Print a Slide in Grayscale

1. Click the **File** tab.
2. Click the **Print** button on the left.
3. For *Settings*, choose the options you need, such as the following:
   a. Which Slides to Print: **Print Current Slide**.
   b. What to Print: **Full Page Slides**.
   c. Print Order: **Collated**.
   d. Color Range: **Grayscale** (Figure 1-71).
4. Enter the number of copies, if you need more than one.
5. Click the **Print** button at the top.

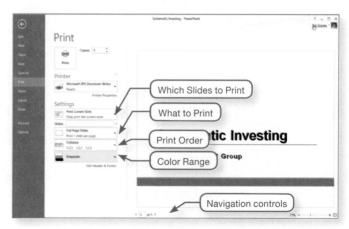

1-71 Print settings for a full-size slide

Print a Handout

Handouts print one to nine slides on a page. You can use these pages as audience handouts or for your own reference during a presentation. Selecting *Scale to Fit Paper* makes the slides larger. *Framing* shows the shape of slides, which is helpful when printing slides with a white background on white paper. Depending on the number of slides, changing the page orientation to landscape can make slides larger.

When preparing handouts for an audience, consider which slides will be important for the audience to have. If not all slides are necessary, you can specify which slides to include and perhaps reduce the number of pages required for printing.

HOW TO: Print a Handout for Selected Slides in Color

1. Click the **File** tab.
2. Click the **Print** button on the left.
3. Select a color printer.
4. For *Settings*, choose the options you need, such as the following:
   a. Which Slides to Print: Enter the specific slides needed (such as **1, 3–4, 6**) in the *Slides* box to print a *Custom Range*.
   b. What to Print: **6 Slides Horizontal, Collated, and Portrait Orientation**.
   c. Color Range: **Color** (Figure 1-72).
5. Enter the number of copies, if you need more than one.
6. Click the **Print** button at the top.

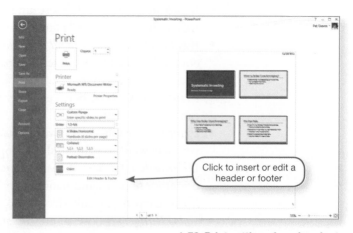

1-72 Print settings for a handout

Print an Outline

If a presentation consists of mostly slides with bulleted lists, printing an outline is a very concise way to display the content. Only the text is shown.

HOW TO: Print an Outline in Pure Black and White

1. Click the **File** tab.
2. Click the **Print** button on the left.
3. For *Settings*, choose the options you need, such as the following:
   a. Which Slides to Print: **Print All Slides**.
   b. What to Print: **Outline**.
   c. What Side: **Print One Sided**.
   d. Print Order: **Collated**.
   e. Orientation: **Portrait Orientation**.
   f. Color Range: **Pure Black and White** (Figure 1-73).
4. Enter the number of copies, if you need more than one.
5. Click the **Print** button at the top.

1-73 Print settings for an outline

Applying Properties

PowerPoint automatically records information in your presentation file, such as the file size, creation date, and number of slides. These *document properties*, also called *metadata*, can help you manage and track files. Click the **File** tab and click the **Info** button to see these properties on the right side of the *Backstage* view. You can edit some of these properties, such as title and author, in this view.

HOW TO: Change Properties Using Backstage View

1. Click the **File** tab.
2. Click the **Info** button.
3. Document properties are listed on the right. Point to the fields to see which ones you can edit (Figure 1-74).
4. Click **Show All Properties** to access additional information.
5. Click in a **field** and type information to edit the document property.

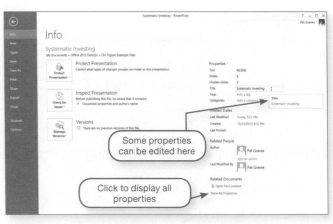

1-74 Document properties on *Backstage* view

Change Document Panel Information

You can change additional properties, such as subject, keywords, or category, using the *Document Properties* panel that appears in the PowerPoint window between the *Ribbon* and the slide area.

HOW TO: Change Properties Using the Document Panel

1. Click the **File** tab.
2. Click the **Info** button.
3. Click the **Properties** list arrow at the top of the *Properties* area.
4. Select **Show Document Panel** (Figure 1-75). The *Backstage* closes, and the *Document Properties Panel* displays (Figure 1-76).
5. Click in the fields and type appropriate information.
6. Click the *Document Properties* **Close** button at the top right of the panel to close the panel.

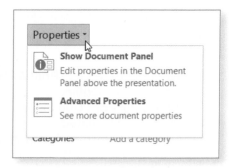

1-75 *Properties* options

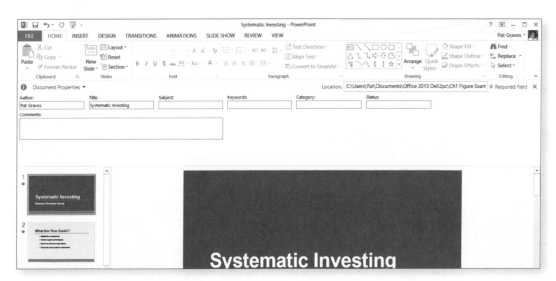

1-76 *Document Properties* Panel

Review Advanced Properties

The *Properties* dialog box displays properties organized in the following five tabs: *General, Summary, Statistics, Contents,* and *Custom.*

HOW TO: Change Properties Using the Properties Dialog Box

1. Click the **File** tab.
2. Click the **Info** button.
3. Click the **Properties** list arrow at the top of the *Properties* area.

4. Select **Advanced Properties**. The *Properties* dialog box is displayed (Figure 1-77).

5. Tabs display properties automatically generated by PowerPoint.

6. Click the **Summary** and **Custom** tabs to add or edit information.

7. Click **OK** to close the *Properties* dialog box.

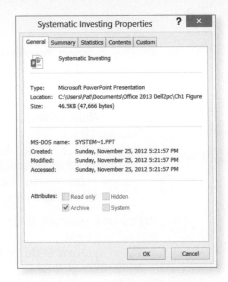

1-77 *Properties* dialog box

ANOTHER WAY

Open the *Advanced Properties* dialog box from the *Document* Panel by clicking **Document Properties** and selecting **Advanced Properties**.

PAUSE & PRACTICE: POWERPOINT 1-3

For this final Pause & Practice project, you finish the presentation about training for a marathon. You insert, resize, and align several pictures, apply transitions, change the presentation properties, and print a handout.

Files Needed: *[your initials] PP P1-2.pptx MarathonInfo-01.pptx, RunnersGroup-01.jpg, RunnerWoman-01.jpg,* and *MarathonSchedule-01.png*
Completed Project File Name: *[your initials] PP P1-3.pptx*

1. Open and rename the *[your initials] PP P1-2* presentation.
   a. Click the **File** tab and click the **Open** button.
   b. Locate your saved files.
   c. Open the *[your initials] PP P1-2* presentation.
   d. Click the **File** tab; then click **Save As**.
   e. Browse to the location on your computer or storage device to save the presentation.
   f. Save this presentation as *[your initials] PP P1-3*.

2. On slide 1, insert, resize, and align a picture on the slide.
   a. Click the **Insert** tab; then click the **Pictures** button.
   b. Locate the folder where your student files are saved.
   c. Select *RunnersGroup-01.jpg* and click **Insert** (or double click the file name) to insert the picture (Figure 1-78). (The .jpg file name extension may not show in your file list.)
   d. Resize the picture using the horizontal sizing arrows so it is **8.5"** wide. Because the picture is already blurred to reflect the speed of running, it looks fine when you stretch the picture.
   e. With the picture selected, click the **Align** button [*Picture Tools Format* tab, *Arrange* group].
      • Select **Align Bottom** (Figure 1-79).
      • Repeat to select **Align Right**.

1-78 Picture of runners inserted

1-79 Picture resized and aligned

3. On slide 6, repeat the process to insert a picture and align it.
   a. Click the **Insert** tab and click the **Pictures** button.
   b. Locate the folder where your files are saved.
   c. Select *RunnerWoman-01.jpg* and click **Insert** (or double click the file name) to insert the picture.
   d. No resizing is required for this picture.
   e. With the picture selected, click the **Align** button [*Picture Tools Format* tab, *Arrange* group] and select **Align Right** (Figure 1-80).

1-80 Picture aligned

4. With slide 6 selected, add a new slide and insert a picture of a table.
   a. Click the **New Slide** list arrow [*Home* tab, *Slides* group].
   b. Select the **Title Only** layout.
   c. Type the title Upcoming Marathons.
   d. Click the **Insert** tab; then click the **Pictures** button.
   e. Locate the folder where your files are saved.
   f. Select *MarathonSchedule-01.jpg* and click **Insert** (or double click the file name) to insert the picture.
   g. Move the table so it is approximately centered in the black area (Figure 1-81).

1-81 Picture of table inserted and positioned

5. On slides 8, 9, and 10, only the large title text appears. Resize the placeholders horizontally on the right side so the text fits in the placeholder without extra horizontal space or word wrapping.

6. On slide 10, change the font color for the word "THERE!" to **Tan, Text 2**.

7. On slides 8, 9, and 10, adjust where the text aligns. Repeat this process for each slide.
   a. Select the title text placeholder and click the **Align** button [*Drawing Tools Format* tab, *Arrange* group].
   b. Click **Align** and select the following alignment:

   Slide 8: **Align Left, Align Top** (Figure 1-82)
   Slide 9: **Align Center, Align Bottom**
   Slide 10: **Align Right, Align Middle**

1-82 Title placeholder aligned top and left

8. Apply one transition to all slides and a different transition to selected slides.
   a. Click the **Slide Sorter** button [*Status bar*].
   b. Press **Ctrl+A** to select all slides.
   c. Click the **Transitions** tab.
   d. Click the **Wipe** transition from the gallery.
   e. Click **Effect Options** [*Transition* tab, *Transition to This Slide* group].
   f. Select **From Left** (Figure 1-83).
   g. Click off a slide to remove the selections.

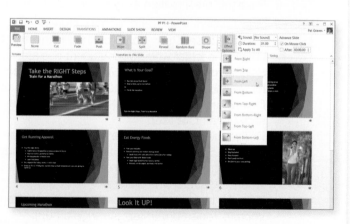

1-83 *Transition Effect* options

h. Select each of the following slides and apply transitions and effect options from the *Transition* tab to emphasize the content with different movements:

Slide 1: **Zoom**, **In**
Slide 7: **Doors**, **Vertical**
Slide 8: **Pan**, **From Bottom**
Slide 9: **Pan**, **From Top**
Slide 10: **Pan**, **From Left**

i. Press **Ctrl+A** to select all slides.
j. Click **Preview** [*Transitions* tab] to see the movements in *Slide Sorter* view.
k. Click the **Slide Show** button [*Status bar*] and click to advance each slide so you can see the movements in *Slide Show* view.

9. Now change some of the presentation properties.
a. Click the **File** tab, then the **Info** button.
b. Under *Properties*, change the *Title* to Train for a Marathon.
c. Click the **Properties** button, then click **Show Document** Panel (Figure 1-84). Type the following information in the respective fields:

Author: Your Name *(unless it already appears)*
Title: Train for a Marathon *(already entered)*
Subject: Athletic Event Promotion
Comments: This presentation will be shown at the Civic Center to explain how to get ready for upcoming marathon events.

d. Click the **Close** button to close the *Document Properties* panel.

1-84 *Document Properties* Panel

10. Print slides as a handout.
a. Click the **File** tab, then the **Print** button on the left.
b. Select the appropriate printer.
c. Change the following *Settings* by clicking the **list arrow** for each option (repeat as necessary to make more than one change) (Figure 1-85):

Which Slides to Print: **Print All Slides**
What to Print: **Handouts, 6 Slides Horizontal, Frame Slides, Scale to Fit Paper**
Print Order: **Collated**
Orientation: **Portrait**
Color Range: **Grayscale** (or **color** if you prefer)

1-85 *Print* settings

d. Preview the handout by clicking the navigation buttons so you can see both pages.
e. Click the **Print** button at the top of the *Backstage* view.

11. Press **Ctrl+S** to save the presentation (or click the **Save** button on the *File* tab or the *Quick Access* toolbar).

Chapter Summary

1.1 Create, open, and save a presentation (p. P1-3).

- You can start creating a presentation with a blank presentation, a *theme*, an existing presentation, or a *template*.
- Different *views* in PowerPoint enable you to look at your content in different ways.
- The *Zoom* feature allows you to adjust the size of the slide on which you are working.
- The standard file format for presentation files has an extension of *.pptx*.
- In *Backstage* view, PowerPoint provides a variety of save and send options. For example, you can save a presentation as a *PDF* file or email a presentation file as an attachment.
- Additional themes and templates are available at Office.com.

1.2 Develop presentation content by adding slides, choosing layouts, moving and resizing placeholders, editing text, and reusing slides from another presentation (p. P1-14).

- Use *placeholders* for presentation text and objects such as pictures, tables, and charts. You can resize, reposition, and align text placeholders on slides.
- The *New Slide* button displays a gallery of slide layouts with placeholders arranged for different content.
- You can make font changes using commands on the *Home* tab or the mini toolbar.
- *Change Case* changes the way words are capitalized.
- In bulleted lists, you can change the bullet symbol, size, and color.
- Use the *Format Painter* to copy formatting from one object and apply it to another object.
- The *Reuse Slides* feature enables you to insert slides from another presentation.
- Although potential spelling errors are automatically marked, you also can use the *Spelling* dialog box to check for errors.
- Use the *Thesaurus* to find synonyms for words in your presentation.

1.3 Rearrange presentation content by moving, copying and pasting, duplicating, and deleting slides (p. P1-22).

- You can move selected slides using a variety of methods to rearrange their sequence.
- *Copy*, *paste*, *duplicate*, and *delete* slides using the *Slides* tab or *Slide Sorter* view.

1.4 Modify a theme to change slide size and use the Slide Master to change theme colors and fonts (p. P1-26).

- Presentation *themes* provide a cohesive look through the consistent use of backgrounds, designs, colors, and font treatments.
- Consider the topic and tone of your presentation when choosing theme colors and fonts.

1.5 Use headers and footers to add identifying information (p. P1-29)

- *Footers* usually appear at the bottom of slides but can appear in other locations. They are applied to all slides or to individual slides.
- Both *headers* and *footers* are used for notes pages and handouts. They are applied to all pages.

1.6 Insert, resize, and align a picture from a file (p. P1-33).

- PowerPoint supports different *graphic file types*; you can insert almost any digital image into slide shows.
- Use *sizing handles* or enter exact dimensions to increase or decrease a picture's size.
- Avoid distortion when resizing pictures by maintaining accurate height and width ratios.
- You can *align* pictures with one another or with the slide.

1.7 Apply and modify transition effects to add visual interest (p. P1-35).

- A *transition* is the visual effect that appears when one slide changes into another slide.
- The *Effect Options* command enables you to control the direction of transition movement.
- You can apply transitions to one slide or to all slides in a presentation.

1.8 Preview a presentation and print slides, handouts, and outlines (p. P1-37).

- *Backstage* view allows you to examine each slide in your presentation before printing.
- The printer you select influences how slides appear in *Backstage* view.
- **Grayscale** shows shades of black.
- **Print settings** control which slides to print, what to print, and the print order, orientation, and color range.

1.9 Change properties (p. P1-39).

- Document properties are automatically recorded in your presentation file.
- You can add properties such as subject, keywords, or category to help manage and track files.
- Edit document properties in *Backstage* view under *Info* or by opening either the *Document Properties* panel or the *Advanced Properties* dialog box.

Check for Understanding

In the **Online Learning Center** for this book (www.mhhe.com/office2013inpractice), there are a variety of resources that can be used to review the concepts covered in this chapter.

The following Online Learning Resources are available in the Online Learning Center:

- Multiple choice questions
- Short answer questions
- Matching exercises

Guided Project 1-1

Jason Andrews is a sales associate for Classic Gardens and Landscaping (CGL) and frequently talks to customers when they visit the CGL showroom. For this project, you prepare a presentation he can use when introducing customers to CGL services.
[Student Learning Outcomes 1.1, 1.2, 1.3, 1.4, 1.5, 1.6]

Files Needed: ***GardenView-01.jpg*** and ***CGLLogo-01.png***
Completed Project File Name: ***[your initials] PowerPoint 1-1.pptx***

Skills Covered in This Project

- Create a new presentation using a theme.
- Change theme colors.
- Change theme fonts.
- Add slides.
- Change font size.
- Rearrange slides.

- Use the Format Painter.
- Insert a footer.
- Check spelling.
- Adjust placeholder position.
- Insert a picture.
- Save a presentation.

---

1. Create a new presentation using a theme.
   a. Click the **File** tab, then click **New**.
   b. Double-click the **Ion** theme (Figure 1-86).

2. Save the presentation as ***[your initials] PowerPoint 1-1***.

3. Change the theme colors.
   a. Click the **Slide Master** button [*View* tab, *Master Views* group].
   b. Select the first layout on the left, **Ion Slide Master**, so your color changes are applied to all slides.
   c. Click the **Colors** button [*Slide Master* tab, *Background* group].
   d. Scroll down the list and click the **Paper** theme.
   e. Click the **Background Styles** button [*Slide Master* tab, *Background* group] and select **Style 3** (Figure 1-87).

4. Change the theme fonts.
   a. Click the **Theme Fonts** button [*Slide Master* tab, *Background* group].
   b. Scroll down the list and click the **Candara** font group.
   c. Click the **Close Master View** button [*Slide Master* tab].

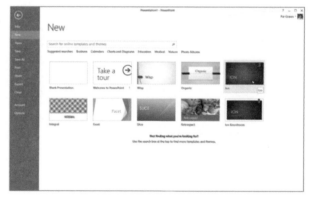

1-86 Ion theme selected

1-87 Background Style 3

5. Type the following text in the placeholders on slide 1:

Title   Creating Beautiful Outdoor Spaces
Subtitle   Jason Andrews, Sales Associate

6. Apply **bold** and a **shadow** [*Home* tab, *Font* group] to both the title and subtitle. Change the title font size to **66 pts**. and the subtitle font size to **28 pts**. [*Home* tab, *Font* group].

7. Add slides.
   a. Click the **New Slide** button [*Home* tab, *Slides* group] to add a new slide that automatically has the **Title and Content** layout. Type the following text for slide 2:

   Slide 2 Title   Our Services
   Bulleted items   Garden center
                     Tree nursery
                     Gift shop
                     Delivery and installation
                     Patios and irrigation systems

   b. Repeat this process to create three new slides with the following text:

   Slide 3 Title   Available Products
   Bulleted items   Shrubs, perennials, annuals
                     Soils and mulches
                     Garden décor including fountains
                     Shade trees and evergreen screening trees
                     Flowering or ornamental trees
                     Trees and plants for Christmas

   Slide 4 Title   Why Sustainable Design?
   Bulleted items   Energy efficiency increased
                     Water efficiency increased
                     Dependency on chemicals decreased
                     Vigor assured through native and hardy plants

   Slide 5 Title   We Make It Easy
   Bulleted items   We can do the entire project or we can assist
   (indent as shown)   You can do as much, or as little, as you like

                     We will provide:
                          Landscape design planning or just advice
                          Soil testing
                          Low-cost delivery
                          Fountain set up

   c. Click the **New Slide** list arrow [*Home* tab, *Slides* group] and click the **Title Slide** layout. Type this text in the placeholders:

   Title   Call for a Consultation
   Subtitle   615-792-8833

8. Move the slide 5 thumbnail before slide 4.

9. Apply bold and use the *Format Painter*.
   a. On slide 2, select the title text and apply **bold**.
   b. Double-click the **Format Painter** button [*Home* tab, *Clipboard* group] so you can apply this change more than one time.

c. Press **Page Down** and click the title text on slide 3 to apply the same change.

d. Repeat for slides 4 and 5.

e. Click the **Format Painter** button or press **Esc** to stop applying formatting.

10. Increase the font size on other slides.

a. On slide 2, select the bulleted text placeholder and click the **Increase Font Size** button [*Home* tab, *Font* group] to increase the font size to **24 pts**.

b. Repeat for slides 3-5. On slide 4, the font size for level 2 bulleted text changes to **20 pts**.

c. On slide 6, increase the font size for the phone number to **32 pts**.

1-88 *Header and Footer* dialog box

11. Create a footer with the company name in the footer text.

a. Click the **Header & Footer** button [*Insert* tab, *Text* group].

b. On the *Slide* tab, select **Date and time** with **Update automatically**, **Slide number**, and **Footer** (Figure 1-88).

c. In the *Footer* text box, type Classic Gardens and Landscapes.

d. Select **Don't show on title slide**.

e. Click the **Apply to All** button.

12. Click the **Spelling** button [*Review* tab, *Proofing* group] and correct any spelling errors you find.

1-89 Completed title slide

13. Make the title slide look more distinctive by adjusting the placeholders and inserting the company logo and a picture.

a. On slide 1, select the subtitle and click the **Change Case** button; then select **Capitalize Each Word**.

b. Click the **Insert** tab; then click the **Pictures** button.

c. Locate the folder where your files are saved.

d. Select **GardenView-01.jpg** and click **Insert** to insert the picture.

e. Align the picture, title, and subtitle as shown in Figure 1-89.

f. Follow the same procedure to insert the logo, which is a picture file named **CGLLogo-01.png**.

14. Resize the logo width to **5.5"** [*Picture Tools Format* tab, *Size* group] and the height will automatically adjust. Position the logo as shown in Figure 1-89.

15. Save and close the presentation (Figure 1-90).

1-90 PowerPoint 1-1 completed

Guided Project 1-2

Solution Seekers, Inc., a management consulting firm, is preparing a series of brief presentations to be used in a training program for new hires. For this project, you develop a presentation about how to get better results when writing email messages.
[Student Learning Outcomes 1.1, 1.2, 1.3, 1.6, 1.7, 1.8, 1.9]

Files Needed: **EmailResults-01.pptx**, **EmailContent-01.pptx**, and **AtSymbol-01.jpg**
Completed Project File Name: **[your initials] PowerPoint 1-2.pptx**

Skills Covered in This Project

- Open a presentation.
- Change bullets.
- Reuse slides from another presentation.
- Rearrange slides.
- Check spelling.
- Adjust placeholder position.

- Insert a picture.
- Apply transitions.
- Preview a presentation.
- Change presentation properties.
- Print a handout.
- Save a presentation.

---

1. Open and rename a presentation.
   a. Open the **EmailResults-01** presentation from your student files.
   b. Press **F12** to open the *Save As* dialog box and save this presentation as **[your initials] PowerPoint 1-2**.

2. On slide 2, change the bullets to emphasize them more.
   a. Select the bulleted text.
   b. Click the **Bullets** list arrow [*Home* tab, *Paragraph* group].
   c. Select **Bullets and Numbering**.
   d. Click the **Color** button and select **Brown**, **Text 2** (Figure 1-91).
   e. Change the size to **80%** of text.
   f. Click the **Customize** button and change the font (if necessary) to **Wingdings 2** (Figure 1-92).
   g. Select the bold **X** (Character code 211) and click **OK** to close the *Symbol* dialog box.
   h. Click **OK** again to close the *Bullets and Numbering* dialog box.

3. Reuse slides from another presentation.
   a. Click the **New Slide** list arrow and select **Reuse Slides**.
   b. On the *Reuse Slides* pane, click **Browse**; then select **Browse file** and locate your student files.
   c. Select the presentation **EmailContent-01** and click **Open**. (This presentation has spelling errors that you will fix later.)

1-91 Change bullet color

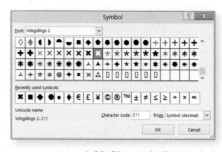

1-92 Change bullet symbol

d. On the *Reuse* Slides pane (Figure 1-93), click all four slides to insert them.
e. Close the *Reuse Slides* pane.

1-93 *Reuse Slides* pane

4. On the *Slides* tab, rearrange the six slides in this order: "Getting Results with Email," "Ask These Questions, Why?," "Write a Meaningful Subject Line," Organize It!," and "Keep It Short."

5. Click the **Spelling** button [*Review* tab, *Proofing* group] and correct each of the spelling errors.

6. Use the *Format Painter* to change bullets.
   a. On slide 2, select the body placeholder with the bulleted text.
   b. Double-click the **Format Painter** button [*Home* tab, *Clipboard* group] so you can apply what you have copied more than one time.
   c. Press **Page Down** and click the list on slide 3 to apply the change for the first-level bullets.
   d. Repeat for slides 4 and 5.
   e. Press **Esc** to end formatting.

7. On slide 3, move the picture down so it does not overlap the listed text.

8. On slide 6, use a different picture and adjust text position.
   a. Delete the picture on the right.
   b. Click the **Insert** tab; then click the **Pictures** button.
   c. Locate the folder where your student files are saved.
   d. Select *AtSymbol-01.jpg* and click **Insert** to insert the picture.
   e. Adjust the size of the title and subtitle placeholders to fit the text; then position them both on the gold shape.
   f. Align the picture, title, and subtitle as shown in Figure 1-94.

1-94 **Completed ending slide**

9. Apply one transition to all slides.
   a. Click the **Slide Sorter** button [*Status bar*].
   b. Press **Ctrl+A** to select all slides.
   c. Click the **Transitions** tab.
   d. Click the **Switch** transition from the gallery.

10. Change the movement direction.
    a. With all slides selected, click **Effect Options** [*Transition* tab, *Transition to This Slide* group] (Figure 1-95).
    b. Select **Left**.

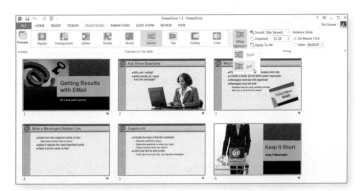

1-95 *Effect Options*

11. Preview the presentation.
    a. Click **Preview** [*Transitions* tab] to examine the movements in *Slide Sorter* view.
    b. Click off a slide to remove the selections.
    c. Click the **Slide Show** button [*Status bar*] and advance through the slides to see the movements in *Slide Show* view.

12. Change some of the presentation properties.
   a. Click the **File** tab, then the **Info** button.
   b. Click the **Properties** button; then click **Show Document Panel**. Type this information in the respective fields.

   Author: Your Name *(unless it already appears)*
   Title: Getting Results with Email *(already entered)*
   Subject: Writing
   Comments: This presentation is for the new hire seminar.

   c. Click the **Close** button to close the *Document Properties* panel.

13. Print slides as a handout.
   a. Click the **File** tab, then the **Print** button on the left.
   b. Select the appropriate printer.
   c. Change the following *Settings* by clicking the button list arrow for each option:

   Which Slides to Print: **Print All Slides**
   What to Print: **Handouts, 6 Slides Horizontal, Frame Slides, Scale to Fit Paper**
   Print Order: **Collated**
   Orientation: **Portrait**
   Color Range: **Grayscale** (or **Color** if you prefer)

   d. Click the **Print** button at the top of the *Backstage* view.

14. Save and close the presentation (Figure 1-96).

1-96 PowerPoint 1-2 completed

Guided Project 1-3

At Placer Hills Real Estate, realtors are always thinking of ways to help sellers make their homes more marketable and help buyers find the right home. For this project, you prepare a presentation for realtors to use when they speak with individual clients to explain how sellers can provide an added-value benefit by offering a home warranty.
[Student Learning Outcomes 1.1, 1.2, 1.5, 1.6, 1.7, 1.9]

Files Needed: *PHRELogo-01.png* and *HomeWarranty-01.pptx*
Completed Project File Name: *[your initials] PowerPoint 1-3.pptx*

Skills Covered in This Project

- Create a new presentation using an online template.
- Change font size.
- Adjust picture position.
- Insert a picture.
- Reuse slides from another presentation.

- Check spelling.
- Insert a footer.
- Apply transitions.
- Change presentation properties.
- Save a presentation.

---

1. Create a new presentation using an online template.
   a. Click the **File** tab; then click **New**.
   b. In the search box, type the search term real estate and click the **Start Searching** button or press **Enter**.
   c. Select the **For sale design template** (Figure 1-97) and click **Create** to download it. Although it is called a template, it contains only background graphics and no content that you need to remove. This template uses the 4:3 aspect ratio. (If you are unable to download the file, it is available as the presentation *ForSale-01.pptx* in your student files.)

1-97 Online real estate themes and templates

2. Save the presentation as *[your initials] PowerPoint 1-3*.

3. Type the following text in the placeholders on slide 1:

Title	Gremlin-Proof Sales
Subtitle	Angie O'Connor
	Sales Associate

4. Increase the font size of the title to **60 pts**. and move the placeholder down slightly.

5. Insert the PHRE company logo.
   a. Click the **Picture** button [*Insert* tab, *Images* group] and locate your student files.
   b. Select *PHRELogo-01.png* and click **Insert** (or double-click the file name) to insert the picture.
   c. Position this logo in the upper left as shown in Figure 1-98.

1-98 Completed title slide

6. Reuse slides from another presentation.
   a. Click the **New Slide** list arrow and select **Reuse Slides**.
   b. On the *Reuse Slides* pane, click **Browse**. Select **Browse file** and locate your student files.
   c. Select the presentation *HomeWarranty-01* and click **Open**.
   d. On the *Reuse Slides* pane (Figure 1-99), click slides 2–6 to insert them.
   e. Close the *Reuse Slides* pane.

7. Click the **Spelling** button [*Review* tab, *Proofing* group] and correct any spelling errors.

8. On slide 6, resize the picture on the top to stretch it to the top of the slide.

9. Add a footer to all slides except the title slide.
   a. Click the **Header & Footer** button [*Insert* tab, *Text* group].
   b. On the *Slide* tab, select *Slide number* and *Footer*.
   c. In the *Footer* text box, type Placer Hills Real Estate.
   d. Select *Don't show on title slide*.
   e. Click the **Apply to All** button.

10. Apply one transition to all slides.
    a. Click the **Slide Sorter** button [*Status bar*].
    b. Press **Ctrl+A** to select all slides.
    c. Click the **Transitions** tab.
    d. Click the **More** button to open the gallery; then click the **Box** effect.
    e. Click **Effect Options** [*Transitions* tab, *Transition to This Slide* group].
    f. Select **From Bottom** (Figure 1-100).
    g. Click **Preview** [*Transitions* tab] to see the movements in *Slide Sorter* view.
    h. Click the **Slide Show** button [*Status bar*] and advance through the slides to see the movements in *Slide Show* view.
    i. Double-click slide 1 to return to *Normal* view.

1-99 *Reuse Slides* pane

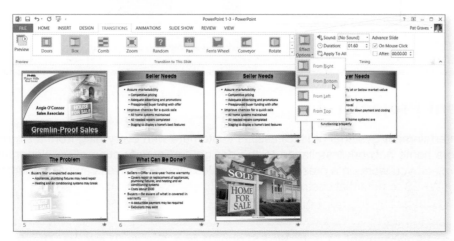

1-100 Transition Effect Options

11. Change some of the presentation properties.
    a. Click the **File** tab; then click the **Info** button.
    b. Click the **Properties** button; then click **Show Document Panel**. Type the following information in the respective fields:

Author	Angie O'Connor
Title	Gremlin-Proof Sales
Subject	Sales Strategies
Comments	Seller can offer a home warranty to encourage buyer purchase.

    c. Click the **Close** button to close the *Document Properties Panel*.

12. Save and close the presentation (Figure 1-101).

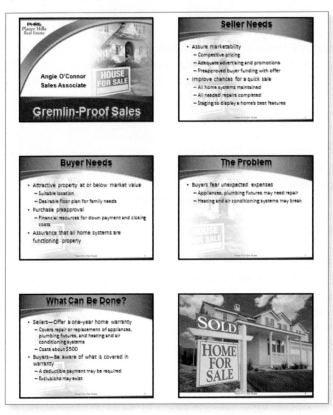

1-101 PowerPoint 1-3 completed

Independent Project 1-4

Wilson Home Entertainment Systems (WHES) assists customers with everything from a single television purchase to a home network installation to the design and construction of an elaborate home theater. In this project, you work on a presentation that sales representatives can use to demonstrate the capabilities of WHES to potential customers.
[Student Learning Outcomes 1.1, 1.2, 1.4, 1.6, 1.7, 1.9]

Files Needed: *SpecialEnvironment-01.pptx*, *WHESLogo-01.png*, *Family-01.jpg*, and *Theater1-01.jpg*
Completed Project File Name: *[your initials] PowerPoint 1-4.pptx*

Skills Covered in This Project

- Open a presentation.
- Add slides.
- Apply a theme.
- Change theme colors.
- Insert a picture.

- Adjust placeholders.
- Check spelling.
- Apply transitions.
- Change presentation properties.
- Save a presentation.

1. Open the presentation **SpecialEnvironment-01**.

2. Save the presentation as **[your initials] PowerPoint 1-4**.

3. After slide 1, insert two new slides. Type the following text for slides 2 and 3:

Slide 2 Title	Our Residential Services
Bulleted items	Design
	Sales
	Installation
	Maintenance

Slide 3 Title	Sales
Bulleted items	Authorized dealer for the highest-quality home theater technology in the industry
	Televisions
	Video Projectors
	Blu-Ray Players
	Audio Systems

4. Apply a theme and change theme colors.
    a. Select the **Integral** theme and the third **Variant** (Figure 1-102).
    b. Click the **View** tab then the **Slide Master** button.
    c. Scroll to the top of the layouts and select the first layout, *Integral Slide Master Layout* on the left so your color changes are applied to all slides.
    d. Click the **Colors** button.
    e. Scroll down the list and click the **Orange Red** theme colors.
    f. Click the **Close Master View** button.

1-102 Change Variant

5. On slide 1, insert different pictures.
    a. Delete the popcorn picture.
    b. Delete the subtitle placeholder.
    c. From your student files, insert **Family-01.jpg** and **WHESLogo-01.png**.
    d. Increase the family picture size (height **5"** and width **7.52"**) and align it on the top right (Figure 1-103).
    e. Align the logo on the bottom right.
    f. Move the title placeholder up and resize it so it fits in the red area on the left and word wraps as shown. Make the text **bold**, change the font color to **White**, increase the font size to **66 pts.**, and apply a **shadow**.

1-103 Completed title slide

6. Click the **Spelling** button and correct any spelling errors you find.

7. On slide 2, increase the text size and insert a picture.
    a. Select the bulleted text placeholder and change the font size to **40 pts**.
    b. From your student files, insert **Theater1-01.jpg** and increase the picture size (height **5"** and width **7.52"**) and align it on the bottom right.

8. On slide 6, increase the picture size (height **2.18"** and width **9"**) and center it horizontally in the space below the text.

9. Apply one transition to all slides.
   a. In *Slide Sorter* view, select all the slides and apply the **Cube** transition.
   b. Apply the **From Right** effect option.
   c. Double-click slide 1 to return to *Normal* view.

10. Insert the following presentation properties using the **Document Properties Panel:**

Author	Liam Martin
Title	Create Your Special Environment
Subject	Residential Services

11. Save and close the presentation (Figure 1-104).

1-104 PowerPoint 1-4 completed

Independent Project 1-5

The Advising Offices in the Sierra Pacific Community College (SPCC) District work to assist students throughout the completion of their academic programs. Because SPCC has a large population of students who are retraining themselves for different types of employment, job-related information is especially important. For this project, you prepare a presentation about writing resumes.
[Student Learning Outcomes 1.1, 1.2, 1.3, 1.4, 1.7, 1.8]

File Needed: ***ResumeUpdates-01.pptx***
Completed Project File Name: ***[your initials] PowerPoint 1-5.pptx***

Skills Covered in This Project

- Open a presentation using an online template.
- Add slides.
- Reuse slides from another presentation.
- Rearrange slides.
- Change theme colors.

- Change bullets.
- Adjust placeholders.
- Check spelling.
- Apply transitions.
- Print a handout.
- Save a presentation.

1. Create a new presentation from an online template.
   a. Click the **File** tab; then click **New**.
   b. In the search box, type business woman design template and press **Enter**.
   c. Select the **Business woman design template** (Figure 1-105) and click **Create** to download it. This template uses the 4:3 aspect ratio. (If you are unable to download the file, it is available as the presentation **Business-01.pptx** in your student files.)

2. Save the presentation as *[your initials]* **PowerPoint 1-5**.

1-105 Online business woman themes and templates

3. On slide 1, type the following text:

   Title   Resume Updates
   Subtitle   Your First Impression

4. After slide 1, insert two new slides. Type the following text for slides 2 and 3:

   Slide 2 Title   Accomplishments, Not Duties
   Bulleted items   Include only the most impressive details about your career
                    Quantify your day-to-day tasks
                        How many times?
                        What was the result?
                        How much money was saved?

   Slide 3 Title: Proofread
   Bulleted items   Employers take spelling and grammar errors as signs of carelessness
                    Ask a trusted friend or colleague to look at your resume

5. Reuse slides from another presentation.
   a. Click the **New Slide** list arrow and select **Reuse Slides**.
   b. On the *Reuse Slides* pane, click **Browse** and select **Browse file**. Locate the student file **ResumeUpdates-01** and click **Open**.
   c. On the *Reuse Slides* pane, click all three slides to insert them.
   d. Close the *Reuse Slides* pane.

6. Move the slide 3 (*Proofread*) thumbnail to the end of the presentation.

7. Change theme colors.
   a. Click the **View** tab; then the **Slide Master** button.
   b. Select the first *Master Layout* on the left so your color changes are applied to all slides.
   c. Click the **Colors** button and select the **Blue II** theme colors (Figure 1-106).
   d. Click the **Close Master View** button.

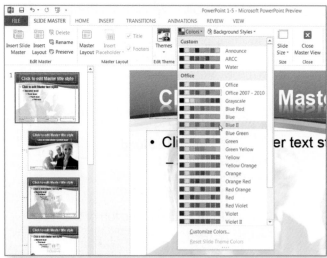

1-106 Change theme colors

8. On slide 2, change the bullets to emphasize them more.
   a. Select the level 1 bulleted text.
   b. Click the **Bullets** list arrow and select **Bullets and Numbering**.
   c. Click the **Color** button and select **Dark Teal**, **Text 2**.
   d. Change the size to **80%** of text if necessary.
   e. Click the **Customize** button and change the font to **Wingdings 2** (Figure 1-107).
   f. Select the large diamond (Character code 191) and click **OK** to close the *Symbol* dialog box.
   g. Click **OK** again to close the *Bullets and Numbering* dialog box.

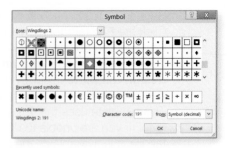

1-107 Change bullet symbol

9. On slide 2, resize the top of the bulleted text placeholder by dragging it down so the text does not overlap the decorative blue title area. Repeat for all other slides.

10. Use **Format Painter** to change the level 1 bullets on all other slides.

1-108 Completed title slide

11. On slide 1, change the title and subtitle placeholders to **Left alignment**; then align both placeholders on the left (but not to the slide) (Figure 1-108).

12. Click the **Spelling** button and correct any spelling errors you find.

13. Apply one transition to all slides.
    a. Click the **Transitions** tab and apply the **Reveal** transition.
    b. Apply the **Through Black from Right** effect option.
    c. Click **Apply To All**.

14. Print slides as an outline (Figure 1-109).
    a. Click the **File** tab; then click the **Print** button on the left.
    b. Select the appropriate printer.
    c. Change the following *Settings* by clicking the list arrow for each option as necessary:

    Which Slides to Print: **Print All Slides**
    What to Print: **Outline**
    Print Side: **Print One Sided**
    Print Order: **Collated**
    Orientation: **Portrait**
    Color Range: **Grayscale**

    d. Click the **Print** button at the top of the *Backstage* view.

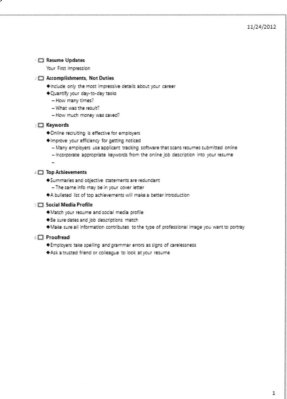

1-109 Outline

15. Save and close the presentation (Figure 1-110).

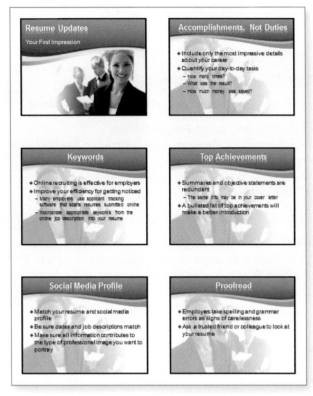

1-110 PowerPoint 1-5 completed

Independent Project 1-6

At the Hendersonville Civic Center, workshops are given for the community to address fitness, health, and wellness issues. For this project, you develop a presentation for an upcoming series about helping families become more active.
[Student Learning Outcomes 1.1, 1.2, 1.3, 1.4, 1.5, 1.6, 1.7, 1.9]

Files Needed: **PedestrianSafety-01.pptx**, **Walk1-01.jpg**, and **Walk2-01.jpg**
Completed Project File Name: **[your initials] PowerPoint 1-6.pptx**

Skills Covered in This Project

- Create a new presentation using a theme.
- Change case.
- Reuse slides from another presentation.
- Check spelling.
- Change theme colors.
- Change theme fonts.

- Rearrange slides.
- Insert a picture.
- Adjust placeholders.
- Insert a footer.
- Apply transitions.
- Change presentation properties.
- Save a presentation.

1. Create a new presentation and select the **Retrospect** theme and **Green** variant.

2. Save the presentation as *[your initials] PowerPoint 1-6*.

3. On slide 1, type the following text:

Title	Pedestrian Safety Matters
Subtitle	Keeping That New Year's Resolution To Be More Active

4. Select the subtitle text and change the case to **Capitalize Each Word**.

5. Click the **New Slide** list arrow and select **Reuse Slides**.
   a. On the *Reuse Slides* pane, click **Browse**. Select **Browse file** and locate your student file *PedestrianSafety-01*. Click **Open**.
   b. On the *Reuse Slides* pane, click all slides to insert them.
   c. Close the *Reuse Slides* pane.

6. Click the **Spelling** button [*Review* tab, *Proofing* group] and correct any spelling errors.

7. Click **View**, then **Slide Master**, and change theme colors and fonts.
   a. Change the colors to **Yellow Orange** and the background style to **Style 6**.
   b. Change the font to **Arial Black-Arial** (the font pairs are not listed in alphabetical order).
   c. Click **Close Master View**.

8. Adjust slide order to match the sequence shown in Figure 1-111.

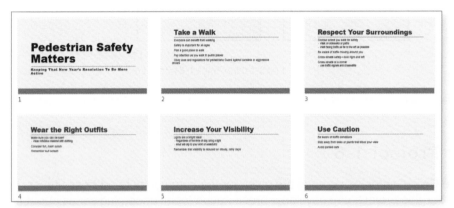

1-111 Slide order

9. On slide 1, insert a picture and resize the placeholders.
   a. From your student files, insert the picture *Walk1-01.jpg*.
   b. Change the picture height to **7.5"** and align it to the slide on the top right.
   c. Adjust the size of the title and subtitle placeholders so the text wraps as shown in Figure 1-112.

10. On slide 2, put your insertion point in front of the word "Guard" and press **Enter**.

1-112 Completed title slide

11. Add a footer to all slides except the title slide.
    a. Click the **Header and Footer** button.
    b. On the *Slide* tab, select *Slide number* and *Footer*.
    c. In the *Footer* text box, type Pedestrian Safety Matters.
    d. Select **Don't show on title slide**.
    e. Click the **Apply to All** button.

12. On slide 6, insert a picture and resize the placeholder.
    a. From your student files, insert the picture **Walk2-01.jpg**.
    b. Change the picture height to **7.5"** and align it to the slide on the top right.

13. Apply one transition to all slides.
    a. In *Slide Sorter* view, select all the slides.
    b. Select the **Push** transition and apply the **From Right** effect option.

14. Preview the transitions in *Slide Show* view.

15. Change these presentation properties using the *Document Properties* panel.

    Author   Anna Lorenzo
    Title   Pedestrian Safety Matters
    Subject   Active Lifestyle

16. Click the **Close** button to close the *Document Properties* panel.

17. Save and close the presentation (Figure 1-113).

1-113 PowerPoint 1-6 completed

Improve It Project 1-7

For this project, you revise a presentation for Margaret Jepson, insurance agent at Central Sierra Insurance. You apply a design theme, adjust its appearance, and add other information to the slide show, including a picture.
[Student Learning Outcomes 1.1, 1.2, 1.3, 1.4, 1.5, 1.6, 1.7, 1.8, 1.9]

Files Needed: *TotaledCar-01.pptx*, *Cars-01.jpg*, and *CSILogo-01.png*
Completed Project File Name: *[your initials] PowerPoint 1-7.pptx*

Skills Covered in This Project

- Open a presentation.
- Change theme colors.
- Check spelling.
- Insert a picture.
- Adjust placeholders.

- Insert a footer.
- Apply transitions.
- Change presentation properties.
- Print a handout.
- Save a presentation.

1. Open the presentation *TotaledCar-01*.

2. Save the presentation as *[your initials] PowerPoint 1-7*.

3. Use the *Slide Master* to change the theme colors and fonts.
   a. Theme colors: **Yellow**
   b. Theme background style: **Style 6**
   c. Theme font: **Gil Sans MT**

4. Check spelling and correct any spelling errors.

5. On slide 1, make text changes and insert a picture and logo (Figure 1-114).
   a. Change the title font size to **66 pts.**, make the text fit on two lines, and position the placeholder on the right of the slide beside the picture.
   b. Delete the subtitle placeholder.
   c. Insert *Cars-01* and align it on the left of the slide.
   d. Insert *CSILogo-01*, change the width to **5"**, and position it below the title text on the lower right of the slide.

1-114 Completed title slide

6. On slide 5, make the following changes:
   a. Change the slide layout to **Title Only**.
   b. Change the font size to **54 pts**. and apply right alignment.
   c. Align the placeholder on the middle right of the slide.

7. Add header and footer text and slide numbering to all slides except the title slide.

Slide footer text:	The Totaled Car
Handout header text:	Central Sierra Insurance

8. Apply the **Reveal** transition to all slides with the **Through Black from Right** effect option.

9. Change the effect option on slide 5 to **Through Black from Left**.

10. Preview the transitions.

11. Change these presentation properties using the **Document Properties Panel**.

    Author: Margaret Jepson
    Title: Totaled Car? What Next?
    Subject: Accident Insurance

12. Print a handout with 6 slides on a page, horizontal, framed, and sized to fit paper.

13. Save and close the presentation (Figure 1-115).

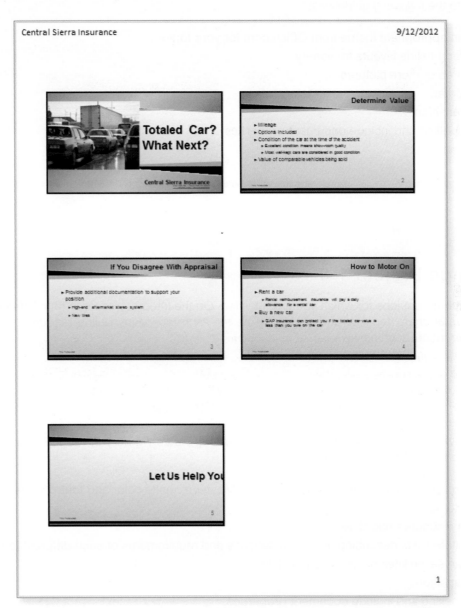

1-115 PowerPoint 1-7 completed

Challenge Project 1-8

For this project, tell the story of your favorite vacation. Create six slides that introduce the topic and describe your main points with bulleted lists. Insert photographs to illustrate locations and resize them to fit with related text.
[Student Learning Outcomes 1.1, 1.2, 1.4, 1.5, 1.6, 1.7, 1.8, 1.9]

File Needed: None
Completed Project File Name: *[your initials] PowerPoint 1-8.pptx*

Create a new presentation and save it as *[your initials] PowerPoint 1-8*. Modify your presentation according to the following guidelines:

- Select an appropriate theme from Office.com for your topic.
- Use different slide layouts for variety.
- Insert three or more pictures.
- Add a footer.
- Apply transitions.
- Check spelling and include document properties.
- Print a handout.

Challenge Project 1-9

Think about different jobs for which you are qualified. On the Internet, research four different jobs and identify several characteristics and requirements for each job. Many online resources provide job-related information, such as www.careerbuilder.com.
[Student Learning Outcomes 1.1, 1.2, 1.3, 1.4, 1.5, 1.6, 1.7, 1.8, 1.9]

File Needed: None
Completed Project File Name: *[your initials] PowerPoint 1-9.pptx*

Create a new presentation and save it as *[your initials] PowerPoint 1-9*. Modify your presentation according to the following guidelines:

- Select an appropriate theme and use the Slide Master to make color and font changes as needed for your topic.
- Create a distinctive title slide.
- Write bulleted lists describing the characteristics and requirements of each different job with no more than seven lines of text on each slide.
- Apply transitions.
- Check spelling and include document properties.
- Print handouts with six slides on a page.

Challenge Project 1-10

For this project, develop a presentation about how a presenter can manage nervous tendencies when presenting in front of an audience. Include information from your own experiences and refer to online resources, such as www.presentationmagazine.com.
[Student Learning Outcomes 1.1, 1.2, 1.3, 1.4, 1.5, 1.6, 1.7, 1.8, 1.9]

File Needed: None
Completed Project File Name: *[your initials] PowerPoint 1-10.pptx*

Create a new presentation and save it as *[your initials] PowerPoint 1-10*. Modify your presentation according to the following guidelines:

- Select an appropriate theme and use the Slide Master to make color and font changes as needed for your topic.
- Create a distinctive title slide.
- Write bulleted lists describing typical causes of nervousness and suggest ways to control nervousness when presenting.
- Insert pictures to illustrate concepts.
- Apply transitions.
- Check spelling and include document properties.
- Print an outline of the presentation.

Illustrating with Pictures and Information Graphics

CHAPTER OVERVIEW

In our world today, we are surrounded by information graphics. We see them in television programming, web sites, and published material of all kinds. We interpret signage that helps us get from place to place and readily recognize many iconic images that help us with everyday tasks. These graphics communicate visually and can be more effective than long passages of text.

PowerPoint gives you the ability to create information graphics—to visually display information in ways that help an audience quickly grasp the concepts you are presenting. You can choose from many options, such as adding shapes or color for emphasis, pictures to illustrate, diagrams to show processes, and charts to show data relationships.

STUDENT LEARNING OUTCOMES (SLOs)

After completing this chapter, you will be able to:

SLO 2.1 Work with shapes, select theme colors and standard colors, and apply styles (p. P2-67).

SLO 2.2 Create interesting and eye-catching text with *WordArt* styles and text effects (p. P2-75).

SLO 2.3 Search for pictures and illustrations, modify picture appearance, and compress picture file size (p. P2-78).

SLO 2.4 Organize information in a grid format using tables and customize the arrangement of columns and rows (p. P2-85).

SLO 2.5 Emphasize portions of a table by applying styles, colors, and effects (p. P2-90).

SLO 2.6 Show processes and relationships with *SmartArt* graphics (p. P2-94).

SLO 2.7 Improve the appearance of *SmartArt* graphics by applying styles, colors, and effects (p. P2-97).

SLO 2.8 Create charts that show relationships between data values and emphasize data in different ways (p. P2-101).

SLO 2.9 Enhance a chart by applying preset styles or manually customizing individual chart elements (p. P2-105).

CASE STUDY

Classic Gardens and Landscapes (CGL) is a landscape design company that creates beautiful and low-maintenance landscapes for outdoor living spaces. Frank and Sandra Hunter recently bought a home with minimal landscaping from a builder. They contacted Gerod Sunderland, a landscape designer for CGL, to discuss improvements.

POWERPOINT

Gerod visited the property and designed plans with several options for trees, shrubs, and plants. You have been asked to prepare a presentation illustrating his key points for his meeting with the Hunters.

Pause & Practice 2-1: Add visual interest with picture enhancements and creative text designs.

Pause & Practice 2-2: Prepare a table.

Pause & Practice 2-3: Create an organization chart and convert text to a *SmartArt* graphic.

Pause & Practice 2-4: Create column and pie charts with an enhanced appearance.

SLO 2.1 — Working with Shapes, Colors, and Styles

Shapes can emphasize key points. For example, an arrow can point to an object, or a line can connect two related objects. You can draw a variety of shapes using PowerPoint's **Shapes** gallery; each shape has both an outline and fill color. The **Quick Style**, **Color**, and **Effects** galleries make it easy to customize shapes and the other objects you use to illustrate your slides.

Shapes and Text Boxes

To insert a shape, select the shape you want from the *Shapes* gallery [*Insert* tab, *Illustrations* group] and use the following features to draw and adjust your shape:

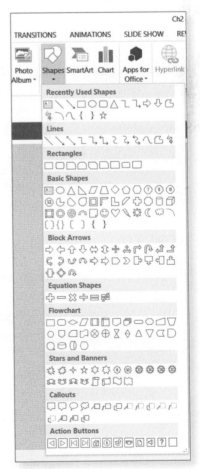

2-1 *Shapes* gallery

- **Crosshair:** A large plus sign used to draw the shape
- **Sizing handles:** Squares on the corners and sides of the shapes used to change shape size
- **Rotation handle:** Circular arrow on the top used to make shapes angle
- **Adjustment handle:** Squares used to change curves or points

You can add text to shapes and format the text as you do text in a placeholder or in a text box. However, the text in shapes or in text boxes does not appear in *Outline* view.

The *Shapes* gallery (Figure 2-1) is on the *Home* tab, the *Insert* tab, and the *Drawing Tools Format* tab. Shapes are grouped in the following categories:

- *Recently Used Shapes*
- *Lines*
- *Rectangles*
- *Basic Shapes*
- *Block Arrows*
- *Equation Shapes*
- *Flowchart*
- *Stars and Banners*
- *Callouts*
- *Action Buttons*

HOW TO: Insert a Shape

1. Click the **Insert** tab.
2. Click the **Shapes** button [*Illustrations* group] to display the *Shapes* gallery.
3. Select the shape you want and your pointer becomes a crosshair (Figure 2-2).
4. Click and drag to draw the shape in the approximate size you need (Figure 2-3). The shape appears with sizing handles and a rotation handle. It may have adjustment handles.
5. Press the **Shift** key while you drag to make oval shapes round, make rectangles square, and make lines straight.
6. Add text if needed.
7. Resize the shape if necessary and move it to the appropriate position on the slide.

2-2 Crosshair and crosshair drawing a shape

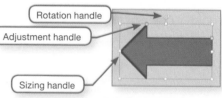

2-3 Shape with handles

When you need more than one of the same shape, you can efficiently draw them using *Lock Drawing Mode*.

HOW TO: Insert Multiple Shapes

1. Click the **Insert** tab.
2. Click the **Shapes** button [*Illustrations* group] to display the *Shapes* gallery.
3. Right-click the shape you want, and click **Lock Drawing Mode** (Figure 2-4).
4. Draw the first shape. Repeat to draw more of the same shape.
5. When you are finished, press **Esc** to turn off **Lock Drawing Mode**.

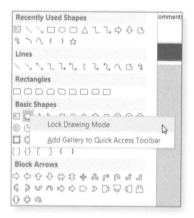

2-4 *Lock Drawing Mode*

When you select an existing shape, the *Drawing Tools Format* tab opens and the *Shapes* gallery is displayed on the left. If the existing shape does not fit your purpose, you can easily change the shape.

HOW TO: Change a Shape to Another Shape

1. Select the shape to be changed.
2. Click the **Edit Shape** arrow [*Drawing Tools Format* tab, *Insert Shapes* group] (Figure 2-5).
3. Select **Change Shape** and click a different shape from the *Shapes* gallery.
4. Click **Undo** to return to your original shape.
5. Click a blank area of the slide to deselect the shape.

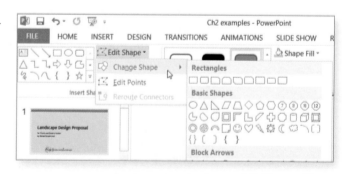

2-5 Change Shape

Using *text boxes*, you can add text anywhere on a slide without using placeholders. For example, you can add notations to identify slide objects or insert brief phrases you want to emphasize. Text boxes can be sized and moved around like any other shape.

HOW TO: Insert a Text Box

1. Click the **Insert** tab.
2. Click the **Text Box** button and your pointer changes to an insertion point. Create a text box using one of the following methods:
   - Begin typing at the insertion point and the text box grows to fit the text you type in it. The *Home* tab opens.
   - Click to change the pointer to a crosshair and draw a text box (Figure 2-6) in the approximate width you need. The *Home* tab opens. The text box height adjusts as you type text.
3. Resize if necessary by dragging sizing handles or entering height and width sizes [*Drawing Tools Format* tab, *Size* group] (Figure 2-7).
4. Click and drag the text box to move it to an appropriate position on the slide.

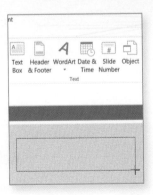

2-6 Draw a text box

2-7 Size measurements

Style Galleries

Different *Style* galleries provide collections of preset effects for shapes, pictures, or other objects. You can customize all effects using the related button such as **Shape Effects**, **Picture Effects**, or **Text Effects** to access drop-down galleries. You can choose from *Shadow, Reflection, Glow, Soft Edges, Bevel,* or *3D Rotation*. These options are described in the following table. The *Transform* effect is only available for **Text Effects**. You can also apply one or more effects without first using styles from a gallery.

Style Effect Options

Effect	Options
Shadow	**Shadow** effects appear in three groupings. An **Outer** shadow shows behind an object from different directions. An **Inner** shadow makes part of the object looked raised. A **Perspective** shadow makes an object "float" with the shadow below.
Reflection	A **Reflection** shows a mirror image below an object, like a reflection on a shiny surface or on water. You can control how close the reflection is to the object.
Glow	**Glow** provides a colored area around an object that fades into the background color on your slide. It is not available for text. Glow colors by default are based on the current theme colors but you can use other colors. The size of the *Glow* is measured in points.
Soft Edges	Some objects, such as pictures or text boxes, have a straight edge on all sides. **Soft Edges** creates a feathered edge that gradually blends into the background color. The size of the blending area is measured in points from the edge of the object inward. The larger the point size, the less you see of the object.
Bevel	**Bevel** effects add light and dark areas to create a dimensional appearance. Objects or text can look raised or inset.
3D Rotation	**3D Rotation** effects include **Parallel, Perspective,** and **Oblique** options that create an illusion of depth by rotating an object from front to back.
Transform	**Transform** is a *Text Effect* used to change the shape of words. It is not available for shapes.

The width of your PowerPoint window affects how galleries are displayed on the various tabs where they appear. If you have a narrow PowerPoint window, you need to click a quick style button to open a gallery. If your window is wide, part of a gallery is displayed and you click the **More** button to open the complete gallery.

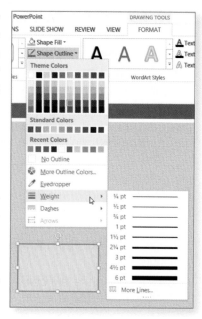

Adjust Outline Weight and Style

You can emphasize an outline by making it wider with a contrasting color; you can deemphasize an outline by making it thinner. You can choose to show no outline or match its color to the shape to make the outline disappear. Select a shape and click the **Shape Outline** button [*Drawing Tools Format* tab, *Shape Styles* group]. Choose one of the following options to see drop-down lists of options (Figure 2-8):

2-8 *Shape Outline Weight*

- **Weight:** Displays line thickness measured in points
- **Dashes:** Displays lines made with various combinations of dots and dashes (Figure 2-9)
- **Arrows:** Displays arrowheads or other shapes for both ends of a line.

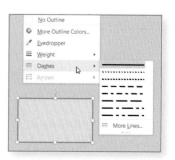

At the bottom of each drop-down list, select **More Lines** to open the *Format Shape* pane (Figure 2-10) where you can customize the following *Line* options:

- **Color:** Provides color choices
- **Transparency:** Adjusts transparency percentages
- **Width:** Controls the thickness of lines measured in points
- **Compound type:** Provides outlines with two or more lines in different thicknesses
- **Dash type:** Displays lines made with various combinations of dots and dashes
- **Cap type:** Controls the look (*Square, Round,* or *Flat*) of the ends of lines; it is usually applied to single lines or arrows
- **Join type:** Controls the look (*Round, Bevel, Miter*) for the connection point where two lines meet (for example, at the corner of a rectangle or square)
- **Begin and End Arrow type:** Controls the shape for both ends of an arrow
- **Begin and End Arrow size:** Controls the size of the shape at both ends of an arrow

2-9 *Shape Outline Dashes*

The *Format Shape* pane is a convenient place to change many options. Figure 2-10 shows the *Fill & Line* tab with *Line* options displayed because a line was selected when the pane opened. Different options appear if you have a shape selected or if you choose a *Gradient* line. Above *Line* you can select *Fill* to change shape colors. You can click the arrow in front of these options to expand or collapse each list.

2-10 *Format Shape* pane

Additional tabs include *Effects, Size & Properties,* and *Picture* with related options on each tab. Click the buttons at the top of the pane to select different tabs.

► **ANOTHER WAY**

Right-click a shape and then select **Format Shape** from the shortcut menu to open the *Format Shape* pane.

Themes and Standard Colors

As you learned in Chapter 1, each PowerPoint *Theme* starts with a set of *Theme Colors* that provide background and accent colors. When you apply *Theme Colors* for shapes and text, these colors automatically change when you select a different set of *Theme Colors*.

Consider all of the colors used throughout your presentation when you make color choices because some colors seem more appropriate than others. This section explains how colors are arranged in PowerPoint and describes different ways to "mix" custom colors. The same techniques for choosing colors apply to color fills or outline colors.

Change Solid and Gradient Fill Colors

To change the color of a selected shape, click the **Shape Fill** button [*Drawing Tools Format* tab, *Shape Styles* group] to open the **Theme Colors** gallery (Figure 2-11). Notice the colors arranged in the first row. The first four colors represent background and text colors; however, you can use these colors for other slide objects as well. The remaining six colors represent accent colors. These colors appear when viewing gallery styles and some effects. Beneath each color on the first row is a column of lighter and darker shades (shown as percentages) of that color. When you point to any color, a ScreenTip shows its name.

Below the *Theme Colors* is a single row of **Standard Colors** arranged in the order of a rainbow. When standard colors are used, they remain in effect even if *Theme Colors* change.

Gradient colors blend two or more colors together. Using the *Format Shape* pane, you can select from preset colors or customize your own gradient color by changing the colors and how they blend.

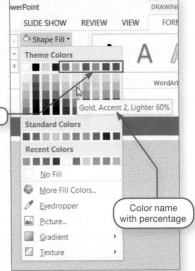

2-11 *Theme Colors* gallery

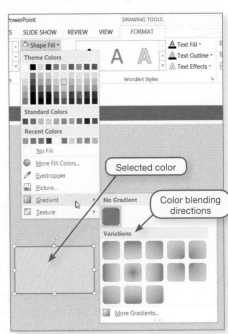

2-12 Gradient color variations for the selected color

HOW TO: Change Gradient Colors Using the Format Shape Pane

1. Select a slide object and click the **Shape Fill** button [*Drawing Tools Format* tab, *Shape Styles* group].
2. Select **Gradient** to select from a gallery of light and dark variations of the current fill color that blend the colors in different directions (Figure 2-12).

3. Click **More Gradients** at the bottom of the gallery to open the *Format Shape* pane to customize the colors.

4. Under *Fill* options, select **Gradient fill** and make selections from the following:
   - *Preset gradients:* Theme color variations (Figure 2-13)
   - *Type: Linear, Radial, Rectangular,* or *Path*
   - *Direction:* Options change based on the selected *Type.*
   - *Angle:* The percentage changes with each *Type* and *Direction.*
   - *Gradient stops:* Shapes on the gradient bar slider that you can move to control where colors change (Figure 2-14)

5. Each *Gradient stop* can be changed in the following ways to control color blending:
   - *Delete a stop:* Click the **Remove Gradient Stop** button or drag the stop off the slider.
   - *Add a stop:* Click the **Add Gradient Stop** button and click on the slider where you want it to appear.
   - *Color:* Select the stop; then change the color.
   - *Position:* Enter a different percentage or drag the stop on the slider to change its position.
   - *Transparency:* Click the arrows to change the percentage. When *Transparency* is 0%, the color is opaque (solid); as the percentage increases, the color becomes increasingly transparent and more of the background color shows through.
   - *Brightness:* Click the arrows to change the percentage. As the percentage decreases from 100%, the color softens.

6. Check **Rotate with shape** to maintain the color settings when a shape or text is rotated so it angles on the slide.

7. Under *Line* options, *select* **No line** or **Solid line** to control whether or not an outline shows around a shape or text.

8. Click **Close** and the new color is applied.

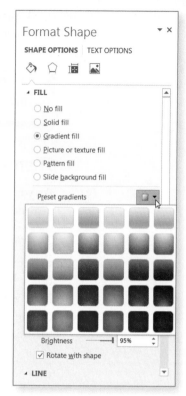

2-13 Preset gradients based on theme colors

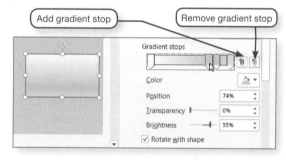

2-14 Gradient stops

> MORE INFO
>
> To apply gradient colors to *WordArt,* click the **Text Fill** button [*Drawing Tools Format* tab, *WordArt Styles* group] and select **Gradient** or select **Text Options,** then **Gradient fill** on the *Format Shape* pane.

Select Custom Colors

The *Colors* dialog box provides many solid color options on two tabs so you can either pick from displayed colors or mix a custom color. The new color appears on the lower right so you can compare it to the original color. Custom colors are not affected by any changes made to theme colors.

HOW TO: Use the Standard Tab to Select a Color

1. Select a shape and click the **Shape Fill** button [*Home* tab or *Drawing Tools Format* tab, *Shape Styles* group].
2. Click **More Fill Colors** to open the *Colors* dialog box.
3. On the *Standard* tab (Figure 2-15), colors are arranged in a honeycomb shape with colors blending from white to black below.
4. Click a color to apply it and notice the *New* color that appears on the right above the *Current* color.
5. Adjust the *Transparency* as needed.
6. Click **OK** to apply the new color.

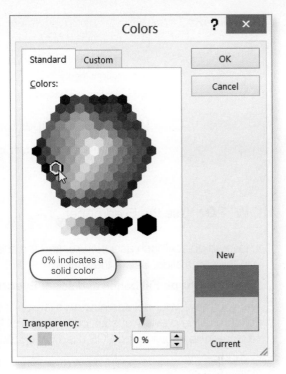

2-15 *Standard* tab on *Colors* dialog box

When you need more precision in selecting a color, use the *Custom* tab on the *Colors* dialog box. Colors are arranged like a rainbow and you drag a crosshair to select a different color. You drag the crosshair up or down to change the color intensity and then move a slider to adjust how light or dark the color appears. **Color model** information is shown on the *Custom* tab also. The **RGB** model is typically used for computer displays and colors are formed by blending values of the three numbers for *Red*, *Green*, and *Blue*. Highly saturated colors at the top have higher number values (255 maximum). You can use these numbers to match colors in different shapes and in different presentations.

HOW TO: Use the Custom Tab to Mix a Color

1. Select a shape and click the **Shape Fill** button [*Home* tab or *Drawing Tools Format* tab, *Shape Styles* group].
2. Click **More Fill Colors** to open the *Colors* dialog box.
3. On the *Custom* tab (Figure 2-16), a crosshair is positioned for the *Current* color.
   - Drag the crosshair to select a different color.
   - When the crosshair is at the top, colors are highly **saturated** (intense and vibrant).
   - As you move the crosshair down, colors become less saturated (duller and less intense).
4. Use the slider on the right to adjust the amount of white and black in the color to raise and lower the **luminosity** (lightness).
5. The current color and the new color appear in the lower right.
6. Adjust the *Transparency* as needed.
7. Click **OK** to apply the new color.

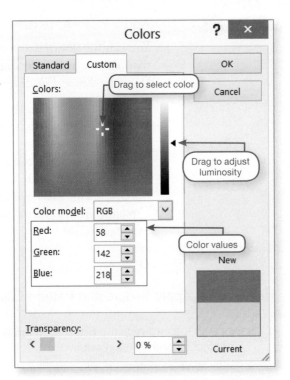

2-16 *Custom* tab on *Colors* dialog box

► **MORE INFO**

Use the *Custom* tab if you need to match a specific color such as one of the colors in a business or college logo.

Use the Eyedropper for Color Matching

You can match the exact color of an object in PowerPoint with the *Eyedropper* and apply it to a shape.

HOW TO: Use the Eyedropper

1. Have an object, such as a picture, and the shape to be changed on the same slide. Select the shape.
2. Click the **Shape Fill** button and select **Eyedropper**.
3. As you move your pointer (now an eyedropper) around the picture, a live preview of each color appears. Pause to see a ScreenTip showing the *RGB* (Red Green Blue) values (Figure 2-17).
4. Click to select the color.

Or

5. Press **Esc** to cancel the eyedropper without selecting a color.

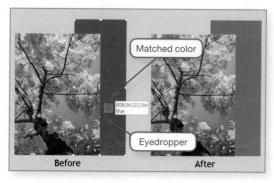

2-17 *Eyedropper* live preview and *RGB* colors

To match a color anywhere on your computer screen, left-click and hold as you drag the eyedropper pointer to other areas of the screen outside of PowerPoint.

Apply Picture, Texture, or Pattern Fills

You can fill *WordArt* and other shapes with more than colors. The following options are available from the *Shape Fill* drop-down list or from the *Format Shape* pane.

- *Texture:* Applies an image such as woven fabric or wood
- *Pattern:* Applies a mixture of two colors in various dotted or crosshatch designs
- *Picture:* Fills the *WordArt* or shape with a picture from a file or from the *Office.com Clip Art* collection

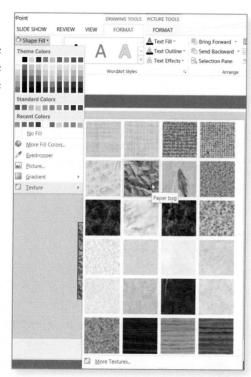

2-18 *Texture* fills

HOW TO: Apply Texture and Pattern Fills

1. Select a shape and click the **Shape Fill** button [*Drawing Tools Format* tab, *Shape Styles* group].
   - Select **Texture** to open the gallery (Figure 2-18).
   - Click a texture to apply it.

2. Select a shape and right-click. Click **Format Shape** from the callout menu to open the *Format Shape* pane.
   - Select **Pattern fill** (Figure 2-19).
   - Click a pattern to apply it.
   - Change *Foreground* and *Background* colors as needed.

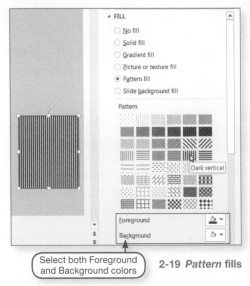

You can also use the *Format Background* pane to insert textures and adjust how they are positioned. Inserting pictures from the *Office.com Clip Art* collection is covered in *SLO 2.3 Working with Pictures*.

Select both Foreground and Background colors

2-19 *Pattern* fills

SLO 2.2

Adding Text Effects and WordArt

You can apply interesting ***text effects*** for many purposes. For example, you can make slide titles more attractive and easier to read, or you can provide a bold focal point on a slide. One way is to start by inserting ***WordArt***.

HOW TO: Apply Text Effects with WordArt

1. Click the **WordArt** button [*Insert* tab, *Text* group] to choose a style from the *WordArt Quick Styles* gallery (Figure 2-20).

2. The gallery has preset text effects showing a variety of solid, gradient, and pattern fill colors.

3. Click to select a *WordArt* style.

4. A text box is inserted on your slide with sample text that you edit to create a *WordArt* object (Figure 2-21).

5. Use the *Font* group [*Home* tab] to make the following changes:
   - Select a different font or attribute such as bold or italic.
   - Change the font size by entering a point size or using the **Increase Font Size** and **Decrease Font Size** buttons.
   - Click the **Character Spacing** button to make letters fit more closely or to spread letters apart.

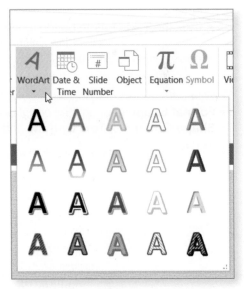

2-20 *WordArt Quick Styles* gallery

2-21 *WordArt as it first appears*

▶ MORE INFO

When using text in a large size, tight character spacing conserves space yet keeps the text easy to read.

You can also start with text in a placeholder or text box and then apply text effects. With either method, you use commands on the *WordArt Styles* group [*Drawing Tools Format* tab] (Figure 2-22) to customize your text. These commands—*Text Fill, Text Outline, and Text Effects*—are similar to the *Shape* commands.

2-22 *WordArt Styles* group

HOW TO: Apply Text Effects to Existing Text

1. Select a *WordArt* object or text in a placeholder or text box.
2. Click the **More** button [*Drawing Tools Format* tab, *WordArt Styles* group] to open the *Quick Styles* gallery (Figure 2-23).
3. Point to a style to see a live preview applied to your text.
4. Click a style to apply it.
5. Use the *WordArt Styles* group [*Drawing Tools Format* tab] to make the following changes:
   - Click the **Text Fill** button to select **Theme** or other color options.
   - Click the **Text Outline** button to select **Theme** or other color options as well as line weight and style.
   - Apply different *Text Effects* (*Shadow, Reflection, Glow, Bevel, 3D Rotation,* or *Transform*).
6. With the WordArt object selected, right-click and then click **Format Shape** to open the *Format Shape* pane. Select **Shape Options** or **Text Options** and make adjustments as needed.

2-23 *WordArt* with style changed

▶ MORE INFO

If the *WordArt Quick Styles* gallery is not open on your *Drawing Tools Format* tab, click the **Quick Styles** button.

Changing the text outline color and increasing line weight emphasizes the outline just as it does on shapes. Different line styles can create interesting effects. Using pictures or patterns as fill colors can add a creative touch when text is shown in a large size. A variety of different color and effects are shown in Figure 2-24.

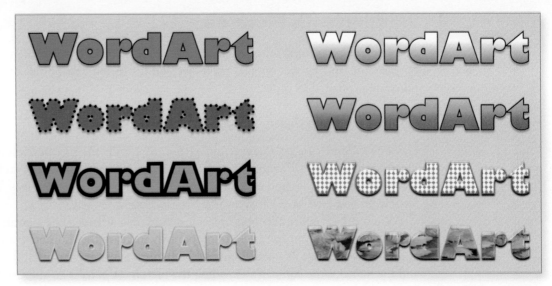

2-24 Sample fill and line effects

> ### ANOTHER WAY
>
> Select the text in a *WordArt* object and right-click. Click **Format Text Effects** from the shortcut menu to open the *Format Shape* pane with *Text Options* listed.

Transform effects are unique to text and make a word or phrase warp to fit different shapes or follow a path. For example, text can angle, flow in a circle, and arc up or down. As you point to different *Transform* effects, a live preview shows how your text will look in that shape. Once a *Transform* effect has been applied, text size is not limited to the font size because you can drag the *WordArt* sizing handles. Some *Transform* effects also provide one or more pink adjustment handles that control the slant of letters or the curve of text.

HOW TO: Apply a Transform Effect

1. Select a *WordArt* object.
2. Click the **Text Effects** button [*Format* tab, *WordArt Styles* group].
3. From the drop-down list, select **Transform** (Figure 2-25).
4. On the *Transform* gallery, point to an effect to see a live preview applied to your text.
5. Click an effect to apply it.
6. Adjust as needed using sizing and adjustment handles.

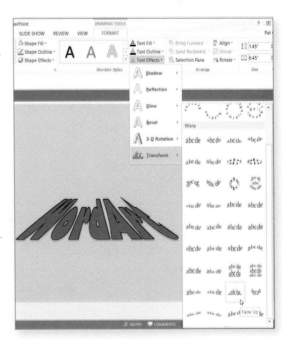

2-25 *Transform Fade Up* effect

SLO 2.3

Working with Pictures

In Chapter 1, you learned how to insert pictures from files, change their size, and align them on the slide. In this section, you use PowerPoint's search capabilities to find images to help illustrate presentation concepts.

Online Pictures and Illustrations

Use PowerPoint's *Insert Pictures* dialog box to search for pictures (digital photographs or illustrations) in the *Office.com Clip Art* collection. You can search the web using *Bing Image Search* but pictures you find may have licensing restrictions or require fees. You can also browse for images you have saved in your *SkyDrive* location.

When the search results appear, each picture has a ScreenTip identifying its name and a magnifying button you can click to temporarily increase the thumbnail size.

On the lower left of the dialog box, the picture name appears with its dimension in pixels and the name of the company providing the picture. A *pixel* is an abbreviated term for *picture element*, a single unit of information about color.

HOW TO: Search for and Insert a Picture or Illustration

1. On a slide, click the **Online Pictures** button [*Insert* tab, *Images* group] (Figure 2-26) to open the *Insert Pictures* dialog box.

2. In the *Search* box, type the search word (Figure 2-27).

3. Click the **Search** button (or press **Enter**) to activate the search.

4. Thumbnails of all the pictures that match your search word appear (Figure 2-28).

5. Click to select the picture you want.

6. Press **Ctrl** while you click to select more than one picture.

7. Click the **Insert** button. The picture will download and the *Insert Pictures* dialog box will close.

2-26 *Online Pictures* button

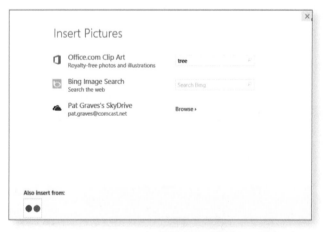

2-27 *Insert Pictures* dialog box

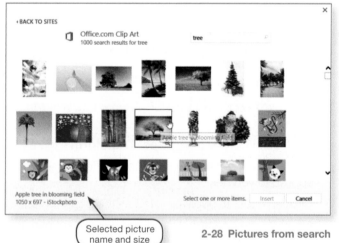

Selected picture name and size

2-28 **Pictures from search**

> **MORE INFO**
>
> You can open the *Insert Pictures* dialog box when creating a new slide by clicking the **Online Pictures** button on the content placeholder.

> **MORE INFO**
>
> Be careful to select images that are appropriate for your topic. Some cartoon-like illustrations look amateurish and may not be appropriate for academic or business situations.

Apply Picture Quick Styles

When you have selected a picture, the *Picture Tools Format* tab becomes available. Different quick styles allow you to frame pictures, give them a 3D appearance, add a reflection, or apply other treatments. You can customize each of these options using the *Picture Effects* drop-down galleries.

When you use multiple pictures in a presentation, try to maintain consistency and use the same or a similar style for each of them. If you use different styles, be sure you have a reason for making them look different so the effects do not appear random.

HOW TO: Apply a Picture Style

1. Select a picture and click the **Picture Tools Format** tab.
2. Click the **More** button on the gallery [*Picture Styles* group] to see the pre-defined effects (Figure 2-29).
3. Drag your pointer over the styles to see a live preview applied to your picture. A ScreenTip showing the style name appears.
4. Click a style to apply it to your picture.
5. To change to a different style, simply select a different one.

2-29 Picture style applied

Picture Effects are similar to *Shape Effects*. Each different effect has many options you can adjust.

HOW TO: Apply or Modify Picture Effects

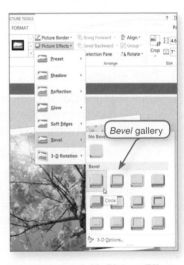

1. Select a picture and click the **Picture Effects** button [*Picture Tools Format* tab, *Picture Styles* group].
2. As you point to each effect, a drop-down gallery (Figure 2-30) provides many variations. Select **Options** at the bottom of each *Effects* drop-down gallery and make the needed changes to fine-tune a specific effect.
3. You can also right-click the picture and select **Format Picture** from the shortcut menu to open the *Format Picture* pane where you can make changes.
4. To remove a picture style, select the picture and click the **Reset Picture** button [*Picture Tools Format* tab, *Adjust* group].

2-30 *Picture Effects*

Crop a Picture

You can *crop* (trim) unwanted areas of a selected picture by dragging black *cropping handles* on the corners and sides of the picture that appear when **Crop** is selected. When you point to these handles, your pointer changes to a shape that resembles the handle. Be careful when dragging to be sure you are moving a cropping handle and not a sizing handle.

HOW TO: Crop a Picture

1. Select a picture and click the **Crop** button [*Picture Tools Format* tab, *Size* group].
2. Drag one or more cropping handles toward the center of the picture; the area to be removed from the edges is grayed out (Figure 2-31).
3. When you are satisfied, click the **Crop** button again to accept this change.

Always check your pictures to be sure they have a strong focal point. Excess detail clutters a picture and does not help your viewers quickly grasp what you want them to see.

2-31 Cropped area of a picture

Change Picture Colors

Pictures are digital photographs usually made up of many colors to achieve the realism that they portray. If an image is faded or if you want a muted image for a background area so text is easy to read, PowerPoint's *Color* feature allows you to apply different color options.

HOW TO: Change Picture Colors

1. Select a picture you want to change.
2. Click the **Color** button [*Picture Tools Format* tab, *Adjust* group].
3. A gallery appears showing different color options (Figure 2-32). The current option within each group is highlighted.
4. Click an option to apply it.
5. Click **Picture Color Options** to open the *Format Picture* pane with the **Picture Color** options listed where you can make your selections.
6. Options include the following:
   - **Color Saturation:** Colors are more muted as you move from the center to the left as saturation becomes lower; colors are more intense as you move from the center to the right as saturation increases.

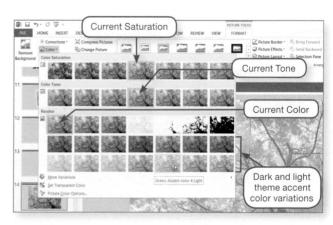

2-32 *Color* gallery

- **Color Tone:** Colors on the left have cool tones and lower temperature values; colors on the right have warm tones and higher values.
- **Recolor:** Options on the first row include *Grayscale, Sepia, Washout,* and percentages of *Black and White.* The second and third rows display dark and light monotone variations of accent colors.

Set a Transparent Color

An image with a white background works well on a slide with a white background (or on a typical Word document) because you see just the image. However, a white background can detract from an image if you place it on a slide background with a contrasting color.

Use the ***Set Transparent Color*** feature to remove a single-color background. Because this feature removes only one color, it does not work well for pictures that have a lot of detail and many colors.

HOW TO: Set a Transparent Color

1. Select a picture.
2. Click the **Color** button [*Picture Tools Format* tab, *Adjust* group].
3. Click **Set Transparent Color** and your pointer changes to a pen tool.
4. Point to the area of the picture you want to remove, and click.
5. All of the pixels with that color value disappear, revealing what is behind the picture (Figure 2-33).

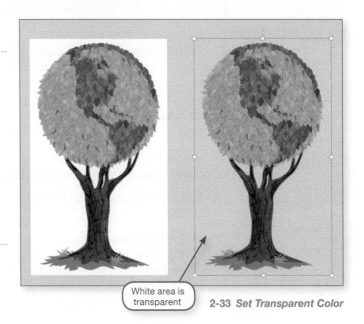

White area is transparent

2-33 Set Transparent Color

Compress Pictures

Pictures can greatly increase your presentation file size. You can **compress** single pictures or all pictures at one time to reduce the picture resolution depending on the quality you need. For print you generally need a higher resolution, and for on-screen viewing a lower resolution is usually fine. Resolution options are expressed in *pixels per inch (ppi)—Print (220 ppi), Screen (150 ppi),* and *E-mail (96 ppi).* The ppi measurement for viewing on screen is very different from the *dots per inch* (*dpi*) print measurement for printing on paper. An inexpensive printer can produce 1,200 or more *dpi,* which produces crisp, clear letterforms that are easy to read on paper.

Deleting cropped areas of pictures removes unused information and, therefore, reduces file size. Compression only affects how the pictures display in the presentation file and not the original picture files.

HOW TO: Compress Picture File Size

1. Select a picture.

2. Click the **Compress Picture** button [*Picture Tools Format* tab, *Adjust* group].

3. On the *Compress Pictures* dialog box (Figure 2-34), deselect **Apply only to this picture** if you want the compression to apply to all pictures in the presentation.

4. If you have cropped pictures, select **Delete cropped areas of pictures**.

5. Select the appropriate *Target output*.

6. Click **OK** to close the dialog box.

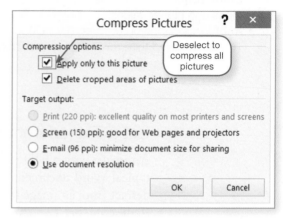

2-34 *Compress Pictures* dialog box

PAUSE & PRACTICE: POWERPOINT 2-1

When Gerod Sunderland shares his landscaping proposal with homeowners, he provides detailed printed information and uses a presentation to illustrate concepts. In this project, you add pictures and other objects to his presentation and apply a variety of styles and colors to enhance the content.

File Needed: *LandscapingProposal-02.pptx*
Completed Project File Name: *[your initials] PP P2-1.pptx*

1. Open the presentation *LandscapingProposal-02*.

2. Save the presentation as *[your initials] PP P2-1*.

3. Add a rectangle.
   a. On slide 1, click the **Shapes** button [*Insert* tab, *Illustrations* group].
   b. Select the rectangle shape.
   c. Click and drag to draw a rectangle across the slide.
   d. Change the rectangle height to **.4"** and width to **13.33"** [*Drawing Tools Format* tab, *Size* group].
   e. Click the **Shape Fill** button [*Drawing Tools Format* tab, *Shape Styles* group] and select **Brown, Accent 5, Darker 25%**.
   f. Click the **Shape Outline** button and select **No Outline**.
   g. Position the rectangle below the white line as shown in Figure 2-35.

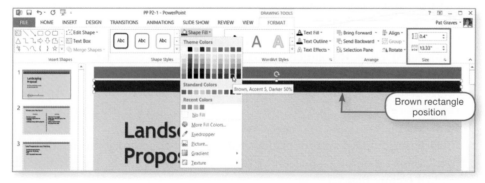

2-35 Change *Shape Fill* color

4. Add text effects.
   a. On slide 1, select the title and click the **Text Effects** button [*Drawing Tools Format* tab, *Word Art Styles* group].
   b. Select **Bevel** and then **Circle**.
   c. Repeat to select **Shadow** and then **Offset Diagonal Bottom Right** (Figure 2-36).

5. Add a frame shape.
   a. On slide 3, click the **Shape** button [*Insert* tab, *Illustrations* group] and select the **Frame** shape under the *Basic Shapes* heading.
   b. Click and drag to draw a frame.
   c. In the frame shape type Allow three days.
   d. Change the font size to **24 pts**.
   e. Adjust the frame size with a height of **1"** and width of **3.3"** [*Drawing Tools Format* tab, *Size* group].

6. Change to a different shape and color.
   a. Click the **Edit Shape** button arrow [*Drawing Tools Format* tab, *Insert Shapes* group] and select **Change Shape**.
   b. Click the **Bevel** shape under the *Basic Shapes* heading.
   c. Change the *Shape Fill* to **Tan, Background 2, Darker 25%**.
   d. Position this shape below the bulleted text (Figure 2-37).

7. On slide 8, add *WordArt* text.
   a. Click the **WordArt** button [*Insert* tab, *Text* group].
   b. Select the style **Gradient fill - Green, Accent 4, Outline - Accent 4.**
   c. In the *WordArt* text box type Thank you for your business!
   d. Move the *WordArt* object so it is at the top of the picture (Figure 2-38).
   e. Change the *Character Spacing* [*Home* tab, *Font* group] to **Tight**.

8. Change the *WordArt* gradient fill and outline colors.
   a. Click the **Text Fill** button [*Drawing Tools Format* tab, *WordArt Styles* group] and select **Gradient**.
   b. Click **More Gradients** to open the *Format Shape* pane.
   c. Select the second gradient stop (at Position **4%**) and click the **Remove gradient stop** button.
   d. Select the left gradient stop (at Position **0%**) and change the color to **Green, Accent 4, Lighter 40%**.
   e. Select the right gradient stop and change the color to **Green, Accent 4, Darker 50%** (Figure 2-39).
   f. Close the *Format Shape* pane.
   g. Click the **Text Outline** button and change the outline color to **Black, Text 1**.

2-36 Apply *Text Effects*

2-37 Text box positioned below list

2-38 *WordArt* with gradient

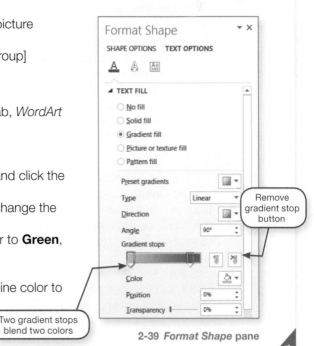

Two gradient stops blend two colors

2-39 *Format Shape* pane

9. Apply a *Transform* effect to the *WordArt*.
   a. Click the **Text Effects** button [*Format* tab, *WordArt Styles* group]. From the drop-down list, select **Transform**.
   b. On the *Transform* gallery, click the **Deflate Bottom** effect (Figure 2-40).
   c. Resize the *WordArt* to fit across the top of the picture (Figure 2-41).

10. Apply effects and use the *Format Painter.*
   a. On slide 2, select the left list heading placeholder.
   b. Change the text to **bold**.
   c. Click the **Shape Fill** button [*Drawing Tools Format* tab, *Shape Styles* group] and select **Texture**.
   d. Click the **Parchment** option.
   e. Click the **Format Painter** button [*Home* tab, *Clipboard* group]. Click the list heading placeholder on the right to apply the same changes.

11. On slide 3, search for and insert a picture.
   a. Click the **Online Pictures** button [*Insert* tab, *Images* group] to open the *Insert Pictures* dialog box.
   b. In the *Office.com* search box, type the word soil.
   c. Click **Search** (or press **Enter**) to activate the search.
   d. Locate the picture shown in Figure 2-42.
   e. Click **Insert**.

12. On slide 3, resize and crop the picture.
   a. Resize the picture to a height of **6"** and the width automatically adjusts to **4.01"** [*Picture Tools Format* tab, *Size* group].
   b. Click the **Crop** button [*Picture Tools Format* tab, *Size* group] and crop a little space from all four edges to focus more on the plant.
   c. Click the **Crop** button again to accept the crop.
   d. Click the **More** button [*Picture Tools Format* tab, *Picture Styles* group] and select the **Rotated**, **White** picture style.
   e. Position the picture on the right (Figure 2-43).

13. On slide 1, insert a picture.
   a. Click the **Online Pictures** button [*Insert* tab, *Images* group] to open the *Insert Pictures* dialog box.
   b. In the *Office.com* search box, type the word leaf.
   c. Locate the picture of a red maple leaf on a white background (Figure 2-44).

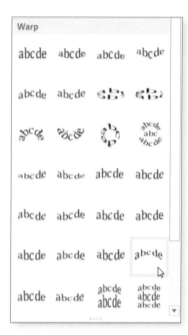

2-40 *WordArt Transform* gallery

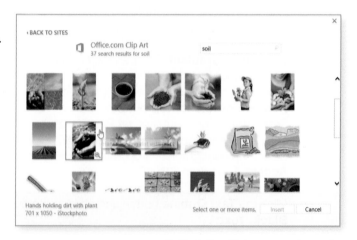

2-41 *Deflate Bottom Transform* effect applied and adjusted

2-42 *Online Pictures* search results

d. Select the thumbnail and click **Insert**.

e. On the *Picture Tools Format* tab, change the leaf height to **5"** and the width automatically adjusts.

f. With the leaf selected, click **Color** [*Picture Tools Format* tab, *Adjust* group].

g. Select **Set Transparent Color** and your pointer changes to a pen tool.

h. Click the white area around the leaf so it becomes transparent.

i. Position the leaf on the right (Figure 2-44).

14. Compress a picture file size.

a. Select the leaf and click **Compress Pictures** [*Picture Tools Format* tab, *Adjust* group].

b. Deselect **Apply only to this picture**.

c. For the *Target output,* select **Use document resolution**.

d. Click **OK**.

15. Save and close your presentation.

2-43 Completed slide 3

2-44 Completed slide 1

Creating a Table

Tables show data in an organized and easy-to-read way because information is arranged in *columns* (vertical) and *rows* (horizontal). The intersection of a column and row is a *cell*. *Border* lines and *shading* show the table structure. Working with PowerPoint tables is much like working with tables in Word.

Once you create a table, you can change its size as well as column width and row height. Use table formatting to emphasize the contents in different ways and help your audience interpret the data. If you plan to project your slides on a large screen, be sure your table information is concise so you can use a minimum font size of 20 points. If a table requires a lot of detailed information, then prepare the table as a full-page handout with body text at an 11–12 point size. You can prepare a PowerPoint slide to reference the handout as you explain the table, or perhaps show on a slide only a portion of the table.

Insert and Draw Methods

You can create a table using the **Table** button [*Insert* tab, *Tables* group]. As you drag over the columns and rows to select them, the table dimensions (such as *3×4 Table*) are shown at the top of the drop-down list. The first number represents columns and the second number represents rows. By default, columns and rows appear on the slide with even sizing, but you can adjust column width and row height as you add information.

HOW TO: Insert a Table and Select Columns and Rows

1. Display the slide where you want the table.
2. Click the **Insert** tab.
3. Click the **Table** button [*Tables* group] to open the drop-down list (Figure 2-45).
4. Drag across and down to select the number of columns and rows you need.
5. Click to insert the table.

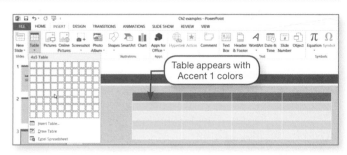

2-45 **Table cells selected**

By using the **Insert Table** command [*Insert* tab, *Tables* group], you can create a table by entering a specific the number of columns and rows.

HOW TO: Insert a Table and Enter the Number of Columns and Rows

1. Display the slide where you want to insert the table.
2. Click the **Insert** tab.
3. Click the **Table** button [*Tables* group] to open the drop-down list.
4. Click **Insert Table** and the *Insert Table* dialog box opens (Figure 2-46).
5. Specify the number of columns and rows you need.
6. Click **OK** to close the *Insert Table* dialog box and insert the table.

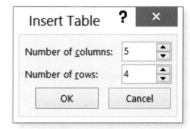

2-46 *Insert Table* dialog box

> **ANOTHER WAY**
>
> When you add a new slide, click the **Table** icon in the empty content placeholder and enter the number of columns and rows to create a table. The table width will be slightly wider than when you click the **Insert** button to create a table.

The final way to create a table is by drawing the table area and dividing it into columns and rows.

HOW TO: Draw a Table

1. Display the slide where you want the table.
2. Click the **Insert** tab.
3. Click the **Table** button [*Tables* group] to open the drop-down list.

4. Click **Draw Table** and your pointer changes to a pen tool.

5. Drag to create the table size you want.

6. Click the **Draw Table** button [*Table Tools Design* tab, *Draw Borders* group] to activate the pen tool again, and drag the pen within the table to insert horizontal and vertical lines that divide the table into rows and columns (Figure 2-47).

7. Press **Esc** to turn off the pen tool.

2-47 Draw Table

Regardless of the method you use to create a table, the *Table Tools Design* tab (Figure 2-48) and *Table Tools Layout* tab (Figure 2-49) are available when the table is active.

2-48 Table Tools Design tab

2-49 Table Tools Layout tab

Move and Select

Your insertion point indicates where you are within a table to add text. To move from cell to cell, use one of the following methods:

- Press **Tab** to move to the next cell on the right (or the first cell in the next row).
- Press **Shift+Tab** to move to the next cell on the left.
- Click a cell to move the insertion point to that cell.
- Use arrow keys to move in different directions from the current cell.

Where you point within a table influences whether you select individual cells, columns, rows, or the entire table. Your pointer changes to a selection pointer (a black arrow that points in different directions based on what you are selecting).

HOW TO: Select Cells, Columns, Rows, and the Table

1. To select a cell, point inside the left border and click when your pointer turns into a black arrow.

2. To select a column, use one of the following methods:

   - Point above its top border and click when your pointer turns into a downward-pointing black arrow (Figure 2-50).
   - Move your insertion point to any cell in the column. Click the **Select** button [*Table Tools Layout* tab, *Table* group] and click **Select Column**.

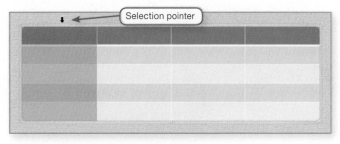

2-50 Select table column

3. To select a row, use one of the following methods:

- Point outside the table to the left of a row and click when your pointer turns into a right-pointing black arrow (Figure 2-51).
- Move your insertion point to **any cell** in the row. Click the **Select** button [*Table Tools Layout* tab, *Table* group] and click **Select Row**.

4. To select multiple cells, columns, or rows, use one of the following methods:

- Drag across adjacent cells.
- Press **Shift** as you click additional adjacent cells.

5. To select an entire table, use one of the following methods:

- Drag across all cells in the table.
- Move your insertion point to any cell in the table. Click the **Select** button [*Table Tools Layout* tab, *Table* group] and click **Select Table**.

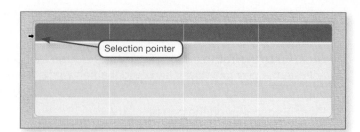

2-51 **Select table row**

Insert and Delete Rows and Columns

After you begin entering table content, you may need to add rows or columns. You can change a table's structure in several ways:

- Insert rows above or below the current row.
- Insert columns to the left or right of the current column.
- Delete rows and columns.

HOW TO: Insert and Delete Rows and Columns

1. Click inside the table.
2. Click the **Table Tools Layout** tab.
3. Insert a row or column.

- Click in a table cell next to where you want to add a column or row.
- Click the **Insert Above** or **Insert Below** buttons [*Rows & Columns* group] to add rows.
- Click the **Insert Left** or **Insert Right** buttons [*Rows & Columns* group] to add columns.

4. Delete a row or column.

- Click in a table cell where you want to delete a column or row.
- Click the **Delete** button and select **Delete Columns** or **Delete Rows** [*Rows & Columns* group] (Figure 2-52).

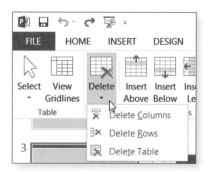

2-52 *Delete* button

> **ANOTHER WAY**
>
> Right-click a row or column and insert or delete rows and columns by selecting the appropriate option from the mini toolbar.

Merge and Split Cells

You can *merge* (combine) two or more cells in a row or column. For example, you can combine all the cells in the top row of a table so a title spans all columns (see Figure 2-53). You can *split* (divide) any single cell into two or more cells.

HOW TO: Merge and Split Cells

1. Select the cells to be merged.
   - Click the *Table Tools Layout* tab.
   - Click the **Merge Cells** button [*Merge* group] to combine those cells into one cell.
2. Select the cell (or cells) to be split.
   - Click the *Table Tools Layout* tab.
   - Click the **Split Cells** button [*Merge* group] to open the *Split Cells* dialog box and enter the number of columns and rows that you need.
   - Click **OK** to close the dialog box.

> **ANOTHER WAY**
>
> Click the **Eraser** button [*Table Tools Design* tab, *Draw Borders* group] and your pointer turns into an eraser. Click a border within the table to remove it and merge cells.

Adjust Sizing

You often need to resize tables to fit information appropriately. Column widths will vary based on content, but row height should usually be consistent.

HOW TO: Resize a Table, Cells, Columns, and Rows

1. Resize a table.
   - Enter sizes in the *Height* and *Width* boxes [*Table Tools Layout* tab, *Table Size* group].
   - Click and drag table sizing handles as you would to resize a shape.
2. Resize a cell, column, or row.
   - Point to a cell, column, or row inside a border. When your pointer changes to a splitter (Figure 2-53), click and drag to make the cell, column, or row larger or smaller.
   - Select the cell, column, or row you want to change; then enter the size you want in the *Height* and *Width* boxes [*Table Tools Layout* tab, *Cell Size* group].
3. To resize a column to fit the text within it, point to a border and double-click when your pointer changes to a splitter.
4. To evenly distribute column width or row height,
   - Select the columns or rows to be changed.
   - Click the **Distribute Rows** or **Distribute Columns** buttons [*Table Tools Layout* tab, *Cell Size* group].

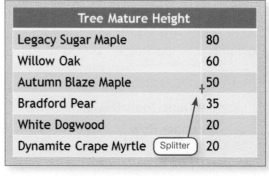

Tree Mature Height	
Legacy Sugar Maple	80
Willow Oak	60
Autumn Blaze Maple	50
Bradford Pear	35
White Dogwood	20
Dynamite Crape Myrtle (Splitter)	20

2-53 Change column width

> **MORE INFO**
>
> To maintain column width proportions, press **Shift** as you drag table sizing handles or select **Lock Aspect Ratio** before entering *Height* or *Width* sizes.

SLO 2.5

Enhancing a Table

You can format text in a table as you can any other text such as changing alignment and applying *WordArt Quick Styles*. You can also change cell margins and text direction. The following are table formatting options:

- Apply a *Table Style*.
- Customize the style by changing effect options.
- Add shading, borders, and other effects to cells, columns, or rows.

Table Style Options and Effects

On the *Table Tools Design* tab, **Table Styles** provide a gallery of built-in options for a table's design. The first style on each row of options is shown in black and white while the other six styles are in theme accent colors. Table styles are arranged in the following categories:

- *Best Match for Document*
- *Light*
- *Medium*
- *Dark*

Each table style is influenced by the features checked for **Table Style Options** [*Table Tools Design* tab]. Fill colors that emphasize table cells vary depending on which of the following options you select:

- **Header Row** or **Total Row:** The first or last row has a darker color and has bold text in a contrasting color.
- **First Column** or **Last Column:** The first or last column has a darker color and has bold text in a contrasting color.
- **Banded Rows** or **Banded Columns:** The rows or columns have alternating colors. *Banded Rows* makes reading across the table easier. *Banded Columns* emphasizes the separate columns.

HOW TO: Apply a Table Style with Header Row and Banded Rows

1. Click anywhere in the table you want to change.
2. Click the **Table Tools Design** tab.
3. Check **Header Row** and **Banded Rows** [*Table Style Options* group].
4. Click the **More** list arrow in the *Table Styles* group to see the complete gallery. The current style is highlighted.
5. Point to a style to see a live preview (Figure 2-54). ScreenTips identify each style name.
6. Click a style to apply it.

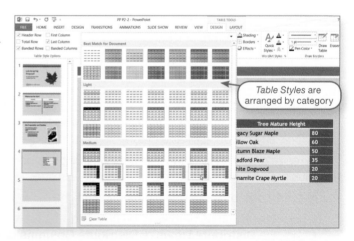

2-54 *Table Styles*

If you want to clear table formatting, click the **More** button [*Table Tools Design* tab, *Table Styles* group] and click **Clear Table**. To emphasize the table or cells within the table, such as a heading row, you can apply effects.

HOW TO: Apply Table Effects

1. Select the table, or the cells, to be changed.
2. Click the **Effects** button [*Table Tools Design* tab, *Table Styles* group (Figure 2-55).
3. Click one of the following effects and select a specific option:
   - **Cell Bevel**
   - **Shadow**
   - **Reflection**

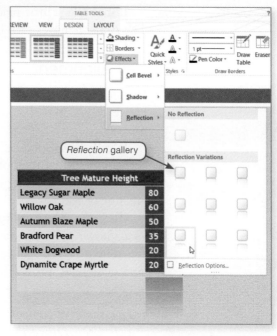

2-55 *Reflection Effects*

Shading and Border Colors

After you apply a built-in table style, you can change colors to emphasize your content or better match other aspects of your presentation. Select the cells you want to change and use the **Shading** button [*Table Tools Design* tab, *Table Styles* group] to select a different color (Figure 2-56). The icon for this button is the same as a **Shape Fill** button.

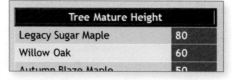

2-56 Row shading emphasizes text

Border lines separate cells and outline the edge of the table. Some table styles do not show border lines. To add lines, use the **Borders** button [*Table Tools Design* tab, *Table Styles* group] and each available option shows where the border line will be applied when that option is selected (Figure 2-57). Make sure to select the appropriate area before you apply the border change. If you want to make the border lines thicker, increase the **Pen Weight** [*Table Tools Design* tab, *Draw Borders* group] before you apply the border change. You can remove borders from selected cells by clicking the **Borders** button and selecting **No Border**.

Also, you can apply, change, and remove borders using the *Pen* tools [*Table Tools Design* tab, *Draw Borders* group].

- *Pen Color:* Change line color.
- *Pen Style:* Choose a different line style.
- *Pen Weight:* Change line thickness.
- *Draw Table:* Draw table area as well as column and row border lines.
- *Eraser:* Remove border lines.

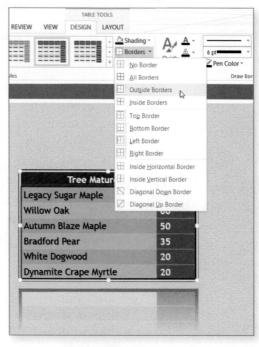

2-57 Border color and weight changed

It may take a little practice to use the pen to change table lines and not start a new table. The *Eraser* removes each line you click.

Cell Alignment

Within cells, text is aligned on the left by default, which is appropriate for words and phrases. However, numbers should usually be right-aligned to make it easy for your audience to interpret values.

If cells have a single line of text, center the text vertically in the cells. If some cells contain more text than other cells, top alignment generally works best because it imposes consistency. Bottom alignment works well for column headings when they have more than one line of text.

Click the **Align** buttons [*Table Tools Layout* tab, *Alignment* group] and choose from the following horizontal and vertical alignment options:

- *Horizontal alignment: Align Text Left, Center, Align Text Right*
- *Vertical alignment: Align Top, Center Vertically, Align Bottom*

Cell Margins and Text Direction

Some space is needed between the border lines that define a cell and the text that goes in the cell. The default *Internal Margin* spacing is *Normal*. You can change the spacing by clicking the **Cell Margins** button [*Table Tools Layout* tab, *Alignment* group] and choose from one of the following options (Figure 2-58):

- *Normal:* **.05"** top/bottom, **.1"** left/right
- *None:* **0"** all sides
- *Narrow:* **0.05"** all sides
- *Wide:* **0.15"** all sides

Click **Custom Margins** to open the *Cell Text Layout* dialog box to enter other measurements.

If text becomes too long to fit in a cell, you can change from the default horizontal direction. Be careful when using this option because your text may not be as easy to read. Click **Text Direction** and choose one of the following four options (Figure 2-59):

- **Horizontal**
- **Rotate all text 90°**
- **Rotate all text 270°**
- **Stacked**

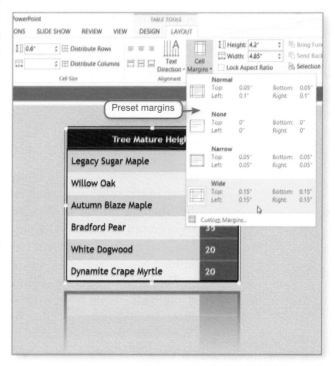

2-58 *Cell Margins increased*

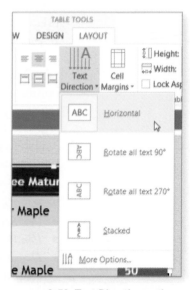

2-59 *Text Direction options*

For this project you create a table of costs, insert a row of data, and format the table to blend with other colors used in the landscaping presentation. You also add a text box to show an alternative cost.

File Needed: *[your initials] PP P2-1.pptx*
Completed Project File Name: *[your initials] PP P2-2.pptx*

1. Open the presentation *[your initials] PP P2-1* and save it as *[your initials] PP P2-2*.

2. Create a table.
   a. On slide 4, click the **Table** button on the content placeholder.
   b. On the *Insert Table* dialog box, enter 4 columns and 5 rows. Click **OK** to close the dialog box.
   c. Type the following table text. It will first appear as shown in Figure 2-60.

Item	Quantity	Cost Each	Totals
Trees—shade	3	500	1,500
Trees—ornamental	3	150	450
Perennials	30	12	360
Hydroseeding sq. ft.	8,000	,10	800

Item	Quantity	Cost Each	Totals
Trees—shade	3	500	1,500
Trees—ornamental	3	150	450
Perennials	30	12	360
Hydroseeding sq. ft.	8,000	,10	800

   2-60 Table as it first appears

   d. Select all table **cells** and change the font size to **20 pts**.

3. Adjust table sizing and alignment.
   a. Make each column the appropriate size for its content by pointing to each line separating the columns, including the right side of the table, and double-clicking when your pointer changes to a splitter.
   b. Select the "Quantity," "Cost Each," and "Totals" columns and click the **Align Right** button [*Table Tools Layout* tab, *Alignment* group].

4. Insert rows and add text.
   a. Click in the "Perennials" cell and click the **Insert Above** button [*Table Tools Layout* tab, *Rows & Columns* group].
   b. Add the following row text:
      Shrubs   10   40   400
   c. Click in the "Hydroseeding" cell and click the **Insert Below** button [*Table Tools Layout* tab, *Rows & Columns* group].
   d. On this new row, select the last three cells and click the **Merge Cells** button [*Table Tools Layout* tab, *Merge* group].
   e. Add the following row text:
      Total   3,510

5. Select styles, options, and shading.
   a. Click the **More** button [*Tables Tools Design* tab, *Table Styles* group] and select the **Medium Style 3, Accent 4** style.
   b. Select **Header Row**, **Total Row**, and **Banded Rows** [*Tables Tools Design* tab, *Table Style Options* group].

c. Select each of the rows with gray shading and click the **Shading** button [*Table Tools Design* tab, *Table Styles* group]; then select **Green**, **Accent 4**, **Lighter 80%**.

d. Select the last row and click the **Shading** button and select **Green**, **Accent 4**, **Lighter 60%**.

e. Select the first row and click the **Effects** button [*Table Tools Design* tab, *Table Styles* group], click **Cell Bevel**, and select **Circle** (Figure 2-61).

Item	Quantity	Cost Each	Totals
Trees—shade	3	500	1,500
Trees—ornamental	3	150	450
Shrubs	10	40	400
Perennials	30	12	360
Hydroseeding sq. ft.	8,000	.10	800
Total			3,510

2-61 Style, row shading, and *Bevel* effect applied

6. Add borders and a shadow effect.
   a. Select the first column.
   b. Click the **Pen Color** button [*Table Tools Design* tab, *Draw Borders* group] and select **Black**.
   c. Click the **Pen Weight** button [*Table Tools Design* tab, *Draw Borders* group] and select **1 pt**.
   d. Click the **Border** button [*Table Tools Design* tab, *Table Styles* group] and select **Left Border**.
   e. Select the last column.
   f. Click the **Border** button and select **Right Border**.
   g. Select the table and click the **Effects** button [*Table Tools Design* tab, *Table Styles* group]. Click **Shadow** and select **Offset Diagonal Bottom Right**.

7. Move the table so it is centered on the slide.

8. Insert a text box.
   a. Click the **Text Box** button [*Insert* tab, *Text* group] and click the slide to start a text box. Type the following text:
      Sod cost for 8,000 sq. ft. @ .60 = $4,800
   b. Change the font size to **20 pts** [*Home* tab, *Font* group].
   c. Click the **Shape Fill** button [*Home* tab, *Drawing* group] and select **Green**, **Accent 4**, **Lighter 60%**.
   d. Resize the text box as necessary so the text fits on one line. Move it to the lower right of the slide (Figure 2-62).

Costs Include Planting/Installation

Item	Quantity	Cost Each	Totals
Trees—shade	3	500	1,500
Trees—ornamental	3	150	450
Shrubs	10	40	400
Perennials	30	12	360
Hydroseeding sq. ft.	8,000	.10	800
Total			3,510

Sod cost for 8,000 sq. ft. @ .60 = $4,800

2-62 Completed table

9. Save and close your presentation.

Creating a SmartArt Graphic

To clearly illustrate concepts such as processes, cycles, or relationships, you can create a diagram using ***SmartArt graphics*** to help your audience see connections or sequences. This is a very important communication strategy; the shapes of the diagram are concisely labeled for each concept and the shapes you use can help people recognize relationships. For example, you can show subtopics radiating from a central topic or sequential steps in a work flow.

The *SmartArt Tools Design* tab (Figure 2-63) provides options for the overall design and styles of the *SmartArt* graphics. You can add shapes and rearrange the order of shapes.

2-63 *SmartArt Tools Design* tab

The *SmartArt Tools Format* tab (Figure 2-73) provides options to customize shape and text styles, fill colors, outline colors, and effects.

2-64 *SmartArt Tools Format* tab

SmartArt Layouts

SmartArt layouts (diagrams) are organized by type in the *Choose a SmartArt Graphic* dialog box; each type is described in the following table. When you select a layout, PowerPoint provides more information about using that specific layout.

SmartArt Graphic Types and Purposes

Type	Purpose
List	Illustrates non-sequential or grouped information
Process	Illustrates sequential steps in a process or workflow
Cycle	Illustrates a continuing sequence or concepts related to a central idea
Hierarchy	Illustrates a decision tree or top-to-bottom relationship such as an organizational chart
Relationship	Illustrates concepts that are connected such as contrasting, opposing, or converging
Matrix	Illustrates the relationship of four parts to the whole
Pyramid	Illustrates proportional or interconnected relationships
Picture	Shows pictures as integral parts of many different diagrams
Office.com	Shows diagrams from layouts on Office.com

HOW TO: Create a SmartArt Graphic

1. Display the slide where you want to insert the *SmartArt* graphic.
2. Click the **Insert** tab.
3. Click the **SmartArt** button [*Illustrations* group] to open the *Choose a SmartArt Graphic* dialog box.
4. Select a type from the list on the left (Figure 2-65).
5. Click a layout in the gallery to select it.
6. Click **OK** to close the dialog box. The *SmartArt* graphic appears on the slide with sample text.

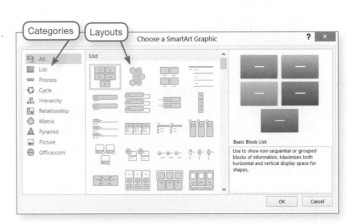

2-65 *Choose a SmartArt Graphic* dialog box

▶ ANOTHER WAY

To insert a *SmartArt* graphic on a new slide, click the **Insert SmartArt Graphic** button on the content placeholder to open the *Choose a SmartArt Graphic* dialog box.

When you insert a *SmartArt* graphic using the **SmartArt** button on the *Insert* tab, the initial size of the *SmartArt* frame may be different than if you inserted the *SmartArt* graphic using the content placeholder on a new slide with a Title and Content layout. You may need to resize the frame for your content and to fit appropriately on your slide.

If the layout you choose has picture placeholders on the shapes, such as the *Continuous Picture List* layout shown in Figure 2-66, click each picture icon to open the *Insert Pictures* dialog box. Locate the picture you want to insert and click **Insert**. The picture is sized automatically and shaped to fit the current picture placeholder.

2-66 SmartArt Continuous Picture List layout

Add Text

Keep text very concise because space is limited for each shape within the *SmartArt* frame. *List* layouts often work well if you have both Level 1 and Level 2 information (shown as indented text in a bulleted list).

Use the Text Pane

You can enter text using the **Text Pane** [*SmartArt Tools Design* tab, *Create Graphic* group] just as you would a bulleted list. As you enter text in the *Text Pane*, it also appears in the *SmartArt* shapes. Text becomes smaller in the shapes as you enter more text. You can resize or move the *Text Pane*.

Typically, only a few words appear in each shape. After the first bulleted text is entered (Level 1 text), press **Enter** to add a second bullet. If the layout you are using has enough space, press **Tab** to indent for Level 2 text. Notice in Figure 2-67 that Level 1 text is in a shape and Level 2 text is in a bulleted list below the shape.

HOW TO: Type SmartArt Text Using the Text Pane

1. Open the *Text Pane,* if necessary, by using one of the following methods:
   - Click the **Text Pane** button [*SmartArt Tools Design* tab, *Create Graphic* group].
   - Click the **Text Pane** control on the left side of the *SmartArt* frame.
2. Type text after the first bullet to add Level 1 text.
3. Press **Enter** to add a new item. Another shape appears in your diagram, and shape sizes automatically adjust.
4. Press **Tab** to indent for Level 2 text (Figure 2-67).
5. Use arrow keys to move through the listed items.
6. To remove a shape, delete the related bulleted text in the *Text Pane.*

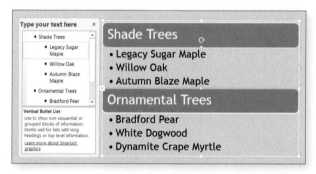

2-67 SmartArt Text Pane

Enter Text in SmartArt Shapes

You can type text directly into each *SmartArt* shape.

HOW TO: Type Text in SmartArt Shapes

1. Close the *Text Pane* by clicking the **Close** button in the top-right corner of the pane.
2. Click each *SmartArt* shape to select it and type your text. A dashed border appears as you type or edit your text.
   - Pressing **Tab** does not move your insertion point between shapes.
   - You cannot drag text into a *SmartArt* shape, but you can paste copied text.
3. Press **Delete** to remove a selected shape.
4. Click outside the *SmartArt* frame, or press **Esc**, when you are finished (Figure 2-68).

2-68 Completed picture *SmartArt* graphic

Convert Text to a SmartArt Graphic

You can change bulleted text to a *SmartArt* graphic.

HOW TO: Convert Text to a SmartArt Graphic

1. Select the bulleted text placeholder or the text within the placeholder that you want to convert to a *SmartArt* graphic.
2. Click the **Home** tab.
3. Click the **Convert to SmartArt Graphic** button [*Paragraph* group] (Figure 2-69). The gallery displays layouts that are designed to show listed information.
4. Select the layout you want and click **OK** to close the dialog box and insert the *SmartArt* graphic.

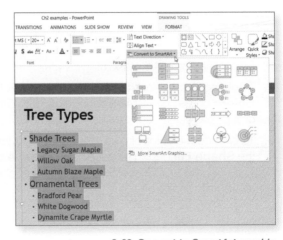

2-69 Convert to *SmartArt* graphic

SLO 2.7

Enhancing a SmartArt Graphic

When you create a *SmartArt* graphic, by default it appears using the first accent color in the current color theme. You can customize many style options and colors using the *SmartArt Tools Design* tab as well as rearrange shape order, add shapes, or change layouts.

SmartArt Styles

The **SmartArt Styles** gallery provides different effects for emphasizing the diagram shapes. In the **3-D** category, the layouts have a dimensional effect. When choosing these layouts, be sure that your diagram is not distorted or difficult to interpret.

HOW TO: Apply SmartArt Styles

1. Select the *SmartArt* graphic.
2. Click the **SmartArt Tools Design** tab.
3. Click the **More** button [*SmartArt Styles* group] to open the *SmartArt Styles* gallery (Figure 2-70).
4. Point to a style to see a live preview.
5. Click a style to apply it.

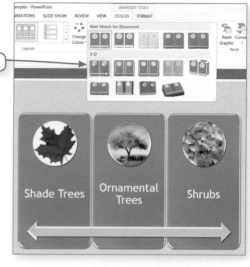

2-70 *SmartArt* graphic styles

Change Colors

How color is applied can help to differentiate between the various parts of a *SmartArt* graphic. The **Change Colors** gallery provides a quick way to change all the colors at the same time. Color options are arranged in categories; some show variations of the same color while others have different colors.

Individual shape colors within a *SmartArt* graphic can be changed as you would any other shape.

HOW TO: Change SmartArt Colors

1. Select the *SmartArt* graphic.
2. To change colors for the entire diagram, click the **Change Colors** button [*SmartArt Tools Design* tab, *SmartArt Styles* group] and select a gallery option (Figure 2-71) to apply it.
3. To change the color of a selected shape within a diagram, click the **Shape Fill** button or the **Shape Outline** button [*SmartArt Tools Format* tab, *Shape Styles* group] and choose an appropriate color.

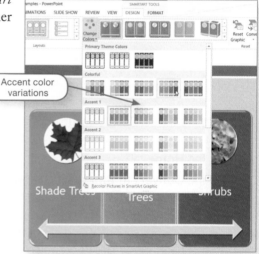

2-71 *SmartArt* graphic *Change Colors* options

Change Layouts

You may find that the *SmartArt* layout you have chosen does not fit your particular process or the relationship you are trying to show. Or you might need a layout that would better fit two levels of information.

HOW TO: Change Layouts

1. Select the *SmartArt* graphic.
2. On the *SmartArt Tools Design* tab, click the **More** button [*Layouts* group] to open the *Layouts* gallery (Figure 2-72).

2-72 *SmartArt* layouts

3. Point to a layout to see a live preview of the current layout.
4. Click **More Layouts** to open the *Choose a SmartArt Graphic* dialog box.
5. Select an appropriate type from the list on the left.
6. Double-click a **layout** to apply it, or select the layout and then click **OK**.

Add Shapes

The ***Add Shape*** button on the *SmartArt Tools Design* tab inserts shapes in relation to the selected shape. The available options include the following:

- *Add Shape After*
- *Add Shape Before*
- *Add Shape Above*
- *Add Shape Below*
- *Add Assistant*

Being able to control where a new shape appears is important. For example, you can add shapes to an organization chart as new employees are hired. Adding a shape before or after a selected shape could show a new managerial position at the same level. Adding a shape above a selected shape could show a director position above a managerial position. Adding a shape below a selected shape could show a subordinate position reporting to a manager. An Assistant shape is only available for organization charts.

HOW TO: Add Shapes

1. Select the shape closest to where you want to add a shape.
2. Click the **SmartArt Design Tools** tab.
3. Click the **Add Shape** button list arrow [*Create Graphic* group] (Figure 2-73) and select the position where you want to add the new shape.

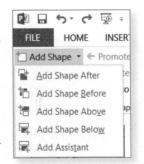

2-73 *Add Shape* options

To change the flow of a diagram, click the **Right to Left** button [*SmartArt Tools Design* tab, *Create Graphic* group].

PAUSE & PRACTICE: POWERPOINT 2-3

For this project you create an organization chart showing the CGL employees who will be managing various aspects of the landscaping for Frank and Sandra Hunter. You also convert one of the existing lists to a *SmartArt* graphic and rearrange slide objects for an interesting appearance. The *SmartArt* styles applied blend with other colors in the presentation.

File Needed: **[your initials] PP P2-2.pptx**
Completed Project File Name: **[your initials] PP P2-3.pptx**

1. Open the presentation **[your initials] PP P2-2** and save it as **[your initials] PP P2-3**.

2. Create a new slide.
   a. On slide 1, click the **New Slide** button list arrow and select the **Title and Content** layout.
   b. Type the slide title Your CGL Team.
   c. Click the **Insert a SmartArt Graphic** button on the content placeholder to open the *Choose a SmartArt Graphic* dialog box.
   d. Select the *Hierarchy* type from the list on the left.
   e. Click the **Organization Chart** layout and click **OK** to close the dialog box and insert the *SmartArt* graphic.

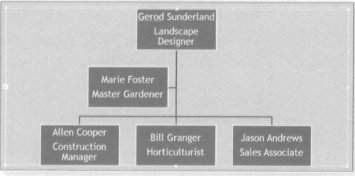

2-74 Organization chart

3. Add the text displayed in Figure 2-74 to the shapes. Press **Enter** after each name and let the job titles word wrap as needed.

4. Make changes to the organization chart using the *SmartArt Tools Design* tab.
   a. Change the flow by clicking the **Right to Left** button [*Create Graphic* group].
   b. Click the **More** button [*SmartArt Styles* group] and select the **Inset** effect (Figure 2-75).
   c. Click the **Change Colors** button [*SmartArt Styles* group] and select **Gradient Loop, Accent 4** (Figure 2-76).

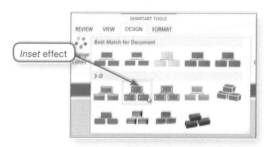

2-75 SmartArt graphic styles

5. Change bulleted text to *SmartArt*.
   a. On slide 4, select the bulleted text and click the **Convert to SmartArt** button [*Home* tab, *Paragraph* group].
   b. Click the **Vertical Bullet List**. The *SmartArt* list fills the slide and is too large since other objects are already on the slide (Figure 2-77).

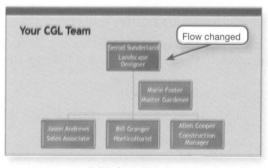

2-76 Completed organization chart

6. Make changes to the *SmartArt* graphic so it fits on the slide with the other objects.
   a. Select all shapes and change the font to **24 pts**.
   b. Select the *SmartArt* frame and resize it to better fit the text as shown (Figure 2-78).
   c. Change the style to **Inset** [*SmartArt Tools Design* tab, *SmartArt Styles* group].

2-77 SmartArt graphic shapes as they originally appear

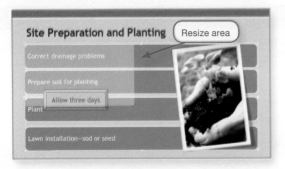

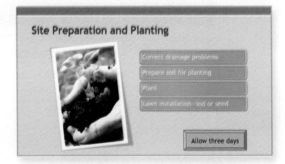

2-78 Resize the *SmartArt* graphic   2-79 Completed slide

d. Click the **Change Colors** button [*SmartArt Tools Design* tab, *SmartArt Styles* group] and select **Colored Fill - Accent 4**.

e. Rearrange slide objects as displayed in Figure 2-79. Be careful to point to the *SmartArt* frame when moving it so the whole diagram moves and not just an individual shape within the frame.

7. Save and close your presentation.

Creating a Chart

Charts help viewers interpret data and make comparisons. If you have lots of data, then create your chart in Excel and copy it to a PowerPoint slide. However, for most situations, Power-Point's *Chart* feature will provide all the options you need.

To insert a chart in PowerPoint 2013, click the **Insert Chart** button on a new slide content placeholder or click the **Insert** tab and then click the **Chart** button [*Illustrations* group] to add a chart to an existing slide. You can choose a chart type to control how data is represented such as with columns, bars, lines, or pie slices. The following table lists chart types and describes their purposes.

Chart Types and Purposes

Type	Purpose
Column	Shows a comparison of values or data changes over time. Categories are shown on the horizontal axis and values are shown on the vertical axis. Columns may be clustered to show a range of values or groupings. Columns in a category may be stacked to emphasize the total category value rather than the subsections that make up the category.
Line	Shows data changes over time; works well to show trends with data plotted at even intervals. Categories are shown on the horizontal axis and values are shown on the vertical axis.
Pie	Shows the values in a data series in proportional sizes that make up a whole pie. Values cannot be negative or zero values. Percentages or actual values can be displayed near or on pie slices. This category also includes *Doughnut* charts that also show parts of a whole but can contain more than one data series as rings.
Bar	Similar to column charts except bars are horizontal; works well for comparison of values.
Area	Shows data changes over time; emphasizes the total value of a trend.
X Y (Scatter)	Shows the relationships between several data series using values on both the X and Y axes; works well to emphasize where data sets have similar values. This category also includes *Bubble* charts.
Stock	Shows fluctuation of stock prices with high, low, and close values displayed over time.

(continued)

Chart Types and Purposes *(continued)*

Type	Purpose
Surface	Shows the differences between two sets of data. Instead of values, the color bands represent the same range of values as in a topographic map showing land elevations.
Radar	Shows the combined values of several data series with values relative to a center point.
Combo	Combines two charts such as a column chart with a line chart displayed over it.

> **MORE INFO**
>
> Use *Help* to search for "chart types" to see examples and get tips on how to arrange data in a worksheet.

The *Chart Tools Design* tab (Figure 2-80) and the *Chart Tools Format* tab (Figure 2-81) are available when a chart is active.

2-80 *Chart Tools Design* tab

2-81 *Chart Tools Format* tab

When you insert a chart in PowerPoint, a ***spreadsheet*** opens with sample data in rows and columns. A group of data values from each column is a ***data series;*** a group of data values from each row is a ***category.*** You can edit the sample data by entering your own information or you could copy and paste data from Excel, Word, or Access. If you need to revise the data in Excel, click the **Excel** button in the spreadsheet title bar.

Because the spreadsheet and PowerPoint chart are linked, the changes you make to the spreadsheet are automatically reflected in the chart.

HOW TO: Insert a Chart

1. Click the **Insert** tab; then click the **Chart** button [*Illustrations* group]. You can also click the **Insert Chart** button on a new slide content placeholder.

2. In the *Insert Chart* dialog box (Figure 2-82), chart categories are listed in the left pane and a variety of chart layouts for each category appear in the right pane. A ScreenTip identifies chart names.

2-82 *Insert Chart* dialog box

3. Click a layout to select a chart.

4. Click **OK** to close the dialog box.

5. A spreadsheet automatically opens showing sample data that you edit (Figure 2-83).

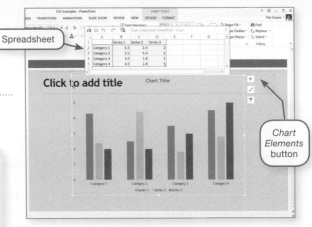

2-83 Spreadsheet linked to a chart

> **MORE INFO**
>
> The chart frame that appears on your slide when it is inserted using the *Insert* tab may be sized differently than when you insert a chart on a new slide from the *Title and Content* placeholder. Resize the chart frames as needed.

The chart frame displays ***chart elements***, the objects that make up the chart. Chart elements vary based on the type of chart used. You can see which chart elements are shown by clicking the **Chart Elements** button, the top button on the right of the chart frame. You can add or remove elements by changing selections from the list. Other chart elements appear in the list box in the *Current Selection* group on the *Chart Tools Format* tab and in the *Format* pane when you are working on the chart. The following table defines chart elements.

Chart Elements and Definitions

Element	Definition
Y-Axis (Vertical)	Also called the *Value Axis;* displayed vertically with numbers usually arranged on the left of a chart
X-Axis (Horizontal)	Also called the *Category Axis;* displayed horizontally with word or number labels across the bottom of the chart
Axis Titles	Both the Y-Axis and the X-Axis can include titles
Chart Area	The background area where the entire chart is displayed in a frame
Chart Title	A chart may include a title
Data Labels	Used to identify series and category names; may include values
Data Markers	The graphical representation of values shown as columns, bars, slices, or data points
Data Table	The data that creates the chart shown in table format below the chart
Error Bars	Used to show margins of error or standard deviation amounts
Gridlines	Lines that appear behind a chart to help the viewer judge values
Legend	The key that identifies the data series by color
Plot Area	The rectangle between the vertical and horizontal axes that is behind the data markers
Tick Marks	Used to identify the categories, values, or series on each axis
Trendline	Shows averages on 2-D charts that are not stacked and can extend beyond actual data to predict future values

Enter Data and Edit

After you replace the spreadsheet sample data with your data, you can close the spreadsheet. If you need to revise the data as you work on the chart in PowerPoint, you can open the spreadsheet again.

HOW TO: Edit Data in the Spreadsheet

1. Select the chart you want to modify.

2. Click the top of the **Edit Data** button [*Chart Tools Design* tab, *Data* group] (Figure 2-84) to open the spreadsheet. (If you need to modify the data in Excel, click the **Edit Data** button list arrow and choose **Edit Data in Excel 2013**.)

3. Resize the spreadsheet window, if necessary, to display all of your data.

4. Replace cell contents (Figure 2-85) by clicking in the **cell** and typing your data.

5. To move around in the spreadsheet,

   - Press **Enter** to move the insertion point down one row.
   - Press **Tab** to move the insertion point to the next cell on the right.
   - Press **Shift+Tab** to move to the next cell on the left.
   - Press arrow keys to move in any direction.

6. Click the spreadsheet **Close** button to return to PowerPoint.

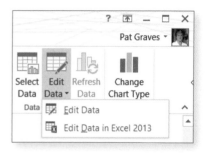

2-84 *Edit Data* button

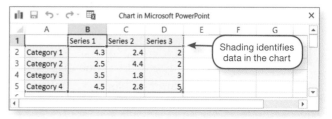

2-85 Default spreadsheet data

> **MORE INFO**
>
> Remove the sample data on the spreadsheet by clicking the **Select All** button (above the row 1 heading and to the left of the column A heading) and pressing your keyboard **Delete**.

Rows and columns on the spreadsheet may need adjustments.

- If a cell displays number signs (#) rather than the data you entered, the cell is not wide enough to display cell contents. You need to make the column wider.
- Be sure the shading correctly identifies the category, series, and data cells. If necessary, drag the sizing handles to adjust.
- If you need to add new columns or rows, edit the spreadsheet in Excel.

HOW TO: Modify the Spreadsheet

1. Select the chart you want to modify.

2. Click the top of the **Edit Data** button [*Chart Tools Design* tab, *Data* group].

3. Adjust column width. Position your pointer on the vertical line to the right of the column heading (Figure 2-86); then use one of these methods:

   - Drag to the correct width.
   - Double-click and the column automatically expands to fit the widest data entered in that column.

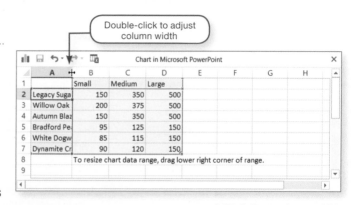

2-86 Adjust column width

- Right-click and select **Column Width**, then width number on the *Column Width* dialog box. Click **OK** to close the dialog box.

4. To add columns and rows, click the **Edit Data** button list arrow [*Chart Tools Design* tab, *Data* group] and choose **Edit Data in Excel 2013**.
   - Click in the column to the right of where you want to add a column.
   - Click in the row below where you want to add a row.
   - Click the **Insert Cells** button [*Home* tab, *Cells* group] and select the option you need to insert cells, columns, or rows.

5. If necessary, resize the shaded areas on the spreadsheet so the data is accurately represented on your chart.

In PowerPoint, switch the data series by clicking the **Switch Row/Column** button [*Chart Tools Design* tab, *Data* group].

Change Chart Type

Click the **Change Chart Type** button [*Chart Tools Design* tab, *Type* group] to open the *Change Chart Type* gallery where you can choose from the many different layouts. For example, Figure 2-87 shows data in a line chart and Figure 2-88 shows the same data in a clustered column chart.

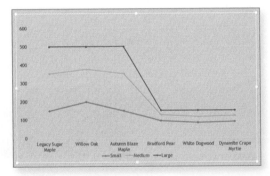
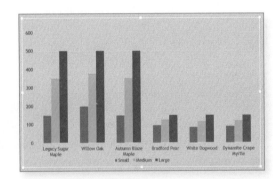

2-87 Line Chart   2-88 Clustered column chart

> **MORE INFO**
> If your PowerPoint window is narrow, you may need to click the **Quick Styles** button [*Chart Tools Design* tab] to open the *Chart Styles* gallery.

SLO 2.9

Enhancing a Chart

You can change the look of a chart by applying preset styles or manually customizing individual chart elements.

Chart Styles

The *Chart Styles* gallery [*Chart Tools Design* tab] provides preset effects for chart elements including the chart background. Click the **More** button to see styles arranged by number. Click a style to apply it (Figure 2-89).

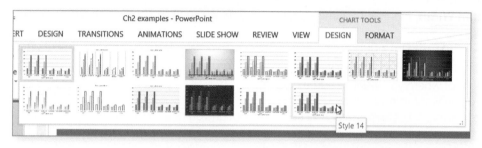

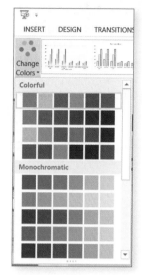

2-89 *Chart Styles* gallery

Click the **Change Colors** button [*Chart Tools Design* tab] to select *Colorful* or *Monochromatic* (shades of one color) combinations based on theme colors (Figure 2-90). The colors you choose then show in all the available chart styles. Be careful when selecting colors so the chart shapes (columns, bars, lines, or pie slices) are easy to distinguish for value comparisons. The colors also need to coordinate with your overall presentation (Figure 2-91).

If possible, avoid arranging red and green colors together. People who have difficulty recognizing different colors are most likely to have problems with red and green because they can look beige or gray.

2-90 *Chart Colors* gallery

> **ANOTHER WAY**
>
> You can also access *Chart Styles* and *Chart Colors* using the **Chart Styles** button on the right of each chart.

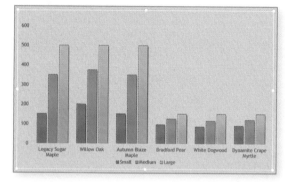

2-91 Chart style applied

Format Chart Elements

You can select chart elements (objects) and apply formatting in several ways.

HOW TO: Format a Chart Element

1. Use one of these methods to select a chart element and open the appropriate *Format* pane:
   - Select an element directly on the slide then double-click or right-click to open the appropriate *Format* pane for that element.
   - Click the **Chart Elements** button on the right of the chart, select a particular element, then click **More Options** to open the appropriate *Format* pane.
   - Use the *Chart Elements* list box [*Chart Tools Format* tab, *Current Selection* group] to select the element you need to change and then click **Format Selection** to open the *Format* pane for that element.

2. Use one or more of these commands on the *Chart Tools Format* tab:
   - Click the **More** button [*Shape Styles* group] and select a style.
   - Click the **Shape Fill**, **Shape Outline**, or **Shape Effects** buttons [*Shape Styles* group] and choose appropriate colors and effects (Figure 2-92).
   - When text is selected, click the **WordArt Quick Styles** button and select from the gallery of effects. You can also click the **Text Fill**, **Text Outline**, or **Text Effects** buttons [*WordArt Styles* group] and choose appropriate colors and effects.

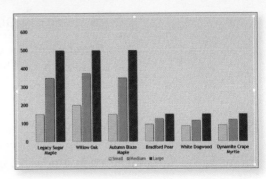

2-92 Colors changed on data series

To change the chart area size, point to any handle (the white squares on the chart frame) and resize by dragging. You can resize chart elements, but be careful not to distort size relationships.

HOW TO: Change the Chart Background

1. Select the chart.
2. Click the **Chart Tools Format** tab.
3. Click an element in the *Chart Elements* list box [*Current Selection* group].
4. Click the **Format Selection** button and the appropriate pane opens with options specific to each different element. Some options are available for 3-D charts only.
5. Chart background elements will vary based on the chart type. They may include:
   - *Chart Area*
   - *Plot Area*
   - *Back Wall*
   - *Side Wall*
   - *Walls*
   - *Floor*

You can fill elements of a chart with pictures. While a chart area picture might provide an interesting background, be careful when using pictures to avoid making the chart cluttered or the text difficult to read. The goal is always to create a chart that is easy to interpret.

In Figure 2-93, the plot area has a gradient fill with the darkest color at the bottom which helps to emphasize the height of the columns. In Figure 2-94, the chart type is a *3-D Column Chart*. The column heights (especially for the shorter columns) are not as easy to compare in this chart as they are in Figure 2-93.

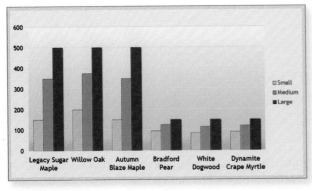

2-93 Chart plot area with gradient fill

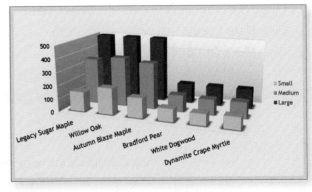

2-94 Chart with *3-D Rotation*

Legends and Labels

The *legend* identifies each data series by color. It is usually displayed on the right, but you can move it to other positions, display it horizontally above or below the plot area, or remove it.

HOW TO: Change Legend Position and Colors

1. To change the selected legend's position, use one of the following methods:
   - Click the **Chart Tools Format** tab, select **Legend** in the *Current Selection* list box, and click **Format Selection** to open the *Format Legend* pane.
   - Right-click the legend and choose **Format Legend** to open the *Format Legend* pane and select a different position. Deselect **Show the legend without overlapping the chart** if you want the legend to appear over the plot area that can be resized if necessary (Figure 2-95).
   - Click the **Chart Elements** button beside the chart, select the **Legend** list arrow, and then select the appropriate position.
   - Select the legend and drag it to another position within the chart area.

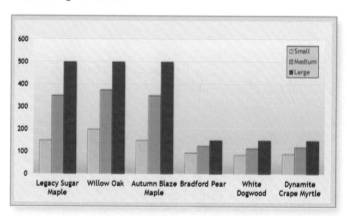

2-95 Legend moved

2. To change the selected legend's fill and outline colors, use one of the following methods:
   - Click the **Chart Tools Format** tab, click the **Shape Fill** or **Shape Outline** buttons, and select different colors.
   - Right-click the legend and choose **Format Legend** to open the *Format Legend* pane. Click the **Fill & Line** tab and then select appropriate fill and border colors. Click **Close**.

3. To remove a selected legend, use one of the following methods:
   - Click the **Chart Elements** button beside the chart and deselect the **Legend**.
   - Press **Delete**.

Labels appear in different places based on the chart style. Use the *Format Data Labels* pane to customize labels.

HOW TO: Change Chart Labels

1. Select the chart and then click the **Chart Element** button beside the chart.
2. Click **Data Labels** and select the position.
3. Click **More Options** to open the *Format Data Labels* pane.
4. Change *Label Options* to control what is displayed as well as the position.
5. Change *Text Options* to control fill and outline colors.

Using data labels above or inside columns enables the viewer to see the exact data value as well as the size relationships that the columns represent. However, the columns must be wide enough to display the numbers without overlapping. If they are too narrow (Figure 2-96), using a data table for this purpose will be more effective (Figure 2-97).

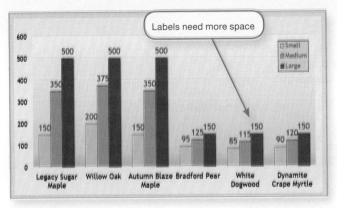

2-96 Data labels

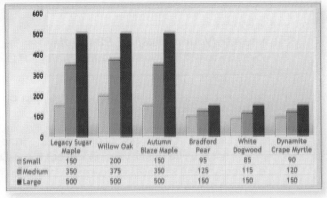

2-97 Data table

Separate a Pie Slice

You can separate pie chart slices (called **exploding**) by drag-ging the pie slices away from the center. However, when all slices are separated, no single slice is emphasized. To empha-size just one slice, it is best to first design a pie chart as you want it to look and then pull that slice away from the pie. Consider, also, how your colors are applied so the most noticeable or brightest color is used for the slice that you want to emphasize (Figure 2-98).

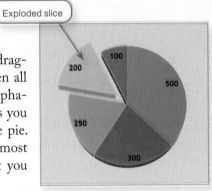

2-98 3-D pie chart with exploded slice

HOW TO: Explode a Pie Slice

1. Click a pie to select the pie object.
2. Click again to select just one pie slice. Check the handles to be sure you have selected the correct slice and not a label on the slice.
3. Drag slightly away from the center of the pie so the slice is emphasized.

As you drag a pie slice away from the center, the remainder of the pie becomes smaller. You may need to make the whole pie larger by resizing the plot area. Removing the legend creates more space for the pie, too. Pie charts are easier to interpret when short labels are shown directly on or beside slices instead of in a legend.

PAUSE & PRACTICE: POWERPOINT 2-4

For this project you create a pie and two clustered column charts showing the cost distribution for CGL landscaping, cost comparisons for tree sizes, and the height of mature trees being considered for the new landscape.

File Needed: *[your initials] PP P2-3.pptx*
Completed Project File Name: *[your initials] PP 2-4.pptx*

1. Open the presentation file *[your initials] PP P2-3* and save it as *[your initials] PP P2-4.*

2. Create a 3-D pie chart.
   a. On slide 6, "Cost Distribution," click the **Insert Chart** button on the content placeholder.
   b. Select the **Pie** chart type then select the **3-D Pie** layout. Click **OK.**
   c. Replace the spreadsheet sample data with the data in the following list and resize the columns as needed:

	Cost
Trees—Shade	1,500
Trees—Ornamental	450
Shrubs	400
Perennials	360
Hydroseeding sq. ft.	800

3. Be sure all chart data is selected. Resize the spreadsheet so you can proof all entries (Figure 2-99).

4. Close the spreadsheet.

5. Make changes to the chart.
   a. In the chart area, delete the *Cost* chart title because it duplicates the slide title.
   b. Click **Style 3** [*Chart Tools Design* tab, *Chart Styles* group].
   c. Select **Chart Area** [*Chart Tools Format* tab, *Current Selection* group] and click the **Shape Fill** button [*Chart Tools Format* tab, *Shape Styles* group]; then select **No fill**.
   d. Select the **Series "Cost" Data Labels** [*Chart Tools Format* tab, *Current Selection* group] and increase the font size to **20 pts**. [*Home* tab].
   e. Select the **Legend** and increase the font size to **20 pts**. [*Home* tab].
   f. Move the legend to the upper right of the **Chart Area.**
   g. Select the **Plot Area** and increase the size of the plot area to make the pie larger (Figure 2-100).
   h. Select the single slice for "Trees—Ornamental" and explode that slice by dragging it down slightly.

6. Create a clustered column chart.
   a. On slide 7, "Tree Size Cost Comparisons," click the **Insert Chart** button on the content placeholder.
   b. Click the **Clustered Column** layout and click **OK.**
   c. Replace the spreadsheet data with the following data:

	Small	Medium	Large
Legacy Sugar Maple	150	350	500
Willow Oak	200	375	500
Autumn Blaze Maple	150	350	500
Bradford Pear	95	125	150
White Dogwood	85	115	150
Dynamite Crape Myrtle	90	120	150

2-99 Spreadsheet linked to a chart

Shading defines chart area

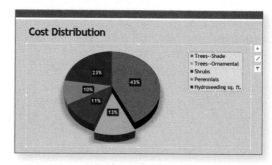

2-100 Slice exploded and legend repositioned

d. Close the spreadsheet. If you need to check the data, click the **Edit Data** button [*Chart Tools Design* tab, *Data* group].

e. Change the chart style to **Style 8** [*Chart Tools Design* tab, *Chart Styles* group] which has a dark fill for the chart area.

7. Click the **Chart Elements** button on the right side of the chart (Figure 2-101). Select the following: **Axes**, **Axis Titles**, **Data Table**, **Gridlines**, and **Legend**. The **Data Table** automatically appears below the columns.

a. Make adjustments to the following chart elements:

Axis Titles: Edit the *Primary Vertical (Y-axis)* rotated text by typing Tree Cost. Delete the *Primary Horizontal (X-axis) title* text below the data table.

Legend: Select the **Legend** and click **Format Selection** [*Chart Tools Format* tab, *Current Selection* group] to open the *Format Legend* pane. Deselect *Show the legend without overlapping the chart* and select the **Right** *Legend Position.* Move the legend to the right of the plot area.

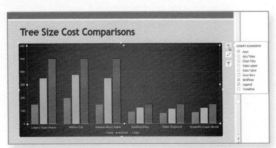

2-101 Clustered column chart with data table, axis title, and legend

b. Select each of the following chart elements and click **Shape Fill** [*Chart Tools Format* tab, *Shape Styles* group] to change the colors:

Chart Area: **Tan**, **Background 2**, **Darker 10%**
Plot Area: **Tan**, **Background 2**
Legend: **Tan**, **Background 2**, **Darker 10%**
Large Series: **Green**, **Accent 4**, **Darker 50%**
Medium Series: **Green**, **Accent 4**
Small Series: **Green**, **Accent 4**, **Lighter 40%**

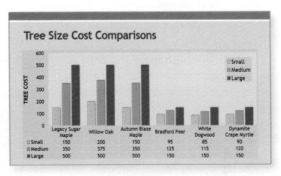

c. Make all text **black**. Increase the font size on the axis title and legend to **20 pts**. Increase the table text and axis number to **18 pts**. The completed slide is shown in Figure 2-102.

2-102 Column fill colors changed

8. Create another clustered column chart.

a. On slide 8, "Growth Potential" click **Chart** [*Insert* tab, *Illustrations* group] because this slide does not have a content placeholder.

b. Click the **Clustered Column** layout and click **OK** to close the dialog box.

c. Replace the spreadsheet data with the following data:

	Height
Legacy Sugar Maple	80
Willow Oak	60
Autumn Blaze Maple	50
Bradford Pear	95
White Dogwood	20
Dynamite Crape Myrtle	20

d. This data is in one data series, so delete the extra columns in the spreadsheet. Be sure you delete the entire spreadsheet columns so the PowerPoint chart columns can expand in the available space (Figure 2-102). An empty column in the spreadsheet creates too much blank space between columns in the PowerPoint chart.

e. Select spreadsheet **Column C** and **Column D** headings and the entire columns are selected.

f. Right-click, then click **Delete**, and the columns appear blank.

g. Check to be sure the data is correctly selected and adjust borders if necessary.

h. Close the spreadsheet.

i. The chart area is smaller than in the previous chart because you inserted the chart directly on the slide rather than inserting it through a content placeholder that is in a larger size.

9. Make changes to the chart.

a. Increase the chart area to a width of **10"** and height of **5.5"** [*Chart Tools Format* tab, *Size* group] and position it evenly on the slide (Figure 2-103).

b. Delete the chart title and the legend.

c. Click the **More** button [*Chart Tools Design* tab, *Chart Styles* group] and change the chart style to **Style 14**.

d. Select the columns and change the color to **Green, Accent 4**.

e. Make the text **black** and increase the font size.

   • *Vertical (Value) Axis:* **bold** and **20 pts**.

   • *Horizontal (Category) Axis:* **bold** and **18 pts**.

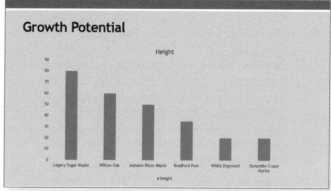

2-103 Column chart as it first appears

10. Select the *Chart Area* and apply a picture fill.

a. Click the **Shape Fill** button [*Chart Tools Format* tab, *Shape Styles* group] and select **Picture** to open the *Insert Pictures* dialog box.

b. In the *Office.com* search box, enter the search word tree and click **Search**.

c. On the *Insert Pictures* dialog box, scroll down the gallery to locate the picture of "Trees with the leaves changing color for autumn" (Figure 2-104) and click **Insert**.

d. If the *Format Chart Area* pane is not open, double-click the picture. Change the *Transparency* percentage to **60%**.

e. Close the *Format Chart Area* pane.

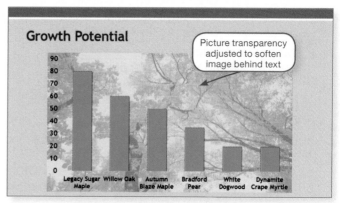

2-104 Chart resized, colors changed, and picture fill

11. Click the **Transitions** tab, apply the **Wipe** transition to all slides, and change the *Effect Options* to **From Left**.

12. Save and close your presentation.

Chapter Summary

2.1 Work with shapes, select theme colors and standard colors, and apply styles (p. P2-67).

- Change shape size by entering exact height and width sizes or by dragging sizing handles.
- Use **Lock Drawing Mode** to draw the same shape multiple times.
- Use **text boxes** to position text anywhere on a slide.
- PowerPoint's various **Styles** galleries provide collections of preset effects for shapes, pictures, or other objects.
- When you apply **Theme Colors** to shapes, the colors change when a different theme is applied.
- **Standard** colors do not change when a different theme is applied.
- Highly **saturated** colors are intense and vibrant; colors that are not saturated are muddy and dull.
- **Luminosity** is a measure of lightness that is adjusted by the amount of white or black in the color.
- Computer screens use the **RGB** color model that displays colors by blending values for *red, green,* and *blue.*
- The **Eyedropper** is used to match any color on your computer screen.

2.2 Create interesting and eye-catching text effects with *WordArt* (p. P2-75).

- The **WordArt Styles** gallery shows a collection of preset **Text Effects**.
- The **Transform** effect makes text warp into different shapes or follow a path.
- You can fill *WordArt* with solid or gradient colors, textures, patterns, or pictures.
- **Line Weight** is the line thickness measured in points.
- **Dashes** show lines with a combination of dots and dashes.
- Use the **Line Style** option on the **Format Shape** dialog box to customize line styles.

2.3 Search for pictures and illustrations, modify picture appearance, and compress picture file size (p. P2-78).

- Use the **Insert Pictures** dialog box to search for online pictures and illustrations.
- The **Picture Styles** gallery shows a collection of preset **Picture Effects**.

- To remove a picture style, click the **Reset Picture** button.
- **Cropping** trims unwanted areas of a selected picture.
- Increase **Color Saturation** to make picture colors more vibrant; decrease color saturation to make picture colors more muted.
- **Color Tone** changes a picture's cool or warm tones.
- Select **Color** and then **Recolor** to change a picture's color to a monotone color.
- The **Set Transparent Color** feature can make one color in a picture transparent. This feature works well to remove white backgrounds.
- **Compressing** pictures reduces the file size of your presentation.

2.4 Organize information in a grid format using tables and customize the arrangement of columns and rows (p. P2-85).

- You can insert and delete table **columns** and **rows**.
- Table **cells** can be **merged** or **split** to create multiple cells.
- **Column width** usually varies based on content; **row height** is usually a consistent size.

2.5 Emphasize portions of a table by applying styles, colors, and effects (p. P2-90).

- You can apply **WordArt Styles** to table text.
- **Table Styles** provide options for a table's design using theme accent colors.
- **Table Style Options** control how columns and rows are emphasized to feature areas of the table.
- **Border lines** or **shading** can separate cells.
- Horizontal cell alignment options include **Align Text Left**, **Center**, or **Align Text Right**; vertical cell alignment options include **Align Top**, **Center Vertically**, or **Align Bottom**.

2.6 Show processes and relationships with *SmartArt* graphics (p. P2-94).

- Use **SmartArt graphics** to create diagrams that illustrate concepts such as processes, cycles, or relationships.
- **SmartArt layouts** are organized by categories.
- Each layout includes information about how you can use it or the meaning it conveys.

- Type text directly in each *SmartArt* shape or type in the *Text Pane*.
- Change bulleted text to a *SmartArt* graphic by clicking the **Convert to SmartArt Graphic** button.

2.7 Improve the appearance of *SmartArt* graphics by applying styles, colors, and effects (p. P2-97).

- ***SmartArt Styles*** provide a gallery of effect options.
- The ***Change Colors*** button provides a gallery of color options arranged in categories.
- The ***Add Shapes*** button inserts shapes in relation to the selected shape.
- You can format or individually resize shapes within a *SmartArt* graphic.

2.8 Create charts that show relationships between data values and emphasize data in different ways (p. P2-101).

- Charts in PowerPoint are linked to spreadsheets in Excel; therefore, changes made to data in the worksheet automatically appear in the chart that represents the data.

- A group of data values is a ***data series***.
- ***Chart Layouts*** are arranged in categories including **Column**, **Line**, **Pie**, **Bar**, and **Area**.
- The ***Chart Area*** displays the entire chart including all **Chart Elements**.
- The ***Plot Area*** provides a background for ***Data Markers***, the columns, bars, or slices that represent data.

2.9 Enhance a chart by applying preset styles or manually customizing individual chart elements (p. P2-105).

- ***Chart Styles*** provide a gallery of preset effects for chart elements.
- The ***legend*** is a key that identifies each data series by color.
- The ***Change Colors*** button provides a gallery of colorful or monochromatic colors for chart elements.
- You can customize chart elements individually to enhance their appearance.
- To emphasize a pie slice, you can **explode** it by separating the slice from the rest of the pie chart.

Check for Understanding

In the ***Online Learning Center*** for this text (www.mhhe.com/office2013inpractice), there are a variety of resources that can be used to review the concepts covered in this chapter.

The following Online Learning Resources are available in the Online Learning Center:

- Multiple choice questions
- Short answer questions
- Matching exercises

Guided Project 2-1

Guest satisfaction has always been important to the success of Paradise Lakes Resort (PLR) in Minnesota. The general manager plans to use feedback from social media to identify problems and to guide improvements at the resort. In this project you illustrate a presentation the general manager will use to explain these concepts to employees at BLR.
[Student Learning Outcomes 2.1, 2.2, 2.3, 2.6, 2.7]

File Needed: ***SocialMedia-02.pptx***
Completed Project File Name: ***[your initials] PowerPoint 2-1.pptx***

Skills Covered in This Project

- Insert an online picture.
- Apply a picture style.
- Adjust size dimensions.
- Apply text effects.

- Insert a text box.
- Create a *SmartArt* graphic.
- Apply a *SmartArt* style and effects.

1. Open the presentation ***SocialMedia-02***. This design theme shows slide titles at the bottom of all slides except the title slide.

2. Save the presentation as ***[your initials] PowerPoint 2-1***.

3. On slide 1, search online for a picture.
   a. Click the **Insert** tab.
   b. Click the **Online Pictures** button to open the *Insert Pictures* dialog box.
   c. In the *Office.com* search box, type the word lake and click **Search**.
   d. Locate the picture showing two chairs on a deck facing the lake (Figure 2-105) and click **Insert**.
   e. Apply the **Metal Oval** picture style [*Picture Tools Format* tab, *Picture Styles* group].
   f. Resize the picture width to **6"** and the height automatically adjusts.
   g. Position the picture on the lower left.

2-105 Title slide

4. On slide 1, adjust the title text to complement the wood decking shown in the picture.
   a. Increase the font size to **60 pts**.
   b. Adjust the placeholder so it fits the text and move it up slightly.
   c. Click the **Text Fill** button [*Drawing Tools Format* tab, *WordArt Styles* group], select **Texture**, and select **Medium Wood**.

d. Click the **Text Effects** button, select **Shadow**, and select **Shadow Options**. The *Format Shape* pane opens.

e. Change the following settings:
   Transparency: **20%**
   Blur: **5 pt**.
   Angle: **50°**
   Distance: **3 pt**.

f. Close the *Format Shape* pane.

5. On slide 1, make the subtitle **bold** and increase the font size to **32 pts**. Adjust the placeholder size so it fits the text and move it down.

6. After slide 2, insert a new slide with a *Title and Content* layout.

7. On slide 3, add text and a shape.

   a. Type the slide title Why Social Media?

   b. Type the following bulleted text:

      Revenue

      Market Share

      Guest Satisfaction

      Guest Loyalty

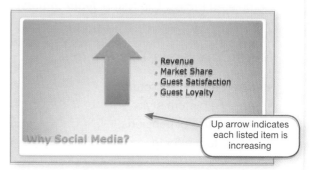

   c. Resize the bulleted list placeholder so it fits the text and move the text to the right (Figure 2-106).

2-106 Slide 3 with a shape

   d. To show that each item in the list is increasing, click the **Shape** button [*Insert* tab, *Illustrations* group] and select the *Up Arrow* shape.

   e. Draw an arrow (height **3.5"** and width **2.5"**); then position the arrow to the left of the text.

   f. With the arrow selected, click the **More** button [*Drawing Tools Format* tab, *Shape Styles* group] and apply the **Intense Effect, Orange, Accent 1**.

8. After slide 4, insert a new slide with a *Blank* layout.

9. On slide 5, create a *SmartArt* graphic using a cycle layout and insert an additional shape.

   a. Click the **Insert** tab.

   b. Click the **SmartArt** button and select the **Cycle** type.

   c. Select the **Continuous Cycle** layout and click **OK**.

   d. Add the following text to each shape starting with the top shape and continuing in a clockwise direction around the circle:

      More Rentals
      Rentals
      Social Media Comments
      Improvements
      Better Social Media Comments

   e. With the Better Social Media Comments shape selected, click the **Add Shape** list arrow [*SmartArt Tools Design* tab, *Create Graphic* group] and select **Add Shape After**.

   f. In the new shape, type Higher Ratings.

   g. Click the **Intense Effect** style [*SmartArt Tools Design* tab, *SmartArt Styles* group].

h. Select all the shapes, change the font size to **20 pts.**, and apply **bold**.

i. With all the shapes selected, resize the shapes horizontally so the word "Improvements" fits on one line (Figure 2-107).

10. Insert a text box.

    a. Click the **Text Box** button [*Insert* tab, *Text* group] and click inside the cycle diagram.

    b. Type the following text on two lines:

       With the help of NewMediaMarketing.com

    c. Change the font size to **20 pts**. and center the text.

    d. Adjust the text box size, if necessary.

11. Click the **Reveal** button [*Transitions* tab, *Transition to This Slide* group] and then click **Apply To All**.

12. Save and close the presentation (Figure 2-108).

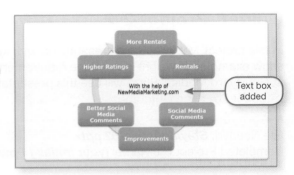

2-107 Slide 4 with *SmartArt graphic and effects added*

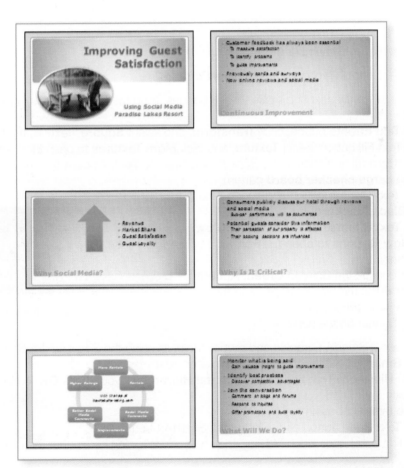

2-108 PowerPoint 2-1 completed

Guided Project 2-2

In this project, you prepare a presentation with key points essential to maintain a healthy lifestyle and show examples of weight loss calorie requirements for men and women at different ages. The doctors at Courtyard Medical Plaza will use this presentation to encourage clients to be more active.
[Student Learning Outcomes 2.1, 2.2, 2.3, 2.4, 2.5, 2.6, 2.7]

File Needed: *StayingActive-02.pptx*
Completed Project File Name: *[your initials] PowerPoint 2-2.pptx*

Skills Covered in This Project

- Apply text effects.
- Create a *SmartArt* graphic.
- Apply a *SmartArt* style and effects.
- Insert an online picture.
- Crop a picture.

- Apply a picture style.
- Adjust size dimensions.
- Insert a text box.
- Insert and format a table.

1. Open the presentation *StayingActive-02.*

2. Save the presentation as *[your initials] PowerPoint 2-2*.

3. On slide 1, select the title text and make these changes using the *Drawing Tools Format* tab, *WordArt Styles* group.
    a. Click the **Text Effects** button, click **Transform**, and select **Square**. Text fills the title placeholder.
    b. Click the **Text Fill** button, select **Texture**, and click **More Textures** to open the *Format Shape* pane.
    c. Select **Pattern fill** and change the *Background Color* to **Teal**, **Accent 6**.
    d. Select the **Large checker board** pattern.
    e. Click the **Text Outline** button and change the color to **Black, Background 1**.
    f. Click the **Text Effects** button and select **Glow**. Select **Glow Options** to open the *Format Shape* pane.
    g. For *Glow,* change the *Color* to **Green, Accent 1, Lighter 60%**; the *Size* to **10 pt.**; and the *Transparency* to **20%** (Figure 2-109).
    h. Close the *Format Shape* pane.

2-109 *Text Effects* **for presentation title**

4. On slide 2, insert a *SmartArt* graphic and modify the style using the *SmartArt Tools Design* tab.
    a. Click the **SmartArt** button on the content placeholder.
    b. Select the **Hierarchy** type and the **Horizontal Hierarchy** layout. Click **OK** to close the dialog box.
    c. Delete the three shapes on the right.
    d. Click the **Text Pane** button on the left of the SmartArt frame.
    e. After the first bullet, type Keep Moving; then type the following items after the indented bullets:

    Moderate Intensity Activity
    Count Steps (Press **Enter** to add another bullet.)
    Combine Aerobic and Strengthening

    f. Close the *Text Pane.*

g. Apply the *Subtle Effect* style [*SmartArt Styles* group].

h. Click the **Change Colors** button and select **Colorful Range, Accent Colors 5 to 6** (Figure 2-110).

5. On slide 3, search for a picture and apply a picture style.

   a. Click the **Online Pictures** button [*Insert* tab, *Images* group] to open *the Insert Pictures* dialog box.

   b. Search for a picture using *Office.com* and the search word **gardening**.

   c. Select the picture "Women smiling while gardening" and click **Insert**.

   d. Resize the picture (height **4.5"** and width will automatically change to the same size since this picture is square).

   e. Move the picture to the right of the slide.

   f. Apply the *Rotated White* picture style [*Picture Tools Format* tab, *Picture Styles* group].

2-110 SmartArt graphic with effects added

6. On slide 5, repeat the process in step 5 to search for a picture using the search word walk.

   a. Select the picture "Family of four walking on the beach" and click **Insert**.

   b. Click the **Crop** button [*Picture Tools Format* tab, *Size* group] and crop the picture on the top and left to focus only on the family. Click **Crop** again to accept your change.

   c. Apply the same style to match the previous picture.

   d. Resize the picture (height **5"** and width will automatically change).

   e. Move the picture to the right of the slide.

7. After slide 6, insert a new slide with a *Title and Content* layout.

8. On slide 7, add text.

   a. Type the title text **Calorie Examples**.

   b. Insert a text box with the text **Gaining 5 pounds a year** and position it below the slide title. Apply **bold** and change the font size to **20 pts**.

9. On slide 7, insert a table, add text, and modify formatting.

   a. Click the **Table** button on the content placeholder and enter **6** columns and **5** rows on the *Insert Table* dialog box. Click **OK** to close the dialog box.

   b. Type the text shown in Figure 2-111 using a font size of **20 pts**.

   c. Resize the last column so the heading text fits on one line.

Shading reflects the same person at two ages

Age	Height	Weight	Maintain	Fat Loss	Extreme Fat Loss
20	5 ft 10 in	200	2,647	2,118	1,600
25	5 ft 10 in	225	2,769	2,215	1,800
30	6 ft 2 in	240	2,916	2,333	1,920
35	6 ft 2 in	265	3,038	2,430	2,120

2-111 Table with formatting changes

   d. Make the column width fit each column by double-clicking the border line between columns.

   e. Select all cells and change to **Center** alignment [*Table Tools Layout* tab, *Alignment* group].

   f. Change the *Pen Color* to **Black** and the *Pen Weight* to **1 pt**. [*Table Tools Design* tab, *Draw Borders* group].

   g. Click the **Borders** button, and select **All Borders** [*Table Tools Design* tab, *Table Styles* group].

   h. Select the top table row and change the *Text Fill* to **Black** [*Table Tools Design* tab, *WordArt Styles* group].

   i. Select the second and third rows and change the *Shading* to **Green, Accent 1, Lighter 80%** [*Table Tools Design* tab, *Table Styles* group].

   j. Select the fourth and fifth rows and change the *Shading* to **Green, Accent 1, Lighter 60%**.

   k. Move the table up slightly and center it on the slide.

10. On slide 7, duplicate the table and edit the text in the second table.
    a. Select the table and press **Ctrl+D** to duplicate it. Position the second table centered near the bottom of the slide.
    b. Edit the table content (Figure 2-112).

Age	Height	Weight	Maintain	Fat Loss	Extreme Fat Loss
20	5 ft 7 in	150	2,041	1,633	1,225
25	5 ft 7 in	175	2,163	1,730	1,400
30	5 ft 9 in	180	2,204	1,763	1,440
35	5 ft 9 in	205	2,325	1,860	1,640

2-112 Table with formatting changes

11. On slide 7, insert and format a shape to label table contents.
    a. Click the **Shapes** button [*Insert* tab, *Illustrations* group] and select the **Oval**. Draw an oval shape and adjust its size (height **0.9"** and width **2"**) [*Drawing Tools Format* tab, *Size* group].
    b. Type the word Female with **black** text and **bold**.
    c. Click the **Shape Outline** button [*Drawing Tools Format* tab, *Shape Styles* group] and change the outline color to **Teal**, **Accent 6**.
    d. Click the **Edit Shape** button [*Drawing Tools Format* tab, *Insert Shapes* group] and select **Change Shape**. Select **Explosion 1**.

2-113 Slide 7 completed tables

    e. Position this shape at the left corner of the bottom table (Figure 2-113).

12. Select the shape and press **Ctrl+D** to duplicate it.
    a. Position the second shape at the left corner of the top table.
    b. Change the text to Male.

13. After slide 7, insert a new slide with a *Title and Content* layout.

14. On slide 8, insert a table and add text.
    a. Type the title Make It Fun.
    b. Click the **Table** button on the content placeholder. Enter 2 columns and 8 rows and click **OK**.
    c. Type the following text:

Exercise Benefits	Motivation
Control weight	Enjoy the activities
Improve health	Keep it a priority
Boost immune system	Vary activities
Control appetite	Share with a friend
Feel more energetic	Enjoy companionship
Be more relaxed	Set realistic goals
Raise self-confidence	Reward yourself

15. On slide 8, make the following changes to the table:
    a. Select the table. If necessary, change the *Pen Color* to **Black** and the *Pen Weight* to **1 pt**. Click **All Borders**.
    b. Change the font size for all text to **20 pts**.
    c. Change the heading row text to **black**.

d. Select all cells and click the **Center Vertically** button [*Table Tools Layout* tab, *Alignment* group].

e. Change the table size (height **4.5"** and width **9"**) and center it horizontally on the slide.

16. Apply the **Cube** transition to all slides.

17. Save and close the presentation (Figure 2-114).

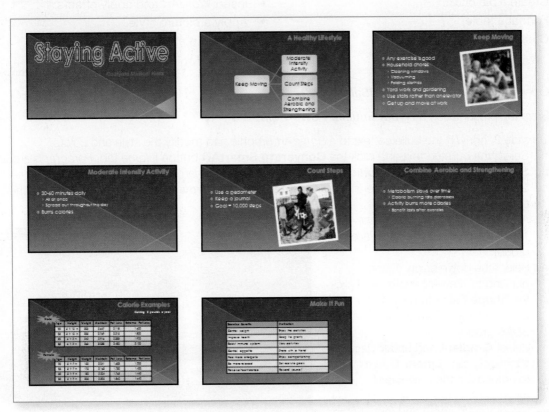

2-114 PowerPoint 2-2 completed

Guided Project 2-3

Solution Seekers, Inc., has been asked to develop a presentation for a meeting of personnel managers about salary trends for information technology workers. In the current economy, some jobs are paying less than they were a few years ago. For this project, you prepare tables and charts showing average salaries and salary changes for selected jobs.
[Student Learning Outcomes 2.1, 2.2, 2.3, 2.5, 2.6, 2.7, 2.8]

File Needed: ***InfoTechSalaries-02.pptx***
Completed Project File Name: ***[your initials] PowerPoint 2-3.pptx***

Skills Covered in This Project

- Convert text to a *SmartArt* graphic.
- Apply a *SmartArt* style and effects.
- Create a pie chart.
- Format a table.
- Create a column chart.

- Apply chart styles.
- Format chart elements.
- Insert *WordArt* and apply effects.
- Apply a picture style.
- Insert and align text boxes.

1. Open the presentation **InfoTechSalaries-02**

2. Save the presentation as **[your initials] PowerPoint 2-3**.

3. On slide 2, convert the bulleted text to a *SmartArt* graphic and modify the style and colors.
    a. Select the bulleted text and click the **Convert to SmartArt** button [*Home* tab, *Paragraph* group].
    b. Select **More SmartArt Graphics** to open the *Choose a SmartArt Graphic* dialog box.
    c. Select the **Relationship** type and the **Counterbalance Arrows** layout. Click **OK** to close the dialog box.
    d. Apply the **Cartoon** style [*SmartArt Tools Design* tab, *SmartArt Styles* group].
    e. Select the down arrow shape pointing to "Fewer Layoffs" and click the **Shape Fill** button list arrow [*SmartArt Tools Format* tab, *Shape Styles* group].
    f. Select **Gradient** and under *Dark Variations,* click **Linear Down** to emphasize the downward movement.
    g. Select the up arrow and repeat step f to apply a **Linear Up** gradient (Figure 2-115).

2-115 Slide 2 *SmartArt graphic* with color changes

4. After slide 2, insert a new slide with a *Title and Content* layout.

5. On slide 3, create a pie chart and modify it.
    a. Type the slide title **Employee Salary Satisfaction**.
    b. Click the **Chart** button in the content placeholder.
    c. Click the **Pie** chart type; then select the **3-D Pie**. Click **OK** to close the dialog box.
    d. Replace the spreadsheet data with the data shown in Figure 2-116. Close the spreadsheet.
    e. Drag the chart title to the top left of the chart area. Increase the font size to **24 pts**. [*Home* tab, *Font* group].
    f. Click the **Chart Elements** button on the right side of the slide and select **Legend**. Click **Right**.
    g. Increase the font size to **20 pts**. and drag the legend to the bottom right of the chart area.

	A	B
1		Satisfaction %
2	Very Satisfied	13
3	Somewhat Satisfied	36
4	Undecided	16
5	Somewhat Dissatisfied	24
6	Very Dissatisfied	11
7		

2-116 Spreadsheet linked to a chart

h. Click the **Chart Elements** button again and select **Data Labels**. Click **Inside End**.

i. Click the **Chart Elements** list box arrow and select **Series "Satisfaction%" Data Labels** [*Chart Tools Format* tab, *Current Selection* group]. Increase the font size to **24 pts**. and apply **bold** (Figure 2-117).

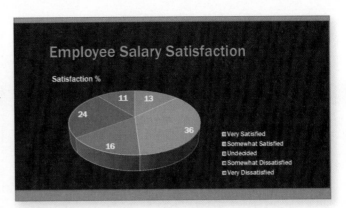

2-117 Slide 3 completed pie chart

6. On slide 4, modify table formatting.
   a. Select the table. Increase the font size to **20 pts**.
   b. Select **Header Row** and **Banded Rows** [*Table Tools Design* tab, *Table Style Options* group].
   c. Apply the **Themed Style 1**, **Accent 2** style [*Table Tools Design* tab, *Table Styles* group].
   d. Increase the table height to **4"** and click the **Center Vertically** button [*Table Tools Layout* tab].
   e. Select columns 2–4 and change to **Right** alignment.

7. After slide 4, insert a new slide with a *Title and Content* layout.

8. On slide 5, create a column chart and modify it.
   a. Type the title **Salary Change, Selected Jobs**.
   b. Click the **Chart** button on the content placeholder.
   c. Select the **3-D Clustered Column** and click **OK**.
   d. Replace the spreadsheet data with the data shown in Figure 2-118. Select **Column D**, right-click, and select **Delete**. By removing the blank column, the chart displays correctly with no blank space. Close the spreadsheet.

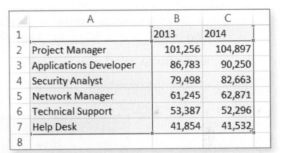

	A	B	C
1		2013	2014
2	Project Manager	101,256	104,897
3	Applications Developer	86,783	90,250
4	Security Analyst	79,498	82,663
5	Network Manager	61,245	62,871
6	Technical Support	53,387	52,296
7	Help Desk	41,854	41,532
8			

2-118 Spreadsheet linked to a chart

   e. Delete the chart title.
   f. Click the **Chart Elements** button on the right side of the chart, select **Legend**, and then click **More Options** to open the *Format Legend* pane. Select **Top Right** and deselect **Show the legend without overlapping the chart**.
   g. Click the **Shape Fill** button [*Table Tools Format* tab, *Shape Styles* group] and change the legend color to **Brown, Accent 2, Darker 50%**.
   h. Click the chart frame to select the **Chart Area** and change the **Shape Fill** color to **Teal, Accent 1, Darker 50%**.
   i. Select the **Legend** and increase the font size to **18 pts**. Repeat to increase the **Vertical (Value) Axis** font size to **18 pts**.
   j. Select the **Horizontal (Category) Axis** and increase the font size to **20 pts**. (Figure 2-119).
   k. On slide 6, apply the *Moderate Frame, Black* picture style [*Picture Tools Format* tab, *Picture Styles* group].

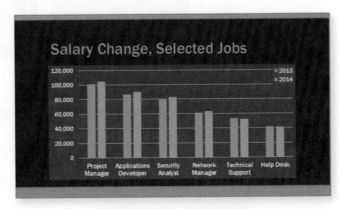

2-119 Slide 5 completed clustered column chart

9. On slide 6, insert *WordArt* text.

   a. Click the **WordArt** button [*Insert* tab, *Text* group] and select the **Fill - White, Text 1, Outline - Background 1, Hard Shadow - Background 1** style (Figure 2-120).

   b. Type the text **Employees Are Valuable** and move this text above the picture.

   c. Click the **Text Effects** button [*Drawing Tools Format* tab, *WordArt Styles* group], select **Shadow**, and click **Offset Diagonal Bottom Right**.

   d. Click the **Text Outline** button [*Drawing Tools Format* tab, *WordArt Styles* group] and select **Black, Background 2**.

   e. Deselect the *WordArt* text.

2-120 Slide 6 picture style, text effects, and text boxes

10. On slide 6, insert text boxes.

   a. Click the **Text Box** button [*Insert* tab, *Text* group] and type the first salary of **$74,270**. Change the font color to **black**, increase the font size to **20 pts.**, and apply **bold**.

   b. Position this salary below the first person on the left of the picture.

   c. With the salary text box selected, press **Ctrl+D** and position the duplicated text box below the second person. Repeat for the remaining figures.

   d. Edit the text boxes to change the salaries to **$62,844**, **$54,340**, and **$48,982**.

   e. Select all of the salary text boxes and click the **Arrange** button [*Drawing Tools Format* tab, *Drawing* group]. Select **Align** and **Align Bottom** (Figure 2-120).

11. Apply the **Blinds** transition to all slides; then apply the **Zoom** transition to slide 6.

12. Save and close the presentation (Figure 2-121).

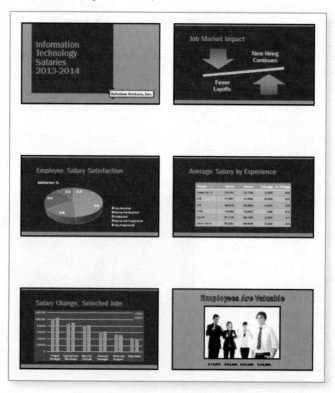

2-121 PowerPoint 2-3 completed

Independent Project 2-4

At Pool & Spa Oasis, sales associates must educate new spa owners about keeping spa water safe with proper maintenance. For this project, you prepare a presentation that emphasizes the routine to follow, explains pH level numbers, and lists available products that are typically used to balance water.
[Student Learning Outcomes 2.1, 2.2, 2.3, 2.4, 2.5, 2.6, 2.7]

Files Needed: **Balancing-02.pptx**
Completed Project File Name: **[your initials] PowerPoint 2-4.pptx**

Skills Covered in This Project

- Insert *WordArt* and apply effects.
- Adjust size dimensions.
- Insert an online picture.
- Apply a picture style.
- Create a *SmartArt* graphic.

- Apply a *SmartArt* style and effects.
- Insert and format a table.
- Insert a text box.
- Change solid and gradient colors.

1. Open the presentation **Balancing-02**.

2. Save the presentation as **[your initials] PowerPoint 2-4**.

3. On slide 1, change the title text arrangement.
   a. Delete the title text "Balancing Act," but leave the word "The" as shown.
   b. Insert *WordArt* with the style **Fill – White, Outline – Accent 1, Glow – Accent 1**.
   c. Type Balancing Act.
   d. Click **Text Effects**, select **Shadow**, and **Offset Right**. Click **Shadow Options** to open the *Format Shape* pane and change the *Transparency* setting to **30%**.
   e. Change the *Character Spacing* to **Tight**.
   f. Apply the *Transform* text effect of **Cascade Up**.
   g. Increase the *WordArt* size to height **3"** and width **9"** and position as shown in Figure 2-122.
   h. Close the *Format Shape* pane.

2-122 Slide 1 with *WordArt*

4. On slide 2, the bulleted list placeholder has a fill color so it cannot be resized without distorting the slide. Adjust text spacing and insert a picture.
   a. On the last bulleted item, place your insertion point in front of the word "such" and press **Shift+Enter**.
   b. Search on *Office.com* using the search word swim and insert the picture "Young woman in swimming pool."
   c. Resize the picture (height **5.5"** and the width will automatically change to **3.71"**).
   d. Apply the **Bevel Rectangle** picture style.
   e. Position the picture as shown in Figure 2-123.

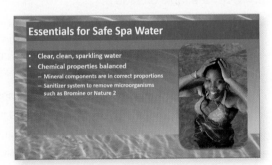

2-123 Slide 2 with inserted picture and picture style

5. On slide 4, insert a *SmartArt* graphic, add text, and change formatting.
   a. Insert a *SmartArt* graphic from the *Process* category with the **Continuous Block Process layout**.
   b. In the three shapes, type Test Water, Add Necessary Products, and Enjoy!
   c. Resize the *SmartArt* graphic (height **5"** and width **9.5"**).
   d. Apply the **Polished** SmartArt style.
   e. Select the arrow and apply **Gradient** colors. Select **More Gradient** to open the *Format Shape* pane. Select a **Linear** type and **Linear Right** direction and three gradient stops.

   First stop: Position **0%**, **Light Turquoise, Background 2, Darker 50%**
   Second stop: Position **40%**, **Light Turquoise, Background 2, Darker 10%**
   Third stop: Position **100%**, **Light Turquoise, Background 2**

   f. Close the *Format Shape* pane.
   g. Apply **bold** to all *SmartArt* text (Figure 2-124).

2-124 Slide 4 *SmartArt graphic* with style and color changes

6. On slide 5, insert a table, add text, and change formatting.
   a. Insert a table with 3 columns and 4 rows.
   b. Select **Header Row** and **Banded Rows**.
   c. Type the following text:

Level	Numbers	Results
High	8.0	Scale, Alkaline
Good	7.2 – 7.6	Ideal pH Range
Low	6.0	Corrosion, Acidic

   d. Change the font size to **20 pts.** for all table text.
   e. Apply the **Themed Style 1, Accent 1** table style.
   f. Select each column and adjust the cell width as follows: left column is **1.5"**, middle column is **2.75"**, and right column is **2.75"**.
   g. Change the alignment on the middle column to **Center**.
   h. Center the table on the slide.

7. On slide 5, insert a text box below the table.
   a. Type Drain and replace spa water every 60-90 days.
   b. Change the font size to **20 pts**.
   c. Change the shape fill to **Turquoise, Accent 3, Lighter 40%**.
   d. Resize the text box, if necessary, to fit the text and position it below the table aligned with the right of the table.

8. Copy the table on slide 5.

9. On slide 6, paste the table and make revisions.
   a. Delete the middle column and make the table **9"** wide.
   b. Delete the table text and add three rows.
   c. Type the following text:

Products	Purpose
Sanitizer	Type needed depends on sanitizer system
Test Strips	Measures chemical levels
Shock Treatment	Breaks down organic or unfiltered material
Total Alkalinity	Increases or decreases to balance pH levels
Calcium Increaser	Balances dissolved calcium
Stain and Scale Prevention	Removes metallic impurities

d. Adjust the column width as needed to avoid word wrapping.

e. Center the table on the slide.

10. Apply the **Ripple** transition with the **From Top-Left** effect option to all slides.

11. Save and close the presentation (Figure 2-125).

2-125 PowerPoint 2-4 completed

Independent Project 2-5

Prospective home buyers need to understand mortgage requirements and how to prepare to apply for a mortgage. Angie O'Connor at Placer Hills Real Estate frequently discusses these issues with clients, so she wants to use a presentation on her notebook computer to help guide her discussions with clients. For this project, you develop the presentation.

[Student Learning Outcomes 2.1, 2.3, 2.4, 2.5, 2.6, 2.7, 2.8]

File Needed: ***PreparetoBuy-02.pptx***
Completed Project File Name: ***[your initials] PowerPoint 2-5.pptx***

Skills Covered in This Project

- Insert an online picture.
- Crop a picture.
- Apply a picture style.
- Adjust size dimensions.
- Insert a chart and edit data.
- Apply chart styles.

- Format chart elements.
- Insert text boxes.
- Insert and format a table.
- Convert text to a *SmartArt* graphic.
- Apply a *SmartArt* style and effects.

1. Open the presentation ***PreparetoBuy-02*** that has a Standard size (4:3 aspect ratio). The slide size is 10" x 7.5" compared to the slide size of 13.333" x 7.5" for the Widescreen (16:9 aspect ratio).

2. Save the presentation as ***[your initials] PowerPoint 2-5***.

3. On slide 1, search at *Office.com* for the picture shown in Figure 2-126 using the search word home.
   a. Insert the picture and crop it slightly on the left to remove part of the sky.
   b. Resize the picture so it is **3"** wide and the height remains in proportion.
   c. Apply the **Moderate Frame, Black** picture style.
   d. Align the picture on the right side of the slide. The black frame portion extends beyond the slide on the right.

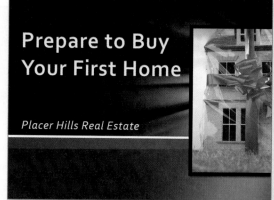

2-126 Slide 1 with inserted picture and picture style

4. On slide 4, insert a chart showing how fixed mortgage rates have changed over time.
   a. Click the **Line** chart type; then select the **Line with Markers** chart layout. Click **OK**.
   b. Replace the spreadsheet data with the data shown in Figure 2-127.
      - Increase the selection area to include *row 10* to avoid error messages.
      - Delete *Column D* so the corresponding chart area is correct with no blank space.
      - Close the spreadsheet.

	A	B	C	
1		Rate	Points	Co
2	1974	9.19	1.2	
3	1979	11.2	1.6	
4	1984	13.88	2.5	
5	1989	10.32	2.1	
6	1994	8.38	1.8	
7	1999	7.44	1	
8	2004	5.84	0.7	
9	2009	5.04	0.7	
10	2014	3.95	0.8	
11				

5. The chart now shows accurate information, but it is difficult to distinguish the data series lines from the gridlines in the background. The data markers that reflect the value of each number can barely be seen (Figure 2-128). The following changes will make the chart easier to interpret.

2-127 Spreadsheet linked to a chart

6. Delete the chart title.

7. Change the chart area *Shape Fill* to **Blue-Gray**, **Accent 5**, **Darker 25%**.

8. Select the "Rate" series line, right-click, and select **Format Data Series** to open the *Format Data Series* pane (Figure 2-129).
   a. Click the **Fill & Line** tab at the top of the pane. Select *Line* options and make one change:
      - *Width:* **3 pt**.
   b. Select *Marker* options and make changes so the marker on the selected series line is more noticeable. Click the option name to access the choices for each option.
      - *Marker Options:* **Built-in**, *Type* **Square**, *Size* **15** (Figure 2-130)
      - *Fill:* **Solid fill, Color Dark Red, Accent 1, Lighter 40%**

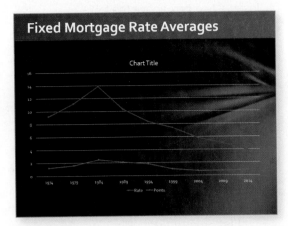

2-128 Line chart as it first appears

9. Select the "Points" series line and make the following similar changes:
   a. For *Line* options, make two changes:
      - *Line Color:* **Solid line, Brown, Accent 3**
      - *Line Style:* **Width, 3 pt**
   b. Click the **Marker** button and make two changes:
      - *Marker Options:* **Built-in** *Type* **Diamond**, *Size* **20**
      - *Marker Fill:* **Solid fill. Brown, Accent 3, Lighter 40%**

10. Close the *Format Data Series* pane.

11. Increase the font size to **16 pts**. and make the text **bold** for the *Horizontal (Category) axis* and the *Vertical (Value) axis*.

12. Move the chart area up slightly to make room for a source notation at the bottom of the slide.
   a. Insert a text box and type the following:

      Information based on Freddie Mac survey data
      http://www.freddiemac.com/pmms

   b. Position the text box as displayed in Figure 2-131.

13. On slide 5, insert a table with 5 columns and 3 rows. Make the following changes:
   a. Type the text shown in Figure 2-132.
   b. Select columns 2–4 and change to **Center** alignment.
   c. In the first row, change to **Bottom** alignment and change the row *Shading* to **Dark Red, Accent 1**.
   d. Align the table in the horizontal and vertical center on the slide.

Click here to open Fill & Line tab

2-129 *Format Data Series* pane

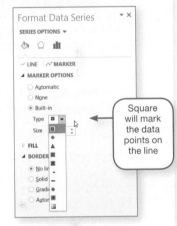

Square will mark the data points on the line

2-130 *Format Data Series* pane with *Marker* options

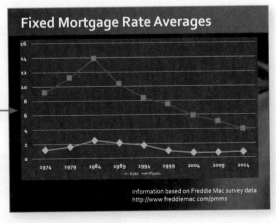

Markers are emphasized and resource information is added

2-131 Slide 4 completed line chart

14. Insert a text box above the table.
    a. Type $250,000.
    b. Change the font to **40 pts**. and **bold**.

15. Insert a text box below the table.
    a. Type the following text on three lines:

       Lender rates are influenced by credit scores.
       Plan for a 20% down payment to avoid cost of points.
       Add taxes and insurance premiums.

    b. Position the text boxes as shown in Figure 2-132.

Sample Fixed Rate Payments

2-132 Slide 5 table with text
boxes added

16. On slide 6, convert the list to a *SmartArt* graphic.
    a. Select the bulleted text and convert it to the **Vertical Curved List** *SmartArt* layout.
    b. Resize the *SmartArt* frame on the right so it fits the longest line of text.

17. Make the following changes to the *SmartArt* graphic:
    a. Change the colors to **Colorful Range, Accent 4 to 5**.
    b. Apply the **Moderate Effect SmartArt** style.
    c. Select all of the white circles and change the *Shape Fill* to **Dark Red, Accent 1** and apply the *Bevel* effect of **Cool Slant**.
    d. Center the *SmartArt* graphic on the slide (Figure 2-133).

2-133 Slide 6 SmartArt graphic
with style and effects changed

18. Apply the **Shape** transition with the **Out** effect option to all slides.

19. Save and close the presentation (Figure 2-134).

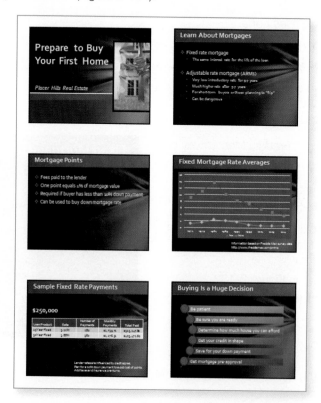

2-134 PowerPoint 2-5 completed

Independent Project 2-6

Kathy Sung, Director of Services at Life's Animal Shelter (LAS), will talk to a luncheon group of businesspeople to explain the important work of LAS and to solicit financial support. For this project you develop the presentation she will use to explain the needs of LAS and describe ways people can contribute through donations or by volunteering their time.
[Student Learning Outcomes 2.1, 2.2, 2.3, 2.4, 2.5, 2.6, 2.7]

Files Needed: ***YouCanHelp-02.pptx, CountryStroll-02.jpg, DayCare-02.jpg, Food-02.jpg, Groom-02.jpg,*** and ***RoyalTreatment-02.jpg***
Completed Project File Name: ***[your initials] PowerPoint 2-6.pptx***

Skills Covered in This Project

- Insert an online picture.
- Apply text effects.
- Apply a picture style.
- Set transparent color.
- Recolor a picture.
- Adjust size dimensions.

- Insert a text box.
- Insert and format a table.
- Convert text to a *SmartArt* graphic.
- Create a *SmartArt* graphic with pictures.
- Apply a *SmartArt* style and effects.

---

1. Open the presentation ***YouCanHelp-02***.

2. Save the presentation as ***[your initials] PowerPoint 2-6***.

3. On slide 1, change the title text fill to **Dark Red, Accent 1, Darker 25%**. Apply the *Bevel* text effect of **Angle**.

4. Change the font size to **80 pts**. and resize the placeholder on the right so one word is on each line.

5. Use the *Insert Pictures* dialog box to search for three pictures from Office.com and insert them on slides. Type the search word dog.
   a. On slide 1, add the picture of a German Shepherd dog with a white background.
   b. On slide 2, add the picture of three boys with a dog on grass.
   c. On slide 3, add the picture of a Golden Retriever dog with a white background.

6. On slide 1, adjust the picture.
   a. Increase the picture size (height **5.9"** and width **4.7"**).
   b. Use *Set Transparent Color* to remove the white area in the picture.
   c. Position the dog picture as shown in Figure 2-135.

7. On slide 2, adjust the picture.
   a. Decrease the picture size (height **5.84"** and width **8"**).
   b. Apply the *Moderate Frame, Black* picture style.
   c. Center the picture horizontally and position it near the top of the slide.

2-135 Slide 1 with picture added, white background removed

8. Insert a text box below the picture and type the following text on two lines:

Our operating funds come through donations and pet adoption fees.

   a. Change the text to **White** and font size to **20 pts**.
   b. Change the *Shape Outline* to **White** and the *Weight* to **3 pts**.
   c. Change the *Shape Fill* to **Black**.
   d. Center the text box horizontally below the picture (Figure 2-136).

9. On slide 3, adjust the picture.
   a. Use *Set Transparent Color* to remove the white area in the picture.
   b. Increase the picture size (height **5.23"** and width **6"**).
   c. Position the picture as shown in Figure 2-137.

10. Select the slide 2 thumbnail and press **Ctrl+C** to copy it.
   a. Put your insertion point after slide 3 and press **Ctrl+V** to paste the copied slide.

11. Make changes to the new slide 4.
   a. In the text box, replace the text with the words **We Need Your Help!**
   b. Resize the text box to fit the text and center it horizontally under the picture.
   c. Select the picture and click the **Color** button.
   d. In the *Recolor* group click the **Orange, Accent color 2, Dark** option (Figure 2-138).

12. On slide 5, convert the list to a *Vertical Bullet List SmartArt* graphic.
   a. Increase the *SmartArt* frame height to **4.7"** so the text size increases.
   b. Reduce the width to **9"**).
   c. Center the *SmartArt* horizontally.
   d. Apply the **Cartoon** *SmartArt* style as displayed in Figure 2-139.

13. On slide 6, convert the list to a **Picture Lineup** *SmartArt* graphic. Click the **Picture** icon on each shape to open the *Insert Pictures* dialog box. Browse to locate your student files and insert the following pictures going from left to right (Figure 2-140):

    1   ***DayCare-02***
    2   ***CountryStroll-02***
    3   ***RoyalTreatment-02***
    4   ***Food-02***
    5   ***Groom-02***

Each picture is automatically resized to fit the SmartArt shape where it is inserted.

2-136 Slide 2 with picture and text box

2-137 Slide 3 with picture added, white background removed

2-138 Slide 4 with picture recolored

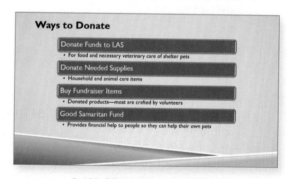

2-139 Slide 5 *SmartArt* graphic converted from bulleted text

14. After slide 6, insert a new slide with a *Title and Content* layout.
    a. Type the title Items We Need
    b. Insert a table with 3 columns and 5 rows.
    c. Type the table text shown in Figure 2-141.
    d. Increase the font size to **20 pts**.
    e. Adjust column width so each column fits the longest line of text.
    f. Center the table on the slide.

15. Apply the *Gallery* transition to all slides.

16. Save and close the presentation (Figure 2-142).

2-140 Slide 6 *SmartArt* graphic picture layout

Cleaning	Paper Products and Bedding	Dog and Cat Play
Bleach	Paper Towels	Dog and Cat Treats
Pine Sol	Paper Plates	Chewies
Mop Heads	Plastic Containers with Lids	Collars
Towels	Blankets	Leashes

2-141 Table text

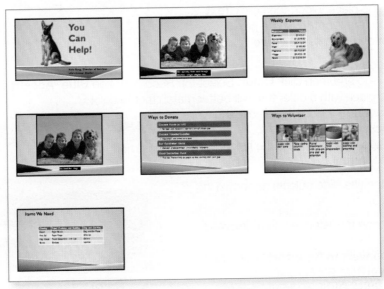

2-142 PowerPoint 2-6 completed

Improve It Project 2-7

The Hamilton Civic Center needs a presentation to explain benefits of yoga and encourage members to join yoga classes. In this project you revise a presentation to give it a cohesive look and illustrate it with pictures, a *SmartArt* graphic, and a table. You apply various styles and effects for a contemporary appearance.
[Student Learning Outcomes 2.2, 2.3, 2.4, 2.5, 2.6, 2.7]

File Needed: ***Yoga-02**.pptx*
Completed Project File Name: ***[your initials] PowerPoint 2-7**.pptx*

Skills Covered in This Project

- Apply text effects.
- Insert an online picture.
- Apply a picture style.
- Reposition slide objects.
- Convert text to a *SmartArt* graphic.
- Apply a *SmartArt* style and effects.
- Format a table.
- Compress pictures.

1. Open the presentation **Yoga-02** that has a Standard size (4:3 aspect ratio). The slide size is 10" x 7.5" compared to the slide size of 13.333" x 7.5" for the Widescreen (16:9 aspect ratio).

2-143 Title slide

2. Save the presentation as **[your initials] PowerPoint 2-7**.

3. Make the title slide more dynamic.
   a. Search online at Office.com and insert a yoga picture.
   b. Apply a **Bevel Rectangle** picture style.
   c. Select the title placeholder; then click **Text Effects** from the *WordArt Styles* group. Select **Transform** and then select **Wave 1**.

4. Recolor the logo.
   a. Select the logo and then click **Color**. Select the *Recolor* option **Blue, Accent color 5 Light** to replace the black with a color that will better match theme colors.
   b. Use *Set Transparent Color* to remove the white so your background color shows.
   c. Make the logo width **2.5"** and the height will automatically adjust.

5. Size and position title slide objects as shown in Figure 2-143.

6. On slide 3, change the listed text to a *SmartArt* graphic.
   a. Click the **Convert to SmartArt** button and select the **Vertical Block List**.
   b. Apply the **White Outline** *SmartArt* style.
   c. Click **Change Colors** and apply the **Colorful Range – Accent Colors 4 to 5** (Figure 2-144).

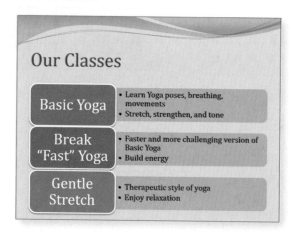

2-144 *SmartArt*

7. On slides 4 and 5, search online at *Office.com* for appropriate yoga pictures and insert them.
   a. Resize and position the pictures appropriately.
   b. With a picture selected, click **Compress Pictures**. Use document resolution, delete cropped areas of pictures, and apply compression to all pictures.

8. On slide 6, modify the table.
   a. Increase the font size to **20 pts**.
   b. Apply the **Medium Style 2 – Accent 4** table style.
   c. Select the title row, click **Cell Bevel,** and apply the **Riblet** effect.
   d. Add a **1 pt** border to all cells using the **Blue, Accent 4, Darker 50%** pen color (Figure 2-145).

9. Apply the **Dissolve** transition to all slides.

10. Save and close your presentation (Figure 2-146).

Classes	Days	Hours
Basic Yoga	Mon/Wed	4:15 – 5:15 p.m.
Break "Fast" Yoga	Tues/Thurs	7:00 – 8:10 a.m.
Gentle Stretch	Fri	10:00 – 11:30 a.m.

2-145 Slide 6 table

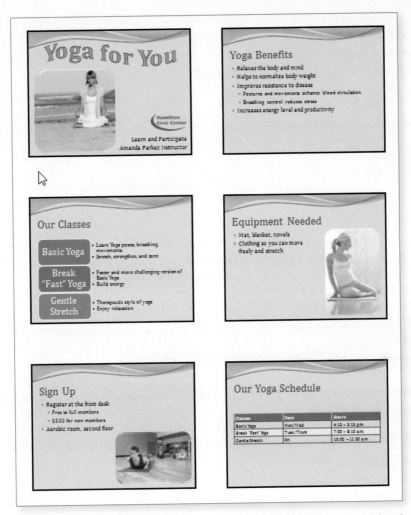

2-146 PowerPoint 2-7 completed

Challenge Project 2-8

For this project, do some online comparison shopping for items you would be likely to buy such as clothing, household products, or automotive supplies. Prepare slides describing the products and apply text effects to the slide titles. Prepare a chart that shows costs either for the same product at several stores or similar products at the same store.

[Student Learning Outcomes 2.1, 2.2, 2.3, 2.4, 2.5, 2.6, 2.7, 2.8]

File Needed: None
Completed Project File Name: *[your initials] PowerPoint 2-8.pptx*

Create a new presentation and save it as *[your initials] PowerPoint 2-8*. Modify your presentation according to the following guidelines:

- Select an appropriate theme and make color and font changes as needed for your topic.
- Prepare a title slide and product description slides.
- Search online for a related image and insert it on the title slide.
- Create a table summarizing some of your findings.
- Create two charts to compare specific items.

Challenge Project 2-9

Using data from the United States Department of Labor published online by the Bureau of Labor Statistics (http://www.bls.gov) prepare a presentation explaining some current trends in the labor force. For example, you could show unemployment rate comparisons from different regions or wage estimates for various occupations in different states.
Student Learning Outcomes 2.1, 2.2, 2.3, 2.4, 2.5, 2.6, 2.7, 2.8]

File Needed: None
Completed Project File Name: *[your initials] PowerPoint 2-9.pptx*

Create a new presentation and save it as *[your initials] PowerPoint 2-9*. Modify your presentation according to the following guidelines:

- Select an appropriate theme and make color and font changes as needed for your topic.
- Create a title slide using a *Transform* text effect.
- Include several bulleted slides describing current trends.
- Search for appropriate pictures, resize as needed, and apply a picture style to each one.
- Prepare a table showing salaries for several jobs in different locations or for data changing over time.
- Prepare a chart comparing employment statistics from your state or region.

Challenge Project 2-10

Using information from one of your favorite coffee or soft drink manufacturers, such as the information you can find at www.thecoca-colacompany.com or www.pepsico.com, prepare a presentation comparing different products. You could show the diversity of the product line or list promotional products with pricing. From financial information provided on the sites, you could feature total revenue, total profits, or other interesting performance data in your presentation.
[Student Learning Outcomes 2.1, 2.2, 2.3, 2.4, 2.5, 2.6, 2.7, 2.8]

File Needed: None
Completed Project File Name: *[your initials] PowerPoint 2-10.pptx*

Create a new presentation and save it as *[your initials] PowerPoint 2-10*. Modify your presentation according to the following guidelines:

- Select an appropriate theme and make color and font changes as needed for your topic.
- Create a distinctive title slide using *WordArt.*
- Search online for appropriate pictures and insert three or more.
- Adjust picture sizes and apply picture styles.
- Prepare slides listing key factors contributing to the company's growth.
- Prepare a *SmartArt* graphic illustrating a specific process or relationship from historical or operational information.
- Create a chart showing comparisons for data such as net revenue or operating profit.

Preparing for Delivery and Using a Slide Presentation

CHAPTER OVERVIEW

In this chapter you learn more methods to help you work with PowerPoint more efficiently and effectively. This chapter teaches you how to create new theme colors customized for your topic, apply animation so selected slide objects appear just at the right time in your presentation, and link to a video from a web site. You also explore PowerPoint's rehearsal features to help you perfect your delivery timing and techniques, project your presentation more effectively, and prepare a presentation to be self-running. Finally, you learn how to save a presentation so it can be distributed on a CD.

STUDENT LEARNING OUTCOMES (SLOs)

After completing this chapter, you will be able to:

SLO 3.1   Create custom theme and background colors (p. P3-139).

SLO 3.2   Apply animation to add interest and reinforce content (p. P3-147).

SLO 3.3   Link to an online video (p. P3-149).

SLO 3.4   Use rehearsal techniques to prepare for presentation delivery (p. P3-156).

SLO 3.5   Control display options for different screen sizes (p. P3-159).

SLO 3.6   Present effectively and professionally using projection equipment (p. P3-164).

SLO 3.7   Use annotation pens to highlight information and save presentation markings (p. P3-167).

SLO 3.8   Prepare a self-running presentation that loops (p. P3-170).

SLO 3.9   Use the *Package Presentation for CD* feature to prepare a slide show for display on other computers (p. P3-171).

CASE STUDY

Specialists at Solution Seekers, Inc., frequently present to both large and small groups as they work with clients to improve business performance. Davon Washington is creating a series of seminars for new hires to help them be more productive and professional. For this project, you work with Davon to finish the presentation he has developed about presentation planning.

Pause & Practice 3-1: Create custom theme and background colors. Add interest with animation and video.

Pause & Practice 3-2: Rehearse a presentation and prepare for a widescreen display.

Pause & Practice 3-3: Practice slide show delivery features.

Pause & Practice 3-4: Prepare a self-running presentation and package a presentation to a folder.

POWERPOINT

Creating Custom Theme and Backgrounds Colors

Themes create a unified appearance for your presentation. When you use themes effectively, the information you present on a topic is seen by your viewers as one "package" and not a collection of random slides. You may need to match specific colors in a company logo or a school's colors, so in this section you will prepare custom theme colors that create a unique palette and help you work more efficiently. Then you will explore different ways to apply pattern, gradient, and picture fills and consider some issues to keep in mind when applying these fills to slide backgrounds.

Custom Theme Colors

As you worked with shapes, colors, and styles in previous chapters, you saw how theme colors are arranged across the top of the *Theme Colors* gallery. Recall that various percentages of each color appear below the top row colors (Figure 3-1). This section takes a closer look at where PowerPoint automatically applies theme colors to various graphics you create.

Four sample slides are shown in Figure 3-2. These samples feature the *Facet* theme and the *Blue* color theme. The background for these slides is white (Background 1) with decorative shapes in Background 2, Text 2, and Accent 1 colors.

- **Slide 1:** The photograph has a border color of Text 2.
- **Slide 2:** The first row of circles shows background and text colors. The second row of circles shows Accent colors 1–6.
- **Slide 3:** The bullets and the *SmartArt* shapes are shown in the Accent 1 color.
- **Slide 4:** Accent 2 color variations are applied to the table; the chart shows Accent colors 1–6 based on the order data is entered on the spreadsheet.

Accent colors (Figure 3-3) appear from left to right in both the *Shape Styles* gallery and the *Table Styles* gallery (Figures 3-4 and 3-5). Other galleries show options in a similar way.

You can boost productivity by creating custom theme colors because the colors you choose are available to you in the galleries as you develop your slide show. When you save custom theme colors, the colors are also available to use again in another presentation. Keep the following guidelines in mind when you create custom theme colors:

- Select your background color first and then select other colors that work well on the background.

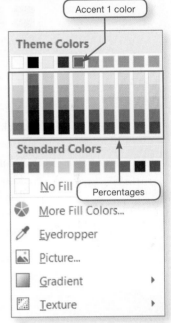

3-1 *Theme Colors* gallery

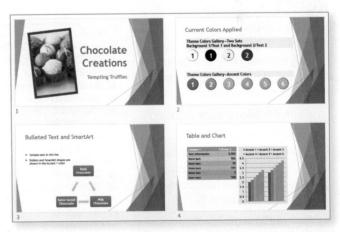

3-2 Sample slides showing graphics with the *Facet* theme

3-3 *Blue* theme accent colors

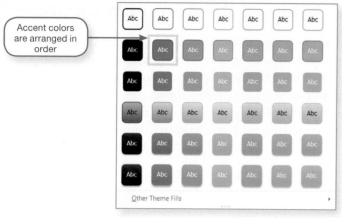

Accent colors are arranged in order

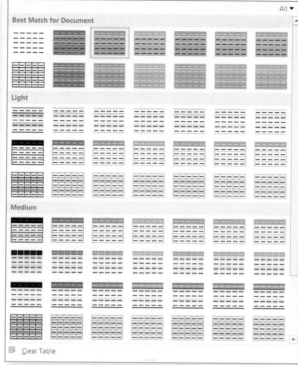

3-4 *Shapes Styles* gallery

3-5 *Table Styles* gallery

- Pick a text color that has a high contrast with your background color so words are easy to read.
- The Accent 1 theme color appears first when you draw shapes and is the first choice in galleries for table and *SmartArt* effects.

The following example illustrates how to change theme colors from the *Design* tab to a new set of colors that is more appropriate for a presentation about chocolate.

HOW TO: Create New Theme Colors

1. Start a new presentation using a design theme or open an existing presentation.
2. Click the **More** button [*Design* tab, *Variants* group].
3. Select **Colors** to open the list of built-in theme colors. The current theme colors are selected (Figure 3-6).
4. Select **Customize Colors** to open the *Create New Theme Colors* dialog box (Figure 3-7). For this example, the *Text/Background – Dark 1* (black) color does not change.
5. Change each color as needed to create your custom theme. This example has a brown and

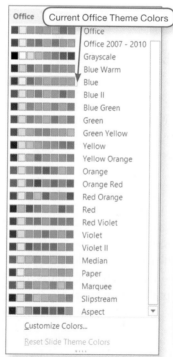

3-6 *Theme Colors* gallery

3-7 *Create New Theme Colors* dialog box showing *Blue* theme colors

yellow color palette that works for a presentation about chocolate (Figure 3-8).

- Click the **list arrow** on a color button to open the *Theme Colors* gallery.
- Click **More Colors** to open the *Colors* dialog box.
- Click the *Standard* or *Custom* tab, choose a color, and click **OK**.
- Repeat for each of the colors you want to change.

6. Name the new custom theme.

7. Click the **Save** button. The new custom theme is automatically applied and the name will appear in the *Custom* section of your list of available theme colors so you can use it again.

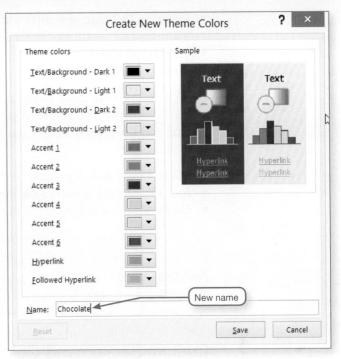

> **ANOTHER WAY**
>
> Use the *Design* tab when you need to customize colors and fonts. When you also need to change background graphics or insert pictures such as a company logo, use the *Slide Master* tab to make all changes.

3-8 *Create New Theme Colors* dialog box showing custom colors

Figure 3.9 shows sample slides with the new colors. Controlling color this way is much more efficient than using an existing theme and having to select a custom color each time you create various illustrations. If any slide text, such as a slide title, retains the original colors, click the **Reset** button [*Home* tab, *Slides* group] to update the colors.

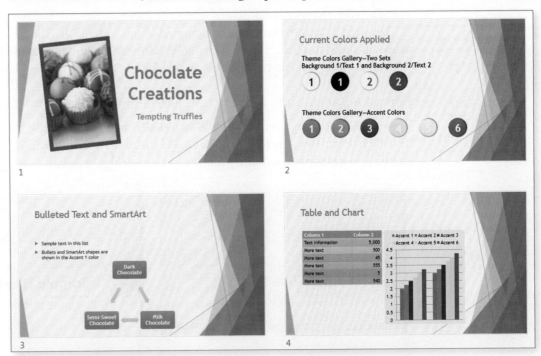

3-9 Chocolate theme colors applied to sample slides

Color combinations influence the tone of your presentation. Your options are endless, but you may want to consider a few of the following tonal effects:

- Varied and vibrant, or similar with subtle differences
- Soothing and tranquil, or lively and energetic
- Youthful or mature
- Historic or high tech

When you think about colors for your topic, consider your audience and be respectful of cultural differences. People tend to assign meaning to colors based on their cultural background and life experiences. A few examples of colors that have symbolic meaning include the following:

- **White:** Purity and cleanliness in the American culture, death in some other cultures
- **Red:** Health (red blood) in the medical field, loss (negative values) in the financial field
- **Green:** Sickness (infection) in the medical field, wealth (money) in the financial field

 MORE INFO

To examine this concept further, look online for information about color meaning, symbolism, or the psychology of color.

Custom Background Colors

The *Format Background* pane has options similar to those you have used on the *Format Shape* pane (*See SLO 2.1: Working with Shapes, Colors, and Styles*). When you change background colors, text colors do not change. Also, the position of placeholders or the graphic shapes that are included on some design themes do not change.

When you choose colors and creative effects for backgrounds, remember that your color choices will fill the entire slide area behind everything else you design on a slide. These changes are visible throughout the presentation if you apply them to all slides, so you should examine your changes at full screen size to be sure you are satisfied with the results.

You need to consider how your background affects text, too. If a theme or template has graphic shapes included in a background, then a solid color background fill is a good choice. Select a color that has a strong contrast from the color used for text (light on dark or dark on light).

Format a Background with Pattern and Gradient Fills

Two colors (the *Foreground* and the *Background*) create pattern fills. Two similar colors make a subtle pattern; two contrasting colors make the pattern more obvious. Notice the differences in two title slides prepared using the *Whisp* theme (Figure 3-10).

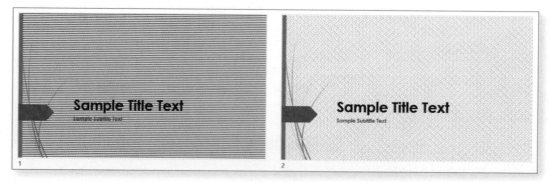

3-10 *Whisp* theme title slide with two background patterns

- **Slide 1 (Left):** Contrasting colors in a bold pattern make the title text difficult to read.
- **Slide 2 (Right):** The same colors with a subtle pattern improve the appearance.

HOW TO: Add a Background Pattern Fill

1. Point to the slide background and right-click to open the shortcut menu.
2. Click **Format Background** to open the *Format Background* pane.
3. Select the **Pattern fill** option.
4. Choose an appropriate *Foreground Color* and *Background Color*.
5. Choose one of the patterns.
6. By default, this change is applied to the current slide only. Click **Apply to All** to apply this change to the entire presentation.
7. If you want to restore the background's original design, click **Reset Background**.
8. Close the *Format Background* pane.

> **ANOTHER WAY**
>
> To open the *Format Background* pane, click the **Format Background** button on the *Design* tab or click the **Background Styles** list arrow [*Slide Master* tab, *Background* group] and then click **Format Background**.

You can use preset gradient colors based on theme colors or select custom colors. You first choose the type of gradient such as *Linear, Radial, Rectangular, Path,* or *Shade from title.* Then you choose the direction of color change. Based on these choices, gradient stops appear on the color bar. Move, delete, or add gradient stops to control how the colors blend. The color change is more gradual with more distance between the stops. Compare the title slides of the *Whisp* design theme shown in Figures 3-11 and 3-12. These two slides started with the same preset gradient fill of *Bottom Spotlight – Accent 4* with a type of *Linear.* The settings were changed differently.

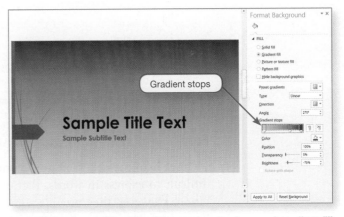

3-11 *Whisp* theme title slide with a custom background gradient fill

Figure 3-11

- *Linear Up* direction
- Three gradient stops are used

Figure 3-12

- *Linear Diagonal – Top Left to Bottom Right* direction
- The three gradient stops on the left of the color bar are close together for a defined color change; the three right stops are spread apart for a more gradual color change.

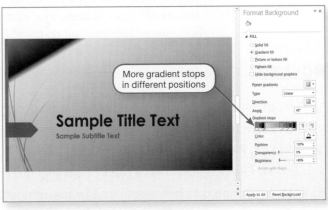

3-12 *Whisp* theme title slide with a custom background gradient fill showing different gradient stops

HOW TO: Add a Background Gradient Fill

1. Point to the slide background and right-click to open the shortcut menu.
2. Click **Format Background** to open the *Format Background* pane.
3. Select the **Gradient fill** option.
4. Click the **Preset gradients** list arrow and select a color style.
5. Click the **Type** list arrow and choose one of the options: *Linear, Radial, Rectangular, Path*, or *Shade from title*.
6. Click the **Direction** list arrow and choose a direction for color blending if one is available.
7. The **Angle** degree is available only for the *Linear* type and it automatically adjusts based on the direction you choose. You can type a different number or click the spin box to change the number in 10 degree increments.
8. Add or remove gradient stops.
   - To add gradient stops, click the **Add gradient stop** button.
   - To remove gradient stops, click the **Remove gradient stop** button or drag the gradient stop off the color bar.
9. Change colors by selecting a gradient stop and clicking the **Color** button. Choose a different color.
10. To change color blending, select the gradient stop and drag it to a different position on the color bar. If you want to change the order, drag the stops to rearrange them. For precise adjustments, change percentages for each stop position.
11. Adjust *Brightness* and *Transparency* as needed.
12. By default, this change is applied to the current slide only. Click **Apply to All** to apply this background to every slide in your presentation.
13. Close the *Format Background* pane.

> ### ANOTHER WAY
>
> You can access various *Background Styles* [*Design* tab, *Variants* group or *Slide Master* tab, *Background* group] that show light and dark color combinations based on theme colors.

Format a Background with Picture and Texture Fills

Pictures help you tell your story, communicate without words, and convey emotions that are difficult to express in words. Pictures can provide a dramatic background for your presentation. However, they provide some special challenges when text is displayed over pictures because of the many colors that are used in pictures. Textures have similar issues if they use many colors or show a lot of detail. Pictures in a small size can be used as textures to fill a slide with many small pictures. The examples in this section will show you several ways to combine background pictures and text.

HOW TO: Add a Background Picture Fill

1. Point to the slide background and right-click to open the shortcut menu.
2. Click **Format Background** to open the *Format Background* pane.
3. Select the **Picture or texture fill** option.
4. Click the **File** button to insert a picture from your collection.
5. Click the **Online** button to search for a picture using the *Insert Picture* dialog box.
   - Type your search word and click the **Search** button or press **Enter**.
   - Select the picture you want to use and click **Insert**.

6. To soften the picture colors so text and other objects on the slide are easy to see, use one of the following methods:
   - On the *Format Background* pane, increase the *Transparency* percentage. This setting mutes the colors but the original colors are still evident.
   - Click **Picture** at the top of the *Format Background* pane; then click **Picture Color**. Click **Presets** to choose from different saturation levels or click **Recolor** to choose from dark and light accent colors for a monotone effect. If you decide not to change colors, click the **Reset** button to restore the picture to its original state.

7. By default, this change is applied to the current slide only. Click **Apply to All** to apply this background to every slide in your presentation.

8. To restore the background to its original state, click the **Reset Background** button.

9. Close the *Format Background* pane.

> MORE INFO
>
> You can change a slide background at any time while you are working on a presentation.

The following figures show some options you can explore using the *Format Background* pane to soften background pictures or use placeholder fill colors to make text over pictures or textures easy to read. In these examples, a single flower that is almost a square image (Figure 3–13) is used in different ways. In Figures 3-13–3-17, the first slide illustrates a problem while the other two slides show possible solutions.

Notice the following characteristics for the slides shown in Figure 3-14:

522 x 529 pixels @ 72 ppi

3-13 A flower used in backgrounds

- *Slide 1 (Left):* Because this picture is almost square (522 × 529 pixels) when it is stretched to fit the width of a widescreen display (height 7.5" and width 13.333"), part of the flower is cut off at the top and bottom. This is not necessarily a problem, just something that happens if you use a square picture. The title text, however, is not easy to read over the dark colors of the flower. This is a problem as your slide text should be legible no matter what designs you use.
- *Slide 2 (Center):* The title placeholder is the same width as the slide. A dark red fill is applied and the white text has a shadow so now the text is easy to read.
- *Slide 3 (Right):* The title placeholder treatment is the same as slide 2. The picture was recolored using the preset *Black and White: 25%* color. This creates a more abstract image.

3-14 A large square picture used as a background fill with color changes

Notice the following characteristics for the three slides shown in Figure 3-15:

- **Slide 4 (Left):** The actual size of this large flower does not fill the slide, so now the complete flower is displayed. The *Tile picture as texture* option was selected with *Alignment* changed to *Center. **Tiling** causes the picture to be repeated to fill the slide area so parts of the flower are shown around the center flower. Like slide 1 in Figure 3-14, the text is difficult to read.
- **Slide 5 (Center):** The title placeholder resembles slide 2 in Figure 3-14, but this time the fill color transparency is 30%. More of the flower shows through, yet the text is still easy to read.
- **Slide 6 (Right):** The picture was recolored with preset *Gray – 25%, Background color 2 Light*. Black text is used with no shadow. (This was done because black text with a black shadow makes the text look blurred.)

3-15 A large square picture used as a tiled background fill with color changes

If you tile a picture or texture that is small, many images fill the screen for an effect like wallpaper. If these images still seem too large, you can adjust the *Tiling Options* and reduce the *Scale* percentage to display each image in a smaller size. *Offset* points control how much the tiled images are indented from the left (*Offset X*) and top (*Offset Y*).

Notice the following characteristics for the three slides shown in Figure 3-16:

- **Slide 7 (Left):** The *Tile picture as texture* option was selected so many of these small flower images (200×203 pixels) fill the screen. For an appropriate fit on the slide, *Alignment* was changed to *Top left;* then *Offset* and *Scale* were adjusted. Like slide 4 in Figure 3-15, the text is difficult to read.
- **Slide 8 (Center):** The flower picture was recolored with preset *Grayscale*. The title placeholder colors were changed to a black fill with red text. The placeholder size was increased, too, for greater emphasis.
- **Slide 9 (Right):** The repeating picture for this slide is a small rectangle (40 by 77 pixels) with a bevel effect to make it look like a real tile. The title text is left aligned and the placeholder is filled with a gold color. A rectangle was added on the right so the date would be easy to read and to help create an asymmetrical focal point with the single large flower. This flower has a transparent background rather than white as in the previous examples.

3-16 Small pictures tiled for a background fill with color changes

Textures available on the *Format Background* pane are small images, so it is generally best to tile them because the effect is more pleasing. When stretched to fill a slide, the textures will appear blurred. Notice the following characteristics for the slides shown in Figure 3-17:

- **Slide 10 (Left):** The *Paper bag* texture was applied and it is blurred.
- **Slide 11 (Center):** The same texture was tiled so multiple small images repeat and no other change was made.
- **Slide 12 (Right):** The same texture was tiled and the *Mirror type* changed to *Both* so this creates an interesting pattern with horizontal and vertical mirror images.

3-17 The same texture used as a background fill with different settings

SLO 3.2

Applying Animation

Animation is the movement of objects on a slide. Animation can make your presentation more dynamic and keep your audience focused on concepts.

You can observe creative animation techniques by noticing how objects and text move in movies or in television commercials. As you decide what effects to use, try to select movements that enhance your content and support your message. Animation can be overdone when it is not used skillfully. Be sure you are applying animation for the right reasons and not just for entertainment value. Use animation sparingly because too much can be distracting.

When planning movement, also consider the transitions (the movement between slides). When a presentation is supporting a speaker, you want to keep the transitions calmer and apply animation effects to draw attention to information on selected slides only.

Add Entrance, Exit, and Emphasis Effects

Animation effects are arranged in three categories that are shown in different colors on the gallery (Figure 3-18):

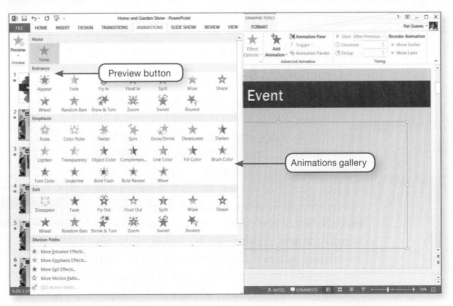

3-18 *Animations* gallery

- *Entrance:* A movement that occurs when an object appears on the slide (green)
- *Emphasis:* A movement that calls attention to an object that remains on the slide (yellow)
- *Exit:* A movement that occurs when an object leaves the slide (red)

Note that some effects are for text only. When animating objects, those effects are gray in the gallery and are not available.

HOW TO: Apply an Animation Effect

1. Select the text or object to be animated.
2. Click the **Animations** tab.
3. Click the **More** button on the *Animations* gallery to see all available effects.
   Or
   If the *Animations* gallery is not open because your PowerPoint window is narrow, click the **Add Animation** button [*Advanced Animation* group] to open the gallery.
4. Click an effect to apply it. A number appears on the slide, showing that the object is animated.
5. Click the **Preview** button to test the animation.
6. Repeat to animate additional objects as desired. Each animated object is numbered in sequence to show animation order.
7. To remove an animation, click the animation number and press **Delete**.

> **MORE INFO**
> Animation numbers are displayed only when the *Animations* tab is open.

Effect Options, Timing, and Duration

Each different animation effect has options that control the direction of movement.

HOW TO: Change Effect Options

1. Select the animated object.
2. Click the **Effect Options** button [*Animations* tab, *Animation* group].
3. Select an appropriate **Direction** and **Sequence** if it is available.

For the *Float In* effect shown in Figure 3-19, two directions are available. Other effects have many different options. You select only one direction for each animation.

The sequence shown in this figure is *By Paragraph.* Animation numbers display before each bulleted text item so they appear individually. If you choose *As One Object,* only one animation number displays and the complete list appears at the same time. If you choose *All at Once,* the same animation number displays for each text item and the complete list appears at the same time.

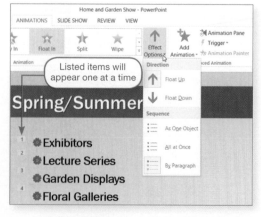

3-19 Animation and effect options applied

Some people are critical of animating text because viewers cannot read text until it stops moving. If you are going to spend significant time discussing each item in a list, adding each item as you start talking about it makes sense. However, animating a list has no value if you are only making brief statements or discussing the complete list in general terms.

You can adjust animation *timing* using the following commands on the *Animations* tab in the *Timing* group:

- **Start:** This controls when animation begins. With *On Click* the speaker controls the timing; *With Previous* or *After Previous* makes animation occur automatically.
- **Duration:** By default, the time to complete each animation ranges from .50 to 2.00 seconds depending on the movement. Increasing the duration seconds extends the time an object is moving so the movement appears slower.
- **Delay:** The default is no delay, but you can enter seconds in the spin box to make the animation begin after a specified time.
- **Reorder Animation:** When multiple objects are animated, click *Move Earlier* or *Move Later* to adjust the sequence of animation.

HOW TO: Adjust Animation Timing and Duration

1. Select the animated object.
2. Click the **Start** list box arrow [*Animations* tab, *Timing* group] and select from *On Click*, *With Previous*, or *After Previous* (Figure 3-20).
3. Increase or decrease **Duration** by editing the time or clicking the spin box arrows.
4. Enter seconds or click the **Delay** spin box to specify the time (in seconds) before the animation starts.
5. Click the **Preview** button to test the animation.
6. Reorder animation if necessary using the *Move Earlier* and *Move Later* buttons.

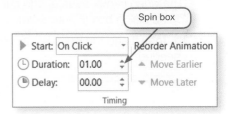

3-20 *Animations* tab, *Timing* group

When you animate several objects, check the animation numbers to be sure the objects will appear in the order you want (Figure 3-21).

If your presentation is designed to support you as a speaker, coordinate the animation timing with your speaking. This technique usually works best in small segments only because precise timing is almost impossible to predict when you are presenting in real time to

3-21 Numbers indicate animation order

an audience. If you are designing a self-running presentation for a trade show exhibit, for example, your animation can be much more dramatic and extensive because the slide show is not dependent on a speaker's pace.

SLO 3.3

Linking to an Online Video

Many videos are available online, but not all of them can be played within PowerPoint. When you search for a video using the *Insert Video* dialog box, the videos found from YouTube are most likely to play within PowerPoint as long as you have Internet access. You click **Insert** to put the video on your slide, but the actual video is not saved in your presentation.

An image of the video will appear and the necessary information to link to it is saved in your presentation.

When you search for videos, you may find a compelling interview or demonstration that will enliven your presentation, but be sure the video fits your topic and adds value.

HOW TO: Link a Presentation to an Online Video

1. Be sure your computer has Internet access. Select the PowerPoint slide where you want to show the video.
2. Click the **Insert** tab.
3. Click the **Video** button list arrow [*Media* group] and select **Online Video** (Figure 3-22) to open the *Insert Video* dialog box (Figure 3-23). The search options that appear depend on how your software is installed.
4. Type a search word in one of the search boxes, *Bing Video Search* or *YouTube* if it is available, and click the **Search** button.
5. Available video clips (brief video segments) appear with ScreenTips that identify names.
   • The video name, source, and number of minutes appear in the lower left corner of the dialog box (Figure 3-24). You may want to use this information in a source notation.
6. Click **Insert** and the video will appear on your slide. Below the video, add the appropriate source information as needed.

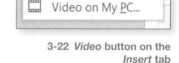

3-22 *Video* button on the *Insert* tab

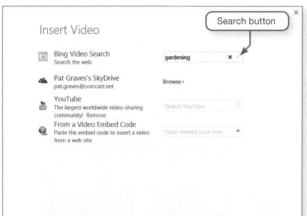

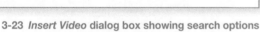

3-23 *Insert Video* dialog box showing search options

3-24 *Insert Video* dialog box showing search results

> **MORE INFO**
> A linked video will not play in a presentation that you send by email.

Play the Online Video

To play an online video in PowerPoint, the computer used to display your presentation must have Internet access.

The clarity you see in playback depends on the resolution of the original video and how it was compressed for online distribution. Resolution is expressed in pixel width and height. With more pixels, image clarity and detail improve.

As with all computer technology, video capabilities continue to improve and many videos can be played at full-screen size from their online source. However, video sharing sites often provide video in the standard definition size (640×480 pixels) or even smaller. Be careful when increasing the video size on your slide to avoid degrading image quality. Test how the video plays before you use it in your presentation.

HOW TO: Play an Online Video

1. In *Normal* view, select the video object.

2. If you wish, increase the size of the video by using one of these methods:
   - Drag handles.
   - Enter specific **Height** and **Width** measurements [*Video Tools Format* tab, *Size* group].
   - Click the *Size* launcher to open the *Format Video* pane (Figure 3-25). Click the *Size & Properties* option at the top of the pane. Adjust size by changing **Height** and **Width** measurements or changing the **Scale Height** and **Scale Width** measurements.

3. On the *Format Video* pane, check **Lock aspect ratio** and **Relative to original picture size** to maintain dimensions as your resize.

4. Check **Best scale for slide show** to select a different resolution.

5. Reposition the video as needed.

6. Notice the clarity of the video as you test it in the next steps. If the image is degraded, click the **Reset** button on the *Format Video* pane. You can also click the **Reset Design list arrow** [*Video Tools Format* tab, *Adjust* group] and click **Reset Design & Size** to restore the video to its original dimensions.

3-25 *Format Video* pane

7. To play the video in *Normal* view:
   - Click the **Play** button [*Video Tools Playback* tab, *Preview* group] to activate the video.
   - If the video can play within PowerPoint, a timeline will appear below the video with playback controls you can use to pause, mute, and access other options (Figure 3-26).
   - Click the **Play** button on the video to play it.

8. To play the video in *Slide Show* view:
   - Click the **Slide Show** button [*Status* bar] to start your slide show on the current slide.
   - Click the **Play** button on the video.
   - The same timeline described in step 7 appears at the bottom of the video as it plays.
   - Press **Esc** to stop the slide show and return to *Normal* view.

3-26 Video playing in *Normal* view

9. To make the video start automatically in *Slide Show* view:
   - Click the **Start** list box arrow [*Video Tools Playback* tab, *Video Options* group] and select **Automatically**.
   - If the video can be played at full screen size, select **Play Full Screen** [*Video Tools Playback* tab, *Video Options* group].
   - Click the **Slide Show** tab and the **From Beginning** button [*Start Slide Show* group]. Advance to the slide with the video to test that it begins playing automatically.

10. Move your pointer so it does not appear on the video while it is playing.

11. When the video is complete, advance to the next slide.

> **MORE INFO**
>
> If you find an online video that you want to use in PowerPoint, you may be able to link to it without searching for it in PowerPoint. You can copy the video's embed codes (the host web address, name of the video, and playback size information) that are included with a video in a sharing section on the host page. Then open the *Insert Video* dialog box and paste the embed codes. Information to link to the video is saved in your presentation, so Internet access is required to play the video.

Obtain Permission

Linking to a video for classroom purposes falls under the guidelines of ***fair use*** for education, and crediting the source may be sufficient. However, business use is different. Just like television programming or movies in a theater, videos are copyrighted by the creator. You need permission before you link to, display, or distribute video that is copyrighted. Obtaining permission is time consuming and can be expensive. If the creator does not give you permission, you must find another video and start the process again.

HOW TO: Obtain Permission to Use an Online Video

1. From the web site where the video is posted, identify the user name of the creator.
2. Click a link to go to more profile information or, in some cases, another web site.
3. Look for terms of use and find contact information.
4. Send an email message explaining the following:
   - How you want to use the video
   - What portion of the video you will use
   - When you will use the video
   - How you will show credits on the slide where the video is displayed such as in Figure 3-26
   - Your contact information for the creator's response

With the dynamic nature of the web, a video you find may be available for only a limited time. You may need to request a high resolution copy of the video, and the creator may charge you for this service.

> **MORE INFO**
>
> The ***Copyright Act of 1976*** is the primary basis of copyright law in the United States. It specifies fair use that permits limited use for such purposes as research, teaching, and scholarship. The ***Digital Millennium Copyright Act of 1998*** addresses issues of online copyright infringement.

PAUSE & PRACTICE: POWERPOINT 3-1

Davon Washington has almost finished the slide show for his seminar on presentation planning. In this project you create custom theme colors that better match the Solution Seekers, Inc., logo, modify a background style, animate several slide objects, and link to a video on a web site. You will later change the slide size from standard to widescreen.

File Needed: ***PresentationPlanning-03.pptx***
Completed Project File Name: ***[your initials] PP P3-1.pptx***

1. Open the presentation
   PresentationPlanning-03.

2. Save the presentation as ***[your initials]***
   PP P3-1.

3. Create new theme colors.
   a. Click the **More** button [*Design* tab,
      Variants group].
   b. Select **Colors** and click **Customize**
      Colors to open the *Create New Theme*
      Colors dialog box (Figure 3-27).
   c. Change four colors. For each change,
      click the **color list arrow** and select
      More Colors. Click the **Custom** tab
      and enter the numbers for *Red*, *Green*,
      and *Blue* from the following table.

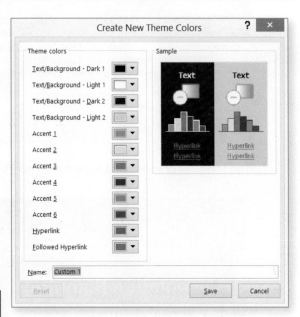

3-27 **Original theme colors**

	Text/Back- ground – Light 2	Accent 1	Accent 2	Accent 3
Red	234	3	102	181
Green	214	110	0	139
Blue	184	131	51	128

   d. Name the new custom theme Planning
      (Figure 3-28).
   e. Click the **Save** button. The new custom
      theme is saved in the *Custom* section of
      your list of available theme colors.

4. On slide 1, apply a gradient fill.
   a. Point to the slide background and
      right-click.
   b. Select **Format Background** to open the
      Format Background pane.
   c. Select the **Gradient fill** option.
   d. Click the **Type** list arrow and choose
      Linear.
   e. Click the **Direction** list arrow and
      Linear Diagonal – Top Right to
      Bottom Left.
   f. The *Angle* percentage automatically adjusts
      to 135°.
   g. If necessary, click the **Add gradient**
      stop button so you have four gradient
      stops.

3-28 *Planning* **theme colors**

h. Click each gradient stop from left to right (Figure 3-29) and adjust the *Color*, *Position*, *Brightness*, and *Transparency* to the values shown in the following table:

Gradient Stops	Stop 1	Stop 2	Stop 3	Stop 4
Color	Dark Teal, Accent 1	Dark Teal, Accent 1, Lighter 60%	Tan, Text 2	Tan, Text 2, Darker 50%
Position	0%	30%	70%	100%
Transparency	0%	50%	0%	0%
Brightness	0%	0%	0%	−50%

i. The title slide gradient fill is shown in Figure 3-30.

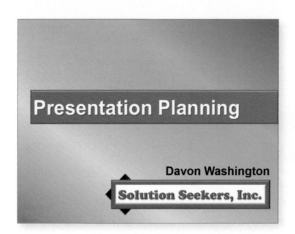

3-30 Title slide with new design

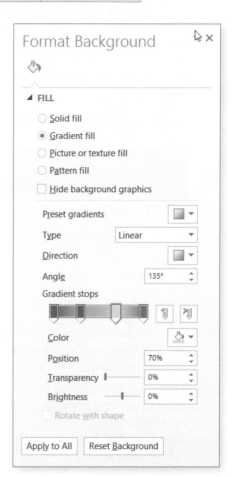

3-29 Gradient stops adjusted

5. On slide 14, create a *Picture fill* background.
   a. On the *Format Background* pane, select **Picture or texture fill** and click the **Online** button to open the *Insert Pictures* dialog box.
   b. In the *Office.com Clip Art* search box, type audience and click **Search**.
   c. Select the picture "Instructor speaking to a group of students" (Figure 3-31) and click **Insert**.

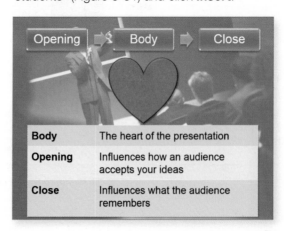

3-31 Background picture fill

d. Click the **Picture** button at the top of the *Format Background* pane and then select **Picture Color**.
e. Click the **Recolor** list arrow, and choose **Brown**, **Accent color 3 Light**.
f. Close the *Format Background* pane.

6. On slide 4, select the text box "Possible body sequence" and change the *Shape Fill* color to **Tan**, **Background 2**, **Darker 50%** and the *Shape Outline* color to **Dark Teal**, **Accent 1** (Figure 3-32).

7. On slide 13, change the *Text fill* color for the text at the top of the slide to **Brown**, **Text 2**, **Lighter 50%**.

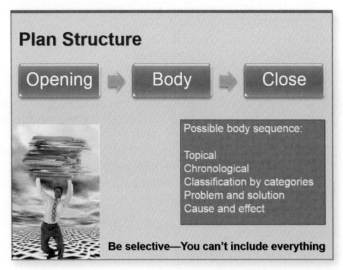

3-32 *SmartArt* resized and text box colors changed

8. Apply a transition.
   a. Click the **Transitions** tab and apply the **Wipe** transition.
   b. Click the **Effect Options** button and select **From Left**.
   c. Click **Apply to All** [*Timing* group].

9. Apply animation.
   a. Click the **Animations** tab and repeat steps b–g for each object in the following table.
   b. Select the **text or object** to be animated.
   c. Click the **More** button on the *Animation* gallery or click the **Add Animation** button [*Advanced Animation* group] if the gallery is not open.
   d. Click an **effect** to apply it.
   e. Click the **Effect Options** button and select the listed **Direction** and **Sequence** or **Amount**.
   f. Adjust settings for *Start*, *Duration*, and *Delay*.
   g. Click the **Preview** button or **Slide Show** button to test the animation.

Slide	Object	Animation Effect	Effect Options	Start	Duration	Delay
4	Possible body sequence text box	Fade (Entrance)	As One Object	On Click	02.00	None
5	First impression text	Wave (Emphasis)	By Paragraph	After Previous	00.50	None
7	Quoted text	Bounce (Entrance)	As One Object	After Previous	02.00	01:00
8	Road picture	Grow & Turn (Entrance)	None	With Previous	02.00	01:00
13	Prepare text	Float In (Entrance)	Float Up	After Previous	01.00	None
13	Slide show text	Float In (Entrance)	Float Up, By Paragraph	After Previous	01.00	01:00
14	Heart	Spin (Emphasis)	Clockwise, Two Spins	With Previous	02.00	None

10. Insert a new blank slide after slide 14.

11. On slide 15, click the **Video** button list arrow [*Insert* tab, *Media* group] and select **Online Video** to open the *Insert Video* dialog box.
    a. In the *Bing Video Search* box (or the *YouTube Search* box if it is available), type the search words presentation skills and click **Search**.
    b. From the search results, select an appropriate video from *YouTube* and click **Insert**.
    c. The video appears in a small size. Increase the size so the width is approximately **5"** wide.
    d. Center the video on the slide.
    e. Click the **Play** button [*Video Tools Playback* tab, *Preview* group] to activate the video.
    f. Click the **Play** button on the video to test it.
    g. If necessary, reduce the size of the video for a clear image.
    h. Add source information below the video.

12. Test all of your transitions and animations in your presentation.

13. Save and close the presentation.

SLO 3.4 — Using Rehearsal Techniques

Everyone, no matter how experienced, can benefit from rehearsing a presentation. Practicing your delivery ensures that each slide's information supports what you are saying. Practice builds confidence, too.

Speaker Notes

Speaker notes help you remember what you need to say in your presentation, but they should never include text that would tempt you to read to your audience. Notes should be your personal reminders, such as items to emphasize or terminology to define. Notes should not be a script for everything you are going to say. For example, you could include statistics you want to mention, a quote you want to say but not show on a slide, a list of upcoming events, or additional resources for your audience. Even if you don't use the speaker notes you prepare, having them available while you present can be comforting and help to reduce nervousness.

As you think about what to include in your notes, plan for smooth and logical transitions between the various topics of your presentation. You can compose your notes using the *Notes* pane in *Normal* view or you can change to *Notes Page* view.

HOW TO: Use the Notes Pane in Normal View

1. In *Normal* view, the *Notes* pane is below the slide.

2. If the *Notes* pane is not showing, click the **Notes** button [*View* tab, *Show* group].

3. You can expand the *Notes* pane by dragging the border up (Figure 3-33).

4. If you drag the border too low and the *Notes* pane disappears, click the **Notes** button or the **Normal** button to restore it.

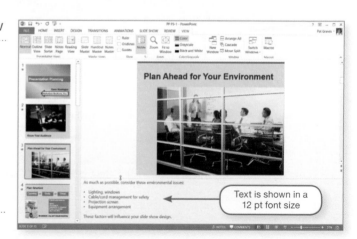

3-33 Increased *Notes* pane size

The *Notes Page* view provides much more space to type text than you have when using the *Notes* pane in *Normal* view.

HOW TO: Use Notes Page View

1. Click the **Notes Page** button [*View* tab, *Presentation Views* group] to show a slide as it will print.
2. Type your text in the text box below the slide to add notes (Figure 3-34).

You may want to increase the font size before you print the pages because large text is easier for you to see on a lectern or podium while you are speaking. You will need your notes to be visible even if overhead lighting is dimmed so slide colors display better on the projection screen.

> **ANOTHER WAY**
>
> Some people find that printed handouts with a few handwritten reminders work well for speaker notes.

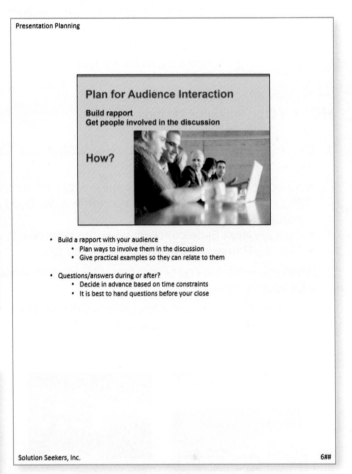

3-34 *Notes Page* view with slide and text

HOW TO: Print Notes Pages

1. Click the **File** tab and click **Print**.
2. For *Print Layout*, choose **Notes Pages** and check **Scale to Fit Paper** to make the slide images larger (Figure 3-35).
3. Omit the **Frame Slide** option for *Notes Pages*. A single-line border around the entire page is unnecessary.
4. Click the **Print** button.

Rehearse Timings

PowerPoint's ***Rehearse Timings*** feature makes it easy to judge the pace of your presentation. When you use this feature to rehearse, the time you spend on each slide is recorded as you move through the presentation. The timings that you save from

3-35 Print settings for *Notes Pages*

rehearsing appear below each slide in *Slide Sorter* view. This view enables you to see the "big picture" aspect of your presentation. You can compare the time spent on each slide and make decisions to spend less time on some slides and more time on other slides where the content takes longer to explain. You can save the timings to automate the presentation and make it self-running. If you are presenting to an audience, remove the timings so you can control when the slides advance.

HOW TO: Rehearse Timings

1. Click the **Rehearse Timings** button [*Slide Show* tab, *Set Up* group] and your slide show will start.

   - A *Recording* dialog box appears in the upper left corner (Figure 3-36). It shows the time each slide is displayed and the total elapsed time.
   - Click the **Next Slide** button (or press the **spacebar**) to advance.
   - Click the **Pause** or **Repeat** buttons as needed.

   3-36 Current slide time and total elapsed time

2. When you reach the end of your presentation, a message will ask if you want to save your timings.

3. Click **Yes** and the timings, in seconds, will display below each slide in *Slide Sorter* view (Figure 3-37). (The seconds shown in this example are brief because they were recorded when testing the presentation. The times would be much longer in an actual presentation.)

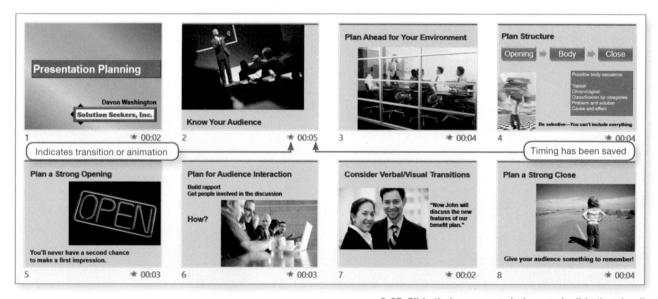

3-37 Slide timings appear below each slide thumbnail

In rehearsal, go through your presentation and practice what you will say while each slide is displayed. Use printed notes pages while you are practicing. If possible, stand to replicate more closely the experience you will have when speaking to your audience. Sometimes knowing how and where to stand in relation to the keyboard and monitor you are using takes a little practice. Your body posture is important. Good posture makes you appear confident and it positively affects how your voice projects. If possible, rehearse with the equipment you will use to deliver the presentation.

Set Timings Manually

You can enter all timings manually, but it is quicker to rehearse your presentation, save the timings, and adjust the time as needed for individual slides.

HOW TO: Modify Timings

1. Click the **Transitions** tab and be sure the **After** option is selected [*Transitions* tab, *Timing* group] and second numbers are showing (Figure 3-38).

2. For each slide, change the number of seconds as needed to increase or decrease the amount of time the slide is displayed.

3. If you want the slides to advance automatically, deselect the **On Mouse Click** option.

4. To remove the timings, click the **Record Slide Show** button list arrow [*Slide Show* tab, *Set Up* group], select **Clear**, and then select **Clear Timing on Current Slide** or **Clear Timings on All Slides** (Figure 3-39).

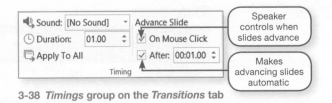

3-38 *Timings* group on the *Transitions* tab

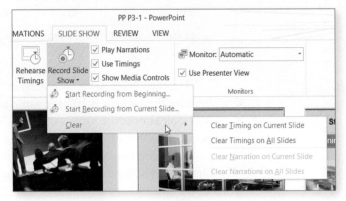

3-39 *Clear Timings* options

Prepare for Mishaps

Be sure you have backup copies of your presentation in case you experience equipment failure and you need to switch to a different computer. In a worst-case situation, where both your computer and projector have malfunctioned, you can present using your handouts to support what you say. All experienced presenters encounter such problems at some time during their careers.

SLO 3.5 | Controlling Display Options

As you learned in Chapter 1, themes and templates that you obtain online are available in different sizes called ***Standard*** and ***Widescreen***. The default sizing for PowerPoint 2013 is *Widescreen* but for previous versions of PowerPoint it was *Standard*. Therefore, you may encounter files that require updating to fit your current screen size, or you may need to adjust the size of your presentation to fit an older projection screen in a room where you will give your presentation.

Adjust Slide Size

Today widescreen computers (like television screens) use a 16:9 or 16:10 aspect ratio (the ratio of width to height). A slide show designed in the 16:9 aspect ratio takes advantage of this wide horizontal space because it fills the screen. A slide show designed in the 4:3 aspect ratio (more square) and displayed on a widescreen will be positioned in the center of the screen with black areas on both sides. Both of these slide sizes are available on the *Design* tab in the *Customize* group and you can change from one to the other by clicking the **Slide Size** button and choosing **Standard (4:3)** or **Widescreen (16:9)**. Two other sizes are available on the *Slide Size* dialog box and you can create a custom size if necessary. These sizes are listed in the following table and illustrated as blue and green thumbnails in Figure 3-40:

Slide Sizes

Aspect Ratios	Width in Inches	Height in Inches
Standard 4:3	10	7.5
16:9	10	5.625
16:10	10	6.25
Widescreen 16:9	13.333	7.5

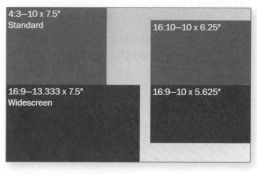

3-40 Screen sizes

The two wide sizes available in the *Slide Size* dialog box look smaller in Figure 3-40 because their width is 10", the same as the Standard 4:3 width. On your computer screen they will look almost the same as the *Widescreen* size, but ruler measurements and object sizes will be different because of the difference in width and height.

Changing between slide show sizes is a simple process, but necessary adjustments after the change can be time consuming. You need to consider how the change affects the text and graphics on your slide. Both *Standard* and *Widescreen* sizes have the same vertical measurement, so the width is what changes and adjustments are usually needed to make slide objects fit appropriately.

If you change from 4:3 to one of the other sizes (16:9 or 16:10), the vertical size is reduced, which compresses the slide vertically. Pictures or text in placeholders may not fit appropriately.

Be aware of these height and width differences when changing slide sizes. If you think you may need to change back to your original size, save the original presentation as a separate file before you begin making changes for the new size. By doing this, you can avoid all the resizing changes that would be necessary to return to the original size.

HOW TO: Change the Aspect Ratio

1. Click the **Design** tab.
2. Click the **Slide Size** button [*Customize* group]; then click either **Standard (4:3)** or **Widescreen (16:9)**.
3. Click **Custom Slide Size** to open the *Slide Size* dialog box. Sizes for printing and four sizes for on-screen viewing are available. You can choose from the following:
   - ***On-screen Show (4:3):*** 10×7.5" (Standard)
   - ***On-screen Show (16:9):*** 10×5.625"
   - ***On-screen Show (16:10):*** 10×6.25"
   - ***Widescreen (16:9):*** 13.333×7.5"
4. Click **OK** (Figure 3-41).

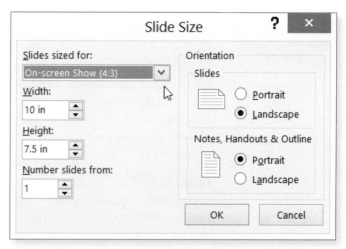

3-41 *Slide Size* dialog box

Presenter View

Presenter View allows you to display your presentation on the screens of two monitors or a monitor and a projector. PowerPoint can automatically detect when two monitors are connected and will recognize one monitor as your main monitor for *Presenter View* and extend the display to the second monitor for your full-screen slide show. Using *Presenter View* is helpful because while you are speaking you can:

- View the current slide and see the next slide in your presentation.
- Click thumbnails to display slides out of sequence.
- Have speaker notes available on the monitor for easy reading instead of needing printed notes.
- Make the screen that's visible to your audience black yet still have speaker notes available to you.
- Magnify sections of a slide.
- Use convenient navigation and pen tools.

Your monitor shows your view of the presentation and includes the displayed slide, the navigation tools, the next slide, and an area for notes. When you are using a second monitor (or projector), only the slide is displayed on that monitor for your audience. You can click the **Display Settings** button to swap between the monitors used for *Presenter View* and your full-size slide show.

If you do not have two monitors connected to your computer, you can still use *Presenter View* by pressing **Alt+F5**.

HOW TO: Use Presenter View

1. Click the **Slide Show** tab.
2. Select **Use Presenter View** [*Monitors* group] (Figure 3-42).

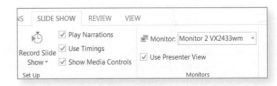

   - If you are using two monitors, confirm that the monitor you want your audience to see the slide show on appears in the *Show Presentation On* list box. Click the **From Beginning** button to start your slide show.
   - If you are using one monitor, press **Alt+F5**.

3-42 *Use Presenter View* option on the *Slide Show* tab

3. Review your slide show using *Presenter View* (Figure 3-43).

   - Click the **Advance to the next slide** button in the navigation area to move through your slides.
   - Click the **See all slides** button to see slide thumbnails. Click a thumbnail to display a different slide out of sequence.
   - Click the **Zoom into the slide** button, then drag the selection area over an object or text you want to magnify, and then click. That portion of the screen is displayed for your audience. Click the same button again (now **Zoom out**) to return to normal screen size.
   - Notice the slide show time displayed above the slide.
   - Press **Esc** to exit the slide show.

3-43 *Presenter View*

For this project, you add speaker notes, print notes pages, and rehearse a presentation. You will save the presentation in its original standard size and then resave it in the widescreen size. For the widescreen version, you will adjust object positioning as needed and then use *Presenter View* to display your slide show.

File Needed: *[your initials] PP P3-1.pptx*
Completed Project File Name: *[your initials] PP P3-2a.pptx* and *[your initials] PP P3-2b pptx*.

1. Open the presentation *[your initials] PP P3-1*.

2. Save the presentation as *[your initials] PP P3-2a*.

3. Create a visual transition between topics. Insert a new slide with the *Section Header* layout after slides 3, 9, and 15. On each of these new slides, delete the subtitle placeholder and type the title text as follows:

    a. Slide 4 title: Presentation Structure (Figure 3-44).
    b. Slide 10 title: Presentation Practice.
    c. Slide 16 title: Summary.

4. Prepare speaker notes for two slides that do not have notes.

    a. On slide 11, click the **Notes Page** button [*View* tab, *Presentation Views* group].
    b. Add the following text with blank space for easy reading (Figure 3-45):
        - Print slide with discussion points below
            - Make notes brief (like cue cards)
            - Keep text large so it is easy to read
        - Can be a "safety net" (builds confidence)
        - Use to rehearse a presentation
        - Do not read during a presentation
    c. On slide 12, add the following text:
        - Experience is the best teacher
        - Identify strengths and develop them
        - Identify weaknesses and work to overcome them
        - Reduce tendency to be nervous
    d. Click the **Normal** button [*View* tab, *Presentation Views* group].

5. Print notes pages for slides 11 and 12.

    a. Click the **File** tab and click **Print**.
    b. Select the appropriate printer and make sure that you are printing just one copy.
    c. For *Slides,* type 11–12 to print a Custom Range.
    d. For *Print Layout,* choose **Notes Pages** and select **Scale to Fit Paper** (Figure 3-46).
    e. Click the **Print** button.

Presentation Structure

3-44 *Section Header* slide layout

- Print slides with discussion points below
    - Make notes brief (like cue cards)
    - Keep text large so it is easy to read
- Can be a "safety net" (builds confidence)
- Use to rehearse a presentation
- Do not read during a presentation

3-45 *Notes Page* view with text

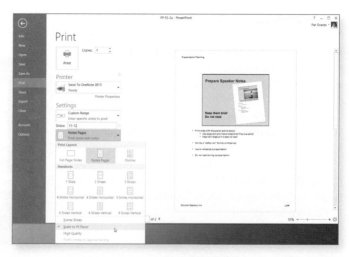

3-46 Print settings for *Notes Pages*

6. Rehearse your presentation and save timings.
   a. Click the **Slide Show** tab.
   b. Click the **Rehearse Timings** button [*Set Up* group].
   c. Using the *Recording* dialog box, click the **Next Slide** button to advance each slide after approximately 3–5 seconds (for the purpose of practicing this feature).
   d. At the end of your presentation, click **Yes** to save your timings.
   e. Click the **Slide Sorter** button [*Status bar*] to see the timings displayed below each slide.

7. Beginning with slide 1, change how slides advance and modify presentation timings.
   a. Click the **Transitions** tab.
   b. Deselect **On Mouse Click** [*Transitions* tab, *Timing* group].
   c. Change the *After* timing to **3** seconds (shown as 00:03:00).
   d. Click the **Apply To All** button.
   e. Change the *After* timing on the *Section Header* slides (slides 4, 10, and 16) to **1** second (shown as 00:01) (Figure 3-47).

3-47 Rehearsal timings modified

8. Save the presentation to preserve the standard size (4:3 aspect ratio, 10×7.5") on the ***[your initials] PP P3-2a*** file.

9. Save the presentation again as ***[your initials] PP P3-2b*** to create a separate file for a widescreen size (16:9 aspect ratio, 13.333×7.5").

10. Click the **Slide Size** button [*Design* tab, *Customize* group] and select **Widescreen (16:9)**.

11. Slide objects are not aligned as they were in the standard size (Figure 3-48). Slide title text remains in the same position, but space has been added to both sides of the slide to stretch slides from 10" wide to 13.333" wide.

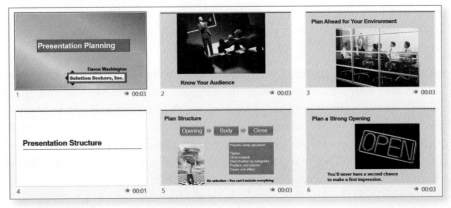

3-48 Slide object alignment changed with widescreen size

12. On some slides, the new object position is acceptable. Double-click Slide 1 to return to *Normal* view. Change the following slides as described (Figure 3-49):
    a. **Slide 1:** Increase the size of the title placeholder by dragging the right sizing handle to the edge of the slide (*Width* **11.2"**). Move the logo and name to the right.
    b. **Slide 2:** Left align the picture. Move the text to the left about **.5"** from the edge of the slide.
    c. **Slide 3:** Right-align the picture.
    d. **Slide 9:** Right-align the picture and the text below it. Move the slide title down.
    e. **Slide 12:** Right-align the picture. Resize the title placeholder so it fits the text and move the title down so it is closer to the picture.

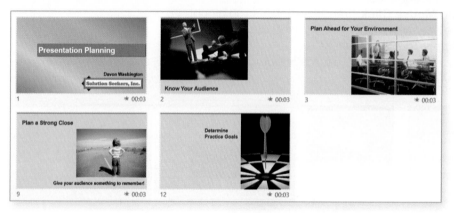

3-49 Alignment adjusted on selected slides

13. Review your presentation using *Presenter View*.
    a. Click the **Slide Show** tab.
    b. Click **Use Presenter View** [*Monitors* group].
    c. Review your slides.
       • If you have two monitors, click the **From Beginning** button [*Start Slide Show* group].
       • If you have one monitor, press **Alt+F5**.

14. Save and close the presentation.

Presenting Using Projection Equipment

When facing the front of a presentation room, the ideal location for a speaker is to the left of the projection screen. People are conditioned to read from left to right, so it is natural for the audience to first look at you and then at the projection screen. Many situations are less than ideal, however, so be flexible when you cannot control the speaker area. Keep the following guidelines in mind:

• Become familiar with your equipment so you won't feel awkward using it.
• If possible, load your slide show before the audience enters the room so you are not seen scrambling around with preliminary preparations. Arrive early and test your presentation to be sure all content works correctly.
• Allow time to relax before your presentation starts. Almost everyone feels nervous before a presentation begins. This reaction is normal and just shows you are respectful of the situation. Harness your nervous energy in a positive way.
• Have your title slide displayed as people enter the room.
• If possible, greet people to make them feel welcome. Let people know that you are glad to have the opportunity to share with them.

Position Equipment

Using a computer while you speak creates some challenges. You may have a tablet computer to control your slide show, but it must work with your projector. If you are using a desktop or notebook computer, you must see the computer screen when facing the audience and be able to access the computer to advance slides. In some presentation rooms, you may need to place your computer on a table. A podium (or lectern) may be available to hold your computer and/or printed notes pages. Be careful, however, that the podium does not create a barrier between you and the audience. Move away from it when you can.

3-50 Poor electrical connections

Even if your computer has a wireless Internet connection and is running on battery power, you may need to manage power cords for other equipment. Connections may not be convenient. (Figure 3-50). Be sure to keep cables and cords away from the area where you and audience members will be walking or tape cords to the floor.

Navigate in a Slide Show

You have advanced through a slide show by pressing the spacebar or clicking on a slide. You can use other methods to advance, to go to specific slides, or to end a slide show.

During a slide show, navigation buttons are on the lower left of each slide. They are barely noticeable unless you point to that area. Use buttons (Figure 3-51) to move between slides or to bring up a shortcut menu of presentation options.

3-51 Slide show navigation buttons

Control Slide Display

The audience needs to focus on you, the speaker. Slides support your message, but you may not want a slide displayed all the time. Also, going from a blank screen to your next slide can seem more dramatic.

Blank Slides

If you know in advance that you need to discuss something unrelated to your slides, then plan ahead and place one or more slides with a black background in specific places in your slide show.

During a presentation, you can blank the screen by pressing **B** to display an empty black screen or **W** to display an empty white screen. Be careful about using the white option, however, because an all-white screen can create glare that will be unpleasant for your audience.

Hide and Reveal Slides

Hiding a slide is helpful when you have information that is not essential to your presentation but you want to have that slide available if you need it depending on time and audience interest. For example, you could hide slides containing information such as:

- References
- Additional pictures
- Additional details about a topic
- Optional charts, diagrams, or tables

To hide the current slide, click the **Hide Slide** button [*Slide Show* tab, *Set Up* group] (Figure 3-52). You can hide multiple slides by selecting thumbnails on the *Slides* pane or in *Slide Sorter* view. In *Normal* and *Slide Show* views, the slide thumbnail for a hidden slide appears grayed out with a diagonal line through the slide number.

During a slide show, you can display a hidden slide by typing the slide number and pressing **Enter**.

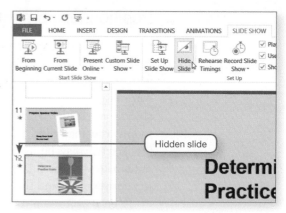

3-52 *Hide Slide* button and hidden slide 12

> **MORE INFO**
>
> You can print hidden slides. Click the **File** tab and then select **Print**. Click the **Print All Slides** option and select **Print Hidden Slides**.

Use Keyboard Shortcuts

Keyboard shortcuts are convenient if you have easy access to your keyboard while speaking.

Slide Show Navigation Shortcuts

Press	Action
N, spacebar, right arrow, down arrow, **Enter**, or **Page Down**	Advance to the next slide.
P, **Backspace**, left arrow, up arrow, or **Page Up**	Go to the previous slide.
Slide number, then **Enter**	Go to a particular slide.
Ctrl+S	Open *All slides* dialog box, select slide, and click **Go To**.
B or period	Blanks the screen to black.
W or comma	Blanks the screen to white.
S	Stop or restart an automatic show.
plus sign	Zoom in.
minus sign	Zoom out.
H or slide number, **Enter**	Go to a hidden slide.

The presentation shortcut menu is available during a slide show by right-clicking when you point anywhere on a slide.

Remote Control and Laser Pointer

A *remote control* enables you to move away from your computer as you are presenting. If you do this, you can interact with your audience more naturally because you don't need to stay close to your computer to control how slides advance. Remote control devices come in many styles from small clickers to clickers that resemble pens with USB storage. When presenting, be sure you have extra batteries available for the remote control.

Some remote controls have a built-in *laser pointer*, or you can purchase a separate pointing device. A laser pointer shows a small dot (usually red) on the slide where you point. PowerPoint's laser pointer feature resembles this dot. To use this feature, press **Ctrl** while you are pointing on the screen and your pointer changes to a dot that can be red, green, or blue.

HOW TO: Change Laser Pointer Color

1. Click the **Set Up Slide Show** button [*Slide Show* tab, *Set Up* group] to open the *Set Up Show* dialog box (Figure 3-53).

3-53 Changing laser pointer color

2. Click the **Laser pointer color** list box arrow and select **green or blue**.

3. Click **OK**.

A dot on the screen directs audience attention to a particular location. Be sure you show the dot long enough for your audience to find it and keep the dot steady. Do not bounce it around on the screen with random movements because this distracts viewers. A very small pointer movement on your computer screen makes a large movement on a projection screen.

SLO 3.7

Using Annotation Pens

During a presentation, you can call attention to information by writing or drawing on slides. These markings are called *ink annotations*. While controlling the pointer to write with a hand-held mouse is a little awkward, you can record audience feedback and make simple drawings on slides. When you reach the end of your presentation, you can save ink annotations. All markings, even if you draw a rectangle, are saved as lines and not as shapes.

Select Pen Style and Ink Color

To write or draw on a slide, use the *Pen*. To add a color overlay on text, use the *Highlighter* just as you would mark text to highlight information on paper. When you change *Ink Color*, be sure the color you select contrasts with the slide background so it is easy to see.

HOW TO: Use the Pen and Highlighter

1. Start a slide show and go to the slide you want to annotate.
2. Select the *Pen* or *Highlighter* using one of the following methods:
   - Click the **Pen** button in the navigation area (Figure 3-54) to open the shortcut menu. Select an option as desired.

Or

   - Right-click anywhere on the slide to open the shortcut menu and select **Pointer Options**. Select an option as desired (Figure 3-55).
3. Begin writing or drawing on one or more slides.
4. To remove markings, select the **Eraser** options from the shortcut menu. Click markings to delete each continuous pen stroke (Figure 3-56).
5. To change annotation color, select the **Ink Color** option from the shortcut menu and then select a different color.
6. At the end of a presentation, click **Keep** to save ink annotations. The markings are saved as lines that you can edit.

3-54 **Navigation area**

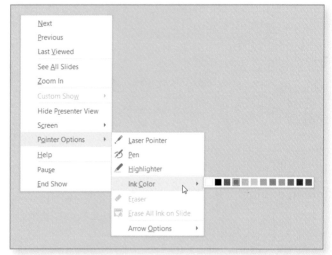

3-55 **Shortcut menu**

3-56 **Ink annotations and the *Eraser* tool**

Pen tools are available in *Presenter View*, also. You can control many of these options during a slide show using keyboard shortcuts summarized in the following table:

Ink Markup Shortcuts

Press	Action
Ctrl+P	Changes the pointer to a pen.
Ctrl+A	Changes the pointer to an arrow.
Ctrl+E	Changes the pointer to an eraser.
Ctrl+M	Shows or hides ink markup.
E	Erases markings on the screen.

For this project, you use PowerPoint features to present more effectively. You hide and reveal slides, blank slides, practice with the laser pointer, change pen colors, use the pen and highlighter, and save annotations.

File Needed: *[your initials] PP P3-2b.pptx*
Completed Project File Name: *[your initials] PP P3-3.pptx*

1. Open the presentation *[your initials] PP P3-2b*.

2. Save the presentation as *[your initials] PP P3-3*.

3. Click the **Transitions** tab and change the slide transitions.
   a. Select **On Mouse Click** and deselect **After** [*Timing* group].
   b. Click **Apply To All** [*Timing* group].

4. Select slide 4 and click the **Hide Slide** button [*Slide Show* tab, *Set Up* group].
   a. Start a slide show from slide 3 to confirm that you automatically advance directly from slide 3 to slide 5.
   b. On slide 6, type 4 and press **Enter** to show the hidden slide.

5. In *Slide Show* view, practice blanking slides.
   a. Press **B** to blank a slide to black. Press **B** to return to the slide.
   b. Press **W** to blank a slide to white. Press **W** to return to the slide.
   c. Press **Esc** to exit *Slide Show* view.

6. Change the laser pointer color.
   a. Click the **Set Up Slide Show** button [*Slide Show* tab, *Set Up Slide Show* group] to open the *Set Up Show* dialog box.
   b. Click the **Laser Pointer** list box arrow and select **blue**.
   c. Click **OK**.
   d. In *Slide Show* view, press **Ctrl** while you move your pointer to practice using the laser pointer.

7. Use the pen and highlighter.
   a. In *Slide Show* view, go to slide 7.
   b. Right-click to open the shortcut menu, select **Pointer Options**, and then select **Ink Color**. Select the standard color **Blue**.
   c. Use the **Pen** to draw a rectangle around the word "How" (Figure 3-57).
   d. Right-click to open the shortcut menu, select **Pointer Options**, and then select **Ink Color**. Select **Yellow**.
   e. Right-click to open the shortcut menu, select **Highlighter**, and then highlight the word "involved."
   f. Type 13 and press **Enter** to go to slide 13. Use the **Highlighter** to highlight the words "Get help" and "feedback."
   g. Type 17 and press **Enter** to go to slide 17. Use the **Highlighter** to highlight the words "heart," "how an audience," "accepts," "what the audience," and "remembers."
   h. Right-click to open the shortcut menu, select **Pointer Options**, and then select **Eraser**. Click to remove the highlights from the words "how an audience" and "what the audience."
   i. Advance to the end of the presentation and click **Keep** to save your annotations.

8. Save and close your presentation.

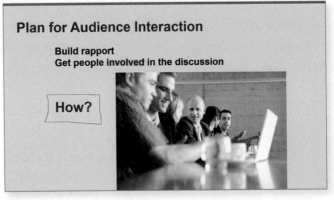

3-57 Pen color changed

SLO 3.8 — Preparing a Self-Running Presentation

A self-running slide show, also referred to as a *kiosk presentation*, can be set up to run continuously without someone being present to advance the slides of the presentation. This type of presentation works well for trade shows or open house events where people walk up to a computer screen and watch the slide show. For example, self-running presentations can be used for marketing products to customers or to educate patients in medical office waiting rooms. You can record narration to accompany the slides. You can also set up the slide show to *loop* so it will automatically repeat and cycle continuously from beginning to end.

Record a Slide Show with Narration

To record voice narration for your presentation, your computer must have a microphone and sound card. Like rehearsal, you can use this feature to practice what you will say during a presentation and evaluate your vocal qualities. You can also make a narrated slide show available as a complete presentation to distribute on CDs or DVDs or to post online for viewers.

Prepare carefully to decide what you will say as each slide is displayed. Use notes pages or other resources as references.

HOW TO: Record Narration

1. Click the **Slide Show** tab.
2. Click the **Record Slide Show** button list arrow [*Set Up* group] and then select **Start Recording from Beginning** or **Start Recording from Current Slide** to open the *Record Slide Show* dialog box.
3. Select **Slide and animation timings**.
4. Select **Narrations and laser pointer**. (This option is available only if your computer has a microphone.)
5. Click **Start Recording** (Figure 3-58).
6. A *Recording* box appears in the top left corner of the screen. You can advance, pause, or resume recording in the same way you do when you rehearse a presentation (see *Section 3.4: Using Rehearsal Techniques*).
7. Speak clearly into your microphone as each slide is displayed.
8. At the end of the presentation, the narration and slide timings will automatically be saved.
9. Separate audio files are recorded on each slide and an audio icon appears in the lower right. Review your slide show and listen to your narration.
10. Save your presentation.

3-58 *Record Slide Show* dialog box

Press **Esc** if you need to end the slide show before reaching the last slide. You can clear timing or narration on the current slide or all slides. When you play back a narration, the recording is synchronized with the presentation.

HOW TO: Clear Timings or Narration

1. Click the **Slide Show** tab.
2. Click the **Record Slide Show** button list arrow [*Set Up* group] and then select **Clear**.
3. Select from these options:

Clear Timing on Current Slide	*Clear Timings on All Slides*
Clear Narration on Current Slide	*Clear Narrations on All Slides*

If you need to display the slide show without narration, click the **Set Up Show** button [*Slide Show* tab, *Set Up* group]. Select **Show without narration** and click **OK**.

Set Up a Kiosk Presentation with Looping

Depending on how you plan to use it, a kiosk presentation may need different design guidelines than a slide show that is shown by a presenter. While other presentations provide minimal text because the slides support the speaker's message, a kiosk presentation may contain more information because it is a stand-alone product. If your kiosk presentation is displayed in a public place with a lot of distractions, then splashy graphics can be used to grab attention. On the other hand, if your kiosk presentation is for educational purposes in a quiet setting such as a doctor's office, the slides might be designed more like pages in a book with smaller text and more detailed information.

HOW TO: Set Up a Kiosk Presentation

1. Click the **Slide Show** tab.
2. Click the **Set Up Slide Show** button [*Set Up* group] to open the *Set Up Show* dialog box (Figure 3-59).
3. Choose the following settings:
   - For *Show type,* select **Browsed at a kiosk (full screen)**.
   - For *Show options*, **Loop continuously until 'Esc'** is automatically selected and grayed out because you chose a kiosk.
   - For *Show slides,* select **All** or enter the first and last slide numbers you want to display.
   - For *Advance slides*, **Use timings**, **if present** is automatically selected for a kiosk.
   - If you are using more than one monitor, select the appropriate monitor for the slide show.
   - For *Resolution*, select **Use Current Resolution** or the highest resolution possible for your equipment.
   - For a kiosk presentation, **Use Presenter View** is not available.
4. Click **OK**.
5. Save the presentation with these changes.

3-59 *Set Up Show* dialog box

Packaging a Presentation to a CD or Folder

The *Package Presentation for CD* feature allows you to easily transport one or more presentations for use on another computer. You can copy your presentation file and any linked files to a blank CD (CD-R, recordable or CD-RW, rewritable) or to a folder on your computer, network location, or removable drive.

HOW TO: Save a Presentation to a CD or Folder

1. Insert a CD in your CD/DVD drive if you are saving to that location.
2. Click the **File** tab and select **Export**.

3. Select **Package Presentation for CD**. Click the **Package for CD** button to open the *Package for CD* dialog box.

4. Type a name for the CD (Figure 3-60).

5. Click the **Options** button to open the *Options* dialog box (Figure 3-61) and choose from the following options:

   - **Linked Files:** Preserves links and copies any external files such as audio or video files.
   - **Embedded TrueType fonts:** Assures that the fonts used in your presentation are available on the playback computer.
   - **Password:** Enhances security for opening or modifying a presentation.
   - **Inspect:** Checks for inappropriate or private information.

6. Click **OK**.

7. To save the presentation use one of the following methods:

   - Click the **Copy to CD** button and click **Yes** to verify that you want to include linked files.
   - Click the **Copy to Folder** to open the *Copy to Folder* dialog box (Figure 3-62). Type a name for the folder and browse for the location to save the presentation. Select the option to **Open folder when complete** if you want to see all the files that are copied. Click **OK**.

8. When the packaging process is complete, click **No** to indicate that you don't need to make another copy. Click **Close**.

9. Test the presentation by loading it from the folder or from the CD.

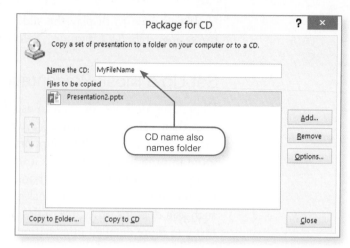

3-60 *Package for CD* dialog box

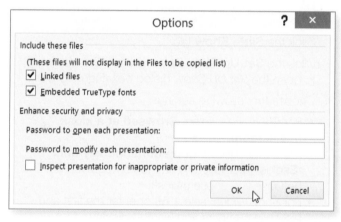

3-61 *Options* dialog box

3-62 *Copy to Folder* dialog box

> MORE INFO
>
> If file size requirements exceed the storage capacity of a CD, you can convert your slide show to a video and then use DVD burning software to save the files to a DVD. PowerPoint does not support direct burning to DVDs.

This project consists of two parts. You record a presentation with audio in Part A if you have a microphone connected to your computer. In Part B, you prepare a kiosk presentation, set it up to loop so it is self-running, and then use the *Package Presentation for CD* feature to save it to a folder.

File Needed: *[your initials] PP P3-2b.pptx*
Completed Project File Name: *[your initials] PP P3-4b.pptx*

Part A (Microphone Required)

1. Open the presentation *[your initials] PP P3-2b*.

2. Save the presentation as *[your initials] PP P3-4a* and change to *Slide Sorter* view.

3. For the purpose of this project, you need only slides 1–5. Delete all other slides in the presentation.

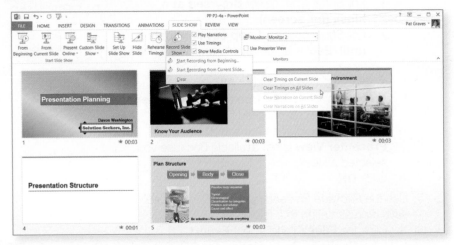

4. Remove the timings.
   a. Click the **Record Slide Show** button list arrow [*Slide Show* tab, *Set Up* group] and select **Clear**.
   b. Select **Clear Timings on All Slides** (Figure 3-63).

3-63 Clear timings on all slides

5. Click the **Notes Page** button and add notes to two slides.
   a. For slide 2, add four items after the first line of text:
      • What is their background?
      • What is their educational level?
      • How familiar are they with your topic?
      • Are they likely to be accepting of your ideas or resistant?
   b. For slide 3, add two items to the bulleted text:
      • Overall cleanliness and organization of the room
      • Temperature level for comfort
   c. Print the notes pages.

6. Using the notes pages as a reference, click the **Record Slide Show** button list arrow [*Slide Show* tab, *Set Up* group] and select **Start Recording from Beginning**.
   a. Select **Slide and animation timings** and **Narrations and laser pointer** (Figure 3-64).
   b. Click **Start Recording**.
   c. Speak clearly into your microphone as you go through the slide show.
   d. At the end of the presentation, click **Yes** to save your timings and narration.

3-64 *Record Slide Show* dialog box

7. Review the presentation and listen to the narration.

8. Save and close the presentation.

Part B

1. Open the presentation *[your initials] PP P3-2b*.

2. Save the presentation as *[your initials] PP P3-4b*.

3. For the purpose of this project, apply timing so slides change rapidly.

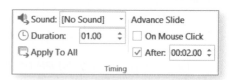

3-65 *Timing* group on the *Transitions* tab

   a. Confirm that **On Mouse Click** [*Transitions* tab, *Timing* group] is not selected.
   b. Change the *After* seconds to **00:02:00**.
   c. Click **Apply to All** (Figure 3-65).

4. Click the **Set Up Slide Show** button [*Slide Show* tab, *Set Up* group] to open the *Set Up Show* dialog box.

   a. Select the following settings (Figure 3-66):
      - For *Show type*, select **Browsed at a kiosk (full screen)**.
      - For *Show options*, **Loop continuously until 'Esc'** is automatically checked for a kiosk.
      - For *Show slides*, select **All**.
      - For *Advance slides*, **Use timings, if present** is automatically checked for a kiosk.
   b. Select the appropriate monitor. **Use Presenter View** is not available because you selected a kiosk.
   c. Click **OK**.

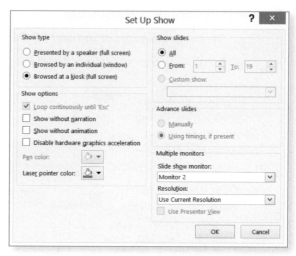

3-66 *Set Up Show* dialog box

5. Use the *Package Presentation for CD* feature to save a presentation to a folder.

   a. Click the **File** tab and select **Export**.
   b. Click **Package Presentation for CD** and click the **Package for CD** button to open the *Package for CD* dialog box.
   c. Type Planning for the name of the CD.

6. Click the **Options** button to open the *Options* dialog box and select the following:
   - Choose **Linked Files** to preserve links and copy any external files such as audio or video files.
   - Choose **Embedded TrueType fonts** to assure that the fonts you use in your presentation are available on the playback computer.

7. Click **OK** and the dialog box closes.

8. Click the **Copy to Folder** button to open the *Copy to Folder* dialog box. The name you typed for the CD automatically appears.

   a. Click **Browse** to open the *Choose Location* dialog box and find the place where you want to save the presentation. Click **Select** and the dialog box closes.
   b. Select the option to **Open folder when complete**.
   c. Click **OK** and the dialog box closes.
   d. If you receive a message about including linked files, click **Yes**.

9. A *File Explorer* window opens showing the files in the open *Planning* folder.

10. Close the *Package for CD* dialog box.

11. Close your original *[your initials] PP P3-4b* presentation.

12. Test the saved presentation by loading it from the *Planning* folder. Double-click the *[your initials] PP P3-4b* file name.

13. Close the presentation and folder.

Chapter Summary

3.1 Create custom theme colors and background styles (p. P3-139).

- Design themes create a unified appearance for your presentation.
- The Accent 1 theme color is the color that appears, by default, each time you draw a shape.
- Create custom theme colors by selecting different colors for background, text, and accent colors. Select the background color first and then select other colors that work well on that background.
- Modify backgrounds using the *Format Background* dialog box to apply a custom pattern, gradient, or picture fill.
- Carefully control how text is placed over background pictures and other fills so text is easy to read.

3.2 Apply animation to add interest and reinforce content (p. P3-147).

- Animation adds movement to slide objects and text.
- Animation is applied through **Entrance**, **Exit**, and **Emphasis** effects.
- If more than one animation is used, each animation is numbered in sequence.
- **Effect Options** control the direction and sequence of movement.
- Animation can start **On Click**, **With Previous**, or **After Previous**.
- **Duration** is the time that it takes to complete an animation.

3.3 Link to an online video (p. P3-149).

- Search for an online video using the *Insert Video* dialog box.
- You need Internet access and a video must currently be available online if you want to link to it during a PowerPoint presentation.
- Some video can be played at full screen size.
- Playback controls appear at the bottom of the video.

3.4 Use rehearsal techniques to prepare for presentation delivery (p. P3-156).

- Type speaker notes using the *Notes* pane or *Notes Page* view.

- Print speaker notes for reference during a presentation.
- Use **Rehearse Timings** to practice and judge the pace of your presentation.
- You can manually adjust timings to increase or decrease the time a slide is displayed.
- Prepare backup copies of your presentation and your notes.

3.5 Control display options for different screen sizes (p. P3-159).

- The shape of your slides varies based on the aspect ratio (the ratio of width to height) you use.
- PowerPoint's default aspect ratio is *Widescreen 16:9;* the *Standard 4:3* is available.
- *Presenter View* displays the current slide, next slide, notes, and navigation controls on one monitor, while the slide show displays on a second monitor or projection screen.
- *Presenter View* can be used with one monitor.

3.6 Present effectively and professionally using projection equipment (p. P3-164).

- Use the slide show toolbar, shortcut menu, or keyboard shortcuts to navigate to different slides in a presentation.
- To blank a slide to black, press **B**; to blank a slide to white, press **W**.
- When you **Hide** a slide, it is still in the presentation but will not display during a slide show unless you go to that specific slide.
- Use **remote controls** to advance slides so you can move away from your computer.
- Use PowerPoint's **laser pointer** to place a dot on the slide during a slide show.

3.7 Use annotation pens to highlight information and save presentation markings (p. P3-167).

- Use the **Pen** or **Highlighter** to mark or draw on a slide during a slide show.
- Use the **Eraser** to remove markings during a slide show.
- These markings, called **ink annotations**, can be saved at the end of the presentation.

3.8 Prepare a self-running presentation that loops (p. P3-170).

- If your computer has a microphone, you can include narration in a presentation.
- A self-running presentation, a *kiosk presentation*, is set to automatically loop so it runs continuously.
- Use the *Set Up Show* dialog box to set up a kiosk presentation.

3.9 Use the *Package Presentation for CD* feature to prepare a slide show for display on other computers (p. P3-171).

- The *Package Presentation for CD* feature saves linked files to a CD or other location.
- To assure that the fonts you used to create your presentation are available on the computer you will use to display your presentation, select *Embedding TrueType Fonts*.

Check for Understanding

In the *Online Learning Center* for this text (www.mhhe.com/office2013inpractice), there are a variety of resources that can be used to review the concepts covered in this chapter.

The following Online Learning Resources are available in the Online Learning Center:

- Multiple choice questions
- Short answer questions
- Matching exercises

Guided Project 3-1

One of the community colleges in the Sierra Pacific Community College District has finished construction of a new building for its business program. A dedication ceremony and open house is planned. In this project, you finalize the presentation for this special program and prepare a kiosk presentation to be displayed on monitors throughout the building while people tour after the opening ceremony. You save the standard slide size version in Part A and then change to a widescreen version in Part B.
[Student Learning Outcomes 3.1, 3.2, 3.4, 3.5, 3.6, 3.8]

File Needed: **Dedication-03.pptx**
Completed Project File Names: **[your initials] PowerPoint 3-1a.pptx** and **[your initials] PowerPoint 3-1b.pptx**

Skills Covered in This Project

- Apply a background picture fill.
- Apply animation and effect options.
- Create and print notes pages.
- Rehearse a presentation and save timings.
- Change to a widescreen slide size.

- Use *Presenter View*.
- Use slide show navigation tools, use keyboard shortcuts, and insert blank slides.
- Prepare a kiosk presentation.

Part A

1. Open the presentation **Dedication-03** that has a standard size (4:3 aspect ratio, 10 x 7.5").

2. Save the presentation as **[your initials] PowerPoint 3-1a**.

3. Apply a background picture fill with a softened effect to all slides.
   a. Right-click to open the shortcut menu. Click **Format Background** to open the *Format Background* pane.
   b. Select the **Picture or texture fill** option.
   c. Click the **Online** button to open the *Insert Pictures* dialog box.
   d. In the *Office.com Clip Art* search box, type the word building and click the **Search** button (or press **Enter**).
   e. Select the picture, "Office building with reflection" shown in Figure 3-67 and click **Insert**.
   f. Click the **Picture** button at the top of the pane and then click **Picture Color**. Click the **Recolor** list arrow and select **Blue, Accent color 2, Dark**.
   g. Click **Apply to All** so this slide is used as the background for all slides.

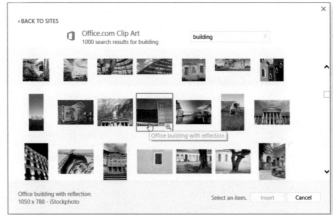

3-67 *Insert Picture* dialog box with search results

4. On slides 1 and 2, restore the background picture to its original color. On the *Format Background* pane under *Picture Color*, click the **Reset** button for each slide.

5. On slide 2, delete the subtitle placeholder and move the title down slightly (Figure 3-68).

3-68 Slide title moved down

6. On slide 6, change the background color to black.
   a. On the *Format Background* pane, click **Fill** at the top of the pane if it is not selected. Select the **Solid fill** option.
   b. Click the **Color** list arrow and select **Black, Background 1**.
   c. Close the *Format Background* pane.

7. Select slide 2 and press **Ctrl+D** to duplicate. Move the new slide to the end of the presentation so it becomes slide 9. Change the slide 9 title text to Take a Tour.

8. Apply a transition to all slides.
   a. Click the **Transitions** tab and apply the **Shape** transition.
   b. Click the **Effect Options** button and select **Diamond**.
   c. Click **Apply to All** [*Timing* group] (Figure 3-69).

3-69 *Transition Effect Options*

9. Apply animation on four slides and change effect options as shown in the following table.
   a. Select the text or object to be animated.
   b. Click the **More** button on the *Animation* gallery. If the *Animation* gallery is not displayed, click the **Add Animation** button [*Animations* tab, *Advanced Animation* group].
   c. Click an effect to apply it.
   d. Click the **Effects Options** button [*Animations* group] to apply *Direction*, *Sequence*, or *Amount* settings.
   e. Adjust settings for *Start* and *Duration*.
   f. Click the **Preview** button or **Slide Show** button to test the animation.

Slide	Object	Animation Effect	Effect Options	Start	Duration
1	Text box for agenda	Wipe (Entrance)	From Bottom, By Paragraph	On Click	00.50
3	Picture	Shape (Entrance)	Out, Diamond	After Previous	02:00
7	Text box for space design	Zoom (Entrance)	Object center, As One Object	On Click	00:50
7	Text box for wireless access	Zoom (Entrance)	Object center, As One Object	On Click	00:50
8	Text box for donors	Wipe (Entrance)	From Bottom, All At Once	After Previous	00:50

10. Prepare speaker notes on two slides.
   a. Click the **Notes Page** button [*View* tab, *Presentation Views* group].
   b. Click the **Zoom** button and increase the *Percent* to **150%** so you can more easily see the text. Click **OK**.
   c. Add the following text with a blank line between each item on two notes pages (Figure 3-70):

   Slide 1: Welcome the audience.
   Review today's agenda—go through animation.

   Slide 9: The tours will now begin and last until 4 p.m.
   Student leaders are available outside this auditorium to guide small groups.
   Or tour on your own.

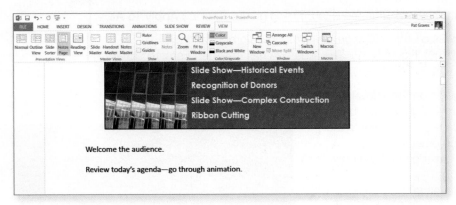

3-70 *Notes Page* view showing speaker notes

   d. Click the **Normal** button to return to *Normal* view.

11. Print notes pages for slides 4 and 5.
   a. Click the **File** tab and click **Print**.
   b. Select the appropriate printer and make sure that you are printing just one copy.
   c. For *Slides*, type 4–5 to print a *Custom Range*.
   d. For *Print Layout*, choose **Notes Pages** and check **Scale to Fit Paper** (Figure 3-71).
   e. Click the **Print** button.

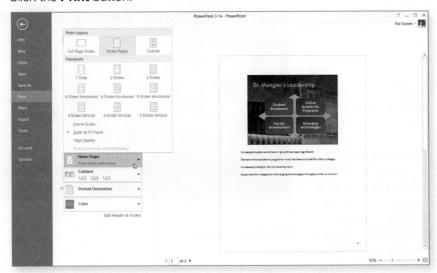

3-71 Print view of notes page

12. Rehearse and save timings.
    a. Click the **Rehearse Timings** button [*Slide Show* tab, *Set Up* group].
    b. Using the *Recording* dialog box, click the **Next Slide** button to advance each slide after approximately 3–5 seconds.
    c. At the end of your presentation, click **Yes** to save your timings. The timings are displayed below each slide in *Slide Show* view.

13. Save the presentation to preserve the current standard (4:3) slide size.

Part B

14. Resave the presentation as *[your initials] PowerPoint 3-1b*.

15. Deselect the **After** timings [*Transitions* tab, *Timing* group] and click **Apply To All**.

16. Click the **Slide Size** button [*Design* tab, *Customize* group] and click **Widescreen (16:9)** (Figure 3-72). The slide size has changed from 10" to 13.333" wide.

3-72 *Slide Size*

17. Reposition objects on the following slides to fit the widescreen size:
    a. ***Slide 1:*** Right-align the text box.
    b. ***Slide 2:*** Move the slide title to the left to match other slide titles.
    c. ***Slide 7:*** Right-align both text boxes (Figure 3-73).
    d. ***Slide 8:*** Move the text at the top of the slide to the left. Right-align the text box.
    e. ***Slide 9:*** Move the slide title to the left to match other slide titles.

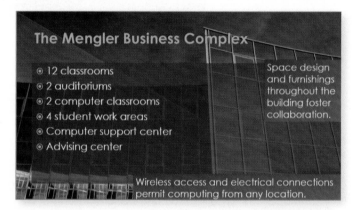

3-73 *Text boxes right-aligned*

18. Use *Presenter View* to review your presentation.
    a. Click the **Slide Show** tab.
    b. Click **Use Presenter View** [*Monitors* group].
    c. Start your presentation.
       • If you have two monitors, click the **From Beginning** button [*Start Slide Show* group].
       • If you have one monitor, press **Alt+F5**.
    d. Click the **Presenter View** right arrow button to advance slides as you review them.
    e. Click the **Zoom into the slide** button to magnify a section of the slide. Click **Zoom Out** to return to the normal slide size (Figure 3-74).
    f. Click the **See all slides** button to view thumbnails of all slides. Click to display different slides.
    g. Press **Esc** to exit *Presenter View*.

3-74 *Presenter View*

19. In *Slide Show* view, practice use of navigation tools, keyboard shortcuts, and blanking slides.
    a. Click the **right arrow** button in the slide navigation area to advance slides.
    b. Click the **Menu** button in the slide navigation area to open the shortcut menu and go to a specific slide.
    c. Right-click to open the shortcut menu and go to a specific slide.
    d. Press **N** to advance to the next slide; press **P** to go to the previous slide.
    e. Type 6 and press **Enter** to go to slide 6.
    f. Press **B** to blank a slide; press **B** to view the screen again.

20. Prepare a kiosk presentation with looping.
    a. Select the **After** timing [*Transitions* tab, *Timing* group] and click **Apply To All** so timings will be available for the kiosk presentation.
    b. On slides 1 and 7, select each animated object and change **Start** [*Animations* tab, *Timing* group] to **After Previous**.
    c. Click the **Set Up Slide Show** button [*Slide Show* tab, *Set Up* group] to open the *Set Up Show* dialog box.
    d. Select the following settings:
       - *For Show type*, select **Browsed at a kiosk (full screen)**.
       - *For Show options*, **Loop continuously until 'Esc'** is automatically selected for a kiosk.
       - *For Show slides*, select **All**.
       - *For Advance slides*, **Use timings**, **if present** is automatically selected for a kiosk.
    e. Select the appropriate monitor.
    f. Click **OK**.

21. Test the presentation to make sure slide transitions and animations work correctly.

22. Save and close the presentation (Figure 3-75).

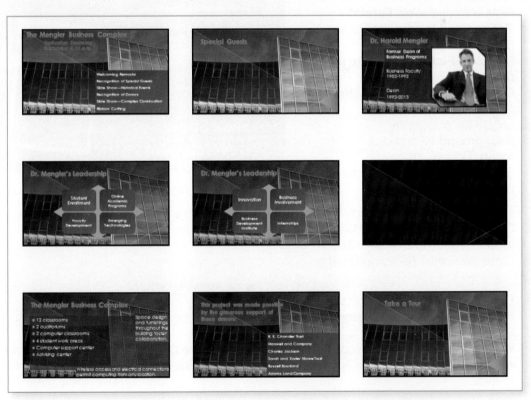

3-75 PowerPoint 3-1 completed

Guided Project 3-2

For the second training session for new hires on presenting effectively, Davon Washington, Management Consultant at Solution Seekers, Inc., is preparing guidelines for designing slides and developing content in a visual way. For this project, you finish the presentation that Davon has prepared and save it on a CD so participants can refer to it after the session.
[Student Learning Outcomes 3.1, 3.2, 3.3, 3.4, 3.7, 3.9]

Files Needed: *SlideShowDevelopment-03.pptx*, *Background-03.jpg*, and *Applause-03.jpg*
Completed Project File Names: *[your initials] PowerPoint 3-2.pptx* and folder *Develop Slides*

Skills Covered in This Project

- Apply a background picture fill.
- Create custom theme colors.
- Apply animation and effect options.
- Link to an online video.

- Create and print notes pages.
- Add ink annotations.
- Use the *Package Presentation for CD* feature.

---

1. Open the presentation *SlideShowDevelopment-03*.

2. Save the presentation as *[your initials] PowerPoint 3-2*.

3. Apply a background picture fill to all slides.
    a. Right-click and select **Format Background** to open the *Format Background* pane.
    b. Select the **Picture or texture fill** option.
    c. Click the **File** button to open the *Insert Pictures* dialog box.
    d. Locate the student file *Background-03* and click **Insert** (Figure 3-76).
    e. Click **Apply to All** so this picture is the background for all slides.

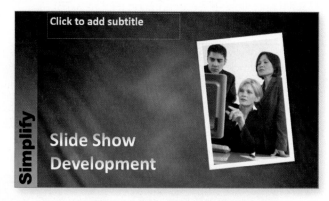

3-76 Title slide with new background picture fill

4. On slide 12, repeat step 3 to apply a different background picture, *Applause-03*, for this slide only.
    a. Change the *Offset left* to **−9%** and the *Offset top* to **−5%** for better picture positioning. (*Offset right* is 0% and *Offset bottom* is −9%.)
    b. Close the *Format Background* pane.

5. Prepare a new custom color theme to blend with the background picture.
    a. Click the **More** button [*Design* tab, *Variants* group].
    b. Select **Colors** and click **Customize Colors** to open the *Create New Theme Colors* dialog box.
    c. Change five accent colors.
        - For each change, click the color list arrow and select **More Colors** to open the *Colors* dialog box.
        - Click the **Custom** tab and enter the numbers for *Red*, *Green*, and *Blue* shown in the following table.

	Accent 1	Accent 2	Accent 3	Accent 4	Accent 5
Red	255	157	255	38	95
Green	247	175	217	203	30
Blue	220	210	82	236	60

d. Name the new custom theme Development (Figure 3-77).

e. Click the **Save** button.

6. Adjust text and object colors on the following selected slides:

a. *Slide 3:* Change the black text on the *SmartArt* shapes to white.

b. *Slide 4 and 5:* Click **Reset** [*Home* tab, *Slides* group] so the list bullet updates for the new *Accent 1* color.

c. *Slide 7 and 11:* Change the *SmartArt* graphic color. Click the **Change Colors** button [*SmartArt Tools Design* tab, *SmartArt Styles* group] and select the **Colored Fill – Plum, Accent 5** style (Figure 3-78).

d. *Slide 12:* Change the text box *Shape Fill* to **Plum, Accent 5**.

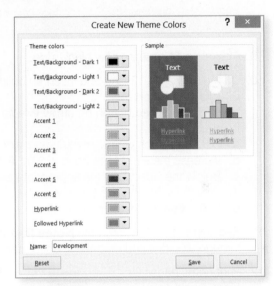

3-77 New theme colors

7. Apply a transition to all slides.

a. Click the **Transitions** tab and apply the **Reveal** transition.

b. Click the **Effect Options** button and the select **Smoothly from Right**.

c. Change the *Duration* to **02:00** [*Timing* group].

d. Click **Apply to All**.

8. Apply animation on four slides and change effect options as shown in the following table.

a. Select the text or object to be animated.

b. Click the **Animations** tab and click the **More** button on the *Animation* gallery. (Click the **Add Animation** button [*Advanced Animation* group] if the gallery is not open.)

c. Click an effect to apply it.

d. Click the **Effects Options** button to apply *Direction*, *Sequence*, or *Amount* settings.

e. Adjust settings for *Start and Duration* as needed to match the table.

f. Click the **Preview** button or **Slide Show** button to test the animation.

3-78 *SmartArt* recolored

Slide	Object	Animation Effect	Effect Options	Start	Duration
2	Ducks	*Fly In* (Entrance)	*From Left*	*On Click*	02.00
2	Slide Show Development text box	*Bounce* (Entrance)	None	*After Previous*	02.00
4 and 5	Up text box	*Float In* (Entrance)	*Float Up*	*After Previous*	01.00

(Continued)

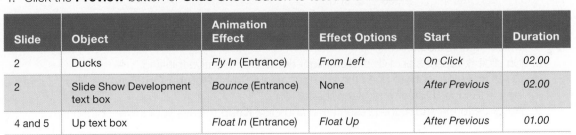

Slide	Object	Animation Effect	Effect Options	Start	Duration
4 and 5	Down text box	*Float In* (Entrance)	*Float Down*	*After Previous*	*01.00*
6	Color wheel	*Spin* (Emphasis)	*Clockwise, Two Spins*	*After Previous*	*03.00*
12	Text box	*Wheel* (Entrance)	*2 Spokes, As One Object*	*After Previous*	*02.00*

9. After slide 11, insert a new blank slide.

10. On the new slide 12, find and insert an online video.
    a. Click the **Insert** tab.
    b. Click the **Video** button list arrow [*Media* group] and select **Online Video** to open the *Insert Video* dialog box.
    c. Use the search words presentation slide design and select an appropriate video. Click **Insert**.
    d. Increase the size of the video (*Width* **6.5"**) if the quality remains acceptable.
    e. Below the video, add the appropriate source information.
    f. Play the video in *Slide Show* view, by clicking the **Start** button on the video.
    g. Press **Esc** to exit *Slide Show* view.

11. Beginning on slide 1, click the **Notes Page** button [*View* tab, *Presentation Views* group] and advance through all slides and read the speaker notes to review tips for slide design.

12. Print notes pages for slides 7 and 11.
    a. Click the **File** tab and click **Print**.
    b. Select the appropriate printer and make sure that you are printing just one copy.
    c. For *Slides,* type 7, 11 to choose a *Custom Range*.
    d. For *Print Layout,* choose **Notes Pages** and check **Scale to Fit Paper** (Figure 3-79).
    e. Click the **Print** button.

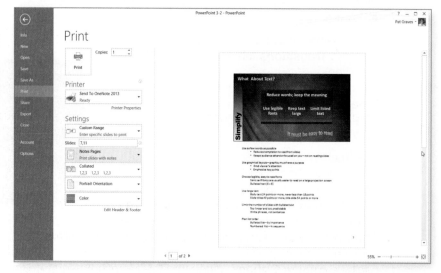

3-79 Print *Notes Pages*

13. Add ink annotations on slides 4, 5, and 7.
    a. In *Slide Show* view, go to slide 4.
    b. Right-click to open the shortcut menu and select **Pointer Options** and **Highlighter**. Highlight the word "organization."
    c. On slide 5, repeat step 14b and highlight the words "creative thinking."
    d. On slide 7, right-click to open the shortcut menu. Select **Pointer Options** and **Pen**. Circle the words "Reduce words" and "keep the meaning."
    e. Advance to the end of the presentation and click **Keep** to save your ink annotations.

14. Save the presentation (Figure 3-80).

15. Use the *Package Presentation for CD* feature to save the presentation to a folder.
    a. Click the **File** tab and select **Export**.
    b. Click **Package Presentation for CD** and click the **Package for CD** button to open the *Package for CD* dialog box.
    c. Type Develop Slides to name the CD.
    d. Click the **Options** button to open the *Options* dialog box and select **Linked Files** and **Embedded TrueType fonts**.
    e. Click **OK**.
    f. Click the **Copy to Folder** button to open the *Copy to Folder* dialog box. The folder name appears and is the same name you typed for the CD. Deselect the **Open folder when complete** option (Figure 3-81).
    g. Browse for the location to save the presentation and click the **Select** button.
    h. Click **OK** to close the *Copy to Folder* dialog box.
    i. A message appears asking if you want to include linked files. Click **Yes**.
    j. Another message appears telling you that ink annotations will not be included. Click **Continue**.
    k. Close the *Package for CD* dialog box.
    l. Close the presentation.

16. Test the presentation.
    a. Open the folder where you "packaged" the presentation. Notice that additional files have been saved in this folder.
    b. Double-click the file name in the folder to open the presentation. If you receive a security warning, click the **Enable** button. Test the presentation and then close it.
    c. To show the presentation from a different computer, the online video link will be broken. You will need to delete the existing video and insert the video again from the presentation computer.

3-80 PowerPoint 3-2 completed

3-81 *Package for CD* and *Copy to Folder* dialog boxes

Guided Project 3-3

At an upcoming meeting of the American River Cycling Club, Eric Salinas is giving a presentation about the importance of knowing your target heart rate and exercising with your heart rate at an appropriate target level. For this project, you finalize the presentation.
[Student Learning Outcomes 3.1, 3.3, 3.4, 3.5, 3.8]

Files Needed: **HeartRateARCC-03.pptx** and **RiderAir.jpg**
Completed Project File Name: **[your initials] PowerPoint 3-3.pptx**

Skills Covered in This Project

- Create custom theme colors.
- Apply a background picture fill.
- Link to a video on a web site.
- Use *Presenter View*.

- Create and print notes pages.
- Record a presentation with narration.
- Prepare a kiosk presentation.

---

1. Open the presentation **HeartRateARCC-03**.

2. Save the presentation as **[your initials] PowerPoint 3-3**.

3. Prepare a new custom color theme to blend with the heart picture on slide 3.
   a. Click the **More** button [*Design* tab, *Variants* group].
   b. Select **Colors** and click **Customize Colors** to open the *Create New Theme Colors* dialog box.
   c. For each change, click the **Color** list arrow and select **More Colors** to open the *Colors* dialog box. Click the **Custom** tab and enter the numbers for *Red*, *Green*, and *Blue* shown in the following table for four colors.

	Text/Background – Dark 2	Accent 1	Accent 2	Accent 3
Red	24	36	204	227
Green	66	99	0	108
Blue	77	116	0	9

   d. Name the new custom theme ARCC (Figure 3-82).
   e. Click the **Save** button and the new colors will automatically be applied to all slides.

4. Format the title slide by adding a background picture fill.
   a. Right-click and select **Format Background** to open the *Format Background* pane.
   b. Select the **Picture or texture fill** option.
   c. Click the **File** button to open the *Insert Pictures* dialog box.
   d. Locate the student file **RiderAir-03** and click **Insert**.

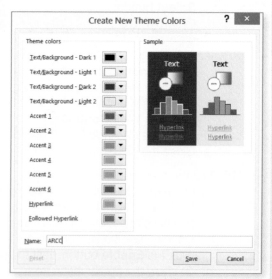

3-82 New ARCC color theme

e. Click **Picture** at the top of the pane and select **Picture Color**. Click the **Recolor** list arrow and select **Black and White**, **25%** (Figure 3-83).

f. Close the *Format Background* pane.

3-83 Completed title slide

5. On the title slide, increase the subtitle font size to **36 pt.** and resize the placeholder so one word fits on each line.

6. On slide 5, find and insert an online video.
   a. Click the **Insert** tab.
   b. Click the **Video** button list arrow [*Media* group] and select **Online Video** to open the *Insert Video* dialog box.
   c. Use the search words Col de la Madone and select an appropriate video. Click **Insert**.
   d. Position the video to the left of the picture and increase the video size (*Width* **5.5"**) if the quality remains acceptable.
   e. Below the video, add the appropriate source information.
   f. Play the video in *Slide Show* view by clicking the **Start** button in the middle of the video.

7. Apply a transition. Choose the **Cube** [*Transitions* tab, *Transition to This Slide* group] with the **From Right** effect options. Click **Apply To All**.

8. Use *Presenter View* to review your presentation.
   a. Click the **Slide Show** tab.
   b. Click **Use Presenter View** [*Monitors* group].
   c. Start your presentation.
      - If you have two monitors, click the **From Beginning** button [*Start Slide Show* group].
      - If you have one monitor, press **Alt+F5**.
   d. Click the **Presenter View** right arrow button to advance slides as you review them.
   e. If the notes text seems too small, click the **Make the text larger** button to adjust the text size in the *Notes* pane and then scroll to read the text (Figure 3-84).
   f. Press **Esc** to end the slide show.

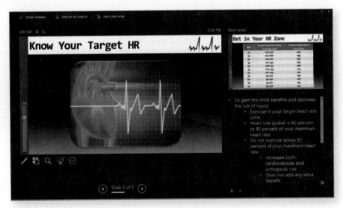

3-84 *Presenter View*

9. Print notes pages for slides 3 and 4.
   a. Click the **File** tab. Click **Print**.
   b. Select the appropriate printer and make sure that you are printing just one copy.
   c. For *Slides,* type 3–4 to choose a *Custom Range.*
   d. For *Print Layout,* choose **Notes Pages** and select **Scale to Fit Paper**.
   e. Click the **Print** button.

10. Record a slide show with narration.
    a. Click the **Record Slide Show** button [*Slide Show* tab, *Set Up* group] and select **Start Recording from Beginning** to open the *Record Slide Show* dialog box.

b. Select both options and click **Start Recording** (Figure 3-85). The *Recording* dialog box appears.

c. Speak clearly into your microphone as each slide is displayed.

d. Click the **Next Slide** navigation button to advance each slide.

11. Prepare a kiosk presentation with looping.

a. Click the **Set Up Slide Show** button [*Slide Show* tab] to open the *Set Up Show* dialog box.

3-85 *Record Slide Show* dialog box

b. Select the *Show type* **Browsed at a kiosk (full screen)**.

c. For *Show slides* select **All**.

d. Select the appropriate monitor.

e. Click **OK**.

12. Save and close your presentation (Figure 3-86).

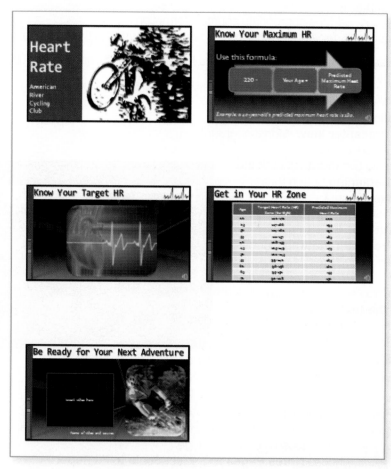

3-86 PowerPoint 3-3 completed

Independent Project 3-4

The sales representatives at Wilson Home Entertainment Systems review acceptable viewing distances when talking with clients who are in the early stages of planning a home theater or media room. They discuss options for televisions or projection systems for the spaces being planned. For this project, you complete a presentation to prepare clients for an in-home consultation.
[Student Learning Outcomes 3.1, 3.2, 3.4, 3.6, 3.7, 3.8]

File Needed: **ScreenSizes-03.pptx**, **TVCabinet-03.jpg**, and **Projector-03.jpg**
Completed Project File Name: **[your initials] PowerPoint 3-4.pptx**

Skills Covered in This Project

- Apply a background picture fill.
- Apply animation and effect options.
- Create and print notes pages.
- Rehearse a presentation and save timings.
- Use slide show navigation tools, keyboard shortcuts, and blank slides.
- Hide and reveal slides.
- Use the laser pointer feature.
- Use annotation pens.
- Prepare a kiosk presentation.

---

1. Open the presentation **ScreenSizes-03**.

2. Save the presentation in its current standard slide size as **[your initials] PowerPoint 3-4**.

3. Using the *Format Background* pane, change the background fill on three slides to a picture fill.
   a. **Slide 5:** Insert **TVCabinet-03** from your student files.
   b. **Slide 6:** Search *Online* using the *Insert Pictures* dialog box and the search word television. Locate a picture of a wall-mounted flat screen television (Figure 3-87).
   c. **Slide 7:** Insert **Projector-03** from your student files.
   d. Close the *Format Background* pane.

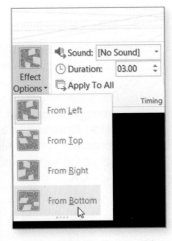

3-87 Background picture fill

4. Apply the **Vortex** transition with the **From Bottom** effect option. Change the *Duration* to **3.00**. Apply these settings to all slides (Figure 3-88).

5. Apply animation on four slides and change effect options as shown in the following table:

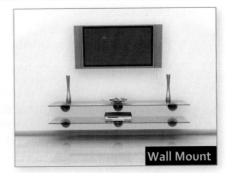

3-88 *Vortex* transition

Slide	Object	Animation Effect	Effect Options	Start	Duration
2	Question mark	Spin (Emphasis)	Clockwise, Two Spins	After Previous	02.00
5, 6, 7	Text box	Fly In (Entrance)	From Top-Left, As One Object	After Previous	00.50

6. Prepare speaker notes on the following three slides. Insert blank space between each item.
   a. **Slide 5:** Provides storage for related equipment and media.
      Select appropriate height for viewing.
      Some cabinets have a lift to hide TV when not in use.
   b. **Slide 6:** Creates an uncluttered, contemporary look.
      Where will you keep related equipment?
   c. **Slide 7:** Most equipment is concealed in some way.
      Projector
      Receiver
      Sound system
      DVD player
      Remote controls operate equipment.
      Wires and cables are in the walls.

7. Print notes pages for slides 5, 6, and 7 (Figure 3-89).

8. Rehearse the presentation and save timings.

9. Modify the timings to advance each slide after approximately 3–5 seconds.

10. Hide slide 4.

11. In *Slide Show* view, practice the following slide show features:
    a. Use the navigation area buttons.
    b. Right-click and use the shortcut menu.
    c. Use keyboard shortcuts.
    d. Blank slides.
    e. Go to the hidden slide 4.
    f. Point to slide objects with the laser pointer.

3-89 Notes page

12. Use the *Set Up Show* dialog box to change *Advance Slides* to **Manually**. Click **OK**.

13. Add annotations on slides 3 and 4 using the **Pen** with **Red** ink and keep annotations. Use *Presenter View* and practice making annotations on the presenter slide.
    a. **Slide 3:** Circle the "55-60" and "100" screen sizes.
    b. **Slide 4:** Go to this hidden slide and circle the following phrases in the bulleted items: "level with the middle," "reduce color clarity," and "visibility at all seats."
    c. Keep ink annotations.

14. Use the *Set Up Show* dialog box to prepare a kiosk presentation with looping.
    a. For *Advance Slides*, select **Use timings, if present**.
    b. Select **Browsed at a kiosk (full screen)** and show **All** slides.
    c. Select the appropriate monitor.
    d. Click **OK**.

15. Save and close the presentation (Figure 3-90).

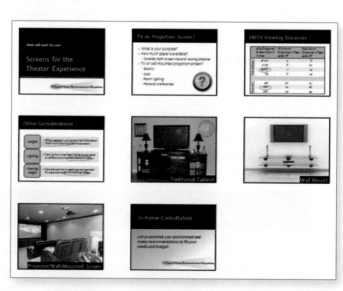

3-90 PowerPoint 3-4 completed

Independent Project 3-5

For the third training session for new hires on presenting effectively, Davon Washington, Management Consultant at Solution Seekers, Inc., is preparing guidelines for delivering a presentation with projection equipment. For this project, you finish the presentation that Davon has prepared.
[Student Learning Outcomes 3.1, 3.2, 3.4, 3.5, 3.7, 3.8]

File Needed: ***PresentationDelivery-03.pptx***
Completed Project File Name: ***[your initials] PowerPoint 3-5.pptx***

Skills Covered in This Project

- Apply a background picture fill.
- Apply animation and effect options.
- Create and print notes pages.
- Hide and reveal slides.

- Rehearse a presentation and save timings.
- Use *Presenter View.*
- Use ink annotation pens.
- Record a presentation with narration.

1. Open the presentation ***PresentationDelivery-03***.

2. Save the presentation as ***[your initials] PowerPoint 3-5***.

3. On slide 3, make the following changes:
   a. From the *Block Arrows* category in the *Shapes* gallery, select the **right arrow** and draw an arrow (*Height* **1.7"** and *Width* **4"**). The **Shape Fill** color is **Dark Red**, **Accent 1**.
   b. Apply the *Shape Effect* of **Shadow**, **Offset Bottom**.
   c. Adjust the arrow position as shown in Figure 3-91.
   d. Delete the "Answer" text box.

4. Apply the **Fade** transition with the **Smoothly** effect option. Change the *Duration* to **01.00**. Apply these settings to all slides.

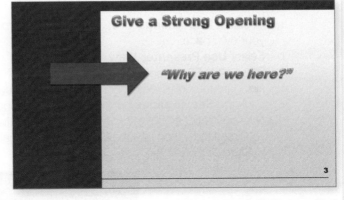

3-91 Shape added

5. Apply animation on five slides and change effect options as shown in the following table.

Slide	Object	Animation Effect	Effect Options	Start	Duration
2	Text, You get only one . . .	*Bounce* (Entrance)	*As One Object*	*After Previous*	*02.00*
5	Butterfly image	*Grow & Turn* (Entrance)	*None*	*After Previous*	*02.00*
7	Graphic	*Wipe* (Entrance)	*From Left*	*After Previous*	*02.50*
11	Text, Make it memorable	*Bounce* (Entrance)	*As One Object*	*After Previous*	*02.00*
12	Success shape	*Grow/Shrink* (Emphasis)	*Both, Larger*	*After Previous*	*02.50*

6. Prepare speaker notes on two slides. Apply bullets and indent the bulleted text (Figure 3-92).

   a. **Slide 2:** Never underestimate the importance of a first impression
      If possible, welcome people as they arrive for your presentation

   b. **Slide 9:** Be careful with how you use humor
      - Use humor only if it is appropriate
      - Avoid jokes—you could unintentionally offend someone
      Humor works best when it fits the presentation and seems natural
      - Break the ice
      - Be yourself; be real
      - Make your audience feel comfortable
      Choose stories or examples from your own experience

7. Print notes pages for slides 5, 6, and 7.

8. Hide slide 8.

9. Review the presentation to check transitions and animations.

   a. On the *Transitions* tab, deselect **On Mouse Click**.

   b. Change *After* to **00:03:00** seconds.

   c. Click **Apply To All**.

   d. Start your slide show from the beginning and review all slide movements.

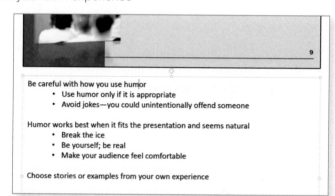

3-92 Notes with bullets and indents

10. Use *Presenter View* to review your presentation and make ink annotations.

    a. Deselect **Use Timings** [*Slide Show* tab, *Set Up* group] so you can advance through the slides at your own pace.

    b. Select **Use Presenter View**.

    c. Press **Alt+F5** to begin the presentation.

    d. Navigate through slides using the *Presenter View* arrow buttons.

    e. Click the **See all slides** button and click thumbnails to move to different slides.

    f. Add annotations on the following slides using the **Pen** with **Blue** ink. If you are not satisfied with your markings, then use the **Eraser** and try again.

       - **Slide 2:** Circle the words "Be professional."

       - **Slide 4:** Draw a rectangle around the words "Eye Contact" and "Smile" (Figure 3-93).

       - **Slide 7:** Circle the words "Avoid monotone."

       - **Slide 10:** Circle "End on time."

    g. At the end of the presentation, click **Keep** to save annotations.

3-93 *Presenter View* showing ink annotations

11. If you have a microphone on your computer, record a slide show with narration.
    a. Print notes pages for additional slides where you need reminders of what to discuss.
    b. On the *Slide Show* tab, click **Record Slide Show** and select both **Slide and animation timings** and **Narrations and laser pointer**.
    c. Begin on the first slide and speak clearly into your microphone as each slide is displayed.
    d. Save and close your presentation (Figure 3-94).

3-94 PowerPoint 3-5 completed

Independent Project 3-6

At the Hamilton Civic Center (HCC), classes are offered for a variety of fitness activities. For this project, you complete a presentation to promote the water aerobics classes at several community events. It will also be used as a self-running presentation at the HCC front desk.
[Student Learning Outcomes 3.1, 3.2, 3.3, 3.4, 3.5, 3.6, 3.8]

File Needed: ***WaterAerobics-03.pptx***
Completed Project File Names: ***[your initials] PowerPoint 3-6a.pptx*** and ***[your initials] PowerPoint 3-6b.pptx***

Skills Covered in This Project

- Create custom theme colors.
- Modify background fill colors.
- Change object colors on selected slides.
- Apply animation and effect options.
- Change to a widescreen slide size.

- Hide and reveal a slide.
- Use slide show navigation tools, keyboard shortcuts, and blank slides.
- Link to an online video.
- Prepare a kiosk presentation.

---

1. Open the presentation **WaterAerobics-03**.

2. Save the presentation as **[your initials] PowerPoint 3-6a**.

3. Use the *Create New Theme Colors* dialog box to create a custom theme. Change four colors according to the *Red*, *Green*, and *Blue* numbers shown in the following table. Name the custom theme Water and save it (Figure 3-95).

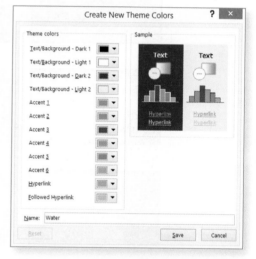

	Text/ Background - Dark 2	Accent 1	Accent 3	Accent 5
Red	7	53	16	255
Green	55	151	89	51
Blue	99	241	100	153

3-95 *Water* theme colors

4. Change the background colors.
   a. Click the **More** button [*Design* tab, *Variants* group] and select **Background Styles**. Click **Style 2** so a light blue is applied to all slides in the presentation.
   b. On slides 1 and 8, use the *Format Background* pane to change the **Solid Fill** to **Dark Blue**, **Text 2**.
   c. On slides 1 and 8, change the color for the text at the bottom of these slides to **White, Background 1** (Figure 3-96).

5. Change the color for the following two objects to **Pink, Accent 5:**
   a. **Slide 3:** *Text Fill for* "Fun"
   b. **Slide 4:** *Shape Fill* for the table heading row

3-96 Title slide in standard slide size

6. Type the following speaker notes on slide 4 (Figure 3-97):

   Swimming classes, scuba classes, and the local swim team practice sessions are scheduled at other times.
   Check with the front desk for unscheduled time when the pool is open.
   Each class is 6 weeks long.

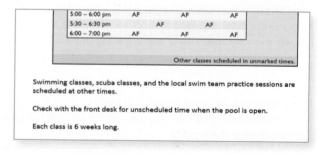

7. Apply the **Ripple** transition with the **From Top-Left** effect option. Apply this transition to all slides.

3-97 Notes page

8. Apply animation on four slides and change effect options as shown in the following table:

Slide	Object	Animation Effect	Effect Options	Start	Duration
2	Bulleted list	*Fly In* (Entrance)	*From Bottom-Right, By Paragraph*	*After Previous*	*01.00*
3	Bulleted list	*Fly In* (Entrance)	*From Bottom, As One Object*	*After Previous*	*01.00*
3	*WordArt* "Fun"	*Bounce* (Entrance)	*As One Object*	*After Previous*	*02.50*
5	Text box	*Wipe* (Entrance)	*From Left, As One Object*	*After Previous*	*02.00*

9. Save the presentation to preserve the file in the **Standard 4:3** slide size.

10. Resave the presentation as *[your initials] PowerPoint 3-6b*.

11. Click the **Design** tab and change *Slide Size* to **Widescreen 16:9**.

   a. Make the following adjustments so objects better fit the wider screen size:

   3-98 Title slide in widescreen slide size

   - *Slide 1:* Increase the picture size (*Height* **4"** and *Width* **6"**). Move the picture and text as shown in Figure 3-98.
   - **Slide 4:** Resize the text box on the right so the text fits on four lines (Figure 3-99). Align it to the slide on the right.
   - **Slide 4:** Right-align the text box at the bottom of the slide and then extend the left end of the box to fit across the bottom of the slide.
   - **Slide 5:** Repeat the same alignment and size increase process for the text box at the bottom of the slide.

12. Hide slide 5.

13. Use *Slide Show* view to practice the following features:

   a. Use the navigation buttons.
   b. Right-click and use the shortcut menu.
   c. Use keyboard shortcuts.
   d. Blank slides.
   e. Go to the hidden slide 5.
   f. Point to slide objects with the laser pointer.

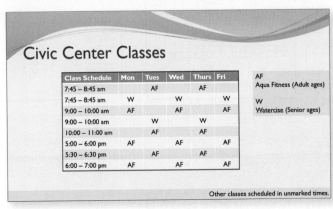

3-99 Text boxes adjusted

14. After slide 4, insert a new slide with the *Title Only* layout. Type the title Learn Online.

15. On slide 5, use the *Insert Video* dialog box to find and insert an online video.
    a. Use the search words water aerobics exercises and select an appropriate video. For referencing purposes, write down the name of the video and online source from the lower left of the dialog box. Click **Insert**.
    b. Increase the video size if the quality remains acceptable.
    c. Below the video, add the name of the video and online source.
    d. Test the video in *Slide Show* view to be sure it plays correctly.

16. Rehearse the presentation and save timings.
    a. Modify the timings to advance each slide after approximately 3–5 seconds.

17. Set up a kiosk presentation so it automatically loops.
    a. Show all slides and use timings.

18. Test the presentation and make any needed timing adjustments.

19. Save and close the presentation (Figure 3-100).

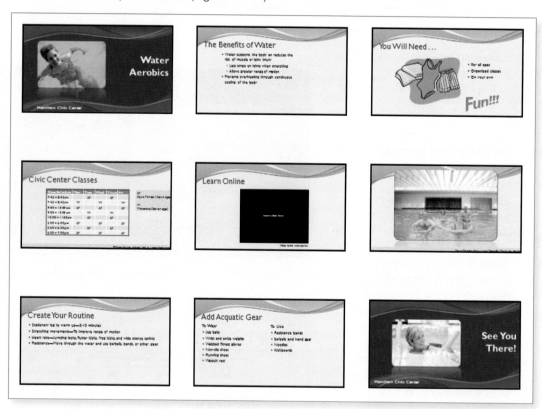

3-100 PowerPoint 3-6 completed

Improve It Project 3-7

Delivering news that employees may perceive as bad news is a difficult task. Improve this text-only presentation about presenting news to employees. Use existing slide text to create notes pages. Create custom theme colors. To communicate the message in a more visual way, add *SmartArt* graphics, brief text, and appropriate pictures. The figures in this section provide slide examples; your slides may differ slightly from these examples.
[Student Learning Outcomes 3.1, 3.2, 3.4, 3.8]

File Needed: *Announcement-03.pptx*
Completed Project File Names: *[your initials] PowerPoint 3-7.pptx*

Skills Covered in This Project

- Create custom theme colors.
- Modify slide content using pictures. *SmartArt,* and text boxes.
- Create and print notes pages.
- Apply appropriate transitions.
- Rehearse a presentation and save timings.
- Prepare a kiosk presentation.

1. Open the presentation **Announcement-03**.

2. Save the presentation as **[your initials] PowerPoint 3-7**.

3. Create custom theme colors. Change five colors and save the custom theme with the name Announce.

	Text/Background - Dark 2	Text/Background - Light 2	Accent 1	Accent 2	Accent 3
Red	38	255	255	124	204
Green	19	230	153	26	236
Blue	0	193	0	26	255

4. On slide 1, make the text more distinctive.
   a. Apply bold to the slide placeholders.
   b. Increase the title text **66 pts**. and "Big" to **96 pts**. Change the font color to **Orange**, **Accent 1**, **Lighter 40%**.
   c. Increase the subtitle text to **32 pts**. and "You" to **48 pts**. (Figure 3-101).

3-101 Revised title slide

5. On slide 2, use the existing bulleted text to create a notes page.
   a. Click the **Notes** button so you can see the *Notes* pane in *Normal* view. Increase the size of the *Notes* pane so you can see it while you are working on each slide.
   b. Copy the existing bulleted text and paste it in the *Notes* pane. Arrange this text neatly (Figure 3-102).

6. On slide 2, show that "change" can be perceived as both good and bad (Figure 3-103).
   a. Replace the bulleted text with three short items: Fear, Dread, Be resistant. Resize the body placeholder and move it to the lower right.

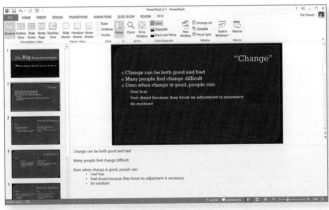

3-102 *Notes* pane expanded

b. Use the search word anxiety to find a similar picture and insert it. Apply the **Rounded Corner Diagonal**, **White** picture style and change the **Picture Border** to **Black**, **Background 2**.

c. Insert a *SmartArt* **Opposing Arrows** layout from the *Relationship* category. Type the text Good and Bad. Apply the **Inset** *SmartArt Style.*

d. Resize chart objects and position them as shown in Figure 3-103.

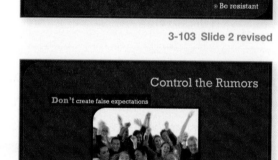

3-103 Slide 2 revised

7. Prepare the remaining notes pages on slides 3-6:

a. Cut the existing bulleted text and paste this text on notes pages for each slide. Also include the words "Do" and "Don't."

b. On each slide, delete the title and heading placeholders.

8. On slide 3, using a picture, emphasize what you should and should not do to control rumors (Figure 3-104).

a. Insert a text box and type Don't create false expectations. Change the font size to **24 pts**. and emphasize the word "Don't" by increasing the font size to **32 pts**. and changing the color to **Orange**, **Accent 1**. Change the shape fill color to **Black**, **Background 2** (this is a very dark brown).

b. Duplicate this text box and change the text to Do explain things in a positive way.

c. Use the search word excitement to find a similar picture and insert it. To match the picture on slide 1, apply the **Rounded Corner Diagonal**, **White** picture style and change the **Picture Border** to **Black**, **Background 2**.

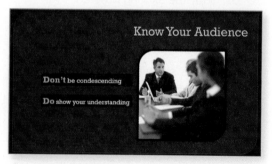

3-104 Slide 3 revised

9. On slide 4, using a picture, emphasize what you should and should not do in your delivery of bad news (Figure 3-105).

a. Copy the "Don't" and "Do" text boxes from slide 3 and paste them on slide 4. Change the slide 4 text boxes to: Don't be insincere or "slick" and Do be confident and caring.

b. Use the search word relax to find a similar picture and insert it. Apply the same picture style.

c. Resize the picture and position objects as shown.

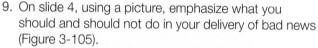

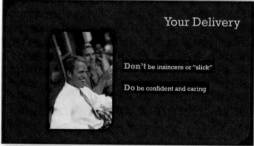

3-105 Slide 4 revised

10. On slide 5, using a picture, emphasize what you should and should not do to reflect your understanding of your audience (Figure 3-106).

a. Copy the "Don't" and "Do" text boxes from slide 4 and paste them on slide 5. Change the slide 5 text boxes to: Don't be condescending and Do show your understanding.

b. Use the search word meeting to find a similar picture and insert it. Apply the same picture style.

c. Resize the picture and position objects as shown.

3-106 Slide 5 revised

11. On slide 6, using a picture, provide a strong summary statement (Figure 3-107).

    a. Insert a text box and type this text: Treat people as you would like to be treated.

    b. Make the text bold, increase the font size to **32 pts**., and change the shape fill to **Black, Background 2**.

    c. Use the search word meeting to find a similar picture and insert it. Apply the same picture style.

    d. Resize the picture and position objects as shown.

3-107 Slide 6 revised

12. Apply the **Gallery** transition to all slides.

13. Print notes pages for slides 2-5.

14. Rehearse the presentation and save timings.

15. Modify the timings and change the *After* seconds to **00:03:00**.

16. Set up the slide show for a kiosk presentation.

17. Save and close the presentation (Figure 3-108).

3-108 PowerPoint 3-7 completed

Challenge Project 3-8

For this project, explain the benefits of tablet computing and factors to consider when purchasing a tablet. Using sources such as www.pcmag.com, list some of the top-rated products and their prices. Describe common features, applications, and accessories.
[Student Learning Outcomes 3.1, 3.2, 3.3, 3.4, 3.5, 3.9]

File Needed: None
Completed Project File Name: *[your initials] PowerPoint 3-8.pptx*

Create a new presentation and save it as *[your initials] PowerPoint 3-8*. Modify your presentation according to the following guidelines:

- Select an appropriate theme and create custom theme colors for a high-tech appearance.
- Change to a widescreen format.
- Include pictures from www.pcmag.com or other sources and credit the source below each picture.
- Animate approximately three objects for emphasis and apply appropriate effects.
- Rehearse the presentation and save timings.
- Link to an online video.
- Prepare a slide listing your references and include it as the last slide in your presentation.
- Use *Package Presentation for CD* to save the presentation to a folder.

Challenge Project 3-9

Prepare a presentation to promote a student or civic organization. Use pictures and very brief text to convey the aim and purpose of the organization. Consider using an organization chart to illustrate the officer or committee structure. Apply styles and text treatments consistently.
[Student Learning Outcomes 3.1, 3.2, 3.3, 3.4, 3.6, 3.9]

File Needed: None
Completed Project File Name: *[your initials] PowerPoint 3-9.pptx*

Create a new presentation and save it as *[your initials] PowerPoint 3-9*. Modify your presentation according to the following guidelines:

- Select an appropriate theme and then create custom theme colors for your topic.
- Modify backgrounds by applying a gradient fill to all slides and a picture fill to one slide.
- Design slides with a variety of illustration techniques and minimal text.
- Add transitions and animations with appropriate effects.
- Create and print notes pages.
- Include an online video if one is available and credit your source.
- Prepare a slide listing your references and include it as the last slide in your presentation.
- Rehearse the presentation and use a variety of navigation techniques.
- Use *Package Presentation for CD* to save your presentation to a folder.

Challenge Project 3-10

Create a presentation about living green. Focus on ways to conserve water and other resources. Use web sites such as www.mygreenside.org and others. Prepare a slide listing your references and include it as the last slide in your presentation.
[Student Learning Outcomes 3.1, 3.2, 3.3, 3.4, 3.6, 3.8]

File Needed: None
Completed Project File Name: *[your initials] PowerPoint 3-10.pptx*

Create a new presentation and save it as *[your initials] PowerPoint 3-10*. Modify your presentation according to the following guidelines:

- Create custom theme colors that fit the "green" topic.
- Modify backgrounds and use at least one picture fill.
- Design slides with a variety of illustration techniques and minimal text.
- Add transitions and animations with appropriate effects.
- Create and print notes pages.
- Include an online video about "green" living and credit your source.
- Hide slides and blank slides.
- Rehearse the presentation, save timings during the rehearsal and then modify timings.
- Prepare a kiosk presentation.

Customizing Images, Illustrations, and Themes

CHAPTER OVERVIEW

An original, well-designed theme will make your presentation unique. While you can find many PowerPoint theme options online, it is often a good idea to create and incorporate custom images, illustrations, and themes. This chapter focuses on some of the PowerPoint illustration features that you can use to customize images and illustrations. You will learn how to apply these features to design a creative new theme and template using *Slide Masters*. You will also learn how to capture and edit images to improve their appearance, apply artistic effects, and create photo albums.

STUDENT LEARNING OUTCOMES (SLOs)

After completing this chapter, you will be able to:

SLO4.1 Customize and work with shapes (p. P4-203).

SLO4.2 Work with objects to align, distribute, and group; convert *SmartArt* to text or shapes (p. P4-208).

SLO4.3 Use a *Slide Master* to create a custom theme with new colors, fonts, and background graphics (p. P4-220).

SLO4.4 Capture screen images with a screenshot or a screen clipping (p. P4-229).

SLO4.5 Edit pictures to make photo corrections, apply artistic effects, and remove backgrounds; recolor illustrated images (p. P4-230).

SLO4.6 Create a photo album and adjust picture order, layout, and captions; apply and customize a photo album theme (p. P4-238).

SLO4.7 Create and use a custom template (p. P4-241).

CASE STUDY

Paradise Lakes Resort (PLR) is a vacation company with four resorts located throughout northern Minnesota. To increase awareness of the natural resources of this area and promote bookings, the resort managers are preparing a tourism presentation entitled "PLR in the Land of 10,000 Lakes."

Pause & Practice 4-1: Create original graphics including a business logo.

Pause & Practice 4-2: Use *Slide Masters* to create a unique theme with original graphics and custom colors.

Pause & Practice 4-3: Modify pictures and apply interesting effects.

Pause & Practice 4-4: Create a photo album presentation with a custom design theme and save the presentation as a template.

Customizing Shapes

In Chapter 2, you worked with several simple shapes. The *Shapes* gallery displays shapes in 10 different categories. The *Drawing Tools Format* tab and the *Format Shape* pane provide many options to customize shapes. When drawing shapes, press **Shift** or **Ctrl** as you drag to *constrain* the shape. Constraining keeps your lines straight, your circles round, and your rectangles square. When you are resizing shapes, you can press **Shift** and **Ctrl** while you drag sizing handles to constrain shapes in the following ways:

- **Shift** preserves height and width proportions.
- **Ctrl** keeps the center in the same place.
- **Ctrl+Shift** keeps the center of the shape in the same place and maintains height and width proportions.

Adjust Text and Spacing within Text Boxes and Shapes

Text that is arranged horizontally is easy to read, but you may want to arrange text in different directions for special purposes. Note that the same alignment and direction adjustments apply to both text boxes and shapes with text; however, the default settings vary.

HOW TO: Change Text Direction and Alignment

1. Select a text box or shape that contains text.
2. Click the **Text Direction** list arrow [*Home* tab, *Paragraph* group] and select from the following choices (Figure 4-1):
   - **Horizontal:** The default direction
   - **Rotate all text 90°:** Makes text read from the top down
   - **Rotate all text 270°:** Makes text read from the bottom up
   - **Stacked:** Arranges text in a one-letter column
3. Click the **Align Text** list arrow [*Home* tab, *Paragraph* group] and select from the following choices that vary based on text direction:
   - **Horizontal:** Top, Middle, or Bottom
   - **Rotate all text 90°:** Right, Center, or Left
   - **Rotate all text 270°:** Left, Center, or Right
   - **Stacked:** Left, Center, or Right
4. To open the *Format Shape* pane, you can click **More Options** from both the **Text Direction** and the **Align Text** options lists. Figure 4-2 illustrates the settings for the horizontal text box in Figure 4-1.

4-1 Text direction examples

Alternatively, you can right-click a text object and select **Format Shape** from the shortcut menu to open the *Format Shape* pane. Additional options on this pane allow you to control how text fits in the text box or shape. For example, you can increase the space between the text and the edge of the shape or arrange the text in columns.

4-2 Text box size options

HOW TO: Control Text Resizing, Margins, Wrapping, and Columns

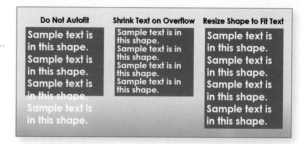

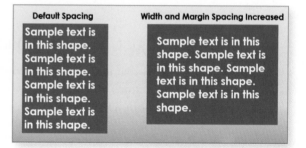

4-3 Text resizing examples

1. Select a text box or shape, right-click, and select **Format Shape** to open the *Format Shape* pane.

2. Click **Text Options** at the top of the pane and then click the **Textbox** button. Choose one of the following options to control text resizing if there is too much text to fit in a text box or shape (Figure 4-3):

   - **Do not Autofit:** Text size remains the same and text extends beyond the shape.
   - **Shrink text on overflow:** Text size is reduced so all text displays in the shape.
   - **Resize shape to fit text:** Text size remains the same but the shape size increases to contain all text.

3. Margin spacing for **Left**, **Right**, **Top**, and **Bottom** is expressed in inches. (You can enter numbers in points, but PowerPoint converts those numbers to inches. One inch contains 72 points.)

   - This option inserts space around the text so it is not too close to the border of a text box or shape (Figure 4-4).
   - This options works especially well when you have selected the *Resize shape to fit text* option.

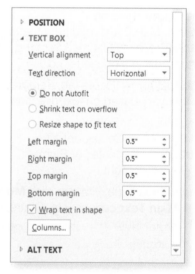

4-4 Margin spacing examples

4. Select **Wrap text in shape** to maintain the width of a text box or shape. The height increases as you enter more text.

5. Click the **Columns** button to arrange the text in two or more columns with the space you need between columns. When this option is selected, text fills the first column and word wraps to the second column (Figure 4-5). The settings for the sample in Figure 4-5 are entered at the bottom of the *Format Shape* pane (Figure 4-6).

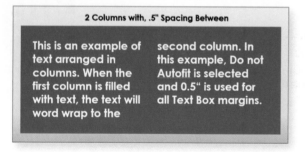

4-5 Column example with word wrap

4-6 Margin size options

Flip and Rotate Shapes

You can use the ***Flip*** and ***Rotate*** commands with many PowerPoint objects. These commands are useful when you want to make objects point in a different direction, angle on the slide, or create a mirror image of a picture. The ***rotation handle*** provides quick movements; you can enter precise rotation degrees by using the *Format Shape* pane.

HOW TO: Flip and Rotate

1. Select a shape.
2. Click and drag the **rotation handle** to make the shape angle.
3. Click the **Rotate** button [*Drawing Tools Format* tab, *Arrange* group] and choose from one of the following (*Figure 4-7*):

   - *Rotate Right 90°*
   - *Rotate Left 90°*
   - *Flip Vertical*
   - *Flip Horizontal*

4. Select **More Rotation Options** to open the *Format Shape* pane and enter specific rotation numbers.

4-7 Rotation options

A creative way to rotate individual letters of a word on a title slide is shown in Figure 4-8.

Shape Adjustment Handles

Some shapes, such as arrows or stars, have *adjustment handles* (yellow squares) that you drag to change the shape dimension in some way. When text is warped with the *Transform* text effect, it also has adjustment handles (pink squares).

Figure 4-9 shows two variations of a 16-point star. The example on the left is the original shape with the adjustment handle in the default position at the top. On the right, the adjustment handle has been moved toward the center, and the star looks quite different with long, narrow points.

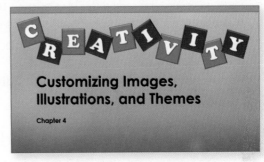

4-8 Individual letters rotated

4-9 Star shape changed using the adjustment handle

Edit Shape Points

Although you can't see them when drawing, all shapes that you draw have small black squares called *points* that control where lines curve or change direction such as in the corners of a diamond shape. A point is also called a *vertex*. More points are used when lines curve compared to straight lines.

You can see these points on the border of a shape when you use the *Edit Points* command. You can drag the points to move the border into different positions.

When you click a point, two lines appear that are attached to the point with white squares on each end to create handles. Dragging the handles changes the curvature of the line between two points. Handles are used in many computer graphics programs to create smooth curves, and practice is required to use them skillfully. Both the length of the handle and the distance of movement affect the curve that is made.

HOW TO: Edit Points

1. Draw a shape.
2. Click the **Edit Shape** button [*Drawing Tools Format* tab, *Insert Shapes* group] and click **Edit Points** (Figure 4-10).
3. Click a point and drag. For example, elongate a diamond shape by dragging the top point up and bottom point down (Figure 4-11).
4. Click on a line to add a point. Remove a point by right-clicking to open the shortcut menu and clicking **Delete Point**.
5. Click a point and drag the handles to change the curve of the line between two points. For example, change the shape of a heart (Figure 4-12).
6. Adjust the length of the handle to change how the line curves when you drag the handle.
7. Press **Esc** or click off the line to turn off **Edit Points**.

4-10 *Edit Points* command

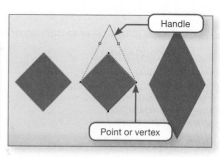

4-11 Drag points to change a shape

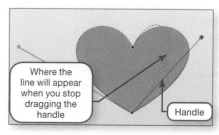

4-12 Rotate handles to change curves between points

Curved Lines and Freeform Shapes

The *Shapes* gallery has three line tools for drawing curved lines and freeform shapes. Each of these tools works differently. With the ***Curve*** line, your pointer changes to a crosshair. You click to begin drawing the line and continue clicking as you extend the line. It automatically curves as you change direction and will draw with smooth curves. An edit point is added each time the direction changes.

HOW TO: Draw Curved Lines

1. Click the **Shapes** button [*Insert* tab, *Illustrations* group] to open the *Shapes* gallery.
   - The *Shapes* gallery is also available on the *Home* tab and the *Drawing Tools Format* tab.
   - On each of these tabs, click the **More** button to open the complete gallery.
2. Select the **Curve** line (Figure 4-13).
3. Click to begin drawing with the crosshair pointer and click to extend the line in the direction you need (Figure 4-14).
4. Press **Esc** or double-click to end the line.
5. Click the **Edit Shape** button [*Drawing Tools Format* tab, *Insert Shapes* group] and select **Edit Points** to adjust the curves using the points and handles (Figure 4-15).
6. Select a point, right-click to open the shortcut menu, and click **Smooth Point** to make the curve more even or click **Delete Points** to remove the point. Press **Esc** to turn off **Edit Points**.

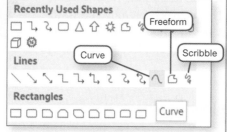

4-13 Part of the *Shapes* gallery

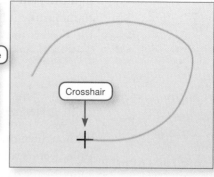

4-14 Curved line with smooth curves

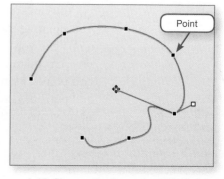

4-15 Change the line using *Edit Points* and drag the handle on a point

With the *Scribble* line, your pointer changes to a pen. You click to begin drawing and you drag the pointer as though you are writing on paper to create a continuous line. This tool is easier to use with a tablet pen or stylus than with a mouse. Many edit points will be added because the line direction changes so many times.

HOW TO: Draw Scribble Lines

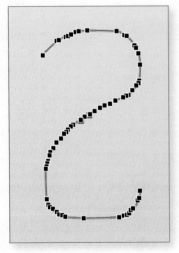

1. Click the **More** button [*Home* tab, *Drawing* group] to open the *Shapes* gallery.
2. Select the **Scribble** line (see Figure 4-13) and your pointer changes to a pen.
3. Click and hold the left mouse button to begin drawing and drag the pointer. Release the button to end the line.
4. Click the **Edit Shape** button [*Drawing Tools Format* tab, *Insert Shapes* group] and select **Edit Points**.
5. Many points will appear based on how curved your line is; it may be difficult to adjust the curves using points and handles (Figure 4-16).
6. To remove a selected point, right-click to open the shortcut menu and click **Delete Point**.
7. Press **Esc** or click off the line to turn off **Edit Points**.

4-16 Scribble line showing points

With the *Freeform* line, your pointer changes to a crosshair to draw both straight and curved lines. When you drag the crosshair, the line will curve like the *Scribble* tool. You can click to draw straight lines between points and to change directions with the line as you draw. An edit point is added each time you click. When the end of the line you draw touches the beginning of the line, a shape is created using your *Accent 1* fill color. You can change fill and outline colors like any other shape.

HOW TO: Draw a Freeform Shape

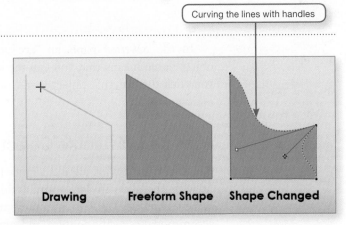

4-17 Freeform shapes

1. Click the **More** button [*Home* tab, *Drawing* group] to open the *Shapes* gallery.
2. Select the **Freeform** shape and your pointer changes to a crosshair.
3. Click to begin drawing curved or straight lines.
   - Press **Shift** to keep the line straight or change direction (Figure 4-17).
   - Press the left mouse button while you move the crosshair to draw a scribble line.
4. When your crosshair touches the beginning point, a shape is created.
5. You can change fill and outline options.
6. As with the other lines, click the **Edit Shape** button [*Drawing Tools Format* tab, *Insert Shapes* group] and select **Edit Points** to adjust the position of points or use handles to adjust the curves between points.
7. Select a point and right-click to open the shortcut menu to choose **Smooth Point** or **Delete Point**.

Working with Multiple Objects

In this section, you explore ways to combine objects in interesting ways and to work efficiently as you align and position objects. The following list previews some of the ways you can work with PowerPoint objects:

- Align multiple objects and evenly distribute the space between them.
- Use guides and grids to align objects.
- Layer objects and adjust their stacking order.
- Group, ungroup, and regroup shapes.
- Merge shapes to create an original shape.
- Convert *SmartArt* graphics to text and shapes that you can use in different ways.
- Use connector lines to create unique diagrams.

You can select multiple objects in several ways. Always confirm that all objects show sizing handles to be sure your selection is complete.

HOW TO: Select Multiple Objects

1. Use one of the following methods to select multiple objects:
    - Select the first object and press **Shift** or **Ctrl** as you click additional objects.
    - Click and drag to draw a selection rectangle over multiple objects and release your left mouse button (Figure 4-18).
    - On the *Home* tab, click **Select** [*Editing* group] and choose from **Select All, Select Objects**, or **Selection Pane**.
    - Click the **Selection Pane** button [*Drawing Tools Format* tab, *Arrange* group] to open the *Selection* pane (Figure 4-19) and press **Ctrl** to select multiple objects. Selected object names are highlighted.

2. When you have selected multiple objects, you can remove an individual object from the selection by pressing **Ctrl** as you click the object.

4-18 Selection rectangle over multiple shapes

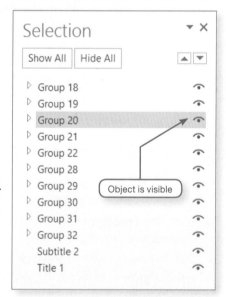

4-19 Selection pane

In the *Selection* pane, an "eye" icon beside each object name means that you can see it on the slide. If you click the eye, that object is still on the slide but is no longer visible.

Align and Distribute Objects

All objects on a slide should align with other objects or with the slide in some way. Using similar alignment techniques throughout a presentation provides consistency; however, alignment should accommodate specific content, and some design variety is good if it is used in a purposeful way.

HOW TO: Align Multiple Objects

1. Select multiple objects.
2. Align the objects with each other.
    - If the *Home* tab is open when you position an object, click the **Arrange** button [*Drawing* group], and click **Align**.
    - If the *Drawing Tools Format* tab is open when you position an object, click the **Align** button [*Arrange* group].

3. On the drop-down list, select one of the following options:
   - *Align Selected Objects* to align objects with each other
   - *Align to Slide* to align objects to the slide
4. Click the alignment you need. Your options include:
   - *Align Left*
   - *Align Center*
   - *Align Right*
   - *Align Top*
   - *Align Middle*
   - *Align Bottom* (Figure 4-20).

4-20 Multiple objects aligned with each other

The ***Distribute*** feature creates even spacing between multiple slide objects.

HOW TO: Distribute Multiple Objects

1. Position the first object on the left.
2. Position the last object on the right.
3. Select all objects.
4. Click **Distribute Horizontally** (Figure 4-21).

4-21 Multiple aligned objects with space distributed evenly

Use Gridlines and Guides

Gridlines are evenly spaced vertical and horizontal lines that aid in object alignment. ***Guides*** are indicated by one vertical and one horizontal line in the middle of the slide. You can move guides to consistently align similar objects across several slides. *Gridlines* and *Guides* are not visible in *Slide Show* view.

HOW TO: Display and Customize Guides and Gridlines

1. Select **Guides** [*View* tab, *Show* group] (Figure 4-22). One dashed vertical and one horizontal line appear at the center of the slide (Figure 4-23).
   - Point to one of the lines and your pointer changes to a splitter. Drag to reposition the line. The number that appears on the guide indicates the distance away from the horizontal or vertical center (Figure 4-24).
   - Remove guides from the slide area by deselecting **Guides** on the *View* tab.
2. Select **Gridlines** [*View* tab, *Show* group]. Dotted vertical and horizontal lines appear on the slide (Figure 4-25).

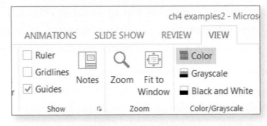

4-22 *View* tab with *Guides* selected

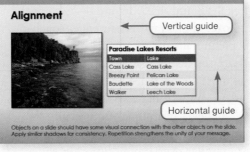

4-23 *Guides* displayed as vertical and horizontal lines

4-24 *Guide* position changed

- In addition to *Gridlines,* Figure 4-25 also shows *Smart Guides* that temporarily appear when objects are aligned and when objects are spaced evenly.
- Remove *Gridlines* from the slide area by deselecting **Gridlines** from the *View* tab.

3. Click the launcher [*View* tab, *Show* group] to open the *Grid and Guides* dialog box (Figure 4-26). Select from the following options:

4-26 *Grid and Guides* dialog box

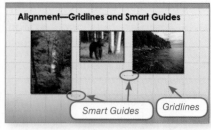

4-25 *Gridlines* and *Smart Guides*

- **Snap to:** As you drag an object to position it, the object automatically moves from dot-to-dot (Figure 4-27) on the *Gridlines.* You can see this movement better when your view is zoomed at 100% or more. If you want to move an object smoothly and position it between grid dots, press **Alt** as you drag.
- **Grid settings:** Enter different spacing amounts for the grid dots and select **Display grid on screen**.
- **Guide settings:** Select **Display drawing guides on screen** to make the guides appear. Select **Display smart guides when shapes are aligned** to see the temporary guides that help you align vertically and horizontally with other objects on the slide.

4. Click **OK** to close the *Grid and Guides* dialog box.

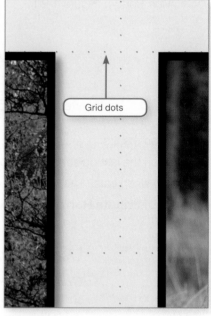

4-27 Top of shapes aligned to the grid

Layer Objects and Adjust Stacking Order

When working with multiple shapes and objects, you can combine them in interesting ways by arranging one object on top of another object. This layering is also called *stacking*. Use the *Selection* pane or click the **Bring Forward** or **Send Backward** commands [*Drawing Tools Format* tab, *Arrange* group] to rearrange the stacking order.

- *Bring Forward:* Moves the object up one layer at a time.
- *Bring to Front:* Moves the object in front of all other objects.
- *Send Backward:* Moves the object back one layer at a time.
- *Send to Back:* Moves the object behind all other objects.

Compare the alignment used on the slides in Figures 4-28 and 4-29. Figure 4-28 shows two text boxes aligned with their edges touching the picture in an asymmetrical way. In Figure 4-29, the text boxes overlap the picture and seem more connected. The technique that looks best to you is a matter of personal preference. Whichever technique you use, aim for consistency and repeat the same alignment pattern or similar overlapping on other slides

4-28 Text boxes touch picture edges

in your presentation. Notice how the shadows on the text boxes match the *Drop Shadow Rectangle* picture style.

When multiple objects are layered, it can be difficult to select one object within the stack, especially if a larger object covers a smaller object. Use the *Selection* pane to choose from the objects on the slide. You can also select any object and press **Tab** several times to cycle through each object until the object you want is selected. When you arrive at the desired object, you can move it or adjust its stacking order.

4-29 Text boxes overlap picture edges

Group, Ungroup, and Regroup Objects

The *Group* command is available on several tabs. When you group two or more objects, they are connected as one object. Sizing handles appear around the group and not the individual objects. Colors, sizes, and effects can change for individual objects or all objects in a group. The *Ungroup* command separates objects so you can modify them independently. The *Regroup* command connects the objects again.

HOW TO: Group, Ungroup, and Regroup

1. Select the objects you want to group. Sizing handles appear around all of the individual shapes on the left in Figure 4-30.

2. Click the **Group** button [*Drawing Tools Format* tab, *Arrange* group] and select **Group** to combine the multiple shapes into one object. One set of sizing handles appear around the entire group on the right in Figure 4-30.

   * If the *Picture Tools Format* tab is open, click the **Group** button [*Arrange* group] and select **Group**.
   * If the *Home* tab is open, click the **Arrange** button [*Drawing* group] and select **Group**.

3. Resize the group by dragging the sizing handles.

4. Select an individual object within the group to resize the object, change its color, or adjust its position.

5. If you need to modify individual objects independently, click the **Group** button [*Drawing Tools Format* tab, *Arrange* group] and select **Ungroup** to separate the shapes.

   * Make your changes (colors or sizing) and click **Regroup** to reconnect the shapes.
   * If you change layering of grouped objects, click **Group** to reconnect the shapes.

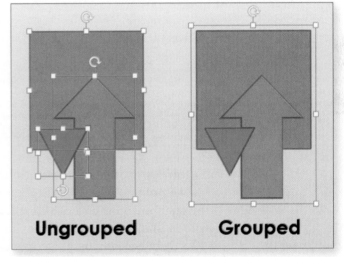

4-30 Three shapes ungrouped and grouped

Save Grouped Objects as a Picture

When text is included in a grouped object, it is not always easy to get good results when you attempt to resize the group. Text sizes do not change by dragging unless you have applied the *Transform* text effect so resizing the group affects text alignment. In Figure 4-31, a company logo is shown in the original size on the left. The center logo is resized by 80%; the letters extend beyond the background shape and bottom text is not centered. The right logo is resized by 120%; the large letters no longer fill the background shape and the bottom text is not centered.

4-31 Grouped logo is distorted with resizing

To prevent this kind of problem, save your grouped objects as a picture. Once you have done this, you can resize the picture without distortion. This also helps you to maintain color consistency. For example, if you use theme colors to design a logo with grouped objects and later use the logo in a different presentation that has different theme colors, the logo colors will change. But if you save the logo as a picture, all the colors will remain the same.

HOW TO: Save Grouped Objects as a Picture

1. Select the grouped objects and right-click to open the shortcut menu.
2. Click **Save as Picture** to open the *Save as Picture* dialog box.
3. Select the appropriate location to save the file.
4. Type your file name.
5. Select an appropriate file type. The png or jpeg file types generally work well in presentations.
6. Click **OK** to close the dialog box.

> **MORE INFO**
>
> Review the *Graphic File Formats* table in *SLO 1.6: Working with a Picture from a File* for a discussion about graphic file formats.

Merge Shapes

The *Merge Shapes* tool combines two or more shapes that are usually stacked in some way. Unlike grouping where the shapes are merely connected and can be moved or recolored within the group, merging creates a completely new shape with one color that is the top shape color with most merge options. Shapes must be selected to be merged, but they cannot be grouped. Also, merging works only with shapes; you cannot merge shapes with pictures or other objects.

HOW TO: Merge Shapes

1. Select two or more shapes that overlap.
2. Click the **Merge Shapes** button [*Drawing Tools Format* tab, *Insert Shapes* group] (Figure 4-32).
3. Choose from one of the following options to join multiple selected shapes into a new shape (Figure 4-33):

   • *Union:* All shapes are combined as one (top shape color).
   • *Combine:* The joined shape has transparent areas where the separate shapes originally overlapped. Individual shape outlines are retained (top shape color).

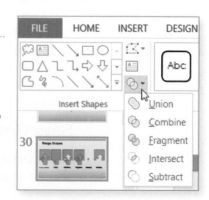

4-32 *Merge Shapes* button

- *Fragment:* The joined shape shows individual shape outlines (top shape color). The shape is sliced into pieces where the shapes originally overlapped. The pieces can be removed or recolored.
- *Intersect:* Only the shape where all original shapes overlapped remains (top shape color).
- *Subtract:* The joined shape (bottom shape color) has transparent areas indicating the places where the other shapes overlapped the bottom shape.

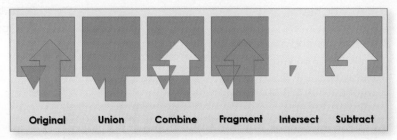

4-33 Original shapes and *Merge Shapes* options

If you arrange *WordArt* text over a shape and apply the *Combine* or *Subtract* merge option, the text becomes transparent and looks cut out because the background shows in the letters (Figure 4-34). Be careful to make your shape fit the text appropriately before merging; once merged, the text is no longer editable and resizing the shape distorts the text.

After shapes are merged, even if they are spaced apart, you can edit points to adjust the new shape.

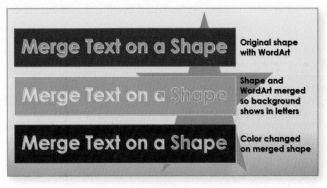

4-34 Merged shape and WordArt showing a cut-out effect

Connector Lines

In the *Shapes* gallery, **Connector Lines** are available in a variety of shapes: *Straight Connectors, Elbow Connectors* (90° angle), or *Curved Connectors.* You can use these lines to connect two or more shapes for custom diagrams. Some connector lines have arrowheads on the ends.

HOW TO: Connect Shapes

1. Draw two or more shapes.
2. Click the **Shapes** button [*Home* tab, *Drawing* group] and select a connector line such as the *Elbow Connector* or the *Curved Arrow Connector* (Figure 4-35).
3. Point to the first shape to be connected and small black squares appear on all four sides of the shape indicating connection sites where the shape and the line can be joined.
4. On the first shape, click the connection site where the connector line will start (Figure 4-36).

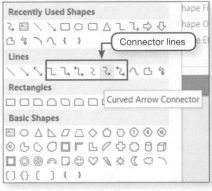

4-35 Part of *Shapes* gallery

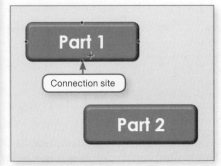

4-36 Connection sites on a shape

5. Your pointer changes to a crosshair and a line forms as you move it. Click a connection site on the next shape.

6. When the shapes are connected, a green circle appears on the end of each line. You can use an adjustment handle to change line curves or angles (Figure 4-37). Once shapes are connected, you can move the shapes and the line between them remains attached.

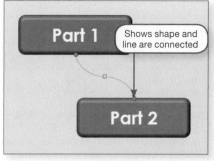

4-37 Line connects shapes

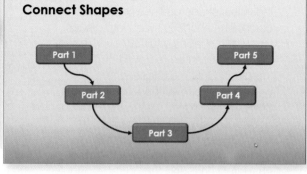

4-38 Line color and width changed

7. By default, the line is very thin. You can increase the line width and color to make the line more obvious (Figure 4-38).

Convert a SmartArt Graphic to Text or to Shapes

You can change a *SmartArt* graphic to bulleted text or to a group of individual shapes.

HOW TO: Convert a SmartArt Graphic

1. Select the *SmartArt* graphic you want to change (Figure 4-39).
2. Click the **Convert** button [*SmartArt Tools Design* tab, *Reset* group].
3. Choose one of the following options:
   - *Convert to Text: SmartArt* text is changed to a bulleted list (Figure 4-40). Edit the text as needed.
   - *Convert to Shapes: SmartArt* shapes are changed to a group of shapes. Click **Arrange** [*Home* tab, *Drawing* group] and then select **Ungroup** to rearrange and modify the shapes individually (Figures 4-41 and 4-42).

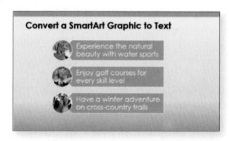

4-39 *SmartArt* original design

4-40 *SmartArt* converted to text

4-41 *SmartArt* shapes rearranged

4-42 *SmartArt* shapes changed and rearranged

In Figure 4-41 the shapes are staggered evenly and made slightly longer, and the pictures are moved to the right of each shape. Figure 4-42 emphasizes the pictures more by making them bigger; the text and shapes fill the slide in a staggered arrangement. The shapes have been changed to rounded rectangles and the text is adjusted to fit around each picture.

For this project you work with shapes to create interesting designs for a presentation promoting Paradise Lakes Resort. You change text direction, use adjustment handles, and adjust layering. You flip, ungroup, and merge shapes and group a series of shapes. You also add connector lines to reinforce the flow of ideas, and convert *SmartArt* graphics to text and to shapes. Finally, you create a business logo for PLR.

File Needed: **PLRPromotion-04.pptx**
Completed Project File Names: **[your initials] PP P4-1.pptx** and **PRGLogo2.png**

4-43 Text direction rotated

1. Open the **PLRPromotion-04** presentation from your student files.

2. Save this presentation as **[your initials] PP P4-1**.

3. Change text direction and alignment in a text box.
   a. On slide 1, select the "Minnesota" text box.
   b. Click the **Text Direction** list arrow [*Home* tab, *Paragraph* group] and select **Rotate all text 270°**.
   c. Click the **Align** button [*Drawing Tools Format* tab, *Arrange* group] and select **Align Left**. Be sure **Align to Slide** is selected.
   d. Repeat to select **Align Bottom** (Figure 4-43).

4. Create a shape, modify it using adjustment handles, and change stacking order.
   a. On slide 2, click the **Shapes** button [*Insert* tab, *Illustrations* group] (Figure 4-44) to open the *Shapes* gallery.
   b. Select the **24-Point Star** and draw a star shape (*Height* **1.5"** and *Width* **2"**) on a blank area of the slide.
   c. Drag the adjustment handle toward the center to make the star points longer.
   d. Change the shape fill color to **Blue, Accent 4, Darker 50%**.
   e. Change the shape outline color to **Dark Blue, Background 2, Darker 50%**.
   f. Select **Gridlines** [*View* tab, *Show* group].
   g. Move the list placeholder down so the top is even with the third horizontal grid line.
   h. Press **Enter** after the first bulleted item to add blank space and press **Backspace** to remove the bullet.
   i. Move the star shape over "PLR" and click **Send Backward** twice [*Drawing Tools Format* tab, *Arrange* group] to move the shape behind the text.
   j. Adjust the shape position as necessary (Figure 4-45) and deselect **Gridlines** [*View* tab, *Show* group].

5. Layer text boxes to identify the four locations of Paradise Lakes Resort.
   a. On slide 3, select the four location name shapes.

Numbers indicate how many star points

Stars and Banners

Callouts

24-Point Star

4-44 Part of *Shapes* gallery

Find Your Perfect Northwoods Getaway

▶ **PLR**—An ideal vacation spot

▶ Try your hand at fishing for walleye

▶ Rent one of our well-equipped boats

▶ Cozy up in a traditional "Up North" cabin

▶ Visit when the temperature drops

4-45 Gridlines displayed and shape behind text

b. Click the **Edit Shape** list arrow [*Drawing Tools Format* tab, *Insert Shapes* group] and select **Change Shape**.

c. In the gallery, select the *Line Callout 1* shape (Figure 4-46). A line appears to the left of each text box. The line is part of the shape, but it looks better when it is attached to the shape outline.

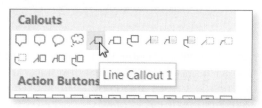

4-46 Part of *Shapes* gallery

d. Click the **Zoom** button on the *Status bar* to increase your viewing percentage to **150%** so detailed positioning is easier.

e. Adjust each line so it touches the outline of each shape (Figure 4-47).

f. For the "Walker" shape, move the line so it connects to the right side of the shape.

g. Drag the shapes to the right so they are on top of the Minnesota map.

h. Position each name as shown in Figure 4-48 and extend the lines as necessary to point to the specific locations.

4-47 Shapes adjusted

6. Modify, flip, ungroup, and merge shapes.

a. On slide 4, select the oval only and click **Edit Shape** [*Drawing Tools Format* tab, *Insert Shapes* group], select **Change Shape**, and select **Rectangle**.

b. Change the rectangle fill color to **Blue, Accent 4** and the shape outline color to **No Outline**.

c. Select the fish. Click the **Rotate** list arrow [*Drawing Tools Format* tab, *Arrange* group] and select **Flip Horizontal**.

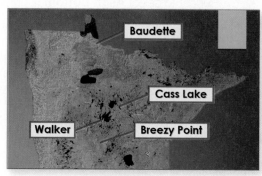

d. With the fish selected, click **Group** [*Drawing Tools Format* tab, *Arrange* group] and select **Ungroup** (Figure 4-49). (Grouped shapes cannot be merged.)

e. With the ungrouped fish shapes still selected, press **Shift** and click the rectangle to add it to the selection. (If you have deselected the fish shapes, draw a selection rectangle to select all the shapes again.)

4-48 Shapes positioned on the map

f. Click the **Merge Shapes** button [*Drawing Tools Format* tab, *Insert Shapes* group] and select **Combine** (Figure 4-50). The new shape adopts the top color, so change the rectangle fill color to **Blue, Accent 4**.

g. Click the **Size Launcher** [*Drawing Tools Format* tab, *Size* group] to open the *Format Shape* pane and select **Lock aspect ratio** so the shape resizes proportionally. Decrease the height to **1"** and the width automatically changes.

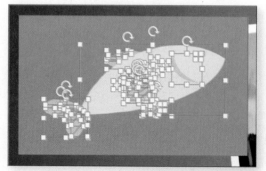

4-49 Ungrouped shapes

4-50 Merged shape

7. Duplicate, align, and distribute shapes.
   a. On slide 4, select the merged shape and press **Ctrl+D**. Position the duplicated shape so it overlaps the first shape.
   b. Repeat this step to create six more shapes. Each new shape is positioned as the second shape was positioned.
   c. Select all eight shapes (Figure 4-51). Click **Align** [*Drawing Tools Format* tab, *Arrange* group] and select **Align to Slide**. Repeat this step to select **Align Left** and to select **Distribute Vertically** (Figure 4-52).
   d. Click **Group** [*Drawing Tools Format* tab, *Arrange* group] and select **Group**.

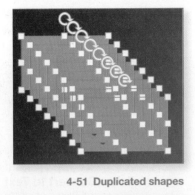

4-51 Duplicated shapes

8. Apply connector lines.
   a. On slide 4, move the picture to the left and position the text boxes as shown in Figure 4.53.
   b. Click the **Shapes** gallery **More** button [*Home* tab, *Drawing* group], and select the **Curved Arrow Connector**.
   c. Connect the right side of the "Fishing" text box to the top of the "Family" text box. You know the ends are connected when a green circle appears at each end of the line.
   d. Repeat to connect the bottom of the "Family" text box to the top of the "Fun!" text box. As you draw the line to make this connection, draw over the picture so this line has a curve with an adjustment handle. Adjust the curve of the line if necessary.
   e. Select both connector lines, click **Shape Outline** [*Drawing Tools Format* tab, *Shape Styles* group], and change the weight to **6 pt**.

4-53 Shapes with connector lines

4-52 Aligned and distributed shapes

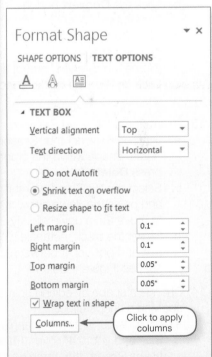

4-54 Format Shape pane

9. Resize a shape to fit text and adjust text box spacing for two columns.
   a. On slide 7, right-click the text placeholder and select **Format Shape** to open the *Format Shape* pane. If necessary, click **Text Options** and click the **Textbox** button (Figure 4-54).
   b. Select **Resize shape to fit text**. The text box extends below the slide.

c. Click the **Columns** button to open the *Columns* dialog box. Select **2** columns with **.3"** spacing. Click **OK**.

d. Resize the text box (*Height* **5"** and *Width* **8.5"**) (Figure 4-55).

10. Convert a *SmartArt* graphic to text.
   a. On slide 15, select the *SmartArt* graphic on the left.
   b. Click the **Convert** button [*SmartArt Tools Design* tab, *Reset* group].
   c. Select **Convert to Text** to change text to a bulleted list (Figure 4-56).
   d. Increase the font size to **20 pt**.

11. Adjust a table.
   a. On slide 15, move the table to the right so it does not overlap the listed text.
   b. For the table title on the first row, change the font color to **Dark Blue, Background 2**.

12. Convert a *SmartArt* graphic to shapes.
   a. On slide 6, select the *SmartArt* graphic.
   b. Click the **Convert** button [*SmartArt Tools Design* tab, *Reset* group].
   c. Click **Convert to Shapes** to change to grouped shapes (Figure 4-57). Click **Arrange** [*Home* tab, *Drawing* group] and **Ungroup**.
   d. Click on the slide background to deselect the shapes.

13. Rearrange ungrouped *SmartArt* shapes.
   a. On slide 6, select the "Seasonal Rates" shape within the graphic and press **Delete**.
   b. Select the "Fall" and "Winter" shapes and press the down arrow 10 times to move them down slightly.
   c. Select the black rectangle with white text and position it between the shapes (Figure 4-58).

14. Change a shape by editing points and applying a shape effect.
   a. On slide 18, draw a rectangle (*Height* **3.5"** and *Width* **4"**) over "Paradise Lakes Resort" (the three words are in separate text boxes). Click **Send Backward** and select **Send to Back** [*Drawing Tools Format* tab, *Arrange* group].
   b. Change the shape fill color to **Blue, Accent 4, Darker 50%** and the shape outline color to **No Outline**.

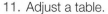

4-55 Text box with columns

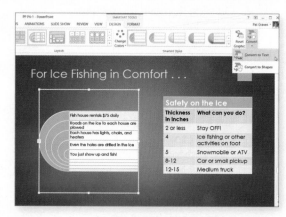

4-56 Convert *SmartArt graphic* to text

4-57 *SmartArt graphic* converted to shapes and ungrouped

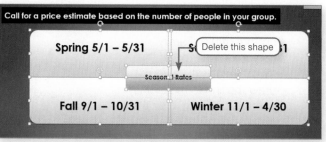

4-58 *SmartArt graphic* shapes adjusted

c. With the rectangle selected, click **Edit Shape** [*Drawing Tools Format* tab, *Insert Shapes* group] and select **Edit Points**. The four corners now have black squares that are points.

d. Click a black square to make the handles active for that point. These are straight lines extending from the edit point ending in a white square.

e. Drag the white squares at the end of the handles to make the line between the points curve. Drag the black point to change the position of where the curve begins and ends.

f. Click on a line to add another point. You started with four points on the rectangle corners; the shape shown in Figure 4-59 has six points.

g. Continue to adjust the position of the points and the line curves so the shape behind "Paradise Lakes Resort" resembles the irregular shape of a lake.

h. Right-click the points and select **Smooth Points**.

i. With the shape selected, click **Shape Effects** [*Drawing Tools Format* tab, *Shape Styles* group], select **Bevel**, and click **Cool Slant**.

4-59 Edit points to change the shape

15. Group objects and save the group as a picture to create a logo.

a. On slide 18, select all text (three words) and the shape, and click **Group** [*Drawing Tools Format* tab, *Arrange* group].

b. With the group selected, right-click. Select **Save as picture** (Figure 4-60).

c. Select the location where you want to save the logo. For *Save as type,* select **PNG Portable Network Graphics Format** so the area around the logo remains transparent.

d. Name the picture PLRLogo2 and click **Save**.

16. On slide 17, insert the ***PLRLogo2*** and position it on the lower right overlapping the picture.

17. On slide 1, insert the ***PLRLogo2***. Resize it (*Height* approximately **1.9"**) so the logo fits on the lower left of the picture.

18. Use *Gridlines* and *Guides* to check placeholder alignment and make any needed adjustments.

4-60 Shape is grouped before saving as a picture

19. Save and close the presentation.

Using Slide Masters to Create a Custom Theme

In *SLO 1.4: Working with Themes,* you learned how to use the *Slide Master* to create custom theme colors. In this section of the chapter, you learn to add background graphics, customize layouts, and change theme fonts to create a unique theme.

Using the *Slide Master* effectively is important to your productivity because the *Slide Master* controls many things that occur automatically when you develop slides. Changes made to *Slide Master* layouts display on all slides that use those layouts.

Change Background Graphics

PowerPoint themes often have graphic accents such as shapes with different fill colors. Using the *Slide Master,* you can customize a background with graphics chosen to support your message. If you have a text-only presentation, you may want your background to be more decorative. If your presentation has a lot of graphic content, you will want to keep the background simple so it does not compete with your content.

Because PowerPoint's *Eyedropper* enables you to precisely match colors, you can choose an original combination for custom theme colors based on an important picture or a graphic image of a particular product you are promoting. Once you have made your initial choice, you can add shapes colored in different ways to emphasize the slide title area or to divide the slide in some way.

> **MORE INFO**
>
> Some online themes cannot easily be changed because of the way they are made. Use *Slide Master* view to determine if you can make changes.

To illustrate the concepts of this section, five slides from the **PLRPromotion-04** presentation (Figure 4-61) have been used to create a separate summer promotion for PLR. The custom theme colors were created based on the PLR logo and the picture of a family in a canoe (Figure 4-62).

Now that the new colors are selected, shapes are added on the *Slide Master* to redesign the background. Placeholders are adjusted to fit the new shapes, and the PLR logo is positioned so it displays on all slides.

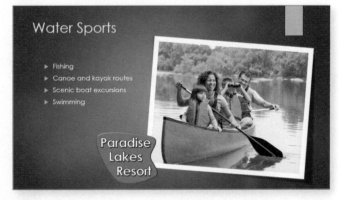

4-61 Original *Ion* theme colors

4-62 *Summer* custom theme colors

HOW TO: Add Background Shapes

1. With your presentation open, click the **Slide Master** button [*View* tab, *Master Views* group] to open the *Slide Master* tab.

2. The left pane shows the layouts for the particular theme you are using. When you point to a slide layout, a ScreenTip identifies it and indicates which slides use that layout.

3. Scroll to the top of the layouts and select the first one. Changes made to this layout affect all slides.

   - The example in Figure 4-63 shows the *Slide Master* and layouts for PowerPoint's *Ion* theme.
   - When you point to the first layout, a ScreenTip shows *Ion Slide Master: used by slide(s) 1-5*.

4. Modify or delete existing shapes.

   - The example in Figure 4-64 shows the blue shape behind the slide number placeholder stretched across the top of the slide so it is behind the slide title placeholder.
   - Another rectangle was added on the left with a fill color slightly lighter than the slide background to define that area for bulleted text.

5. Send shapes behind all text placeholders.

6. If appropriate, you can add a business logo or other picture to the first layout so it appears on all slides.

7. Repeat steps 4–6 to add shapes to other layouts as needed.

8. Click the **Close Master View** button. The changes you have made appear on your slides.

4-63 *Ion Slide Master:* used by slide(s) 1-5

4-64 **Shapes added to the** *Slide Master* **layout behind text placeholders**

> **MORE INFO**
>
> Remember to save frequently as you are working.

Adjust Slide Layout Placeholders

As you have worked on different PowerPoint presentations, you have used slide layouts that control what is placed on a slide and where various objects are positioned. As discussed in *SLO 1.2: Adding and Editing Presentation Text*, the most common layouts include the following:

- *Title Slide*
- *Title and Content*
- *Section Header*
- *Two Content*
- *Comparison*
- *Title Only*
- *Blank*

In the *Slide Master*, these layouts are displayed in order under the first layout, which you use to make global changes that affect the entire presentation. Other layouts are displayed, too. When you customize your *Slide Master*, you can delete any extra layouts that you do not plan to use.

Placeholders on the *Slide Master* layouts are positioned differently based on the theme. Therefore, as you change the background by adding shapes or pictures, you must adjust placeholder positioning. Once you have customized your theme colors and added shapes for the background, evaluate how the placeholder sizing works with the text and objects on your slides. You may want to adjust shape sizing to better fit your text, or adjust text placeholder sizing to better fit your shapes.

HOW TO: Adjust Placeholder Positions

1. With your presentation open, click the **Slide Master** button [*View* tab, *Master Views* group] to open the *Slide Master* tab.
2. Scroll to the top of your layouts and select the first layout. Notice the ScreenTip that shows the current theme name.
3. Modify shape size, if necessary, to fit the text such as a title that needs two lines.
4. Change the bulleted text placeholder size, if necessary, and position it to fit appropriately with shapes.
5. Adjust text color as needed.
6. The completed *Slide Master* layout is shown in Figure 4-65. Notice how the placeholders are now positioned to fit on the shapes, compared to their default position in Figure 4-64.
7. Click the **Close Master View** button.
8. Once your *Slide Master* is complete, check existing slides to be sure slide content fits with the new layouts.
9. Figure 4-66 shows slide 2 after placeholder size and positions were changed on the *Slide Master*. The text has automatically adjusted to fit the new placeholder positions.

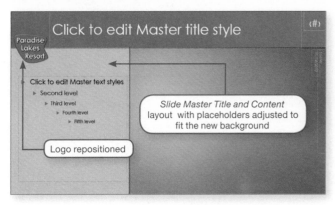

4-65 *Slide Master* placeholders adjusted   4-66 Slide 2 content with placeholders changed

Create New Theme Fonts

The theme font pairs available on the *Slide Master* tab have been selected to work well together. Some use the same font for headings and for body (bulleted text and text box default fonts). Others use two different fonts. In addition to using the available theme fonts, you can create your own theme fonts as well.

The two major categories of fonts are serif (which include details at the ends of letter strokes) and sans serif (which do not include details at the ends of letter strokes) (Figure 4-67). For presentation slides, a sans serif font usually works well because the letters are easier to read from a distance. This becomes very important when lighting conditions in a presentation room are less than ideal.

4-67 Font categories

Some fonts appear larger than others, even when the same point size is used, because of the way letters are designed. You might choose a very thick font for short heading text or choose a more decorative font that appears like handwriting or printing. Examples of a few different fonts, all in the same point size, are shown in Figures 4-68 and 4-69.

Notice the differences in the horizontal space these fonts use. As you select fonts for a new theme, consider both the size differences and how legible and easy to read they will be when projected on a large screen. Some fonts are suitable for printing purposes but may not work well for slides. Also consider the tone a font creates so it is appropriate for your topic. A whimsical font might not be appropriate for a serious business presentation, for example. Make sure when using two fonts that they blend well together.

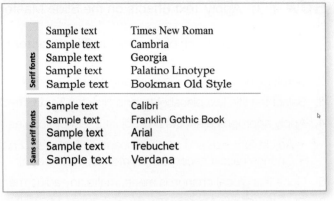

4-68 Fonts available in the *Theme Fonts* list

4-69 Fonts for special uses

HOW TO: Create New Theme Fonts

1. With your presentation open, click the **Slide Master** button [*View* tab, *Master Views* group] to open the *Slide Master* tab.

2. Click the **Fonts** button and choose **Customize Fonts** from the drop-down list to open the *Create New Theme Fonts* dialog box.

3. Select a *Heading font* and select a *Body font*; then name your font pair (Figure 4-70). Click **Save** and this new theme font is saved in the *Custom* category of your *Theme Fonts* list.

4. Click the **Close Master View** button.

5. Check your slides and make font or word wrapping adjustments as needed.

4-70 *Create New Theme Fonts* dialog box

Apply Text Effects

Consistent text treatments for color, effects, and font size create a hierarchy of importance that will help your audience understand and prioritize your content. The most important text should be emphasized the most. Slide titles should be larger than body text, and they could also have a shadow or bevel effect to emphasize them more. A shadow effect can help to define letters and improve the contrast between the text color and the slide background color. Always strive for options that make the text easier to read. For consistency across multiple slides in your presentation, apply text effects using the *Slide Master*.

HOW TO: Apply Text Effects on the Slide Master

1. With your presentation open, click the **Slide Master** button [*View* tab, *Master Views* group] to open the *Slide Master* tab.
2. Scroll to the top of your layouts and select the first layout.
3. Select the title text placeholder and click the **Text Effects** button [*Drawing Tools Format* tab, *WordArt Styles* group].
4. Apply appropriate effects and adjust effect options as needed. Title text on all slides automatically changes.
   - Adjust font size and color as needed [*Home* tab, *Font* group].
   - Change case if necessary [*Home* tab, *Font* group].
5. Once this global change is made, make any adjustments that you want for individual slide layouts.
6. Click the **Close Master View** button [*Slide Master* tab, *Close* group].
7. Check your slides to be sure all changes are appropriate.

Change List Bullets and List Indent

In *SLO 1.2: Adding and Editing Presentation Text,* you changed list bullets by selecting different characters and adjusting the character color and size. You can also apply picture bullets from online sources or insert your own picture file. A picture bullet can add a creative accent to support the topic of your presentation. Although you could use an actual photograph in a tiny size, most likely it would not be recognizable. A simple line art image usually works best, and you may want it to be larger than your text size. Changing bullets once on the *Slide Master* is much more efficient than changing bullets on multiple slides.

HOW TO: Change Bullets to Pictures

1. With your presentation open, click the **Slide Master** button [*View* tab, *Master Views* group] to open the *Slide Master* tab.
2. Scroll to the top of your layouts and select the first layout.
3. Select the bulleted text placeholder.
4. Click the **Bullets** list arrow [*Home* tab, *Paragraph* group].
5. Click **Bullets and Numbering** to open the *Bullets and Numbering* dialog box (Figure 4-71).
6. Change the bullet *Size* to a percentage that is appropriate for your picture.
7. Click the **Picture** button to open the *Insert Picture* dialog box.
8. Browse to find a picture you have saved, or search for an appropriate bullet.
9. Select a picture and click **Insert**.
10. Click **OK** to close the *Bullets and Numbering* dialog box.

4-71 *Bullets and Numbering* dialog box

A picture bullet is often larger than a character bullet, so text may wrap unevenly after the bullet. You may need to change the distance between the bullet and the text so the text aligns correctly. This distance is called an ***indent*** and its spacing is controlled on the ***Ruler***.

When you select the *Ruler* on the *View* tab, a ruler displays above the slide and on the left side. If no text is selected, ruler numbering begins at the center and extends to the edge of the slide. Markers on the ruler show the current margin and indent. Default ***Tab stops*** are spaced every one-half inch. When you select text in a placeholder, the ruler adjusts and the slide area not used is grayed out.

HOW TO: Increase the Indent After a Bullet

1. With your presentation open, click the **Slide Master** button [*View* tab, *Master Views* group] to open the *Slide Master* tab.

2. Scroll to the top of your layouts and select the first layout.

3. Click the **Ruler** button [*View* tab, *Show* group] and the ruler displays (Figure 4-72).

4. Drag the **Zoom** slider to **200%** to make working with the ruler easier. Adjust the slide position so you can see the text and the ruler above.

5. Click in the first line of text in the bulleted text placeholder where spacing needs to increase.

6. **Indent Markers** appear on the horizontal ruler (Figure 4-73).

   - *First-line indent marker* (triangle pointing down): Appears on the left-most position indicating no indention
   - *Left indent marker* (triangle pointing up): Shows the first indention position on the *Ruler*
   - *Double marker* (rectangle below left indent marker): Moves both indent markers

7. Drag the **Left indent marker** to the right to the 1" position on the *Ruler* (Figure 4-74). You may need less or more space, depending on the size of your picture bullet, to achieve even alignment for all the text that follows a bullet.

8. The picture size in Figure 4-74 was increased to **130%** for the first line of bulleted text.

9. Repeat step 7 for second-level bullets or other list levels that you may use.

10. Click the **Close Master View** button [*Slide Master* tab].

11. Click the **Fit slide to current window** button on the *Status bar* (Figure 4-75).

12. Adjust placeholder size on individual slides if needed.

4-72 Incorrect word wrap after the bullet

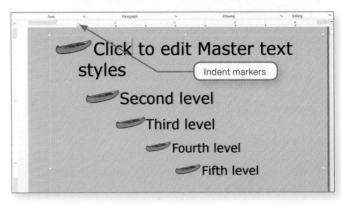

4-73 Text word wraps under the picture bullet

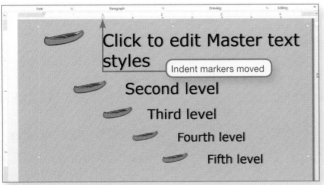

4-74 Text word wraps evenly after the picture bullet

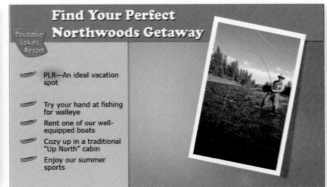

4-75 Slide 2 with corrected indent

The Handout Master

The *Handout* feature is a printing option that allows you to share a paper copy of your presentation with your audience. It displays several slides on each page in fixed positions based on the number of slides you select. You can use the *Handout Master* to rearrange header and footer placeholders or to change fonts or add graphics.

It works well to include some design element from the presentation in the handout. Handouts provide a convenient place for people to take notes during a presentation and can be a useful resource for them after the presentation.

HOW TO: Customize the Handout Master

1. Click the **View** tab and click the **Handout Master** button [*Master Views* group] to open the *Handout Master* tab.

2. In the *Page Setup* group, click these options to make changes (Figure 4-76):

   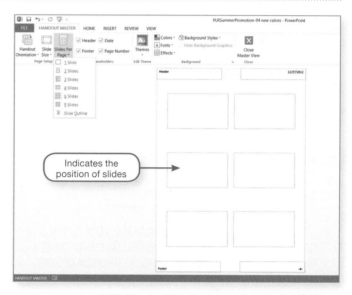

   4-76 *Handout Master* tab and page placeholders

   - *Handout Orientation:* Portrait (default) or landscape orientation.
   - *Slide Size:* Widescreen (default) or Standard slide size. Be very careful when changing slide size. The miniature slides in standard size may fit the handout better than widescreen size, but a change here also affects the slide show. You may not want the slide show changed, especially if extensive editing is required to make slide content fit the different slide size.
   - *Slides Per Page:* 1, 2, 3, 4, 6, 9 slides or the slide outline can be shown. Lines for writing notes appear beside each slide if you choose 3 slides.

3. In the *Placeholders* group, select each of the placeholders you want to appear on the page. Remove placeholders by deselecting the name or by deleting them on the page.

4. In the *Background* group, click options to make choices from the available galleries.

   - Click the **Background Styles** button and select **Format Background** to open the *Format Background* pane where you can change fill options. Do not click the **Apply to All** button. If you do, the changes you make for the handout will affect your slide show.
   - While color backgrounds may look attractive on handouts, printing full-color pages can be expensive and may make note taking on the pages more difficult. A plain page background is usually effective.

5. Select each placeholder and edit it using one or more of the following techniques. Increase the **Zoom** as needed to work with detailed areas of the page.

   - Change the font, apply text effects, or change alignment [*Home* tab].
   - Insert text in a placeholder or replace the data or slide number element that is displayed.
   - Resize a placeholder.
   - Drag a placeholder to a different location.

6. Click the **Insert** tab to add a picture, such as a company logo, or other objects that you want to appear on all printed pages (Figure 4-77).

   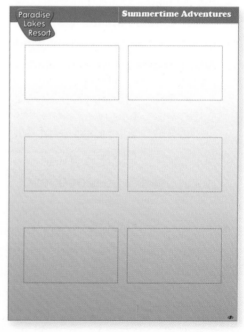

   4-77 Handout master changed

7. Click the **Close Master View** button [*Handout Master* tab].

P4-226

To create a PLR summer promotion presentation, you use the *Slide Master* to add background shapes and the PLR logo. The current theme colors have already been customized. You adjust placeholder positioning, customize fonts, and insert a picture bullet for a unique theme.

Files Needed: ***PLRPromotionSummer-04.pptx*** and ***PLRLogo2.png***
Completed Project File Name: ***[your initials] PP P4-2.pptx***

1. Open the ***PLRPromotionSummer-04*** presentation.

2. Save the presentation as ***[your initials] PP P4-2***.

3. Click the **Slide Master** button [*View* tab, *Master Views* group] to open the *Slide Master* tab.

4. Scroll to the top of your layouts and select the first layout.

5. Change theme fonts.
   a. Click the **Fonts** button [*Slide Master* tab, *Background* group] and select **Customize Fonts** to open the *Create New Theme Fonts* dialog box.
   b. For the *Heading* font select **Cooper Black**. For the *Body* font select **Verdana**.
   c. Name this font group Summer. Click **Save**.
   d. Select the bulleted text placeholder. Select the **Font** list arrow [*Home* tab, *Font* group] and choose **Verdana (Body)** (Figure 4-78). The body placeholders on all other slide master layouts will update accordingly.

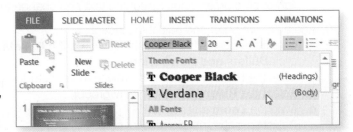

4-78 Applying the correct *Theme Fonts* style

6. Apply a shadow style to title text.
   a. Select the title placeholder and click the **Text Effects** button [*Drawing Tools Format* tab, *WordArt Styles* group]. Select **Shadow** and click **Shadow Options** to open the *Format Shape* pane.
   b. For *Presets,* select **Offset Diagonal Bottom Right** (in the *Outer* group).
   c. Reduce the shadow transparency to **30%**. Increase the *Blur* to **6 pt.** and the *Distance* to **6 pt.**
   d. Close the *Format Shape* pane.

7. Modify and insert background shapes.
   a. Select the blue rectangle at the top of the slide and stretch it on the left and right to the width of the slide (**13.33"**).
   b. With the blue rectangle selected so the *Drawing Tools Format* tab is open, click the **Rectangle** (*Insert Shapes* group). Draw a second rectangle (*Height* **7.5"** and *Width* **5"**) anywhere on the slide.
   c. Click the **Shape Fill** button [*Drawing Tools Format* tab, *Shape Styles* group] and change the **Fill** color to **Olive Green Background 2, Lighter 40%**.
   d. Click the **Shape Outline** button [*Shape Styles* group] and choose **No Outline**.
   e. Click the **Shape Effects** button [*Shape Styles* group] and select **Shadow** and **Offset Right** (in the *Outer* group).
   f. Click the **Send Backward** list arrow [*Arrange* group] and choose **Send to Back**. Click the **Align** button and choose **Align Left** and repeat to choose **Align Top**.

8. Insert a logo.
   a. Click the **Pictures** button [*Insert* tab, *Images* group] and locate your saved files. Select the ***PLRLogo2*** that you created in *Pause & Practice: PowerPoint 4-1* and insert the logo.
   b. Move the logo to the upper left of the slide master layout and resize it (*Height* approximately **1.2"**). Position this small logo on the left partially over the blue rectangle (Figure 4-79).

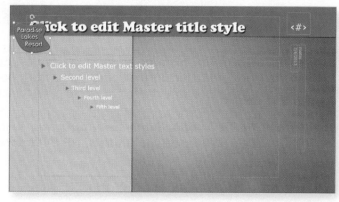

4-79 Inserted logo shown in its original size

9. Adjust placeholder positions.
   a. Move the title placeholder up to fit on the blue rectangle at the top of the slide beside the PLR logo.
      • Resize the title placeholder so it has the same height as the blue rectangle.
      • Click the **Align Text** button [*Home* tab, *Paragraph* group] and choose **Middle** so the text will be centered vertically in the title placeholder.
   b. Move the bulleted text placeholder to the left and resize it so all text fits on the rectangle with the lighter olive green color. Select the text and change the color to **black**.

10. Add a picture bullet and adjust the indent.
    a. Select the bulleted text placeholder. Click the **Bullets** button [*Home* tab, *Paragraph* group] and click **Bullets and Numbering**.
    b. Click the **Picture** button and browse to your student files. Select **CanoeBlue-04** and click **Insert**.
    c. Select the **Ruler** [*View* tab, *Show* group].
    d. Drag the **Zoom** slider to **200%**. Adjust your slide position so you can see the top of the bulleted area.

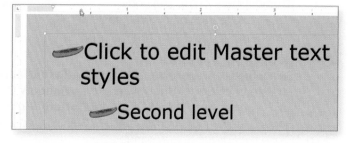

    e. Click to position your insertion point at the beginning of the first bulleted item. Drag the first line indent marker (Figure 4-80) to the **0.5"** position.
    f. Click to position your insertion point at the beginning of the second bulleted item. Drag the first line indent marker to the **1"** position. Deselect the **Ruler**.

4-80 The bullet indent is adjusted using the *Ruler*

    g. Click the **Fit slide to current window** button on the *Status bar*.

11. Modify the title slide layout.
    a. Select the title slide layout. Move the footer and date placeholders to the right of the slide.
    b. Resize the title placeholder to fit on the darker green area.
    c. Resize the subtitle placeholder to fit on the darker green area. Click the **Change Case** button [*Home* tab, *Font* group] and select **Capitalize Each Word**. Increase the font size to **28 pt.** and apply **bold**. Resize the subtitle placeholder to fit the text.

12. Insert the PLR logo.
    a. On the title slide layout, click the **Pictures** button [*Insert* tab] and locate your student files. Select the ***PRGLogo2*** and click **Insert**.
    b. Move the logo to the upper left to cover the smaller logo behind it and decrease the size to be as wide as the rectangle that it is over (Figure 4-81).

13. Click the **Slide Master** tab and click the **Close Master View** button.

14. On slide 1, if necessary, click the **Reset** button [*Home* tab, *Slides* group].

15. Check each slide to be sure that all slide objects fit appropriately and adjust if necessary.

16. Save and close the presentation.

4-81 Completed title slide

Inserting a Screenshot or Screen Clipping

When you need an image of your computer screen, you can capture it using PowerPoint's **Screenshot** feature to copy the entire application window or the **Screen Clipping** feature to copy a portion of the window. These features are very useful, especially if you need to reference a web site during a presentation in a location where there is no Internet access. The document or web page you want to capture must be open at the same time you are working on your PowerPoint presentation.

HOW TO: Insert a Screenshot

1. Open the document or Internet web page you want to capture.
2. In PowerPoint, go to the slide where you want the captured image to appear.
3. Click the **Screenshot** button [*Insert* tab, *Images* group] and a gallery appears showing all available (open) windows (Figure 4-82).
4. Click the window you want to show in PowerPoint and the entire window of the application or web page is displayed on the current slide as a picture. It will automatically be sized to fit the vertical size of your slide (Figure 4-83).
5. Use the *Picture Tools Format* tab to customize the picture by cropping or applying picture effects.

4-82 *Screenshot* button and available windows

4-83 *Screenshot* inserted showing full application window

▶ ANOTHER WAY

You can capture a screen image by pressing **Print Screen**, and a copy of your computer screen is placed on the *Clipboard*. Press **Alt+Print Screen** to copy only the current window. In both cases, press **Ctrl+V** to paste these images from the *Clipboard*. They will appear on the slide at full size.

The ***Screen Clipping*** feature also shows a gallery of *Available Windows*. In the gallery, the first window on the left is the most recently opened window. It is the one from which a clipping can be made. Therefore, you should view the document or web page you plan to capture right before moving to the slide in PowerPoint where you intend to put the screen clipping.

HOW TO: Insert a Screen Clipping

1. Open the document or web site that contains the information you want to capture.
2. In PowerPoint, go to the slide where you want the captured image to appear.
3. Click the **Screenshot** button list arrow [*Insert* tab, *Images* group] and click **Screen Clipping**.
4. Your screen becomes gray and your pointer changes to a crosshair.
5. Click and drag to reveal the portion of the screen you want to capture (Figure 4-84).
6. Release the mouse button and your screen clipping is displayed on your slide as a picture such as the one shown on the left in Figure 4-85.
7. In Figure 4-85, the screen clipping on the right has picture effects applied. Rounded corners better match this particular image and a shadow makes it more defined.

Drag crosshair to reveal captured area

4-84 *Screen Clipping* to capture a portion of the screen

4-85 *Screen clipping* as it first appears on the left and with picture effects applied on the right

---

SLO 4.5

Editing Pictures

PowerPoint provides many photo editing features that allow you to improve your pictures or arrange them in creative and artistic ways.

Make Corrections

If a picture lacks detail because it is too dark or if colors are washed out from bright sunshine, you can improve the pictures using *Corrections*. The *Corrections* gallery opens with the current image positioned in the middle of available options.

- *Sharpen or Soften*: Sharpen makes picture details more evident; soften creates a blending effect. In the *Corrections* gallery, the options change in 25 percent increments; softer colors are on the left and sharper colors are on the right.
- *Contrast and Brightness*: Contrast affects the difference between the picture's lightest and darkest colors. Increasing brightness lightens a picture by adding white while decreasing brightness darkens the picture by adding black. In the *Corrections* gallery, the options change in 20 percent increments for both adjustments. Darker variations are on the left and lighter variations are on the right.

If these percentages make bigger changes than you want, you can open the *Format Picture* pane to make precise adjustments using **Picture Corrections** options.

HOW TO: Use Corrections

1. Select the picture you want to change.
2. Click the **Corrections** button [*Picture Tools Format* tab, *Adjust* group] to open the gallery.
3. As you point to various effects in the *Sharpen/Soften* category or in the *Brightness/Contrast* category, the live preview shows you the effect on your picture.
4. Click an effect to apply it.
    - Figure 4-86 shows the original picture, and the one on the right has **Sharpen: 50%** applied.
    - Figure 4-87 shows the original picture, and the one below has **Brightness: 0% (Normal) Contrast: +40%** applied.
5. To restore the picture to its original colors, click the **Reset Picture** button.

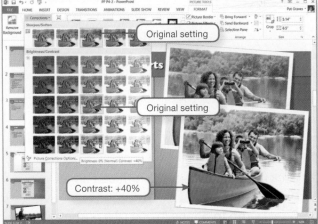

4-86 Original picture and picture with *Sharpen* effect applied   4-87 Original picture and picture with *Contrast* effect applied

Artistic Effects

With the *Artistic Effects* gallery, you can transform your picture using various effects that resemble painting techniques. The effects include *Pencil Sketch, Line Drawing, Watercolor*

Sponge, Glass, Plastic Wrap, and many others. These effects lessen the realism of a picture, but the results can make a picture beautiful in a creative way. Consider using these effects for special situations.

HOW TO: Apply Artistic Effects

1. Select the picture you want to change.

2. Click the **Artistic Effects** button [*Picture Tools Format* tab, *Adjust* group].

3. As you point to various effects, observe the name of the effect and the live preview of that effect on your picture.

4. Click an effect to apply it. Figure 4-88 shows the original picture and the one on the right has the *Cutout* effect applied.

5. To restore the picture to its original appearance, click the **Reset Picture** button.

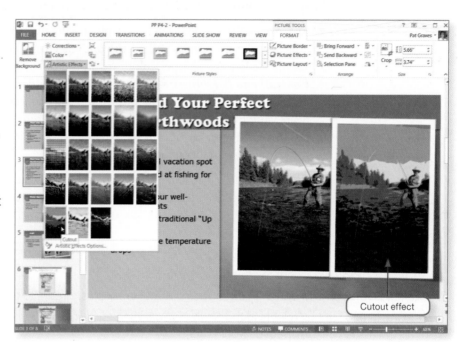

4-88 Original picture and picture with Artistic effect applied

Crop a Picture to a Shape or an Aspect Ratio

As you learned in *SLO 2.3: Working with Pictures,* you crop a picture by dragging the cropping handles from the edge of the picture. You can also crop a picture to a shape from the *Shape* gallery or to a specific aspect ratio.

HOW TO: Crop a Picture to a Shape or Aspect Ratio

1. Select the picture you want to change.

2. Click the **Crop** button [*Picture Tools Format* tab, *Size* group].

3. Select **Crop to Shape** to open the *Shapes* gallery and click a shape for the picture (Figure 4-89).

4. Select **Aspect Ratio** to open a list of sizes organized by orientation: *Square, Portrait,* and *Landscape.*

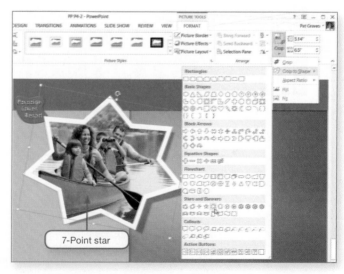

4-89 Picture is cropped to a shape from the *Shapes* gallery

5. Click an *Aspect Ratio* size to apply it. The first number is the horizontal ratio; the second number is the vertical ratio.

   • With each different aspect ratio, the center of the picture remains stable while areas from the edges of the picture are removed to achieve that particular size (Figure 4-90).
   • If you need to adjust the focus of the picture within the shape, point to the picture and drag it so the area you want to keep shows in the crop area.

6. Click the **Crop** button.

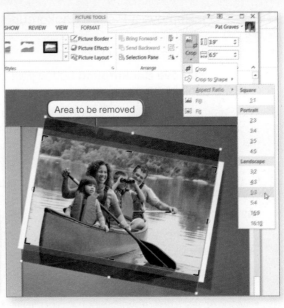

> MORE INFO
>
> Changing the fill on a shape to a picture fill results in the same appearance as cropping a picture to a shape.

4-90 *Aspect Ratio* of 5:3 crops from the picture's middle

Change a Picture

The ***Change Picture*** command replaces one picture with another. It works when you have inserted a picture and even when the picture is cropped. It does not work if you use a picture as a shape fill.

HOW TO: Change a Picture

1. Select a picture and click the **Change Picture** button [*Picture Tools Format* tab, *Adjust* group] (Figure 4-91).

2. On the *Insert Pictures* search box, click **Browse** to search for the file you need.

3. The new picture replaces the original picture but retains the same styles that were applied to the original picture. You will notice a change in size if one picture has a portrait orientation and the other one has a landscape orientation because the width remains the same.

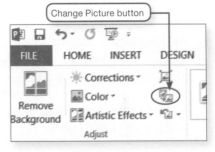

4-91 *Change Picture* button

Apply a SmartArt Picture Layout

When a picture is selected, you can apply a *SmartArt* layout. Click the **Picture Layout** button [*Picture Tools Format* tab, *Picture Styles* group] (Figure 4-92). The *SmartArt* layouts that appear all have pictures in them.

Remove a Picture Background

As you learned in *SLO 2.3: Working with Pictures*, it is easy to remove the background that is a solid fill by using the *Set Transparent Color* feature. You can use the ***Background Removal*** feature to remove detailed areas of a background to focus on just one element of the picture. The area removed appears transparent on the slide. Depending on the complexity of the picture, it may take more than one attempt to get good results.

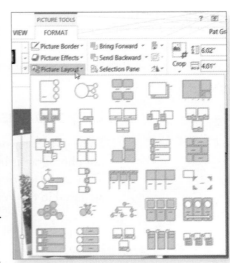

4-92 *SmartArt* layouts available for pictures

HOW TO: Remove a Picture Background

1. Select the picture you want to change.
2. Click the **Remove Background** button [*Picture Tools Format* tab, *Adjust* group].
3. The *Background Removal* tab opens with editing tools. A rectangle suggests the part of the picture you may want to choose. Only part of the picture is in color; the rest of the picture has a magenta color that indicates the area to be removed (Figure 4-93).
4. First, adjust the rectangle to fit the area of the picture that you want to keep (Figure 4-94). Increase the **Zoom** percentage so you can work more easily with details.
5. Use the following editing tools and click various areas of the picture to keep or remove areas:
   - *Mark Areas to Keep:* Selects colors to keep and places a small circle with a plus sign on that area
   - *Mark Areas to Remove:* Selects colors to remove and places a small circle with a minus sign on that area
   - *Delete Mark:* Removes keep or remove marks
   - *Discard All Changes:* Restores the picture to its original colors
6. Once you have marked areas on your picture to keep or remove, click **Keep Changes** to accept your selections and remove the background (Figure 4-95).
7. If you are not satisfied with the result, click the **Remove Background** button again to make more adjustments. You can continue to make changes to the picture until you save your presentation. Only the modified picture remains when you open the presentation again.
8. Your original picture file is not affected by removing the background in PowerPoint. However, if you want to preserve the transparent area for future use, right click and select **Save As Picture**. Rename the picture and select the *.png* format. Save the picture in an appropriate location and you can use it again.

4-93 *Background Removal* showing the selected area before editing

4-94 *Background Removal* area is changed and areas to keep are marked

4-95 The background is removed

> **MORE INFO**
>
> The *.jpg* format does not support transparency. If you have removed a picture's background and save the picture using the *.jpg* format, the removed area will be displayed as white.

Ungroup Illustrations and Recolor

Some of the artwork you find by searching in PowerPoint can be ungrouped. These images are not photographs but are line drawings or simple illustrations created with drawing programs. They are made of different shapes that are combined to form the image. Often these images are saved in the Windows Metafile format (*.wmf*), which is a vector-based graphic file format.

When this type of image is ungrouped, it becomes a PowerPoint drawing and must be ungrouped again before you can select individual parts of the image. Once you ungroup it, you can change fill and outline colors for individual parts or delete parts of the image to better match your presentation.

> **MORE INFO**
>
> If an illustration cannot be ungrouped, you will receive an error message when you try to ungroup it.

HOW TO: Ungroup an Illustration and Recolor

1. Select an illustrated image.
2. Change the **Zoom** percentage so you can see the image in a larger size to work in detail.
3. Click **Group** [*Picture Tools Format* tab, *Arrange* group] and select **Ungroup**. A dialog box asks if you want to convert this picture to a Microsoft Office drawing object (Figure 4-96). Click **Yes**. The *Drawing Tools Format* tab opens instead of the *Picture Tools Format* tab. One set of handles appears around the illustration.

4-96 Warning message that appears when ungrouping an illustrated image

4. Click the **Group** button [*Drawing Tools Format* tab, *Arrange* group] and click **Ungroup** again. Selection handles appear on the many shapes in the illustrated image (Figure 4-97). Often these shapes have a blank shape behind them that should be removed if you are deleting part of the image to be used in a different way.
5. Click anywhere on the slide to turn off handles. Now you can select individual parts of the image and delete parts you do not want, change fill or line colors, or rearrange shapes.
6. If you are deleting a large area with multiple parts, draw a selection rectangle so more parts are selected at once. Press **Delete**.
7. When your changes are complete, select all of the remaining shapes. Click the **Group** button [*Drawing Tools Format* tab, *Arrange* group] again and click **Regroup**. Figure 4-98 shows the modified image.

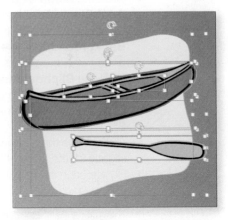

4-97 Ungrouped image showing handles for multiple shapes

> **ANOTHER WAY**
>
> If you have difficulty selecting individual shapes of a detailed illustration that you have ungrouped, press **Tab** to move between the shapes.

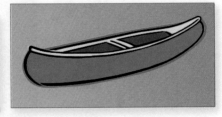

4-98 Modified image

For this project you improve several images for a PLR winter promotion by making picture corrections and applying artistic effects. You change picture shapes by cropping to a shape and removing a background. You also ungroup an illustrated image, recolor it, and regroup the image.

Files Needed: **PLRPromotionWinter-04.pptx, SnowBackground1-04.jpg, Minnesota-04.wmf (from office.com templates)** and **SnowBranch-04.jpg**
Completed Project File Name: **[your initials] PP P4-3.pptx**

1. Open the **PLRPromotionWinter-04** presentation.

2. Save the presentation as **[your initials] PP P4-3**.

3. On slide 1, copy the snowflake.

4. Use the *Slide Master* to change the background.
   a. Click the **View** tab and click the **Slide Master** button [*Master Views* group].
   b. Select the first *Slide Master* layout (*Office Theme Slide Master: used by slides 1–6*).
   c. Insert a background picture.
      • Click the **Background Styles** list arrow [*Slide Master* tab, *Background* group] and choose **Format Background** to open the *Format Background* pane.
      • Select **Picture or texture fill** and click **File**. Locate your student files and select **SnowBackground1-04**. Click **Insert**.
   d. Change the font.
      • Click the **Fonts** list arrow [*Slide Master* tab, *Background* group], scroll down, and choose the **Arial Black, Arial** theme font.
      • Select both the slide title and bulleted text placeholders and change the font color to **White, Background 1** [*Home* tab, *Font* group] and click the **Shadow** button.
   e. Arrange three snowflakes.
      • Click the **Clipboard Launcher** button [*Home* tab, *Clipboard* group]. The snowflake image you copied is displayed in the *Clipboard* list.
      • Click the snowflake image three times and change each snowflake to a different size (*Height* **2", 1",** and **3"**).
      • Arrange the three snowflakes on the right with the top and bottom snowflakes extending slightly off the edge of the slide.
      • Rotate each snowflake slightly so they are not aligned in the same way (Figure 4-99).

4-99 *Slide Master* view showing background picture fill and snowflakes

5. Close the *Clipboard* pane.

6. Click the **Close Master View** button [*Slide Master* tab].

7. On slide 1, delete the original snowflake image.

8. On slide 1, insert an illustrated image and modify it as follows.

   a. Click the **Online Pictures** button [*Insert* tab, *Images* group] to open the *Insert Pictures* dialog box. In the *Office.com Clip Art* search box, type Minnesota.

   b. Select the map of Minnesota (Figure 4-100) and click **Insert**. (Note: If this map does not appear in your search, insert the image, **Minnesota-04**, from your student files.) Resize the map (*Height* approximately **7"**). Ensure proportions are maintained.

4-100 *Insert Picture* dialog box with search results

   c. Click the **Group** button [*Picture Tools Format* tab, *Arrange* group] and choose **Ungroup**. You need to make this a drawing object, so click **Yes**.

   d. Click the **Group** button [*Drawing Tools Format* tab, *Arrange* group] and choose **Ungroup**. Now many handles appear on all the shapes that make up the drawing object (Figure 4-101).

   e. Click on the slide background to turn off shape handles.

   f. Select the small blue and black circles on the map and press **Delete**.

   g. Select the black map that looks like a shadow and press **Delete**.

   h. Click just below the map to select the transparent shape that is behind the map. Click **Delete** to remove it. Only one shape of the Minnesota map remains.

4-101 Ungrouped shape

9. On slide 1, move the map and apply a picture fill.

   a. Select the map and move it to the left side of the slide.

   b. On the *Format Shape* pane, click **Fill**, select **Picture or texture fill**, and click the **File** button. Locate your student files and select the file **SnowBranch-04.jpg**.

   c. Move the picture to better fit the shape by changing the following *Offset* percentages: *Offset left* **–12%** and *Offset bottom* **–6%**.

d. Close the *Format Picture* pane.

e. Click the **Shape Outline** button [*Drawing Tools Format* tab, *Shape Styles* group] and select **Black, Text 1**. Repeat to select **Weight** and **3 pt**.

f. Click the **Shape Effects** button [*Drawing Tools Format* tab, *Shape Styles* group], select **Shadow**, and select **Offset Diagonal Bottom Right** (in the *Outer* group).

10. On slide 1, modify the text.

a. Change the title font size to **66 pt**. and resize the title placeholder so the text appears as shown in Figure 4-102.

b. Change the subtitle text to **White, bold,** and **36 pt**. Align the subtitle with the bottom of the slide.

4-102 Title slide completed

11. For pictures on three slides, make changes using the following options [*Picture Tools Format* tab, *Adjust* group]:

Slide 3	Snowmobile	Corrections	Sharpen: 50%
Slide 4	Girl/Snowboard	Corrections	Brightness: 0% (Normal) Contrast: +20% Sharpen: 50%.
Slide 6	Snowman	Artistic Effects	Cutout

12. Review the slide show.

13. Save and close the presentation.

SLO 4.6 # Creating a Photo Album

To create a presentation consisting mainly of pictures, use the ***Photo Album*** feature. In a photo album, one or more pictures appear on as many slides as you need to display them. When you create the photo album, you can set up many options for display. To make changes, you can edit the photo album. You can control the following options using the *Photo Album* dialog box:

- Select pictures and adjust picture order.
- Select a caption text box for each picture.
- Adjust brightness, contrast, and rotation.
- Insert text boxes to create a text placeholder between pictures.
- Use special layout options.
- Apply a theme and customize *Slide Masters*.

Select Pictures

Pictures for an album can come from any storage location. It is practical to place all pictures in one file folder before creating a photo album. A new presentation is created when you start a photo album.

1. If PowerPoint is not open, start a new, blank presentation so you can access the *Insert tab*.

2. Click the **Photo Album** list arrow [*Insert* tab, *Images* group] and click **New Photo Album** to open the *Photo Album* dialog box.

3. Click the **File/Disk** button.

4. On the *Insert New Pictures* dialog box, locate your first picture and select its file name. Press **Ctrl** while you click additional file names to select them or press **Ctrl+A** to select all pictures at once.

5. Click **Insert**. All the names for the selected pictures appear in the picture list (Figure 4-103).

6. Click the box in front of each picture to select it for individual changes.

   - Reorder the pictures as needed using the **Up** and **Down** arrows below the picture list (Figure 4-104).
   - Click **Remove** when a picture is highlighted to remove it from the album.

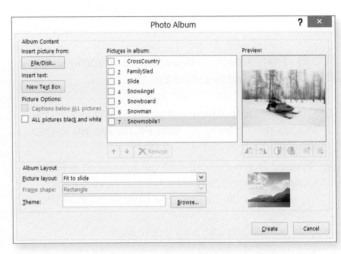

4-103 *Photo Album* dialog box with pictures inserted

7. Below the *Preview* image for each selected picture, click to use the following editing functions:
   - *Rotate Left* or *Rotate Right*
   - *Contrast Up* or *Contrast Down*
   - *Brightness Up* or *Brightness Down*

8. Click **Create** and a new presentation is created with a title slide and each of your pictures on separate slides (Figure 4-105).

9. Save the photo album.

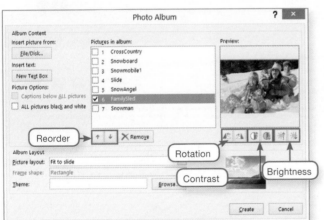

4-104 Reorder pictures

4-105 Photo album created

Adjust Album Layout, Frame Pictures, and Apply a Theme

You can adjust how pictures appear when you are creating a photo album or you can make adjustments later using the *Edit Photo Album* dialog box. Choosing the appropriate settings for a photo album can save editing time because the settings apply to all pictures in the album. If you need to make additional changes, you can modify individual pictures later.

The *Picture Layout* default fills each slide with a picture. You can change this option to display more pictures on a slide. The pictures automatically resize for each option. Just as with any other presentation, you can apply a theme to a photo album to create an attractive consistent background.

HOW TO: Adjust Picture Layout, Frame Pictures, and Apply a Theme

1. Click the **Photo Album** list arrow [*Insert* tab, *Images* group] and click **Edit Photo Album** to open the *Edit Photo Album* dialog box.

2. Select a *Picture Layout.* The default option is **Fit to slide** so each picture fills your slide height. Click the list box arrow to see other options such as the following:
   - *1 picture, 2 pictures, or 4 pictures*
   - *1 picture, 2 pictures, or 4 pictures with titles* (a slide title)

3. Select a *Frame shape.* The default option is **Rectangle**; this shape works for many situations. Click the list box arrow to see other options such as the following:
   - *Rounded Rectangle*
   - *Simple Frame, White*
   - *Simple Frame, Black*
   - *Compound Frame, Black*
   - *Center Shadow Rectangle*
   - *Soft Edge Rectangle*

4. Select a *Theme.* Click the **Browse** button to open the **Choose Theme** dialog box. Select a presentation theme and click **Select** (Figure 4-106). The theme name appears in the *Theme* list box (Figure 4-107).

5. Click **Update** to apply these settings.

4-106 *Choose Theme* dialog box

4-107 *Edit Photo Album* dialog box with changes

> **ANOTHER WAY**
>
> Apply a theme using the *Design* tab after you have created the photo album.

Add Photo Album Text

Use the *Edit Photo Album* dialog box to add text placeholders to your photo album in two ways: as text boxes or as captions below each picture. If you want to add captions, you must use a picture layout other than *Fit to slide* so space is available for caption text. *Picture Options* can also display pictures in black and white.

HOW TO: Add Captions and Text Boxes

1. Click the **Photo Album** list arrow [*Insert* tab, *Images* group] and click **Edit Photo Album** to open the *Edit Photo Album* dialog box.

2. Add text boxes on separate slides.
   - Select the box for a picture name where you would like to add a text box. If you have two or four pictures on a slide, the text box fits in the space of a picture. If you have one picture on a slide, the text box appears on a separate slide.
   - Click the **New Text Box** button and a new slide appears in the *Pictures in album* list. Repeat as needed.
   - When you click **Update**, separate text boxes are inserted.

3. Add text captions below each picture.
   - Adjust *Picture Options* by selecting **Captions below ALL pictures**. This option is not available if the *Picture Layout* is *Fit to slide*.
   - When you click **Update**, the file name appears in a text box below each picture. Edit that text as appropriate and make any needed font changes (Figure 4-108).

4-108 *Album Layout* options adjusted, text box added, captions added

Plan ahead to work efficiently when making changes to the entire photo album or to individual slides. First create and edit the album before making changes on individual slides.

Modify and reposition the pictures in an album just as you do in any other presentation. Add other content as needed. Apply appropriate transitions and animations.

SLO 4.7

Creating and Using a Custom Template

You can save any presentation as a **template**. This is an effective technique once you have developed a unique design using the *Slide Master* that you would like to use again. For example, you might develop a presentation that contains graphics, such as your company logo, or text that may be appropriate for many different presentations. A template can make developing a presentation more efficient and provide design consistency for multiple presentations.

In *SLO 4.3: Using Slide Masters to Create a Custom Theme*, you learned to customize background shapes and fonts for your presentation. You can also customize existing layouts by deleting or adding placeholders. Click the **Insert Placeholder** button [*Slide Master* tab, *Master Layout* group] to add placeholders for the type of slides that you need. Also, you can delete any unused layouts to streamline the available options. You have the option of including sample content that will be especially helpful for other people who may use your template.

Save a Presentation as a Template

A template file has a *.potx* file extension, while a presentation file has a *.pptx* file extension.

You can save a template in any location, such as on your *SkyDrive* or a removable drive if you are working away from your own computer. If you store your templates on your computer in Microsoft's *Templates* folder, they will be easy to access when you start a new presentation.

A template file, with the *.potx* file extension, is automatically saved in a storage location on your computer for this purpose, the folder called *Custom Office Templates*, in the *My Documents* folder. The file path will look something like this: *Libraries/Documents/My Documents/Custom Office Templates*.

HOW TO: Save a Presentation as a Template

1. Complete all changes to your presentation and save it as a presentation file (*.pptx* file extension) in case you want to make changes to the presentation file in the future.

2. Resave the presentation as a template. Click the **File** tab and click **Save As**. Click the **Browse** button to open the *Save As* dialog box.

3. Type an appropriate name in the *File Name* box.

4. In the *Save As Type* list box, choose **PowerPoint Template** (Figure 4-109).

5. The default path to Microsoft's *Custom Office Template* folder appears. You can save the file there so it is easily available and all templates are in one location or you can save it to a different file location.

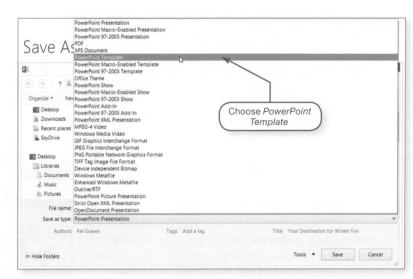

4-109 *Save As* dialog box, *Save as type* selected

6. Click **Save** and the presentation is saved as a template (*.potx* file extension).

Apply a Template

If you save a template to the default storage location, the *Custom Office Templates* folder, it appears in the list of files in that folder when you start a new presentation. You can also browse to this folder to apply the template to an existing presentation.

HOW TO: Apply a Custom Template to a New or Existing Presentation

1. Apply a custom template to a new presentation.
   - Click **File** and click **New**.
   - At the top of the thumbnails, click **Personal**.
   - Click the **Custom Office Templates** folder (Figure 4-110) to open it.
   - Select your template and click **Create**.

2. Apply a custom template to an existing presentation.
   - Open the presentation.
   - Click the **More** button [*Design* tab, *Themes* group] and click **Browse for Themes**.
   - Click the **Custom Office Templates** folder (or other folder if you have saved the template at a different location).
   - Select the template and click **Apply**.

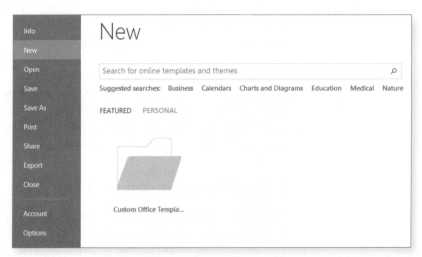

4-110 Custom Office Template and Document Themes folders

When you start a presentation using a template, save the presentation with a different name to avoid modifying your template file.

> **MORE INFO**
> Open a presentation or template when viewing a list of files or thumbnails by double-clicking the file name or thumbnail.

PAUSE & PRACTICE: POWERPOINT 4-4

For this project you create a photo album using seven pictures of snow scenes for Paradise Lakes Resort. You customize the photo album with a picture background and modify an illustrated image for a decorative effect. Once you have edited the photo album, you resave the presentation as a template and apply a custom template.

Files Needed: **SnowScenes-04 folder: Forest.jpg, IcyTrees.jpg, SnowScene1.jpg, SnowScene2.jpg, SnowyTrees.jpg, Stream.jpg, WinterLake.jpg; SnowBackground2-04**, and **Snowflake2-04**
Completed Project File Names: **[your initials] PP P4-4.pptx** and **Winter.potx**

1. Select pictures for a photo album.
   a. With PowerPoint open, click the **Insert** tab and click the **Photo Album** button to open the *Create Photo Album* dialog box.
   b. Click the **File/Disk** button, locate your student files, and open the folder *SnowScenes-04*.
   c. Press **Ctrl+A** to select all of the pictures. Click **Insert**. The file names are listed (Figure 4-111).
   d. Click **Create**. The default sizing of *Fit to slide* makes each picture as large as possible with the height the same as the slide height. By default, the slide background is black.

2. Save the presentation as **[your initials] PP P4-4**.

3. Edit the photo album to reorder slide sequence, add captions, and change slide size.
   a. Click the **Insert** tab and click the **Photo Album** list arrow. Select **Edit Photo Album** to open the *Edit Photo Album* dialog box.
   b. Click the **SnowScene1** file name to put a check in the box that precedes the slide number and name. Click the up arrow twice to move this picture to the top of the list. Deselect this picture.
   c. Select the **SnowyTrees** picture and click the up arrow one time. Deselect this picture.
   d. Select the **Stream** picture and click the **Increase Contrast** button six times and the **Increase Brightness** button six times.
   e. Under *Album Layout,* click the **Picture layout** list arrow and select **1 picture**.
   f. For *Frame Shape,* click the list arrow and select **Center Shadow Rectangle**.
   g. Under *Picture Options,* select **Captions below ALL pictures** (Figure 4-112).
   h. Click **Update**. (This completes changes to the photo album editing.)

4-111 Pictures added to photo album list

4-112 Photo album edits complete

4. The pictures now appear in a smaller size with the file names as captions below each picture. The picture and file names are grouped. The shadow you applied is not yet evident because the background is black.

5. Edit each of the captions as follows to change the text or add a space between words:

   Slide 2   The Road to PLR
   Slide 3   A Quiet Forest
   Slide 4   Icy Trees
   Slide 5   Snowy Trees
   Slide 6   New Snow
   Slide 7   Woodland Stream
   Slide 8   Winter Lake

6. Insert a picture background.
   a. On slide 1, point to the background and right-click. Click **Format Background** to open the *Format Background* pane.
   b. Select **Picture or texture fill**. Click the **File** button.
   c. From your student files, select **SnowBackground2-04**. Click **Insert**.
   d. On the *Format Background* pane, click the **Picture** button and click **Picture Color**.
   e. Click the **Recolor** button and select **Blue, Accent color 5 Dark**.
   f. Click **Picture Corrections** to access the following options:
      • Click the **Sharpen/Soften Presets** button and choose **Sharpen: 50%**.
      • Click the **Brightness/Contrast Presets** button and choose **Brightness: -20% Contrast: +20%** (Figure 4-113).
   g. Click **Apply to All**.
   h. Close the *Format Background* pane.

4-113 Adjust *Brightness* and *Contrast*

7. On the *Slide Master,* change the font for slide titles.
   a. Click the **Slide Master** button [*View* tab, *Master Views* group].
   b. On the first *Slide Master* layout, select the title placeholder and change the font to **Gill Sans Ultra Bold** [*Home* tab, *Font* group]. Click the **Shadow** button.
   c. On the *Title Slide* layout, change the title font size to **66 pt.** and choose **Align Left**.
   d. Change the subtitle placeholder font size to **40 pt.** and choose **Align Left**. Click the **Bold** and the **Shadow** buttons.
   e. Select **Gridlines** [*View* tab, *Show* group].
   f. Resize the title and subtitle placeholders and align them on the gridlines as shown in Figure 4-114.

4-114 *Slide Master, Title Slide* layout

8. On the *Title Slide* layout, insert a snowflake picture on the right and remove the picture background.
   a. Click the **Pictures** button [*Insert* tab, *Images* group] and locate your student files.
   b. Select **Snowflake2-04**. Click **Insert**.

c. Click the **Remove Background** button [*Picture Tools Format* tab, *Adjust* group].

d. Resize the selection area so the entire snowflake appears.

e. Click the **Zoom In** button on the *Status bar* several times for **200%** so you can easily see the detail.

f. Click the **Mark Areas to Remove** button [*Background Removal* tab, *Refine* group] and delete blue areas within the snowflake that should not appear (Figure 4-115).

g. Click the **Keep Changes** button [*Background Removal* tab, *Close* group].

h. Click the **Fit slide to current window** button on the *Status bar*.

i. Resize the snowflake to approximately **6.5"** square. Move the snowflake to the right.

j. Click the **Close Master View** button [*Slide Master* tab, *Close* group].

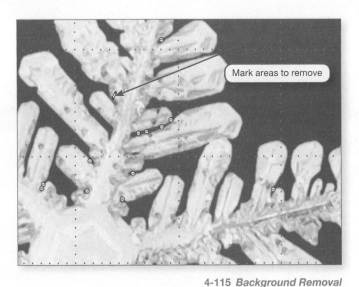

4-115 *Background Removal*

9. On slide 1, insert the following text:
   Title   Dressed in White
   Subtitle   Paradise Lakes Resort

10. Select the slide 1 thumbnail and press **Ctrl+C**. After slide 8, press **Ctrl+V**.

11. Edit the text on slide 9 as follows:
    Title   Paradise Lakes Resort
    Subtitle   1256 Raymond Drive
                   Cass Lake, MN 56633
                   218-339-5551
                   www.PLR.com

12. On slide 9, resize the placeholders as necessary so the title remains at **66 pt.** and the subtitle at **40 pt.** (Figure 4-116).

13. Deselect **Gridlines** [*View* tab, *Show* group].

14. Click the *Transitions* tab and apply the **Glitter** transition with the **Diamonds from Top** effect options. Change the *Duration* to **03.00**. Click **Apply to All**. Review the transitions.

4-116 **Completed presentation**

15. Save the presentation.

16. Resave the presentation as a template.
    a. Click the **File** tab and click **Save As**.
    b. Select **Computer** and click **Browse**.
    c. Type the file name Winter.
    d. For the *Save as type,* select **PowerPoint template**. The default folder *Custom Office Templates* will open unless you have selected a particular location (Figure 4-117).

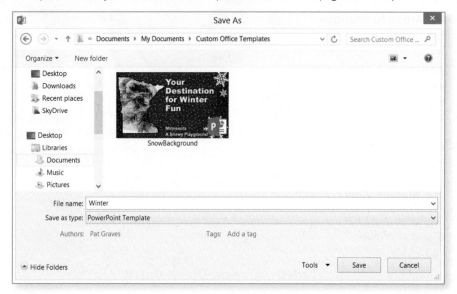

4-117 *Save As* dialog box

    e. Click **Save**.
    f. Close the template but keep PowerPoint open.

17. Apply a custom template.
    a. Click the **File** tab and click **New**.
    b. Click the **Personal** button.
    c. Click the **Custom Office Template** folder to open it.
    d. Select the **Winter** theme.
    e. Click the **Create** button. Now you have the option of replacing the pictures, adding new content, and revising the text to create a different presentation.
    f. Close the presentation without saving.

Chapter Summary

4.1 Customize and work with shapes (p. P4-203).

- Press **Shift** to preserve an object's proportions as you resize. Press **Shift** when drawing to make a rectangle square, an oval round, or lines straight.
- You can rotate or stack text in a text box.
- Use the **rotation handle** to make an object angle.
- Use the **adjustment handle** to change the dimension of a shape such as an arrowhead.
- You can change the curve of a line or shape by **editing points**.
- With the **Curve** line tool, a line is formed each time you click and the line curves as you change direction.
- With the **Scribble** line tool, a line is formed as you drag your pointer, similar to writing.
- With the **Freeform** line tool, a solid fill is applied when the end point of your line touches the beginning point.

4.2 Work with objects to align, distribute, and group; convert *SmartArt* to text or shapes (p. P4-208).

- Select multiple objects by pressing **Shift** as you click, drawing a selection rectangle, or using the *Selection* pane.
- You can align objects to each other or to the slide.
- Use **Distribute** to create even spacing between multiple slide objects.
- **Gridlines** are evenly spaced vertical and horizontal lines that aid in object alignment.
- **Guides** are one horizontal and one vertical line in the middle of the slide that you can move to check for consistent alignment.
- Adjust the stacking order of layered objects by clicking **Bring Forward, Bring to Front, Send Backward**, or **Send to Back** options.
- You can connect multiple shapes by **grouping**. Shapes within a group can be recolored or resized.
- Save grouped shapes as a picture to maintain accurate sizing and colors.
- Create a new shape by **merging** two or more overlapping shapes.
- **Connector lines** connect two or more shapes for custom diagrams.
- You can convert a *SmartArt* graphic to bulleted text or to grouped shapes.

4.3 Use a *Slide Master* to create a custom theme with new colors, fonts, and background graphics (p. P4-220).

- Background graphics added on the **Slide Master** can affect placeholder positioning on side layouts.
- You can change **Theme Colors** and **Theme Fonts** on the *Slide Master* tab and the *Design* tab.
- Changes made to *Slide Master* layouts affect all slides in the presentation that use those layouts.
- Small pictures can be used as list bullets.
- For presentation consistency, use design elements from the *Slide Master* on your *Handout Master*.

4.4 Capture screen images with a screenshot or a screen clipping (p. P4-229).

- The **Screenshot** feature copies an entire application window and displays it on a slide.
- The **Screen Clipping** feature copies the portion of an application window that you select and displays it on a slide.

4.5 Edit pictures to make photo corrections, apply artistic effects, and remove backgrounds; recolor illustrated images (p. P4-230).

- **Sharpen** is a picture correction option that makes details more evident; **Soften** is a picture correction option that creates a blending effect.
- Adjusting the **Contrast** picture correction affects the difference between a picture's lightest and darkest colors.
- **Brightness** lightens a picture by adding white and darkens a picture by adding black.
- The **Artistic Effects** gallery provides many options to apply creative effects.
- You can crop a picture to a shape from the *Shapes* gallery.
- The **Change Picture** command enables you to replace one picture with another while retaining the same size and effects.
- The **Remove Background** feature deletes portions of a picture on a slide without affecting the original picture. The areas you remove become transparent; save the picture using the *.png* format to preserve the transparent area for future use.
- Some line drawings or simple illustrations can be ungrouped and modified.

4.6 Create a photo album and adjust picture order, layout, and captions; apply and customize a photo album theme (p. P4-238).

- You can use the **Photo Album** command to prepare a presentation featuring pictures.
- After selecting pictures for a photo album, you can adjust their order and rotation as well as change contrast and brightness.
- A photo album can include text captions under pictures and text-only slides between picture slides.
- Various picture layout options are available for a photo album.
- You can apply a theme to a photo album presentation and customize it using the *Slide Master*.

4.7 Create and use a custom template (p. P4-241).

- Use the **Save As** dialog box to save a presentation as a template.
- A presentation template has the file extension of *.potx*.
- You can start a new presentation from a template, or apply a template to an existing presentation.
- When you start a presentation using a template, resave the presentation with a different name to avoid modifying your template file.

Check for Understanding

In the **Online Learning Center** for this text (www.mhhe.com/office2013inpractice), there are a variety of resources that can be used to review the concepts covered in this chapter.

The following Online Learning Resources are available in the Online Learning Center:

- Multiple choice questions
- Short answer questions
- Matching exercises

Guided Project 4-1

A presentation about current services created for the Living Good Income Tax and Accounting firm needs improvement. For this project, you rearrange background graphics *on Slide Master l*ayouts and apply an *Artistic Effect* to a photograph of company representatives. You also convert *SmartArt* graphics to shapes that you rearrange in different ways and to text that you arrange in a two-column format. [Student Learning Outcomes 4.1, 4.2, 4.3]

File Needed: ***AccountingServices-04.pptx***
Completed Project File Name: ***[your initials] PowerPoint 4-1.pptx***

Skills Covered in This Project

- Use text box columns.
- Flip and rotate a shape.
- Use adjustment handles.
- Select and distribute multiple objects.
- Ungroup objects.

- Convert a *SmartArt* graphic to text.
- Convert a *SmartArt* graphic to shapes.
- Use the *Slide Master* to change background shapes and slide layouts.
- Apply an artistic effect to a picture.

1. Open the presentation ***AccountingServices-04***. Save the presentation as ***[your initials] PowerPoint 4-1***.

2. Customize the first *Slide Master* layout.
   a. Click the **Slide Master** button [*View* tab, *Master Views*] group.
   b. Select the first layout, *Office Theme Slide Master: used by slides 1-6*.
   c. Select the rectangle below the title placeholder.
   d. Click the **Align** button [*Drawing Tools Format* tab, *Arrange* group] and select **Align Bottom**.
   e. Click the **Send Backward** list arrow [*Drawing Tools Format* tab, *Arrange* group] and choose **Send to Back** so the rectangle is behind the slide footer placeholders.
   f. Select the title placeholder and change the font to **Cooper Black** at **44 pt**. [*Home* tab, *Font* group]. Click the **Shadow** button and change the font color to **Plum, Accent 5**.
   g. Click in the first line of the bulleted text placeholder.
   h. Click the **Bullets** list arrow [*Home* tab, *Paragraph* group] and select **Bullets and Numbering** to open the *Bullets and Numbering* dialog box.
   i. Change the bullet color to **Plum, Accent 5** and click **OK** (Figure 4-118).

4-118 First *Slide Master* layout complete

3. Customize the *Title and Content* layout on the *Slide Master.*
   a. Select the *Title and Content* layout (third layout).
   b. Select the group of shapes below the title placeholder and click **Ungroup** [*Drawing Tools Format* tab, *Arrange* group].
   c. Select the green rectangle and resize it [*Drawing Tools Format* tab, *Size* group] (*Height* **1.5"** and *Width* **13.33"**).
   d. Click the **Align** button [*Drawing Tools Format* tab, *Arrange* group] and choose **Align Top**. Repeat to select **Align Center**.
   e. Click the **Send Backward** list arrow [*Drawing Tools Format* tab, *Arrange* group] and choose **Send to Back** so the rectangle is behind the title placeholder.
   f. Select the purple square and resize it (*Height* and *Width* **1.5"**).
   g. Click the **Align** button [*Drawing Tools Format* tab, *Arrange* group] and choose **Align Top**. Repeat to select **Align Left**.
   h. Resize the title placeholder on the left so it fits on the green rectangle.
   i. Select the thin rectangle (plum color) and resize it (*Height* **.1"** and *Width* **13.33"**).
   j. Center this thin rectangle at the bottom of the green title area (Figure 4-119).

4-119 *Slide Master Title and Content* layout complete

4. Customize the *Title Slide* layout on the *Slide Master.*
   a. Select the *Title Slide* layout (second layout).
   b. Select the title placeholder and click the **Shadow** button [*Home* tab, *Font* group].
   c. Select the grouped squares and resize the group (*Height* **7.5"** and *Width* **2.5"**).
   d. Click the **Align** button [*Drawing Tools Format* tab, *Arrange* group] and choose **Align Left**.
   e. Click the **Send Backward** list arrow [*Drawing Tools Format* tab, *Arrange* group] and choose **Send to Back** so the grouped squares are behind the picture.
   f. Select the picture and click the **Artistic Effects** button [*Picture Tools Format* tab, *Adjust* group] and choose the **Cutout** effect (first column, last row) as shown in Figure 4-120.

4-120 *Slide Master Title Slide* layout complete

5. Click the **Slide Master** tab and click **Close Master View**.

6. Convert a *SmartArt* graphic to shapes and rearrange shapes.
   a. On slide 2, select the *SmartArt* graphic and click the **Convert** button [*SmartArt Tools Design* tab, *Reset* group]. Choose **Convert to Shapes**.
   b. With the *SmartArt* shapes selected, click **Ungroup** [*Drawing Tools Format* tab, *Arrange* group].
   c. Select the three shapes with text and click the **Edit Shape** button [*Drawing Tools Format* tab, *Insert Shapes* group]. Choose **Change Shape** and select the **Rectangle**.

d. Resize the three shapes so the bulleted text fits on one line. Each rectangle should have a consistent height (**1.2"**) [*Drawing Tools Format* tab, *Size* group] but their width will vary.

e. Position the "Professionalism" rectangle on the left of the slide (Figure 4-121).

f. Position the "Quality" rectangle on the lower right of the slide.

g. Select the "Responsiveness" rectangle and click the **Align** button [*Drawing Tools Format* tab], and select **Align Center**.

4-121 Custom diagram

h. Select all three rectangles, click the **Align** button [*Drawing Tools Format* tab], and select **Distribute Vertically**.

i. Select the circular arrow and press **Delete**.

7. Add shapes to show the connection between concepts.
   a. On slide 2, click the *Shapes* gallery **More** button [*Home* tab, *Drawing* group] and choose the **Left-Up Arrow** (in the *Block Arrows* category).
   b. Draw an arrow and adjust the size [*Drawing Tools Format* tab, *Size* group] (*Height* and *Width* **1.5"**).
   c. Use the adjustment handle on the inside corner where the arrows join. Drag it slightly to make the arrow narrower.
   d. Click the **Rotate** button [*Drawing Tools Format* tab, *Arrange* group] and select **Rotate Right 90°**.
   e. Position this arrow between the first and second rectangles.
   f. Press **Ctrl+D** to duplicate this arrow and position the duplicated arrow between the second and third rectangles.
   g. Refer to Figure 4-121 for placement.

8. Change a *SmartArt* graphic to a different layout.

4-122 *SmartArt* graphic modified

   a. On slide 3, select the *SmartArt* graphic and click the **More** button [*SmartArt Tools Design* tab, *Layouts* group].
   b. Choose **Bending Picture Caption List** because it better fits the content.
   c. Click the **Change Colors** button [*SmartArt Tools Design* tab, *SmartArt Styles* group] and select the **Colored Fill – Accent 5** (Figure 4-122).

9. Convert a *SmartArt* graphic to text and reformat text.
   a. On slide 4, select the *SmartArt* graphic and click the **Convert** button [*SmartArt Tools Design* tab, *Reset* group] and choose **Convert to Text**. Now the text appears in a placeholder.
   b. Resize the placeholder to be **11"** wide [*Drawing Tools Format* tab, *Size* group].
   c. Select the text and increase the font size to **28 pt**. [*Home* tab, *Font* group].
   d. Click the **Bullets** button [*Home* tab, *Paragraph* group] and select **None** to remove the bullets.
   e. Click the **Columns** button [*Home* tab, *Paragraph* group] and select **Two Columns**.
   f. Resize the placeholder from the bottom until the columns are as evenly spaced as you can make them.
   g. Move the placeholder so the text is approximately centered on the slide.

10. Save and close your presentation (Figure 4-123).

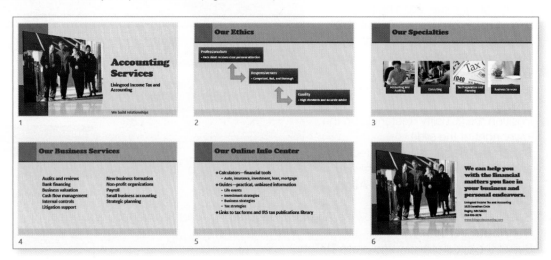

4-123 PowerPoint 4-1 completed

Guided Project 4-2

At the four colleges of the Sierra Pacific Community College District, concerts are held throughout the year by their respective music programs. In the summer, free outdoor concerts are performed by current students and alumni at each different college. For this presentation, you use the *Slide Master* to prepare an elegant background using decorative graphics and fonts for a concert of love songs from well-known movies to be held at American River College. Once your background is prepared, you modify other slide elements to blend with this new design.
[Student Learning Outcomes 4.1, 4.2, 4.3, 4.5, 4.7]

File Needed: *LoveSongs-04.pptx* and *Vine1-04.wmf, Vine2-04.wmf, Note-04.png,* and *Violin-04.jpg (from Office.com)*
Completed Project File Names: *[your initials] PowerPoint 4-2.pptx*
[your initials] PowerPoint 4-2.potx

Skills Covered in This Project

- Flip and rotate a shape.
- Align objects with *Gridlines*.
- Layer objects and adjust stacking order.
- Use the *Slide Master* to change background shapes and slide layouts.
- Use the *Slide Master* to change theme fonts and text effects.
- Apply picture bullets.
- Remove a picture background.
- Save a presentation as a template.

1. Open the presentation **LoveSongs-04**. Save the presentation as **[your initials] PowerPoint 4-2**.

2. Click the **Slide Master** button [*View* tab, *Master Views* group]. For this project you will make changes to four different layouts.

3. Align placeholders with *Gridlines;* then change size, color, and fonts.
   a. Select the first layout, *Office Theme Slide Master: used by slides 1-5*.
   b. Select **Gridlines** [*View* tab, *Show* group].
   c. Select the title placeholder and press the down arrow several times so the top of it is even with the first horizontal grid line.
   d. Change the title placeholder size [*Drawing Tools Format* tab, *Size* group] (*Height* **1"** and *Width* **13.33"**).
   e. Click the **Align** button [*Drawing Tools Format* tab, *Arrange* group] and choose **Align Center**.
   f. Change the *Shape Fill* to **Dark Red, Accent 6, Darker 50%** [*Drawing Tools Format* tab, *Shape Styles* group].
   g. Change the font to **Lucida Handwriting** [*Home* tab, *Font* group] at **44 pt**. Click **Bold** and **Shadow**.

4. Insert and rotate a decorative image
   a. On the first layout, click the **Online Pictures** button [*Insert* tab, *Images* group]. Enter the search word vine in the *Office.com Clip Art* search box and press **Enter**.
   b. Select the "Vine scrollwork decoration" (Figure 4-124). Click **Insert**. (If this image does not appear in your search, use **Vine1-04** in your student files.)
   c. Increase the decorative image height to **4.5"** and the width will automatically adjust.
   d. Click the **Rotate** button [*Picture Tools Format* tab, *Arrange* group] and choose **Flip Horizontal**. Repeat to choose **Rotate Left 90°**.
   e. Click the **Align** button [*Picture Tools Format* tab, *Arrange* group] and choose **Align Top**. Repeat to choose **Align Right** (Figure 4-125).

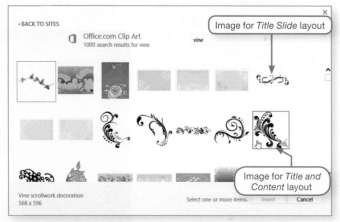

4-124 *Insert Pictures* dialog box with search results

5. Add a rectangle and adjust stacking order.
   a. Select the *Title Slide* layout (the second layout).
   b. Click the **Shapes** button, select the **Rectangle** tool [*Home* tab, *Drawing* group], and draw a rectangle (*Height* **4.5"** and *Width* **13.33"**).
   c. Click the **Align** button [*Drawing Tools Format* tab, *Arrange* group] and select **Align Top**. Repeat to select **Align Center**.
   d. Change the **Shape Fill** [*Drawing Tools Format* tab, *Shape Styles* group] to **Black**.
   e. Change the **Shape Outline** [*Drawing Tools Format* tab, *Shape Styles* group] to **No Outline**.
   f. Click the **Send Backward** list arrow [*Drawing Tools Format* tab, *Arrange* group] and select **Send to Back**.

4-125 First *Slide Master* layout completed

6. Adjust placeholders.
   a. On the *Title Slide* layout, select the title placeholder and click the **Align** button [*Drawing Tools Format* tab, *Arrange* group]. Select **Align Top**.
   b. Change the **Shape Fill** [*Drawing Tools Format* tab, *Shape Styles* group] to **No Fill**.
   c. Select the subtitle placeholder and click the **Bring Forward** list arrow [*Drawing Tools Format* tab, *Arrange* group]. Select **Bring to Front**.
   d. Press the up arrow several times until the third text line is positioned on the thin rectangle.

7. Insert a decorative image and use *Gridlines*.
   a. On the *Title Slide* layout, click the **Online Pictures** button [*Insert* tab, *Images* group] and enter the search word vine in the *Office.com Clip Art* search box. Click **Search**.
   b. Select the "Vine scrollwork decoration" identified in *Figure 4-124*. (It has the same name as the first vine image, but this one has a horizontal shape.) Click **Insert**. (If this image does not appear in your search, use **Vine2-04** in your student files.)
   c. Drag the top and side sizing handles to increase the decorative image size (approximate *Height* **2.47"** and *Width* **10.7"**).
   d. Move the vine image to the bottom of the slide. Using the gridlines to judge spacing, move the vine image to be centered on the gray area at the bottom of the slide. Because the image has extra space on the left, the handles will not appear centered (Figure 4-126).

4-126 *Title Slide* **layout completed**

8. Apply a *Picture* bullet.
   a. Select the *Title and Content* layout.
   b. Select the first two bulleted items.
   c. Click the **Bullets** list arrow [*Home* tab, *Paragraph* group] and choose **Bullets and Numbering**.
   d. Click the **Picture** button and search in the *Office.com Clip Art* search box for note.
   e. Select the "Musical note icon button" image. Click **Insert**. (If necessary, use **Note-04** in your student files.)

9. Use *Gridlines,* align placeholders, and change text.
   a. Select the *Section Header* layout.
   b. Select the *Title* placeholder and make the following changes:
      • Change its size (*Height* **3.5"** and *Width* **9.65"**).
      • Click the **Align** button [*Drawing Tools Format* tab, *Arrange* group] and select **Align Right**.
      • Move the title placeholder up so the top is even with the second horizontal gridline.
      • Change the font to **Lucida Handwriting** at **28 pt**. [*Home* tab, *Font* group].
      • Click the **Align Text** button [*Home* tab, *Paragraph* group] and select **Align Middle**.
   c. Select the *Subtitle* placeholder and make the following changes:
      • Change the font to **Lucida Handwriting** at **28 pt**. [*Home* tab, *Font* group]. Click **Bold** and **Shadow**.
      • Click the **Align Text** button [*Home* tab, *Paragraph* group] and select **Align Middle**.
      • Resize the subtitle placeholder and align it on the *Gridlines* as shown in Figure 4-127.

    d. Click the **Rectangle** tool [*Home* tab, *Drawing* group] and draw a rectangle (*Height* **.3"** and *Width* **13.33"**).

- Click the **Align** button [*Drawing Tools Format* tab, *Arrange* group] and select **Align Center**.
- Change the **Shape Fill** [*Drawing Tools Format* tab, *Shape Styles* group] to **Black**. Repeat to change the **Shape Outline** to **No Outline**.
- Move this shape to fit above the title placeholder.

4-127 *Section Header* layout completed

10. Copy an image from one layout and paste it on another layout.
    a. On the first layout, select the vine shape and press **Ctrl+C**.
    b. Select the *Section Header* layout. Press **Ctrl+V**.
    c. Using the rotation handle, rotate the image and position it on the lower left.

11. Click the **Slide Master** tab and click the **Close Master View** button.

12. Slides 1 and 2 are complete with the changes made to the *Slide Master*. Notice that the slide 2 list now shows the round note picture bullets.

13. On slide 3, select the *SmartArt* graphic. Click the **Change Colors** button [*SmartArt Tools Design* tab, *SmartArt Styles* group] and select **Dark 2 Fill**.

14. Modify a table.
    a. On slide 4, select the table and click the **More** button [*Table Tools Design* tab, *Table Styles* group]. Select **Medium Style 2**.
    b. Select the table text and change the font to **Lucida Handwriting** [*Home* tab, *Font* group].
    c. Resize the table slightly to align with the *Gridlines* as shown in Figure 4-128.

4-128 Table aligned on *gridlines*

15. Deselect the **Gridlines** [*View* tab, *Show* group].

16. Insert and align a picture
    a. With slide 4 selected, create a new slide with the **Title Only** layout.
    b. On slide 5, type the slide title Enjoy the Show!

c. Click the **Online Pictures** button [*Insert* tab, *Images* group] and search *Office.com Clip Art* using the search word violin.

d. Select the violin picture (the name is "music, musical instruments, photographs, violins") shown in Figure 4-129. Click **Insert**. (If necessary, use **Violin-04** in your student files.)

e. Resize the violin (*Height* **5.75"** and *Width* automatically changes to **3.83"**).

f. Click the **Align** button [*Picture Tools Format* tab, *Arrange* group] and choose **Align Left**. Repeat to choose **Align Bottom**.

4-129 Picture with background removed

17. Remove the picture background.

a. On slide 5, select the picture.

b. Click the **Remove Background** button [*Picture Tools Format* tab, *Adjust* group].

c. Increase the selection area size by dragging the handles to the edge of the photograph so the violin retains its original size.

d. Click the **Mark Areas to Keep** button and click on the violin areas until they appear.

e. Click the **Mark Areas to Remove** button and click the small area on the left of the violin until it is removed.

f. Click **Keep Changes**.

18. Review all slides and make adjustments if necessary.

19. Save the presentation (Figure 4-130).

20. Resave the presentation as a template and close the template file.

4-130 PowerPoint 4-2 completed

Guided Project 4-3

Creative Gardens and Landscaping maintains a woodlands area to showcase natural and seasonal plantings. In the spring, plantings of tulips and other spring flowers are featured. This woodlands area is open to the public daily. In this project, you create a photo album using pictures of tulips to illustrate the annual Tulip Extravaganza.
[Student Learning Outcomes 4.1, 4.3, 4.5, 4.6, 4.7]

Files Needed: *TulipPictures-04Folder:CandyCane.jpg*, *CGL-Logo.png*, *DynastyPink.jpg*, *GardenParty.jpg*, *PinkWhite.jpg*, *RedRhapsody.jpg*, *SunshineFire.jpg*, *Tulip1.jpg*, *Tulip2.jpg*, and *Watermelon.jpg*
Completed Project File Names: *[your initials] PowerPoint 4-3.pptx* and *[your initials] PowerPoint 4-3.potx*

Skills Covered in This Project

- Rotate a picture.
- Use the *Slide Master* to add a background shape and adjust placeholders.
- Use the *Slide Master* to change theme fonts and text effects.
- Remove a picture background.
- Select pictures to create a photo album.
- Edit photo album settings to change order and add captions.
- Save a presentation as a template.

1. Open PowerPoint.
2. Select pictures for a photo album.
   a. Click the **Insert** tab and click **Photo Album**.
   b. Click the **File/Disk** button, locate your student files, and open the folder *TulipPictures-04*.
   c. Press **Ctrl+A** to select all of the pictures and click **Insert**.
3. Adjust picture order and select photo album options.
   a. On the *Photo Album* dialog box, select the **Tulip1, Tulip2,** and **CGL-Logo** picture names and click the **Remove** button.
   b. Select the **SunshineFire** picture name and click the up arrow four times until it is the second picture. Deselect this picture.
   c. Select the **RedRhapsody** picture name and click the down arrow once.
   d. Under *Album Layout,* click the **Picture layout** list arrow and select **1 picture**.
   e. For *Frame Shape,* click the list arrow and select **Center Shadow Rectangle**.
   f. Under *Picture Options,* select **Captions below ALL pictures** (Figure 4-131). Click **Create**.
   g. This completes the photo album setup. If you need to recheck your settings, select **Edit Photo Album** to make changes.

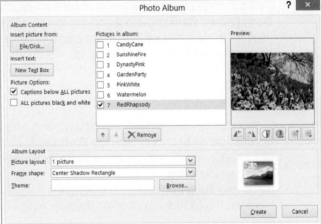

4-131 Picture names in album and options selected

4. The pictures now appear with the file names as captions below each picture. The picture and file names are grouped.

5. Save the presentation as *[your initials] **PowerPoint 4-3***.

6. Adjust picture captions.
   a. For each picture caption, click the **Align Right** button [*Home* tab, *Paragraph* group].
   b. Revise each of the picture captions as follows:
      Slide 2   Candy Cane
      Slide 3   Sunshine and Fire
      Slide 4   Dynasty Pink
      Slide 5   Garden Party
      Slide 6   Purity and Romance
      Slide 7   Watermelon
      Slide 8   Red Rhapsody

7. Click the **Slide Master** button [*View* tab, *Master Views* group].

8. Adjust the *Slide Master* background and text effects.
   a. Select the first layout, *Office Theme Slide Master: used by slides 1-8,* to adjust the placeholders and fonts.
   b. Click the **Colors** button [*Slide Master* tab, *Background* group] and select the **Paper** theme colors.
   c. Click the **Background Styles** button [*Slide Master* tab, *Background* group] and select **Style 3**.
   d. Select the title placeholder, change the font to **Pristina** [*Home* tab, *Font* group]. Click **Bold** and **Shadow**.
   e. Select both the title and body text placeholders and change the font color to **Light Yellow, Text 2** [*Home* tab, *Font* group].

9. Add a shape and adjust placeholder text.
   a. On the *Title Slide* layout, click the **Rectangle** tool [*Home* tab, *Drawing* group] and draw a rectangle (*Height* **2"** and *Width* **13.33"**).
   b. Click the **Align** button [*Drawing Tools Format* tab, *Arrange* group] and select **Align Center**.
   c. Change the **Shape Fill** [*Drawing Tools Format* tab, *Shape Styles* group] to **Light Yellow, Text 2**.
   d. Change the **Shape Outline** [*Drawing Tools Format* tab, *Shape Styles* group] to **No Outline**.
   e. Click the **Send Backward** list arrow [*Drawing Tools Format* tab, *Arrange* group] and select **Send to Back**. Arrange the rectangle evenly behind the title placeholder.
   f. Select the title placeholder and change the font color to **Dark Green, Background 2** and the font size to **66 pt**. [*Home* tab, *Font* group]. Resize the placeholder to fit the text. Click the **Align Left** button [*Home* tab, *Paragraph* group].
   g. Move the subtitle down slightly and increase the font size to **32 pt**. Click the **Align Right** button [*Home* tab, *Paragraph* group].

4-132 Background removed

10. Insert two pictures and remove the background on each.
    a. On the *Title Slide* layout, click the **Pictures** button [*Insert* tab, *Images* group] and open the ***TulipPictures-04*** folder in your student files.
    b. Select the **Tulip1** picture and click **Insert**.
    c. Increase the picture height to **6"** [*Picture Tools Format* tab, *Size* group].
    d. Click the **Remove Background** button [*Picture Tools Format* tab, *Adjust* group].
    e. Adjust the selection area size by dragging the handles to fit the single tulip and the stem only (Figure 4-132).

f. Click the **Mark Areas to Keep** button and click on the tips of the petals and the stem.

g. Click **Keep Changes**.

h. Click the **Crop** button [*Picture Tools Format* tab, *Size* group] and resize the picture area to better fit the tulip. Click the **Crop** button again.

i. Position the **Tulip1** picture on the left side of the yellow rectangle. Move the title placeholder near the **Tulip1** picture.

j. Repeat this process to insert the **Tulip2** picture and remove the background. No size change is needed. Align the **Tulip2** picture on the right.

11. Insert a logo.
    a. On the *Title Slide* layout, resize the subtitle placeholder to fit the text and move it down.

    b. Click the **Pictures** button [*Insert* tab, *Images* group] and locate your student files.

    c. Select **CGL-Logo**. Click **Insert**.

    d. Position the logo below the title placeholder (Figure 4-133).

4-133 *Slide Master Title Slide* layout completed

12. Copy, paste, and arrange pictures.
    a. On the *Title Slide* layout, select the **Tulip1** image and press **Ctrl+C**.

    b. Select the **Blank Slide** layout and press **Ctrl+V**.

    c. Move the tulip to the lower left of the slide, extending slightly off the slide.

    d. Press **Ctrl+D** and move the second tulip to the upper right. Rotate this tulip and make it extend slightly off the slide (Figure 4-134).

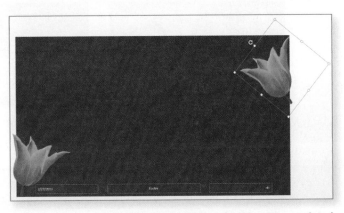

4-134 *Slide Master Blank Slide* layout completed

13. Click the **Slide Master** tab and click the **Close Master View** button.

14. Edit text.
    a. On slide 1, select the title placeholder and type the title Tulip Extravaganza.
    b. Change the subtitle text to Tour Our Woodland Gardens.

15. Copy and paste a slide; then edit text.
    a. Select slide 1 and press **Ctrl+C**.
    b. After slide 8, press **Ctrl+V**.
    c. On slide 9, change the subtitle font size to **28 pt**. [*Home* tab, *Font* group] and click **Align Left** [*Home* tab, *Paragraph* group]. Increase the placeholder size as needed and edit the subtitle text as follows:

    Subtitle: 400 Powell Avenue
                 Brentwood, TN 38522
                 615-792-8833

16. Click the **Transitions** tab and apply the **Wind** transition with the **Right** effect options. Click **Apply to All**. Review the transitions.

17. Save the presentation (Figure 4-135).

18. Resave the presentation as a template and close the template.

4-135 PowerPoint 4-3 completed

Independent Project 4-4

At Wilson Home Entertainment Systems, employees work with homeowners to design home theater spaces. Subcontractors are used if home remodeling is required. However, the Wilson employees help with paint color and carpet selections that will work well with large-screen projected images. They also plan storage space for all of the necessary equipment. Wilson can provide high-end cabinetry and durable seating to fit the room design and family needs.

For this project you create a seating plan for a proposed home theater, remove a picture background to feature an equipment rack, and prepare a creative title slide design. You also create a new Wilson logo using the *Merge* feature.

[Student Learning Outcomes 4.1, 4.2, 4.3, 4.5]

Files Needed: ***HomeTheater-04.pptx***, ***EquipmentRack-04.jpg***, and ***Family-04.jpg***
Completed Project File Names: ***[your initials] PowerPoint 4-4.pptx*** and ***WHESLogo2.png***

Skills Covered in This Project

- Rotate a shape.
- Align multiple objects.
- Layer objects and adjust stacking order.
- Group, ungroup, and regroup objects.
- Merge shapes.

- Save grouped shapes as a picture.
- Use the *Slide Master* to add background shapes.
- Remove a picture background.
- Ungroup an illustration and recolor.

---

1. Open the presentation *HomeTheater-04*. Save the presentation as *[your initials] PowerPoint 4-4*.

2. Add background shapes on a *Slide Master* layout.
   a. Click the **Slide Master** button and select the **Title and Content** layout (third).
   b. Draw a rectangle (*Height* **1.5"** and *Width* **13.33"**). Align it with the slide top and center. Change the *Shape Fill* to **Black** with no outline.
   c. Click the **Send Backward** button and select **Send to Back** so this rectangle is behind the title placeholder.
   d. Draw a horizontal line (*Width* **13.33"**). Change the *Shape Outline* to standard **Dark Red** and *Weight* to **6 pt**. Center this line on the slide and position it at the bottom of the black rectangle.
   e. Close *Slide Master* view.

3. Add, layer, ungroup, and arrange shapes.
   a. On slide 7, complete a room layout with theater seating for nine people.
   b. Draw a rectangle (*Height* **6"** and *Width* **10"**) that represents the size of the room.
   c. Change the **Shape Fill** to **Tan, Accent 2, Lighter 40%**.
   d. Click the **Send Backward** list arrow and select **Send to Back**. Align this rectangle with the slide bottom and slide center.
   e. Three types of seating (chair, sofa, and theater seats) are shown with cup holders on the arms. These illustrations are grouped separately with the three groups combined in a larger group. Ungroup the combined group.
   f. Select the chair (one seat with a cup holder on both sides). Duplicate the chair.

4. Add, layer, rotate, group, and position shapes.
   a. On slide 7, prepare a rectangle to represent a raised platform for the back row of seating.
   b. Draw a rectangle (*Height* **1.5"** and *Width* **6"**), position it near the bottom, and center it in the room area.
   c. Change the *Shape Fill* to **Gray-50%, Accent 1, Darker 25%**.
   d. Select the row of four seats and click the **Bring Forward** button. Position this group of seats on the "raised platform."
   e. Adjust the seating objects with the chairs rotated as shown in Figure 4-136.
   f. Group the seating arrangement, including the platform.

5. Add, duplicate, and position shapes.
   a. On slide 7, draw a thin rectangle (*Height* **.1"** and *Width* **3.6"**) representing the projection screen. Change the *Shape Fill* to **White** and position it at the top of the room area.

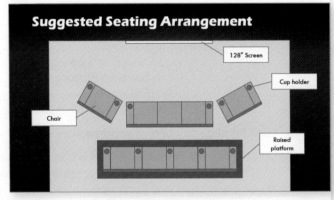

4-136 Room arrangement with theater seating

b. Position the cup holder callout box on the right to point to the chair cup holder.

c. Duplicate this callout three times and edit the text for the 128" Screen, Chair, and the Raised Platform. Adjust the callout position and where the line points to label these objects.

6. Insert a picture and remove the background.
   a. On slide 6, insert the ***EquipmentRack-04*** picture from your student files.
   b. Select the picture and click the **Remove Background** button [*Picture Tools Format* tab]. Resize the selection area to fit the black equipment rack.
   c. Use the **Mark Areas to Remove** button to delete the area around the equipment rack. Click **Keep Changes**.
   d. Crop the picture to remove blank space. Apply a **Simple Frame, White** picture style so the image can be seen on the black background. Change the height to **6.5"** and position the rack on the right side of the slide.

7. Draw, layer, merge, and recolor shapes.
   a. On slide 8, text is grouped for the logo. Increase your **Zoom** to about **150%** so you can work in detail.
   b. Select the **Flow Chart: Merge** shape (in the *Flowchart* category) and draw a triangle (*Height* and *Width* **1.5"**).
   c. Draw a rectangle shape (*Height* **.5"** and *Width* **2.8"**). Overlap these shapes. The outline around the rectangle shape is evident.
   d. Select the triangle and the rectangle and click **Send Backward**. Position the shapes behind the grouped text as shown in Figure 4-137.
   e. With the triangle and rectangle selected (not the text), click the **Merge Shape** button [*Drawing Tools Format* tab, *Insert Shape* group] and select **Union**.
   f. Now change the *Shape Fill* to the standard **Dark Red**. Change the *Shape Outline* to **Black**. Compare how the line now appears around the single merged shape rather than around two separate shapes (see Figure 4-137).

4-137 Logo shapes behind text

   g. Draw another rectangle shape (*Height* **.5"** and *Width* **2.8"**). Change the *Shape Fill* to **Black** with **No Outline**.
   h. Click **Send to Back**. Check alignment and make adjustments if needed (Figure 4-138).
   i. Select all shapes and text in the logo and group.

8. Save the grouped logo as a picture.
   a. Point to any handle on the grouped logo and right-click. Choose **Save as Picture**.
   b. Name the logo ***WHESLogo2***. Save using the *png* file type. Click **Save**.

4-138 Shapes merged and logo complete

9. Click **Fit slide to current window** button.

10. Ungroup and recolor an illustrated image; then layer images and text for a concluding slide.
    a. On slide 9, resize the theater screen image (*Height* **6.5"** and *Width* **9.35"**).
    b. Ungroup the image to convert it to a drawing object. Ungroup it again.
    c. Select the shapes on the bottom half of the image that represent rows of seats and delete them.
    d. Select all other lines that are around the center screen and change them to **Black**.
    e. Change the color of the three background shapes to these three colors going from left to right: **Gray – 50%, Accent 1**, **Gray – 25%, Text 2**, and **Tan, Accent 3**.

f. Regroup all of the theater screen shapes.

g. Resize the movies image (*Height* and *Width* **1.5"**). Click **Bring Forward** and then select **Bring to Front**.

h. Position the movies image on the theater screen.

i. Select the text, "Family Night," click **Bring Forward**, and then select **Bring to Front**. Move it to the bottom of the theater image (Figure 4-139).

11. Insert a picture, remove a background, and apply an artistic effect.

a. On slide 1, right-click and select **Format Background** to open the *Format Background* pane. Select **Picture or texture fill** and click the **File** button. Locate your student files, choose *Family-04*, and click **Insert**.

b. Click the **Pictures** button [*Insert* tab, *Images* group] and select the **Family-04** again. Click **Insert** and the pane on the right changes to the *Format Picture* pane.

c. Resize this picture to fit the height of the slide (**7.5"**).

d. Click the **Crop** button and crop the picture on all four sides as shown in Figure 4-140. Click **Crop**.

e. Resize the picture again until it fits over the background image and aligns with that image.

f. Click **Remove Background** and adjust the selection area to fit the family. Mark areas to keep or remove as needed (Figure 4-141). Click **Keep Changes**.

g. Click an area of the background to open the *Format Background* pane. Click the **Effects** button. Click the **Artistic Effects** list arrow and choose the **Line Drawing** effect (first row, last effect). Change the **Pencil Size** to **10** (Figure 4-142). Now the background has a decorative effect while the family remains in focus.

h. Insert the *WHESLogo2* you saved and position it on the lower right.

i. Close the *Format Background* pane.

12. Delete slide 8 since the company logo is complete and you have saved the logo on this slide.

13. Check the slides that you changed to be sure spacing is appropriate.

14. Select the **Fall Over** transition and apply it to all slides.

4-139 Illustrated image recolored

4-140 Inserted family picture cropped

4-141 Background removed on family picture

4-142 Title slide completed

15. Save and close the presentation (Figure 4-143).

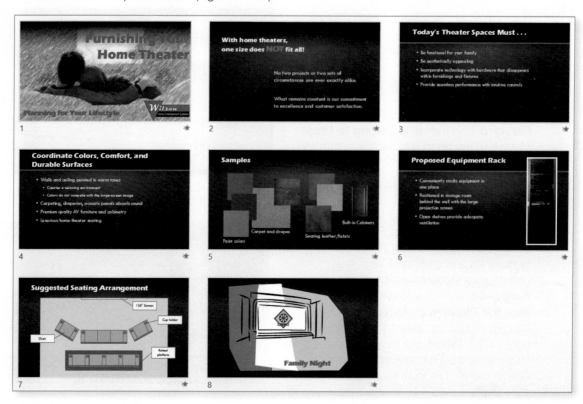

Independent Project 4-5

Life's Animal Shelter rescues dogs and cats, provides medical services, and finds both foster care and forever homes. For this project, you prepare a presentation to be shown at the shelter and at other local sites to promote pet adoption.
[Student Learning Outcomes 4.1, 4.2, 4.3, 4.4, 4.5, 4.7]

Files Needed: **PetAdoption-04.pptx**, **PawPrintBackground-04.jpg**, **PawPrint-04.png**, **Adoption Application-04.docx**, and **Gabriel-04.jpg**
Completed Project File Names: **[your initials] PowerPoint 4-5.pptx** and **[your initials] PowerPoint 4-5.potx**

Skills Covered in This Project

- Change text direction.
- Use adjustment handles.
- Work with layered objects.
- Convert a *SmartArt* graphic to text.
- Use the *Slide Master* to create a custom theme with a tiled background picture and adjusted layouts.

- Apply a picture bullet.
- Crop a picture to a shape.
- Apply artistic effects to a picture.
- Save a presentation as a template.

1. Open the presentation **PetAdoption-04**. Save the presentation as **[your initials] PowerPoint 4-5**.

2. Insert a tiled background picture on the first *Slide Master* layout.
   a. Click the **Slide Master** button to open *Slide Master* view and select the first *Slide Master* layout.
   b. Select the tan rectangle and delete it. Repeat to delete the shape that has a thin black outline with no fill.
   c. Change the title placeholder font to **Forte** and the bulleted text placeholder to **Century Gothic**.
   d. On the *Slide Master* tab, click **Background Styles** and select **Format Background** to open the *Format Background* pane.
   e. Select **Picture or texture fill**. Click the **File** button, locate your student files, and select **PawPrintBackground-04**. Click **Insert**.
   f. On the *Format Background* pane, check **Tile picture as texture** and change the **Scale X** and **Scale Y** percentages to **30%**. Click **Apply to All** (Figure 4-144).

4-144 Background picture tiled and scaled to 30%

4-145 *Slide Master Title and Content* layout complete

3. Add and copy a shape; then apply a picture bullet.
   a. Select the *Title and Content* layout and draw a rectangle.
   b. Change rectangle fill to **White** and increase the size (*Height* **6.7"** and *Width* **11.3"**). Click **Send to Back** and align this shape on the slide bottom and right. Press **Ctrl+C** to copy the rectangle.
   c. Select the first line of text in the bulleted text placeholder and make it bold.
   d. Click the **Bullets** list arrow and select **Bullets and Numbering**. Change the *Size* to **150%** of text. Click the **Picture** button and browse to your student files. Select **PawPrint-04** and click **Insert**.
   e. Resize both placeholders and move them to the right to fit on the white rectangle (Figure 4-145).

4. Delete three *Slide Master* layouts that you are not using in this presentation: *Section Header Layout, Two Content Layout,* and *Comparison Layout* (Figure 4-146).

5. Paste a shape and change text direction.
   a. Select the *Title Only* layout and press **Ctrl+V** to paste the white rectangle.
   b. Click **Send to Back** and align the rectangle on the slide bottom and right.
   c. Select the title placeholder. Click the **Text Direction** button [*Home* tab], and choose **Rotate all text 270°**. Resize the placeholder (*Height* **6.5"** and *Width* **1.5"**) and move the placeholder to the left side of the white rectangle.

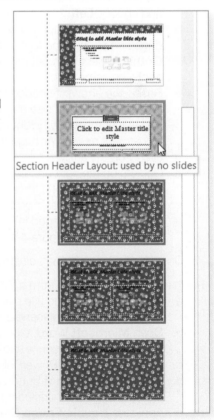

4-146 Unused *Slide Master* layouts to delete

6. Modify text; then resize and reposition placeholders.
   a. Select the *Title Slide* layout.
   b. Change the title slide placeholder font to **Forte** and **Align Left**. Change the subtitle font size to **28 pt., Bold**, and **Align Left**.
   c. Delete all layout objects except the title, subtitle, and white rectangle.
   d. Resize the white rectangle (*Height* **4.5"** and *Width* **10.5"**).
   e. Resize the title and subtitle placeholders and position them as shown on Figure 4-147.

4-147 *Slide Master Title Slide* **layout completed**

7. All changes to the *Slide Master* are complete. Close *Slide Master* view.

8. Close the *Format Background* pane.

9. On slide 1, click the **Reset** button [*Home* tab, *Slides* group].

10. On slide 2, move the *SmartArt* graphic down slightly. Change the text to **Century Gothic**.

11. On slide 3, convert the *SmartArt* graphic to a list using the **Convert** button on the *SmartArt Tools Design* tab.

12. Change fonts, shape size, and adjust alignment.
    a. On slide 4, select the title placeholder, click the **Align Text** button [*Home* tab, *Paragraph* group], and choose **Left**.
    b. Select both paragraphs describing the dogs and change the font to **Century Gothic**. Select both pet names and apply the same font.
    c. Resize the arrows if needed to fit the text. Keep the point size the same and adjust the arrow height using the adjustment handle. Arrange the text evenly on the arrows.
    d. Objects on the right are aligned with the slide on the right. Other objects are aligned with each other on the left.
    e. Pet names are arranged in varied ways over the pictures (Figure 4-148).

4-148 **Pet pictures and text arrangement**

13. On slides 5–7, repeat the adjustments you made to slide 4 in the previous step.

14. Insert a screen clipping from a Word document.
    a. On slide 8, adjust the title placeholder size so the text fits on three lines and position it on the right. Delete the content placeholder.
    b. Open **Microsoft Word**. Open the ***AdoptionApplication-04*** for Life's Animal Shelter. Only the first page of the application is shown in this file. Adjust the *View* size to **100%**.
    c. Return to slide 8 in PowerPoint.
    d. Click the **Screenshot** button [*Insert* tab] and select **Screen Clipping**. Capture the top portion of this application form including the contact information.
    e. Apply the **Double Frame Black** picture style. For *Picture Effects,* choose **3-D Rotation** and select the **Perspective Right** effect (Figure 4-149).

15. Crop a picture to a shape.
    a. On slide 9, select the picture. Click **Crop** and **Crop To Shape**. Choose the **Heart** shape.
    b. Apply a picture border with the color **Dark Red** and make the border weight **6 pt.** (Figure 4-150).

16. On slide 9, move the slide title below other text.

17. Change a picture and apply an artistic effect.
    a. On slide 1, select the picture and click the **Change Pictures** button. Locate your student files and select the picture *Gabriel-04*. Click **Insert**.
    b. Resize the width to **7.5"** and click **Align Top** and **Align Right**.
    c. Stretch the picture on the bottom so it ends evenly with the white rectangle.
    d. Click the **Artistic Effects** button and choose **Pencil Sketch** (Figure 4-151).

18. Save the presentation.

19. Resave the presentation as a template and close the template.

4-149 *Screen* Clipping inserted

4-150 Picture cropped to a shape

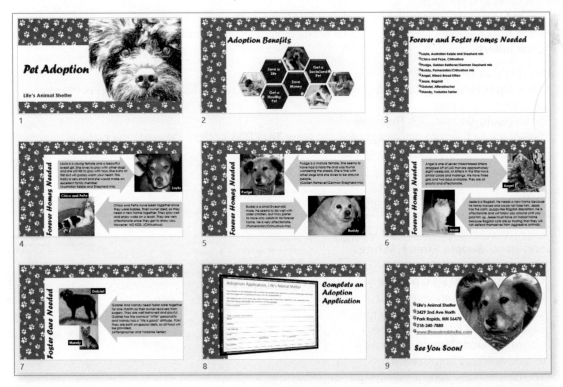

4-151 **PowerPoint 4-5 completed**

Independent Project 4-6

At Placer Hills Real Estate, a screen is set up in the lobby displaying news, available property listings, and promotional events for visitors. This project provides home pictures and location addresses for the four homes featured in an upcoming open house. You create a photo album presentation to be shown in the office lobby featuring these images.
[Student Learning Outcomes 4.2, 4.3, 4.6, 4.7]

Files Needed: *RealEstatePictures-04 folder: House1-04.jpg*, *House2-04.jpg*, *House3-04.jpg*, *House4-04.jpg*, *OpenHouse-04.jpg*, *PlacerHillsSold-04.jpg*, and *Sold-04.jpg*; and *PHRELogo-04.png*
Completed Project File Names: *[your initials] PowerPoint 4-6.pptx* and *[your initials] PowerPoint 4-6.potx*

Skills Covered in This Project

- Layer objects and adjust stacking order.
- Use the *Slide Master* to change background shapes and slide layouts.
- Select pictures to create a photo album.
- Edit photo album settings to change order, add captions, and insert text boxes on slides.
- Use the *Slide Master* to apply and customize a design theme.
- Save a presentation as a template.

1. With PowerPoint open, click the **Photo Album** button on the *Insert* tab.

2. Add pictures to a photo album.
   a. On the *Photo Album* dialog box, click the **File/Disk** button.
   b. Locate your student files and select all seven pictures in the *RealEstatePictures-04* folder. Click **Insert**.

3. Select photo album options.
   a. Click **OpenHouse-04** to put a check before the picture name. Move it to the top of the list. Deselect the picture.
   b. Select **Sold-04** and click **Remove**.
   c. Select the first picture name and click the **New Text Box** button. Deselect the picture.
   d. Repeat to add a text box following all pictures in the album.
   e. Under *Album Layout,* click the **Picture layout** list arrow and select **2 pictures**.
   f. For *Frame shape,* click the list arrow and select **Simple Frame, White**.
   g. Under *Picture Options,* select **Captions below ALL pictures**.
   h. Click the first picture again and click the **New Text Box** button. Select this text box and move it above the **OpenHouse-04** picture (Figure 4-152). Click **Create**.
   i. The pictures now appear on the right of each slide with a text box on the left.

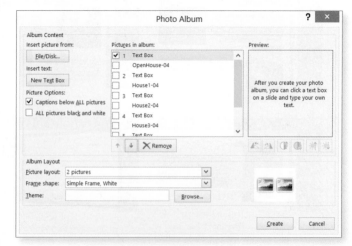

4-152 *Photo Album* pictures and options selected

4. Save the presentation as *[your initials] PowerPoint 4-6.*

5. Apply the **Frame** theme and select the **Variant** on the right with the dark brown and gray colors.

6. Customize a *Slide Master* layout with shapes, a logo, and font changes.
   a. Click the **Slide Master** button and select the first *Slide Master* layout.
   b. Click the **Fonts** button and choose the **Trebuchet MS** font pair.
   c. Select the rectangle on the right, resize it (*Height* **0.83"** and *Width* **13.33"**), and reposition it to align at the top and center of the slide. Change the *Shape Fill* to **Brown, Background 2, Darker 50%** with no outline.
   d. Select the rectangle behind the title text on the left. Change the *Shape Fill* to **Brown, Accent 4, Lighter 40%** with no outline. Select the title placeholder and change the font color to **Black**.
   e. Draw a rectangle to fit below the title placeholder. Change the *Shape Fill* to **Brown, Accent 4, Lighter 80%** with no outline.
   f. Insert the ***PHRELogo-04*** from your student files. Make the logo slightly smaller and position it on the new rectangle (Figure 4-153).

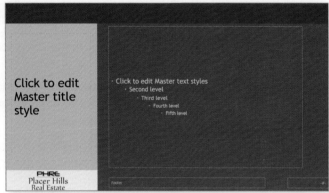

4-153 First *Slide Master* layout completed

7. Adjust shapes and fonts.
   a. Select the *Title Slide* layout.
   b. Select the large rectangle on the left. Change the *Shape Fill* to **Brown, Accent 4, Lighter 40%** with no outline.
   c. Select the rectangle on the right. Change the *Shape Fill* to **Brown, Background 2, Darker 50%** with no outline.
   d. Select the title placeholder. Change the font color to **Brown, Background 2, Darker 50%** and click **Bold** and **Shadow**. Change the title font size to **60 pt**. Resize the title placeholder for a width of **3.5"** and center it horizontally on the rectangle.
   e. Select the subtitle placeholder. Change the font color to **Gold, Accent 3, Darker 50%** and click **Bold**. Increase the font size to **28 pt**.

8. Close the *Slide Master* tab.

9. Copy a picture and paste it on a different slide.
   a. On slide 2, copy the picture.
   b. On slide 1, paste the picture.
   c. Delete slide 2.

10. Adjust text.
    a. For the slide 1 title, type Open House.
    b. For the subtitle, type Sunday 1-4 p.m.
    c. Insert a text box and type Placer Hills Real Estate. Change the font size to **32 pt.** and the font color to **Brown, Background 2**.
    d. Delete the caption below the picture.
    e. Position the picture and text as shown in Figure 4-154.

4-154 Title slide completed

11. Remove a placeholder and adjust text.
    a. On slide 2 (House1-04), delete the *Text Box* placeholder and change the *Slide Layout* to **Title Only**. (The text box served the purpose of controlling the size and spacing for two objects on the slide; using the *Title Only* layout changes the text color and displays the background shapes.)
    b. Increase the caption font size to **28 pt**.
    c. Move the caption down slightly so that it does not overlap the picture.

12. Repeat this process on slides 3–5 to prepare the slides for text.

13. On slides 2–5, insert text.
    a. Replace the caption (file name) under each picture with the city name and adjust the caption alignment.
    b. Type the following listing information in the title placeholder on the left. (Resize this placeholder, if necessary, so each street address fits on one line.)

Slide	Caption	Listing Information
2	Lincoln (Align Right)	615 Silver Hill Court 1,600 sq ft 3 br, 2 ba $339,600
3	Roseville (Align Left)	1720 Grey Owl Circle 2,182 sq ft 3 br, 2 ba $389,900
4	Roseville (Align Right)	1917 Oak Crest Dr. 3397 sq ft 4 br, 3 ba $368,505
5	Auburn (Align Left)	863 Holly Hills Drive 2,876 sq ft 3 br, 2 ba $349,900

14. Insert, color, size, and layer a shape.
    a. On slide 2, insert a diamond shape and adjust its position with the picture.
    b. Apply a *Shape Fill* of **Brown, Accent 4, Lighter 80%** and no outline.
    c. Adjust the size (*Height* and *Width* **7"**).
    d. Click **Send to Back**.
    e. Adjust the shape and picture positions as shown in Figure 4-155 to feature the city name.

15. Add and position a shape on multiple slides.
    a. Copy the diamond shape on slide 2 and paste it on slides 3–5.
    b. On each slide, click **Send to Back**.
    c. The city names alternate between left and right alignment below each picture. Position the diamond so it fits behind the picture on the other side.

4-155 Slide 2 completed

16. Reposition a picture.
    a. On slide 6, increase the picture size (*Width* approximately **9"**).
    b. Delete the text box.
    c. Delete the caption text (not the caption placeholder) below the picture.
    d. Center the picture on the slide.

17. Apply an automatic transition and make the presentation loop.
    a. On the *Transitions* tab, select the **Gallery** transition.
    b. Deselect **On Mouse Click**. For *After,* type 00:03.00. Click **Apply To All**.
    c. On the *Slide Show* tab, click the **Set Up Slide Show** button and select **Browsed at a kiosk (full screen)** so the presentation will loop continuously.
    d. Select **Show all slides** and select the appropriate monitor. Click **OK**.

18. Save the presentation (Figure 4-156).

19. Resave the presentation as a template and close the template.

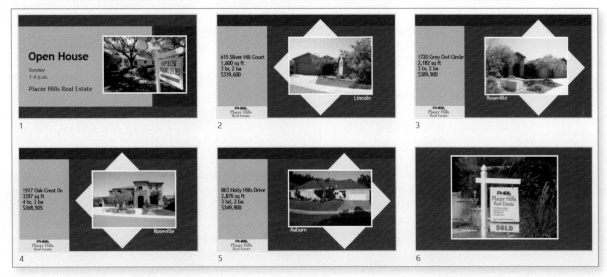

4-156 PowerPoint 4-6 completed

Improve It Project 4-7

At Courtyard Medical Plaza, nurse practitioners frequently provide educational seminars for patients as part of the CMP Women's Wellness Program. In this presentation, you enhance a presentation about three important fitness requirements for women. You make the title slide more interesting with additional graphics and customized illustrations and you add two pictures, adjust contrast and brightness, and remove backgrounds.
[Student Learning Outcomes 4.1, 4.2, 4.5]

Files Needed: ***BalancedFitness-04.pptx, Fitness1-04.jpg***, and ***Fitness2-04.jpg***
Completed Project File Name: ***[your initials] PowerPoint 4-7.pptx***

Skills Covered in This Project

- Edit shape points.
- Align and distribute multiple objects.
- Layer objects and adjust stacking order.
- Make sharpen, contrast, and brightness picture corrections.

- Remove a picture background
- Group, ungroup, and regroup.

---

1. Open the presentation *BalancedFitness-04*. Save the presentation as *[your initials] PowerPoint 4-7*.

2. Ungroup, modify, regroup, duplicate, and align an illustrated image.
   a. On slide 1, select the heart rate image.
   b. Increase your **Zoom** to about **150%** so you can work in detail.
   c. Click **Ungroup** to change this image to a drawing object; click **Ungroup** again so you can work with individual parts.
   d. Delete all shapes in the object except the three white shapes. **Regroup** them.
   e. Click the **Fit slide to current window** button so you can see the entire slide again.
   f. Increase the object size (*Height* **3.5"** and *Width* **4.64"**).
   g. Duplicate the grouped object two times. Position one object on the left of the slide and one object on the right.
   h. Select all three objects. Align them on the top and distribute them horizontally. If you notice an overlap, resize one or more of the objects horizontally and redistribute them until the three objects fit across the slide.
   i. Group the three heart rate objects (Figure 4-157).

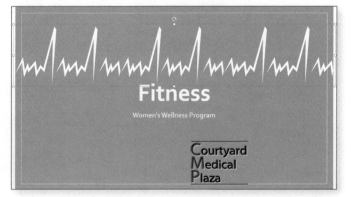

4-157 Heart rate image modified

3. Apply text effects and group.
   a. Insert a text box and type 3. Increase the font size to **96 pt.** and make the text **Bold**. Change the *Text Fill* to **Turquoise, Accent 1, Darker 25%**.
   b. Click the **Text Effects** button, select **Transform**, and choose the **Square** effect (*Warp* category).
   c. Resize the text by dragging (*Height* **6.5"** and *Width* **6"**) and position it evenly on the slide (refer to Figure 4-158).
   d. Group the heart rate group and the large **3**.

4. Layer title placeholders and adjust text size.
   a. Select the title placeholder and click **Bring to Front**.

4-158 Title slide completed

b. Increase the font size to **96 pt.** Make the placeholder better fit the text.

c. Position the text in the middle of the large **3**.

d. Select the subtitle placeholder and click **Bring to Front**.

e. Increase the font size to **32 pt.** Make the placeholder better fit the text.

f. Position the text below the word **Fitness**.

5. Insert a picture, make corrections, and remove the background.

a. On slide 1, insert the **Fitness1-04** picture from your student files and align it on the right.

b. Click **Corrections** and select **Sharpen: 50%**.

c. Repeat to select **Brightness: 0% (Normal) Contrast: +20%**.

d. Click **Remove Background**. Adjust the selection area and mark areas to keep or remove. Keep changes.

6. If necessary, adjust the position of the Courtyard Medical Plaza logo so it does not overlap other slide objects.

7. Draw a shape and edit shape points.

a. On slide 3, draw a heart shape (*Height* **2.5"** and *Width* **3"**).

b. Change the *Shape Fill* to **Dark Red** and the *Shape Outline* to **Dark Teal, Text 2**.

c. Edit shape points to stretch the heart vertically and make it more narrow.

d. Position the heart in the upper right corner of the slide (Figure 4-159).

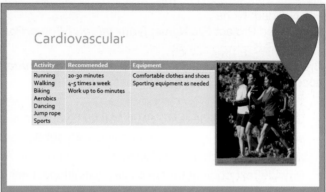

4-159 Heart with points edited

8. Insert a picture, make corrections, crop, and remove the background.

a. On slide 7, insert the **Fitness2-04** picture from your student files and align it on the right.

b. Click **Corrections** and select **Sharpen: 50%**.

c. Repeat to select **Brightness: +20% (Normal) Contrast: +20%**.

d. Crop the picture to include only the woman in the middle.

e. Click **Remove Background**. Adjust the selection area and mark areas to keep or remove. Keep changes.

f. Click the **Rotate** button and choose **Flip Horizontal**.

g. Position the picture on the right side of the slide.

9. Save and close the presentation (Figure 4-160).

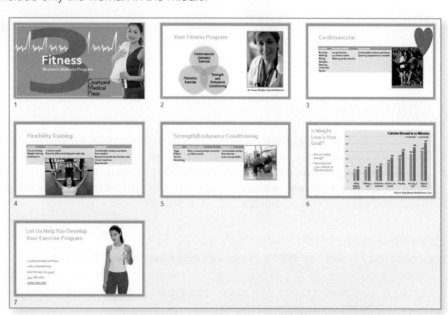

4-160 PowerPoint 4-7 completed

P4-273

Challenge Project 4-8

Today's Internet and cellular technology have made visual content accessible to the masses. Explore some emerging trends for visual communication and information graphics. These topics are quite broad, so look online for a specific idea that interests you. Consider topics such as why information graphics matter, what makes information graphics successful, tips for design, ethical representation of information, or how information graphics are impacting marketing strategies. Show how some of these concepts can be applied in PowerPoint to present content in a visual way that is pleasing to the eye and more interesting than plain text.
[Student Learning Outcomes 4.1, 4.2, 4.3, 4.4, 4.5]

File Needed: None
Completed Project File Name: *[your initials] PowerPoint 4-8.pptx*

Create a new presentation and save it as *[your initials] PowerPoint 4-8*. Modify your presentation according to the following guidelines:

- Customize a theme using *Slide Master* layouts to create a unique background. Add simple shapes that are layered in some way with subtle color differences. Select a title font with a bold appearance such as Arial Black for slide titles and Arial for body text.
- Provide text content for necessary definitions. Limit use of bulleted text.
- Create one *SmartArt* graphic that you convert to shapes. Design your own diagram.
- Design a timeline showing several key dates as information graphics continues to evolve.
- Locate an effective illustration online and insert a screen clipping on a slide. Credit the source.
- Using the drawing concepts of this chapter, recreate several aspects of this illustration on one or more slides.
- Create a merged shape.
- Prepare an interesting title slide with artistic effects applied to a picture.

Challenge Project 4-9

For this project, identify strategies you can use to budget for an upcoming life event or major purchase. For example, perhaps a wedding is in your near future or you need to purchase a new car. Locate a variety of worksheets online to record planned and actual spending. Develop a presentation describing various methods for keeping track of expenditures and setting aside money for future needs.
[Student Learning Outcomes 4.1, 4.2, 4.3, 4.4, 4.5, 4.7]

File Needed: None
Completed Project File Name: *[your initials] PowerPoint 4-9.pptx*

Create a new presentation and save it as *[your initials] PowerPoint 4-9*. Modify your presentation according to the following guidelines:

- Create a custom theme that reflects a goal-oriented approach to saving money.
- Use *Slide Master* layouts and include background images or shapes. Use *Gridlines* to control alignment consistency. Arrange rotated text as part of the design with a color that blends with the background.
- Apply a modern-looking font for slide titles and apply appropriate text effects. Apply a simple font for body text. Be sure all text is easy to read.
- Insert a picture to represent the upcoming event or major purchase for which you are saving.
- Locate two budget worksheets online and insert a screen clipping of each one on its own slide.
- Compare the differences in what the worksheets track or how they work. Prepare a comparison slide or table listing similarities or differences. Credit the sources.
- Save the presentation as a template.

Challenge Project 4-10

Prepare a photo album presentation featuring pictures you have from an event such as a wedding, family reunion, or organization activity. Design an appropriate custom background for this topic that helps to communicate the mood of the presentation. Add captions and text boxes as well as illustrations to design the presentation like a scrapbook that can be viewed on a tablet or notebook computer. [Student Learning Outcomes 4.1, 4.2, 4.3, 4.4, 4.5, 4.6]

File Needed: None
Completed Project File Name: *[your initials] PowerPoint 4-10.pptx*

Create a new presentation and save it as *[your initials] PowerPoint 4-10*. Modify your presentation according to the following guidelines:

- Create a photo album with six or more pictures. Include captions for each picture and text boxes inserted as needed. Adjust the album order and select a picture layout. Edit the photo album if necessary before other changes are made to individual slides.
- Create a custom theme appropriate for your topic. Use *Slide Master* layouts to design background graphics and colors. Using the drawing concepts of this chapter, include creative elements for a unique design.
- Use *Gridlines* to assure alignment consistency.
- Insert additional slides to provide supporting information such as a text box with a list of brief terms or statements that are arranged in columns.
- Insert a screen clipping from a related document or a web site that has appropriate information. Credit the source.
- Check each picture and make corrections as needed.
- Select one picture to feature in a creative way using artistic effects.
- Crop one picture to a shape.

Working with Advanced Animation, Hyperlinks, and Rich Media

CHAPTER OVERVIEW

With PowerPoint 2013, you can integrate many forms of media into your presentations. The term *rich media*, also called *multimedia*, encompasses a broad range of digital media that includes text, pictures, audio, and video combined with dynamic motion and interactivity. This chapter explores how to work with audio and video content, add motion through complex animations, and provide interactivity with hyperlinks. You will learn how to arrange and link content in your presentations to actively engage your audience.

STUDENT LEARNING OUTCOMES (SLOs)

After completing this chapter, you will be able to:

SLO 5.1   Apply multiple animation effects and create complex animation sequences in a presentation (p. P5-277).

SLO 5.2   Add hyperlinks and action buttons to a presentation to assist with navigation and link to other sources (p. P5-289).

SLO 5.3   Insert audio and video content in a presentation (p. P5-294).

SLO 5.4   Adjust audio and video playback settings using bookmark, trim, and fade options (p. P3-298).

SLO 5.5   Record an audio clip and add sound to an animation (p. P5-302).

SLO 5.6   Format, optimize, and compress media in a presentation (p. P5-303).

SLO 5.7   Integrate rich media in a presentation effectively (p. P5-306).

CASE STUDY

Allen Wilson, owner of Wilson Home Entertainment Systems (WHES), was recently asked to speak to the "Leaders Under 40" annual recognition ceremony about the success of his family-owned business and the services WHES provides. In the Pause & Practice projects in Chapter 5, you apply the concepts of the chapter to complete his presentation.

Pause & Practice 5-1: Apply animation to multiple slide objects and create complex animations.

Pause & Practice 5-2: Create a menu of presentation topics with hyperlinks and action buttons to control navigation.

Pause & Practice 5-3: Insert video and audio files, adjust playback settings, and record audio.

Applying Advanced Animation

Animation in your presentation helps you to tell your story. Using animation, you can break a concept down into small increments that you **build** on a slide at just the right time to focus attention. Building can help your audience see the connections between concepts as you reveal them; therefore, building is referred to as ***progressive disclosure***. Animation works well for comparison situations, too, such as showing before and after pictures or presenting two lists independently. You can control animation timing as you present, or animation can occur automatically.

In *SLO 3.2: Applying Animation*, you explored animation with *Entrance* effects that make an object appear, *Emphasis* effects that apply a movement or color change to call attention to an object, or *Exit* effects that make an object leave the slide. In this chapter, you will work with animations that are more complex with multiple effects and synchronized timings. Be sure you save your presentations frequently while you are working.

Motion Path animation allows you to vary the direction of movement. As with other types of animation, PowerPoint provides many *Motion Path* effects in the gallery, or you can click **More Motion Paths** to access additional effects. You can also draw your own path using the ***Custom Path*** option. Sound effects are possible with animation as well.

Animation effects should not be used simply to attract attention. Animation quickly loses its novelty when you overuse it. A little goes a long way. Remember that presentations are for sharing information; they are usually not intended to be entertainment events. Judge carefully what is best to include in each individual presentation situation. Make object movements match what you need to say and appear naturally to aid meaning.

Animation can be effective for the following:

- Progressive disclosure.
- Featuring or emphasizing content.
- Reinforcing or supporting content.
- Showing change.
- Illustrating dynamic concepts or objects in motion.

Animate a List and Dim Text

You can add movement and control animation settings for selected objects with commands on the *Animations* tab. Recall from *SLO 3.2: Applying Animation* that an ***animation tag***, a small numbered box, appears on the slide next to an animated object when the *Animations* tab is active. If you want to remove an animation, delete this animation tag. The *Animation Pane* offers additional options you can use to fine-tune settings or coordinate complex sequences.

Remember that audience members won't read text until it stops moving. And some people find constant movement distracting. So animate text sparingly. When animating lists, consider choosing a color to dim text for the items you have already presented. This text is still readable but not emphasized as much as the new text that you are introducing.

HOW TO: Animate a List and Use Dim Text

1. Select the bulleted list to be animated.
2. To open the *Animation* gallery (Figure 5-1), click the **More** button [*Animations* tab, *Animation* group] or click the **Add Animation** button [*Animations* tab, *Advanced Animation* group].
3. Click an **Animation** effect to apply it or click one of the options at the bottom of the gallery to open a dialog box with more effects for each animation type. *Entrance* effects are shown in Figure 5-2.

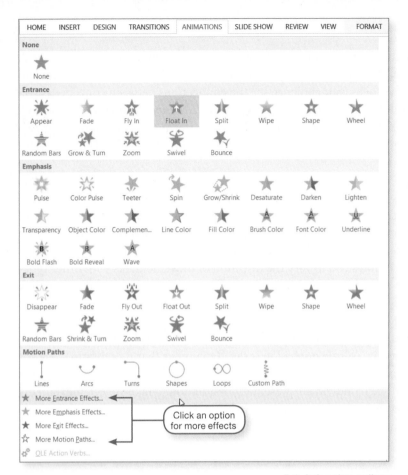

5-1 Animation gallery

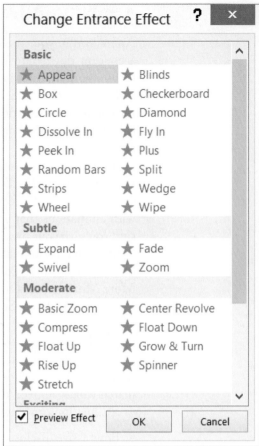

5-2 More *Entrance* effects

4. Once an animation is applied, click the **Effect Options** button [*Animations* tab, *Animation* group] to control options such as *Direction* or *Sequence*. The options vary based on the selected animation effect. Choose from one of the following for *Sequence* options (Figure 5-3):

5-3 Animated list *Effect Options*

- *As One Object:* All text appears at one time
- *All at Once:* All text appears at once but the animation effect is applied to each part individually
- *By Paragraph:* Each bulleted item and related subpoints appear together

5. Click the **Preview** button [*Animations* tab, *Preview* group] to test the animation.

6. Click the launcher [*Animations* tab, *Animation* group] to open a dialog box with additional effect options that vary based on the selected animation. The animation effect name appears in the title bar (Figure 5-4).

7. Click the **After animation** list arrow to select a different color for the text after it has been animated. Select a color that enables the text to still be readable but deemphasizes it compared to the color used on the new text.

8. Click the **Animate text** list arrow and choose from *All at once*, *By word*, or *By letter*.

9. Click **OK** to close the dialog box.

10. To remove an animation, delete the animation tag or select **None** in the *Animations* gallery.

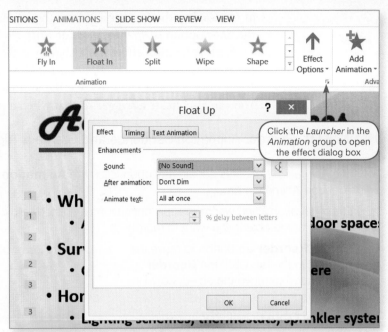

5-4 *Float Up* dialog box

> MORE INFO
>
> The difference between the *As One Object* and the *All at Once* sequence is very subtle for many animation effects. These options are more evident with effects that grow or rotate in some way.

You can use the same keyboard shortcuts (described in the following table) to move between animations that you use for moving to the next or previous slides.

Animation Shortcuts

Press	Action
N, **Enter**, **Page Down**, right arrow, down arrow, or spacebar	Start the next animation.
P, **Page Up**, left arrow, up arrow, or **Backspace**	Start the previous animation.

> MORE INFO
>
> You can test animation in *Slide Sorter* view by clicking the animation icon below each slide that has animation effects.

The Animation Pane

While you can control most animation effects on the *Animations* tab, the *Animation Pane* is useful when you are preparing animation for multiple objects and multiple effects. Typically, one animation effect occurs after another. By default, animation occurs with the *Start* option of *On Click* so the speaker activates the animation. To make animation happen automatically, the *Start* option is *After Previous* or *With Previous*.

Each animation effect has a slightly different duration time. Recall from *SLO 3.2: Applying Animation* that a longer *Duration* time makes the movement appear more slowly. The *Delay* option enables you to have the animation start after the number of seconds you enter. You can also create a ***trigger*** so that when a particular object is clicked, the animation starts.

HOW TO: Reorder Animation Sequence and Create a Trigger

1. If the *Animation Pane* it is not already open, click the **Animation Pane** button [*Animations* tab, *Advanced Animation* group].

2. In the *Animation Pane* where multiple animations are listed, click the name of the animated object you want to reorder.

3. Click the **Reorder up** button to move the object up in the list. Click the **Reorder down** button to move the object down in the list (Figure 5-5).

4. Click **Play From** to test your animations.

5. If an animation has multiple parts, such as a bulleted list that is animated by paragraph, you can expand the list on the *Animation Pane* to show each of the individual items by clicking the **chevron** icon that appears with the name in the animation list.

6. Right-click the effect in the *Animation Pane* and select **Effect Options** (Figure 5-6) or **Timing**. The same dialog box opens with tabs where you can control more settings at once.

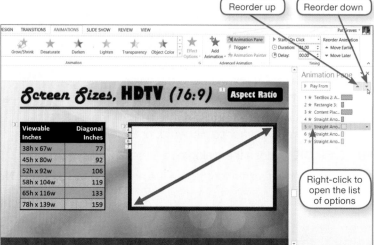

5-5 Reorder list in the *Animation* pane

7. On the *Timing* tab, you can adjust these options:

   - Select *Start*, *Delay*, and *Duration* options.
   - Click the **Repeat** list box arrow and choose an appropriate number.
   - Select **Rewind when done playing**, if appropriate.
   - Click the **Triggers** button and choose **Start effect on click of** to select a particular object on your slide to begin the animation (Figure 5-7). By default, the animation being applied is considered part of an animation sequence.
   - The option, **Start effect on play of** is available only when a video or audio object is on a slide.

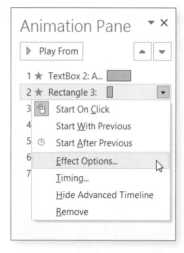

5-6 Open the *Animation Effect* dialog box from the animation list

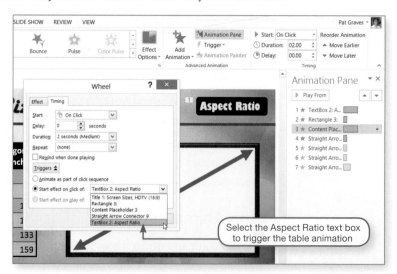

5-7 Choose a *trigger*

8. Click **OK** to close the dialog box.

9. On the *Animation Pane*, the colored bar following each object name reflects the duration for that animation effect (Figure 5-8). Click the **Play From** button to test animation. At the bottom of the pane, the elapsed seconds will show while the animation plays.

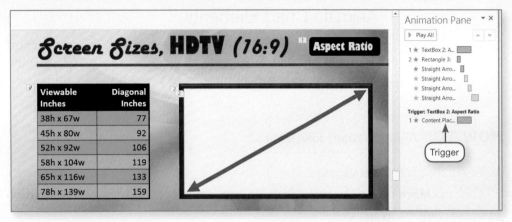

5-8 *Trigger* assigned and other timing adjusted

> **ANOTHER WAY**
>
> The *Animations* tab shows options for *Trigger, Start, Duration, Delay,* and *Reorder Animation*.

When working with complex animations, make the *Animation Pane* wider to see when each animation begins and ends. You can resize the pane after you finish making changes. When you close the *Animation Pane* and then open it again, the size will be the same as when you closed it.

The Animation Painter

The ***Animation Painter*** copies animation settings and applies them to another object in the same way the *Format Painter* copies format settings. Using *Animation Painter* is especially helpful when you have created a complex animation sequence and you want to apply those settings again.

HOW TO: Use Animation Painter

1. On the slide, select the object with the animation you need and click the **Animation Painter** button [*Animations* tab, *Advanced Animation* group] (Figure 5-9).

2. Click another object to apply this animation.

3. If you need to apply the same animation to multiple objects, double-click the **Animation Painter** button and it will remain active. Press **Esc** to turn off the *Animation Painter*.

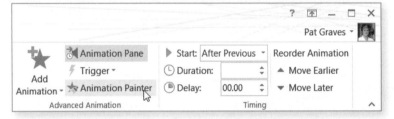

5-9 *Animation Painter* button

When you add animation to a selected object, the selection handles are replaced with the animation tag. You can add a second animation to that object even though it has no handles; the animation tag shows it is selected. However, you must click the **Add Animation** button to open the gallery so you can select another effect. If you simply choose a different effect from the open gallery, the previous effect is replaced with the current effect. You can click anywhere on the slide background to deselect the animated object. When you click the animated object again to select it, handles will appear.

Animate Chart Elements

Animation effects for charts add movement by making the entire chart appear as one object or by making chart data appear by series or category. Chart animation can be a powerful way to help your audience absorb content as you gradually introduce comparison data.

HOW TO: Animate Chart Elements

1. Select the chart to be animated.
2. Click the **More** button [*Animations* tab, *Animation* group] or click the **Add Animation** button [*Animations* tab, *Advanced Animation* group] to open the gallery.
3. Choose an animation effect or click one of the **More** options at the bottom of the gallery to select from additional effects.
4. Once an animation effect is applied, click the **Effect Options** button [*Animations* tab, *Animation* group] and choose a particular sequence for how your chart will build (Figures 5-10 and 5-11).

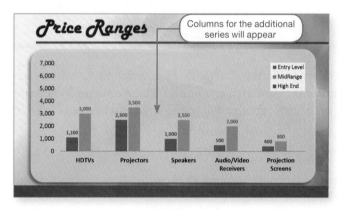

5-10 Chart being animated *By Series*

5-11 Chart being animated *By Category*

5. By default, the *Start* option is set for *On Click*. You can change this option to *After Previous* with an appropriate time for *Delay* to better focus on either the series or the categories as they appear.

   • On the *Animation Pane*, click the **chevron** icon below an item name to expand the animation list and show the multiple parts such as series data displayed in columns with different colors (Figure 5-12).
   • Adjust individual items in the expanded list (Figure 5-13).
   Click the **chevron** again to collapse the list.

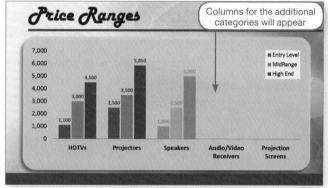

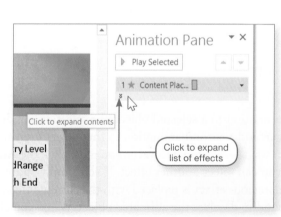

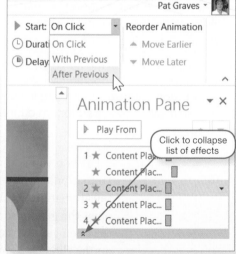

5-12 Expand animation list   5-13 Adjust timing for chart series or category

6. Click the **Animations Pane** button [*Animations* tab, *Advanced Animation* group]. Select the chart object in the *Animation Pane* list. Right-click and choose **Effect Options** to open the dialog box for the animation effect you chose.

- Click the **Chart Animation** tab (Figure 5-14).
- For the *Group Chart* option, note that the same *Effect Options* are available.
- Deselect the option for **Start animation by drawing the chart background**. This change makes the chart background appear at the time the slide appears. Click **OK**.

7. In the *Animation Pane*, the *Play* button name changes based on what is selected (see Figures 5-12 and 5-13). One of the following options appears:

- *Play Selected* when an animated object is selected on the slide
- *Play From* when an animated object is selected in the animation list
- *Play All* when no object is selected

5-14 *Animation Effects* dialog box

8. Test this effect and then try the animation with a different sequence to see which one you prefer.

Animate a SmartArt Graphic

When you apply animation to a *SmartArt* graphic, you can control the direction and the sequence to make shapes appear in phases. Use the *Timing* group options [*Animations* tab] or the *Animation Pane* to control other settings for how the animation starts and timings for duration and delay.

> **MORE INFO**
>
> Some animation effect dialog boxes do not have options available in the *Group Chart* list box.

HOW TO: Animate a SmartArt Graphic

1. Select the *SmartArt* graphic you want to animate. Be sure you select the *SmartArt* frame so the entire *SmartArt* graphic is selected and not an individual shape within the frame.

2. Click the **More** button [*Animations* tab, *Animation* group] or click the **Add Animation** button [*Animations* tab, *Advanced Animation* group] to open the gallery.

3. Choose an animation effect or click one of the **More** options at the bottom of the gallery to select from additional effects.

4. Once an animation effect is applied, click the **Effect Options** button [*Animations* tab, *Animation* group] and choose a *Direction*, a *Sequence*, or one of the other options that are available based on the selected animation. The *Effect Options* of *One by One* builds the *SmartArt* graphic one shape at a time. Figure 5-15, which was captured during animation, shows how each shape and related picture swivel together. When animating SmartArt graphics, animation effects that grow or rotate in some way will look quite different using the *One by One* option versus the *As One Object* option.

5. To test the animation, click the **Preview** button [*Animations* tab], the **Play Selected** button [*Animation Pane*], or view the slide in *Slide Show* view.

5-15 *Swivel* animation with *One by One* sequence

▶ MORE INFO

Connecting lines in a *SmartArt* graphic are not animated individually. They are associated with shapes.

To create a more complex animation, you can first show the completed *SmartArt* to provide an overview, apply an exit animation so the *SmartArt* disappears, and then apply an *Entrance* effect to make the *SmartArt* appear in stages as you discuss each part.

Not all diagrams benefit from animation, so use animation selectively for *SmartArt* graphics. If you need more control over how the individual shapes appear, convert the *SmartArt* graphic to shapes. Once you have done this, you can regroup the shapes as needed and animate them in a way that works best for your message.

Create Motion Path Animation

With a **Motion Path** animation, you can make an object move from one position to another following a predesigned path. PowerPoint provides many different *Motion Path* effects, or you can select **Custom Path** to draw your own.

A *Motion Path* animation effect has a green marker for the beginning point, and most of the effects have a red marker for the ending point. You can drag these markers to adjust them and use resizing handles to change the area that contains the movement. Paths can also be modified by *editing points*. To make an object begin movement off the slide and then enter the slide, you must place the object away from the slide for its beginning position. The position after animation is the end of the movement.

HOW TO: Apply Motion Path Animation

1. Change your *Zoom* to **50%** so you can use the blank area around your slide for object placement.

2. Select the object you want to animate.

   - The current object position may be where the animation starts or where it ends, depending on the effect you choose.
   - If you want an animated object to move onto the slide, drag the object off the slide for its start position on the blank area outside the slide. Then select the animation effect.

3. With the object selected, click the **Add Animation** button [*Animations* tab, *Advanced Animation* group] to open the gallery. In the *Motion Paths* category (Figure 5-16), select from the following options:

   - Choose one of the effects shown.
   - Click the **Custom Path** to draw the path an object will follow.
   - Choose **More Motion Paths** to open the *Add Motion Path* dialog box and view more options (Figure 5-17). Select a specific animation from one of the three categories: *Basic*, *Lines-Curves*, or *Special*.

4. Click **OK**.

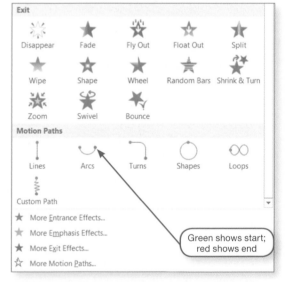

5-16 *Animation* gallery showing *Motion Path* effects

5. A line appears that is attached to your object. The shape of the line varies based on the particular path you selected. A green triangle marker indicates the beginning point of the *Motion Path* animation. The center of your object will move along the path.

   - Figure 5-18 shows a *Swoosh Motion Path* effect (*Special* category) applied to the first grouped object. This effect begins and ends in the same position.
   - You can drag the sizing handles to make the movement cover a larger area.

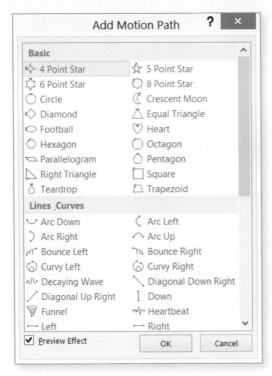

5-17 *Motion Path* dialog box

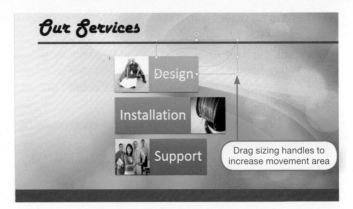

5-18 *Motion Path Swoosh* effect as it first appears

5-19 *Motion Path Zigzag* effect as it first appears

6. Depending on which *Motion Path* effect you choose, the effect may have a red marker that indicates the ending point of the *Motion Path* animation.

   - Figure 5-19 shows a *Zigzag Motion Path* effect applied to the second grouped object. The markers are in the middle of the object in the start and end positions. In this case, the movement is from left to right.
   - Click the **Effect Options** button [*Animations* tab, *Animation* group] and choose **Reverse Path Direction**. This change makes the second object move from right to left so its final position aligns with the first object on the slide.

7. To move an object's start and end position, point to the appropriate marker. When your pointer changes to a four-tipped arrow, you can drag the marker to a different position. The object you are moving shows in a transparent color while you move it.

8. To prepare a *Custom Path* animation where an object enters the slide during animation, change your *Zoom* to **50%** so you can use the blank area outside the slide.

   - Select the object to be animated and move it to an appropriate start position off the slide in the blank area.
   - Select the *Custom Path Motion Path* effect and your pointer changes to a crosshair. Draw the line that your object will follow. Double-click at the end of the line.
   - Figure 5-20 shows an example. A car is in its start position on the right of the slide, the custom path the car will follow is on the road, and the car end position is by the stop sign on the left. When played, this animation makes the car move along the curve of the road.
   - When you are drawing a custom path to make an object exit the slide during animation, the end position must be in the blank area outside the slide.

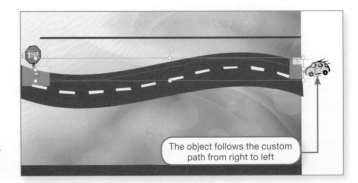

5-20 *Motion Path Custom Path* effect

9. To have an object with motion path animation invisible until the motion starts, follow these steps:
   - Select the animated object.
   - Click the **Add Animation** button [*Animations* tab, *Advanced Animation* group] and apply an *Entrance* effect.
   - In the *Animation Pane*, move the *Entrance* effect above the *Motion Path* effect.
   - On the *Motion Path* effect, change the *Start* option to *With Previous* so the entrance and movement happen together.

10. Click **Preview** [*Animations* tab] to test each movement.

11. Some movements can be too rapid. Adjust *Duration* as needed to make the movements occur more slowly.

When working with complex animations, increase the size of the *Animation Pane* so you can see the color bars showing when each animation plays. Test each portion of the animation and adjust as necessary before working on the next part. If your sequence becomes lengthy, you may want to work in stages by duplicating your slide and adding additional animation to the duplicated slide. Then you can always go back to the previous slide and start again if you have problems getting the sequences and timing to work as you need. Save your presentation frequently.

Test the animation on the computer used for delivery. You may need to adjust timings if the computer you are using to project the presentation has a different processing speed from the computer you used to develop the presentation.

PAUSE & PRACTICE: POWERPOINT 5-1

For his presentation for the "Leaders Under 40" annual recognition ceremony, Allen Wilson has prepared a slide show about the success and services of his family-owned business, Wilson Home Entertainment Systems. The presentation features a theater-like, count-down effect leading to a red curtain that opens as a transition to the title slide. For this project, you apply animation to multiple slide objects and create complex animations.

File Needed: ***BringingHollywoodHome-05.pptx***
Completed Project File Name: ***[your initials] PP P5-1.pptx***

1. Open the ***BringingHollywoodHome-05*** presentation and resave it as ***[your initials] PP P5-1***.

2. Animate a list and dim text.
   a. On slide 5, select the bulleted list placeholder.
   b. Click the **Add Animation** button [*Animations* tab, *Advanced Animation* group] to open the gallery. Choose the **Float In** *Entrance* effect.
   c. Click the **Effect Options** button [*Animations* tab, *Animation* group] and note that *By Paragraph* is already selected. Each bulleted item and related subpoints will appear together.
   d. Click the launcher [*Animations* tab, *Animation* group] to open the *Float Up* dialog box.

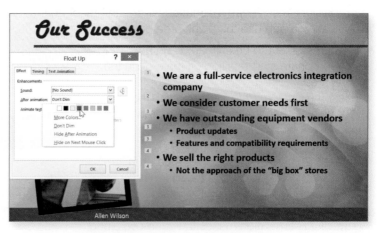

5-21 Text color dimmed to the selected color after animation

e. Click the **After Animation** list arrow and select the **dark gray** color (Figure 5-21).
f. Click **OK** to close the dialog box.

3. Use the *Animation Painter*.
   a. Select the animated list on slide 5 and click the **Animation Painter** button [*Animations* tab, *Advanced Animation* group].
   b. Press **Page Down** so the *Animation Painter* remains active.
   c. On slide 6, click the list to apply this animation.

4. Rearrange the animation order using the *Animation Pane*.
   a. On slide 1, click the **Animation Pane** button [*Animations* tab, *Advanced Animation* group].
   b. Ten text boxes with large numbers are stacked in the center of the slide on a circular shape.
   c. In the *Animation Pane*, the animation names indicate that each item is a "TextBox" followed by two numbers. The first number was assigned as each text box was created. After the colon, the second number shows the text in each box, which is also a number.
   d. The timing has been set to create a count-down sequence, but the numbers are not in the correct order.
   e. Select the animated objects and click the **Reorder Up** and **Reorder Down** buttons as necessary to rearrange the animations in descending order (**TextBox11:10** to **TextBox 2:1**) (Figure 5-22).
   f. Select **TextBox 11:10** in the animation list and click the **Preview** button [*Animations* tab, *Preview* group] to test the animation.

5-22 Animated objects are arranged in descending order

5. Create a trigger to start the animation sequence.
   a. In the *Animation Pane*, select **TextBox 11:10** in the animation list, right-click, and choose **Timing** to open the *Fade* dialog box.
   b. Click the **Triggers** button. By default, **Animate as part of click sequence** is applied.
   c. Choose **Start effect on click of** and click the list box arrow. Scroll down and select **5-Point Star 12** (Figure 5-23).
   d. Click **OK** to close the dialog box.
   e. In the *Animation Pane*, select **TextBox 10:9** and change the delay to 04.00 [*Animations* tab, *Timing* group].
   f. Select the remaining text boxes and change the delay to 00.50.
   g. Test the animation in *Slide Show* view by clicking the star on the lower left of the slide.

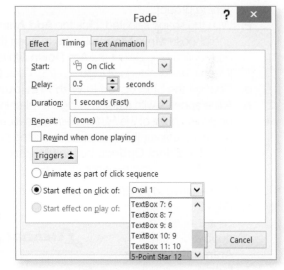

5-23 The *Trigger* is the *5-Point Star 13*

6. Animate chart elements.
   a. On slide 7, select the area chart. This chart has one data series and the area for that series is filled with a picture.
   b. Click the **Add Animation** button [*Animations* tab, *Advanced Animation* group] to open the gallery. Select the **Wipe** *Entrance* effect.
   c. Click the **Effect Options** button [*Animations* tab, *Animation* group] and choose the *Direction* of **From Bottom**. Click the **Effect Options** button again and choose the *Sequence* of **By Series**. This option makes the chart background elements appear before the data series area appears.
   d. Change the *Duration* to **5.00** seconds [*Animations* tab, *Timing* group].

e. Select the arrow on the chart and click the **Add Animation** button. Select the **Wipe** *Entrance* effect with the **From Bottom** option. Change the *Start* option to **After Previous**.

f. With the arrow still selected, repeat step 6e to apply the **Teeter** *Emphasis* effect (Figure 5-24).

g. Click **Preview** [*Animations* tab] to test the animation.

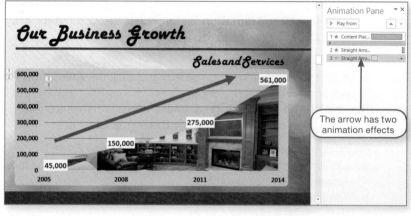

5-24 Completed chart animation

7. Animate a *SmartArt* graphic.

a. On slide 9, select the *SmartArt* graphic.

b. Click the **Add Animation** button [*Animations* tab, *Advanced Animation* group] to open the gallery. Select the **Grow & Turn** *Entrance* effect.

c. Click the **Effect Options** button [*Animations* tab, *Animation* group] and choose the *Sequence* of **One By One**.

d. Click **Preview** [*Animations* tab] to test the animation.

8. Apply two animation effects that display together.

a. On slide 11, select the "Receiver" shape. Click the **Add Animation** button [*Animations* tab, *Advanced Animation*] group to open the gallery. Select the **Grow & Turn** *Entrance* effect.

b. Change the *Start* option to **With Previous** [*Animations* tab, *Timing* group].

c. With the shape selected, click the **Add Animation** button again and choose **More Motion Paths** to open the *Add Motion Path* dialog box. Select the **Arc Down** *Motion Path* effect [*Lines-Curves* category] (Figure 5-25). Click **OK**.

d. Change the *Start* option to **With Previous**.

e. A line appears with a green triangle marker indicating the beginning point of the *Motion Path* animation (its original position) and a red marker that indicates the ending point of the *Motion Path* animation (moving from left to right).

f. Click the **Effect Options** button [*Animations* tab, *Animation* group] and choose **Reverse Path Direction** (moving from right to left).

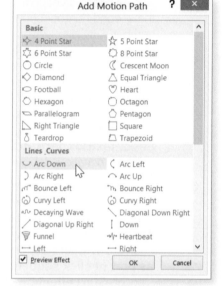

5-25 *Add Motion Path* dialog box

9. Use the *Animation Painter* to create an animation sequence.

a. With the animated shape selected, double-click the **Animation Painter** button.

b. Click all other shapes to apply the same animation effects. Each shape moves as you apply the animation to it (Figure 5-26).

c. Press **Esc** to turn off the *Animation Painter*.

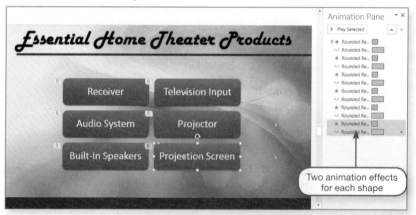

5-26 The animation sequence plays automatically

10. Create an animated sequence including a custom path.

    a. On slide 14, select the text on the right (Figure 5-27) and click the **Add Animation** button [*Animations* tab, *Advanced Animation* group]. Select the **Grow & Turn** *Entrance* effect.

5-27 Animation sequence with a custom motion path

    b. Select the red oval positioned over "Peoria" on the map.

       • Click the **Add Animation** button and select the **Appear** *Entrance* effect. Change the *Start* option to **After Previous**.

       • Click the **Add Animation** button again and select the **Spin** *Emphasis* effect. Click the **Effect Options** button [*Animations* tab, *Animation* group] and choose **Full Spin**. Change the *Start* option to **With Previous**, *Duration* to 02.00, and the *Delay* to 01.00.

    c. Select the car and move it near "Waukegan" at the top of the map.

       • Click the **Add Animation** button and select the **Appear** *Entrance* effect. Change the *Start* option to **After Previous**.

       • Click the **Add Animation** button again, scroll down the gallery, and select the **Custom Path** *Motion Paths* effect.

       • Draw a path going left to "De Kalb" and then down to the oval around "Peoria" and double click to stop drawing the path (see Figure 5-27). Change the *Start* option to **With Previous** and the *Duration* to **05.00**.

11. Test the animation in *Slide Show* view.

12. Save the presentation.

Adding Hyperlinks

A *hyperlink* is a connection between two locations. It enables you to move quickly to a different slide, different presentation, different application, or even a web site. You can use different methods to link in PowerPoint and you can assign the linking action to text, action buttons, or objects.

You can use a hyperlink, for example, to access a series of slides that you plan to show during a presentation only if there is audience interest or if time permits. Hyperlinks enable interactivity either for the presenter or for an individual viewing a slide show independently.

This feature is especially valuable for kiosk presentations where an individual user can control how the presentation is viewed. For example, you can create a slide with a table of contents or list of presentation topics using text or shapes. When you assign a hyperlink action to each of the items, you create a menu of choices. When a user clicks one of these items during the presentation, the user is taken directly to the series of slides for that topic. At the end of the slides for that topic, a link can return the user to the menu slide where he or she can choose another topic. This navigation ability is available throughout the presentation if the linking action to return to the menu is created on the *Slide Master*.

Create Text Hyperlinks

You can create a text hyperlink from one word or several words. During the slide show, a user can click this text to jump to the destination. With text hyperlinks, the linked text automatically has an underline and the text displays in a different color than other text. After a user clicks a text hyperlink, the text color changes again because the text is a "followed hyperlink." You cannot change these two colors directly on the slide. You can use the *Create New Theme Colors* dialog box to change colors for the *Hyperlink* and *Followed Hyperlink* options.

HOW TO: Create and Use Text Hyperlinks

1. Select the text for your link and click the **Hyperlink** button [*Insert* tab, *Links* group] (or press **Ctrl+K**) to open the *Insert Hyperlink* dialog box.

2. Under *Link to* on the left side, choose **Place in This Document** (Figure 5-28). In the *Select a place in this document* list box, choose the slide number and title to which you want to link. Click **OK**.

3. The linked text is underlined and displays in a different color.

4. If you are creating a table of contents or menu slide, repeat this process for each item in your list.

5. In *Slide Show* view, test each link to be sure the correct slide displays.

6. To return to your menu slide, type the slide number for that slide and press **Enter**.

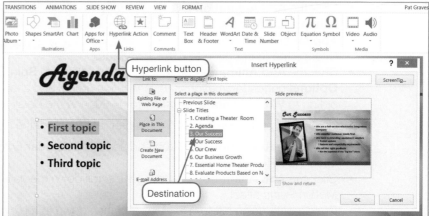

5-28 *Insert Hyperlink* dialog box

Add Hyperlinks with ScreenTips to Objects

You can add hyperlinks to objects such as shapes or pictures. For example, you can create a series of shapes with identifying text to serve as a table of contents or a menu for your topics. Each shape or object can include hyperlinks to the appropriate slides in your presentation.

You can also add a **ScreenTip** to a hyperlink. A ScreenTip is text that displays when the user points to a hyperlink. A ScreenTip can provide more information than the shape displays or indicate where the link will go. Grouped objects cannot be hyperlinked.

HOW TO: Hyperlink from Objects and Display ScreenTips

1. Select the first shape or picture to be linked. Click the **Hyperlink** button [*Insert* tab, *Links* group] or press **Ctrl+K** to open the *Insert Hyperlink* dialog box.

2. Under *Link to* on the left side, choose **Place in This Document**. In the *Select a place in this document* list box, choose the slide number and title to which you want to link.

3. Click the **ScreenTip** button in the upper right corner of the dialog box. The *Set Hyperlink ScreenTip* dialog box opens (Figure 5-29).

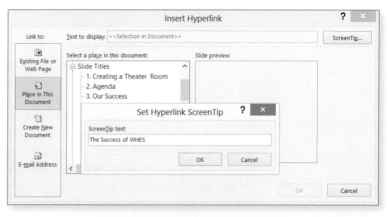

5-29 *Set Hyperlink ScreenTip* dialog box

4. Type appropriate text in the *ScreenTip* box. This text will appear when you point to the hyperlink during a slide show (Figure 5-30).

5. Click **OK** to close the *Set Hyperlink ScreenTip* dialog box; click **OK** again to close the *Insert Hyperlink* dialog box.

6. Repeat steps 1–5 for each shape that should link in your presentation.

7. Test each link to be sure the correct slide opens.

8. Type the slide number for your menu slide and press **Enter** to return to your menu slide to test another link.

5-30 *ScreenTip* example

Create Action Buttons

The *Shapes* gallery includes a category of shapes called **Action Buttons**. You can draw and format these as you would any other shape, but usually action buttons are shown in a small size. As soon as you draw a shape, the *Action Settings* dialog box automatically opens with a suggested hyperlink destination. For example, you can choose shapes for *Previous, Next, Beginning, Home,* and others. You can customize these options and control what happens during a slide show if the shape is clicked (called *Mouse Click)* or if you just point to the shape (called *Mouse Over*).

A common use for action buttons is to provide a way to move quickly back to a menu where a user can select another topic choice. You can place the buttons on the last slide in a series, or you could place them on a *Slide Master* layout, where they are visible throughout a presentation.

HOW TO: Create Action Buttons

1. Select the slide where you want to create an action button.

2. Click the **Shapes** button [*Insert* tab, *Illustrations* group] to open the *Shapes* gallery. Select one of the action buttons (Figure 5-31).

5-31 *Action Buttons* in the *Shapes* gallery

3. Draw a small rectangle such as the *Home* shape shown in Figure 5-32. The *Action Settings* dialog box automatically opens.

   - On the *Mouse Click* tab, select **Hyperlink to:** and click the list box arrow. Choose **Slide** to open the *Hyperlink to Slide* dialog box.
   - Select the slide for your link.
   - Click **OK**.

4. Click **OK** again to close the *Action Settings* dialog box.

5. If you have several slides that will include this same link, copy the action button and paste it on each slide.

6. If you want to provide navigation options throughout a slide show, create the action buttons on the appropriate *Slide Master* layout.

7. View your slide show and check the links to be sure they function correctly.

8. If you need to make changes, select the action button and click the **Action** button [*Insert* tab, *Links* group] to open the *Action Settings* dialog box.

5-32 *Action Settings* dialog box

> **ANOTHER WAY**
>
> You can set up an action button to open a different program and display a document or worksheet.

Link to Other Sources

Your slide show can link to other sources such as a different presentation, files from another application, or a web page.

HOW TO: Link to Other Sources

1. On the slide where you want to include a link, select the text or shape for your hyperlink.
2. Click the **Hyperlink** button [*Insert* tab, *Links* group] or press **Ctrl+K**. The *Insert Hyperlink* dialog box opens.
3. Under the *Link to* heading on the left, choose **Existing File or Web Page** (Figure 5-33).
4. To link to a file, follow these steps:
   - In the *Look in* box, navigate to the file location and select the file you want to open.
   - The file name is added to your list. Note that the application icon precedes the file name.

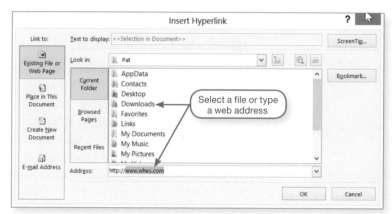

5-33 *Insert Hyperlink* dialog box

5. To link to a web page, follow these steps:
   - Copy the entire web address for the page to which you want to link.
   - On the *Insert Hyperlink* dialog box, in the *Address* list box, paste the address from the web page.
6. Click the **ScreenTip** button and type appropriate text.
7. Click **OK** to close the *Set Hyperlink ScreenTip* dialog box. Click **OK** again to close the *Insert Hyperlink* dialog box.
8. View your slide show and check the links to be sure that they work correctly and the appropriate applications open.
9. After working in a different application or web page, click the PowerPoint button on the *Taskbar* to return to your slide show.

If you display your presentation on a different computer, links can be broken. It is a good idea to save all presentation files in the same folder. Then you can copy the entire folder for use on a different computer. If you are linking to other application files or to web pages, you need to reestablish the links after you open your slide show on the different computer.

PAUSE & PRACTICE: POWERPOINT 5-2

For this Pause & Practice project, you continue to work with the Wilson Home Entertainment Systems (WHES) presentation and create a menu of presentation topics with object hyperlinks to the appropriate slides, add action buttons on the *Slide Master* to control navigation, and include a text hyperlink to a web page.

File Needed: *[your initials] PP P5-1.pptx*
Completed Project File Name: *[your initials] PP P5-2.pptx*

1. Open the **[your initials] PP P5-1** presentation and save it as **[your initials] PP P5-2**.

2. On slide 4, assign hyperlinks to shapes to create a menu of presentation topics on the "Agenda" slide. Be sure to select each shape and not just the text on the shape.

   a. Select the "Our Success" shape and click the **Hyperlink** button [*Insert* tab, *Links* group] or press **Ctrl+K** to open the *Insert Hyperlink* dialog box.

   b. Under *Link to* on the left side, choose **Place in This Document**. In the *Select a place in this document* list box, choose slide title **5. Our Success**. Click **OK**.

   c. Repeat steps 2 a–b to hyperlink each of the remaining menu shapes on slide 4 to its respective slide in the presentation (Figure 5-34):

Menu Shape	Hyperlink to Slide
Our Services	9. Our Services . . .
Home Theater Products	11. Essential Home Theater Products
How to Find Us	14. Slide 14

   d. Test each link to be sure the correct slide opens. To return to the menu slide, type 4 and press **Enter**.

5-34 *Insert Hyperlink* dialog box

3. Create navigation controls with *Action Buttons* on the *Slide Master*.

   a. Click the **Slide Master** button [*View* tab, *Master Views* group].

   b. Select the first *Slide Master* layout.

   c. Click the **Shapes** button [*Insert* tab, *Illustrations* group] to open the *Shapes* gallery. Select the **Forward or Next** action button (Figure 5-35) and draw a small rectangle (*Height* **.5"** and *Width* **.5"**) anywhere on the slide. You will move it into position later.

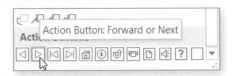

5-35 *Forward or Next Action Button* in the *Shapes* gallery

   d. The *Action Settings* dialog box automatically opens. On the *Mouse Click* tab, the **Hyperlink to** list box automatically shows **Next Slide**.

   e. Click **OK** to close the *Action Settings* dialog box.

   f. Repeat step 3 c–e to create two more action buttons:

Action Button	Hyperlink to
Previous	Previous Slide
Home	Slide . . ., and then choose 4. Agenda

   g. Move the three action buttons to the bottom of the slide and arrange them evenly on the right (Figure 5-36).

   h. Click the **Close Master View** button [*Slide Master* tab, *Close* group].

   i. View your slide show and check the links to be sure that movements are correct.

4. Create a text hyperlink with a ScreenTip to link to a web page.

   a. On slide 6, select the text "CEDIA (Custom Electronic Design and Installation Association)."

5-36 *Action Buttons* arranged on the *Slide Master* layout

b. Click the **Hyperlink** button [*Insert* tab, *Links* group]. The *Existing File or Web Page* option should be selected.

c. In the *Address* box, type http://www.cedia.org/.

d. Click the **ScreenTip** button in the upper right corner of the dialog box. The *Set Hyperlink ScreenTip* dialog box opens.

e. In the **ScreenTip** text box, type Link to CEDIA @ http://www.cedia.org.

f. Click **OK** to close the *Set Hyperlink ScreenTip* dialog box. Click **OK** again to close the *Insert Hyperlink* dialog box.

g. In *Slide Show* view, test the *ScreenTip* and the hyperlink to the CEDIA web page.

5. Save and close the presentation.

SLO 5.3

Inserting Audio and Video Content

Including an audio recording in your presentation can be an effective way to share a speech, a testimony, or a discussion from an expert with your audience. Or you may want to play music before your presentation as people enter the room.

Seeing a video may be the best way for your audience to understand your message. Video is effective for showing time-based and situation-based conditions. Video can also convey non-verbal information that is impossible to portray in a text-only presentation. Video combines both audio and visual components, and it can appeal to emotions and stimulate responses.

When you use video, remember to avoid visual clutter and keep your slide designs as simple as possible. Use text to label and credit sources when appropriate. Any formatting you apply should work well with your background graphics and other consistently used elements in your presentation.

Your computer system must have a sound card and speakers if you want to present audio or video content. Audio and video files greatly increase your presentation file size. Digital video is made of individual frames (like pictures) that are played back at the rate of approximately 30 frames per second to create the illusion of real-time motion. (You may have noticed these frames on YouTube videos when the slider at the bottom of the video is dragged.) Both digital audio and video are encoded to standardize data for storage and transmission. The files are compressed to reduce file size. Different file formats are used for different purposes.

PowerPoint supports many different audio and video file formats, which are listed in the following table. For best results, use *.m4a* audio files and *.mp4* videos files. If you use a file conversion program, you can convert audio and video files from a different format to one that will play in PowerPoint. Problems can occur if the required *codec* (compressor/decompressor) is not installed on your computer or if a file is not recognized by your version of Microsoft Windows. In *SLO 5.6: Format, Optimize and Compress Media*, you learn about some new PowerPoint features to improve playback.

Supported Audio and Video File Formats

File Format	Extension	More Information and Common Uses
Audio		
MPEG-4 file	.m4a, .mp4	Moving Pictures Expert Group, encoded with Advanced Audio Coding.
MP3 file	.mp3	MPEG Audio Layer 3. Files are compressed.
WAV file	.wav	Windows Audio File. Sounds are stored as waveforms and file sizes can vary significantly.

WMA file	.wma	Windows Media Audio. Files are compressed with Microsoft Windows Media Audio codec; commonly used to distribute recorded music on the web.
MIDI file	.mid or .midi	Musical Instrument Digital Interface. Standard format used for musical instruments, synthesizers, and computers.
AIFF file	.aiff	Audio Interchange File Format. Files are not compressed so file sizes are large.
AU file	.au	UNIX Audio. Used for UNIX computers and the web.
Video		
MP4 file	.mp4, .m4v, .mov	Video file, encoded with H.264 video (MPEG-4 AVC) and Advanced Audio Coding audio.
Movie file	.mpg or .mpeg	Moving Pictures Experts Group. An evolving set of standards for video and audio compression.
Windows Media file	.asf	Advanced Streaming Format. Stores synchronized data used to stream audio and video content.
Windows Media Video file	.wmv	Windows Media Video. Uses a codec to compress audio and video content requiring minimal storage space.
Windows Video file	.avi	Audio Video Interleave. Common format that compresses audio and video content with a wide variety of codecs (some .avi files require additional codecs).
Adobe Flash file	.swf	Adobe Flash Media file. Common format for web graphics with animations and interactivity.

Insert an Audio or Video File

The methods for inserting digital audio and video are very similar. When you insert audio or video files, they become objects in your presentation and are saved with the presentation. Audio and video objects can play automatically when a slide appears, or a user can activate them with a click.

HOW TO: Insert an Audio or Video File

1. Select the slide where you want to insert audio or video.
2. Click the *Audio* or *Video* button [*Insert* tab, *Media* group] and choose *Audio on My PC* or *Video on My PC*.
3. Locate the place on your computer where the audio or video file is stored, select the file, and click **Insert**.
   - **Audio:** An icon that looks like a speaker appears on your slide. When the speaker icon is selected, a playback bar displays (Figure 5-37).
   - **Video:** The first frame or a black fill displays in a rectangle on your slide. When the rectangle is selected, a playback bar

5-37 Audio object with the playback control bar

5-38 Video object with the playback control bar

   displays (Figure 5-38). The size and shape of the rectangle vary depending on the resolution and aspect ratio of the video.
4. Drag the audio or video object to an appropriate position on the slide.
5. Depending on how a video was made, you may be able to increase its size without experiencing too much distortion. Experiment until you are satisfied with the results.

Insert an Online Audio or Video Clip

On the *Insert Audio* dialog box, you can search *Office.com Clip Art* for royalty-free sound clips. Many of these clips are event sounds such as a door closing or an alarm sound. They are small files (usually with the extension *.wav* or *.mid*). The *.mid* files are brief music clips that usually play more seconds and, therefore, may have a larger file size.

HOW TO: Search for and Insert an Online Audio Clip

1. Select the slide where you want to insert audio.

2. Click the **Audio** button [*Insert* tab, *Media* group] and select **Online Audio**. The *Insert Audio* dialog box opens.

3. Enter a search word in the *Office.com Clip Art* list box and click **Search**.

4. The search results display an audio icon and a name for each clip (Figure 5-39). When you point to the clip, you can hear the sound, and information about the file appears in the lower left. The file extension does not appear.

5. Select the audio clip you want to include in your presentation and click **Insert**.

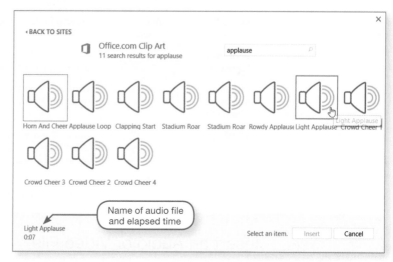

5-39 Audio online search results

On the *Insert Video* dialog box, you can search the web using *Bing Video Search*, browse your *SkyDrive* or other online location, or search YouTube. Depending on how your software is set up on your computer, you may or may not have a search box for YouTube; however, YouTube videos will appear when searching using the *Bing Video Search* box. Recall that in *SLO 3.3: Linking to an Online Video*, you learned how to link to files from YouTube.

HOW TO: Search for and Insert an Online Video Clip

1. Select the slide where you want to insert video.

2. Click the **Video** button [*Insert* tab, *Media* group] and select **Online Video**. The *Insert Video* dialog box opens.

3. Enter a search word in one of the search boxes (*Bing Video Search*, your *SkyDrive*, or YouTube) and click **Search**.

4. The search results display the first frame for each video (Figure 5-40). When you point to the video, the name appears. If you

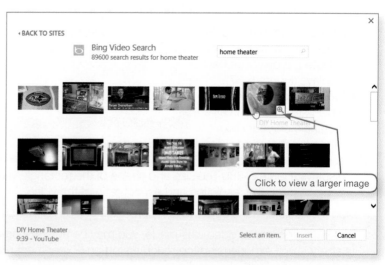

5-40 Video online search results

click the **View Larger** button, the video is shown in a larger size with a **Play** button so you can view it before inserting it into your presentation (Figure 5-41).

5. Select a video and click **Insert**. The link to this video is inserted in your presentation.

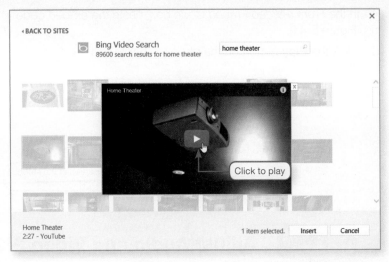

5-41 View larger before clicking the *Insert* button

On the *Insert Video* dialog box, you can also paste embed codes to link to videos from web sites. If you find a video you want to use at a web site, you can copy the embed code (if this has been made public). The embed code contains linking information with instructions for how the video displays. It will play within your presentation when the link is activated as long as you have Internet access.

Some videos that you find when searching provide buttons to share or embed the video.

- **Share:** Allows you to post the video to different social media sites or to copy the URL so you could send the video's address (Figure 5-42).
- **Embed:** Allows you to copy the embed code that enables linking to and displaying a site within PowerPoint. An Internet connection is required (Figure 5-43).

5-42 Share options

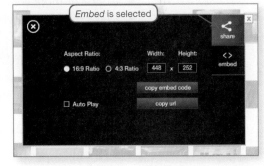

5-43 Copy embed codes

HOW TO: Insert a Video Using Embed Codes

1. On the appropriate web site, display the video you want to use and right-click. Select **Copy embed html**. If this command is not available, the video owner has not made the video available for public use. The embed code is sometimes shown below the video and can be copied from there also. You may need to use the old embed code.

2. In PowerPoint, display the slide where you want to insert the video.

3. Click the **Video** button [*Insert* tab, *Media* group] and select **Online Video**. The *Insert Video* dialog box opens.

4. In the *From a Video Embed Code* box, paste the embed code (Figure 5-44).

5. Click the **Play** button on the playback bar to test the video.

A small portion of the embed code is displayed

5-44 **Paste copied embed code**

SLO 5.4 Adjust Audio and Video Playback Settings

By default, audio and video files play when you click their object on the slide; therefore, when this option is used, the audio or video object must be visible on the slide. When you point to these objects during your slide show, the *playback bar* becomes visible. It displays a *timeline* with *Play/ Pause, Move Back, Move Forward*, and *Mute/Unmute* buttons. The *Elapsed time* appears also.

With both audio and video objects, two tabs become available for editing. The *Audio Tools Format* tab and the *Video Tools Format* tab provide options that are similar to the *Picture Tools Format* tab. Both the *Audio Tools Playback* tab and the *Video Tools Playback* tab provide unique options for handling changes to audio and video objects. If the audio or video object is used in conjunction with animation effects, you can adjust the playback sequence on the *Animation Pane*. Editing options for both audio and video objects include the following:

- Specify *Automatic* or *On Click* playback.
- Bookmark to designate specific locations.
- Trim to reduce playback time.
- Fade to make the object gradually appear or disappear.
- Adjust or mute volume.
- Make the object invisible while the presentation is displayed in *Reading* view or *Slide Show* view.
- Specify *Continuous Play* or *Rewind*.

With video files, you can specify playback at full-screen size. Video clarity depends on how the video was created and its resolution.

Add and Remove Bookmarks

You can add a *Bookmark* to an audio or video object at a specific location so you can jump to a point of interest to focus on that content rather than starting playback at the beginning. A *Bookmark* can also activate animation effects.

HOW TO: Add and Remove Bookmarks

1. Select the audio or video object, and the *Audio Tools Playback* tab or the *Video Tools Playback* tab (Figure 5-45) automatically opens.

5-45 *Video Tools Playback* tab

2. On your playback bar, move your pointer over the timeline without clicking and you can see how the timing seconds change (Figure 5-46).

3. Click on the timeline to advance the audio or video object to that position (Figure 5-47). To the left of where you click, the timeline becomes gray. If you click the *Play* button, the audio or video will begin playing from this position.

5-46 *Timeline* showing video seconds from the start

5-47 *Timeline* showing seconds at a new start position

4. Click the *Move Back* or *Move Forward* buttons on the playback bar to adjust the stopped position of the audio or video object. These buttons move the stopped position in increments of .25 seconds.

5. Click the **Add Bookmark** button [*Audio Tools Playback* tab or *Video Tools Playback* tab, *Bookmarks* group], and a bookmark dot appears on the timeline. Yellow shows the bookmark is selected (Figures 5-48 and 5-49).

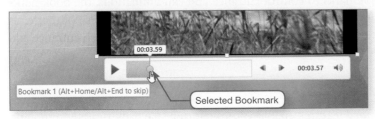

5-48 *Timeline* showing a video *Bookmark*

5-49 *Timeline* showing an audio *Bookmark*

6. You can also add a bookmark while the audio or video is playing. The audio or video object stops when you click the **Add Bookmark** button.

7. Repeat if you want to add a second bookmark. Bookmarks are numbered in sequence.

8. To remove a bookmark, select the bookmark and click the **Remove Bookmark** button [*Audio Tools Playback* tab or *Video Tools Playback* tab, *Bookmarks* group].

A ***trigger*** starts an animation sequence. A trigger is either an object on the slide that is clicked or a bookmark. For example, if you create two bookmarks on a video, the first one can trigger an object's entrance effect and a second bookmark can trigger the object's exit effect. The object, or text, enters and leaves the video at preplanned times. You can use this technique to call attention to key parts of the video.

HOW TO: Trigger an Animation with a Video Bookmark

1. Create one or more animation effects on the slide where you display your video.

2. Create a bookmark on the timeline where you want the animation effect to begin and a second one if you want the animation to end at a specific timeline position.

3. Click the **Animation Pane** button [*Animations* tab, *Advanced Animation* group] to open the *Animation Pane*.

4. Select the animation effect that you want to start when the video playback reaches the bookmark.

5. Click the **Trigger** button [*Animations* tab, *Advanced Animation* group], select **On Bookmark**, and select the bookmark that will start the animation (Figure 5-50).

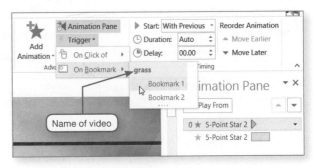

5-50 *Bookmark 1* is the animation *Trigger*

6. The *Start* option changes to **On Click** because the trigger controls the animation.

7. Test the animation trigger by playing the video (Figure 5-51).

8. You can add an animation exit effect triggered with another bookmark to make the animation end before the video ends.

5-51 The animation plays with the video

You can use the procedure just described to trigger animation sequences with bookmarks on audio objects.

If you are using several bookmarks to control entrance and exit animations, the bookmarks may get out of sequence if you make corrections. The bookmark numbering does not matter as long as the bookmark for the beginning and ending positions correctly match each entrance and exit effect.

Trim and Fade

The ***Trim Audio*** and ***Trim Video*** features enable you to shorten playback time by removing seconds from the beginning or end of an audio or video object. You cannot trim seconds from within an audio or video object. Trimming only affects the way an object plays in your slide show; the original object file is not affected.

HOW TO: Trim Audio and Video

1. Select the audio or video object you want to edit, and click the **Trim** button [*Audio Tools Playback* tab or *Video Tools Playback* tab, *Editing* group].

2. On your timeline, adjust the green start marker or the red end marker to remove seconds. Use one of the following methods:

   - Drag the start or end marker on the timeline (Figures 5-52 and 5-53).
   - Type the specific number of seconds (or click the spin box arrows) in the *Start Time* or *End Time* boxes.
   - Select the marker and click the *Previous Frame* or *Next Frame* buttons.

5-53 *Trim Video* dialog box

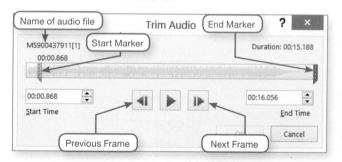

5-52 *Trim Audio* dialog box

Fade In causes an audio to gradually reach full volume or a video to gradually come into focus. *Fade Out* causes an audio to gradually decrease in volume or a video to gradually blur out. *Fading* is typically used at the beginning and end of playback, but these settings can occur within an audio or video object as well. You can change the *Fade In* or *Fade Out* duration seconds by typing a number or clicking the spin box arrows (see Figure 5-45). By increasing the duration seconds, you make the fade more gradual.

You can use fading effects to vary volume levels in interesting ways. For example, if you have a long audio clip, you can fade the volume in the middle to create a silent period during which you can make comments. You can have the volume return to its normal level after your comments at the appropriate point in the timeline.

Hide, Loop, and Rewind

Additional options on the *Audio Tools Playback* tab and the *Video Tools Playback* tab control volume and determine if audio and video objects start automatically or on click. Video can be expanded to fill the entire screen. Audio can play in the background while several slides change and can loop to restart if the audio ends before the last slide displays. If you set the audio to play automatically, you can hide the sound icon so it does not appear on the screen during your slide show.

HOW TO: Hide, Loop, and Rewind

1. Select the audio or video object.
2. Choose an appropriate volume, start, and playback style [*Audio Tools Playback* tab, *Audio Options* group or *Video Tools Playback* tab, *Video Options* group] from the following options (Figure 5-54):
   - **Volume:** *Low*, *Medium*, *High*, or *Mute*.
   - **Start:** *On Click* or *Automatically*.
   - **Play Across Slides:** Audio plays throughout the presentation as slides advance. This option has the same effect as *Play in Background* [*Audio Tools Playback* tab, *Audio Styles* group].
   - **Play Full Screen:** Video expands to fill the screen.
3. Choose from the following hide, loop, and rewind options [*Audio Tools Playback* tab, *Audio Options* group or *Video Tools Playback* tab, *Video Options* group]:
   - **Hide During Show**: The audio icon is invisible in *Reading* view or *Slide Show* view and the video is invisible when it is not active. This option is usually appropriate when you have the audio or video play automatically.
   - **Loop until Stopped**: The audio or video repeats until you stop it.
   - **Rewind after Playing**: The audio or video starts from the beginning each time it is played.

5-54 *Audio Options*

If you need audio to play only while a specific sequence of slides is displayed, you can click the launcher [*Animation* tab, *Animation* group] to open the *Play Audio* dialog box. Select from *On click*, *After current slide*, or *After* where you can enter the specific number of slides to show before the audio stops.

The video shortcuts listed in the following table work with an inserted video file but not with an online video file:

Video Shortcuts

Press	Action
Alt+Q	Stop playback.
Alt+P	Play or pause.
Alt+End	Go to the next bookmark.
Alt+Home	Go to the previous bookmark.
Alt+Shift+Page Down	Seek forward.
Alt+Shift+Page Up	Seek backward.
Alt+Up	Increase sound volume.
Alt+Down	Decrease sound volume.
Alt+U	Mute sound.

SLO 5.5

Record an Audio Clip and Add Sound to Animation

You must have a sound card, microphone, and speakers installed on your computer to record and test audio. You will need external speakers to amplify the audio in a large room.

Record Audio on a Slide

If you have a microphone with your computer, you can use *Record Audio* to create an audio clip of your own voice.

HOW TO: Record Audio

1. Select the slide where you want to insert the audio.
2. Click the **Audio** button [*Insert* tab, *Media* group] and select **Record Audio** to open the *Record Sound* dialog box (Figure 5-55).
3. In the **Name** box, type a name for your audio clip.
4. Click the **Record** button to begin recording and speak into the microphone.
5. When your recording is complete, click **OK**. The audio object appears on your slide.
6. Click the **Play** button to review your recording.
7. Test the audio in *Slide Show* view by clicking the audio object.

5-55 *Record Sound* dialog box

Add Sound to an Animation

In the dialog box for each animation effect, you can name an audio file to play with the animation effect. When audio is included with an animated object, the audio playback is controlled by how the object is animated such as to begin playing when the animated object appears on the slide. An audio object does not show on the slide and the audio does not show as a separate object in the *Animation Pane* list.

HOW TO: Add Sound to an Animation

1. Select the object to be animated.
2. Click an animation effect from the gallery or click the **Add Animation** button [*Animations tab, Advanced Animation* group] and choose an effect.
3. Click the launcher [*Animations* tab, *Animations* group] to open a dialog box for the particular animation effect that you chose (Figure 5-56). The available options can vary.
4. On the *Effect* tab, click the **Sound** list box arrow and scroll down the list to select one of the default sounds. Click **Other Sounds** at the bottom of the list to open the *Add Audio* dialog box (Figure 5-57).
5. By default, the file type is *Audio Files* and all file formats in your collection may not be shown. Change the file type to *All Files* (Figure 5-58).

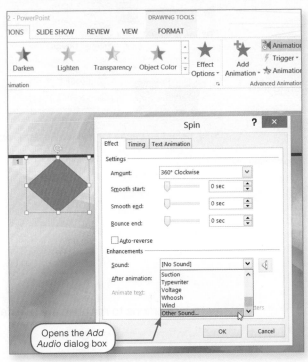

5-56 *Spin Animation* dialog box

5-57 *Add Audio* dialog box showing *.wav* files only

5-58 *Add Audio* dialog box showing all files

6. Locate and select the file you want to use. Click **OK** to close the dialog box and insert the file. You will hear the audio.
7. Check the volume level by clicking the **Volume** button beside the audio name and adjust it if necessary.
8. Make other adjustments as needed to *Settings* or *Timing*. Click **OK** to close the dialog box.
9. Test your animation to make sure your sound plays appropriately.

SLO 5.6

Format, Optimize, and Compress Media

You can position, resize, and format audio and video objects using the *Audio Tools Format* tab or the *Video Tools Format* tab. Several options, however, apply only to video and how it displays. When your presentation is complete, you can optimize media compatibility and compress the media to reduce the file size of your presentation.

Format an Audio and Video Object

The *Video Tools Format* tab provides options that are similar to the *Picture Tools Format* tab to change the appearance of audio and video objects with color changes, styles, borders, shapes, and cropping. Audio objects are usually small, so the changes you make to them may be less obvious. However, you can substitute a different picture for the default speaker icon to feature the audio in an interesting way.

With a video, you can add a *Poster Frame*, which is a picture displayed at the beginning of the video. *Video Styles* are very similar to *Picture Styles*. You can crop a video to a shape or layer a video with other objects on the slide.

HOW TO: Format a Video

1. Select the video object you want to format.
2. Select the *Video Tools Format* tab.
3. From the *Adjust* group, select from the following options:

   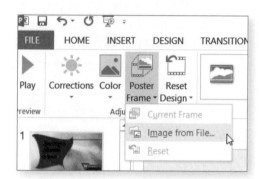

   • **Corrections:** To change contrast and brightness.
   • **Color:** To change to a monotone shade of theme colors.
   • **Poster Frame:** To insert a picture that will display as a preview image of the video before it plays (Figure 5-59).
   • **Reset Design:** To remove changes to the video by restoring it to its original design.

   5-59 Select an image for a video *Poster Frame*

4. From the *Video Styles* group, select from the following options:

   • **Video Styles:** To select a preset style.
   • **Video Shape:** To crop the video to a shape from the *Shapes* gallery.
   • **Video Border:** To change border color or weight.
   • **Video Effects:** To customize effects.

5. From the *Arrange* group, select from the following options:

   • *Bring Forward*, *Send Backward*, or *Selection Pane*
   • *Align*, *Group*, or *Rotate*

6. From the *Size* group, select from the following options:

   • **Crop:** To remove areas from the edges of the video.
   • **Size:** To adjust video size. Be careful to adjust width and height in accurate proportions to maintain the original aspect ratio.

Optimize Media Compatibility

When you use audio and video in your presentation, you may face problems if you change computers to deliver your presentation. To avoid playback issues, you can optimize the media files for compatibility.

HOW TO: Optimize Media Compatibility

1. Click the **File** tab and select **Info**.
2. The **Optimize Compatibility** option appears when files can be optimized. It shows a summary of files that can be optimized (Figure 5-60).

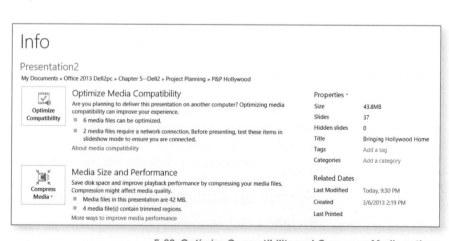

5-60 *Optimize Compatibility* and *Compress Media* options

3. Click the **Optimize Compatibility** button.

4. When optimization is complete, a summary is provided (Figure 5-61). Click **Close**.

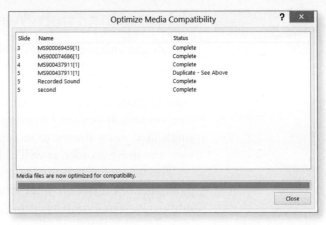

5-61 *Optimize Media Compatibility* dialog box showing results

Compress Media

Audio and video files greatly increase the file size of your presentation. Compress the files to improve playback performance and to reduce presentation file size. Different levels of quality are available.

HOW TO: Compress Media

1. Before you perform a compression, be sure to save a copy of your original file in case you are not satisfied with the result of a compression.

2. Click the **File** tab and select **Info**.

3. If files can be compressed, the **Compress Media** option appears showing the total media file size and how compression could be helpful (see Figure 5-60). The way you want to present and display your slide show dictates the level of compression you should choose. Click the **Compress Media** button and choose from the following options (Figure 5-62):

   • *Presentation Quality*
   • *Internet Quality*
   • *Low Quality*

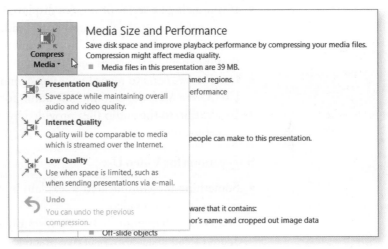

5-62 *Compress Media* options

4. When compression is complete, a summary of the results is provided. In the example shown in Figure 5-63, the file size was reduced 11.4 MB using *Presentation Quality*. Although not shown, other options for the same presentation resulted in greater reduction (*Internet Quality* reduced 24.8 MB; *Low Quality* reduced 32.2 MB).

5. Click **Close**.

6. Test your presentation to determine if the clarity of your slides is satisfactory for the way you plan to display them.

7. If you are not satisfied, close the presentation without saving and return to your original file.

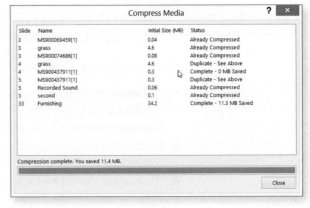

5-63 *Compress Media* dialog box

Integrating Rich Media

Sounds and images can enrich a presentation. Animation can reinforce content through movement and timing. The first step in using media effectively in PowerPoint is carefully selecting content specifically for your presentation. You may find online content to use at no cost, or you may need to purchase suitable content. For some situations, you may want to create your own content. If you are preparing an educational or informative presentation designed for a single user, you will want to incorporate interactivity so the user can choose which content to view and in what order, as well as link to other related sources.

The following lists provide some ideas for using rich media in your presentations, some guidelines to consider if you capture your own video content, and suggestions for effectively introducing video content during a presentation.

Suggestions for Audio Use

- Recorded sound must be loud enough for your audience to hear. Therefore, the effective use of sound in a presentation depends on a number of factors. For example, you use sound differently when you are presenting to a large group in a conference room and when you are speaking to an individual using your tablet or notebook computer.
- Use music to energize or create a relaxing mood.
- Usually it is best to use music when you are not speaking during your presentation. It is very difficult to talk over music.
- If you include a series of images displayed as a photo album, you might choose to play music softly in the background as the slides change.
- Sometimes sound can add a bit of humor. Carefully consider what you use, however, so that it generates the right reaction.
- Use *Record Audio* to record your voice, or a colleague's voice, to be played on one slide. Use *Record Slide Show* to include audio for every slide in the presentation.
- In addition to the audio files provided by Microsoft, many commercial collections are available online.

Suggestions for Video Use

- Something too complicated to explain in words can sometimes be instantly understood when you show a video.
- Sometimes showing is better than simply telling. For example, when training employees about effective customer service practices, a series of video clips of transaction examples, both good and bad, might be helpful.
- For sales purposes, record a video displaying product information or customer testimonials to support your product.
- Video clips from different locations can be sent electronically and inserted in your presentation.

Interactivity and Animation

- An interactive presentation is set up to respond to user input.
- A menu with hyperlinks and other navigation options allows users to have control over how they view the content.
- Interaction can help users to learn because they are actively engaged with the presentation content.
- Animation should be logical, intuitive, and not disorienting.

Video Quality

- The quality of a video depends on the hardware, software, and type of compression used to capture the video.
- Video clips are recorded at different pixel resolutions and play back at a rate of approximately 30 frames per second to show smooth, realistic movement. Depending on how the video is recorded, it may or may not be clear when displayed at full-screen size. Be sure the video is large enough for the entire audience to see.
- The video should contain enough information for the audience to understand the point that you are making without showing unnecessary information. If possible, limit a video to no more than one minute. If you need to show a clip that is longer, consider breaking it into multiple parts.

Delivery Techniques When Using a Video

- Unless you are using a video for its surprise factor, introduce the video to your audience before you play it.
- Be sure that you face your audience when you introduce a video. Let your audience know what to look for in a video clip. Point out highlights or a change you want them to observe.
- Always have your playback settings prepared so the video begins playing from the correct location and ends appropriately.
- Move your pointer away from the video so the pointer is not on screen while the video plays.
- Refrain from looking at the projection screen when the video is playing. It's better for you to watch the response of your audience so you can react to this when the video is finished.
- After the video is finished, review what your audience should have seen. Be sure your audience understands why you played the video. Engage the audience in discussion about the video.

PAUSE & PRACTICE: POWERPOINT 5-3

For *Pause & Practice PowerPoint 5-3*, you insert a video file that was created *from Pause & Practice PowerPoint 4-4* into the Wilson Home Entertainment Systems (WHES) presentation. You also insert an online audio file and adjust playback settings, bookmark the video and make the bookmark a trigger for the audio, record audio on a slide, and add sound to an animation.

Files Needed: *[your initials] PP P5-2.pptx*, *Furnishing-05.mp4*, and *WHES-Start-05.jpg*
Completed Project File Name: *[your initials] PP P5-3.pptx*

---

1. Open the file *[your initials] PP P5-2* and save it as *[your initials] PP P5-3*.

2. Insert a video.
   a. On slide 16, click the **Video** button [*Insert* tab, *Media* group] and choose **Video on My PC**.
   b. Locate your student video files, select *Furnishing-05*, and click **Insert**. This video clip is 32.47 seconds long.

c. Decrease the video's size (*Height* **3.06"**).

d. Drag the video object over the white area of the projection screen in the picture. Drag a sizing handle on the side of the video (*Width* approximately **6.16"**) so the video fits the white area (Figure 5-64).

5-64 Video inserted and resized

3. Format the video object with a *Poster Frame*.

   a. Select the **Furnishing-05** video object.

   b. Click the **Poster Frame** button [*Video Tools Format* tab, *Adjust* group] and click **Image from file**.

   c. Locate your student files, select **WHES-Start-05**, and click **Insert** (Figure 5-65).

   d. View the slide in *Slide Show* view and click the **Play** button on the video timeline to test the video.

4. Insert an online audio clip to play while the video plays.

   a. On slide 16, click the **Audio** button [*Insert* tab, *Media* group] and select **Online Audio**. The *Insert Audio* dialog box opens.

   b. Type the search word music in the *Office.com Clip Art* list box and click **Search**.

5-65 Video with *Poster Frame*

   c. From the search results, select a music clip of your choice that is at least 17.00 seconds long such as **Inroads** (Figure 5-66). Click **Insert**. This audio clip is 17.23 seconds long.

   d. Select **Loop until Stopped** and **Hide During Show** [*Audio Tools Playback* tab, *Audio Options* group].

5. Trim the audio to remove blank time at the end. This adjustment will make the music sound better when the audio repeats.

   a. On slide 16, select the audio object and click the **Trim Audio** button [*Audio Tools Playback* tab, *Editing* group].

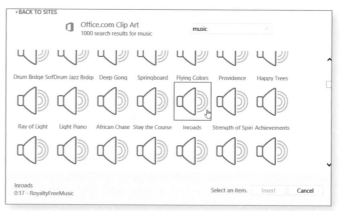

5-66 *Insert Audio* dialog box

   b. Click the **End Time** spin box down arrow so the time is 00:16.00. Click **OK**. The music will play twice during the video playback.

6. Add a bookmark to the video.

   a. On slide 16, select the video object and click the **Video Tools Playback** tab.

   b. On your playback bar timeline, move your pointer to approximately 02.00 seconds and click to stop the video in that position. Click the *Move Back* or *Move Forward* buttons if necessary.

   c. Click the **Add Bookmark** button [*Audio Tools Playback* tab or *Video Tools Playback* tab, *Bookmarks* group] and a bookmark dot appears on the timeline.

7. Trigger the audio to play when the video playback reaches the bookmark.

   a. Click the **Animation Pane** button [*Animations* tab, *Advanced Animation* group] to open the *Animation Pane*.

   b. Select the audio object.

   c. Click the **Trigger** button [*Animations* tab, *Advanced Animation* group], select **On Bookmark**, and then select **Bookmark 1** (Figure 5-67).

   d. Test the audio trigger by playing the video.

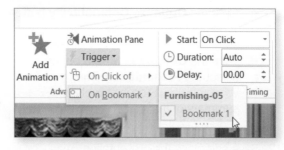

5-67 *Trigger*

8. Make the video start automatically, rewind, and fade out.

   a. On slide 16, select the video object. For the *Start* option [*Video Tools Playback* tab, *Video Options* group], choose **Automatically** and click **Rewind after Playing**.

   b. Click the **Fade Out** spin box up arrow so the duration is 02.00 [*Video Tools Playback* tab, *Editing* group].

9. Record an audio clip. (Skip this step if your computer cannot record sound.)

   a. On slide 8, click the **Audio** button [*Insert* tab, *Media* group] and select **Record Audio** to open the *Record Sound* dialog box.

   b. In the **Name** box, type Dream as the name for your audio.

   c. Click the **Record** button and speak into your microphone as you read the quoted text on the slide.

   d. When your recording is complete, click **OK**. The audio object appears on your slide.

   e. Click the **Play** button to review your recording [*Audio Tools Playback* tab, *Preview* group].

   f. Change the *Start* option to **Automatically** and select **Hide During Show**.

10. Animate text to appear after the audio plays.

    a. On slide 8, select the "If you can dream it . . ." text box.

    b. Click the **Wipe** *Entrance* effect [*Animations* tab, *Animation* group]. Click **Effect Options** and choose **From Left**.

    c. Change the *Start* option to **With Previous** [*Animations* tab, *Timing* group].

    d. Change the *Delay* to 02.00.

    e. Click the **Animation Pane** button [*Animations* tab, *Advanced Animation* group].

    f. Move the *Dream* audio effect above the *TextBox* in the list (Figure 5-68).

    g. Test your animation in *Slide Show* view to make sure your sound plays appropriately.

    h. Close the *Animation Pane*.

5-68 **Animation settings**

11. Optimize and compress the media.

    a. Click the **File** tab and select **Info**.

    b. The **Optimize Compatibility** option shows a summary of files that can be optimized (Figure 5-69).

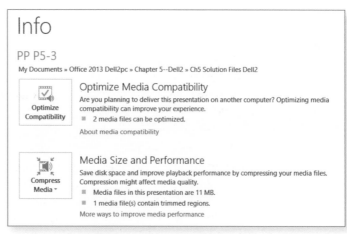

5-69 *Optimize Compatibility* and *Compress Media* options

c. Click the **Optimize Compatibility** button.

d. When optimization is complete, a summary is provided. Click **Close**.

e. Click the **Compress Media** button and select the **Presentation Quality** option.

f. When compression is complete, a summary of the results is provided (Figure 5-70). Click **Close**.

12. Save and close the presentation.

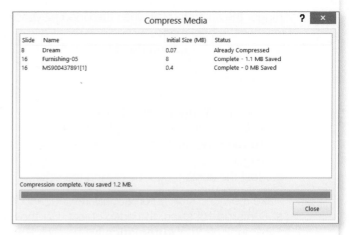

Slide	Name	Initial Size (MB)	Status
8	Dream	0.07	Already Compressed
16	Furnishing-05	8	Complete - 1.1 MB Saved
16	MS900437891[1]	0.4	Complete - 0 MB Saved

Compression complete. You saved 1.2 MB.

5-70 *Optimize Media Compatibility* dialog box showing results

Chapter Summary

5.1 Apply multiple animation effects and create complex animation sequences in a presentation (p. P5-277).

- You can apply multiple animation effects and synchronize their timing.
- Dialog boxes for each animation effect provide additional options not available on the *Animations* tab.
- Adjust animation sequence using the **Animation Pane**.
- When applied to an object, a **trigger** can make animation start.
- The **Animation Painter** copies animation settings and applies them to another object.
- You can animate chart elements by series or by category.
- You can animate *SmartArt* graphics so the shapes appear in phases.
- With *Motion Path* animation, you apply a predesigned path or a custom path to make an object move from one position to another.

5.2 Add hyperlinks and action buttons to a presentation to create navigation and to link to other sources (p. P5-289).

- A **hyperlink** is a connection between two locations. In PowerPoint, you can hyperlink to another slide, presentation, application, or web page.
- Both text and objects such as shapes or pictures can hyperlink.
- A menu or table of contents created with text or shapes and hyperlinks makes a presentation interactive by giving the viewer control over how the presentation is viewed.
- A **ScreenTip** provides text information that appears when you point to a hyperlink.
- **Action buttons** have preset hyperlinks that you can customize.
- When you click a PowerPoint hyperlink to a web page, the default browser opens and the web page appears. You click the PowerPoint button on the task bar to return to PowerPoint.
- Hyperlinks to external sources will be broken if you move your presentation to a different computer.

5.3 Insert audio and video content in a presentation (p. P5-294).

- PowerPoint supports a variety of audio and video file formats.
- Online audio clips are short sounds such as event sounds or brief pieces of music.
- Inserted audio or video files become objects in your presentation and are saved with the presentation.
- Online video clips are linked to the online source; only the linking information is saved with the presentation.
- If an online video owner has made the **embed code** public, you can paste the code on the *Insert Video* dialog box to create a link to that video.

5.4 Adjust audio and video playback settings using bookmark, trim, and fade options (p. P5-298).

- By default, audio and video files play when clicked but can be made to play automatically.
- You can **bookmark** a video to designate specific locations for start times or to trigger an animation sequence.
- **Trimming** audio and video files reduces playback time by removing seconds from the beginning or end of the file.
- **Fading** causes audio and video files to gradually appear or disappear.
- Playback changes made for an audio or video file do not affect the original file.

5.5 Record an audio clip and add sound to animation (p. P5-302).

- You must have a sound card, microphone, and speakers installed on your computer to record and test sounds.
- You can record your own voice with **Record Audio**.
- When you make an audio recording, an audio icon appears on the slide.
- You can add sound to animation using the dialog box for each different animation effect. An audio object does not display on the slide.

5.6 Format, optimize, and compress video in a presentation (p. P5-303).

- Formatting options for video and audio are similar to the options for formatting pictures.
- A *Poster Frame* provides a preview image for a video.
- Crop video objects to remove unneeded areas or crop to a shape.
- To change the appearance of a video, apply a *Video Style* and change the border and effects as needed.
- Use *Optimize Media Compatibility* to avoid playback issues if you change computers.
- Use *Compress Media* to reduce media size and, therefore, presentation file size.

5.7 Integrate rich media content in a presentation effectively (p. P5-306).

- Carefully select audio and video content to enhance and add value to your presentation message.
- Add interactive elements when designing for user control.
- Apply animation effects that are logical and aid meaning.

Check for Understanding

In the *Online Learning Center* for this text (www.mhhe.com/office2013inpractice), there are a variety of resources that can be used to review the concepts covered in this chapter.

The following Online Learning Resources are available in the Online Learning Center:

- Multiple choice questions
- Short answer questions
- Matching exercises

Guided Project 5-1

An associate at Central Sierra Insurance is giving a talk to a student organization about common disasters and what individuals can do to prepare themselves. For this presentation, you work with animation effects and timings as well as insert and format an online audio. You include hyperlinks to other sources and optimize and compress the revised presentation.
[Student Learning Outcomes 5.1, 5.2, 5.3, 5.4, 5.6, 5.7]

File Needed: **DisastersHappen-05.pptx**
Completed Project File Name: **[your initials] PowerPoint 5-1.pptx**

Skills Covered in This Project

- Animate a list and dim text.
- Reorder an animation sequence.
- Create a trigger.
- Use the *Animation Painter*.
- Create a hyperlink.
- Create an action button.

- Hyperlink to another source.
- Insert an online audio clip.
- Trim, fade, and bookmark an audio object.
- Format an audio object.
- Optimize media compatibility.
- Compress media.

1. Open the presentation **DisastersHappen-05** and save the presentation as **[your initials] PowerPoint 5-1**.

2. Apply two animation effects that display together.
   a. On slide 2, select the "Will you be prepared?" text. Click the **Add Animation** button [*Animations* tab, *Advanced Animation* group] to open the gallery. Click **More Entrance Effects** and select the **Flip** effect [*Exciting* group]. Click **OK**.
   b. No change is required for *Effect Options*.
   c. Change the *Start* to **With Previous** [*Animations* tab, *Timing* group]. The *Duration* time is automatically 01.00.
   d. With the same text selected, click the **Add Animation** button again and choose the **Fade** *Entrance* effect.
   e. Change the *Start* to **With Previous** and the *Duration* time to 01.00 so both effects start and end at the same time.
   f. Click the **Preview** button [*Animations* tab, *Preview* group] to test the animation.

3. Animate a list and dim text.
   a. On slide 6, select the bulleted list placeholder.
   b. Click the **More** button [*Animations* tab, *Animation* group] to open the *Animation* gallery. Choose the **Random Bars** *Entrance* effect.
   c. No change is required for *Effect Options*.
   d. Click the *Animation Effect* launcher [*Animations* tab, *Animation* group] to open the *Random Bars* dialog box.
   e. Click the **After Animation** list arrow and select the **orange** color (last color on the right).
   f. Click **OK** to close the dialog box and the color change appears.
   g. Click the **Preview** button [*Animations* tab, *Preview* group] to test the animation.

4. Use the *Animation Painter*.
   a. On slide 6, select the animated list. Double-click the **Animation Painter** button [*Animations* tab, *Advanced Animation* group].
   b. Press **Page Down** so the *Animation Painter* remains active, and click the list on slide 7. Continue to press **Page Down** and apply the animation to the lists on slides 8 and 9.
   c. Press **Esc** to turn off the *Animation Painter*.

5. Fade and trim an audio file.
   a. On slide 3, select the audio object on the left. Its duration is too long for this slide.
   b. Change the *Fade In* and *Fade Out* times to 02.50 [*Audio Tools Playback* tab, *Editing* group].
   c. Click **Trim Audio** [*Audio Tools Playback* tab, *Editing* group] to open the *Trim Audio* dialog box.
   d. Drag the *End* marker to 00:08.00 on the audio timeline (or type 00.08 in the spin box) (Figure 5-71).
   e. Click **OK** to close the dialog box.
   f. Click the **Play** button [*Audio Tools Playback* tab, *Preview* group] to test the audio.

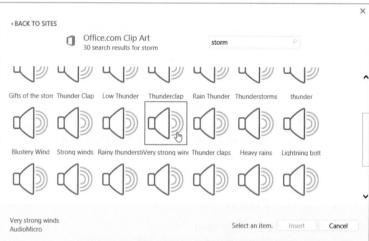

5-71 *Trim Audio* dialog box

6. Insert an online audio clip.
   a. Note that the content arrangement on slide 5 matches the design of slides 3 and 4. Pictures and rotated text are grouped. The pictures are aligned with slide edges, so the picture frame extends beyond the slide in some places. The two groups are animated separately using the *Blinds* animation effect.
   b. On slide 5, click the **Audio** button list arrow [*Insert* tab, *Media* group] and select **Online Audio**. The *Insert Audio* dialog box opens.
   c. Type the search word storm in the *Office.com Clip Art* list box and click **Search**.
   d. As you point to each audio object, the sound plays. From the search results, select a storm sound such as **Very Strong Winds** (Figure 5-72) and click **Insert**.
   e. Move the audio object to the left of the slide.

5-72 *Online Audio* search results

7. Fade, trim, and bookmark an audio object.
   a. On slide 5, select the audio object.
   b. Change the *Start* time to **Automatically** [*Audio Tools Playback* tab, *Audio Options* group].
   c. Change the *Fade In* and *Fade Out* times to 03.00 [*Audio Tools Playback* tab, *Editing* group].

d. Click **Trim Audio** [*Audio Tools Playback* tab, *Editing* group] to open the *Trim Audio* dialog box.

e. Drag the **End** marker to 00:16.00 on the audio timeline (or type 00:16 in the spin box).

f. Click **OK** to close the dialog box.

g. Point to the audio object timeline and click at approximately 00:08.00 (Figure 5-73).

h. Click the **Add Bookmark** button [*Audio Tools Playback* tab, *Bookmark* group].

i. Click the **Play** button [*Audio Tools Playback* tab, *Preview* group] to test the audio.

8. Rearrange the animation order and apply a trigger.

a. Click the **Animation Pane** button [*Animations* tab, *Advanced Animation* group].

b. Select **Group 8** in the animation list (left group on the slide) and click the **Reorder Up** button so it is above *Group 5*. Change the *Start* time to **With Previous** [*Animations* tab, *Timing* group].

c. Select **MS91022051** (the audio object) and click the **Reorder Up** button twice so it is at the top of the animation list. Change the *Start* time to **With Previous**.

d. Select **Group 5** in the animation list (right group on the slide). The *Start* time is **On Click**.

e. In the *Animation Pane* list, right-click **Group 5** and select **Timing** to open the *Blinds* dialog box.

f. Click the **Triggers** button, select **Start effect on play of**, and **Bookmark 1** (with the name of the audio object) automatically appears (Figure 5-74).

g. Click **OK** to close the dialog box.

h. Close the *Animation Pane*.

i. Click the **Slide Show** button on the *Status bar* to test the animation in *Slide Show* view. The sound plays through the animation of both groups.

9. Format an audio object.

a. On slide 5, select the audio object.

b. Click **Change Picture** [*Format* tab, *Adjust* group] to open the *Insert Pictures* dialog box.

c. In the *Office.com Clip Art* search box, type storm.

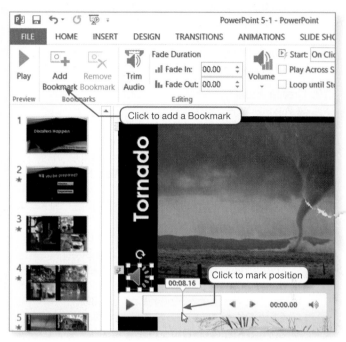

5-73 *Bookmark* the audio object

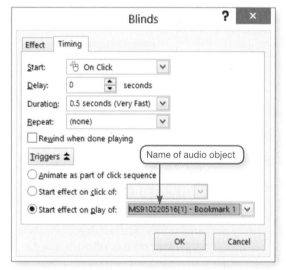

5-74 The *Trigger* controls when animation starts

d. From the search results, select the "Lightening and rain from cloud" image and click **Insert**.

e. Increase the audio object size (*Height* and *Width* **1"**) and position the object in the black area on the left of the slide (Figure 5-75).

10. Create a text hyperlink with a ScreenTip to link to a web page.
    a. On slide 10, select the text "Federal Emergency Management Agency."
    b. Click the **Hyperlink** button [*Insert* tab, *Links* group]. The **Existing File or Web Page** option is selected.
    c. In the *Address* box, type http://www.fema.gov.
    d. Click the **ScreenTip** button in the upper right corner of the dialog box. The *Set Hyperlink ScreenTip* dialog box opens.
    e. In the *ScreenTip* text box, type Link to FEMA @ http://www.fema.gov (Figure 5-76).
    f. Click **OK** to close the *Set Hyperlink ScreenTip* dialog box; click **OK** again to close the *Insert Hyperlink* dialog box.

5-75 **Audio object with new picture**

11. Select the text "American Red Cross" and repeat steps 10 b–f.

Address	http://www. redcross.org
ScreenTip	Link to American Red Cross @ http://www. redcross.org.

12. In *Slide Show* view, test the ScreenTip and the hyperlink to both web pages.

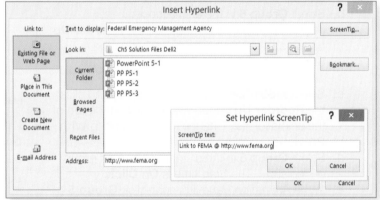

5-76 *Insert Hyperlink* dialog box

13. Assign hyperlinks to shapes to create links to presentation topics.
    a. On slide 2, select the "Disasters" shape and click the **Hyperlink** button [*Insert* tab, *Links* group] or press **Ctrl+K** to open the *Insert Hyperlink* dialog box.
    b. Under *Link to* on the left side, choose **Place in This Document**. In the *Select a place in this document* list box, choose **Slide 3**. Click **OK**.
    c. Repeat steps 13 a–b to hyperlink the "Preparedness" shape to **Slide 6. Food Supplies**.
    d. In *Slide Show* view, test each link to be sure the correct slide opens. To return to the menu slide, type 2 and press **Enter**.

14. Insert an action button on the *Slide Master*.
    a. Click the **Slide Master** button [*View* tab, *Master Views* group].
    b. Select the first *Slide Master* layout.
    c. Click the **Shapes** button [*Insert* tab, *Illustrations* group] to open the *Shapes* gallery. Select the **Home** button and draw a small rectangle (*Height* and *Width* **.5"**) in the lower left corner of the slide.

d. The *Action Settings* dialog box will automatically open. On the *Mouse Click* tab, in the *Hyperlink to* list box, select **Slide**. On the *Hyperlink to Slide* dialog box, select **Slide 2** (Figure 5-77).

e. Click **OK** to close each dialog box.

f. Click the **Close Master View** button [*Slide Master* tab, *Close* group].

g. View your slide show and check the links to be sure that movements are correct.

15. Optimize and compress the media.

a. Click the **File** tab and select **Info**.

b. The **Optimize Compatibility** option shows a summary of files that can be optimized (Figure 5-78).

c. Click the **Optimize Compatibility** button.

d. When optimization is complete, a summary appears. Click **Close**.

e. Click the **Compress Media** button and select the **Presentation Quality** option.

f. When compression is complete, a summary of the results appears (Figure 5-79). Click **Close**.

5-77 Action Settings to hyperlink

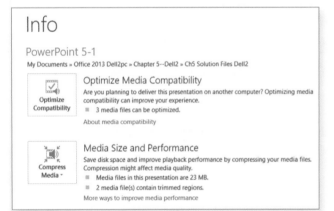
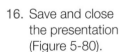

5-78 Optimize and Media Size information

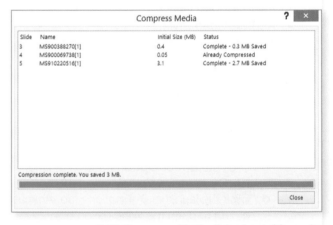

5-79 *Compress Media* dialog box with results

16. Save and close the presentation (Figure 5-80).

5-80 PowerPoint 5-1 completed

Guided Project 5-2

Classic Gardens and Landscaping (CGL) has prepared a presentation about designing and installing custom gardens for a CGL exhibit at a two-day home improvement show. The presentation includes pictures of gardens CGL has installed and features a scale drawing, a photo imaging plan, and a video of installed plantings. You use a variety of animation effects to display pictures and text, insert and format a video, and add music to the video playback.
[Student Learning Outcomes 5.1, 5.3, 5.4, 5.6, 5.7]

Files Needed: ***Gardens-05.pptx*** and ***GardenPanorama-05.mp4***
Completed Project File Name: ***[your initials] PowerPoint 5-2.pptx***

Skills Covered in This Project

- Animate a list and dim text.
- Create an animation sequence and rearrange order.
- Use the *Animation Painter*.
- Animate a *SmartArt* graphic.
- Insert a video file.
- Apply a *Video Style*.

- Trim, fade, and bookmark a video object.
- Create a trigger.
- Insert an online audio clip.
- Hide, loop, and rewind video and audio objects.
- Optimize media compatibility.
- Compress media.

1. Open the presentation ***Gardens-05*** and save the presentation as ***[your initials] PowerPoint 5-2***.
2. Animate a list and dim text.
    a. On slide 9, select the bulleted list placeholder.
    b. Click the **Add Animation** button [*Animations* tab, *Advanced Animation* group] to open the gallery. Choose the **Wipe** *Entrance* effect.
    c. Click the **Effect Options** button [*Animations* tab, *Animation* group] and select **From Left** (*By Paragraph* is already selected).
    d. Click the launcher [*Animations* tab, *Animation* group] to open the *Wipe* dialog box.
    e. Click the **After animation** list arrow and select the **dark gold** color (Figure 5-81).
    f. Click **OK** to close the dialog box.
    g. Change *Start* to **After Previous**, *Duration* to 01.00, and *Delay* to 01.00.
3. Apply multiple animation effects.
    a. On slide 2, select the picture on the left. Click the **Add Animation** button [*Animations* tab, *Advanced Animation* group] to open the gallery. Select the **Fade** *Entrance* effect.
    b. Change the *Start* to **After Previous** [*Animations* tab, *Timing* group] and change *Duration* to 02.00.
    c. With the picture selected, click the **Add Animation** button again and choose the **Fade** *Exit* effect.

5-81 Dim text color

d. Change the *Start* to **After Previous**, change *Duration* to 02.00, and *Delay* to 02.00.
e. With the animated shape selected, double-click the **Animation Painter** button.
f. Click the remaining two pictures to apply the same animation effects.
g. Press **Esc** to turn off the *Animation Painter*.
h. Click the **Animation Pane** button and increase its size to see the timeline for all entrance and exit effects for this entire sequence (Figure 5-82).

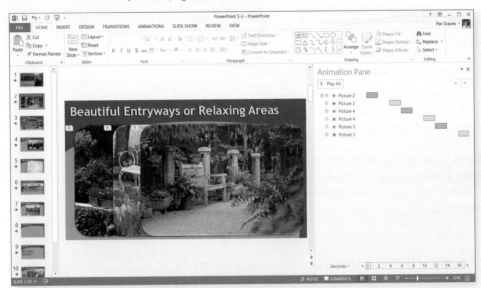

5-82 *Animation Pane* expanded to show duration times for all effects

i. In the *Animation Pane*, select the **Picture 3** *Exit* effect in the list and press **Delete** so that picture remains on the slide until you advance to the next slide.

4. Animate a *SmartArt* graphic.
   a. On slide 10, select the *SmartArt* graphic and click the **Add Animation** button [*Animations* tab, *Advanced Animation* group] to open the gallery. Select the **Pulse** *Emphasis* effect.
   b. Click the **Effect Options** button [*Animations* tab, *Animation* group] and choose the *Sequence* of **Level One By One**.
   c. Change the *Start* to **After Previous**.
   d. Click **Preview** [*Animations* tab] to test the animation.

5. Apply animation effects and rearrange order.
   a. On slide 10, select the larger picture on the right that is behind the top picture (**Picture 2** in the *Animation Pane*).
   b. Click the **Add Animation** button [*Animations* tab, *Advanced Animation* group] and select the **Fade** *Entrance* effect.
   c. Change the *Start* to **After Previous** [*Animations* tab, *Timing* group] and change *Duration* to 02.00.
   d. With the animated picture selected, click the **Animation Painter** button and click the top picture (**Picture 3** in the *Animation Pane*).
   e. In the *Animation Pane*, select **Picture 2** *Entrance* effect and click **Reorder Up** to move it above the *Diagram* effect.
   f. With **Picture 2** selected, click the **Add Animation** button and select the **Fade** *Exit* effect.
   g. Change the *Start* to **After Previous** [*Animations* tab, *Timing* group] and change *Duration* to 02.00.

h. In the *Animation Pane*, select the **Picture 2** *Exit* effect in the *Animation Pane* and click **Reorder Up** to move it above *Picture 3* (Figure 5-83).
i. Click the **chevron** icon to expand the "Diagram" animation contents to see how each shape in the *SmartArt* graphic appears in the timeline (Figure 5-84). Click the **chevron** icon again to collapse the list.
j. Test the animation in **Slide Show** view.

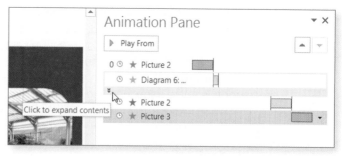

5-83 *Animation Pane showing duration times and a collapsed list*

6. Add an *Exit* animation effect to reveal a picture.
   a. On slide 11, select the picture and press **Ctrl+D** to duplicate it. Place the duplicated picture over the original picture.
   b. With the duplicated picture selected, click the **Artistic Effects** button [*Picture Tools Format* tab, *Adjust* group] and select the **Chalk Sketch** (Figure 5-85).

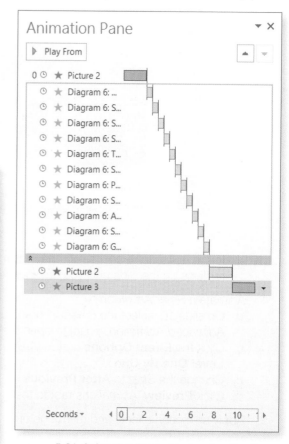

5-84 *Animation Pane showing duration times and an expanded list*

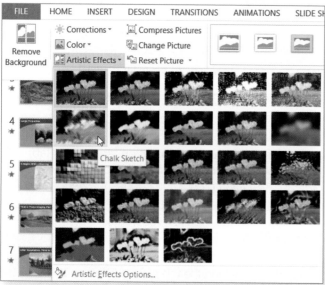

5-85 *Artistic Effects gallery*

c. Select the **Add Animation** button [*Animations* tab, *Advanced Animation* group] and select the **Fade** *Exit* effect.
d. Change the *Start* to **After Previous** [*Animations* tab, *Timing* group] and change *Duration* to 03.00.
e. Click **Preview** [*Animations* tab] to test the animation. The "Chalk Sketch" picture in grayscale gradually fades away revealing the original color picture.

7. Reposition pictures with animation.
   a. On slide 7, select the four overlapping pictures that are animated.
   b. Click the **Align** button [*Picture Tools Format* tab, *Arrange* group] and select **Align Center**.
   c. Repeat to select **Align Middle**.
   d. With the four pictures still selected, move them up slightly and position them evenly on the slide.

e. Check the *Animation Pane* list to be sure the pictures are arranged in ascending order from *Picture 2* to *Picture 5*.

f. Click **Preview** [*Animations* tab] to test the animation.

g. Close the *Animation Pane*.

8. Insert a video and apply a *Video Style*.

a. On slide 8, click the **Video** button list arrow [*Insert* tab, *Media* group] and choose **Video on My PC**.

b. Locate your student video files, select **GardenPanorama-05**, and click **Insert**.

c. Decrease the video's size (*Height* **6"** and the *Width* will automatically adjust) [*Video Tools Format* tab, *Size* group]. Move the video down below the slide title.

d. Click the **More** button on the *Video Styles* gallery [*Video Tools Format* tab, *Video Styles* group] and click the **Beveled Rounded Rectangle** style (*Moderate* category).

9. Adjust video playback options.

a. Click the **Trim Video** button [*Video Tools Playback* tab, *Editing* group] (Figure 5-86).

b. Drag the *Start* marker or type 00:03.00 seconds; drag the *End* marker or type 00:30.00 seconds. Click **OK**. This trim reduces the video from almost 35 seconds to 27 seconds.

c. For both *Fade In* and *Fade Out*, type 03.00.

d. Change the *Start* time to **Automatically**.

e. Select **Rewind after Playing**.

f. Click **Send Backward** [*Video Tools Format* tab, *Arrange* group] and select **Send to Back** so the video is behind the two "cloud" shapes.

g. View the video in *Slide Show* view.

10. Add bookmarks and trigger animated shapes.

a. With the video object selected, click on the timeline at approximately 05.00 seconds. Click the **Add Bookmark** button [*Video Tools Playback* tab, *Bookmarks* group].

b. Repeat to add three more bookmarks at approximately 10.00, 14.00, and 20.00 seconds (Figure 5-87).

c. Select the "cloud" shape on the left with the text, "Video captured in August."

d. Click the **Add Animation** button [*Animations* tab, *Advanced Animation* group] and select the **Fade** *Entrance* effect.

e. Click the **Trigger** button [*Animations* tab, *Advanced Animation* group], select **On Bookmark**, and select **Bookmark 1** (Figure 5-88).

5-86 Trimming the video to remove 8 seconds

5-87 Four bookmarks added to the video timeline

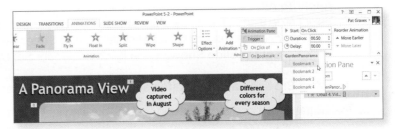

5-88 *Fade* entrance effect triggered by *Bookmark 1*

f. With the same shape selected, click the **Add Animation** button again and select the **Fade** *Exit* effect.

g. Click the **Trigger** button, select **On Bookmark**, select **Bookmark 2**.

h. Repeat steps 10 d–g for the "cloud" shape on the right with the text, "Different colors for every season," to apply the **Fade** *Entrance* and *Exit* effects that are triggered by *Bookmark 3* and *Bookmark 4*.

i. Close the *Animation Pane*.

11. Insert an online audio clip to play while the presentation plays.

a. On slide 1, click the **Audio** button list arrow [*Insert* tab, *Media* group] and select **Online Audio**. The *Insert Audio* dialog box opens.

b. Type the search word soothing in the *Office.com Clip Art* list box and click **Search**.

c. From the search results, select an audio clip of soft-sounding music such as **Words often fail**, and then click **Insert**. This audio clip is 60.00 seconds long but the one you find may have a different length.

d. Change the *Start* to **Automatically**. Click the **Volume** button to change the volume level if necessary [*Audio Tools Playback* tab, *Audio Options* group].

e. Select **Play Across Slides**, **Loop until Stopped**, **Hide During Show**, and **Rewind after Playing** [*Audio Tools Playback* tab, *Audio Options* group] (Figure 5-89).

5-89 *Audio Options*

12. Adjust transition timings and change show type to a kiosk presentation.

a. Click the *Transitions* tab.

b. Deselect **On Mouse Click**. Select **After** and type 03.00 [*Transitions* tab, *Timing* group]. Click **Apply To All**.

c. Select slide **9** and change the *After* time to 00:08.00. Repeat to apply the same time to slide 11.

d. If you wish, check the timings for all slides in *Slide Sorter* view.

e. Click the **Set Up Slide Show** button [*Slide Show* tab, *Set Up* group] to open the *Set Up Show* dialog box.

f. Select **Browsed at a kiosk (full screen)**. Click **OK** to close the dialog box.

13. Test all transitions and animations in *Slide Show* view to be sure all settings are working correctly. Speeds can vary on different computers, so you may need to increase or decrease some animation or transition timings.

14. Optimize and compress the media if options are available.
    a. Click the **File** tab and select **Info**.
    b. Click the **Optimize Compatibility** button. When optimization is complete, a summary appears. Click **Close**.
    c. Click the **Compress Media** button and select the **Presentation Quality** option. When compression is complete, a summary appears. Click **Close**.

15. Save and close the presentation (Figure 5-90).

5-90 PowerPoint 5-2 completed

Guided Project 5-3

American River Cycling Club has many events and racing opportunities that are appropriate for members with different skill and ability levels. This presentation describes racing opportunities and team options. It includes a variety of animation effects and a formatted video.
[Student Learning Outcomes 5.1, 5.2, 5.3, 5.4, 5.6, 5.7]

Files Needed: ***ARCCPromotion-05.pptx*** and ***StartYoung-05.mov***
Completed Project File Name: ***[your initials] PowerPoint 5-3.pptx***

Skills Covered in This Project

- Animate a list and dim text.
- Reorder an animation sequence.
- Create a trigger.
- Animate a *SmartArt* graphic.
- Create motion path animation.
- Hyperlink to another source.

- Insert a video file.
- Hide, loop, and rewind a video.
- Apply a *Poster Frame* and *Video Style*.

- Optimize media compatibility.
- Compress media.

1. Open the presentation **ARCCPromotion-05** and save the presentation as *[your initials] PowerPoint 5-3*.

2. Animate a list and dim text.
   a. On slide 2, select the bulleted list placeholder.
   b. Click the **Add Animation** button [*Animations* tab, *Advanced Animation* group] to open the gallery. Choose the **Zoom** *Entrance* effect.
   c. Click the **Effect Options** button [*Animations* tab, *Animation* group] and choose **Object Center**. The *By Paragraph* option is already selected.
   d. Click the launcher [*Animations* tab, *Animation* group] to open the *Zoom* dialog box.
   e. Click the **After animation** list arrow and select the **blue** color.
   f. Click **OK** to close the dialog box.

3. Apply multiple animation effects and adjust their sequence and timing.
   a. On slide 5, five pictures are each grouped with a text box and arranged on the slide. Select the five picture and text groups.
   b. Click the **Add Animation** button and select the **Wheel** *Entrance* effect. Change the *Start* to **After Previous** and the *Duration* to 02.50. Animation tags appear with each grouped picture and this indicates the grouped pictures are still selected.
   c. Click the **Add Animation** button again and select the **Shrink and Turn** *Exit* effect. Change the *Start* to **After Previous**, the *Duration* to 01.50, and the *Delay* to 3.00.
   d. Click the **Animation Pane** button [*Animations* tab, *Advanced Animation* group]. The *Exit* effects appear below the *Entrance* effects (Figure 5-91).

5-91 *Exit* effects are after *Entrance* effects

5-92 **Animation sequence**

   e. Select each *Exit* effect and click the **Reorder Up** button to rearrange the animations so each group's *Exit* effect follows the *Entrance* effect. If you wish, resize the *Animation Pane* to see the duration for each effect (Figure 5-92); then resize the pane to its regular size.
   f. Select the first group in the list and click the **Preview** button [*Animations* tab] to test the animation.
   g. Close the *Animation Pane*.

4. Animate a *SmartArt* graphic.
   a. On slide 6, select the *SmartArt* graphic. Be sure you have selected the entire *SmartArt* graphic and not an individual shape within the *SmartArt* graphic frame.
   b. Click the **Add Animation** button [*Animations* tab, *Advanced Animation* group] to open the gallery. Select the **Wipe** *Entrance* effect.
   c. Click the **Effect Options** button [*Animations* tab, *Animation* group]; then choose the *Direction* **From Bottom** and the *Sequence* of **As One Object**.
   d. Change the *Start* to **After Previous** and the *Duration* to 01.00.
   e. Click the **Preview** button [*Animations* tab] to test the animation.

5. Apply multiple animation effects that display together on the same object.
   a. On slide 1, select the rider picture and apply three effects. Click the **Add Animation** button [*Animations* tab, *Advanced Animation* group] each time to open the gallery and select an effect. When the animation tags are visible, no handles will appear around the picture. Apply the effects and adjust *Timing* options as shown in the following table:

Animation Effect	Effect Options	Start	Duration	Delay
Appear (Entrance)		*After Previous*	Auto	00.00
Zoom (Entrance)	*Object Center*	*With Previous*	10.00	00.00
S Curve 2 (Motion Path)		*With Previous*	10.00	00.00

   b. Move the green triangle marker (the beginning point) of the *Motion Path* animation to the left of the slide. Move the red marker (the ending point) to the middle of the slide so the rider movement ends beside the title (Figure 5-93).

5-93 *Motion Path* beginning and ending positions

   c. Click **Preview** [*Animations* tab] to test the animation. Adjust the beginning and ending positions if necessary so it looks like the rider is approaching from the distant hill.

6. Create a text hyperlink with a ScreenTip to link to a web page.
   a. On slide 7, select the text "USA Cycling."
   b. Click the **Hyperlink** button [*Insert* tab, *Links* group]. Select the **Existing File or Web Page** option.
   c. In the *Address* box, type http://www.usacycling.org.
   d. Click the **ScreenTip** button in the upper right corner of the dialog box to open the *Set Hyperlink ScreenTip* dialog box.
   e. In the *ScreenTip* text box, type Link to USA Cycling @ http://www.usacycling.org.
   f. Click **OK** to close the *Set Hyperlink ScreenTip* dialog box. Click **OK** again to close the *Insert Hyperlink* dialog box.
   g. In *Slide Show* view, test the ScreenTip and the hyperlink to the USA Cycling web page.

7. Insert a video and apply a style.
   a. On slide 8, click the **Video** button list arrow [*Insert* tab, *Media* group] and choose **Video on My PC**.
   b. Locate your student video files, select *StartYoung-05*, and click **Insert**.

c. Position the video on the right side of the slide.

d. Click the **Crop** button [*Video Tools Format* tab, *Size* group] and remove the black area at the top and bottom of the video.

e. Increase the video's size (*Height* **3.5"** and *Width* will automatically adjust) [*Video Tools Format* tab, *Size* group].

f. Click the **Drop Shadow Rectangle** [*Video Tools Format* tab, *Video Styles* group] (in the *Subtle* group) (Figure 5-94).

g. View the slide in *Slide Show* view and click the **Play** button on the video timeline to test the video.

5-94 Video inserted, cropped, resized, and style applied

8. Add a trigger to make the video play when the title is clicked.

   a. With the video object selected, select **Hide While Not Playing** [*Video Tools Playback* tab, *Video Options* group]. For *Start*, use the default option of **On Click**.

   b. Click the **Trigger** button [*Animations* tab, *Advanced Animation* group], select **On Click of**, and then select **Title 1**. Change the *Delay* to 00.50.

9. View the slide in *Slide Show* view. When the title animation ends, click the title to test that the trigger starts the video.

10. Review the entire presentation in *Slide Show* view to check all animation sequences. Make any necessary adjustments.

11. Optimize and compress the media.

    a. Click the **File** tab and select **Info**.

    b. Click the **Optimize Compatibility** button. When optimization is complete, a summary appears. Click **Close**.

    c. Click the **Compress Media** button and select the **Presentation Quality** option. When compression is complete, a summary appears. Click **Close**.

12. Save and close the presentation (Figure 5-95).

5-95 PowerPoint 5-3 completed

Independent Project 5-4

At Life's Animal Shelter, training sessions are given for newly adopted dogs and their owners. For this project you work on a presentation for one of these introductory training sessions. The presentation includes a variety of animation effects and two brief formatted videos. When the presentation is complete, you optimize media compatibility and compress media to reduce the presentation's file size.
[Student Learning Outcomes 5.1, 5.2, 5.3, 5.4, 5.6, 5.7]

Files Needed: *DogTraining-05.pptx*, *PillowPup-05.mov*, and *Sit-05.mov*
Completed Project File Name: *[your initials] PowerPoint 5-4.pptx*

Skills Covered in This Project

- Animate a list and dim text.
- Reorder an animation sequence.
- Use the *Animation Painter*.
- Create a motion path animation.
- Hyperlink to another source.

- Insert a video file.
- Insert an online audio clip.
- Format a video object.
- Optimize media compatibility.
- Compress media.

---

1. Open the presentation ***DogTraining-05*** and save the presentation as ***[your initials] PowerPoint 5-4***.

2. Animate a list and dim text.
   a. On slide 4, select the bulleted list placeholder and apply the **Float In** *Entrance* effect. Change *Effect Options* to **Float Up**.
   b. Click the launcher to open the *Float Up* dialog box and change the *After animation* effect to a **light blue** color (Figure 5-96). Click **OK** to close the dialog box.
   c. Use the *Animation Painter* to copy this animation and apply it to the lists on slides 5 and 6.

3. Create an animated sequence including a motion path.
   a. On slide 3, the red shape for "Name" is in its final position. Select the shape and click the **Add Animation** button. Click **More Motion Paths** to open the *Add Motion Path* dialog box.
   Select the **Spiral Right** *Motion Path* effect and click **OK**.
   b. Click the **Effect Options** button and select **Reverse Path Direction**. Change the *Start* to **After Previous** and the *Duration* to 04.00.

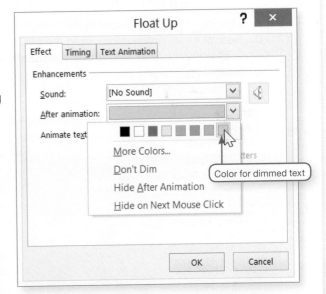

5-96 *Float Up* dialog box

c. Resize the animation area to almost fill the slide. Be sure to keep the animated shape's start position in front of the sentence text (Figure 5-97). The center of the animated object moves on the line.

d. Test the animation to be sure it moves around the slide and ends in its original position.

e. Select the text box and apply the **Wipe** *Entrance* effect. Change the *Effect Options* to **From Left**. Change the *Start* to **After Previous**, the *Duration* to 01.50 and the *Delay* to 01.00.

f. Test the animations in *Slide Show* view.

5-97 *Spiral Right Motion* **Path** animation

4. Create an animated sequence including a color change and an inserted online audio.

a. On slide 7, select the first arrow on the left. Apply a **Wipe** *Entrance* effect and change the *Direction* to **From Left**. Use the *Animation Painter* to apply the same effect to the second and third arrow.

b. Select the first star shape on the right. Click the **Add Animation** button to apply each of the following effects:

- Click the **Add Animation** button and apply the **Appear** *Entrance* effect. Change the *Start* to **After Previous**; the *Duration* is **Auto**.
- Click the **Add Animation** button again and apply the **Fill Color** *Emphasis* effect. Change the *Effect Options* to **Red**, **Accent 5**, **Darker 25%** (second column from the right; second color from the bottom). Change *Start* to **With Previous** and *Duration* to 02.00.

c. Use the *Animation Painter* to apply the same effect to the second and third star shapes.

d. Search for an online audio using the search word dog growl. Find an appropriate sound and insert it. Change the *Start* time to **Automatically** and select the **Hide During Show** option.

e. Search again using the search word dog bark and insert an appropriate sound. Apply the same options as you did in 4d.

f. Position both audio objects on their related arrows (Figure 5-98).

g. Adjust the animation sequence as shown in Figure 5-99. The arrows appear when clicked; all other effects are sequenced to appear in order.

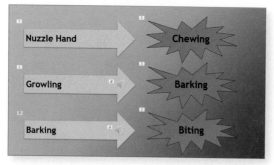

5-98 Animation applied and online audio clips inserted

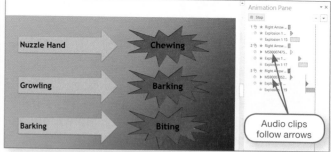

5-99 Animation sequence changed and emphasis effect shown

5. Create a hyperlink to a web page.

a. On slide 11, select the text "Cesar's Way" and prepare a hyperlink to http://www.Cesarsway.com. Add the *ScreenTip* Cesar's Way @ http://www.Cesarsway.com.

b. Select the text "Dog Training Central" and prepare a hyperlink to http://www.dog-obedience-training-review.com. Add the *ScreenTip* Dog Training Central @ http://www.dog-obedience-training-review.com.

6. Insert two video files.
   a. On slide 2, insert the ***PillowPup-05*** video from your student files.

   5-100 Video inserted, cropped, resized, and style applied

   - Crop the black and gray border lines from the top and bottom of the video.
   - Change the video size (*Height* **4.5"** and *Width* automatically adjusts).
   - Add the **Moderate Frame**, **Black** *Video Style*.
   - Position the video as shown in Figure 5-100.
   - Apply the following *Video Options:* Change *Start* to **Automatically** and select **Rewind after Playing**.

   b. On slide 4, insert the ***Sit-05*** video from your student video files.

   - Crop the gray border line at the bottom of the video.
   - Change the video size (*Height* **3.6"** and *Width* automatically adjusts).
   - Add the **Moderate Frame**, **Black** *Video Style*.
   - Position the video on the right so it does not overlap text.
   - Change the *Video Options Start* to **Automatically**.
   - Change the *Animation Start* to **After Previous**.

7. Review the entire presentation in *Slide Show* view to check all animation sequences. Make any needed adjustments.

8. Optimize media compatibility and compress media size using **Presentation Quality**.

9. Save and close the presentation (Figure 5-101).

5-101 PowerPoint 5-4 completed

Independent Project 5-5

The doctors at Courtyard Medical Plaza have opportunities to visit schools to talk to classes and student organizations. One of their goals is to reduce the number of young people who start smoking; therefore, they have developed a presentation to discuss some of the long-range effects of smoking. For this project you add animation and create hyperlinks for a menu slide and navigation. You also insert and format a video.
[Student Learning Outcomes 5.1, 5.2, 5.3, 5.4, 5.5, 5.6, 5.7]

Files Needed: *TeenSmoking-05.pptx*, *Smoking05.mov*, and *Lungs-05.png*
Completed Project File Name: *[your initials] PowerPoint 5-5.pptx*

Skills Covered in This Project

- Create an animation sequence.
- Use the *Animation Painter*.
- Animate chart elements.
- Animate a *SmartArt* graphic.
- Create a hyperlink.
- Create an action button.

- Insert a video file.
- Add and remove bookmarks.
- Format a video object.
- Record an audio clip.
- Optimize media compatibility.
- Compress media.

1. Open the presentation **TeenSmoking-05** and save the presentation as *[your initials] PowerPoint 5-5*.
2. Create an animated sequence.
   a. On slide 2, select the text box with "90%" and apply the **Grow & Turn** *Entrance* effect. Change the *Start* setting to **After Previous**.
   b. Select the callout shape with "13" and apply the **Zoom** *Entrance* effect. Change *Start* to **After Previous**, the *Duration* to 01.00, and the *Delay* to 00.75.
   c. Use the *Animation Painter* to apply this animation to the callout with "12". Change the *Delay* to 00.25.
   d. Use the *Animation Painter* to apply this animation to the remaining callouts continuing in a clockwise order (Figure 5-102).
   e. Test the animation in *Slide Show* view.

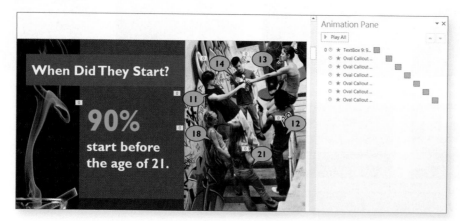

5-102 Animation sequence

3. Create an animated sequence including a chart.
   a. On slide 3, select the pie chart and apply the **Wheel** *Entrance* effect. Change the *Effect Options* to **By Category** (Figure 5-103), the *Start* to **After Previous**, and the *Duration* to 01.50.
   b. Select the text box on the left and apply the **Grow & Turn** *Entrance* effect. Change the *Start* setting to **After Previous**.
   c. Select the text box on the bottom right and apply the **Grow & Turn** *Entrance* effect. Change the *Start* setting to **After Previous** and the *Delay* to 1.00.
   d. Test the animation in *Slide Show* view.

4. Apply two animation effects that display together.
   a. On slide 5, select the "Cool" shape, click the **Add Animation** button, and apply the **Fade** *Entrance* effect. Change the *Start* setting to **After Previous** and the *Duration* to 03.00.
   b. Click the **Add Animation** button again and apply the **Bounce** *Entrance* effect. Change the *Start* setting to **With Previous** and the *Duration* to 03.00 so both effects last the same amount of time.
   c. Use the *Animation Painter* to apply these effects to the "Cool" shape on slide 6.

5. On slide 6, click the **Transitions** tab and apply the **Dissolve** *Transition* effect. Increase the *Duration* to 02.00 to emphasize slide 5 changing to slide 6.

6. Animate a *SmartArt* graphic.
   a. On slide 10, select the *SmartArt* graphic and apply the **Wipe** *Entrance* effect.
   b. Change the *Effect Options* to **From Left** and **Level One by One**. Change *Start* to **After Previous**, and *Duration* to 01.00.

7. Insert, resize, and format a video.
   a. On slide 12, insert the video **Smoking-05** from your student video files. This video is 1:27 minutes long and its size is very small (Figure 5-104).
   b. Increase the size of the video (*Height* **4"** and *Width* automatically adjusts). The video quality is not high enough to display well at a larger size without too much distortion.
   c. Move the video to the center of the slide.
   d. Click the **Poster Frame** button [*Video Tools Format* tab, *Adjust* group] and click **Image from file**.
   e. Locate your student files, select **Lungs-05**, and click **Insert**.

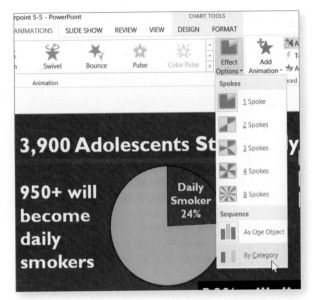

5-103 *By Category Effect Options*

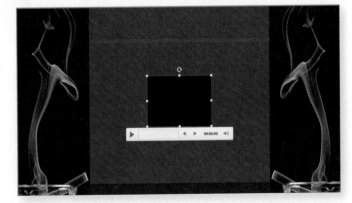

5-104 *Video inserted*

f. Apply the **Beveled Frame**, **Gradient** *Video Style* [*Subtle* group] (Figure 5-105).

g. Select **Rewind after Playing**.

h. Test the video in *Slide Show* view.

8. Prepare a menu slide with hyperlinked shapes.

a. After slide 1, insert a new slide with a *Blank* layout.

b. Draw a rounded rectangle and type Early Smoking Is Dangerous. Increase the font size to **28 pt.** and apply the **Intense Effect – Black, Dark 1** *Shape Style*. Resize the shape to fit the text (Figure 5-106).

c. Press **Ctrl+D** to duplicate this shape and align the second shape below the first one. Edit this text so it reads Smoking-Related Diseases.

d. Select the first shape and hyperlink it to slide 3; select the second shape and hyperlink it to slide 8.

9. Create action buttons on the *Slide Master* to provide navigation.

a. In *Slide Master* view, select the first *Slide Master* layout.

b. In the *Shapes* gallery, select the **Next or Forward** shape (in the *Action Buttons* group) and draw this shape on the slide. Make it link to the **Next** slide. Resize it (*Height* and *Width* **.4"**).

c. Repeat this step to draw the **Previous or Backward** shape and make it link to the **Previous** slide.

d. Repeat this step to draw the **Home** shape and make it link to **Slide 2**.

e. Select the three shapes and apply the **Intense Effect – Aqua, Accent 4** *Shape Style*.

f. *Position* the three shapes at the bottom of the slide near the cigarette (Figure 5-107).

g. Close *Slide Master* view.

10. Record an audio clip. (Skip this step if your computer cannot record sound.)

a. On slide 14, click the **Audio** button [*Insert* tab, *Media* group] and select **Record Audio** to open the *Record Sound* dialog box.

b. In the *Name* box, type Help as the name for your audio (Figure 5-108).

c. Click the **Record** button and speak into your microphone as you read the following text:

Call Courtyard Medical Plaza at 559-288-1600 to set up a consultation appointment. We will help you customize a plan to stop smoking.

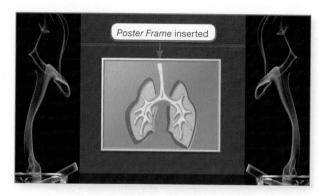

5-105 Video with *Poster Frame* and *Video Style*

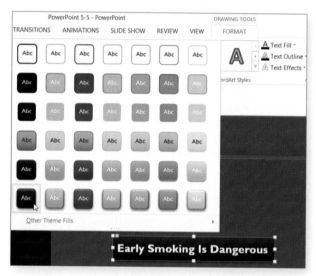

5-106 Shape style

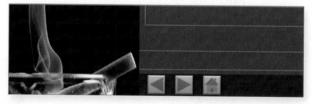

5-107 Action buttons

5-108 *Record Sound* dialog box

d. When your recording is complete, click **OK**. An audio object appears on your slide.
e. Click the **Play** button to review your recording [*Audio Tools Playback* tab, *Preview* group].
f. Change the *Start* time to **Automatically** and select **Hide During Show**.

11. Optimize and compress the media using *Presentation Quality*.

12. Save and close the presentation (Figure 5-109).

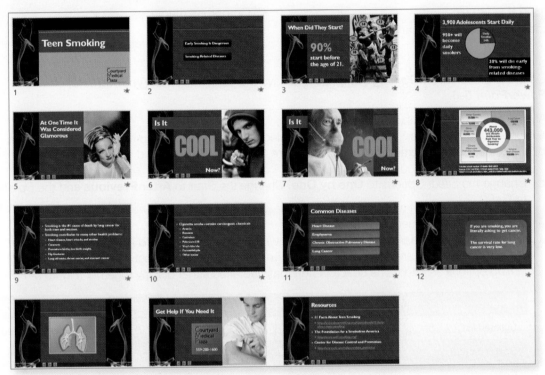

5-109 PowerPoint 5-5 completed

Independent Project 5-6

One of the community colleges in the Sierra Community College District is hosting a two-day training camp for student athletes in grades 6–12. The organizers of this track event plan to distribute a presentation to coaches so they can share it with students before the registration deadline. For this project you add animation sequences, record audio, and insert a video. You also customize video playback options with bookmarks and animated text.
[Student Learning Outcomes 5.1, 5.3, 5.4, 5.5, 5.6]

Files Needed: ***TrainingCamp-05.pptx*** and ***RunningRace-05.m4v***
Completed Project File Name: ***[your initials] PowerPoint 5-6.pptx***

Skills Covered in This Project

- Animate a list and dim text.
- Use the *Animation Painter*.
- Animate a *SmartArt* graphic.
- Create a motion path animation.
- Insert a video file.
- Add and remove bookmarks.

- Create a trigger.
- Record an audio clip.
- Format a video object.
- Optimize media compatibility.
- Compress media.

---

1. Open the presentation *TrainingCamp-05* and save the presentation as *[your initials]* *PowerPoint 5-6*.

2. Animate a *SmartArt* graphic.
   a. On slide 4, select the *SmartArt* graphic showing application and camp registration information.
   b. Click the **Add Animation** button, select **More Entrance Effects**, and select the **Curve Up** *Entrance* effect.
   c. Change the *Effect Options* to **One by One**. Change the *Start* to **After Previous** and the *Duration* to 02.00.

3. Create an animated sequence.
   a. On slide 5, select the slide objects in the following table. Click the **Add Animation** button [*Animations* tab, *Advanced Animation* group] to open the gallery. Select an effect and then adjust *Timing* options as listed. The coach picture has two effects that display together (Figure 5-110).

Object	Animation Effect	Effect Options	Start	Duration	Delay
Bulleted list	*Fly In* (Entrance)	*From Right*	*After Previous*	1.00	00.00
Coach picture	*Spiral In* (Entrance)	*None*	*After Previous*	3.00	00.00
Coach picture	*Dissolve In* (Entrance)	*None*	*With Previous*	3.00	00.00
Other Coaches text box	*Dissolve In* (Entrance)	*As One Object*	*After Previous*	2.00	00.00

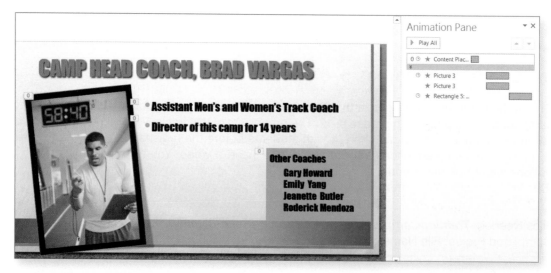

5-110 Animation sequence

4. Create an animated sequence to build a custom diagram.
   a. On slide 3, select the "Nutrition" shape and apply the **Fly In** animation effect. Change the *Effect Options* to **From Top-Right**, the *Start* to **After Previous**, and the *Duration* to 01.00.
   b. With the "Nutrition" shape selected, double-click the **Animation Painter** button and apply the same effect to the other shapes going across the bottom row and then up.
   c. Click the **Effect Options** button and change the *Direction* on three shapes as follows:

Running Mechanics	**From Top**
Racing Tactics	**From Top-Left**
Motivation	**From Top-Left**

   d. Test the animation in *Slide Show* view.

5. Close the *Animation Pane*.

6. Apply a motion-path animation.
   a. On slide 1, change the **Zoom** to about **50%** so you can use the area around the slide.
   b. Select the runner shape and move it off the slide on the left.
   c. Click the **Add Animation** button and select **More Motion Paths**. Select the **Right** *Entrance* effect [*Lines-Curves* group].
   d. Change the *Start* setting to **After Previous** and the *Duration* to 02.00.
   e. Check the *Start* and *End* positions and adjust if necessary so the animation path aligns with the green rectangle on the slide (Figure 5-111).

   5-111 *Motion Path* animation beginning and ending positions

   f. Select the star shape, click the **Add Animation** button, and apply the **Spin** *Emphasis* effects. Change the *Effect Options* to **Two Spins**, the *Start* setting to **After Previous**, and the *Duration* to 02.00.
   g. Test the animation in *Slide Show* view.

7. Insert, resize, and format a video.
   a. On slide 10, insert the video ***RunningRace-05*** from your student video files. This video is 1:28 minutes long and its size is small.
   b. Increase the size of the video object (*Height* **4.5"** and *Width* automatically adjusts).
   c. Position the video above the black text about the Championship winner.
   d. Apply the **Center Shadow Rectangle** *Video Style* [*Subtle* group].

8. Add bookmarks.
   a. Select the video and stop it. Click the **Add Bookmark** button. Repeat for seven bookmarks.
   b. Use the following positions (approximately).
      - 00:05.00
      - 00:15.00
      - 00:26.00
      - 00:39.00
      - 00:50.00
      - 01:02.00
      - 01:25.00

9. Trigger animation with bookmarks to control start and end times.
   a. Select the video and click **Send to Back** so text boxes can be positioned over the video.
   b. Move the four text boxes at the bottom of the slide over the video and position each text box as shown in Figure 5-112. These positions were planned to fit appropriately on the video as it plays.
   c. Select the first text box listed in the following table and apply the effects in this order:

   - Apply the **Appear** *Entrance* effect.
   - Click the **Trigger** button and select *Bookmark 1*.
   - Click the **Add Animation** button and apply the **Fade** *Exit* effect.
   - Click the **Trigger** button and select *Bookmark 2*.

5-112 Text in position to appear with video *Triggers*

   d. Repeat step 9 c for each of the remaining text boxes with the effects and bookmarks in the following table.

Text Box	Appear Entrance Effect Trigger	Fade Exit Effect Trigger
Sydney moves to the inside lane	*Bookmark 1*	*Bookmark 2*
She's in the lead	*Bookmark 3*	*Bookmark 4*
No competition	*Bookmark 5*	*Bookmark 6*
The winner is Sydney	*Bookmark 7*	*None*

10. Adjust video playback settings.
    a. Use the default *Start* of **On Click**.
    b. Select **Rewind after Playing**.
    c. Test the video in *Slide Show* view.

11. Insert an online audio clip to play while the video plays.
    a. On slide 10, click the **Audio** button list arrow [*Insert* tab, *Media* group] and select **Online Audio**. The *Insert Audio* dialog box opens.
    b. Type the search word background in the *Office.com Clip Art* list box and click **Search**.
    c. From the search results, select **In my head** and click **Insert**. This audio clip is almost 50.00 seconds long.
    d. Select **Loop until Stopped** and **Hide During Show** [*Audio Tools Playback* tab, *Audio Options* group].
    e. Click the **Trigger** button [*Animations* tab, *Advanced Animation* group], click **On Bookmark**, and select **Bookmark 1**.
    f. Move the audio object to the bottom of the slide (see Figure 5-113).
    g. Test the audio and video in *Slide Show* view.

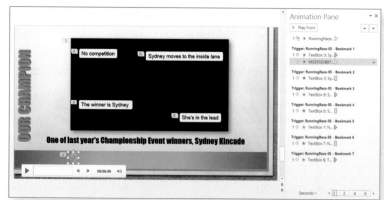

5-113 Text boxes and audio clip are triggered with bookmarks

12. Record an audio clip. (Skip this step if your computer cannot record sound.)
   a. On slide 2, click the **Audio** button [*Insert* tab, *Media* group] and select **Record Audio** to open the *Record Sound* dialog box.
   b. In the *Name* box, type Goal as the name for your audio.
   c. Click the **Record** button and speak into your microphone as you read the following text:

   > Our goal is for campers to leave the camp as more knowledgeable, motivated, and team-oriented runners than when they arrived.

   d. When your recording is complete, click **OK**. An audio object appears on your slide.
   e. Click the **Play** button to review your recording.
   f. Change the *Start* time to **Automatically** and select **Hide During Show**.

13. Optimize and compress the media using *Presentation Quality*.

14. Save and close the presentation (Figure 5-114).

5-114 PowerPoint 5-6 completed

Improve It Project 5-7

For this project you update a presentation for Placer Hills Real Estate by applying animation effects, adding hyperlinks, and recording audio. Adjust the animation effects and timing settings as appropriate.
[Student Learning Outcomes 5.1, 5.2, 5.5, 5.6, 5.7]

File Needed: ***PreparetoBuy-05.pptx***
Completed Project File Name: ***[your initials] PowerPoint 5-7.pptx***

Skills Covered in This Project

- Create an animation sequence.
- Animate a list and dim text.
- Use the *Animation Painter*.
- Animate chart elements.
- Record an audio clip.

- Animate a *SmartArt* graphic.
- Create a motion path animation.
- Hyperlink to another source.
- Optimize media compatibility.
- Compress media.

---

1. Open the presentation ***PreparetoBuy-05*** and save it as ***[your initials] PowerPoint 5-7***.

2. Create an animated sequence.
   a. On slide 1, animate slide objects using three different *Entrance* effects in this order:

Slide title	**Grow & Turn**
Picture	**Zoom**
Placer Hills Real Estate	**Wipe**

   b. Choose appropriate effects and timings (Figure 5-115).

5-115 Title slide with animation effects

3. Animate a list and dim text.
   a. On slide 2, select the bulleted text and apply a **Wipe** *Entrance* effect with **From Left** *Effect Options*. Use the default **By Paragraph** option and change the *Start* to **After Previous**.
   b. Use the **Animation Painter** to apply these effects to the list on slide 3.

4. Animate chart elements.
   a. On slide 4, select the chart and apply a **Wipe** *Entrance* effect. Change the *Effect Options* to **From Left** and **By Series**. Change the *Start* to **After Previous** and the *Duration* to 01.00.
   b. Select the source text below the chart and animate it to appear after the chart. Apply a **Wipe** *Entrance* effect with **From Right** *Effect Options*.

5. Apply a hyperlink.
   a. On slide 4, select the text **Freddie Mac**.
   b. Prepare a hyperlink to the web site http://www.freddiemac.com and include an appropriate *ScreenTip*.

6. Animate a *SmartArt* graphic.
   a. On slide 6, select the *SmartArt* graphic and apply the **Rise Up** *Entrance* effect with **One by One** *Effect Options*.
   b. Select the picture and apply the **Dissolve In** *Entrance* effect. Change the *Start* to **After Previous** and the *Duration* to 02.00.

7. Record audio. (Skip this step if your computer cannot record sound.)
   a. On slide 4, use *Record Audio* to record your voice as you read the text at the bottom of the slide.
   b. Test the audio and make adjustments if needed.

8. On slide 7, use the **Animation Painter** to apply the same animation effects to slide objects that you used for slide 1 objects.

9. Use the *Optimize Compatibility* option if it is available.

10. Use *Compress Media* using *Presentation Quality* to reduce the file size.

11. Save and close the presentation (Figure 5-116).

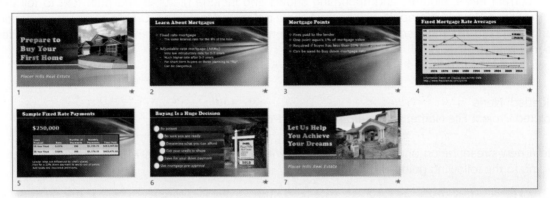

5-116 PowerPoint 5-7 completed

Challenge Project 5-8

For this project, you develop a kiosk presentation to promote an event at a zoo. Using sources such as www.nashvillezoo.org, research some typical zoo events and learning activities to get ideas. Search in *Office.com Clip Art* to find suitable animal pictures and sounds to add interest. Create complex animations and adjust timings so sequences are timed appropriately.
[Student Learning Outcomes 5.1, 5.2, 5.3, 5.4, 5.5, 5.6, 5.7]

File Needed: None
Completed Project File Name: *[your initials] PowerPoint 5-8.pptx*

Create a new presentation and save it as *[your initials] PowerPoint 5-8*. Modify your presentation according to the following guidelines:

- Select an appropriate theme and colors for an outdoor environment.
- Prepare a distinctive title slide to announce the event.
- Tell the story with pictures and brief text to develop interesting slides.
- Create animation sequences including audio files of animal sounds.
- Include a chart or *SmartArt* graphic that is animated.
- Provide a hyperlink to the Association of Zoos & Aquariums at http://www.aza.org.
- Insert a picture of a zoo employee and record an audio file to play while the picture is displayed.
- Select an appropriate transition and check all animation and transition timings.
- Optimize compatibility and compress media.
- Save as a kiosk presentation with automatic looping.
- Credit sources that you use.

Challenge Project 5-9

Prepare a presentation about your favorite musical artist or group. Research information about their history, current news, albums, and upcoming shows and include pictures and brief text to tell their story. Prepare a *SmartArt* graphic with several show dates and locations. Create complex animations and add navigation with hyperlinks and action buttons. If a video performance is available, include a link to it in your presentation.

[Student Learning Outcomes 5.1, 5.2, 5.3, 5.4. 5.5, 5.6, 5.7]

File Needed: None
Completed Project File Name: *[your initials] PowerPoint 5-9.pptx*

Create a new presentation and save it as *[your initials] PowerPoint 5-9*. Modify your presentation according to the following guidelines:

- Select an appropriate theme and colors for the artist or group.
- Prepare a distinctive title slide.
- Tell the story with pictures and brief text to develop interesting slides.
- Create animation sequences with pictures and text boxes.
- Prepare a table of contents or menu slide to link to the major topics of the presentation.
- Include action buttons on the *Slide Master* for navigation.
- Link to or insert a video performance.
- Select an appropriate transition and check all animation and transition timings.
- Optimize compatibility and compress media.
- Credit sources that you use.

Challenge Project 5-10

For this project, assume you work for a property management company that handles rental property. Develop a kiosk presentation to advertise the availability of an apartment or home. Use pictures and descriptions of your own residence or pictures you find online of another residence. Prepare complex animations with at least one motion path animation. If possible, record a brief video showing a feature of interest in your residence that a prospective renter would find interesting. Include soft music that plays in the background as slides automatically advance.
[Student Learning Outcomes 5.1, 5.3, 5.4, 5.6, 5.7]

File Needed: None
Completed Project File Name: *[your initials] PowerPoint 5-10.pptx*

Create a new presentation and save it as *[your initials] PowerPoint 5-10*. Modify your presentation according to the following guidelines:

- Select an appropriate theme and colors for a property management company.
- Prepare a distinctive title slide to announce the availability of a residence.
- Include pictures and brief text to illustrate the residence's features.
- Create animation sequences such as clicking the name of a room to make descriptive text appear.
- Include a chart showing estimated utility costs and other fees.
- Select an appropriate transition and check all animation and transition timings.
- Insert a soft-sounding music clip and have it play while the entire slide show is displayed.
- Set up the slide show as a kiosk presentation with automatic looping.
- Optimize compatibility and compress media.
- Credit sources that you use.

Integrating, Reviewing, and Collaborating

CHAPTER OVERVIEW

Microsoft PowerPoint has many powerful tools you can use to make presentation preparation easy and effective. For example, you can integrate materials into your presentation from other applications such as an Excel chart, a Word document, or other objects. When a presentation becomes lengthy, you can divide it into sections to gain easy access to each topic. Custom shows enable you to create a presentation within a presentation and show only selected slides. Proofing tools help you locate errors, make good word choices, and even translate when necessary. You can incorporate comments from other people in your presentation and work collaboratively to refine presentation content.

STUDENT LEARNING OUTCOMES (SLOs)

After completing this chapter, you will be able to:

SLO 6.1   Add content from other sources to a presentation and work with multiple open windows (p. P6-343).

SLO 6.2   Add sections to organize presentation slides into groups (p. P6-354).

SLO 6.3   Use proofing tools to correct errors, improve word choices, and translate content (p. P6-360).

SLO 6.4   Create a custom slide show of selected slides within a presentation (p. P6-365).

SLO 6.5   Insert, edit, and review comments, compare presentations, and consider reviewer feedback (p. P6-370).

CASE STUDY

For the Pause & Practice projects in this chapter, you improve a presentation to promote the Hope Run, an annual fundraising event sponsored by the Hamilton Civic Center. Everyone participating can select a charity to receive the funds they raise. Kamala Graham is the event coordinator.

Pause & Practice 6-1: Create presentation slides from a Word outline, insert content from other sources, and add sections.

Pause & Practice 6-2: Use proofing tools and create custom shows within a presentation.

Pause & Practice 6-3: Review a presentation and make revisions using comments.

POWERPOINT

Adding Content from Other Sources

PowerPoint can integrate information between the different Office applications. For example, you can create a presentation from a Word outline, insert a document as an image, or link to an Excel worksheet. Working with multiple open windows makes it easy to copy slides and other content from one presentation or document to your current presentation.

Use a Word Outline to Create Slides

If you want to create slides from a Microsoft Word document, the document must be formatted as an outline with heading styles applied to the text. PowerPoint interprets heading styles as follows:

- *Heading 1 style:* The text becomes slide titles.
- *Heading 2 style:* The text becomes first-level bulleted text.
- *Heading 3 style:* The text becomes second-level bulleted text.

You can use documents from other word processing programs, too, if heading styles are supported in that program and the text is in outline form. If no heading styles are used, Power-Point creates an outline based on paragraphs in the document and your results may not be optimal. PowerPoint interprets every item as a slide title, so too many slides may be created.

To efficiently create a Word outline to be used in Power-Point, type each slide title and bulleted text on a separate line (Figure 6-1) and apply heading styles. If you have a lot of bulleted text, first select all the text and apply a Heading 2 style since that style applies to most text. Then apply Heading 1 or Heading 3 styles as needed (Figure 6-2). Save the document and close it. You can use the outline to create slides in a new presentation or to add slides to an existing presentation.

Presentation Title
Presentation Subtitle
Slide 2 Title
Listed item 1
Listed item 2
Listed item 3
Slide 3 Title
Listed item 1
Listed item 1a
Listed item 1b
Listed item 2
Slide 4 Title
Listed item 1
Listed item 2
Listed item 2a
Listed item 2b

6-1 Text for slides in Microsoft Word

6-2 Text for slides in Microsoft Word with heading styles applied

HOW TO: Create Slides from a Word Outline

1. Start a new presentation or select the slide in an existing presentation that you want to precede the new slides.
2. Click the **New Slide** list arrow [*Home* tab, *Slides* group] and select **Slides from Outline** (Figure 6-3) to open the *Insert Outline* dialog box.

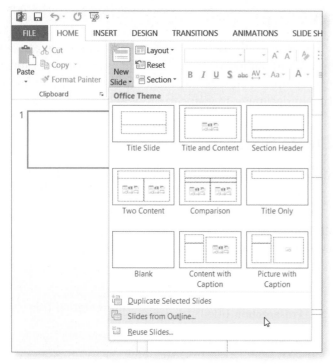

6-3 Create slides from a Word outline

3. Locate the Word file you want to use for slide text.

4. Click **Insert**.

5. All inserted slides use the *Title and Content* layout. The new slides will appear in the current theme (Figure 6-4).

   - You may have a blank slide at the beginning, depending on which slide was selected when you created the new slides. Delete this slide if you do not need it.
   - If your first slide is a title slide, select the *Title Slide* layout [*Home* tab, *Slides* group].
   - Apply a theme and other formatting as needed.

6. Save your presentation.

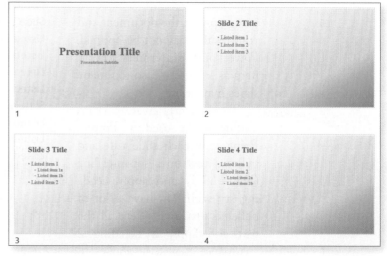

6-4 Slides created from a Word outline

Work with Multiple Open Windows

In Chapter 1, you learned two ways to reuse and edit slides in the *Reuse Slides from Another Presentation* section in *SLO 1.2: Adding and Editing Presentation Text* and in the *Copy, Paste, and Duplicate Slides* section in *SLO 1.3: Rearranging Slides*. The *Reuse Slides* feature requires that you have access to the second presentation, but you do not need to open it. For many situations, however, it is helpful to see more than one presentation at the same time to determine which slides you want to use again. PowerPoint makes this possible by displaying multiple open windows.

You can arrange multiple windows using ***Switch***, ***Cascade***, or ***Arrange All***. These options work differently, depending on whether PowerPoint is maximized to fill your screen or if PowerPoint is used with a floating window.

HOW TO: Work with Multiple PowerPoint Windows

1. Open two presentations or start a new presentation and open an existing one.
2. Click the **Maximize** button [*Title bar*] so PowerPoint fills the screen.
3. In either presentation, click the **View** tab. In the *Window* group, click one of the following options (Figure 6-5):

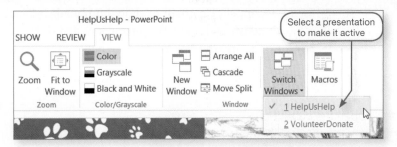

6-5 *Window* group on the *View* tab

- **Switch Windows**: Only one presentation is displayed at a time. Select the presentation you want to be active.
- **Cascade**: Each presentation is displayed in a separate window with its own *Ribbon*. The windows are layered with the presentation name in each title bar. Click a title bar to make that presentation active and bring it to the front (Figure 6-6).
- **Arrange All**: Presentation windows are tiled so you can see them all at the same time. A side-by-side arrangement is used most often when you are working with two presentations. However, you can tile more than two windows. All *Ribbon* options are available with each window. When the window width is narrow, you must expand the groups to access commands (Figure 6-7).
- **New Window**: A duplicate presentation of the active presentation opens in a new window.

6-6 *Cascade* layers all open presentation windows

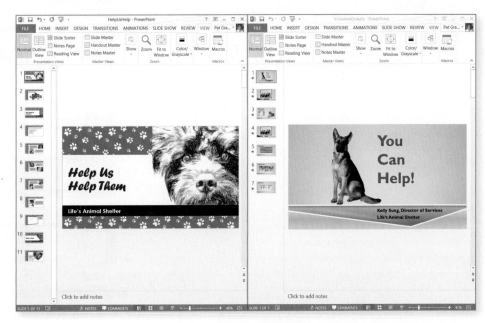

6-7 *Arrange All* shows all open presentation windows

These options make it easy to move back and forth between presentations. Working with multiple presentations gives you the ability to copy slides between presentations. You can copy slide content or slide thumbnails in one active presentation, make the other presentation active, and paste. By default, a pasted slide uses the theme of the slide that precedes it. You can also use the *Format Painter* between presentations.

HOW TO: Copy Slides from Another Presentation

1. Open the current presentation you are developing, and open the one from which you want to copy slides.

2. Click **Arrange All** [*View* tab, *Window* group]. Your current presentation appears on the left and the second presentation is on the right.

3. Move between presentations by clicking the title bar to make a presentation active.

4. Change to *Slide Sorter* view in both presentations and adjust the *Zoom* to **50%**.

5. In the presentation on the right, select one or more slides that you want to insert in your current presentation (Figure 6-8) and press **Ctrl+C**.

6. Make your current presentation active and click to move your insertion point to the location where you want to paste the copied slides. Press **Ctrl+V** to insert the slides in this position. Rearrange slide order if necessary (Figure 6-9).

7. When all slides that you need are copied, save your current presentation and close the second presentation.

8. Edit the new slides as needed. *Paste Options* are discussed on page 351–352.

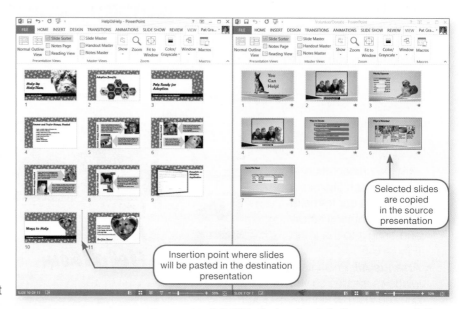

6-8 *Slide Sorter* view in both open presentations

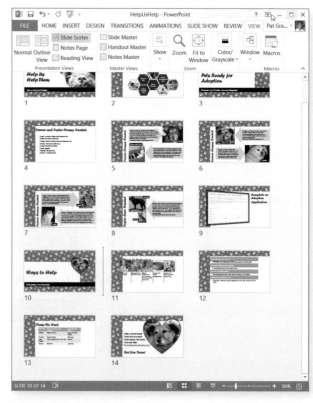

6-9 Pasted slides are rearranged

If you want to copy something from another application such as an Excel spreadsheet or a Word document, you can resize each application window so you can see both applications at the same time.

Link and Embed Objects

Object linking and embedding (*OLE*) is a technology developed by Microsoft to share objects between different Microsoft Office applications. For example, you can place an Excel worksheet in your PowerPoint presentation. When you do this, it is important to know these terms and the following definitions:

- *Source program:* The Office application where the object was created.
- *Source file:* The file where the original content is stored.
- *Destination program:* The Office application where the object is inserted.
- *Destination file:* The file where the object is inserted.

For example, if you want to place an Excel worksheet in your presentation, the worksheet is the object. Excel is the source program and the worksheet is the source file. PowerPoint is the destination program and the presentation is the destination file. When you insert content from another Office application, the way you modify the object within the PowerPoint presentation differs based on whether the object is *embedded* or *linked*.

Embed or Link an Object

When you *embed* an object, PowerPoint makes a connection to the source program and the object retains the formatting from the source program. When you activate the object by double-clicking it, the *Ribbon* for the source program becomes available for editing and replaces the PowerPoint *Ribbon*. Even though you can edit the object using this *Ribbon*, the object in PowerPoint and the source file are independent of each other. Any changes you make to the object displayed in PowerPoint do not affect the original file in the source program.

When you *link* an object, PowerPoint displays a representation of the object with linking information. The object content and formatting are stored in the source file. When you activate the object by double-clicking it, the object opens in a separate window for the source program. You use the source program to make changes and those changes are reflected in the PowerPoint object. You can edit a linked object from either the object file in PowerPoint or the source file, but changes are stored only in the source file.

The process for embedding or linking is essentially the same, but the way you edit the objects is different.

HOW TO: Embed or Link a File

1. Select the slide where you want to insert the embedded file.
2. Click the **Object** button [*Insert* tab, *Text* group] to open the *Insert Object* dialog box (Figure 6-10).
3. Select **Create from File** and click the **Browse** button to open the *Browse* dialog box.
4. Select the file you want to embed and click **OK** to close the dialog box.
5. If you want to link the file to its source program, select **Link**. Click **Display as icon** to show the link in a small size rather than as a full-size image.

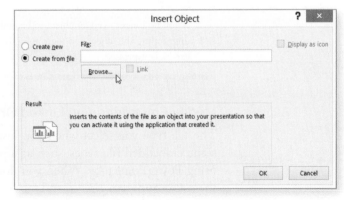

6-10 *Insert Object* dialog box

6. Click **OK** to close the *Insert Object* dialog box and embed or link the file.
   - If you embed the file, a copy of it appears on your slide (Figure 6-11).
   - If you link the file, a representation of it (a picture) appears on your slide.

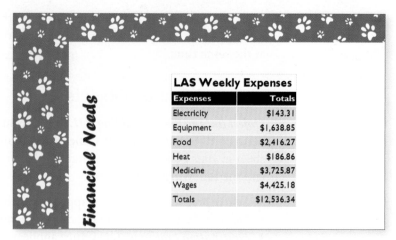

6-11 Embedded Excel object with its size increased

> **ANOTHER WAY**
>
> You can use the **Paste Special** command to embed or link an object from another application. This technique is discussed in the next section.

You can create a new file using another program from within PowerPoint. In the *Insert Object* dialog box, click the **Create new** option to open the source program and create the object. When you complete the embedded object, click outside the object to close the source program.

Embedded objects increase your presentation file size because PowerPoint stores not only the entire object but the information about how to access the source program. A smaller PowerPoint file generally results when objects are linked because only the data needed to display the information is saved.

Use embedding when the source and destination files do not need to remain the same. For example, if you are showing sales data in Excel for a past time period, embedding is a good choice because the data is not expected to change. However, if you are showing projected sales data in Excel, linking is a better option because the information will likely change as time goes by. It is best to keep permanent changes in the source file and update your presentation as needed.

> **MORE INFO**
>
> If you no longer need an object to be embedded, you can reduce your presentation file size by ungrouping the object and regrouping it. This step removes the OLE data and the remaining picture can be compressed.

Modify Embedded and Linked Objects

The file type you select when you insert an object determines how the object is edited. For some embedded file types, such as a picture or Microsoft Office Object, you edit the object using PowerPoint tabs. When you double-click an inserted object with a different file type, the source program *Ribbon* and tabs open. You use these tabs to modify the embedded object. Any changes made to the object in PowerPoint do not affect the original file.

HOW TO: Modify an Embedded Object

1. Double-click the embedded object to open the *Ribbon* from the source program (Figure 6-12).
2. Modify the object as desired. In Figure 6-13, row shading colors are changed.

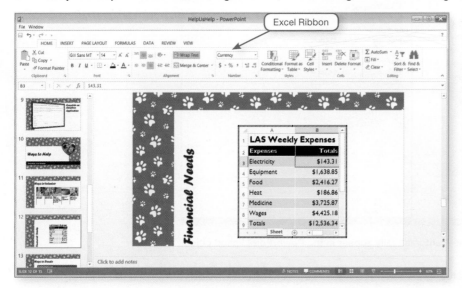

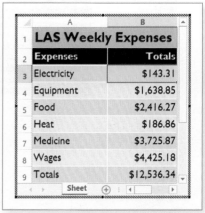

6-13 Object embedded in PowerPoint and edited

6-12 Editing a selected object within PowerPoint using the source program *Ribbon*

3. Click outside the object or press **Esc** to deselect it.

When you open a presentation containing one or more links, a dialog box opens telling you that Microsoft Office has identified a security concern because the presentation has links to other files. You are asked if you want to update the links (Figure 6-14). If you are comfortable with the source of the files, click **Update Links**. The dialog box closes and your links are updated.

When you edit the linked object, the source file opens so you can make changes. After you save the source file, update the linked object to reflect the current data from the source file.

HOW TO: Modify a Linked Object

1. Double-click the linked object to open the source program and file. Alternatively, you can right-click the linked object, select the **object** (such as a document or worksheet), and select *Edit* or *Open* (Figure 6-15) to open the source program and file.
2. Make changes to the source file.
   - Because both files are open, the linked object in PowerPoint is updated (Figure 6-16).

6-14 Update links in the presentation

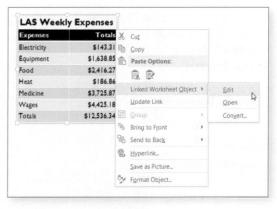

6-15 Use the shortcut menu to edit a linked object

SLO 6.1 Adding Content from Other Sources   P6-349

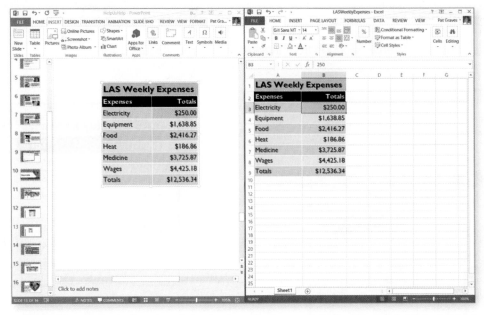

6-16 Changes in the Excel worksheet automatically appear in the PowerPoint linked object

- If the linked object does not update, right-click the linked object and select **Update Link** from the shortcut menu.
3. Save and close the source file.

If changes are made to the source file when the destination file is not open, the next time you open the destination file you will be prompted to update the linked objects in the presentation.

Modify a Link to an Object

If the location of a source or a destination file with a linked object changes, the link is broken. The instructions saved by PowerPoint to connect the source and destination files are no longer valid. You can reestablish the link to a file using the *Links* dialog box.

HOW TO: Modify a Link

1. Open the destination file. When you are prompted to update links in the presentation, click **Update Links**.
2. If you are notified that links could not be found, click **OK** to close the dialog box.
3. Click the **File** tab to open the *Backstage* view.
4. Click the **Info** button on the left.
5. At the bottom of the *Properties* list on the right side of *Backstage* view, click **Edit Links to Files** (Figure 6-17) to open the *Links* dialog box (Figure 6-18).

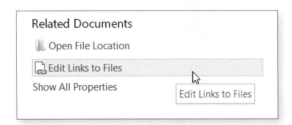

6-17 Edit Links to Files on the Backstage view

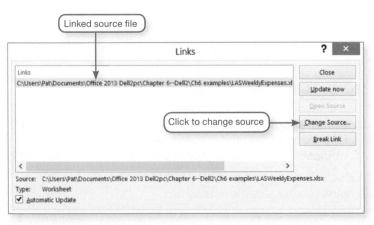

6-18 The Links dialog box

6. In the *Links* area, source files used in the presentation are listed. Select the source file you need to change if more than one is listed.

7. Click the **Change Source** button to open the *Change Source* dialog box (Figure 6-19).

8. Select the source file for the linked objects and click **Open** to modify the link and close the *Change Source* dialog box.

9. Click **Close** to close the *Links* dialog box.

10. Click the **Back** arrow to return to your presentation.

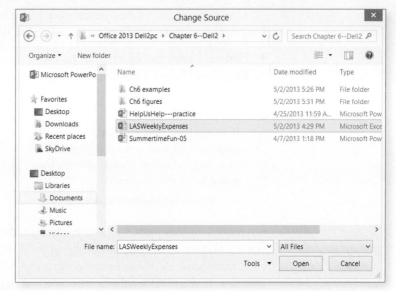

6-19 *Change Source* dialog box

Break a Link to an Object

If you no longer want a linked object connected to the source file, you can break the link between them. The linked object is converted to an embedded object and can be modified independently of the source file.

HOW TO: Break a Link

1. Open the destination file containing the linked object. When you are prompted to update links in the presentation, click **Cancel**.

2. Click the **File** tab to open the *Backstage* view.

3. Click the **Info** button on the left.

4. At the bottom of the *Properties* list on the right side of *Backstage* view, click **Edit Links to Files** (see Figure 6-17). The *Links* dialog box opens.

5. In the *Source file* area, select the source file of the linked object.

6. Click the **Break Link** button (see Figure 6-18) and the source file name is removed automatically.

7. Click **Close** to close the *Links* dialog box.

8. Click the **Back** arrow to return to your presentation.

Paste Options and Paste Special

If you use the *Paste* button [*Home* tab, *Clipboard* group] to insert slides copied from another presentation, they display with the destination theme by default. If you click the *Paste* list arrow, you see the following additional **Paste Options** (Figure 6-20):

6-20 *Paste Options*

- *Use Destination Styles:* Applies the formatting of the destination presentation styles to the material you are pasting.
- *Keep Source Formatting:* Retains theme formatting from the source document (the presentation where the slides were copied) in the material you are pasting.

Context-specific paste options vary based on what you are pasting. For example, you may have options for embedding, retaining styles, or one of the following options:

- **Picture:** Pastes an object, even text, as a picture rather than editable text.
- **Keep Text Only:** Pastes unformatted text.

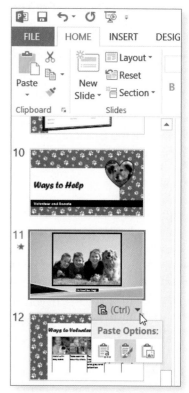

> **MORE INFO**
>
> If you're having trouble with the format of pasted text, try pasting the text using *Keep Text Only*, and format the text *after* you have pasted it into the presentation.

After a slide is pasted in a new location, the *Paste Options* button (Figure 6-21) automatically appears near the pasted slide thumbnail in *Normal* view so you can make a different selection. If you don't see the button, you can right-click a slide thumbnail and select a paste option from the shortcut menu.

To paste objects from other programs on a slide, use the **Paste Special** command. Given the space constraints on a slide, you often will want to show just a portion of an object rather than embedding the entire file. For example, you may need just a chart from an Excel worksheet rather than the entire worksheet. Copy the portion of the source file you want to show in PowerPoint and use the *Paste Special* dialog box to select the file format of the object. Choose *Paste* to embed the object and choose *Paste link* to link to the object.

6-21 *Paste Options* after a slide is pasted

HOW TO: Use Paste Special

1. In your source program, open the source file.
2. Select and copy the portion of this file you want to display in PowerPoint.
3. In PowerPoint, open your presentation (the destination file).
4. Select the slide where you want to insert the copied object.
5. Click the **Paste** list arrow [*Home* tab, *Clipboard* group] and select **Paste Special** (Figure 6-22) to open the *Paste Special* dialog box (Figure 6-23).

6-22 Open the *Paste Special* dialog box

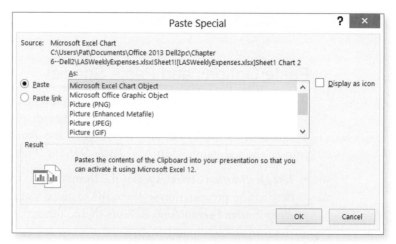

6-23 *Paste Special* dialog box with *Paste* options

6. To embed the object, select **Paste**. In the *As* area, select the appropriate format such as *Microsoft Excel Chart Object*.

- If you select the source program file type, the object retains the connection with the source program and you can edit the object from within PowerPoint.
- If you choose a different file type, such as a *Picture* or *Microsoft Office Graphic Object*, the object does not retain connection with the source program. In PowerPoint, you can edit this type of embedded object as you would a picture.

7. To link to the object, select **Paste link**.

- In the *As* area, only the appropriate format for the object will display (Figure 6-24).
- Changes made in the source file are also made in the linked destination file.

8. Click **OK** to close the *Paste Special* dialog box and a copy of the object appears in the destination file.

9. When you are satisfied with how the object looks, close the source file and program.

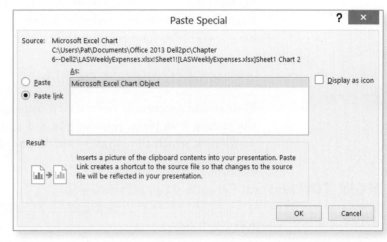

6-24 *Paste Special* dialog box with *Paste link* options

Regardless of the pasting method used (embedding or pasting the link), the object will look the same on the slide, such as the pie chart shown in Figure 6-25.

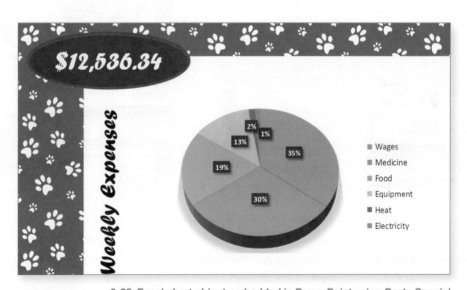

6-25 Excel chart object embedded in PowerPoint using *Paste Special*

> ANOTHER WAY
>
> **Alt+Ctrl+V** opens the *Paste Special* dialog box.

Adding Sections to Organize a Presentation

You can organize your slides into groups using **Sections**. Sections allow you to divide a lengthy presentation. You can also create sections for major topics while developing your presentation. Sections make your presentation easier to work with; you can collapse sections of your presentation and focus on one section at a time as you develop slides. During a slide show, sections are not visible to your audience and they do not interrupt the flow of your presentation.

Add and Rename a Section

You can add a section in *Normal* view using the *Slides* pane as well as in *Slide Sorter* view. Once the section is in place, you can give it a logical name. It is generally easier to work in *Slide Sorter* view, which allows you to see the slides in multiple sections at one time.

HOW TO: Add and Rename a Section

1. You can add a section in two ways:
   - Click between slide thumbnails where you want to add a section. Click the **Section** button [*Home* tab, *Slides* group] and select **Add Section** (Figure 6-26).
   or
   - Right-click between the slide thumbnails where you want to add a section and select **Add Section** from the shortcut menu (Figure 6-27).

6-26 Adding a *Section* using the *Home* tab

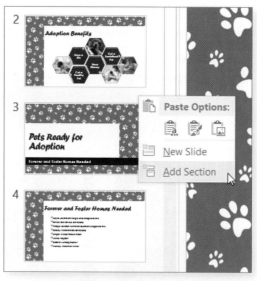

6-27 Adding a *Section* from the shortcut menu

2. The **Untitled Section** name appears and the slides below the name are selected.

3. Point to the **Untitled Section** name and right-click.

4. Select **Rename Section** and a dialog box appears (Figure 6-28).

5. Type the name for your section and click **Rename**.

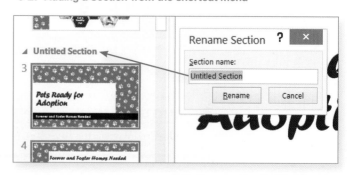

6-28 Rename the *Untitled Section*

Edit Sections

As noted earlier, *Slide Sorter* view generally works best when you are revising slide order or adjusting sections because you can see more slides at one time. You can also reduce the *Zoom* percentage so you can see more slides at one time. Note that slide thumbnails are grouped following each section name (Figure 6-29).

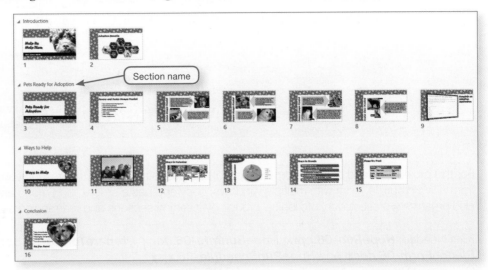

6-29 *Sections* in *Slide Sorter* view

You can move a slide from one section to another by simply dragging the slide or move an entire section by dragging the section title to its new position (drag and drop). Right-click the section title and choose from one of the following options to rearrange sections:

- ***Remove Section:*** Deletes the section title.
- ***Remove Section & Slides:*** Deletes the section title and all slides in that section.
- ***Remove All Sections:*** Deletes all section titles.
- ***Move Section Up:*** Moves up the section title and all slides in that section.
- ***Move Section Down:*** Moves down the section title and all slides in that section.
- ***Collapse All:*** Displays only the section titles with the number of slides in that section.
- ***Expand All:*** Displays the slide thumbnails for all slides in that section.

You can collapse and expand sections by clicking the triangle shape beside each section title (Figure 6-30). Collapsing the titles can help you see the "big picture" of your presentation by

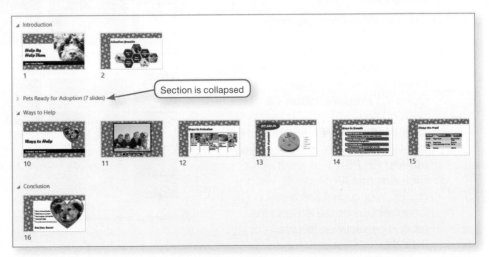

6-30 Move *Section* by dragging the section title to its new position

focusing on major topics. Seeing only the section titles makes it easy to rearrange sections by dragging (Figure 6-31). When you are ready to develop detailed information, you can expand sections one at a time to focus on each topic individually. You can move a section whether or not it is collapsed, but it is easier to see the section order when they are collapsed.

▷ Introduction (2 slides)

Ways to Help (6)

▷ Pets Ready for Adoption (7 slides)

▷ Conclusion (1 slide)

6-31 *Sections* collapsed and rearranged

PAUSE & PRACTICE: POWERPOINT 6-1

For this project you add content from a variety of sources to the *Hope Run* presentation. You create slides from a Word outline, work with multiple windows, copy and paste slides, and embed and link objects. You also organize a presentation into logical groups by inserting sections and rearranging section and slide order.

Files Needed: ***HopeRun-06.pptx***, ***HopeRunInfo-06.docx***, ***PrepareToRun-06.pptx***, ***PledgeForm-06.docx***, and ***HopeRunSchedule-06.xlsx***
Completed Project File Name: ***[your initials] PP P6-1.pptx***

1. Open the ***HopeRun-06*** presentation and save it as ***[your initials] PP P6-1***.

2. Add slides from a Word outline.
   a. Select slide 9. Click the **New Slide** list arrow [*Home* tab, *Slides* group] and select **Slides from Outline** (Figure 6-32) to open the *Insert Outline* dialog box.
   b. Locate your student files and select ***HopeRunInfo-06***.
   c. Click **Insert**. Two slides are inserted.
   d. On the inserted slides 10 and 11, click the **Reset** button [*Home* tab, *Slides* group] so the font changes to the theme font.

3. Arrange two PowerPoint windows side-by-side.
   a. If your window is not already maximized, click the **Maximize** button [*Title bar*] so PowerPoint fills the screen.
   b. Open the ***PrepareToRun-06*** presentation.
   c. Click the **Switch Window** button [*View* tab, *Window* group] and select ***[your initials] PP P6-1*** to make it active.
   d. Click **Arrange All** [*View* tab, *Window* group]. Your current presentation (destination) is on the left, and the second presentation (source) is on the right.

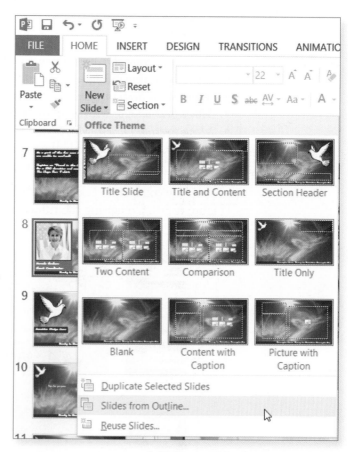

6-32 **Create slides from a Word outline**

4. Copy slides from the source presentation and paste them in the destination presentation.
   a. Change to *Slide Sorter* view in both presentations and adjust the *Zoom* to approximately **40%**.
   b. In the source presentation on the right, select slides 3–6 (Figure 6-33) and press **Ctrl+C**.
   c. Make your current presentation (destination presentation) active and click after slide 12. Press **Ctrl+V** to insert the slides in this position.

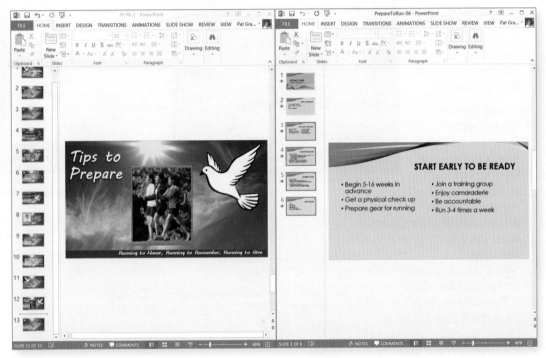

6-33 Two presentation windows displayed using *Arrange All*

   d. The new slides are automatically formatted for the current theme.
   e. Save your current presentation with the new slides and close the **PrepareToRun-06** presentation.
   f. Maximize your PowerPoint window or restore it to the size you prefer.

5. Embed a Word file and modify the embedded object.
   a. Double-click slide 4 to open it in *Normal* view.
   b. Click the **Object** button [*Insert* tab, *Text* group] to open the *Insert Object* dialog box.
   c. Select **Create from File** and click the **Browse** button to open the *Browse* dialog box. Locate your student files and select **PledgeForm-06** (Figure 6-34). Click **OK** to close the dialog box.
   d. Click **OK** to close the *Insert Object* dialog box and embed the file. It currently displays with a transparent background.
   e. Click the **Shape Fill** button [*Drawing Tools Format* tab, *Shape Styles* group] and select **White, Background 1**.
   f. Move the object to the right.
   g. Double-click the embedded object to

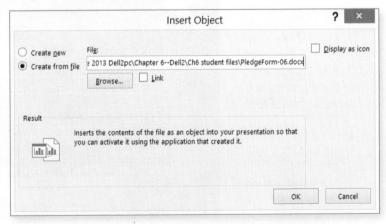

6-34 *Insert Object* dialog box

open the *Ribbon* from the source program.

h. Change the form title to The Hope Run Donation Pledge (Figure 6-35).

i. Click outside of the object or press **Esc** to deselect it.

6. Use *Paste Special* to link to an object.

a. Open Excel. Click **File** and then click **Open**. Locate your student files and select ***HopeRun Schedule-06***. Click **Open** to open the worksheet and close the dialog box.

b. Select the table cells A3:B10 and press **Ctrl+C**.

c. In PowerPoint, select slide 3.

d. Click the **Paste** list arrow [*Home* tab, *Clipboard* group] and select **Paste Special** to open the *Paste Special* dialog box (Figure 6-36).

e. Select **Paste link**. In the *As* area, select **Microsoft Excel Worksheet Object**.

f. Click **OK** to close the *Paste Special* dialog box and the object appears on your slide.

g. Double-click the worksheet to open it in Excel. Change the times on row 4 to 7:15 and on row 8 to 10:30.

h. Save and close the worksheet. Close Excel.

i. On slide 3, increase the size of the linked worksheet so the text is easy to read (Figure 6-37).

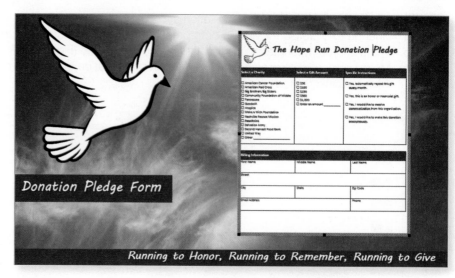

6-35 Embedded Word file revised in PowerPoint

6-36 *Paste Special* dialog box

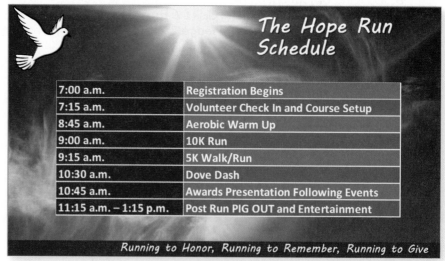

6-37 Linked Excel object revised in PowerPoint

7. Break the link to an object.
   a. Click the **File** tab to open the *Backstage* view.
   b. Click the **Info** button on the left.
   c. At the bottom of the *Properties* list on the right side of *Backstage* view, click **Edit Links to Files**. The *Links* dialog box opens.
   d. In the *Links* area, select the source file of the linked object.
   e. Click the **Break Link** button (Figure 6-38). The source file name is removed automatically.
   f. Click **Close** to close the *Links* dialog box.
   g. Click the **Back** arrow to return to your presentation.

Links

Links
C:\Users\Pat\Documents\Office 2013 Dell2pc\Chapter 6--Dell2\Ch6 student files\HopeRunSchedule-

Close
Update now
Open Source
Change Source...
Break Link

Source: C:\Users\Pat\Documents\Office 2013 Dell2pc\Chapter 6--Dell2\Ch6 student files\HopeRunSchedule-06.xlsx!Shee...
Type: Worksheet
☑ Automatic Update

6-38 *Links* dialog box

8. Add and rename sections.
   a. Click the **Slide Sorter** [*Status bar*] and adjust your *Zoom* percentage to approximately **60%**.
   b. Click after slide 8.
   c. Click the **Section** button [*Home* tab, *Slides* group] and select **Add Section**.
   d. The **Untitled Section** name appears and the slides below the name are selected.

6-39 *Rename Section* in *Slide Sorter* view

   e. Point to the **Untitled Section** name and right-click (Figure 6-39).
   f. Select **Rename Section** and a dialog box appears.
   g. Type Donations and Volunteer Positions (Figure 6-40) and click **Rename**.
   h. Click after slide 11. Repeat steps 8 c–g and rename the section Tips to Prepare.
   i. Rename the *Default Section* before slide 1 Event Details.

Rename Section

Section name:

Donations and Volunteer Positions

Rename   Cancel

6-40 *Rename Section* dialog box

9. Rearrange slides between sections.
   a. Select slide 4 in the *Event Details* section.
   b. Drag and drop slide 4 after slide 10 in the *Donations and Volunteer Positions* section (Figure 6-41).

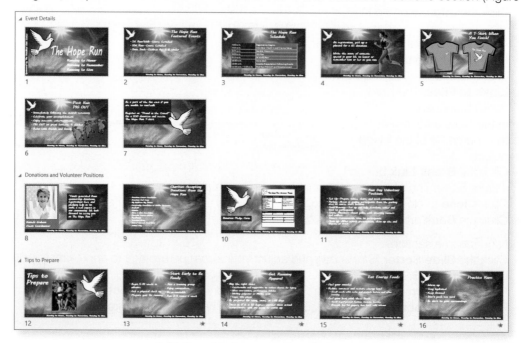

6-41 Completed presentation with inserted *Sections* in *Slide Show* view

10. Save and close the presentation.

Using Proofing Tools

PowerPoint has many built-in features to automatically catch common spelling and typing mistakes. For example, if you type "teh," it is automatically changed to "the." If you type "ANalyze," the word is automatically changed to "Analyze." Similarly, some punctuation marks are changed to ones used in printing for a more modern text appearance.

AutoCorrect and AutoFormat

The *AutoCorrect* feature recognizes and corrects commonly misspelled words. It also makes the following corrections:

- Eliminates two initial capital letters in a word.
- Capitalizes the first letter of a sentence.
- Capitalizes the first letter of table cells.
- Capitalizes the names of days.
- Resolves accidental usage of the **Caps Lock** key.
- Replaces incorrectly spelled words with the correct spelling.

The *AutoFormat* feature applies the following replacements and formatting as you type:

- Changes the keyboard "straight quotes" to "smart quotes."
- Converts fractions (such as 3/4) with a fraction character such as ¾.
- Applies superscript to ordinal numbers such as 1st, 2nd, 3rd, etc.
- Converts two hyphens (--) with no space around them to an em dash (—).

- Converts a single hyphen with a space on either side (-) to an en dash (–).
- Displays URLs (web addresses) as hyperlinks.
- Adds bullets or numbers to listed text in the body text placeholder.
- *AutoFits* text in title and body text placeholders.

You can customize these options in the *AutoCorrect* dialog box. To open the *AutoCorrect* dialog box, click the **AutoCorrect Options** button in the *PowerPoint Options* dialog box. On the *AutoCorrect* tab, you can deselect options or click the **Exceptions** button to list words or spelling that you do not want *AutoCorrect* to change.

The *AutoCorrect* tab has two parallel word lists with the wrong spelling on the left and the correct spelling on the right that is used for the correction. This list also includes a few symbols such as the copyright notation "(c)" that automatically changes to "©." You can add words that you frequently misspell to this list, or add an abbreviation that will change to a lengthy term that you frequently use.

This same list is used in all of your Office programs; therefore, changes you make in PowerPoint will affect other Office application programs as well.

HOW TO: Add a Custom AutoCorrect Entry

1. Click the **File** tab to open the *Backstage* view.
2. Choose the **Options** button to open the *PowerPoint Options* dialog box.
3. Click the **Proofing** button on the left (Figure 6-42).
4. Select the **AutoCorrect Options** button. The *AutoCorrect* dialog box opens.
5. In the *Replace* box, type the misspelled word or abbreviation you want PowerPoint to recognize.
6. In the *With* box, type the word(s) to replace the original text (Figure 6-43).

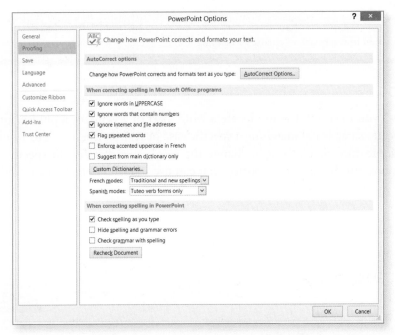

6-42 *Proofing Options* on the *PowerPoint Options* dialog box

6-43 *AutoCorrect* dialog box

7. Click **Add**. This pair of words is added to the *AutoCorrect* list.
8. Click **OK** to close the *AutoCorrect* dialog box.
9. Click **OK** to close the *PowerPoint Options* dialog box.

> **MORE INFO**
>
> In the *AutoCorrect* dialog box, click the **AutoFormat As You Type** tab to customize selections.

When PowerPoint automatically makes a correction or formatting change, you may not notice that a change has been made. A very subtle mark, a short line, appears below the corrected word. If you keep typing, the change is accepted. If you click the short line, a list button appears with several options depending on the correction that was made. For example, when the misspelled word "independant" is typed as the first word in a text box, it is corrected to "Independent." These options (Figure 6-44) appear:

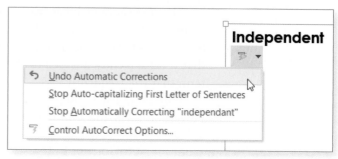

6-44 *AutoCorrect Options*

- *Undo Automatic Corrections*
- *Stop Auto-capitalizing First Letter of Sentences*
- *Stop Automatically Correcting "independant"*
- *Control Auto Correct Options*

You can click one of the options to undo or prevent a correction. Click **Control Auto Correct Options** to open the *AutoCorrect* dialog box.

> **ANOTHER WAY**
>
> Press **Ctrl+Z** or click **Undo** to reverse an automatic correction.

Find and Replace

The ***Find*** feature allows you to search for and locate a word, part of a word, or a phrase. You can also use *Find* to locate occurrences matching a specific case or restrict the search to whole words only. The ***Replace*** feature enables you to change the words that match your specifications. The *Find* dialog box also has a *Replace* button you can use to change the word it finds. Searches begin on the currently selected slide.

HOW TO: Use Find and Replace

1. Select the first slide in your presentation.
2. Click the **Find** button [*Home* tab, *Editing* group] or press **Ctrl+F**. The *Find* dialog box opens (Figure 6-45).
3. In the *Find what* box, type the text you want to locate.
   - Select *Match case* and only words matching the capitalization of the word you type will be found.
   - Select *Find whole words only* if you do not want PowerPoint to find matches for the word you type within a longer word.

6-45 *Find dialog box*

4. Click the **Find Next** button.

5. If the text is in your presentation, PowerPoint will highlight the first occurrence of the matching text (Figure 6-46).

6. Edit the highlighted text if you want to make changes.

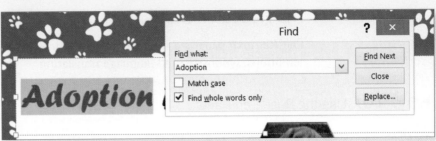

7. Keep clicking the **Find Next** button to move through each matching occurrence in the presentation.

6-46 Use *Find* for whole words only

8. Click the **Replace** button (in the *Find* dialog box or on the *Home* tab) or press **Ctrl+H** to open the *Replace* dialog box (Figure 6-47).

   • Type the word you want to use in the *Replace with* box.
   • Click the **Find Next** button to locate the next word without making a change.
   • Click the **Replace** button to change only the highlighted word.
   • Click the **Replace All** button to change all occurrences of the word.

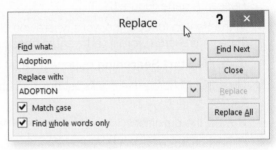

6-47 *Replace* dialog box

9. When the matching process is complete, a dialog box opens identifying the last match. Click **OK** to close the dialog box.

10. Click **Close** to close the *Find* or the *Replace* dialog box.

> ### MORE INFO
>
> It is a good idea to use **Match Case** when replacing acronyms (an abbreviation formed from initials—usually capital letters) with words so the replaced words will not be all uppercase.

You can also use the *Replace* feature to replace one font with another. In the *Replace* box, only the fonts used in your current presentation are listed. After you change fonts, check each slide because text box sizing and alignment with other slide objects may need adjustment.

HOW TO: Use Replace to Change Fonts

1. On any slide in your presentation, click the **Replace** list arrow [*Home* tab, *Editing* group] and select **Replace Fonts**. The *Replace Font* dialog box opens (Figure 6-48).

2. In the *Replace* box, click the arrow to select from the fonts used in the current presentation.

3. In the *With* box, type the name of the font or click the arrow to select a font you want to use.

4. Click the **Replace** button and the text is changed.

6-48 *Replace Font* dialog box

5. If you want to change another font, change both the *Replace* and *With* font names and click **Replace** again.

6. Click **Close** to close the *Replace Font* dialog box.

The Research Pane

The **Research** pane is a useful tool for finding dictionary definitions, synonyms, and language translation.

HOW TO: Use the Research Pane

1. Click in the word you want to check.
2. Click the **Research** button [*Review* tab, *Proofing* group] to open the *Research* pane (Figure 6-49).
3. In the *Search for* box, the word where you clicked will automatically appear. Type your search word if you want to check a different word.
4. Click the **Start Searching** button and a list of definitions appears.
5. Click the *All Reference Books* list box and choose the dictionary or research site you prefer.
6. Review the definitions.
7. Click the **Close** button to close the *Research* pane.

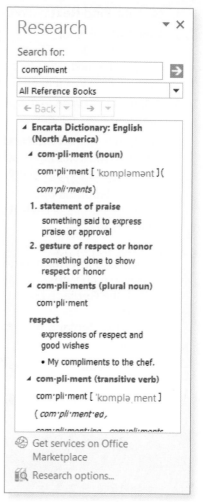

6-49 *Research* pane

Change Proofing Language

If you change the ***Proofing Language*** in PowerPoint, you can type in a different language and the spell checking and grammar rules for that language are applied automatically.

HOW TO: Change Proofing Language

1. Select any text object. Click the **Language** button [*Review* tab, *Language* group].
2. Select **Set Proofing Language** and select a language (Figure 6-50). Click **OK**.
3. Type a word or phrase in the English language and the words will be marked as spelling errors since they are not in the language dictionary you selected.
4. Type a word in the proofing language you selected.
5. No spelling errors are noted.

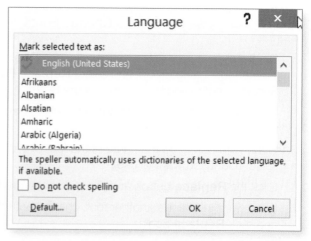

6-50 *Language* dialog box

Translate Words

PowerPoint's *Translate* feature can convert words or phrases to a different language. This translation works best for short passages and is not intended to translate an entire presentation.

HOW TO: Translate Words

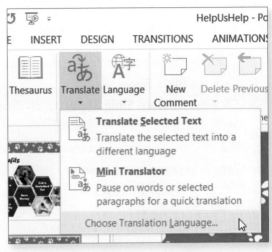

1. Click in the word you want to translate.
2. Click the **Translate** button [*Review* tab, *Language* group].
3. Select **Choose Translation Language** (Figure 6-51) to open the *Translation Language Options* dialog box.
4. Select the language you want to use from the drop-down list (Figure 6-52). Click **OK** to close the dialog box.
5. Click the **Translate** button and choose **Mini Translator**.
6. Point to the word you want to translate and the *Bilingual Dictionary* displays.
   - If you want to insert the translated word, click the **Copy** button on the **Mini Translator** and then click **Paste** where you want the word to display. Some editing may be required.
   - Click the **Expand** button on the **Mini Translator** to open the *Research* pane where you can select different languages.
7. Click the **Translate** button and click **Mini Translator** to turn off the translation feature.

6-51 Choose Translation Language

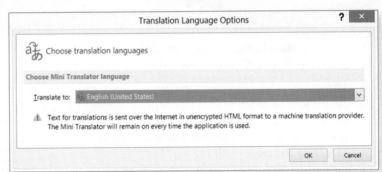

6-52 *Translation Language Options* dialog box

> **ANOTHER WAY**
>
> You can also click the **Translate** button and select **Translate Selected Text** to open the *Research* pane where you can enter the languages you want to use for translation.

SLO 6.4

Creating Custom Slide Shows

The *Custom Slide Show* feature creates a presentation within a presentation. When you set up a custom slide show, you create a list of slides from an open presentation and arrange them in any order you prefer. For example, you could prepare one presentation and then create two custom slide shows with slight variations that make them appropriate for two different audiences. You could prepare hyperlinks to make it easy to start a custom show from a slide in the original presentation. A lengthy presentation could benefit from custom slide shows, too, because you could create a menu slide with hyperlinks to each different topic.

Create, Edit, and Show a Custom Slide Show

To create a custom slide show, you must start with an open presentation so you can access slides by number and slide title. In the *Define Custom Show* dialog box, a list of all the slides in your presentation appears and you select which slides you want to add to your custom show.

HOW TO: Create a Custom Slide Show

1. Open the presentation that contains the slides you want to use in your custom side show.
2. Click the **Slide Show** tab.
3. Click the **Custom Slide Show** button [*Start Slide Show* group], and choose **Custom Shows** (Figure 6-53) to open the *Custom Shows* dialog box.

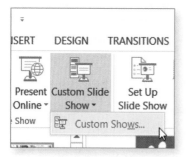

6-53 Select *Custom Shows*

6-54 *Custom Shows* dialog box

4. Click the **New** button to open the *Define Custom Show* dialog box (Figure 6-55).
5. Type a name for the custom show.
6. On the left, all slides in the original presentation are listed under *Slides in presentation*. Select the check box next to each slide that you want to include in the custom show.
7. Click the **Add** button and the slides you have selected are listed on the right under *Slides in custom show* (Figure 6-56).

   - Change the slide order, if necessary, by selecting the slide name and clicking the **Up** and **Down** buttons.
   - Delete a slide from your list by selecting the slide name and clicking the **Remove** button. When you delete a slide from the custom show, your original presentation is not affected.

8. Click **OK** when your list of slides is complete and in the order you want.
9. In the *Custom Shows* dialog box, choose from the following options:

   - *New:* Create another custom show.
   - *Edit:* Revise the selected custom show.
   - *Remove:* Delete a custom show.
   - *Copy:* Copy a custom show.
   - *Show:* Display a slide show starting with the first slide of the custom show.
   - *Close:* Close the *Custom Shows* dialog box.

10. Save your presentation so the custom shows are saved within it.

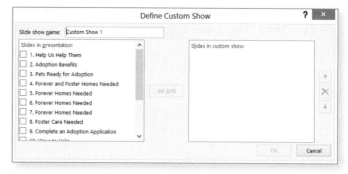

6-55 *Define Custom Show* dialog box

6-56 Slides added to the *Custom Show*

Once a show is created, you can view it using the *Custom Slide Show* button.

HOW TO: Show a Custom Slide Show

1. Open a presentation that includes one or more custom shows.
2. Click the **Slide Show** tab.
3. Click the **Custom Slide Show** button [*Start Slide Show* group] and select the name of your custom show (Figure 6-57).
4. The slide show automatically begins.
5. Test the custom show from beginning to end to verify that the correct slides are displayed in the correct sequence.

6-57 Select a custom show

> ### ANOTHER WAY
> In *Slide Show* view, point to the *Navigation bar*, click the **Navigation** button, click **Custom Show**, and select the show you want to display.

Hyperlink Custom Slide Shows

To make it easy to access custom slide shows within a presentation, you can create a table of contents or menu slide with hyperlinks from text or shapes to link to the custom shows. For more on hyperlinks, see *SLO 5.2: Adding Hyperlinks*.

HOW TO: Hyperlink to a Custom Show

1. Open a presentation that includes one or more custom shows.
2. Type text or prepare shapes with text labels to identify the custom shows and serve as your hyperlink.
3. Select the text or shape for the first show.
4. Click the **Hyperlink** button [*Insert* tab, *Links* group].
5. In the *Insert Hyperlink* dialog box, under *Link to*, click **Place in This Document**.
6. In the *Select a place in this document* list, select the custom show that you want to link to (Figure 6-58) and select the **Show and return** check box. Click **OK**.
7. Repeat steps 3-6 to link to additional custom shows.
8. Test the hyperlinks in *Slide Show* view to make sure each custom show opens and advances correctly.

6-58 Prepare a hyperlink to a custom show

If you want a more subtle approach to link to custom shows, you can accomplish the same linking action by using action buttons designed to be less noticeable on the slide. See *Create Action Buttons* section in *SLO 5.2: Adding Hyperlinks.*

ANOTHER WAY

Click the **Set Up Slide Show** button [*Slide Show* tab, *Set Up* group] to open the *Set Up show* dialog box. Click the *Custom Show* option and select the name of the show you want to display.

PAUSE & PRACTICE: POWERPOINT 6-2

For this project, you continue to work on the *Hope Run* presentation. You use proofing tools and create custom shows within the presentation.

File Needed: ***PP P6-1.pptx***
Completed Project File Name: ***[your initials] PP P6-2.pptx***

1. Open the ***[your initials] PP P6-1*** presentation and save it as ***[your initials] PP P6-2***.

2. Remove sections.
   a. Click the **Section** button [*Home* tab, *Slides* group].
   b. Select **Remove All Sections**.

3. Add a custom *AutoCorrect* entry.
   a. Click the **File** tab to open the *Backstage* view.
   b. Choose the **Options** button to open the *PowerPoint Options* dialog box.
   c. Click the **Proofing** button on the left.
   d. Select the **AutoCorrect Options** button. The *AutoCorrect* dialog box opens.
   e. In the *Replace* box, type Kamila.
   f. In the *With* box, type Kamela (Figure 6-59).
   g. Click **Add**. This pair of words is added to the *AutoCorrect* lists.
   h. Click **OK** to close the *AutoCorrect* dialog box.
   i. Click **OK** to close the *PowerPoint Options* dialog box.

4. Use *Find* and *Replace*.
   a. Select the first slide and click the **Find** button [*Home* tab, *Editing* group] or press **Ctrl+F**. The *Find* dialog box opens.
      • In the *Find what* box, type Honor.
      • Select **Match case** and **Find whole words only**.

6-59 *AutoCorrect* dialog box

b. Click the **Replace** button to open the *Replace* dialog box (Figure 6-60).

- In the *Replace with* box, type HONOR.
- Click the **Replace All** button to change all occurrences of the word.
- Click **OK** to close the dialog box indicating the replacements that were made.

c. Repeat step 4 a-b to change the words Remember to REMEMBER and Give to GIVE.

d. Click **Close** to close the *Replace* dialog box.

6-60 *Replace* dialog box

5. Use the *Research* pane.
   a. Select slide 14 and click the word "camaraderie" to put your insertion point in the word.
   b. Click the **Research** button [*Review* tab, *Proofing* group] to open the *Research* task pane (Figure 6-61).
   c. In the *Search for* box, the word you clicked in is already entered.
   d. Click the **Start Searching** button and a list of definitions appears.
   e. Click the *All Reference Books* list box and choose the **Encarta Dictionary**. (An Internet connection is required for this dictionary to appear.)
   f. Consider the definition shown.
   g. Click the **Close** button to close the *Research* task pane.

6. Create two custom slide shows.
   a. Click the **Slide Show** tab.
   b. Click the **Custom Slide Show** button [*Start Slide Show* group] and select **Custom Shows** to open the *Custom Shows* dialog box.
   c. Click the **New** button to open the *Define Custom Show* dialog box.
   d. For the *Slide show name*, type Event Information.
   e. On the left, click slides 2–11 to select them (Figure 6-62) and click the **Add** button so these slides are also listed on the right under *Slides in custom show*.
   f. Click **OK** to close the *Define Custom Show* dialog box.
   g. Repeat steps 6 c–f using the *Slide show name* Tips to Prepare, and select slides 12–16.
   h. Click **OK** to close the *Define Custom Show* dialog box.
   i. Click **Close** to close the *Custom Shows* dialog box.

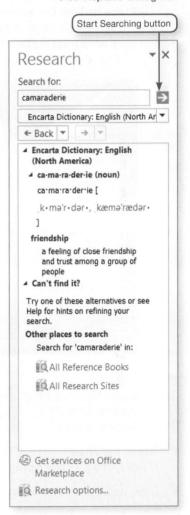

6-61 *Research* pane

6-62 Slides added to the *Custom Show*

7. Hyperlink to the two custom shows.
   a. On slide 1, insert two rectangle shapes (*Height* **.5"**) with the word Event on one and Prepare on the other to identify the custom shows. Make the text white and position these shapes on the lower left (Figure 6-63).
   b. Select the *Event* shape.
   c. Click the **Hyperlink** button [*Insert* tab, *Links* group].
   d. In the *Insert Links* dialog box, under *Link to*, click **Place in This Document**.
   e. In the *Select a place in this document* list, select the **Event Information** custom show (Figure 6-64) and select the **Show and return** check box. Click **OK**.

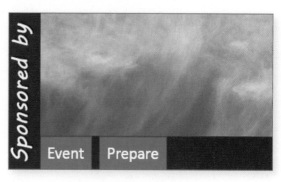

6-63 Shapes for hyperlinks to custom shows

6-64 Prepare a hyperlink to a custom show

   f. Select the *Prepare* shape and repeat steps 7 c–e to create a hyperlink for the Tips to Prepare custom slide show.
   g. Test the hyperlinks in *Slide Show* view to verify that each custom show opens and advances correctly.
8. Select the **Wipe** transition [*Transitions* tab, *Transition to This Slide* group] and apply the **From Left** *Effect Options*. Click **Apply To All** [*Transitions* tab, *Timing* group].
9. Save and close the presentation.

SLO 6.5

Adding and Reviewing Comments

The *Comments* feature provides a way to enter notes about presentation content without affecting the design of slides. You can attach a comment to text, objects, or the slide itself. While developing a presentation, you can use comments to make notes to yourself about revisions or where additional information is needed. If you plan to collaborate with someone else, you can ask questions or comment on specific slides and the person reviewing the presentation can respond with his or her own comments.

When your presentation is ready for review, be sure to save the original. You can share a copy of your presentation as an email attachment or by posting it on a shared location. The person reviewing the presentation can make changes and add comments and return or repost it. You can use PowerPoint's *Compare* feature to merge the reviewed presentation with your original version so you view all the changes and comments at one time and consider edits and suggestions. Once you decide which advice to heed, you can accept or reject any changes that were made.

Insert Comments

When you insert a comment, a comment icon appears on the slide and the *Comments* pane opens. A text box showing your name is available where you type your comment. The time when the comment is made is automatically recorded and updated.

HOW TO: Insert a Comment

1. Select the text or object on the slide that you want to reference.
2. Click the **New Comment** button [*Review* tab, *Comments* group] (Figure 6-65).

6-65 *New Comment* button

   - The comment icon appears near the selected object. If no object is selected, the comment icon appears in the upper left corner of the slide.
   - The *Comments* pane opens showing your name and an empty text box.
   - Type your comment in the text box (Figure 6-66).

6-66 Comment typed in the *Comments* pane

   - The comment time displays first as seconds; it is automatically updated to minutes or hours as time progresses. If the comment was created more than 24 hours ago, the date displays.
   - Press **Enter** or click outside the comment box when you have finished entering your comment.
3. To insert another comment, click the *New Comment* button [*Review* tab, *Comments* group] or the *New* button at the top of the *Comments* pane.
4. When all comments are complete, close the *Comments* pane.

If you are working on a presentation with multiple comments, you can click the **Next** or **Previous** button in the *Comments* group on the *Review* tab (Figure 6-67) to move between comments. You can also scroll through comments by clicking the up or down arrows at the top of the *Comments* pane.

When you close the *Comments* pane, the comment icons remain on the slide. If you want to want to hide comments, click the **Show Comments** button and deselect **Show Markup**.

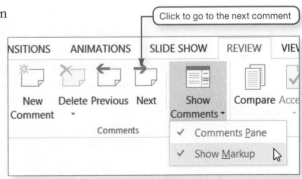

6-67 Move to the next comment

Change User Name

Comments are identified by the user name and initials specified in the *PowerPoint Options* dialog box. When you initially install Microsoft Office on your computer, you are prompted to enter your ***user name*** and ***initials***. Office stores this information to personalize Office on your computer. PowerPoint uses your user name as the ***author*** of each new presentation you create. Similarly, each comment made in PowerPoint is attributed to the user name stored in Office.

On a public computer, such as in a computer lab on your college campus, a generic user name is assigned to Office on that computer. To make sure any comments you make in a presentation are attributed to you, you can change your user name and initials.

HOW TO: Change User Name

1. Click the **File** tab to open the *Backstage* view.
2. Choose the **Options** button to open the *PowerPoint Options* dialog box.
3. Click the **General** button on the left (Figure 6-68).
4. Type your name in the *User name* text box.
5. Type your initials in the *Initials* text box.
6. Click **OK** to close the *PowerPoint Options* dialog box.

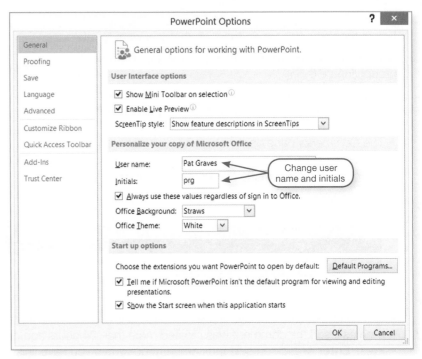

6-68 Change user name in the *PowerPoint Options* dialog box

Edit and Reply to Comments

If the *Comment* pane is not open, double-click the comment icon. You can edit a comment by clicking in the *Comment* pane text box and making revisions. Below each comment is a *Reply* box where you can add a related comment. Using the *Reply* box creates a "discussion thread" about that concept (Figure 6-69).

6-69 Reply to a comment

Compare Presentations

Compare is a collaboration feature that enables you to compare the content of two versions of a presentation. This feature is very useful when you want to consider the feedback from someone who has reviewed the presentation. You can consider all comments and changes and accept or reject the revisions. Be sure you have your original presentation saved because when you use *Compare*, the revised presentation is merged with the original presentation.

More than one reviewer can provide feedback on a presentation as long as all reviewers are adding comments to the same presentation file.

HOW TO: Compare Presentations

1. With your original presentation open, click the **Compare** button [*Review* tab, *Compare* group].

2. Select **Compare**. The *Choose File to Merge with Current Presentation* dialog box opens. Browse to locate the reviewer presentation, select it, and click **Merge**.

3. The two presentations are combined and the *Revisions* pane automatically opens (Figure 6-70).

4. Save this merged version with a different file name so you still have the original presentation.

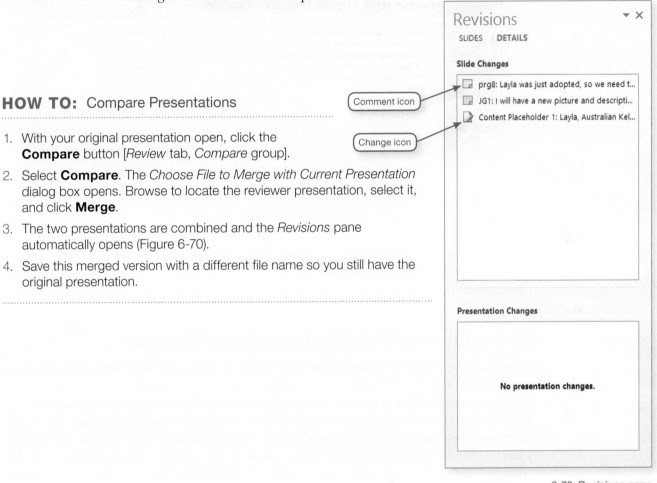

6-70 *Revisions* pane

If the *Revisions* pane closes, reopen it by clicking the **Reviewing Pane** button in the *Compare* group on the *Review* tab (Figure 6-71).

At the top of the *Revisions* pane, the *Details* tab is selected showing *Slide Changes* as you review each slide. In the *Revisions* pane, comments are shown in an abbreviated form and include the initials of the person making the comment. An icon also appears

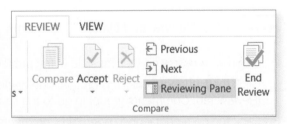

6-71 *Reviewing Pane button*

before the comment in a different color for each person. These comments are the same ones that you see when you review them in the *Comments* pane. If you want to read all of the text for a comment, click the icon or the *Show Comments* button [*Review* tab, *Comments* group] to open the *Comments* pane. Changes made to content placeholders or slide objects are listed with a different icon and a brief explanation for what changed. Click the icon in the *Revisions* pane or on the slide to see the changes that were made by the reviewer (Figure 6-72). As you review changes and comments in a presentation, you can accept, reject, or skip the changes.

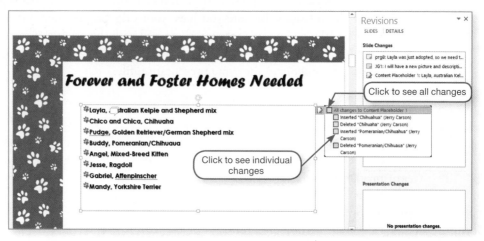

6-72 Changes made to a placeholder by the reviewer

> **MORE INFO**
>
> You can only compare two presentations at a time. If you have multiple presentations to compare, you can perform this process multiple times.

Review Comments and Accept or Reject Changes

After you have compared presentations and you are working with the merged presentation, you can complete the review process in different ways. For example, you can review each comment individually and delete them one-by-one or delete all comments in the presentation when you have finished. Similarly, when you review proposed changes, you can either accept or reject each item individually or accept all the changes at one time. If you only want to view the slides that have either a comment or a change, move to those slides by clicking the *Previous* or *Next* buttons in either the *Comments* group or the *Compare* group on the *Review* tab.

HOW TO: Review and Delete Comments

1. Begin your review on the first slide of the presentation.
2. Click the first comment if it is on this slide or click the **Next** button [*Review* tab, *Comments* group] to go to the first comment.
3. Click the comment icon to open the *Comments* pane.
4. After you consider the comment, use one of the following methods to delete it:
   - Select the comment in the *Comments* pane and click the black **X** (Figure 6-73) or press **Delete**.
   - Right-click a comment icon on the slide and select **Delete Comment** from the shortcut menu.

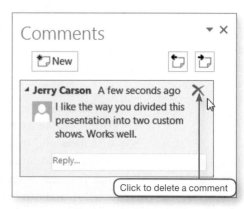

6-73 Delete in the *Comments* pane

- Select a comment icon and click the top half of the **Delete** button [*Review* tab, *Comments* group] (Figure 6-74).
- Click the **Delete** list arrow and select *Delete All Comments and Ink on This Slide* or *Delete All Comments and Ink in This Presentation*.

6-74 Delete options

When you accept an editing or formatting change, the change is applied to the slide, and the change icon is marked. When you reject an editing or formatting change, the text and formatting remain in their original form.

HOW TO: Accept or Reject Changes

1. Begin your review on the first slide of the presentation. If no changes are on this slide, click the **Next** button [*Review* tab, *Compare* group] to go to the first change.
2. Click the first change icon on the slide or in the *Revision* pane to view the change.
3. Click the *Accept* or *Reject* button [*Review* tab, *Compare* group] to accept or reject the change.

   - If you click the *Accept* list arrow, you can choose *Accept Change*, *Accept All Changes to This Slide*, or *Accept All Changes to the Presentation* (Figure 6-75).
   - If you click the *Reject* list arrow, you can choose *Reject Change*, *Reject All Changes to This Slide*, or *Reject All Changes to the Presentation*.
   - You can also click *Next* to skip a comment or revision in the document.

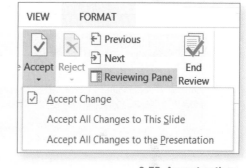

4. When changes on the slide are complete, click the **Next** button to go to the next change.

6-75 *Accept* options

5. If a placeholder has multiple changes, click one or more check boxes before accepting or rejecting.

   - To select all changes, check the box at the top of the list (Figure 6-76).
   - To select individual changes, check the box for the item you want to accept or reject.

6-76 Select changes to accept or reject

6. If a reviewer inserted an object (Figure 6-77), check the box to add the object to the slide (Figure 6-78).

7. If a reviewer made a change to an object such as a table, you first see the original version on the slide (Figure 6-79). Check the box to see the reviewer changes (Figure 6-80).

8. After you accept or reject the last change in the presentation, a dialog box opens confirming the last change and asking if you want to continue reviewing from the beginning. Click **Cancel** (Figure 6-81) to close the dialog box.

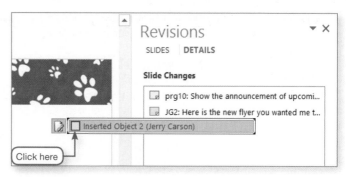

6-77 Click check box to insert the object

6-78 Reviewer object inserted

6-79 Table before reviewer changes

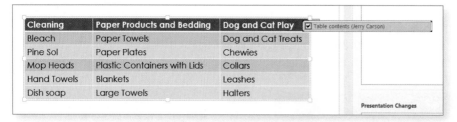

6-80 Table with reviewer changes

6-81 Dialog box that appears after reviewing the presentation

For this project, you insert comments and then compare an original and a reviewed presentation. You consider and delete comments and accept or reject changes made by the reviewer.

Files Needed: *[your initials] PP P6-2.pptx* and ***HopeRunReview-06.pptx***
Completed Project File Names: *[your initials] PP P6-3a.pptx* and *[your initials] PP P6-3b.pptx*

1. Open the *[your initials] PP P6-2* presentation and save it as *[your initials] PP P6-3a*.
2. Change the user name if necessary.
   a. Click the **File** tab to open the *Backstage* view.
   b. Choose the **Options** button to open the *PowerPoint Options* dialog box.
   c. Click the **General** button on the left (Figure 6-82).
   d. Type your name in the *User name* text box.
   e. Type your initials in the *Initials* text box.
   f. Click **OK** to close the *PowerPoint Options* dialog box.

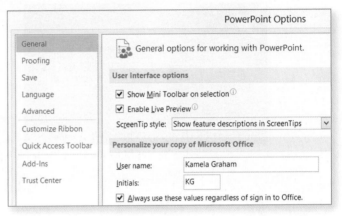

6-82 Change user name in *PowerPoint Options*

3. Insert comments.
   a. On slide 3, click the **New Comment** button [*Review* tab, *Comments* group]. In the *Comments* pane, type Have you verified that these times are all correct? (Figure 6-83).
   b. Move the comment icon above the times in the table.
   c. On slide 9, click the **New** button at the top of the *Comments* pane and type Please check this list to be sure all charities we are using are listed. Move the comment icon near the list.
   d. On slide 10, click the **New** button again and type Be sure we have printed enough copies of this form. Move the comment icon near the form.
   e. Close the *Comments* pane.
   f. Save the presentation.

6-83 Comment inserted

4. Compare presentations.
   a. With *[your initials] PP P6-3a* open, click the **Compare** button [*Review* tab, *Compare* group]. The *Choose File to Merge with Current Presentation* dialog box opens.
   b. Browse to locate your student files, select ***HopeRunReview-06***, and click **Merge**.
   c. The two presentations are combined and the *Revisions* pane automatically opens. Select **slide 1** (Figure 6-84).
   d. Save this merged version as *[your initials] PP P6-3b*.

6-84 *Reviewing* pane showing no changes on slide 1

5. Review and delete comments.
    a. Select slide 3, the first slide with a comment.
    b. Click one of the comment icons to open the *Comments* pane.
    c. Read each comment in the *Comments* pane and click the black **X** (Figure 6-85) to delete each comment.

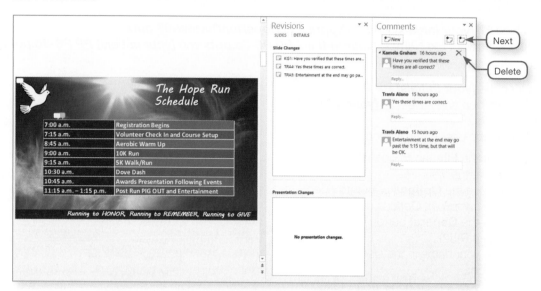

6-85 *Comments* pane with comments on slide 3

6. Click the **Next** button [*Review* tab, *Comments* group or on the *Comments* pane] to go to the next comment on slide 5. Read and delete the comment.

7. Repeat step 6 to review and delete the remaining comments in the presentation.

8. Close the *Comments* pane.

9. Accept and reject changes.
    a. Begin your review on slide 1. Click the **Next** button [*Review* tab, *Compare* group] to go to the first reviewer change.
    b. Click the **Next** button [*Review* tab, *Compare* group] to go to the next reviewer change on slide 6.
        • In the *Revisions* pane, select **Rectangle 1** and click **Accept**.
        • Select **Title2: Post Run PIG OUT** and click **Accept** (Figure 6-86).
        • Select the other two changes to see what they are. Click **Reject** for each one.

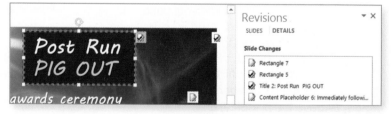

6-86 Accepting three changes to one object

    c. Click **Next** to go to each of the remaining slides with reviewer changes. Accept the changes.
    d. On the dialog box that opens, click **Cancel** to avoid reviewing again from the beginning.
    e. Click the **End Review** button [*Review* tab, *Compare* group] because you have read and deleted all comments and accepted or rejected all changes.
    f. Click **Yes** to close the dialog box. The changes are made and the change icons removed.

10. Save and close the presentation.

Chapter Summary

6.1 Add content from other sources to a presentation and work with multiple open windows (p. P6-343).

- You can create slides from a Word outline with heading styles.
- **Arrange All** enables you to see all open PowerPoint windows at one time.
- **Object linking and embedding (OLE)** allows users to integrate information from other Office applications into PowerPoint.
- When you **embed** a file from a **source program**, you can edit the embedded object in PowerPoint using the *Ribbon* from the source program. The embedded object in PowerPoint and the source file are independent.
- When you **link** a file from a **source program**, it opens in a separate window for editing in the source program. Because PowerPoint retains its connection to the source file, changes you make to a linked file appear in both the object in PowerPoint and the source file.
- You can **edit** a linked object in the source file and **update** the object in the destination file to reflect the changes in the source file.
- You can **modify** or **break** the link between an object in the source and destination files.
- Use the **Paste Special** dialog box to paste an embedded or linked object into the destination file.

6.2 Add sections to organize presentation slides into groups (p. P6-354).

- **Sections** divide slides into groups which is helpful for a lengthy presentation.
- You can add and rename sections in *Normal* view or *Slide Sorter* view.
- Edit and rearrange sections in *Slide Sorter* view.
- You can move slides between sections.
- When you **Collapse** sections, only section titles are visible.

6.3 Use proofing tools to correct errors, improve word choices, and translate content (p. P6-360).

- The **AutoCorrect** feature recognizes and corrects commonly misspelled words and other errors.
- The **AutoFormat** feature makes punctuation corrections and other replacements.

- You can add or delete *AutoCorrect* entries.
- The **Find** feature allows you to search for a word, part of a word, or a phrase.
- The **Replace** feature allows you to search for a word, part of a word, or a phrase and replace it with other information. You can use the *Replace* feature to replace one font with another.
- The **Research** pane is useful for finding dictionary definitions, synonyms, and language translation.
- You can change PowerPoint's **Proofing Language**.
- The **Translate** feature can convert words or phrases to a different language.

6.4 Create a custom slide show of selected slides within a presentation (p. P6-365).

- A **Custom Show** is a list of slides you choose within a presentation that displays in the order you determine.
- You can create more than one custom show in a presentation.
- A **hyperlink** provides a convenient way to start a custom show.

6.5 Insert, edit, and review comments, compare presentations, and consider reviewer feedback (p. P6-370).

- **Comments** allow you to make notes or provide feedback in a presentation without changing the design of slides.
- You can add, edit, reply to, or delete comments. *Comments* appear in the *Comments* pane with a corresponding comment icon on the slide.
- Comments are associated with a Microsoft Office **user name** and **initials**, which you can change in the *PowerPoint Options* dialog box.
- Use the **Previous** and **Next** buttons to review comments in a presentation. You can delete comments individually or delete all comments in the presentation at the same time.
- **Compare Presentations** enables you to merge two versions of a presentation and review comments and changes to obtain reviewer feedback.

P6-379

- The **Revisions** pane displays all of the changes in the presentation. Icon color and user initials distinguish changes made by different reviewers.
- Use the **Previous** and **Next** buttons to review changes in the merged presentation.

- You can accept or reject changes individually or you can accept or reject all of the changes in the merged presentation at once.

Check for Understanding

In the **Online Learning Center** for this text (www.mhhe.com/office2013inpractice), there are a variety of resources that can be used to review the concepts covered in this chapter.

The following Online Learning Resources are available in the Online Learning Center:

- Multiple choice questions
- Short answer questions
- Matching exercises

Guided Project 6-1

For this project, you create a presentation for Margaret Jepson, an insurance agent at Central Sierra Insurance. You add slides from a Word outline and another presentation and embed an Excel file. You prepare custom shows for the presentation's four topics.
[Student Learning Outcomes 6.1, 6.3, 6.4]

Files Needed: ***HomeSafety-06.pptx***, ***PoolSafetyRules-06.pptx***, ***PreventionChecklist-06.docx***, and ***AccidentalDeaths-06.xlsx***
Completed Project File Name: ***[your initials] PowerPoint 6-1.pptx***

Skills Covered in This Project

- Create slides from a Word outline.
- Work with multiple PowerPoint windows.
- Copy slides from one presentation to another.
- Embed a file.
- Use *Replace*.
- Create a custom slide show.
- Hyperlink a custom slide show.

1. Open the presentation ***HomeSafety-06*** and save it as ***[your initials] PowerPoint 6-1***.

2. Create slides from a Word outline.
   a. Select slide 6. Click the **New Slide** list arrow [*Home* tab, *Slides* group] and select **Slides from Outline** to open the *Insert Outline* dialog box.
   b. Locate your student files and select ***PreventionChecklist-06***.
   c. Click **Insert**.

3. Update slide layouts.
   a. If your window is not already maximized, click the **Maximize** button [*Title bar*] so PowerPoint fills the screen.
   b. Change to *Slide Sorter* view and adjust the *Zoom* to approximately **60%** so you can see all 20 slides (Figure 6-87).

6-87 Slides inserted from a Word outline

   c. Select **slides 7–20**, click the **Layout** button [*Home* tab, *Slides* group], and select the **Title and Content** layout. Click the **Reset** button to update the font.

4. Rearrange four slides and delete three extra slides with duplicate titles.

   a. Select **slide 3**, "Preventable Fires" (*Section Header* layout) and move it before slide 7. Delete slide 7 (with the same title but the *Title and Content* layout).

   b. Select **slides 3** and **4**. Move the two slides before slide 10. Delete slide 10.

   c. Select **slide 3** and move it before slide 14. Delete slide 14 (Figure 6-88).

   d. Save your presentation with the new slides.

6-88 Slides rearranged with *Title and Content* layout applied

5. Open a second presentation and arrange two PowerPoint windows side-by-side.

   a. Open the **PoolSafetyRules-06** presentation.

   b. Change to *Slide Sorter* view and adjust the *Zoom* to approximately **60%**.

   c. Click the **Switch Windows** button [*View* tab, *Window* group] and select **[your initials PowerPoint 6-1** to make it active.

   d. Click **Arrange All** [*View* tab, *Window* group]; your current presentation (destination) is on the left and the second presentation (source) is on the right.

6. Copy slides from the source presentation and paste them in the destination presentation.

   a. In the source presentation on the right, select **slides 2–5** (Figure 6-89) and press **Ctrl+C**.

   b. Make your current presentation (destination presentation) active and click after slide 7. Press **Ctrl+V** to paste the slides.

   c. With the pasted slides selected, click the **Reset** button to update the font and bullets.

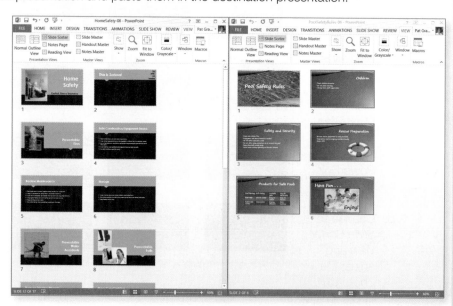

6-89 Two presentation windows displayed using *Arrange All*

    d. Close the ***PoolSafetyRules-06*** presentation.

    e. Maximize your PowerPoint window or restore it to the size you prefer.

    f. Double-click **slide 11** to open it in *Normal* view.

    g. Select the table and apply the **Medium Style 1 – Accent 1** table style [*Table Tools Design* tab, *Table Styles* group].

    h. Save ***[your initials] PowerPoint 6-1*** with the new slides.

7. Embed an Excel file and modify the embedded object.

    a. Select **slide 2**.

    b. Click the **Object** button [*Insert* tab, *Text* group] to open the *Insert Object* dialog box.

    c. Select **Create from File** and click the **Browse** button to open the *Browse* dialog box. Locate your student files and select ***AccidentalDeaths-06***. Click **OK** to close the dialog box.

    d. Click **OK** to close the *Insert Object* dialog box.

    e. Increase the object size (approximate *Height* **4.5"**) and center it horizontally on the slide.

    f. Double-click the embedded object to open the *Ribbon* from the source program.

    g. Change the table title to Accidental Deaths (Figure 6-90).

    h. Click outside the object to deselect it.

8. Use *Replace*.

    a. Select the **first slide** and click the **Replace** button [*Home* tab, *Editing* group] to open the *Replace* dialog box.

       • In the *Find what* box, type Preventable.

       • In the *Replace with* box, type Prevent.

       • Select **Match case** and **Find whole words only** (Figure 6-91).

       • Click the **Replace All** button to change all occurrences of the word.

    b. Click **OK** to close the dialog box identifying the last match.

    c. Click **Close** to close the *Replace* dialog box.

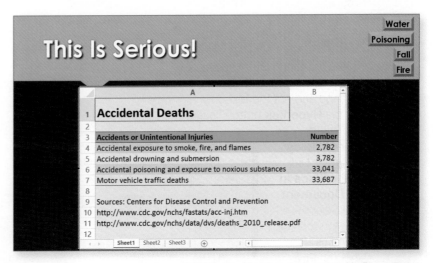

6-90 Embedded Excel file revised in PowerPoint

9. Create four custom slide shows.

    a. Click the **Slide Show** tab.

    b. Click the **Custom Slide Show** button [*Start Slide Show* group] and select **Custom Shows** to open the *Custom Shows* dialog box.

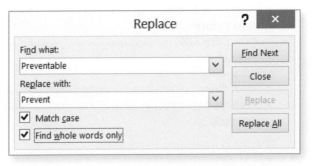

6-91 *Replace* dialog box

c. Click the **New** button to open the *Define Custom Show* dialog box.

d. For the *Slide show name*, type Fire.

e. On the left, click **slides 2–6** to select them and click the **Add** button so these slides are also listed on the right under *Slides in custom show* (Figure 6-92).

f. Click **OK**.

g. Repeat steps 9 c–f for three more shows:

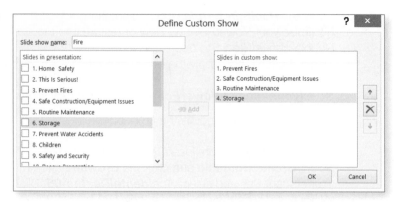

6-92 Slides added to the *Custom Show*

Slide show name	Slides
Water	7–11
Fall	12–16
Poisoning	17–21

h. Click **Close**.

10. Hyperlink to the four custom shows.

a. On slide 2, select the **shape** on the upper right corner with the word "Fire." Be careful to select the shape and not the text only.

b. Click the **Hyperlink** button [*Insert* tab, *Links* group].

c. In the *Insert Hyperlink* dialog box, under *Link to*, click **Place in This Document**.

d. In the *Select a place in this document* list, select the **Fire** custom show (Figure 6-93) and select the **Show and return** check box. Click **OK**.

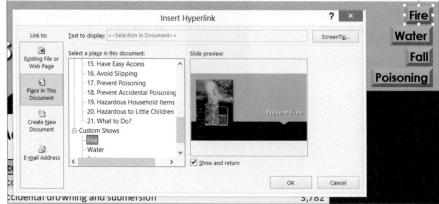

6-93 Hyperlink to a custom show

e. Repeat steps 10 a–d to hyperlink from the remaining three shapes (*Water*, *Fall*, and *Poisoning*) to their respective custom shows.

f. Test the hyperlinks in *Slide Show* view to verify that each custom show opens and advances correctly.

11. Change bulleted lists to columns.

a. On slide 19, select the bulleted text placeholder.

b. Increase the size of the placeholder text to **18 pt.**

c. Click the **Bullets** button to remove the bullets.

d. Click the **Columns** button and select **Two Columns**.

e. Resize the placeholder from the bottom until the columns are as even as possible (Figure 6-94).

f. On slide 20, the text does not require resizing. Repeat steps 11 c–e to change the list to columns.

12. Select the **Fracture** transition [*Transitions* tab, *Transition to This Slide* group] and click **Apply To All** [*Transitions* tab, *Timing* group].

13. Save and close the presentation (Figure 6-95).

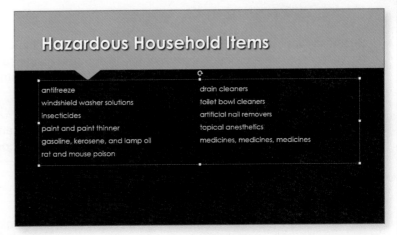

6-94 Bulleted text changed to columns

6-95 PowerPoint 6-1 completed

Guided Project 6-2

Business faculty from the colleges within the Sierra Pacific Community College District are working together to create promotional presentations about available careers in different fields of business. For this project, you embed a file, link an object, divide the presentation into sections, and add comments.
[Student Learning Outcomes 6.1, 6.2, 6.3, 6.5]

Files Needed: ***ITCareers-06.pptx***, ***ITCertifications-06.docx***, and ***ITSalaryChanges-06.xlsx***
Completed Project File Name: ***[your initials] PowerPoint 6-2.pptx***

Skills Covered in This Project

- Create slides from a Word outline.
- Work with multiple PowerPoint windows.
- Copy slides from one presentation to another.
- Embed a file.

- Use *Paste Special* to link an object.
- Break a link to an object.
- Add and rename sections.
- Use *Replace*.
- Insert comments.

1. Open the presentation ***ITCareers-06*** and save it as ***[your initials] PowerPoint 6-2***.

2. Add an object from a Word file.
   a. Select **slide 10**. Click the **Object** button [*Insert* tab, *Text* group] to open the *Insert Object* dialog box.
   b. Select **Create from File** and click the **Browse** button to open the *Browse* dialog box. Locate your student files and select ***ITCertifications-06***. Click **OK** to close the dialog box (Figure 6-96).
   c. Click **OK** to close the *Insert Object* dialog box and embed the file which is a list of certifications with a texture fill and black outline.
   d. Position the list on the right as shown in Figure 6-97.
   e. Click outside of the object or press **Esc** to deselect it.

3. Use *Paste Special* to link to an object.
   a. Open Excel. Click **File** and **Open**. Locate your student files and select ***ITSalaryChanges-06***. Click **Open** to open the worksheet and close the dialog box.
   b. Select the chart and press **Ctrl+C**.

6-96 *Insert Object* dialog box

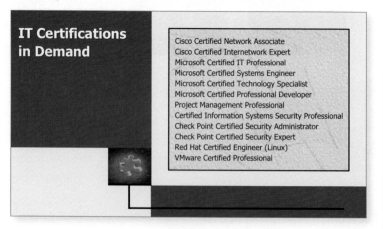

6-97 **Word file embedded in PowerPoint**

P6-386

PowerPoint 2013 Chapter 6 Integrating, Reviewing, and Collaborating

c. In PowerPoint, select **slide 12**.

d. Click the **Paste** list arrow [*Home* tab, *Clipboard* group] and select **Paste Special** to open the *Paste Special* dialog box.

e. Select **Paste link**. In the *As* area, select **Microsoft Excel Chart Object**.

f. Click **OK** to close the *Paste Special* dialog box and the object appears on your slide.

g. Increase the chart size (approximate *Height* **4.5"** and *Width* **7.45"**); then move it to the right side of the slide (Figure 6-98).

h. Close the worksheet and close Excel.

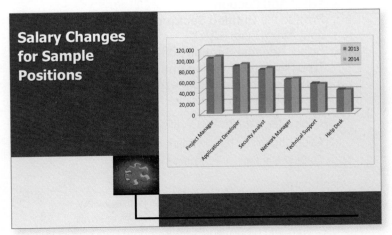

6-98   Linked Excel chart in PowerPoint

4. Break the link to an object.
   a. Click the **File** tab to open the *Backstage* view.
   b. Click the **Info** button on the left.
   c. At the bottom of the *Properties* list on the right side of *Backstage* view, click **Edit Links to Files**. The *Links* dialog box opens.
   d. In the *Links* area, select the source file of the linked object.
   e. Click the **Break Link** button and the source file name is removed automatically.
   f. Click **Close** to close the *Links* dialog box.
   g. Click the **Back** arrow to return to your presentation.

5. Use *Replace*.
   a. Select the **first slide** and click the **Replace** button [*Home* tab, *Editing* group]. The *Replace* dialog box opens.
      - In the *Find what* box, type IT.
      - In the *Replace with* box, type Information Technology.
      - Select **Match case** and **Find whole words only**.
   b. Click the **Find Next** button to go to the first occurrence on slide 10 (Figure 6-99).
      - Click the **Replace** button to change the highlighted word. Resize the text placeholder on the right side so "in Demand" is on the last line of text. Deselect the placeholder.
      - Click the **Find Next** button and a message appears indicating that PowerPoint found no more matches.
   c. Click **OK** to close the message and click **Close** to close the *Replace* dialog box.

6-99 *Replace* dialog box

6. Add and rename sections.
   a. Click the **Slide Sorter** button [*Status bar*] and adjust your *Zoom* percentage to approximately **60%**.
   b. Click after slide 2.

c. Click the **Section** button [*Home* tab, *Slides* group] and select **Add Section**.

d. Point to the **Untitled Section** name that appears and right-click (Figure 6-100).

e. Select **Rename Section** and a dialog box appears.

f. Type Skills and click **Rename**.

g. Repeat steps 6 c–f for three more sections including the one before the first slide:

Click after slide 8	Certifications
Click after slide 10	Salaries
Default Section	Introduction

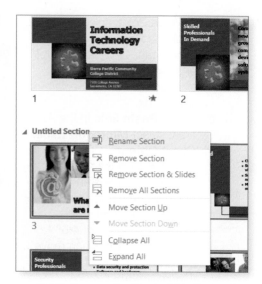

7. Insert comments.

a. Double-click slide 1 to open it in *Normal* view.

b. Click the **New Comment** button [*Review* tab, *Comments* group]. In the *Comments* pane, type Colleges in the District could show their names and addresses on this slide. (Figure 6-101).

c. On slide 12, click the **New** button at the top of the *Comments* pane and type Please verify this data for our area. Move the comment icon near the top of the chart.

d. Close the *Comments* pane.

6-100 *Rename Section* in *Slide Sorter* view

8. Select the **Gallery** transition [*Transitions* tab, *Transition to This Slide* group] and click **Apply To All** [*Transitions* tab, *Timing* group].

9. Save and close the presentation (Figure 6-102).

6-101 Comment inserted

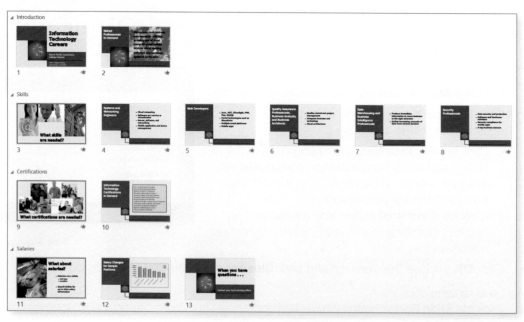

6-102 PowerPoint 6-2 completed with inserted *Sections* in *Slide Show* view

Guided Project 6-3

Hamilton Civic Center offers a summer day camp for children ages 6–12. For this project, you will complete a presentation about the day camp including information on fees, activities, and regulations. You embed a file, link an object, create custom shows, add comments, compare presentations, and accept or reject changes.
[Student Learning Outcomes 6.1, 6.4, 6.5]

Files Needed: ***HCCDayCamp-06.pptx***, ***HCCListedInfo-06.pptx***, ***HCC-SoccerClub-06.pdf***, and ***HCCDayCampReview-06.pptx***
Completed Project File Names: ***[your initials] PowerPoint 6-3a.pptx*** and ***[your initials] PowerPoint 6-3b.pptx***

Skills Covered in This Project

- Work with multiple PowerPoint windows.
- Copy slides from one presentation to another.
- Embed a file.
- Create a custom slide show.
- Hyperlink a custom slide show.
- Insert comments.
- Compare presentations.
- Accept or reject changes.

1. Open the presentation ***HCCDayCamp-06*** and save it as ***[your initials] PowerPoint 6-3a***.

2. If your window is not already maximized, click the **Maximize** button [*Title bar*] so PowerPoint fills the screen. Change to *Slide Sorter* view and adjust the *Zoom* to approximately **60%**.

3. Open a second presentation and arrange two PowerPoint windows side-by-side.
   a. Open the ***HCCListedInfo-06*** presentation.
   b. Change to *Slide Sorter* view and adjust the *Zoom* to approximately **60%**.
   c. Click the **Switch Windows** button [*View tab*, *Window* group] and select **[your initials] PowerPoint 6-3a** to make it active.
   d. Click **Arrange All** [*View tab*, *Window* group]. Your current presentation (destination) is on the left and the second presentation (source) is on the right.

4. Copy slides from the source presentation and paste them in the destination presentation.
   a. In the source presentation on the right, select **slides 2–5** (Figure 6-103) and press **Ctrl+C**.

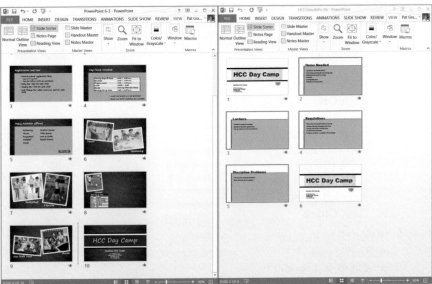

6-103 Two presentation windows displayed using *Arrange All*

b. Make your current presentation (destination presentation) active and click after slide 9. Press **Ctrl+V** to paste the slides.

c. Save your *[your initials] PowerPoint 6-3a* presentation with the new slides and close the *HCCListedInfo-06* presentation.

d. Maximize your PowerPoint window or restore it to the size you prefer.

5. Embed a PDF file.

a. In *Slide Sorter* view, double-click **slide 8** to open it in *Normal* view.

b. Click the **Object** button [*Insert* tab, *Text* group] to open the *Insert Object* dialog box.

c. Select **Create from File** and click the **Browse** button to open the *Browse* dialog box. Locate your student files and select *HCCSoccerClub-06*. Click **OK** to close the dialog box.

d. Click **OK** to close the *Insert Object* dialog box.

e. Change the object size (*Height* **5"**) and position it on the right.

f. Click outside the object to deselect it (Figure 6-104).

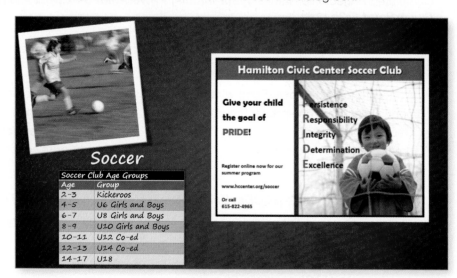

6. Create two custom slide shows.

a. Click the **Slide Show** tab.

b. Click the **Custom Slide Show** button [*Start Slide Show* group] and select **Custom Shows** to open the *Custom Shows* dialog box.

6-104 PDF object embedded in PowerPoint

c. Click the **New** button to open the *Define Custom Show* dialog box.

d. For the *Slide show name*, type HCCInfo.

e. On the left, click **slides 2–4** and **10-13** to select them and click the **Add** button so these slides are also listed on the right under *Slides in custom show* (Figure 6-105).

f. Click **OK**.

g. Repeat steps 6 c–f to create a second custom show named HCCActivities that includes slides 5–9.

h. Click **Close**.

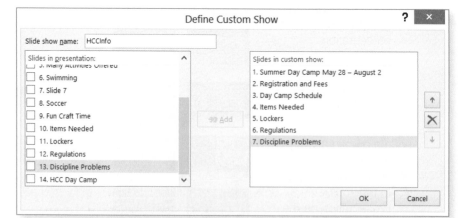

6-105 Slides added to the *Custom Show*

7. Hyperlink to the two custom shows.

a. On slide 1, select the **shape** on the bottom center with the word "Info." Be careful to select the shape and not the text only.

b. Click the **Hyperlink** button [*Insert* tab, *Links* group].

c. In the *Insert Hyperlink* dialog box, under *Link to*, click **Place in This Document**.

d. In the *Select a place in this document* list, select the **HCCInfo** custom show and select the **Show and return** check box (Figure 6-106). Click **OK**.

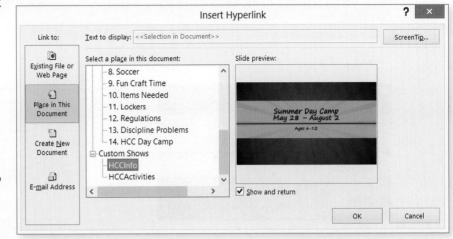

6-106 Hyperlink to a custom show

e. Repeat steps 7 a–d to hyperlink from the "Activities" shape to the **HCCActivities** custom show.

f. Test the hyperlinks in *Slide Show* view to verify that each custom show opens and advances correctly.

8. Change the user name if necessary.
   a. Click the **File** tab to open the *Backstage* view.
   b. Choose the **Options** button to open the *PowerPoint Options* dialog box.
   c. Click the **General** button on the left.
   d. Type your name in the *User name* text box.
   e. Type your initials in the *Initials* text box.
   f. Click **OK** to close the *PowerPoint Options* dialog box.

9. Insert comments.
   a. On slide 2, click the **New Comment** button [*Review* tab, *Comments* group]. In the *Comments* pane, type Please search in Office.com Clip Art to find an appropriate picture of children that will fit on the bottom of this slide. (Figure 6-107).

   b. On slide 4, click the **New** button at the top of the *Comments* pane and type Breakfast is new this year. Should we emphasize it more? Move the comment icon near the top of the table.
   c. Close the *Comments* pane.

10. Save the *[your initials] PowerPoint 6-3a* presentation.

6-107 Comment inserted

11. Compare presentations.
    a. With *[your initials] PowerPoint 6-3a* open, click the **Compare** button [*Review* tab, *Compare* group]. The *Choose File to Merge with Current Presentation* dialog box opens.
    b. Browse to locate your student files, select *HCCDayCampReview-06*, and click **Merge**.
    c. The two presentations are combined and the *Revisions* pane automatically opens.
    d. Save this merged version as *[your initials] PowerPoint 6-3b*.

12. Review and delete comments.
    a. Select **slide 2**, the first slide with a comment.
    b. Click one of the comment icons to open the *Comments* pane.

c. Read each comment in the *Comments* pane and click the black **X** (Figure 6-108) to delete each comment.

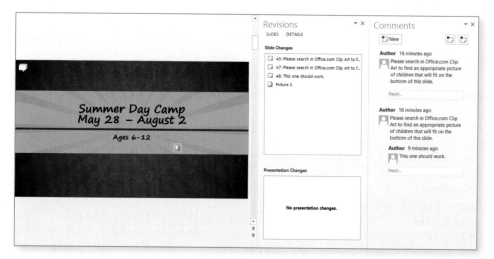

6-108 *Revisions* and *Comments* panes on slide 3

d. Click the **Next** button [*Review* tab, *Comments* group or on the *Comments* pane] to go to the next comment on slide 4. Read and delete the comment.
e. Repeat step 12 d to delete the remaining comments in the presentation.
f. Close the *Comments* pane.

13. Accept and reject changes.
a. Begin your review on slide 1. Click the **Next** button [*Review* tab, *Compare* group] to go to the first reviewer change.
b. On slide 2, select **Picture 3** in the *Revisions* pane and click the **Accept** button [*Review* tab, *Compare* group].
c. Click the **Next** button [*Review* tab, *Compare* group] to go to slide 3. In the *Revisions* pane, select **TextBox 1** and click **Accept**.
d. Click the **Next** button to go to slide 4.
 - In the *Revisions* pane, select **Group 5** and click **Accept**.
 - Select **Content Placeholder 2** in the *Slide Changes* area, then select the **All Changes to Content Placeholder 2** check box and the accepted changes automatically appear (Figure 6-109).
 - Close the *Revisions* pane.

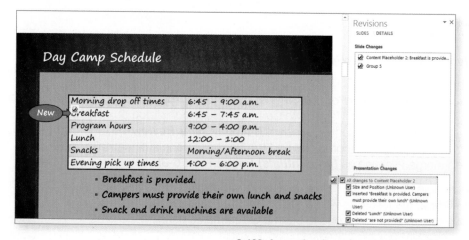

6-109 **Accepting four changes to one object**

14. Select the **Page Curl** transition [*Transitions* tab, *Transition to This Slide* group] and click **Apply To All** [*Transitions* tab, *Timing* group].

15. Save and close the presentation (Figure 6-110).

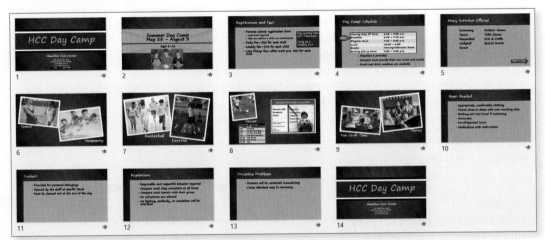

6-110 PowerPoint 6-3 completed

Independent Project 6-4

At the Courtyard Medical Plaza, one of the physicians has been asked to speak to a community college organization about nutrition. For this project, you help the physician complete the presentation by creating slides from a Word outline, using *Paste Special* to embed an object, creating custom shows, and inserting comments.
[Student Learning Outcomes 6.1, 6.3, 6.4, 6.5]

Files Needed: ***Nutrition-06.pptx***, ***Carbohydrates-06.docx***, and ***Calories-06. xlsx***
Completed Project File Name: ***[your initials] PowerPoint 6-4.pptx***

Skills Covered in This Project

- Create slides from a Word outline.
- Work with multiple PowerPoint windows.
- Use *Paste Special* to embed an object.
- Modify an embedded object.

- Use *Replace*.
- Create a custom slide show.
- Hyperlink to a custom slide show.
- Insert comments.

1. Open the presentation ***Nutrition-06*** and save it as ***[your initials] PowerPoint 6-4***.

2. Add slides from a Word outline.
   a. Select **slide 17**. Click the **New Slide** list arrow and select **Slides from Outline** to open the *Insert Outline* dialog box.
   b. Locate your student files and select ***Carbohydrates-06***. Click **Insert**.

3. Update slide layouts.
   a. Select **slide 18**, click the **Layout** button, and select the **Section Header** layout. Click the **Reset** button to update the font.
   b. Select **slides 19–22** and click the **Reset** button again.

4. Use *Paste Special* to embed an Excel chart and modify the embedded object.
   a. Open Excel and open the file ***Calories-06*** in your student files.
   b. Select the **bar chart** and press **Ctrl+C**.
   c. In PowerPoint, double-click slide 6 to return to Normal view.
   d. Click the **Paste** list arrow and select **Paste Special** to open the *Paste Special* dialog box.
   e. Select **Paste**. In the *As* area, select **Microsoft Excel Chart Object**.
   f. Click **OK** to close the *Paste Special* dialog box, and the object appears on your slide.

5. Modify the embedded object.
   a. Increase the chart size (approximate *Height* **5"**) using sizing handles (Figure 6-111).
   b. Double-click the **chart** to open the Excel *Ribbon*.
   c. Select the axis titles, series numbers, and legend and make them **bold**.
   d. Click off the chart to return to PowerPoint.
   e. **Center** the chart on the slide.
   f. Close the worksheet without saving the file and close Excel.

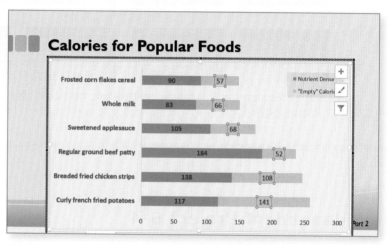

6-111 Editing an embedded Excel chart in PowerPoint

6. Use *Replace*.
   a. Select the **first slide** and click the **Replace** button to open the *Replace* dialog box.
   b. In the *Find what* box, type U. S. (space once after U.) and in the *Replace with* box, type United States.
   c. Select **Match case** and click the **Replace All** button.
   d. Click **OK** to close the dialog box identifying the last match, and click **Close** to close the *Replace* dialog box.

7. Create three custom slide shows.
   a. Click the **Slide Show** tab.
   b. Click the **Custom Slide Show** button and select **Custom Shows** to open the *Custom Shows* dialog box.
   c. Click the **New** button to open the *Define Custom Show* dialog box.
   d. For the *Slide show name*, type Dietary Guidelines.
   e. On the left, click **slides 2–17** and **29** to select them and click the **Add** button. The slides are listed on the right (Figure 6-112).

6-112 Slides added to the *Custom Show*

f. Click **OK** to close the *Define Custom Show* dialog box.

g. Repeat steps 7 c–f for two more shows:

- Slide show name: Carbohydrate. Select **slides 18–24** and click **Add**. Repeat to select **slides 10–17** and click **Add** so this group appears after the first group.
- Slide show name: Farm to Table. Select **slides 15–28** and click **Add**.

h. Click **Close**.

8. Prepare shapes on the title slide to hyperlink to the three custom shows.

a. On slide 1, draw a rectangular shape with the first custom show name, *Dietary Guidelines*.

b. Change the font to **20 pt.** and **Align Left**. Change the shape size (*Height* **.4"** and *Width* **2.4"**).

c. Duplicate this shape twice and edit the text for the remaining custom show names (*Carbohydrates* and *Farm to Table*).

d. Position these shapes on the lower left of the slide.

9. Hyperlink to the three custom shows.

a. Select the "Dietary Guidelines" shape.

b. Click the **Hyperlink** button [*Insert* tab, *Links* group].

c. In the *Insert Hyperlink* dialog box, under *Link to*, click **Place in This Document**.

d. In the *Select a place in this document* list, select the **Dietary Guidelines** custom show (Figure 6-113) and select the **Show and return** check box. Click **OK**.

e. Repeat steps 9 a–d to hyperlink the remaining two shapes (*Carbohydrates* and *Farm to Table*) to their respective custom shows.

f. Click **Close**.

g. Test the hyperlinks in *Slide Show* view to verify that each custom show opens and advances correctly.

10. Insert comments.

a. On slide 3, click the **New Comment** button. In the *Comments* pane, type Please find an image for MyPyramid to put on this slide so people will better recognize the change in recommended proportions. (Figure 6-114).

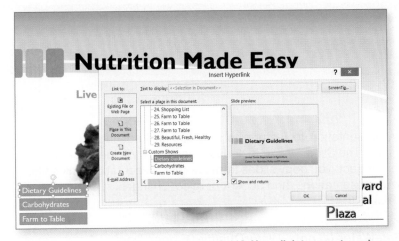

6-113 Hyperlink to a custom show

6-114 Comment inserted

b. On slide 19, click the **New** button at the top of the *Comments* pane and type Put a picture of a food label on this slide.

c. Close the *Comments* pane.

11. Select the **Fade** transition and click **Apply To All**.

12. Save and close the presentation (Figure 6-115).

6-115 PowerPoint 6-4 completed

Independent Project 6-5

The Pool & Spa Oasis has prepared a presentation to feature its services and educate customers about how to maintain their pools and spas. The *Slide Master* includes a background video to emphasize the soothing nature of water. For this project, you copy slides from another presentation, link a file, add sections, insert comments, compare presentations, and accept or reject changes.

[Student Learning Outcomes 6.1, 6.2, 6.3, 6.5]

Files Needed: ***SummerFun-06.pptx***, ***SafeWater-06.pptx***, ***WaterQuality-06.docx***, and ***SummerFunReview-06.pptx***

Completed Project File Names: ***[your initials] PowerPoint 6-5a.pptx*** and ***[your initials] PowerPoint 6-5b.pptx***

Skills Covered in This Project

- Work with multiple PowerPoint windows.
- Copy slides from another presentation.
- Embed a file.
- Add and rename sections.

- Add a custom *AutoCorrect* entry.
- Insert comments.
- Compare presentations.
- Accept or reject changes.

---

1. Open the presentation **SummerFun-06** and save it as **[your initials] PowerPoint 6-5a**.

2. If your window is not already maximized, click the **Maximize** button so PowerPoint fills the screen. Change to *Slide Sorter* view and adjust the *Zoom* to approximately **60%**.

3. Open a second presentation and arrange two PowerPoint windows side-by-side.
   a. Open the **SafeWater-06** presentation.
   b. Change to *Slide Show* view and adjust the *Zoom* to approximately **60%**.
   c. Click the **Switch Windows** button and select **[your initials] PowerPoint 6-5a**.
   d. Click **Arrange All**; your current (destination) presentation is on the left and the second (source) presentation is on the right.

4. Copy slides from the source presentation and paste them in the destination presentation.
   a. In the source presentation on the right, select **slides 1–5** (Figure 6-116) and press **Ctrl+C**.

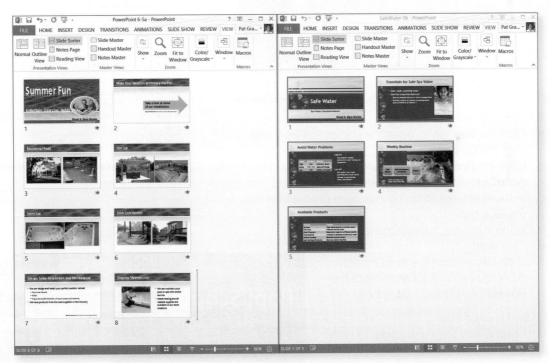

6-116 Two presentation windows displayed using *Arrange All*

   b. Make your current presentation active, click after slide 8, and press **Ctrl+V**.
   c. Save **[your initials] PowerPoint 6-5a** presentation with the new slides and close the **SafeWater-06** presentation.
   d. Maximize your PowerPoint window or restore it to the size you prefer.

5. Edit objects on the pasted slides to blend with the current presentation.
    a. Double-click **slide 8** to open it in *Normal* view.
    b. Select the picture, click the **Format Painter** button [*Home* tab, *Clipboard* group], and click the **picture** on slide 10 to apply the same picture style settings. Move the picture on slide 10 down slightly and away from the slide edge.
    c. Repeat step 5 b to apply the same picture style settings and positioning to the picture on slide 12.
    d. On slide 11, select the **table** and apply the **Themed Style 1 – Accent 1** table style. Move the table slightly to the left.
    e. On slide 13, select the **table** and apply the same **Themed Style 1 – Accent 1** table style. **Center** the table horizontally.
    f. On slide 12, select the *SmartArt* graphic, click the **Change Colors** button, and select the **Colored Fill – Accent 1** style. Select the text box below the *SmartArt* graphic and change the *Shape Fill* to **No Fill** (Figure 6-117).

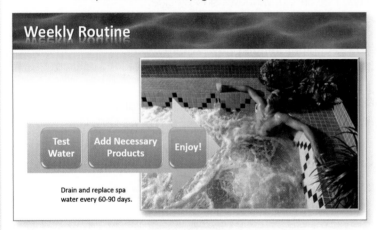

6-117 Slide objects adjusted for the current theme

6. Add a custom *AutoCorrect* entry.
    a. Click the **File** tab to open the *Backstage* view and click the **Options** button.
    b. Click the **Proofing** button and select the **AutoCorrect Options** button.
    c. In the *AutoCorrect* dialog box, type Bromene in the *Replace* box.
    d. In the *With* box, type Bromine (Figure 6-118).
    e. Click **Add**.
    f. Click **OK** to close the *AutoCorrect* dialog box and click **OK** to close the *PowerPoint Options* dialog box.

6-118 *AutoCorrect* dialog box

7. Embed a Word file.
    a. Insert a new slide after slide 13 with the *Title Slide* layout.
    b. Type Pool School! for the slide title and delete the subtitle placeholder (Figure 6-119).
    c. Click the **Object** button [*Insert* tab, *Text* group] to open the *Insert Object* dialog box.

6-119 Embedded Word file

    d. Select **Create from File** and click the **Browse** button to open the *Browse* dialog box. Locate your student files and select **WaterQuality-06**. Click **OK** to close the dialog box.

    e. Click **OK** to close the *Insert Object* dialog box.

    f. Increase the object size (approximate *Height* **7"**) and place it on the right.

8. Add and rename sections.

    a. Click the **Slide Sorter** button [*Status bar*] and adjust your *Zoom* percentage to approximately **60%**.

    b. Click after slide 1.

    c. Click the **Section** button and select **Add Section**.

    d. Point to the **Untitled Section** name that appears and right-click.

    e. Select **Rename Section** and a dialog box appears.

    f. Type Installations (Figure 6-120) and click **Rename**.

    g. Add another section after slide 8 and rename it Safe Water.

    h. Rename the *Default Section* (before slide 1) Introduction.

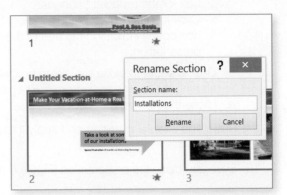

6-120 *Rename Section* dialog box

9. Insert comments.

    a. Double-click **slide 2** to open it in *Normal* view.

    b. Click the **New Comment** button [*Review* tab, *Comments* group]. In the *Comments* pane, type Should we show when this special promotion ends? (Figure 6-121). Move the comment icon near the promotion text.

    c. On slide 5, click the **New** button at the top of the *Comments* pane and type Replace the picture on the right to show the swim spa filled with water and the jets running. Move the comment icon near the top of the picture.

    d. Close the *Comments* pane.

6-121 **Comment inserted**

10. Save the **[your initials] PowerPoint 6-5a** presentation.

11. Compare presentations.

    a. With **[your initials] PowerPoint 6-5a** open, click the **Compare** button. The *Choose File to Merge with Current Presentation* dialog box opens.

    b. Browse to locate your student files, select **SummerFunReview-06**, and click **Merge**.

    c. Save this merged version as **[your initials] PowerPoint 6-5b**.

12. Review and delete comments.

    a. Select **slide 2**, the first slide with a comment.

    b. Click one of the comment icons to open the *Comments* pane.

    c. Read the comments in the *Comments* pane and delete them.

    d. Click the **Next** button on the *Comments* pane to go to the next comment on slide 5. Read and delete the comments.

    e. Close the *Comments* pane.

13. Accept and reject changes.

    a. Begin your review on slide 2.

    b. On slide 2, make the following changes:

      • Select the **Freeform 7** change in the *Revisions* pane and check the box to see the reviewer's change. Leave the items checked to accept them.

      • Select the **TextBox 2** change in the *Revisions* pane and check the box to see the reviewer's change. Click the **Reject** button to keep the text box in its original location.

c. Click the **Next** button in the *Compare* group to go to the next reviewer change on slide 7.

- Check the box for the reviewer change to add another bulleted item to the list (Figure 6-122).
- Click **Next** to move to slide 8. Check the box for the reviewer changes.
- Click the **Next** button and a dialog box opens indicating the end of the presentation.

d. Click **Cancel** to close the dialog box without starting the review again from the beginning.
e. Close the *Revisions* pane.

14. Select the **Ripple** transition and apply it to all slides.

15. Save and close the presentation (Figure 6-123).

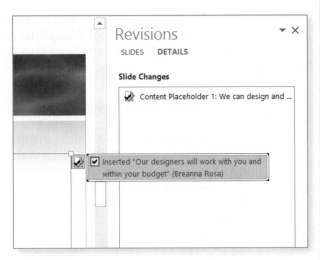

6-122   Accepting a change

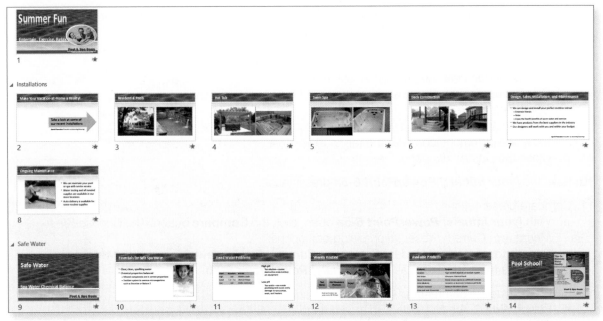

6-123 PowerPoint 6-5 completed with inserted *Sections* in *Slide Show* view

Independent Project 6-6

At Solution Seekers, Inc., one of the consultants has been asked to give a seminar. The clients want to learn more about using color to make their presentations unique. For this project, you paste slides from another presentation, replace fonts, add sections, and create custom shows.
[Student Learning Outcomes 6.1, 6.2, 6.4]

Files Needed: ***ColorChoices-06.pptx*** and ***ColorUse-06.pptx***
Completed Project File Name: ***[your initials] PowerPoint 6-6.pptx***

Skills Covered in This Project

- Work with multiple PowerPoint windows.
- Copy slides from one presentation to another.
- Use *Replace*.
- Add and rename sections.
- Create a custom slide show.
- Hyperlink a custom slide show.

1. Open the presentation ***ColorChoices-06*** and save it as ***[your initials] PowerPoint 6-6***.

2. If your window is not already maximized, click the **Maximize** button [*Title bar*] so PowerPoint fills the screen. Change to *Slide Sorter* view and adjust the *Zoom* to approximately **60%**.

3. Open a second presentation and arrange two PowerPoint windows side-by-side.
   a. Open the ***ColorUse-06*** presentation.
   b. Change to *Slide Sorter* view and adjust the *Zoom* to approximately **60%**.
   c. Click the **Switch Windows** button and select **[your initials] PowerPoint 6-6** to make it active.
   d. Click **Arrange All**; your current (destination) presentation is on the left and the second (source) presentation is on the right (Figure 6-124).

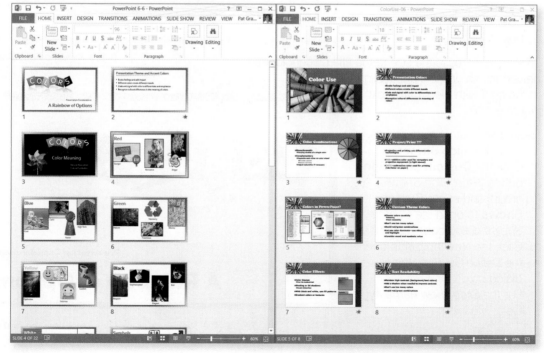

6-124 Two presentation windows displayed using *Arrange All*

4. Copy slides from the source presentation and paste them in the destination presentation.
   a. In the source presentation on the right, select **slides 5**, **6**, and **8**. Press **Ctrl+C**.
   b. Make your current presentation active and click after slide 14. Press **Ctrl+V** to paste the slides.
   c. With the pasted slides selected, click the **Layout** button and choose the **1_Title and Content white** layout.
   d. Save your *[your initials] PowerPoint 6-6* presentation with the new slides and close the *ColorUse-06* presentation.
   e. Maximize your PowerPoint window or restore it to the size you prefer.
   f. Double-click **slide 15** to open it in *Normal* view.
   g. Select the group of pictures and move the pictures slightly to the right.

5. Add and rename sections.
   a. Click the **Slide Sorter** button [*Status bar*] and adjust your *Zoom* percentage to approximately **60%**.
   b. Click after slide 2.
   c. Click the **Section** button and select **Add Section**.
   d. Point to the **Untitled Section** name that appears and right-click.
   e. Select **Rename Section** and a dialog box appears.
   f. Type Color Meaning and click **Rename**.
   g. Add another section after slide 12 and rename it Presentation Colors.
   h. Rename the *Default Section* (before slide 1) Introduction.

6. Replace fonts.
   a. Double-click **slide 1** to open it in *Normal* view.
   b. Click the **Replace** list arrow and select **Replace Fonts**. The *Replace Font* dialog box opens.
   c. In the *Replace* box, select **Corbel**.
   d. In the *With* box, click the **list box arrow** to select **Berlin Sans FB** (Figure 6-125).
   e. Click the **Replace** button and the font changes on all slides.
   f. Click **Close** to close the *Find and Replace* dialog box.

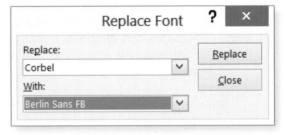

6-125 *Replace Font* dialog box

7. On slide 1, increase the size of the title placeholder so the text fits on one line and it aligns on the right with the subtitle text (Figure 6-126).

8. Create two custom slide shows.
   a. Click the **Slide Show** tab.
   b. Click the **Custom Slide Show** button [*Start Slide Show* group] and select **Custom Shows** to open the *Custom Shows* dialog box.
   c. Click the **New** button to open the *Define Custom Show* dialog box.
   d. For the *Slide show name*, type Color Meaning.

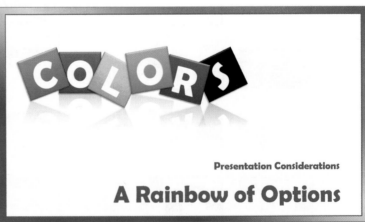

6-126 Placeholder size adjusted after the font change

e. On the left, click **slides 3–12** to select them and click the **Add** button so these slides are also listed on the right under *Slides in custom show* (Figure 6-127).

f. Click **OK**.

g. Click the **New** button again and type the *Slide show name* Presentation Colors. Select **slides 13–24** and click the **Add** button.

h. Click **OK** to close the *Define Custom Show* dialog box and click **Close** to close the *Custom Shows* dialog box.

6-127   Slides added to the *Custom Show*

9. Prepare shapes to hyperlink to the two custom shows.
   a. On slide 2, draw a rectangular shape with the first custom show name, *Color Meaning*.
   b. Change the font to **20 pt.** and **Align Left**.
   c. Apply the *Shape Style* **Intense Effect – Indigo**, **Accent 6**.
   d. Change the shape height to **.4"** and adjust the width so the words fit on one line.
   e. Press **Ctrl+D** to duplicate this shape and edit the text for the show name, *Presentation Colors*. Adjust the width as needed.
   f. Position these shapes on the lower left of the slide.

10. Hyperlink to the two custom shows.
    a. Select the "Color Meaning" shape.
    b. Click the **Hyperlink** button [*Insert* tab, *Links* group].
    c. In the *Insert Hyperlink* dialog box, under *Link to*, click **Place in This Document**.
    d. In the *Select a place in this document* list, select the **Color Meaning** custom show (Figure 6-128) and select the **Show and return** check box. Click **OK**.

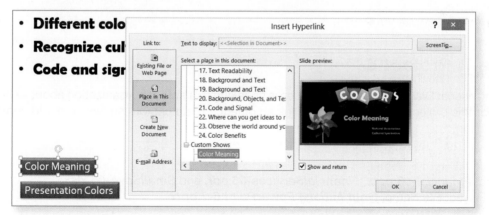

6-128 Prepare a hyperlink to a custom show

    e. Repeat steps 10 a–d to hyperlink from the "Presentation Colors" shape to the *Presentation Colors* custom show.
    f. Test the hyperlinks in *Slide Show* view to verify that each custom show opens and advances correctly.

11. Select the **Wipe** transition with the **From Left** *Effect Option* and click **Apply To All**.

12. Save and close the presentation (Figure 6-129).

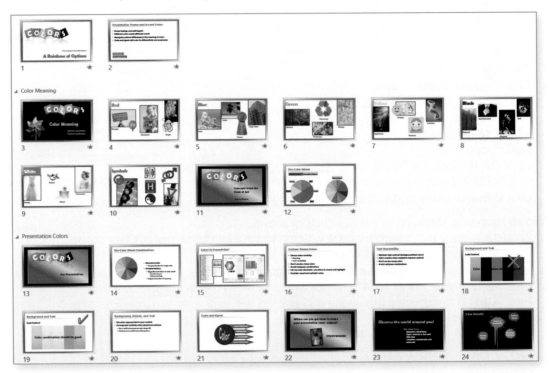

6-129 PowerPoint 6-6 completed with inserted *Sections* in *Slide Show* view

Improve It Project 6-7

A financial adviser at Dawson Financial Services is speaking to a student organization about saving and investing. For this project, you embed a file, link an object, create custom shows, and add comments to a presentation.
[Student Learning Outcomes 6.1, 6.4, 6.5]

Files Needed: *Financial-06.pptx*, *FinancialServices-06.pdf*, and *SmallSave-06.xlsx*
Completed Project File Name: *[your initials] PowerPoint 6-7.pptx*

Skills Covered in This Project

- Embed a file.
- Use *Paste Special* to link an object.
- Create a custom slide show.
- Hyperlink a custom slide show.
- Insert comments.

1. Open the presentation *Financial-06* and save it as *[your initials] PowerPoint 6-7*.

2. Embed a PDF file.
   a. On slide 11, insert the PDF file, *FinancialServices-06*.
   b. Resize and move the object to the right (Figure 6-130).

3. Use *Paste Special* to link to an object.
   a. Open Excel and open the file *SmallSave-06*.
   b. Copy the chart.
   c. In PowerPoint, select **slide 4**.
   d. Click the **Paste** button list arrow and select **Paste Special**.
   e. Select **Paste link**. In the *As* area, select **Microsoft Excel Chart Object**.
   f. Click **OK** to close the *Paste Special* dialog box. The object appears on your slide.
   g. In Excel, make a correction to the "Year" data and type 1,277. Press **Ctrl+S** to save the Excel file and the change is automatically reflected on slide 4. If the chart does not update in PowerPoint, then right-click the chart and select the **Update Link** option from the shortcut menu.
   h. Increase the chart size (approximate *Height* **5"**) and move it slightly to the right (Figure 6-131).
   i. Close the worksheet and close Excel.

6-130   PDF file embedded in PowerPoint

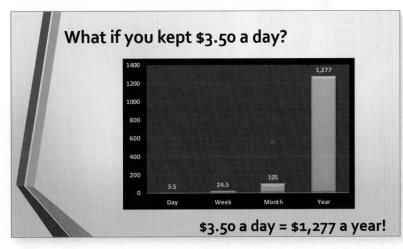

6-131   Linked Excel chart in PowerPoint

4. Break the link to an object.
   a. From the *Backstage* view, select the **Info** button.
   b. Click **Edit Links to Files** to open the *Links* dialog box.
   c. Select the *SmallSave-06* file and click the **Break Link** button.
   d. **Close** the *Links* dialog box.

5. Create two custom slide shows.
   a. Click the **Slide Show** tab and the **Custom Slide Show** button; then select **Custom Shows**.
   b. Click the **New** button to open the *Define Custom Show* dialog box.
   c. In 5c, create a custom show, the student will select slides 2–4 and 7.

    d. Create a second custom show with the name Invest with slides 5, 6, and 8–11.

    e. Click **Close**.

6. Create two shapes that hyperlink to the two custom shows.

    a. On slide 1, delete the subtitle placeholder.

    b. Insert a shape and type text Save. Change the font to **24 pt.** and **bold**. Change the size (*Height* 0.5" and *Width* 1.2"). Apply the **Subtle Effect – Brown**, **Accent 3** *Shape Style*.

    c. Duplicate the "Save" shape and change the text to Invest.

    d. Move both shapes to fit under the camera and align them to the right of the slide.

    e. Create a hyperlink to each custom show and test the hyperlinks.

7. Insert comments.

    a. On slide 4, click the **New Comment** button [*Review* tab, *Comments* group]. In the *Comments* pane, type It would be good to add another chart showing how much $1,277 a year would generate in 10 years with current interest rates.

    b. On slide 7, click the **New** button at the top of the *Comments* pane and type Remind people that their preferences may differ from the images shown here. Move the comment icon near the top of the *SmartArt* graphic.

    c. Close the *Comments* pane.

8. Select the **Window** transition to all slides.

9. Save and close the presentation (Figure 6-132).

6-132 PowerPoint 6-7 completed

Challenge Project 6-8

For this project, search online for information about how mobile apps can support team collaboration. Create a presentation about this topic. Include cautions about sharing private or sensitive data. List some of the products and their prices in a spreadsheet and link to it in PowerPoint. Describe features and capabilities.
[Student Learning Outcomes 6.1, 6.2, 6.3, 6.5]

File Needed: None
Completed Project File Name: *[your initials] PowerPoint 6-8.pptx*

Create a new presentation and save it as *[your initials] PowerPoint 6-8*. Modify your presentation according to the following guidelines:

- Select an appropriate theme and colors.
- Identify the most common categories of mobile apps and describe them.
- Use Excel to list some of the products and their prices.
- In PowerPoint, link to the price list in Excel.
- Add sections to divide the presentation into logical groups.
- Add two or more *AutoCorrect* entries to recognize some of the trade names for web apps or devices.
- Use other proofing options as needed.

Challenge Project 6-9

Video conferencing has become increasingly popular for meetings and job interviews. For this project, search online for information about how to prepare yourself to appear professional when the camera is on you. Discuss both verbal and nonverbal behaviors that are important during a video conference. Share your presentation with a friend or colleague and ask that person to provide feedback with the *Comments* feature of PowerPoint. Compare the presentations and use those comments and any changes to improve your presentation.
[Student Learning Outcomes 6.1, 6.3, 6.4, 6.5]

File Needed: None
Completed Project File Name: *[your initials] PowerPoint 6-9.pptx*

Create a new presentation and save it as *[your initials] PowerPoint 6-9*. Modify your presentation according to the following guidelines:

- Select an appropriate theme and colors.
- Create slides that include information about what you need to do before a video conference to prepare yourself.
- Create slides that include information about behaviors that are important during a video conference.

- Use proofing options as needed.
- Prepare two custom shows within your presentation.
- Create hyperlinks to begin each custom show.
- Insert comments for a reviewer and distribute the presentation for review.
- Compare your original presentation and the reviewed presentation by merging them.
- Consider comments and delete them; consider changes and accept or reject them.

Challenge Project 6-10

Good manners never go out of style. For this project, create a presentation that provides some tips for business etiquette. Use online sources such as emilypost.com, etiquettescholar.com, missmanners.com, netmanners.com, or other similar sites. Work with another student to divide this project into two parts. Each of you should prepare slides, and when they are complete, you can combine them into one presentation. [Student Learning Outcomes 6.1, 6.2, 6.3, 6.4, 6.5]

File Needed: None
Completed Project File Name: *[your initials] PowerPoint 6-10.pptx*

Create a new presentation and save it as *[your initials] PowerPoint 6-10*. Modify your presentation according to the following guidelines:

- Prepare two presentations and combine them by pasting slides from the source presentation into the destination presentation.
- Select an appropriate theme and colors.
- Create slides that include information about behaviors that are important regardless of technology use.
- Create slides that include information about behaviors that are important as a result of technology use.
- If possible, take your own photos to illustrate several good and bad behaviors.
- Use proofing options as needed.
- Rearrange slide order as needed.
- Prepare custom shows for the major topics of the presentation.
- Create hyperlinks to begin each custom show.

Sharing a Presentation

CHAPTER OVERVIEW

PowerPoint has many different collaboration features. For example, when you share your presentation with others, you may want to remove personal information or make sure your presentation meets accessibility standards. You can also control the security of your content by marking a presentation as final so it cannot be accidentally changed or by requiring a password to open the presentation.

Office 2013 also integrates "cloud" technology, which allows you to use your Office files in *SkyDrive*, *SkyDrive* groups, and Office Web Apps. These different cloud services provided by Microsoft let your files and Office settings travel with you. With these features, you are not locked into using Office on only one computer, and you don't have to save your files on a USB drive or portable hard drive to have access to your files. Internet access is the only requirement. However, security settings in computer labs may inhibit some software features.

STUDENT LEARNING OUTCOMES (SLOs)

After completing this chapter, you will be able to:

SLO 7.1 Prepare a presentation for sharing by removing personal information, adapting it for accessibility, and checking compatibility (p. P7-410).

SLO 7.2 Protect a presentation by marking it as final and adding a password (p. P7-413).

SLO 7.3 Export a presentation by creating different file types and by creating a video (p. P7-419).

SLO 7.4 View and modify Office account settings and add an Office app (p. P7-426).

SLO 7.5 Create folders and add, move, copy, and share files in *SkyDrive* (p. P7-429).

SLO 7.6 Create a group in *SkyDrive,* invite a member, and change group options (p. P7-435).

SLO 7.7 Open, create, edit, print, share, use comments, and collaborate on a presentation in Office Web Apps (p. P7-442).

SLO 7.8 Share a presentation by sending it as an email attachment, presenting online, or publishing slides (p. P7-448).

CASE STUDY

For the Pause & Practice projects in this chapter, you use various methods to share a presentation you are creating for the Eye Care Clinic at Courtyard Medical Plaza.

Pause & Practice 7-1: Remove personal information from a presentation, check for accessibility issues, check compatibility, protect a presentation with a password, and mark a presentation as final.

Pause & Practice 7-2: Export a presentation to create a slide picture, a PDF version of a presentation, a presentation video, and a handout in Word.

Pause & Practice 7-3: Use *SkyDrive* and a *SkyDrive* group to save, create, edit, and share a presentation.

Pause & Practice 7-4: Create, save, edit, and share a presentation using PowerPoint Web App.

SLO 7.1

Preparing to Share a Presentation

PowerPoint has features to alert you to potential problems when your presentation is shared with and modified by multiple users. You can inspect your presentation, check accessibility, and check compatibility. All of these options are available on the *Backstage* view (Figure 7-1).

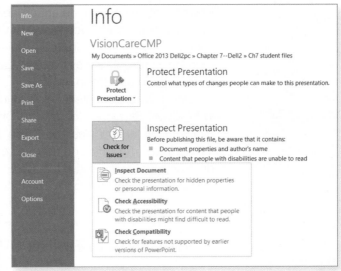

7-1 *Check for issues*

Inspect Document

The **Inspect Document** feature looks for hidden content, properties, or personal information that you may not want to share. When you use the *Inspect Document* feature, PowerPoint generates a report and allows you to choose to remove properties or hidden information from your presentation before sharing it with other users.

Once information is removed using the *Document Inspector* dialog box, you may not be able to restore the removed information if you later need it. Therefore, you may want to make a copy of your presentation before removing the information.

HOW TO: Inspect a Document

1. Click the **File** tab to open the *Backstage* view.
2. Click the **Check for Issues** button and select **Inspect Document** to open the *Document Inspector* dialog box (Figure 7-2).
3. Select the presentation content you want to inspect.

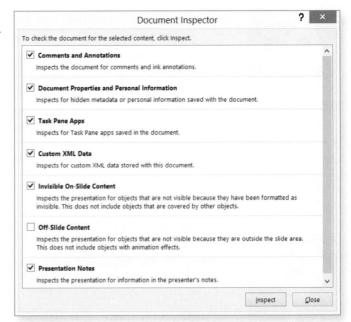

7-2 *Document Inspector* dialog box

4. Click **Inspect**. The inspection results appear in the *Document Inspector* dialog box (Figure 7-3).

5. Click the **Remove All** button for each area that contains content you want to remove from your presentation.

6. If you want to inspect the presentation again after you remove content, click the **Reinspect** button.

7. Click the **Close** button to close the *Document Inspector* dialog box.

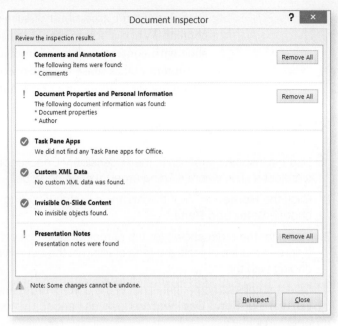

7-3 Document inspection results

Check Accessibility

Users with vision and hearing impairments can have difficulty viewing presentations or hearing audio recordings. When a presentation is distributed on a CD or over the Internet for independent viewing, the difficulties can be limiting. Assistive technologies help with these problems by enlarging screen content for easier viewing or converting text to audio words with screen readers. While converting text to audio works well for many PowerPoint slides, pictures and graphics, such as *SmartArt* or other illustrations, cannot be read.

The ***Check Accessibility*** feature identifies potential issues that users with disabilities may have with your presentation. The *Accessibility Checker* pane displays what is found as errors or warnings and provides tips about other items you might need to check. As you click each item in the list, additional information is shown regarding why the issue has been identified and how you can fix the issue.

HOW TO: Check Accessibility

1. Click the **File** tab to open the *Backstage* view.

2. Click the **Check for Issues** button and select **Check Accessibility** to open the *Accessibility Checker* pane (Figure 7-4).

3. In the *Inspection Results* area, select one of the results.
   - In the *Additional Information* area, information is provided regarding why and how to fix accessibility issues.
   - If a list is collapsed, a white arrow appears before the item name and a number in parentheses follows the item name showing the number of errors (Figure 7-5).

4. Click the **X** in the upper right corner to close the *Accessibility Checker* pane.

7-4 *Accessibility Checker* pane with expanded and collapsed lists

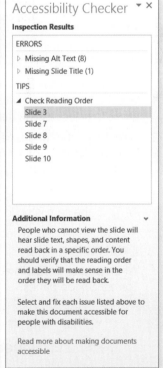

7-5 *Accessibility Checker* pane showing a suggestion

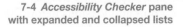

Solutions for accessibility issues may be as simple as revising the reading order for slide content. When a screen reader is used, a slide title is heard before other text. If you have a slide with content such as additional text boxes, you may need to specify the reading order so content makes sense to someone who is only hearing the text rather than seeing the slide. Changing the reading order does not affect how the slide looks.

HOW TO: Change Reading Order

1. Use the inspection results in the *Accessibility Checker* pane as your guide to select a slide where reading order may be an issue.
2. Click the **Home** tab, click the **Arrange** button [*Drawing* group], and then choose **Selection Pane**.
3. Consider the order shown for the names of slide objects (Figure 7-6). With a screen reader, objects are read starting at the bottom of the list and ending with the top object.
4. Select an object name that is not in the correct order and click the **Bring Forward** or **Send Backward** arrows as needed to move the object up or down in the list.
5. Repeat as needed to address other items listed in the *Accessibility Checker* pane.
6. When the order is correct, close the *Accessibility Checker* and the *Selection* panes.

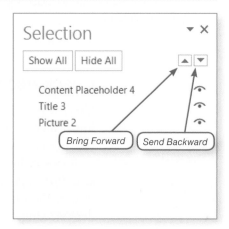

7-6 *Selection* pane

Alt Text (Alternative text) is text that describes pictures or other graphic objects on a slide. *Alt Text* appears in *Slide Show* view when you point to a picture or object. With a screen reader, this descriptive text is read so a person who cannot see the slide can still understand the content of the picture or object.

HOW TO: Add Alt Text

1. Use the inspection results in the *Accessibility Checker* pane as your guide to select a slide that is missing *Alt Text*.
2. Select a picture or shape, right-click, and choose *Format Picture* or *Format Shape*.
3. Click the **Size & Properties** button and click **Alt Text**.
4. Type an appropriate description and title (Figure 7-7). Once you enter *Alt Text,* the item is no longer listed on the *Accessibility Checker* pane.
5. Repeat as needed to address other items listed in the *Accessibility Checker* pane.
6. When all the *Alt Text* is added, close the *Accessibility Checker* and the *Format Shape* panes.

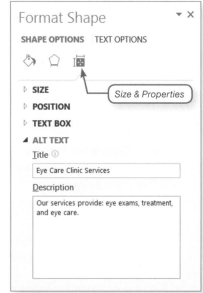

7-7 Add *Alt Text* for a *SmartArt* diagram

Check Compatibility

The **Check Compatibility** feature looks for compatibility issues between the current version of PowerPoint and versions before 2007. This feature is useful if you share presentations with others who are using these earlier versions of PowerPoint.

HOW TO: Check Compatibility

1. Click the **File** tab to open the *Backstage* view.
2. Click the **Check for Issues** button and select **Check Compatibility** to open the *Microsoft PowerPoint Compatibility Checker* dialog box (Figure 7-8).
3. The *Summary* area displays potential compatibility issues.
   - Based on the summary, make changes in your presentation to address issues as needed.
4. Click **OK** to close the dialog box.

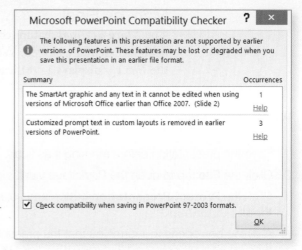

7-8 *Microsoft PowerPoint Compatibility Checker dialog box*

Conversions between PowerPoint 2013 and 2010 or 2007 should work well. However, new features such as transition effects, styles, or video capabilities are not supported in earlier versions and may display differently. If you convert from the current software to the 97-2003 version, additional changes will be evident. For example, *SmartArt* and tables are converted to pictures and soft shadows are converted to solid-color shadows. The appearance of these objects on the slide may be acceptable, but the objects cannot be edited in the older software.

When you open an earlier presentation file in PowerPoint 2013, it opens in compatibility mode. You can preserve this format and continue to work on the presentation in compatibility mode, but many software features will be disabled. Alternatively, you can resave it as a 2013 presentation to take advantage of all current software features.

SLO 7.2

Protecting a Presentation

When your presentation is complete, you may want to protect the content before sharing it with other people. In PowerPoint, you can mark a presentation as a final version, encrypt a presentation with a password, and add a digital signature. All of these options are available on the *Backstage* view (Figure 7-9).

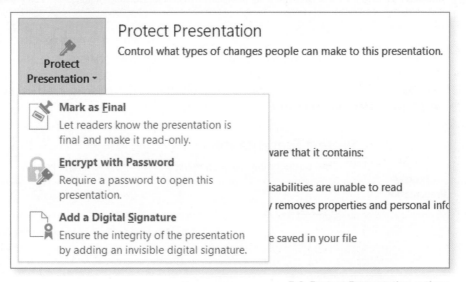

7-9 *Protect Presentation* options

Mark as Final

The *Mark as Final* feature creates a read-only file. This action protects a presentation from being accidentally altered. When a user opens a presentation that has been marked as final, the *Info bar* displays a notification message and a *Mark as Final* icon displays in the *Status bar*.

HOW TO: Mark a Presentation as Final

1. Save the presentation before marking it as final.
2. Click the **File** tab to open the *Backstage* view.
3. Click the **Protect Presentation** button and select **Mark as Final**.
4. A dialog box opens to inform you that the presentation will be marked as final and saved (Figure 7-10). Click **OK**.
5. Another dialog box opens to provide information about the final version (Figure 7-11).

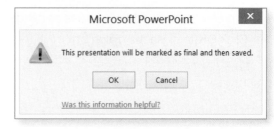

7-10 Dialog box confirms choice to mark as final

7-11 Marked as final informational dialog box

- Check the **Don't show this message again** box if you don't want this informational dialog box to appear again.
- Click **OK**.

6. The *Info bar* between the *Ribbon* and the *Ruler* displays a notation indicating that the presentation has been marked as final (Figure 7-12).

7-12 *Marked as Final* notation in the *Info bar*

- The *Ribbon* is collapsed and the presentation is protected from editing.
- A *Mark as Final* icon displays near slide numbers on the *Status bar*.
- On the *Backstage* view, a notation stating the presentation has been marked as final appears in the *Protect Presentation* area (Figure 7-13).

7-13 *Marked as Final* notation on the *Backstage* view

Mark as Final is not considered a security feature because users can still edit the presentation by turning off *Mark as Final*. You can turn off *Mark as Final* in two ways:

- Click the **Edit Anyway** button in the *Info bar* (see Figure 7-12).
- Click the **File** tab to open the *Backstage* view, click the **Protect Presentation** button, and select **Mark as Final**.

> **MORE INFO**
>
> *Mark as Final* is automatically applied when you add a signature, but a signature is not required to use *Mark as Final*.

Encrypt with Password

You can protect a presentation with the ***Encrypt with Password*** feature. When your presentation requires a password, it can only be opened if a user enters the authorized password when prompted. You must apply this feature before marking a presentation as final.

HOW TO: Encrypt a Presentation with a Password

1. Click the **File** tab to open the *Backstage* view.
2. Click the **Protect Presentation** button and select **Encrypt with Password** to open the *Encrypt Document* dialog box (Figure 7-14).
3. Type a password in the *Password* text box.
   - Passwords are case sensitive.
4. Click **OK**. The *Confirm Password* dialog box opens.
5. Type the password in the *Reenter password* text box and click **OK**.
   - On the *Backstage* view, a notation stating a password is required to open the presentation appears in the *Protect Presentation* area (Figure 7-15).
6. Click the **Back** button to close the *Backstage* view and return to the presentation.

7-14 *Encrypt Document* dialog box

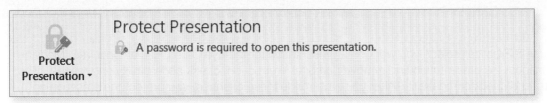

7-15 Password notation on the *Backstage* view

> **MORE INFO**
>
> Be sure to store presentation passwords in a secure location. If you lose your password, you will not be able to open your own file.

After you save and close your password-encrypted presentation, you must enter the password to reopen it. Type the password in the dialog box (Figure 7-16) and click **OK** to open the presentation.

You can remove a password after you open a presentation that is encrypted with a password.

7-16 *Password* dialog box

HOW TO: Remove a Presentation Password

1. Using the appropriate password, open the password-encrypted presentation.
2. Click the **File** tab to open the *Backstage* view.
3. Click the **Protect Presentation** button and select **Encrypt with Password**. The *Encrypt Document* dialog box opens.
4. Delete the password in the *Password* text box and leave the box blank.
5. Click **OK** to close the dialog box and remove the password.
6. Click the **Back** button to close the *Backstage* view and return to the presentation.

Other Protect Presentation Settings

You also can restrict access and add a digital signature to a presentation. Both of these features are useful when you are working with files that contain highly sensitive information.

The *Add a Digital Signature* feature helps you ensure the integrity of a presentation by adding an invisible digital signature to the presentation. The presentation is marked as final and becomes a read-only presentation.

The *Restrict Access* feature controls users' access to a presentation as well as their ability to edit, copy, or print the presentation. To use this feature, you must have a Windows Live ID and set up the Information Rights Management service on your computer.

PAUSE & PRACTICE: POWERPOINT 7-1

For this Pause & Practice project, you work on a presentation for the Eye Care Clinic at Courtyard Medical Plaza. You inspect the presentation and remove personal information, check accessibility and make adjustments, and check compatibility. After you have made these changes, you protect the presentation by encrypting it with a password and marking it as final.

File Needed: ***VisionCarePersonal-07.pptx***
Completed Project File Name: ***[your initials] PP P7-1.pptx***

1. Open the presentation ***VisionCarePersonal-07*** and save it *as **[your initials] PP P7-1***.
2. Inspect the presentation.
   a. Click the **File** tab to open the *Backstage* view.
   b. Click the **Check for Issues** button and select **Inspect Document** to open the *Document Inspector* dialog box.

c. Deselect the **Document Properties and Personal Information** check box.

d. Click **Inspect**. The *Document Inspector* dialog box opens with the inspection results displayed (Figure 7-17).

e. Click **Remove All** in the *Comments and Annotations* area.

f. Click **Close**.

g. Save the presentation.

3. Check accessibility and add *Alt Text.*

a. Click the **File** tab, click the **Check for Issues** button, and select **Check Accessibility**.

b. In the *Accessibility Checker* pane, select **Content Placeholder 3 (Slide 2)** under *Missing Alt Text* (Figure 7-18) and the *SmartArt* graphic is automatically selected on the slide.

c. Right-click the *SmartArt* graphic and choose **Format Object**.

d. Click the **Size & Properties** button and click **Alt Text** (Figure 7-19).

e. Type the title and the description text shown in the first row of the table in step f.

f. Use the other table information to add titles and description text to the remaining items listed under *Missing Alt Text* in the *Accessibility Checker* pane.

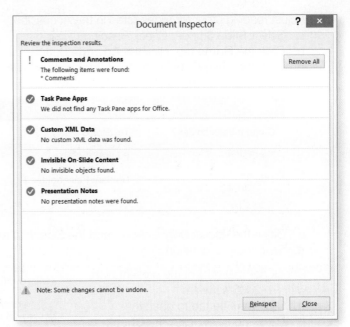

7-17 *Document Inspector* with inspection results displayed

Item	Title Text	Description Text
Content Place-holder 3 (Slide 2)	A Partnership Between Us	This diagram shows that our services and your ongoing care work together.
Picture 1 (Slide 5)	Sunglasses	This picture shows a young couple wearing sunglasses.
Picture 1 (Slide 6)	Eye drops	This picture shows how to look up when adding drops to your eye.
Picture 1 (Slide 7)	Optometrist	This picture shows Dr. David Edward.

g. Close the *Format Picture* pane.

7-18 *Accessibility Checker* with results displayed

7-19 *Alt Text* added

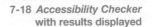

4. Adjust reading order for slides listed in the *Accessibility Checker* pane.
   a. Select **Slide 3** under *Check Reading Order.*
   b. Click the **Home** tab, click the **Arrange** button [*Drawing* group], and choose **Selection Pane**.
   c. Click the *Bring Forward* or *Send Backward* arrows so the content on the four listed slides is in the order shown in the following table:

Slide 3	Slide 5	Slide 6	Slide 7
Content Placeholder 7	TextBox 5	Content Placeholder 3	No change
TextBox 8	Picture 1	Picture 1	
Title 6	Content Placeholder 3	Title 2	
	Title 2		

   d. Close the *Accessibility Checker* and the *Selection* panes.
   e. Save the presentation.

5. Check compatibility of the presentation with 97-2003 software.
   a. Click the **File** tab to open the *Backstage* view, click the **Check for Issues** button, and select **Check Compatibility**.
   b. Note the summary on the *Microsoft PowerPoint Compatibility Checker* dialog box (Figure 7-20).
   c. Click **OK** to close the dialog box.

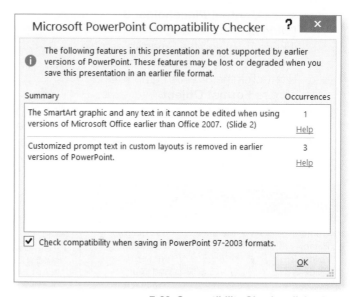

7-20 *Compatibility Checker* dialog box

6. Encrypt the presentation with a password.
   a. Click the **File** tab to open the *Backstage* view, click the **Protect Presentation** button, and select **Encrypt with Password** to open the *Encrypt Document* dialog box (Figure 7-21).
   b. Type the password CMPecc and click **OK** to open the *Confirm Password* dialog box.
   c. In the *Reenter password to confirm* text box, type CMPecc.
   d. Click **OK** to close the dialog box.

7. Mark the presentation as final.
   a. On *Backstage* view, click the **Protect Presentation** button and select **Mark as Final**.
   b. A dialog box opens with the marked as final message. Click **OK**.
   c. Another dialog box opens with the final version message. Click **OK**. (This message will not appear if you previously selected the *Don't show this message again* check box.)
   d. The presentation is automatically saved. Close the presentation.

7-21 *Encrypt Document* dialog box

Saving and Exporting in Different File Types

You can save individual slides as pictures to use the content in different ways such as in a flyer or a report. If PowerPoint is not available to display your presentation or if others cannot view your presentation in PowerPoint, you can create a PDF file or save your presentation as a video file. You can create handouts in Microsoft Word and choose from several layouts not available in PowerPoint.

Save a Slide as a Picture

When you save slides in a picture format, you have the option to save all the slides in the presentation as separate pictures or to save only selected slides.

HOW TO: Save a Slide as a Picture

1. Open the presentation that you want to save as one or more pictures.
2. If you want to save just one slide, select the slide.
3. Click **File** and then choose **Export**.
4. Select **Change File Type** (Figure 7-22).
5. Select one of the following *Image File Types:*
   - *PNG Portable Network Graphics*
   - *JPEG File Interchange Format*
6. Click the **Save As** button to open the *Save As* dialog box.
7. Type the file name for your slide or presentation if you are saving all slides.
8. Confirm the *Save as type* is the one you want (*PNG* or *JPEG*).
9. Click **Save**.
10. In the dialog box that opens (Figure 7-23), click **Just This One** to save the current slide as a picture. Click **All Slides** to save every slide in the presentation as a picture. Pictures will be saved in a folder and individually named and numbered beginning with *Slide 1*.

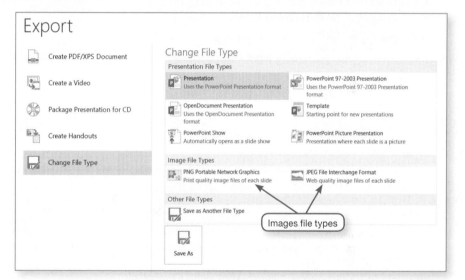

7-22 Export a presentation by changing the file type

7-23 Export one slide or all slides as pictures

> **ANOTHER WAY**
>
> Choose the **Save As** option from the *File* tab and name the file. In the *Save as type* box, select *PNG* or *JPEG* from the available options. Click **Save**.

Create PDF/XPS Documents

When your presentation is finished, you can save it in a PDF or XPS format. PDF (Portable Document Format) is an Adobe format that is viewed using Adobe Reader (available at no cost) or Adobe Acrobat. XPS (XML Paper Specification) is a document format developed by Microsoft.

These PDF and XPS formats create copies of a presentation that can be viewed or printed without PowerPoint. This content is more secure than it is when viewed in PowerPoint because it is not editable. These formats also significantly reduce file sizes, so electronic distribution is easier. You can create a PDF or XPS file from individual slides, handouts, or notes pages.

HOW TO: Save a Presentation as a PDF File

1. Open the presentation that you want to save as a PDF file.
2. Click **File** and choose **Export**.
3. Select **Create PDF/XPS Document** and click the **Create PDF/XPS** button (Figure 7-24) to open the *Publish as PDF or XPS* dialog box.
4. Type the file name for your presentation.
5. Confirm the *Save as type* is **PDF** (Figure 7-25).

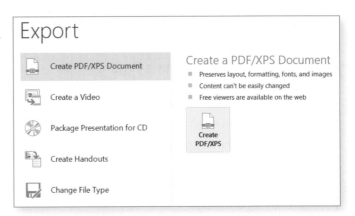

7-24 Export as PDF or XPS Document

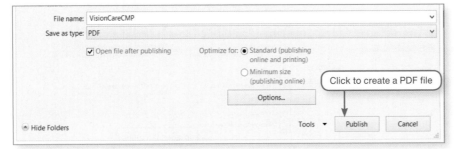

7-25 File type, Optimize choices, and Options on *Save As* dialog box

6. If you want to open the file in its new format, select **Open file after publishing**.
   - The file will open in *Acrobat Reader* if that program is installed on your computer.
7. The *Optimize* option for **Standard (publishing online and printing)** is selected by default. This option results in higher print quality. If you need a smaller file size to make electronic distribution easier or for another reason, select **Minimum size (publishing online)**.
8. Click the **Options** button to open the *Options* dialog box (Figure 7-26).
   - For *Range,* select *All, Current slide,* or *Selection.*
   - For *Publish what,* select *Slides, Handouts, Notes pages,* or *Outline view.*
   - Select other options as needed.
9. Click **OK** to close the *Options* dialog box.

7-26 *Options* dialog box for creating a PDF file

10. Click **Publish**. Figure 7-27 shows a presentation exported as handouts in *Adobe Reader.*

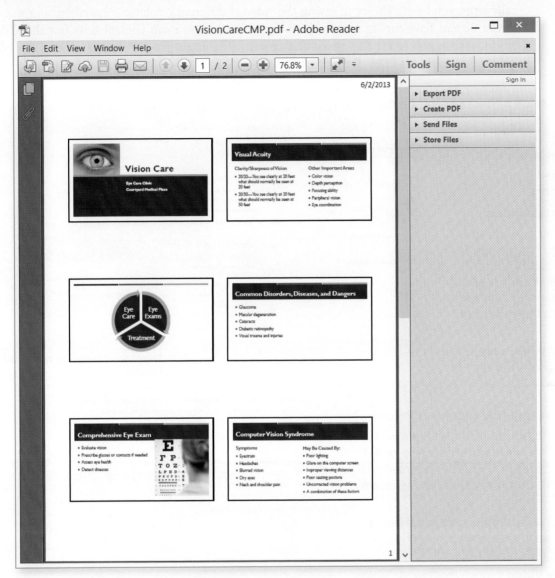

7-27 Exported presentation as a PDF handout shown in Adobe Reader

> **ANOTHER WAY**
> Choose the **Save As** option from the *File* tab and name the file. In the *Save as type* box, select *PDF* or *XPS Document* from the available options. Click **Save**.

Create a Presentation Video

PowerPoint presentations can be saved as video files. When you create a video from your presentation, you can include all recorded timings, narrations, and laser pointer gestures as well as animations, transitions, and media. All of these elements are saved with the slides. People can watch the video on their computers without PowerPoint. You can save the video on a CD or a DVD, or you can share it online using a video sharing site or *SkyDrive*. Video file sizes generally are large.

Video files are created using the Windows media video format. Because file sizes are typically large, you have a choice of saving the video at different resolutions based on your needs. If you do not have timing set within the presentation, you can control how fast the slides advance when you create the video. The process of saving a presentation as a video can take longer than saving in other formats.

HOW TO: Create a Presentation Video

1. Open the presentation that you want to save as a video.
2. Click the **File** tab and then choose **Export**.
3. Select **Create a Video**.
4. On the first list box, click the list arrow and choose one of the three quality options (Figure 7-28). You may need to test more than one option to find results that meet your needs.

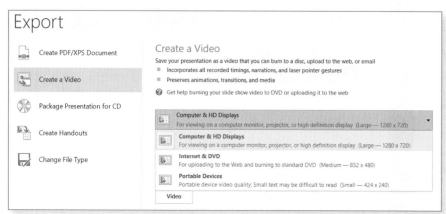

7-28 Select an appropriate video quality

   • *Computer & HD Displays:* Very high quality but large file size
   • *Internet and DVD:* Medium quality and moderate file size
   • *Portable Devices:* Low quality and small file size

5. On the second list box, click the list arrow and choose whether you want to include recorded timings and narrations. The *Use Recorded timings and Narrations* option is grayed out if there are no timings.
6. If you are not using timings, type a number of seconds for each slide (5 seconds is the default time) (Figure 7-29).
7. Click **Create Video** to open the *Save As* dialog box.

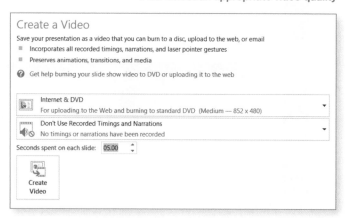

7-29 Select the number of seconds each slide is displayed

8. Type the file name for your presentation.
9. For *Save as type,* select *MPEG-4 Video* or *Windows Media Video.*
10. Click **Save**.

Test your video by adding a blank slide in PowerPoint and inserting your video. Play the video to be sure that it plays correctly (Figure 7-30). If you need to change transitions for selected slides, make the changes, resave your presentation, and then export the video again.

7-30 Test the video in PowerPoint

Create Handouts in Word

If you would like more control over formatting when you create handouts than is available in PowerPoint, you can use Word to revise and print handouts.

HOW TO: Create Handouts in Word

1. Open the presentation that you want to use to create handouts.
2. Click the **File** tab, choose **Export** and select **Create Handouts** (Figure 7-31).

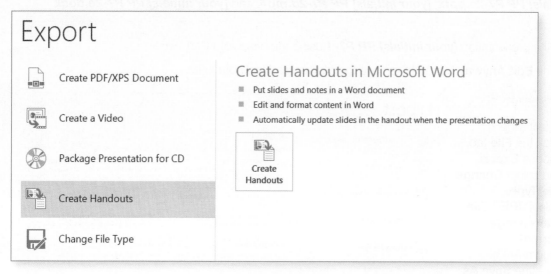

7-31 Export a presentation to create handouts in Microsoft Word

3. Click the **Create Handouts** button to open the *Send to Microsoft Word* dialog box (Figure 7-32).
4. Choose from one of the following page layouts:
   - *Notes next to slides*
   - *Blank lines next to slides*
   - *Notes below slides*
   - *Blank lines below slides*
   - *Outline only*
5. Select one of the following paste options:
   - *Paste* embeds the slides, and the Word Document will remain unchanged if the presentation changes.
   - *Paste link* allows changes made to the presentation to be reflected in the Word document.
6. Click **OK** and Word opens with the slides arranged as you selected.
7. Edit the Word document as needed and save it using an appropriate name.

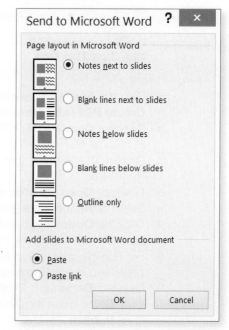

7-32 Page layouts in Word

For this Pause & Practice project, you work on additional presentation materials for the Eye Care Clinic at Courtyard Medical Plaza. You export a presentation to create a slide picture, a PDF version of a presentation, a presentation video, and a handout in Word.

File Needed: *[your initials] PP P7-1.pptx*
Completed Project File Names: *[your initials] PP P7-2a.jpg*, *[your initials] PP P7-2b.pdf*, *[your initials] PP P7-2c.pptx*, *[your initials] PP P7-2d.mp4*, and *[your initials] PP P7-2e.docx*

1. Open the presentation *[your initials] PP P7-1* using the password CMPecc.

2. Click the **Edit Anyway** button to remove the *Marked as Final* notation.

3. Save a slide as a picture.
   a. Select slide 7.
   b. Click the **File** tab, choose **Export**, and select **Change File Type**.
   c. Select **JPEG File Interchange Format** (Figure 7-33).
   d. Click the **Save As** button to open the *Save As* dialog box.
   e. Type the file name [your initials] PP P7-2a.
   f. Click **Save**. In the dialog box that opens, click **Just This One**.

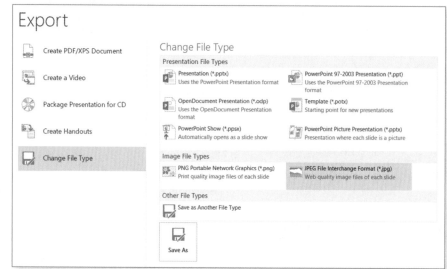

7-33 **Export with the JPEG file format**

4. Create a PDF file.
   a. Click the **File** tab, choose **Export**, and select **Create PDF/XPS Document**.
   b. Click the **Create PDF/XPS** button to open the *Publish as PDF or XPS* dialog box.
   c. Change the file name that appears to [your initials] PP P7-2b.
   d. Deselect **Open file after publishing**.
   e. Select **Minimum size (publishing online)**.
   f. Click the **Options** button to open the *Options* dialog box.
   g. For *Publish what,* select **Handouts** (6 slides per page) and check **Frame slides**.
   h. Deselect **Document Properties** (Figure 7-34).
   i. Click **OK** to close the dialog box.
   j. Click **Publish**.

7-34 *Options* dialog box for saving a PDF file

5. Apply transitions and save the presentation.
   a. On any slide, click the **Transitions** tab and select **Page Curl** [*Transition to This Slide* group]. Click **Apply To All** [*Timing* group].
   b. Select **slides 1** and **2**. Select the **Vortex** transition and select the *Effect Options* **From Right** [*Transition to This Slide* group].
   c. Save the presentation as *[your initials] PP P7-2c*.

6. Create a presentation video.
   a. Click the **File** tab, choose **Export**, and select **Create a Video**.
   b. On the first box, click the list arrow and choose the **Internet and DVD** quality option (Figure 7-35).

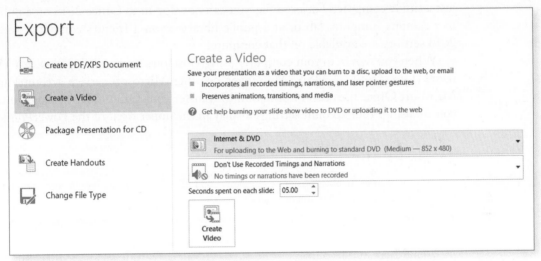

7-35 Options for exporting a video

c. On the second box, use the default setting for **Don't Use Recorded Timings and Narrations**.
d. For *Seconds to spend on each slide,* type 3:00 seconds.
e. Click **Create Video** to open the *Save As* dialog box.
f. Change the file name that appears to [your initials] PP P7-2d.
g. For *Save as type,* select **MPEG-4 Video**.
h. Click **Save**.

7. Create a handout in Word.
   a. Click the **File** tab, choose **Export**, and select **Create Handouts**.
   b. Click the **Create Handouts** button to open the *Send to Microsoft Word* dialog box.
   c. Select the page layout **Blank lines next to slides** and select **Paste** (Figure 7-36).
   d. Click **OK** and Word opens with the slides arranged as you selected. If Word is minimized on the task bar, click the Word button on the task bar to open the Word window.
   e. Save the Word document with the file name *[your initials] PP P7-2e* in your solutions folder.
   f. Close Word.

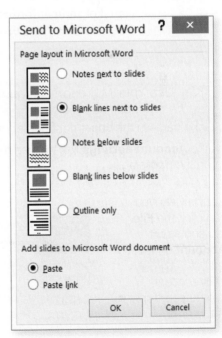

7-36 Options for exporting to Word

8. Close the *[your initials] PP P7-2c* presentation.

Customizing Office Account Options

When you purchase and install Office 2013, you set up your account options. For example, you establish your Microsoft user name and password and choose the Office background. If you upgrade from Office 2010 to Office 2013, many of your settings are automatically transferred for you. You can view and customize your Office account settings on the *Backstage* view.

Microsoft Account Information

One feature that is new in Office 2013 is the portability of your presentations and account settings. Your Office settings and files can travel with you, so you are not restricted to using just a single computer. For example, you can now log in to Office 2013 on a public computer in a campus computer lab or at a public library or on a friend's computer, and your Office 2013 settings are available on that computer.

When you sign in to your computer using Windows 8, you can log in with a Microsoft user name (Live, Hotmail, MSN, Messenger, or other Microsoft service account) and password. Microsoft Office uses this information to transfer your Office 2013 settings to the computer you are using. Your account settings display in the upper right of the PowerPoint window.

> **MORE INFO**
>
> If you are using an older version of Windows and Office 2013, you are prompted to sign in to your Microsoft account when you open an Office 2013 application or file.

Your Microsoft account not only signs you in to Windows and Office, but also signs you in to other free Microsoft online services, such as **SkyDrive, SkyDrive groups,** and **Office Web Apps.** If you don't have a Microsoft account, you can create a free account at www.live.com. For more information on these online Microsoft services, see *SLO 7.5: Using SkyDrive, SLO 7.6: Using SkyDrive Groups,* and *SLO 7.7: Using Office Web Apps.*

HOW TO: Use Your Microsoft Account in Office

1. Click your name in the upper right corner of the PowerPoint window (Figure 7-37).

2. Click the **Account settings** link to open the *Account* area on the *Backstage* view (Figure 7-38).

   - Alternatively, you can click the **File** tab and select **Account** on the left.
   - Your account information displays in this area.

7-37 Microsoft account information

7-38 Office account information and settings

3. If you are not logged in to Office 2013, click the **Switch Account** link. The *Sign In* dialog box opens.

4. Type your Microsoft account email address and click **Next**. Another *Sign in* dialog box opens (Figure 7-39).

   Type your password and click **Sign in**.

   - If you don't have a Microsoft account, click the **Sign up now** link, which will take you to a web page where you can create a free Microsoft account.
   - You also use your Microsoft account to log in to *SkyDrive* where you can create, store, and share files; use Office Web Apps; and create *SkyDrive* groups (see *SLO 7.5: Using SkyDrive*).

5. Click the **back arrow** to return to PowerPoint.

7-39 Sign in to Office using a Microsoft account

> **MORE INFO**
>
> If you are using a public computer, be sure to click the **Sign Out** link in the *Account* area on the *Backstage* view to log out of your Office account.

Office Background and Theme

You can change the Office background and theme in the *General* category in the *PowerPoint Options* dialog box or in the *Account* area on the *Backstage* view. The background displays a graphic pattern in the upper right corner of the application window; the theme determines the colors of the *Ribbon,* the *Backstage* view, and dialog boxes. The background and theme you select apply to all Office applications you use. Click the *Office Background* or *Office Theme* drop-down lists to select from the available options (see Figure 7-38).

Connected Services

Office 2013 has added many features to allow you to connect to online services. In the *Account* area on the *Backstage* view, you can add online services you regularly use by clicking the **Add a service** drop-down list and selecting a service (Figure 7-40). When you add a service, you are usually prompted to enter your user name and password to connect to the online service. The services you are currently connected to are listed in the ***Connected Services*** area.

All of the connected services in your account travel with you when you log in to Office on another computer. The following services are available in the different service categories listed:

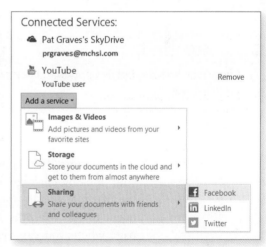

7-40 Add an online service to your Office account

- ***Images & Video:*** Facebook for Office, Flickr, and YouTube
- ***Storage:*** Office365 SharePoint and *SkyDrive*
- ***Sharing:*** Facebook, LinkedIn, and Twitter.

Add and Manage Apps for Office

Another new feature in Office 2013 is the ability to add *apps* (applications) to your Office 2013 program. Just like the apps on your smart phone, apps for Office are programs that add functionality to your Office software. For example, you can add a dictionary, an encyclopedia, a search tool, or many other apps.

HOW TO: Add Apps to Office

1. Click the **Apps for Office** button [*Insert* tab, *Apps* group] to open the *Apps for Office* dialog box.

   - The *Apps for Office* button is a split button. Click the bottom half of the button to see your recently used apps, or select *See All* to open the *Apps for Office* dialog box.
   - Click **My Apps** to display Office apps you have already installed.
   - Click **Featured Apps** to display available apps (Figure 7-41). Use the search text box to look for additional apps.

2. Select an app and click the **Add** button to install the app. The *Apps* pane opens on the right.

   - Depending on the app you select, you may be taken to a web site to add the app.
   - Some apps are free, but you must purchase some apps to receive the full version.

3. If the app does not automatically load in the *Apps* pane, click the **exclamation point** in the upper left corner of the *Apps* pane to display information about the app, and click the *Buy* button or the *Start* button if it is available to activate the app (Figure 7-42).

   - The app is displayed in the *Apps* pane.
   - You must be online for an app to start and load content.

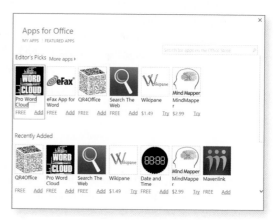

7-41 *Apps for Office* dialog box

7-42 Activate the app in the *Apps* pane

> **MORE INFO**
>
> Regularly check the *Apps for Office* dialog box for new and featured apps.

After installing apps in Office, you can manage your apps by clicking the **Manage My Apps** link in the *My Apps* area in *Apps for Office* dialog box. You are taken to the *My Apps for Office and SharePoint* web page where you can view your apps, hide apps, and search for other apps to install that are appropriate for the program you are using (Figure 7-43).

7-43 Manage your apps online

Using SkyDrive

With Microsoft Office 2013, you can use "cloud" storage space provided by Microsoft called *SkyDrive*. By saving your files to the cloud, you can access them from any computer that is online. You are not tied to one computer, and you don't have to carry your files on a portable storage device. When you sign in to your Microsoft account (Live, Hotmail, MSN, Messenger, or other Microsoft service account), you can access the online services that *SkyDrive* provides.

Your *SkyDrive* is a private and secure online location. You can use *SkyDrive* to store files, create folders to organize stored files, share files with others, and create *SkyDrive* groups. For your *SkyDrive* groups, you can invite people to become members and store and share files. Using Windows 8, you can access your *SkyDrive* files on your own computer or you can access *SkyDrive* online from any computer using an Internet browser web page. For more information on Microsoft accounts, see *SLO 7.4: Customizing Office Account Options*.

> **MORE INFO**
>
> While *SkyDrive* is secure and does require a user name and password to log in, no online accounts are 100 percent secure. Never store highly sensitive documents online.

Use SkyDrive on Your Computer

With Windows 8, *SkyDrive* is one of your storage location folders, similar to your *Documents* or *Pictures* folders you have access to in the dialog boxes that you use when opening and saving files. You can also save and open your files from the *SkyDrive* folder in a *File Explorer* window (called *Windows Explorer* in previous versions of Windows software) (Figure 7-44). You can create folders and rename, move, or delete files from your *SkyDrive* folder. In your *PowerPoint Options*, you can set *SkyDrive* as the default save location.

7-44 *SkyDrive* folder displayed in a File Explorer Window

> **MORE INFO**
>
> To use these features if you are using Windows 7 or a previous version of Windows, you need to download and install the free ***SkyDrive desktop app for Windows*** on your computer. After you do this, the *SkyDrive* folder is available when you open a File Explorer folder. Use an Internet search engine to find, download, and install this program.

The primary difference between the *SkyDrive* folder and other Windows folders is the physical location where the files are stored. If you save a presentation in your *Documents* folder, the file is stored on the hard drive on your computer, and you have access to this file only when you are working on your computer. When you save a presentation in your *SkyDrive* folder, the file is stored on both your computer and the *SkyDrive* cloud storage. You have access to the file from your computer *and* from any other computer with Internet access.

▶ MORE INFO

If you save to your *SkyDrive* folder on your computer when you are offline, your changes sync to your online *SkyDrive* when you reconnect later.

Use SkyDrive Online

The main benefit of using *SkyDrive* to store your files is the freedom it gives you to access your files from any computer with Internet access. In addition to accessing your *SkyDrive* when you open or save files on your computer, you can access your *SkyDrive* files from a web page using an Internet browser. You sign in to the *SkyDrive* web page using your Microsoft account.

HOW TO: Use SkyDrive Online

1. Open an Internet browser Window and go to the *SkyDrive* web site (www.skydrive.com), which takes you to the *SkyDrive* sign in page (Figure 7-45).

   - You can use any Internet browser to access *SkyDrive* (such as Internet Explorer, Google Chrome, or Mozilla Firefox).

2. Type in your Microsoft account email address and password.

   - If you are on your own computer, select the **Keep me signed in** check box to stay signed in to *SkyDrive* when you return to the page.

7-45 Sign in to *SkyDrive* (www.skydrive.com)

3. Click the **Sign In** button to go to your *SkyDrive* web page (Figure 7-46).

   - The different areas of *SkyDrive* (such as *Files, Recent docs,* or *Groups*) are displayed under the *SkyDrive* button in the upper left corner.

4. On the *SkyDrive* page, sort and view options are available in the upper right corner of the window (Figure 7-47).

   - Click the **Sort by** drop-down list to select a sort option.
   - Click the *Details* view or *Thumbnails* view buttons to change how files and folders display. In Figure 7-47, the *Details* view button is selected.

5. Click the **Files** button on the left to display your folders and files in the *Files* area.

6. Check a file or folder box on the left to select it.

   - At the top, buttons and drop-down menus allow you to perform actions on selected files and folders.
   - If you click a folder, the folder opens.
   - If you click a Word, Excel, or PowerPoint file, the file opens in Office Web Apps (see *SLO 7.7: Using Office Web Apps*).

7-46 *SkyDrive* online environment

7-47 *SkyDrive* sort and view options

7. Click the **SkyDrive** drop-down list to navigate between the different areas of your Microsoft Account: Outlook.com, *People* (contacts), *Calendar,* and *SkyDrive* (Figure 7-48).

8. Click your name in the upper right corner and select **Sign out** to sign out of *SkyDrive.*

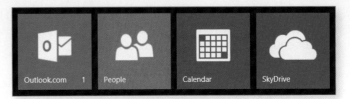

7-48 Microsoft Account areas

> **MORE INFO**
>
> If you are using a public computer, do not select the *Keep me signed in* check box. You do not want your *SkyDrive* files available to the next person who uses the computer.

Create a Folder

In *SkyDrive,* you can create folders to organize your files.

HOW TO: Create SkyDrive Folders

1. Click the **Files** button on the left to display the contents of your *SkyDrive* folder in the *Files* area.

2. Click the **Create** button and select **Folder** from the drop-down list. A new folder is created (Figure 7-49).

3. Type the name of the new folder and press **Enter**.

4. Double-click a folder to open it.
   - You can create a new folder inside an existing folder, or you can upload files to the folder (see the following *Upload a File* section).
   - Click **[your name's] SkyDrive** link above the folder area to return to the main *SkyDrive* folder.

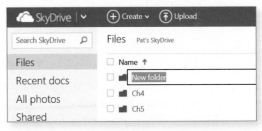

7-49 Add a new *SkyDrive* folder

> **MORE INFO**
>
> When you upload files or create folders online in *SkyDrive,* these changes are reflected in your Windows *SkyDrive* folder on your computer.

Upload a File

You can upload files to your *SkyDrive* from a folder on your computer or a portable storage device. When you upload files to your *SkyDrive,* you are not removing the files from the original location but copying them to *SkyDrive.*

HOW TO: Upload Files to SkyDrive

1. Click **Files** on the left to display your files and folders in the *Files* area.

2. If you are uploading a file to a folder, click the folder to open it.

3. Click the **Upload** button (Figure 7-50). An upload dialog box opens (Figure 7-51). The name of this dialog box varies depending on the browser you use.

- *Google Chrome: Open* dialog box.
- *Microsoft Internet Explorer: Choose File to Upload* dialog box.
- *Mozilla Firefox: File Upload* dialog box.
- The figures in the book use Google Chrome.

4. Select the file or files you want to upload to your *SkyDrive* and click **Open**.

- You can select more than one file. Press **Ctrl** when you click to select non-adjacent files, press **Shift** when you click to select a range of files, or press **Ctr+A** to select all files in a folder.
- You can upload only files, not folders.

5. An upload status window appears in the bottom right corner when you are uploading files.

6. The files you upload appear in the files and folders area of *SkyDrive.*

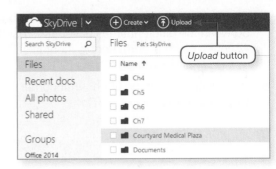

7-50 Upload a file to *SkyDrive*

7-51 Select files to upload to *SkyDrive*

Move, Copy, and Delete Files and Folders

You can also move, copy, and delete files and folders online in *SkyDrive*. When you move a file or folder, it is removed from its location and placed in the new location you select. When you copy a file or folder, it is copied to the new location you select; the file or folder also remains in its original location.

HOW TO: Move, Copy, and Delete SkyDrive Files

1. Check the box to the left of the file or folder you want to move or copy.

2. Click the **Manage** button and select *Move to* or *Copy to* from the drop-down list (Figure 7-52). A window opens (Figure 7-53).

- You can select and move multiple files at the same time.
- You can copy only one file at a time.

7-52 Move a *SkyDrive* file

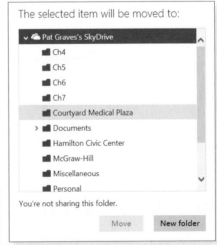

7-53 Select folder where you will move or copy selected items

3. Select the folder where you want to move or copy the selected items.
   - You can place selected items in an existing folder or create a new folder for moved or copied items.
   - Press **Esc** on the keyboard or click away from the move or copy window to cancel the process and close the window.
4. Click the *Move* or *Copy* button to close the window and move or copy the selected items.
5. To delete a file or folder, check the box to the left of the items you want to delete.
6. Click the **Manage** button and select **Delete**.

Download a File

If you are working on a computer in a computer lab or any other public computer, you can download a file or folder from your *SkyDrive* folder and open it in PowerPoint (or another program). After you finish modifying the presentation, you can upload it to your *SkyDrive* folder so the most recent version of your presentation is in *SkyDrive*. When you download files from *SkyDrive*, the files are not removed from *SkyDrive*. The browser you are using and your computer set-up may influence whether file copies go automatically into your *Downloads* folder or if a *Save As* box opens so you can choose the download location.

HOW TO: Download Files from SkyDrive

1. Check the box to the left of the file or folder you want to download.
   - If you select a single file, *SkyDrive* downloads the file.
   - If you select more than one file or a folder to download, a compressed (zipped) folder downloads with the files or folders you selected.
2. Click the **Download** button at the top of the window. The *Save As* dialog box opens (Figure 7-54).
3. Select the location where you want to save the downloaded files.
4. If you want to rename the file, type a file name in the *File name* area.
5. Click the **Save** button to close the *Save As* dialog box and download the selected files.

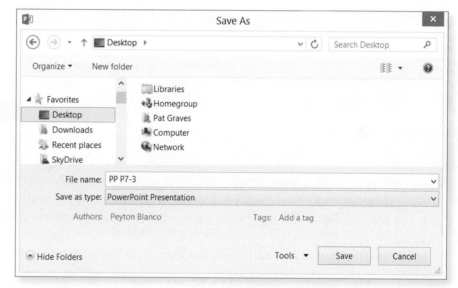

7-54 Save downloaded items from *SkyDrive*

> ### ANOTHER WAY
>
> If your file is saved to the *Downloads* folder when you click the *SkyDrive* **Download** button, then transfer the file from that location to the appropriate folder.

Share a File

SkyDrive allows you to share files or folders with others. When you share files or folders with others, you establish the access they have to the items you share. You can choose whether other users can only view files or view and edit files. When you share a file or folder in your *SkyDrive*, you have the option to send an email with a link to the shared item or generate a hyperlink to share with others that gives them access. If your Windows account is connected to LinkedIn, Facebook, or Twitter, you can also post a link to a shared file in these social networking sites.

HOW TO: Share a SkyDrive File or Folder

1. Select the file or folder you want to share.
   - You can select only one file or folder at a time. You can share as many files or folders as you want, but you have to select and share them one at a time.
   - If you share a folder, shared users have access to all of the files in the folder.
2. Click the **Sharing** button at the top. A sharing window opens listing different sharing options (Figure 7-55).

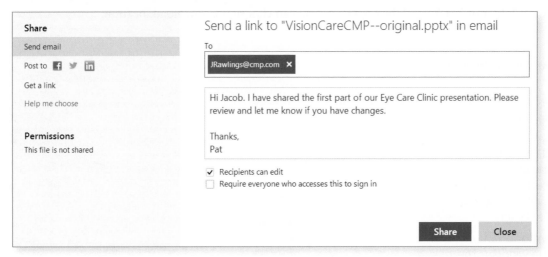

7-55 Send a sharing email

3. To send an email, click **Send email**, type the email address, and type a brief message.
   - Press **Tab** after typing an email address to add another recipient's address.
   - You can click **Get a link** to generate a link you can send to recipients using your own email account.
   - You can post the link on Facebook, Twitter, or LinkedIn.
4. Select the **Recipients can edit** check box if you want the recipient to be able to edit the file.
   - Deselect this check box if you want recipients only to be able to view the file.
   - You can also require recipients to sign in to *SkyDrive* to view or edit the file by selecting the **Require everyone who accesses this to sign in** check box.
5. Click the **Share** button to send the sharing invitation email.
   - The people you have chosen receive an email containing a link to the shared file or folder.
6. Click **Close** in the confirmation window that opens.

You can change the sharing permission or remove sharing on a file or folder. The *Details pane* on the right displays properties of the selected file or folder.

HOW TO: Change or Remove SkyDrive Sharing

1. Select the shared file or folder.
2. Click the **Details** button in the upper right corner. The *Details* pane opens on the right (Figure 7-56).
   - The *Sharing* area lists those who have permission to view or edit the selected item.
3. Click the *Can view* or *Can edit* link to open the *Share* window (Figure 7-57).
   - The display name of this link (*Can view* or *Can edit*) depends on the sharing permission of the file.
4. Select or deselect the **Can edit** check box to change this permission.
5. Click the **Remove permissions** button to remove all sharing permissions.
6. Click the **Close** button to close the *Share* window.
7. Click the **Details** button again to close the *Details* pane.

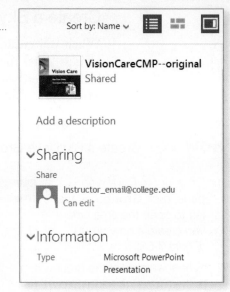

7-56 Change or remove sharing permission in the *Details* pane

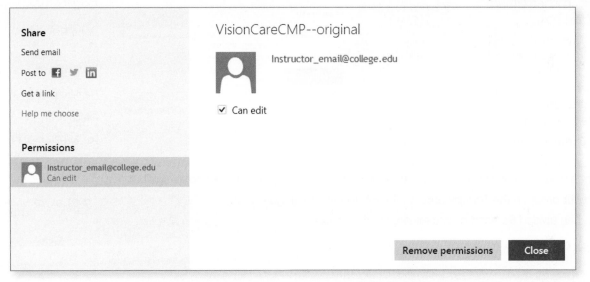

7-57 Change or remove sharing permissions

 SLO 7.6

Using SkyDrive Groups

If you belong to a team at work or school or in an organization, you can create a **SkyDrive group** to store and share presentations and other files with your colleagues. A *SkyDrive* group is another free Microsoft online service that is available from your *SkyDrive* web page. You can invite people to become group members, and members can access groups from their *SkyDrive* web pages.

> **MORE INFO**
>
> If *Groups* are not available on your *SkyDrive* page, you need to activate this feature. Using an Internet browser, search for "create SkyDrive groups." On the *How do I create a group?* Windows page, click the **Groups** link or the **Go to Groups** button on the right to create a *SkyDrive* group.

Create a SkyDrive Group

When you create a *SkyDrive* group, the group has a name, web address, and group email address. After you create a group, you can invite members and establish a role for each member. Members you invite to your group must have a Microsoft account to access the group. Members can store and share presentations or other files in this group on *SkyDrive*.

HOW TO: Create a SkyDrive Group

1. On your *SkyDrive* web page, click **Groups** on the left to open the area where you create a new group (Figure 7-58).

2. Type the name of the group in the *Group name* text box.

3. Type an email address for the group in the *Group email* text box.

   • SkyDrive group email addresses are limited to 24 characters
   • Email addresses can contain only numbers, letters, and hyphens.

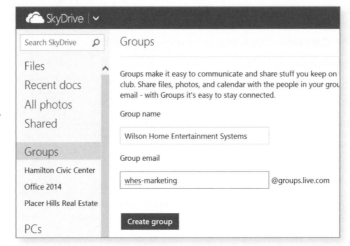

7-58 Create a *SkyDrive* group

4. Click **Create group** to create your group.

   • The new group is listed in the *Groups* area at the left.
   • If the email address is not available, try a different one and click **Create group** again.

5. Click your group in the *Groups* area on the left to select it (Figure 7-59).

   • You can upload files and create folders in your group.

7-59 *SkyDrive* group

People you invite as members receive emails that invite them to join the group. When they accept the invitations, they are listed in the *Group membership* area of the group.

> **MORE INFO**
> You can upload files to your group the same way you upload files to your *SkyDrive* folder.

Invite and Manage SkyDrive Group Members

After you create your group and invite members, you can add new members, remove members, and change roles of members. You can set members' ***roles*** as *Owner, Co-Owner,* and *Member.* Roles control the permission level assigned to a group member. *Owners* and *Co-Owners* have full access to create, edit, and delete files and folders in the group, and to customize group options. *Members* can create files and folders, edit them, and view others' files and folders.

HOW TO: Invite and Manage SkyDrive Group Members

1. On your *SkyDrive* web page, select your group.
2. Click the **Group actions** button at the top and select **Invite People** to open an area where you can invite members (Figure 7-60).

Invite people to join this group

| david@whes.com ✕ | allen@whes.com ✕ | teri@whes.com |

Invite   Cancel

7-60 Invite *SkyDrive* group members

3. Type the email addresses of people you want to invite to the group.
   - Press **Tab** after typing each email address to enter another one.
4. Click **Invite** to send the group invitation.
   - Each person you invite receives an email message inviting him or her to the group.
   - A person has to accept the invitation to join the group.
   - When you invite a person to become a member of a *SkyDrive* group, the person's role (permission level), by default, is *Member.* You can change members' roles.
5. Click the **Group actions** button and select **View membership** to view group membership, change group members' roles, or remove members. The *Membership* area displays.
   - Select a member, click the **Change role** button, and select a membership role (Figure 7-61) for that member.
   - To delete a member, select the **member** and click the **Remove** button.

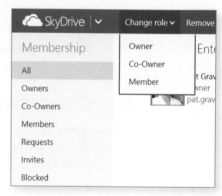

7-61 Change a group member's role

Email SkyDrive Group Members

When you create a group, you choose an email address for the group. You can send emails to the entire group using this email address.

HOW TO: Email SkyDrive Group Members

1. On your *SkyDrive* web page, select your group.
2. Click the **Group actions** button at the top and select **Send an email message**. A new message opens in your Microsoft account email (Figure 7-62).
   - The appearance of this window may vary depending on the type of email address you have (e.g., Live.com, Hotmail, or Outlook.com).
   - The *SkyDrive* group email address is automatically entered in the *To* area. Press **Tab** to type additional addresses in the *To* area.

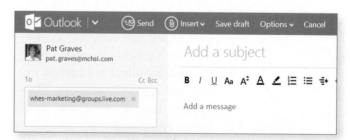

7-62 Send an email to *SkyDrive* group members

3. Type a subject and a message.
4. Click **Send** to send the email message.

MORE INFO

You can view the group email history by selecting **Show email messages** from the *Group actions* drop-down list.

Alternatively, you can create a group email or view email history by clicking on a link in the *Details* pane (Figure 7-63). Click the **Details** button on the upper right to open the *Details* pane. Click the **Group email address** link to create a new group email. Click the **View** link to the left of *Group email history* to view group emails.

ANOTHER WAY

Select **Properties** from the *Group actions* drop-down list to display the *Details* pane.

Change SkyDrive Group Options

If you are the owner or co-owner of a group, you can customize the group options. The following categories are available:

- *General*
- *Email*
- *Group conversations*
- *Personal*
- *Leave group*
- *Delete group*

7-63 *Details* pane

Select a group and click the **Group options** button at the top of the window to display the *Options* page (Figure 7-64). Click one of the categories on the left to display the customization options for that category. When you finish making changes, click the **Save** button at the bottom to save and apply the changes. The *Options* area is where you can leave a group or delete a group.

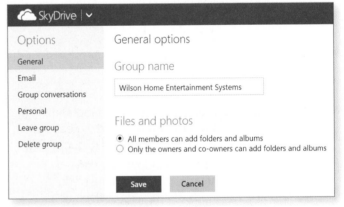

7-64 *SkyDrive* group options

ANOTHER WAY

Click the **Options** link in the *Details* pane to open the *Options* area for the select group.

For this project, you change your Microsoft account settings and add an app. You also upload files to your *SkyDrive* folder and create a folder online, move files, delete a folder, share a file, create a *SkyDrive* group, invite a member, and modify group options.

Note to Instructor and Students:
    General Information*: For this project, you use the* SkyDrive *Windows folder and* SkyDrive *groups. If these are not available on your computer, refer to the instructions in the* More Info *boxes on pages 429 and 435.*
    Students*: For this project, you share* SkyDrive *files with your instructor and invite your instructor to become a member of your* SkyDrive *group.*
    Instructor*: To complete this project, your students need your Microsoft email address. You can create a new Live or Hotmail account for projects in this chapter.*

Files Needed: ***[your initials] PP P7-2c.pptx***, ***VisionCarePart1-07.pptx***, and ***Vision-07.jpg***
Completed Project File Name: ***[your initials] PP P7-3.pptx***

1. Open the presentation ***[your initials] PP P7-2c*** using the password CMPecc.

2. Remove the password and save the file.
   a. Click the **File** tab, choose **Info**, and select **Protect Presentation**.
   b. Select **Encrypt with Password**.
   c. On the *Encrypt Document* dialog box, delete the password. Click **OK**.
   d. Save the presentation as ***[your initials] PP P7-3***.

3. Log in to Office using your Microsoft account. Skip this step if you are already logged in with your Microsoft account. If you don't have a Microsoft account, go to www.live.com and follow the instructions to create a free Microsoft account.
   a. In the upper right corner of the PowerPoint window, click your name and click **Switch Account** to open the Microsoft *Sign In* dialog box.
   b. Type your Microsoft account email address and click **Next**. Enter your password and click **Sign In**.

4. Customize your Office account settings.
   a. Click the **File** tab and select **Account** to display your account information on the *Backstage* view.
   b. Click the **Office Background** drop-down list and select a background of your choice.
   c. Click the **Office Theme** drop-down list and select a theme of your choice.
   d. Click the **Add** a service drop-down list, select **Images & Videos**, and click **YouTube** (Figure 7-65). YouTube is added in the *Connected Services* area.
   e. Click the **Back** button to return to *Normal* view.

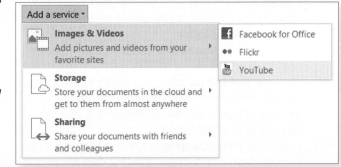

7-65 Add a service

5. Add an Office app.
   a. Click the top half of the **Apps for Office** button [*Insert* tab, *Apps* group] to open the *Apps for Office* dialog box.
   b. Click **Featured Apps** to display the featured apps.

c. Select an app of your choice and click the **Add** link. The *Apps* pane opens on the right.

d. If the app you selected does not automatically load in the *Apps* pane, click the **exclamation point** in the upper left corner of the *Apps* pane to display information about the app, and then click the **Start** button to activate the app.

e. Close the *Apps* pane.

6. Create a folder in your *SkyDrive* folder and save this presentation in the new folder.

a. Open the *Save As* dialog box, select the **SkyDrive** folder on the left, and click **Browse**.

b. Click the **New Folder** button (Figure 7-66).

c. Type Courtyard Medical Plaza as the folder name and press **Enter**. Double-click this name to open the folder.

d. Click **Save**.

7. Close the presentation and exit PowerPoint.

8. Log in to *SkyDrive* online, create a new folder, and upload files.

a. Open an Internet browser window, type www.skydrive.com in the address bar at the top, and press **Enter** to go to the *SkyDrive* log in page.

b. Type your Microsoft email address and password to log in to *SkyDrive.*

c. Click **Files** on the left to display the contents of your *SkyDrive* folder. The new folder you created is displayed in *SkyDrive* (there might be other folders listed as well).

d. Click **Details** view (Figure 7-67), if necessary, so your screen displays file names rather than thumbnail images.

e. Click the **Create** button at the top and select **Folder** from the drop-down list (Figure 7-68).

f. Type CMP Marketing as the name for the new folder and press **Enter**.

g. Click the **CMP Marketing** folder (not the check box) to open it.

h. Click the **Upload** button at the top to open an upload dialog box. Remember, the name of this dialog box varies depending on the Internet browser you are using.

i. Select the **VisionCarePart1-07** and **Vision-07** files from your student data files (use the **Ctrl** key to select non-adjacent files, if necessary) and click **Open.** The two files are added to the *CMP* folder.

9. Move a file.

a. Click **Files** on the left to return to your list of folders.

b. Click the **Courtyard Medical Plaza** folder to open it. The *[your initials] PP P7-3* file is in this folder. If it is not, add the file.

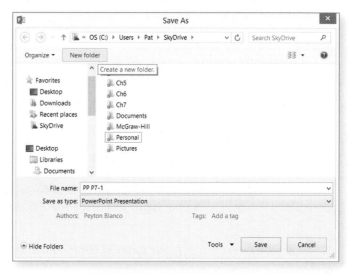

7-66 Create a new *SkyDrive* folder on your computer

7-67 *Details* view button

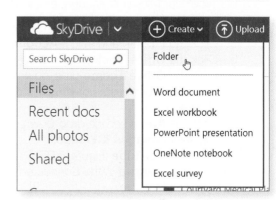

7-68 Create a new *SkyDrive* folder online

c. Check the box to the left of the *[your initials]*
   PP P7-3 file to select it.
d. Click the **Manage** button and select **Move to** from
   the drop-down list. A dialog box opens (Figure 7-69).
e. Select the **CMP Marketing** folder and click **Move**.
f. Click **Files** to return to your list of folders.
g. Click the **CMP Marketing** folder to open it and
   confirm that the file is moved.

10. Delete a folder.
    a. Click **Files** on the left to return to your list of folders.
    b. Check the box to the left of the *Courtyard Medical*
       Plaza folder.
    c. Click the **Manage** button and select **Delete**.

11. Share a folder.
    a. Click **Files** to return to your list of folders.
    b. Check the box to the left of the **CMP Marketing**
       folder.
    c. Click **Sharing** at the top to open the sharing dialog
       box (Figure 7-70).

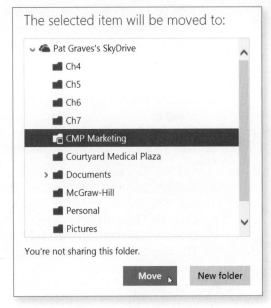

7-69 Move a file to a folder

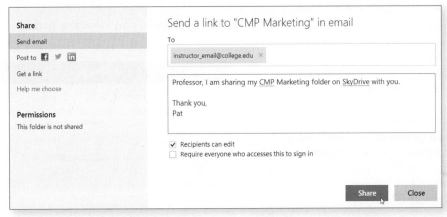

7-70 Share a folder and send an email

d. Select **Send email** on the left.
e. Type your instructor's email address in
   the *To* area.
f. Type a brief message in the body area.
g. Check the **Recipients can edit** box.
h. Click **Share** to send the sharing email
   to your instructor. You may receive
   a message asking you to verify your
   account.
i. Click **Close** in the *Share* window that
   opens.

12. Create a *SkyDrive* group and invite a
    member.
    a. Click **Groups** on the left to open the
       Groups page (Figure 7-71).
    b. Type CMP Eye Care Clinic in the
       Group name text box.

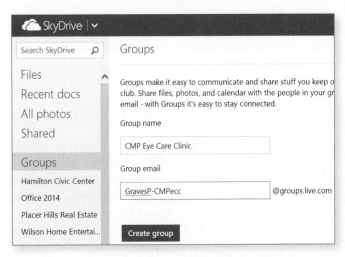

7-71 Create a *SkyDrive* group

c. Type your last name, first initial, and -CMPecc in the email area (for example, *GravesP-CMPecc*).

d. Click **Create group** to create your group. If the email address you choose is already taken, type a different one. After the group is created, you are returned to *SkyDrive* and the *CMP Eye Care Clinic* group is selected.

13. Invite a member to your group.
    a. Confirm that the *CMP Eye Care Clinic* group is selected in the *Groups* area on the left. If it is not, select it.
    b. Click the **Group actions** button at the top and select **Invite people**. An *Invite* window opens.
    c. Type your instructor's email address and click **Invite**.

14. Upload files to your group.
    a. Confirm that the *CMP Eye Care Clinic* group is selected in the *Groups* area on the left. If it is not, select it.
    b. Click the **Upload** button to open an upload dialog box.
    c. Select the ***VisionCarePart1-07*** and ***Vision-07*** files from your student data files and click **Open**. The files are added to your group. (You may need to refresh your browser window to display the files.)

15. Change group options.
    a. With the *CMP Eye Care Clinic* group selected on the left, click the **Group options** button at the top. The *Options* page opens.
    b. Select **Email** on the left if it is not already selected.
    c. In the *Link to group website* area, click the **Only group members can view the group using this link** radio button.
    d. Click the **Save** button. The *Options* page closes and you return to your group.
    e. Click the **Group options** button again to reopen the *Options* page.
    f. Click **Group conversations** on the left.
    g. Click **Turn off group conversations**. The *Options* area closes and you are redirected to your group.
    h. Confirm the two files are in your CMP Eye Care Clinic group folder (Figure 7-72).

16. Click **[your name]** in the upper right corner of the window and select **Sign out** from the *Account* drop-down list.

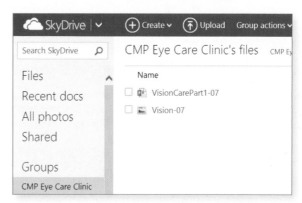

7-72 PP 7-2 completed (*SkyDrive* group displayed)

Using Office Web Apps

Office Web Apps is free online software from Microsoft that works in conjunction with your online *SkyDrive* account. With Office Web Apps, you can work with many different Office files online *without* having Office 2013 installed on the computer you are using. This is a convenient option, for example, when you are using a friend's computer or a public computer that does not have Office 2013 installed.

Office Web Apps is available from your *SkyDrive* web page. Office Web Apps is a scaled-down version of Office 2013. It is not as robust in terms of features, but you can use it to create, edit, print, share, and insert comments on files. If you need more advanced features, you can open Office Web Apps files in their respective Office 2013 programs.

Edit an Office Web Apps File

You can use Office Web Apps to open and edit the Office files you have stored in your *Sky-Drive* or *SkyDrive* groups. The working environment in Office Web Apps is very similar to Microsoft Office and has the familiar *Ribbon,* tabs, and groups. However, not as many tabs and features are available in Office Web Apps.

When you initially open an Office file from either *SkyDrive* or a *SkyDrive* group, the file is displayed in ***read-only mode*** in the browser window where you are viewing it. When you edit the file in the browser window, Office Web Apps opens your file in ***edit mode*** in the appropriate program. For example, if you edit a PowerPoint presentation in *SkyDrive,* your presentation opens in ***PowerPoint Web App***.

HOW TO: Edit an Office Web Apps File

1. Log in to your *SkyDrive* account using the Internet browser of your choice.

2. Click an Office file (in this case a PowerPoint file) to open from *SkyDrive* or a *SkyDrive* group (Figure 7-73). The file displays in read-only mode in an Office Web Apps window (Figure 7-74).

   - You cannot edit a file in read-only mode.
   - Alternatively, you can select a file (check box), click the **Open** button, and select *Open in PowerPoint Web App* or *Open in PowerPoint*.

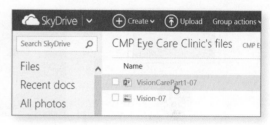

7-73 Open a presentation in PowerPoint Web App

7-74 A presentation opened in Microsoft PowerPoint Web App

3. Click **Edit Presentation** and select **Edit in PowerPoint Web App** (Figure 7-75) to edit the file in your browser.

- Alternatively, you can open an Office Web Apps file in Microsoft Office if Microsoft Office is installed on the computer you are using.
- Click **Edit in PowerPoint** to launch the full version of PowerPoint from your computer.

7-75 Change from *read-only* mode to *edit* mode in Microsoft PowerPoint Web App

4. Make editing and formatting changes in Office Web Apps (Figure 7-76).

7-76 The Microsoft PowerPoint Web App *Ribbon*

- The *File, Home, Insert, Design, Animations, Transitions,* and *View* tabs are on the *Ribbon* in PowerPoint Web App. Other apps will display some different tabs.
- Click **Open in [Office application]** (*Open in PowerPoint*) to open the presentation in Office on your computer.
- You can edit and change formatting, apply styles, and cut, copy, and paste selected text. Font sizing and gallery options are limited. Resizing or rearranging objects will feel a little different than when using the complete version of PowerPoint.
- When you are using Office Web Apps, some advanced formatting such as text boxes, pictures, charts, and *SmartArt* might not be arranged and aligned as they are when you open the presentation in PowerPoint 2013. *Slide Sorter* view is not available.

5. In PowerPoint Web App, your file is automatically saved. Click the **File** tab and choose **Save As** if you want to save to a different location.

6. Click the **X** in the upper right corner to close the presentation and return to your *SkyDrive* folders and files.

- Alternatively, click the **SkyDrive** link at the top of the window to return to your *SkyDrive* folders and files.

> **MORE INFO**
> The PowerPoint Web App *Ribbon* displays in edit mode but not in read-only mode.

Create an Office Web Apps File

You are not limited to editing existing files in Office Web Apps; you can also create new Word documents, Excel workbooks, PowerPoint presentations, and OneNote notebooks. When you create an Office Web Apps file, the document is saved in your *SkyDrive* or *SkyDrive* group folder.

> **MORE INFO**
>
> *OneNote* is a note-taking application that is a part of Microsoft Office. You can use OneNote to create, gather, organize, and share notes.

HOW TO: Create an Office Web Apps File

1. In *SkyDrive* or a *SkyDrive* group, select the folder where you want to create a new file.

2. Click the **Create** button and select the type of file to create (*Word document, Excel workbook, PowerPoint presentation,* or *OneNote notebook*) (Figure 7-77). A dialog box for that Web app opens (in this case, the *New Microsoft PowerPoint presentation*) (Figure 7-78).

3. Type the name of your file and click the **Create** button. The file opens in the selected Web App in edit mode.

4. Type information and apply formatting as desired.

5. In PowerPoint Web App, your file is automatically saved when you close the presentation. In other Web Apps, you click the **File** button or press **Ctrl+S**.

6. Click the **File** tab and choose **Save As** if you want to save to a different location.

7. Click the **X** in the upper right corner to close the current file and return to your *SkyDrive* folders and files.

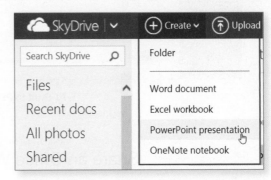

7-77 Create a PowerPoint Web App presentation

7-78 Name a new PowerPoint presentation

> **MORE INFO**
>
> If you edit a PowerPoint Web App file in PowerPoint, you must save your changes before closing the presentation so your online file is updated.

Print an Office Web Apps File

You can print files from Office Web Apps in the same general way you print files in Office. The difference in Office Web Apps is that the program creates a PDF (portable document format) file when you print so the file retains its original format. You can print from either read-only or edit mode.

HOW TO: Print an Office Web Apps File

1. Click a file to open from *SkyDrive* or a *SkyDrive* group.

2. In either read-only or edit mode, click the **File** tab.

3. Select **Print** and click the **Print to PDF** button (Figure 7-79).
4. Click the **Click here to view the PDF of your document** link to open the printable PDF file (Figure 7-80).
   - The printable PDF file opens in a *Print* window with a preview of the document on the right.
   - Choose from the available print options.
5. Click the **Print** button.

7-79 Print to PDF

7-80 Click to view printable PDF file

Share an Office Web Apps File

In addition to sharing a file from *SkyDrive* or a *SkyDrive* group, you can also share a file you are previewing or editing in Office Web Apps. The process for sharing a file in Office Web Apps is similar to sharing a file or folder in *SkyDrive*.

HOW TO: Share an Office Web Apps File

1. Open a file in Office Web Apps.
2. In *read-only* mode, click the **Share** button above the document. The *Share* window opens with different options (Figure 7-81).
   - In either *read-only* or *edit* mode, click the **File** tab and select **Share** on the left. Click the **Share with People** button to open the *Share* window.
3. To send an email, click **Send email**, type the recipient's email address, and type a brief message.
   - Press **Tab** after typing an email address to add another recipient.
   - You can also click **Get a link** to generate a link that you can send to recipients.
4. Check the **Recipients can edit** box if you want the recipient to be able to edit the file.
   - Deselect this check box if you want recipients to be able only to view the file.
   - You can also require recipients to sign in to *SkyDrive* in order to view or edit the file by checking the **Require everyone who accesses this to sign in** box.
5. Click the **Share** button.
   - Recipients receive an email containing a link to the shared file or folder.
6. Click **Close** to close the *Share* window and return to the Office Web Apps document.

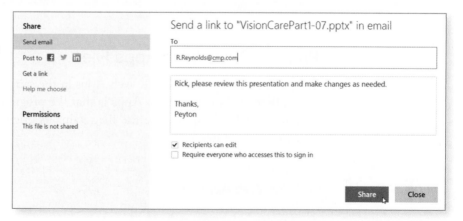

7-81 Share an Office Web Apps file

Collaborate in Office Web Apps

Office Web Apps let you synchronously or asynchronously (at the same time or different times) collaborate on an Office file with others who have access to the shared file. In Excel and PowerPoint Web Apps, updates made by another user are reflected immediately. In Word, you are notified in the *Status bar* that updates are available.

The number of users working on the same file is also displayed in the *Status bar*. This number appears at the bottom left corner of the PowerPoint Web App window (Figure 7-82). Click this number to view the names of users who are currently editing the file.

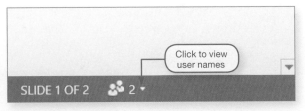

7-82 Collaboration information displayed in the *Status bar*

If a user has edited your file using PowerPoint Web App and you open that file from the *SkyDrive* folder on your computer using PowerPoint, you will be notified in the *Status bar* that updates are available. If you both have the file open, the number of users is displayed also.

Use Comments in PowerPoint Web App

In PowerPoint Web App, you can add comments to a file, review comments from others, reply to comments, and delete comments. When you click the **Comments** button in read-only mode, the *Comments* pane opens where you click **Add Comments**. Then the presentation opens in edit mode where you can insert your comments.

HOW TO: Add Comments in PowerPoint Web App

1. Open a file in PowerPoint Web App.
2. In read-only mode, click the **Comments** button at the top to open the *Comments* pane on the right (Figure 7-83).
3. Click the **Add Comments** button to open the file in edit mode.

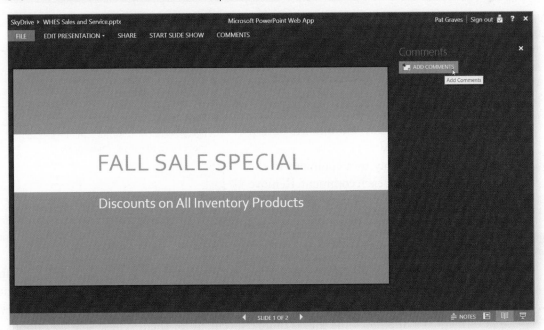

7-83 Using comments in Microsoft PowerPoint Web App

4. In the *Comments* pane, click the **New** button. Your name automatically appears with a space for your comment (Figure 7-84).

7-84 Using comments in Microsoft PowerPoint Web App

5. Type your comment and press **Enter**.
   - A comment icon displays in the upper left corner.
   - If you select a slide object before making a comment, the comment icon appears near the object you selected.

> **ANOTHER WAY**
>
> In *edit* mode, select the slide where you want to add a comment, click the **Insert** tab, and click the **Comment** button.

When reviewing your own comments or comments from others, click a comment icon in the presentation to open the *Comments* pane, which appears on the right (Figure 7-85). Alternatively, you can open the *Comments* pane by clicking the **Show Comments** button [*View* tab, *Show* group].

You can type a reply to a comment in the box that appears below each comment. Remove a comment by clicking the **Delete** button.

7-85 *Comments* pane

SLO 7.8

More Ways to Share

In addition to *SkyDrive* and Office Web Apps, Microsoft provides other options for collaborating. Distance and time are no longer barriers to collaboration because people in remote locations can view your presentation online as you present it or they can review materials you send to them at a different time that is more convenient for them. These sharing options are available by clicking the *Share* button on the *File* tab.

Share with Email

With your PowerPoint presentation open, click the **File** tab, click **Share,** click **Email,** and click **Send as Attachment** (Figure 7-86). Microsoft Outlook automatically opens with your file name as the attachment. Type one or more recipient addresses, add a subject, and type your message before sending. Each recipient will receive a copy of the presentation.

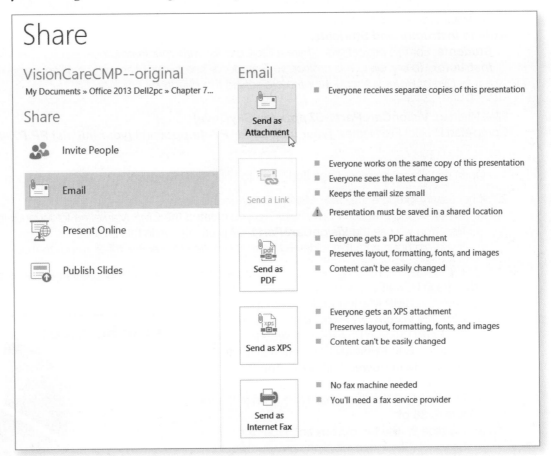

7-86 *Share* options

For the option *Send a Link,* your presentation must be saved in a shared location. When you select the options *Send as PDF* or *Send as XPS,* your presentation is automatically converted to the format you choose and that file name appears when Microsoft Outlook opens. The option *Send as Internet Fax* requires a fax service provider.

Present Online or Publish Slides

The ***Office Presentation Service*** is a free, public service provided with your Microsoft account. Your presentation is saved in an online location with a link created that you can share with people in advance. Invited people can view your presentation remotely in a web browser and can download the presentation if you enable this option.

The ***Publish Slides*** feature stores slides in a shared location such as Microsoft's SharePoint site (which is available for a monthly subscription fee). Several SharePoint products exist that provide cloud-based service for businesses and individuals to create websites and to store, organize, share, and access information.

For this project, you use a file that you uploaded to your *SkyDrive* in *Pause & Practice PowerPoint 7-3*. You edit a presentation in PowerPoint Web App, add comments to the presentation, share a file, create a PowerPoint Web App presentation, and rename files.

Note to Instructor and Students:

> **Students**: For this project, you share a SkyDrive file with your instructor.
>
> **Instructor**: To complete this project, your students need your Microsoft email address. You can create a new Live or Hotmail account for the projects in this chapter.

Files Needed: **VisionCarePart1-07.pptx (on SkyDrive)**
Completed Project File Names: **[your initials] PP P7-4a.pptx** and **[your initials] PP P7-4b.pptx**

1. Open an Internet browser page and log in to your *SkyDrive* account (www.skydrive.com).

2. If necessary, prepare the *CMP Marketing* folder and files.
   a. In *Pause and Practice PowerPoint 7-3* you created the *CMP Marketing* folder and uploaded three files. You will use the **VisionCarePart1-07** presentation in this project.
   b. If you did not create this folder in *Pause & Practice PowerPoint 7-3*, return to that project and complete steps 8 a–i.

3. Edit a file in PowerPoint Web App.
   a. Click the **CMP Marketing** folder to open it.
   b. Click the **VisionCarePart1-07** file to open it in read-only mode in PowerPoint Web App.
   c. Click the **Edit Presentation** button at the top and select **Edit in PowerPoint Web App** from the drop-down list.
   d. On slide 1, select the subtitle and change the font size to **36 pt**.
   e. On slide 2, insert a text box and type Our Services. Change to left alignment, apply bold, and change the font size to **54 pt**. Move this text box to the left (Figure 7-87).
   f. In PowerPoint Web App, the file is saved automatically.

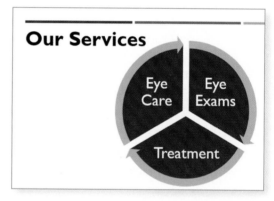

7-87 Text box added

4. Add a comment to the presentation.
   a. On slide 3, click the **Show Comments** button [*View* tab, *Show* group] to open the *Comments* pane.
   b. Click **New** and type We need to develop a separate presentation about eye exams for children. in the box after your name (Figure 7-88).

5. Share the presentation with your instructor.
   a. Click **Share** at the top to open the *Share* window (Figure 7-89).
   b. Select **Send email** on the left.
   c. Type your instructor's email address in the *To* area.
   d. Type a brief message in the body area.
   e. Select the **Recipients can edit** check box.

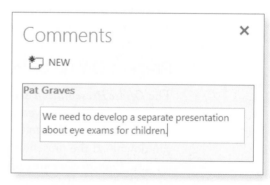

7-88 Add comment

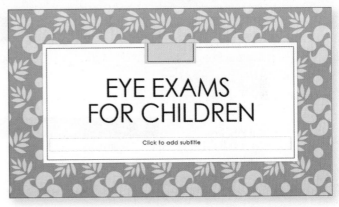

7-89 Share a presentation

f. Click **Share** to send the sharing email to your instructor.
g. Click **Close** to close the *Share* window.
h. Click the **SkyDrive** link at the top to return to your *SkyDrive* folders.

6. Create a new presentation in PowerPoint Web App.
a. Click the **CMP Marketing** folder to open it.
b. Click the **Create** button and select **PowerPoint presentation**. The *New Microsoft PowerPoint presentation* window opens.
c. Type Children Exams as the title of the new presentation and click **Create**. The new presentation opens in PowerPoint Web App in edit mode.
d. Click the **Design** tab, click the **More** button to open the *Themes* gallery, and click the **Savon** theme to apply it.
e. For the slide 1 title, type Eye Exams for Children to fit on two lines (Figure 7-90).
f. Click the **New Slides** button [*Home* tab, *Slides* group], select the **Title and Content** layout, and click **Add Slide**.
g. On slide 2, type Recommended Ages for the slide title.
h. On slide 2, click the **SmartArt** button in the content placeholder. Click the **Basic Chevron Process** layout [*Design* tab, *Layouts* group]. Click the first shape and bullets appear (Figure 7-91). Type the ages, 6 months, age 3, and age 5, after each bullet. When you click anywhere on the slide, the text appears in the three shapes as shown in Figure 7-92.

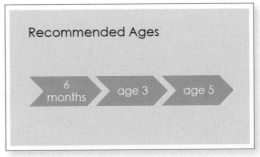

7-90 Title slide

7-91 Typing *SmartArt* text

7-92 Completed *SmartArt* graphic

i. Click the **New Slides** button [*Home* tab, *Slides* group], select the **Title and Content** layout, and click **Add Slide**.

j. On slide 3, type Eyesight Skills for Learning. In the content placeholder, type the following items. Only one bullet will appear when you start typing, but the remaining bullets will appear when the list is complete.
   - Near and distance vision
   - Eye coordination and movement
   - Focusing skills
   - Peripheral awareness
   - Hand-eye coordination

k. On slide 3, increase the list font size to **27 pt**.

l. View the presentation in *SlideShow* view.

m. Close the presentation and return to your *SkyDrive* folders.

7. Rename files.
   a. Click the **CMP Marketing** folder to open it.
   b. Select the ***VisionCarePart1-07*** check box.
   c. Click the **Manage** button and select **Rename** from the drop-down list (Figure 7-93).

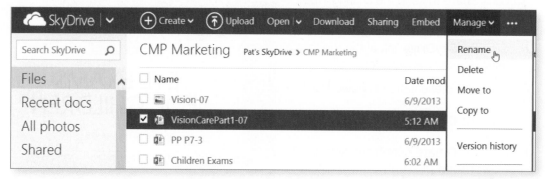

7-93 Rename a file

   d. Type [your initials] PP P7-4a and press **Enter**.
   e. Deselect the **[your initials] PP P7-4a** check box.
   f. Rename the ***Children Exams*** presentation [your initials] PP P7-4b.

8. Select **[your name]** in the upper right corner and select **Sign out** from the *Account* drop-down list.

Chapter Summary

7.1 Prepare a presentation for sharing by removing personal information, adapting it for accessibility, and checking compatibility (p. P7-410).

- The *Inspect Document* feature targets hidden content, properties, or personal information that you may not want to share.
- The *Check Accessibility* feature identifies potential issues in a presentation that may cause problems for users with disabilities.
- *Alt Text* identifies graphic objects for assistive technologies such as screen readers.
- The *Check Compatibility* feature identifies potential problems when a current presentation is saved in a version before 2007.

7.2 Protect a presentation by marking it as final and adding a password (p. P7-413).

- *Mark as Final* creates a read-only file and prevents the file from being accidentally edited.
- *Encrypt with Password* prevents a document from being opened without a password.

7.3 Export a presentation by creating different file types and by creating a video (p. P7-419).

- When you change to an image file type, you can save one slide or all slides as separate pictures in a *.png* or *.jpg* format.
- PDF (Portable Document Format) or XPS (XML Paper Specification) files create copies of a presentation that can be viewed or printed without PowerPoint. Both formats create small file sizes.
- When you save a presentation as a video, you can include all recorded timings, narrations, laser pointer gestures, and animations. Video file sizes can be large.
- Exporting a presentation to create handouts in Word provides additional layout options.

7.4 View and modify Office account settings and add an Office app (p. P7-426).

- The *Account area* on the *Backstage* view provides information and account customization options.
- Your *Office account information and settings* are available whenever you log in to PowerPoint (or any Office application) using your *Microsoft account*. You can obtain your own free Microsoft account through Live, Hotmail, Messenger, or MSN.
- You can change the *Office background* in the *Account* area on the *Backstage* view.
- You can add *connected services* to your account to access online services for *Images & Videos*, *Storage*, and *Sharing*.
- *Apps* (applications) provide additional functionality to Office. The *Apps for Office* window lists available apps for Office.

7.5 Create folders and add, move, copy, and share files in *SkyDrive* (p. P7-429).

- *SkyDrive* is a *cloud storage* area that provides online storage space for your files. If you have a Microsoft account (Live, Hotmail, MSN, Messenger, or other Microsoft service account), you have access to *SkyDrive.*
- You can access your *SkyDrive* files from any computer that has Internet access.
- Log in to *SkyDrive* using your Microsoft account.
- If you use Windows 8, *SkyDrive* is one of your storage options. You can save and edit *SkyDrive* files using a Windows folder in a dialog box, in a *File Explorer* window, or online using an Internet browser.
- In *SkyDrive,* you can add files, create folders, and move, copy, delete, and download files.
- You can share *SkyDrive* files with others. You determine the access other users have to view and/or edit your *SkyDrive* files.

7.6 Create a group in *SkyDrive,* invite a member, and change group options (p. P7-435).

- A *SkyDrive group* is an online workspace you can use to store and share presentations and other documents with other group members.
- *SkyDrive* groups are connected to *SkyDrive;* you can create groups if you have a Microsoft account.
- You can access groups you create or are a member of from your *SkyDrive* page.
- You can invite a person to become a *member* of your *SkyDrive* group and determine each member's role. A member can be an *owner*, a *co-owner*, or a *member*.

- Each *SkyDrive* group has a **web address** and **group email account**. You can send email to all group members using the group email address.
- You can add and edit files and create folders in groups.

7.7 Open, create, edit, print, share, use comments, and collaborate on a presentation in Office Web Apps (p. P7-442).

- **Office Web Apps** is free online software that works in conjunction with your *SkyDrive* account and is available from your *SkyDrive* web page.
- Office Web Apps is similar to Microsoft Office 2013 but its features are less robust.
- You can use Office Web Apps without Office 2013 being installed on your computer.
- You can edit existing files from your *SkyDrive* account in Office Web Apps and create new Office files using Office Web Apps.
- You can share Office Web Apps files with others.

- More than one user can edit an Office Web Apps file at the same time, which allows real-time collaboration on presentations and other documents.
- You can add comments, reply to comments, or delete comments on PowerPoint Web Apps files.

7.8 Share a presentation by sending it as an email attachment, presenting online, or publishing slides (p. P7-448).

- PowerPoint **Share** options include a feature to send presentation files as attachments.
- **Office Presentation Service** is available with your Microsoft account so users from remote locations can view or download your presentation in an Internet browser.
- The **Publish Slides** feature enables you to connect with Microsoft's SharePoint, a cloud-based service available for a subscription fee.

Check for Understanding

In the **Online Learning Center** for this text (www.mhhe.com/office2013inpractice), there are a variety of resources that can be used to review the concepts covered in this chapter.

The following Online Learning Resources are available in the Online Learning Center:

- Multiple choice questions
- Short answer questions
- Matching exercises

Note to Instructor and Students: For most of these projects, you use the SkyDrive Windows folder and SkyDrive groups. If these are not available on your computer, refer to the instructions in the More Info boxes on pages 429 and 435. Security settings in computer labs may inhibit some software features.

Guided Project 7-1

For this project, you inspect a presentation, mark it as final, save a slide as a picture, create a PDF document, create a presentation video, and send an email attachment.
[Student Learning Outcomes 7.1, 7.2, 7.3, 7.8]

Note to Instructor: To complete this project, your students need your Microsoft email address.

File Needed: **Fitness-07.pptx**
Completed Project File Names: *[your initials] PowerPoint 7-1a.pptx*, *[your initials] PowerPoint 7-1b.jpg*, *[your initials] PowerPoint 7-1c.pdf*, and *[your initials] PowerPoint 7-1d.mp4*

Skills Covered in This Project

- Inspect a presentation.
- Mark a presentation as final.
- Save a slide as a picture.
- Create a PDF document from a presentation.
- Create a presentation video.
- Send a presentation as an attachment.

1. Open the presentation **Fitness-07.pptx** and save it as *[your initials] PowerPoint 7-1a*.

2. Inspect the presentation.
   a. Click the **File** tab, choose **Check for Issues**, and select **Inspect Document** to open the *Document Inspector* dialog box.
   b. Deselect the **Document Properties and Personal Information** check box.
   c. Click **Inspect**. The *Document Inspector* dialog box opens with the inspection results displayed (Figure 7-94).
   d. Click **Remove All** in the *Comments and Annotations* and *Invisible On-Slide Content* area.
   e. Click **Close** to close the dialog box.

3. Mark the presentation as final.
   a. From the *Backstage* view, click the **Protect Presentation** button. Select **Mark as Final**.
   b. On the dialog box that opens, click **OK**.
   c. Another dialog box opens with the final version message. Click **OK**.
   d. The presentation is automatically saved.

4. Save a slide as a picture.
   a. Select **slide 6**.

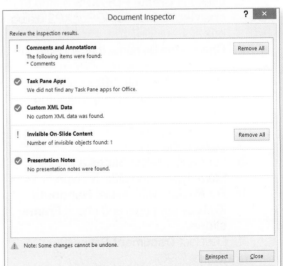

7-94 *Document Inspector* with inspection results displayed

b. Click the **File** tab, choose **Export**, and select **Change File Type**.
c. Select **JPEG File Interchange Format** (Figure 7-95).
d. Click the **Save As** button.
e. On the *Save As* dialog box, type the file name [your initials] PowerPoint P7-1b.
f. Click **Save**. On the dialog box that opens, click **Just This One**.

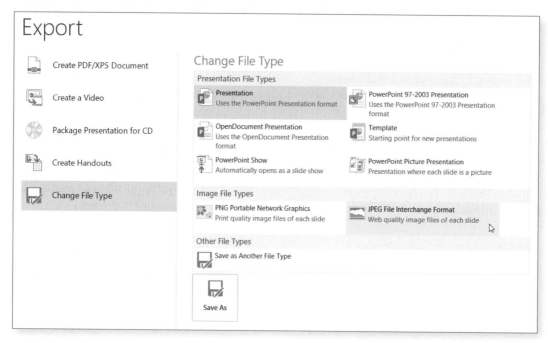

7-95 Export with the JPEG file format

5. Create a PDF file.
   a. Click the **File** tab, choose **Export**, and select **Create PDF/XPS Document**.
   b. Click the **Create PDF/XPS** button to open the *Publish as PDF or XPS* dialog box.
   c. Change the file name that appears to [your initials] PowerPoint P7-1c.
   d. Deselect **Open file after publishing**.
   e. Select **Minimum size (publishing online)**.
   f. Click the **Options** button to open the *Options* dialog box.
   g. For *Range,* select **Slides** and after *From:* type 1 and after *To:* type 6.
   h. For *Publish what,* select **Handouts** (6 slides per page) and check **Frame slides**.
   i. Deselect **Document Properties** (Figure 7-96).
   j. Click **OK** to close the dialog box.
   k. Click **Publish**.

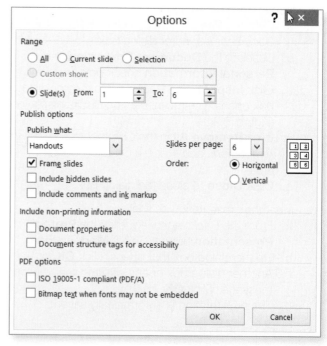

7-96 *Options* dialog box for saving a PDF file

6. Create a presentation video.
   a. Transitions and animations have been applied.
   b. Click the **File** tab, choose **Export**, and select **Create a Video**.
   c. On the first list box, click the **list arrow** and choose the **Internet and DVD** quality options (Figure 7-97).

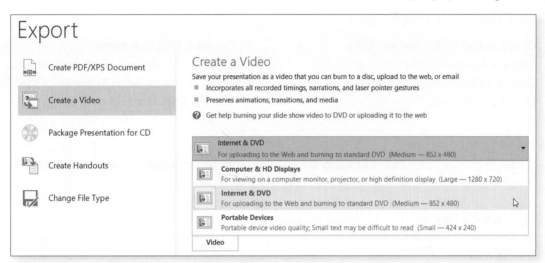

7-97 Options for exporting a video

   d. On the second list box, use the default setting for **Don't Use Recorded Timings and Narrations**.
   e. For *Seconds to spend on each slide,* type 3:00 seconds.
   f. Click **Create Video**.
   g. In the *Save As* dialog box, change the file name that appears to [your initials] PowerPoint 7-1d.
   h. For *Save as type,* select **MPEG-4 Video**.
   i. Click **Save**.

7. Share the presentation with your instructor.
   a. Click the **File** tab, choose **Share**, and select **Email**. Click **Send as Attachment**.
   b. Microsoft Outlook opens. Type your instructor's email address in the *To* area and add an appropriate subject line.
   c. Type a brief message in the body area.
   d. Click **Send**.

8. Close the *[your initials] PP P7-1a* presentation.

Guided Project 7-2

For this project, you check a presentation for compatibility, create a PDF document, create *SkyDrive* folders, upload files, edit a presentation using PowerPoint Web App, and share a presentation.
[Student Learning Outcomes 7.1, 7.3, 7.5, 7.7, 7.8]

Note to Students and Instructor:

Students: *For this project, you share a SkyDrive file with your instructor and invite your instructor to a SkyDrive group.*
Instructor: *To complete this project, your students need your Microsoft email address.*

File Needed: ***HomeStaging-07.pptx***
Completed Project File Names: ***[your initials] PowerPoint 7-2a.pptx***, ***[your initials]***
PowerPoint 7-2b.pdf, and ***[your initials] PowerPoint 7-2c.pptx***

Skills Covered in This Project

- Check presentation compatibility.
- Encrypt a presentation with a password.
- Create a PDF document from a presentation.
- Log in to *SkyDrive.*

- Create a *SkyDrive* folder.
- Upload a file to your *SkyDrive* folder.
- Edit a presentation in PowerPoint Web App.
- Share a *SkyDrive* folder.

1. Open the presentation ***HomeStaging-07*** and save it as ***[your initials] PowerPoint 7-2a*** on your computer in the location where you store your solution files.

2. Check compatibility of the presentation with 97-2003 software.
   a. Click the **File** tab, choose **Check for Issues**, and select **Check Compatibility** to open the *Microsoft PowerPoint Compatibility Checker* dialog box (Figure 7-98). Because this presentation consists of pictures and text only, the issue identified is minor and the file will convert well to the earlier software version.
   b. Click **OK** to close the dialog box.

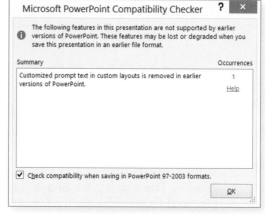

7-98 *Compatibility Checker* **dialog box**

3. Encrypt a presentation with a password.
   a. Click the **File** tab, click the **Protect Presentation** button, and select **Encrypt with Password** to open the *Encrypt Document* dialog box.
   b. Type the password PHRE-hs (Figure 7-99); then click **OK** to open the *Confirm Password* dialog box.
   c. In the *Reenter password to confirm* text box, type PHRE-hs.
   d. Click **OK** to close the dialog box.
   e. Save the presentation.

4. Create a PDF file.
   a. Click the **File** tab, choose **Export**, and select **Create PDF/XPS Document**.
   b. Click the **Create PDF/XPS** button to open the *Publish as PDF or XPS* dialog box.
   c. Change the file name that appears to [your initials] PowerPoint 7-2b. Save this file in the same folder used in step 1.
   d. Select **Open file after publishing**.
   e. Select **Minimum size (publishing online)**.
   f. Click the **Options** button to open the *Options* dialog box.
   g. For *Publish what,* select **Handouts** (9 slides per page) and check **Frame slides**.

7-99 *Encrypt Document* **dialog box**

h. Deselect **Document Properties** (Figure 7-100).
   i. Click **OK** to close the dialog box.
   j. Click **Publish**.
   k. The file opens in *Adobe Reader.* Review the handout page and then close the *Adobe Reader* window.

5. Prepare the presentation for sharing on the *SkyDrive* by removing the password and resaving a new file.
   a. Save the presentation as the [your initials] PowerPoint 7-2c.
   b. Click the **File** tab, click the **Protect Presentation** button, and select **Encrypt with Password**.
   c. Delete the current password and click **OK**.
   d. Save and close the *[your initials] PowerPoint 7-2c* presentation.

6. Open an Internet browser window and log in to your *SkyDrive* account (www.skydrive.com).

7. Create a new folder and upload files to your *SkyDrive.*
   a. Click **Files** on the left to display your *SkyDrive* folders and files.
   b. Click the **Create** button and select **Folder** from the drop-down list.
   c. Type Placer Hills Real Estate as the name for the new folder (Figure 7-101) and press **Enter**.

7-100 *Options* dialog box for saving a PDF file

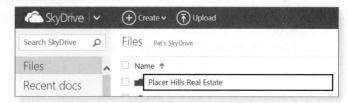

7-101 Name a new folder in *SkyDrive*

8. Upload files to your *SkyDrive* folder.
   a. Click the **Placer Hills Real Estate** folder (not the check box) to open it.
   b. Click the **Upload** button and select the *[your initials] PowerPoint 7-2b* and *[your initials] PowerPoint 7-2c* files from your solution files. Click **Open**. The two files are added to the *Placer Hills Real Estate* folder.
   c. Click **Details** view, if necessary, so your screen displays file names rather than thumbnail images.

9. Edit a file in PowerPoint Web App.
   a. Click the *[your initials] PowerPoint 7-2c* file to open it in PowerPoint Web App in read-only mode.
   b. Click the **Edit Presentation** button at the top and select **Edit in PowerPoint Web App** from the drop-down list. No password is required when opening the presentation in PowerPoint Web App.
   c. On slide 1, select the subtitle and change the font size to **36 pt**. Move the subtitle placeholder to the left as shown in Figure 7-102. Press **Ctrl+D** to duplicate.
   d. Edit the second text box to add the company name, Placer Hills Real Estate. Change the font size to **20 pt**, resize the text box, and position it in the lower right corner.

7-102 Subtitle text duplicated with resizing and font size changes

e. Select slide 7, click the **New Slide** button, and select the *Title and Content* layout. Click **Add Slide**.
f. On slide 8, type the title For Assistance, Call. Change the font color to **white**.
g. Select the bulleted text placeholder and type:

    Emma Cavelli, Listing Agent
    Placer Hills Real Estate
    7100 Madrone Road
    Roseville, CA 95722
    916-450-3300

h. Select the bulleted text placeholder and click the **Bullets and Numbering** button to remove the bullets.

i. Resize the bulleted text placeholder on the left side to make this box smaller and indent the text. While you resize, the text appears condensed but it restores to its correct size when you release the sizing handle.
j. Move both placeholders down and position them as shown in Figure 7-103.
k. View the presentation in *Slide Show* view.

7-103 New slide added

10. Share the presentation with your instructor.
    a. Click **Share** at the top to open the *Share* window (Figure 7-104).
    b. Select **Send email** on the left.
    c. Type your instructor's email address in the *To* area.
    d. Type a brief message in the body area.
    e. Select the **Recipients can edit** check box.
    f. Click **Share** to send the sharing email to your instructor.
    g. Click **Close** to close the *Share* window.
    h. Click the **SkyDrive** link at the top to return to your *SkyDrive* folders. The file is automatically saved and closed.

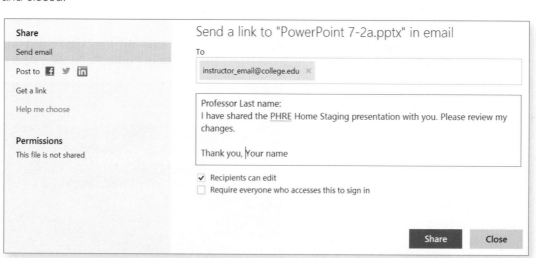

7-104 Share a presentation

11. Click your name in the upper right and select **Sign Out**.

Guided Project 7-3

For this project, you check a presentation for accessibility, add *Alt Text* and adjust reading order, mark as final, save a slide as a picture, create *SkyDrive* folders, upload files, create a *SkyDrive* group, invite a member, and change group options.
[Student Learning Outcomes 7.1, 7.2, 7.3, 7.5, 7.6]

Note to Students and Instructor:
  Students: *For this project, you share a* SkyDrive *file with your instructor and invite your instructor to a* SkyDrive *group.*
  Instructor: *To complete this project, your students need your Microsoft email address.*

Files Needed: ***HealthyLifestyle-07.pptx*** and ***ExerciseProgram-07.jpg***
Completed Project File Names: ***[your initials] PowerPoint 7-3a.pptx*** and
[your initials] PowerPoint 7-3b.png

Skills Covered in This Project

- Check a presentation for accessibility.
- Add *Alt Text* to a presentation and adjust reading order.
- Mark a presentation as final.
- Save a slide as a picture.
- Save a file to your *SkyDrive* folder.
- Log in to *SkyDrive*.
- Create a *SkyDrive* group and invite a member.
- Change *SkyDrive* group options.
- Upload a file to a *SkyDrive* group.

1. Open the presentation ***HealthyLifestyle-07***.
2. Create a *SkyDrive* folder on your computer and save the file.
   a. Click the **File** tab, click **Save As**, and select your ***SkyDrive***.
   b. Click the **Browse** button.
   c. Click the **New Folder** button and type CMP Education. Open this folder.
   d. Change the file name to [your initials] PowerPoint 7-3a.
   e. Click **Save**.
3. Check presentation accessibility and add *Alt Text*.
   a. Click the **File** tab, click the **Check for Issues** button, and select **Check Accessibility**.
   b. In the *Accessibility Checker* pane, select **Content Placeholder 2 (Slide 2)** under *Missing Alt Text*. The *SmartArt* graphic is selected on the slide.
   c. Right-click the *SmartArt* graphic and choose **Format Object**.
   d. Click the **Size & Properties** button and click **Alt Text** (Figure 7-105).

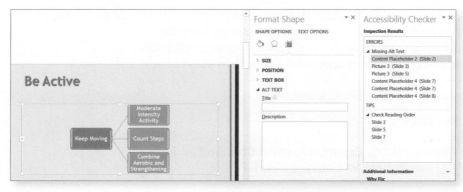

7-105 Add *Alt Text* to describe a *SmartArt* graphic

e. Type the title and the description text for each item listed under *Missing Alt Text* in the *Accessibility Checker* pane as shown in the following table. The items are removed from the list as the *Alt Text* is entered.

Item	Title Text	Description Text
Content Placeholder 2 (Slide 2)	Keep Moving diagram	The diagram emphasizes keep moving with moderate intensity activity, count steps, and combine aerobic and strengthening.
Picture 3 (Slide 3)	Gardening	A mother and daughter planting flowers.
Picture 3 (Slide 5)	Walking	A family walking.
Content Placeholder 4 (Slide 7)	Calorie table	Calories required for weight loss for males at different ages.
Content Placeholder 4 (Slide 7)	Calorie table	Calories required for weight loss for females at different ages.
Content Placeholder 4 (Slide 8)	Exercise	The table shows benefits of exercise.

f. Close the *Format Shape* pane.

4. Adjust the reading order for three items listed in the *Accessibility Checker* pane.
   a. Select **Slide 3** under *Check Reading Order.*
   b. Click the **Home** tab, click the **Arrange** button [*Drawing* group], and choose **Selection Pane**.
   c. Click the *Bring Forward* or *Send Backward* arrow so the content on the three slides is in the order shown in the following table. (A screen reader reads from the bottom up.)

Slide 3	Slide 5	Slide 7
Content Placeholder 2	Content Placeholder 2	Content Placeholder 4
Picture 3	Picture 3	Explosion 1 6
Title 1	Title 1	Content Placeholder 4
		Explosion 1 7
		TextBox 3
		Title 1

   d. Close the *Accessibility Checker* and the *Selection* panes.
   e. Save the presentation.

5. Mark the presentation as final.
   a. Click the **File** tab, click the **Protect Presentation** button, and select **Mark as Final**.
   b. A dialog box opens with the marked as final message. Click **OK**.
   c. Another dialog box opens with the final version message. Click **OK**.
      (Note: This dialog box will not open if the *Don't Show this message again* option was checked earlier.)
   d. The presentation is automatically saved.

6. Save a slide as a picture.
   a. Select slide 7.
   b. Click the **File** tab, choose **Export**, and select **Change File Type**.
   c. Select *PNG Portable Network Graphics* (Figure 7-106).

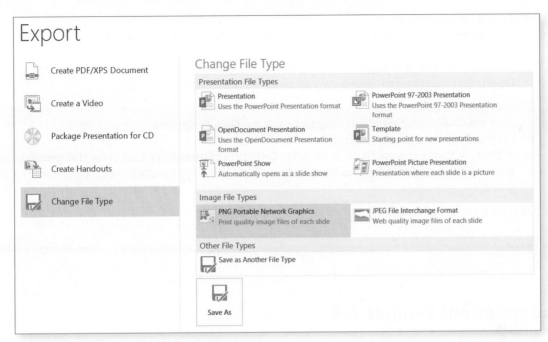

7-106 Export with the PNG file format

   d. Click the **Save As** button to open the *Save As* dialog box.
   e. Click the **CMP Education** folder to open it. Type the file name [your initials] PowerPoint 7-3b.
   f. Click **Save**. On the dialog box that opens, click **Just This One**.
   g. Close the presentation.

7. Open an Internet browser and log in to your *SkyDrive* account (www.skydrive.com).
   a. Click **Files** on the left to display the contents of your *SkyDrive* folder.
   b. The new folder you created in step 2 is displayed (other folders may be listed as well).

8. Create a *SkyDrive* group.
   a. Click **Groups** on the left to open the *Groups* page (Figure 7-107).
   b. Type CMP Seminars in the *Group name* text box.
   c. Type your last name, first initial, and -CMPseminars in the email area (for example, *GravesP-CMPseminars*) (see Figure 7-107).
   d. Click **Create group** to create your group.

9. Invite a member to your group.
   a. In the *SkyDrive* groups area on the left, select *CMP Seminars*.
   b. Click the **Group actions** button at the top and select **Invite people**. An *Invite* window opens.
   c. Type your instructor's email address and click **Invite**.

Groups

Groups make it easy to communicate and share stuff you keep on club. Share files, photos, and calendar with the people in your gro email - with Groups it's easy to stay connected.

Group name

> CMP Seminars

Group email

> GravesP-CMPseminars   @groups.live.com

Create group

7-107 Create a group in SkyDrive

10. Upload files to your group.
    a. Click **Files** on the left and confirm that the *CMP Seminars* group is selected.
    b. Click the **Upload** button.
    c. Select the ***HealthyLifestyle-07*** and ***ExerciseProgram-07*** files from your student files and click **Open**. You may need to refresh your browser window to display the files.

11. Change group options.
    a. With the *CMP Seminars* group selected, click the **Group options** button at the top.
    b. On the *Options* page, select **Email**.
    c. In the *Link to group website* area, click the **Only group members can view the group using this link** radio button. Click the **Save** button. The *Options* page closes and you return to your group.

12. Click your name in the upper right corner and select **Sign out**.

Independent Project 7-4

For this project, you inspect a presentation and check for compatibility. You save a presentation in an earlier PowerPoint format and as a video. You create a *SkyDrive* folder, upload files, and add comments using PowerPoint Web App.
[Student Learning Outcomes 7.1, 7.3, 7.5, 7.7]

Note to Students and Instructor:
Students: *For this project, you share a* SkyDrive *file with your instructor and invite your instructor to a* SkyDrive *group.*
Instructor: *To complete this project, your students need your Microsoft email address.*

File Needed: ***RacingARCC-07.pptx***
Completed Project File Names: ***[your initials] PowerPoint 7-4a.pptx***, ***[your initials]***
PowerPoint 7-4b.ppt, and ***[your initials] PowerPoint 7-4c.mp4***

Skills Covered in This Project

- Inspect a presentation.
- Check presentation compatibility.
- Export a presentation to an earlier version of PowerPoint.
- Create a presentation video.

- Log in to *SkyDrive*.
- Create a *SkyDrive* folder.
- Upload a file to your *SkyDrive* folder.
- Add a comment to a slide in PowerPoint WebApp.

1. Open the presentation ***RacingARCC-07*** and save it as ***[your initials] PowerPoint 7-4a***.

2. Inspect the presentation.
   a. Click the **File** tab, choose **Check for Issues**, and select **Inspect Document**.
   b. Deselect the **Document Properties and Personal Information** check box.
   c. Click **Inspect**.

d. In the *Document Inspector* dialog box (Figure 7-108), click **Remove All** in the *Custom XML Data* area.

e. Click **Close** to close the dialog box.

f. Save the presentation.

3. Check compatibility of the presentation with 97-2003 software.

   a. Click the **File** tab, choose **Check for Issues**, and select **Check Compatibility**.

   b. Note the summary on the *Microsoft PowerPoint Compatibility Checker* dialog box (Figure 7-109).

   c. Click **OK** to close the dialog box.

4. Export the presentation in a PowerPoint 97-2003 file format.

   a. Click the **File** tab, choose **Export**, and select **Change File Type**.

   b. Select **PowerPoint 97-2003 Presentation** (Figure 7-110) and click **Save As**.

   c. Change the file name to [your initials] PowerPoint 7-4b.

   d. The *Compatibility Checker* dialog box opens again. Click **Continue**.

   e. The file name appears in the title bar with *[Compatibility Mode]* following the name.

   f. View this self-running presentation in *Slide Show* view to confirm that slide transitions and animation work well in the earlier software version.

   g. Close the presentation.

5. Create a presentation video.

   a. Open the *[your initials] PowerPoint 7-4a* presentation.

7-108 *Document Inspector* with inspection results displayed

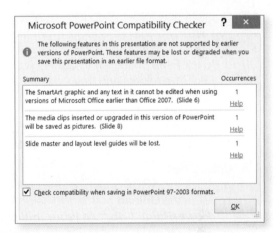

7-109 *Compatibility Checker* dialog box

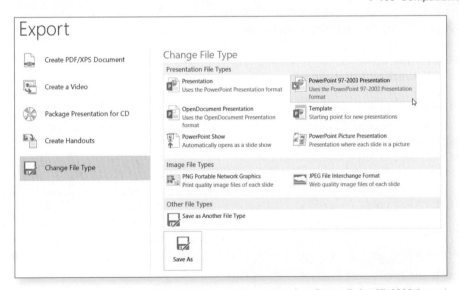

7-110 **Export a presentation in a PowerPoint 97-2003 format**

b. Click the **File** tab, choose **Export**, and select **Create a Video**.

c. On the first box, click the **list arrow** and choose the **Internet and DVD** quality options (Figure 7-111).

d. On the second box, choose **Don't Use Recorded Timings and Narrations**.

e. For *Seconds to spend on each slide,* type 3:00 seconds.

f. Click **Create Video** to open the *Save As* dialog box.

g. Change the file name that appears to [your initials] PowerPoint 7-4c.

h. For *Save as type,* select **MPEG-4 Video**.

i. Click **Save**.

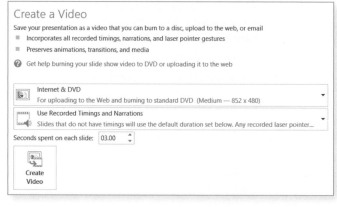

7-111 Options for exporting a video

6. Open an Internet browser window and log in to your *SkyDrive* account (www.skydrive.com).

7. Create a new folder. (Skip this step if you already created this folder in another project.)

a. Click **Files** on the left to display your *SkyDrive* folders and files.

b. Click the **Create** button and select **Folder** from the drop-down list.

c. Type ARCC as the name for the new folder (Figure 7-112) and press **Enter**.

7-112 Name a new folder in SkyDrive

8. Upload files.

a. Click the **ARCC** folder (not the check box) to open it.

b. Click the **Upload** button and select the *[your initials] PowerPoint 7-4a, [your initials] PowerPoint 7-4b*, and *[your initials] PowerPoint 7-4c* files from your solution files. Click **Open**. The three files are added to the *ARCC* folder.

9. Add comments to a presentation in PowerPoint Web App.

a. Click the *[your initials] PowerPoint 7-4a* file to open it in *read-only* mode in PowerPoint Web App.

b. Click the **Edit Presentation** button at the top and select **Edit in PowerPoint Web App** from the drop-down list.

c. On slide 2, click the **Show Comments** button [*View* tab, *Show* group] to open the *Comments* pane.

d. Click **New** and type Do you know of other events we should include? in the box after your name (Figure 7-113).

e. Close the *Comments* pane.

7-113 Add a comment

10. View the presentation in *Slide Show* view.

11. Click the **SkyDrive** link at the top to return to your *SkyDrive* folders. The file is automatically saved.

12. Click your name in the upper right and select **Sign Out**.

Independent Project 7-5

For this project, you upload a file to a *SkyDrive* folder, rename a file, create a *SkyDrive* group and invite a member, and edit a presentation and add comments using PowerPoint Web App.
[Student Learning Outcomes 7.5, 7.6, 7.7]

Note to Students and Instructor:
   Students*: For this project, you share a SkyDrive* file with your instructor.
   Instructor*: To complete this project, your students need your Microsoft email address.*

File Needed: ***Stress-07.pptx***
Completed Project File Names: ***[your initials] PowerPoint 7-5.pptx***

Skills Covered in This Project

- Log in to *SkyDrive*.
- Create a *SkyDrive* group and invite a member.
- Upload a file to a *SkyDrive* group.
- Rename a file.

- Edit a presentation in PowerPoint Web App.
- Add a comment to a slide in PowerPoint Web App.

---

1. Open an Internet browser and log in to your *SkyDrive* account (www.skydrive.com).
   a. Click **Files** on the left to display the contents of your *SkyDrive* folder.
   b. Skip steps 2 and 3 if you have already created a *CMP Seminars* group.

2. Create a *SkyDrive* group.
   a. Click **Groups** on the left to open the *Groups* page.
   b. Type CMP Seminars in the *Group name* text box.
   c. Type your last name, first initial, and -CMPseminars in the email area (for example, *GravesP-CMPseminars*) (Figure 7-114).
   d. Click **Create group** to create your group.

7-114 Create a group in *SkyDrive*

3. Invite a member to your group.
   a. Confirm that the *CMP Seminars* group is selected in the *Groups* area on the left.
   b. Click the **Group actions** button at the top and select **Invite people**. An *Invite* window opens.
   c. Type your instructor's email address and click **Invite**.

4. Upload a file to your group.
   a. Click **Files** on the left and select the *CMP Seminars* group.
   b. Click the **Upload** button.
   c. Select the ***Stress-07*** files from your student files and click **Open**. You may need to refresh your browser window to display the files.
   d. In the file list, check the file ***Stress-07***.

e. Click the **Manage** button and select **Rename** (Figure 7-115).

f. Name the file [your initials] PowerPoint 7-5.

5. Open the file in PowerPoint Web App.

   a. Click the *[your initials] PowerPoint 7-5* file to open it in read-only mode in PowerPoint Web App.

   b. Click the **Edit Presentation** button at the top and select **Edit in PowerPoint Web App** from the drop-down list.

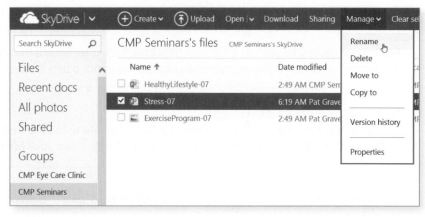

7-115 Rename a file

6. Insert *SmartArt,* apply styles, and adjust object positions.

   a. On slide 2, delete the title placeholder.

   b. In the content placeholder, click the **SmartArt** button. Shapes automatically appear.

   c. In the *SmartArt* gallery, click the **More** button [*SmartArt Tools Design* tab, *Layouts* group] and select the **Diverging Arrows** layout (Figure 7-116).

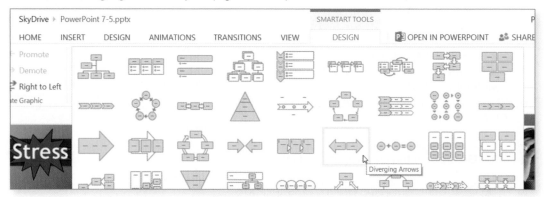

7-116 *SmartArt* layouts in *SkyDrive*

   d. Select the left shape and bullets automatically appear. Type Eustress and Distress after the bullets (Figure 7-117). Click the slide background and the text appears on the two arrow shapes.

   e. Select the *SmartArt*. Click the **More** button [*SmartArt Tools Design* tab, *Layouts* group] and select the **Intense Effect**.

   f. Select the picture of a woman. Click the **Bring Forward** button [*Picture Tools Format* tab, *Arrange* group]. Move the picture to fit between the two arrows (Figure 7-118).

7. Add titles on two slides.

   a. On slide 4, select the title placeholder and type The "Always On" World We Live In.

   b. On slide 6, select the title placeholder and type My Prescription?

7-117 Adding *SmartArt* text

7-118 Picture moved over *SmartArt*

8. Apply a transition.
   a. Click the **Transitions** tab and select the **Fade** transition.
   b. Click **Effect Options** and select **Smoothly**.
   c. Click **Apply to All**.

9. Add comments.
   a. On slide 5, click the **Comment** button [*Insert* tab, *Comments* group] to open the *Comments* pane.
   b. In the comment box, type Should we include other items? We could change this to a two-column layout if necessary. (Figure 7-119).
   c. Close the *Comments* pane.

7-119 Add a comment

10. View the presentation in *Slide Show* view.

11. Send an email message to your instructor.
   a. Click **Share** at the top to open the *Share* window.
   b. Select **Send email** on the left.
   c. Type your instructor's email address in the *To* area.
   d. Type a brief message in the body area.
   e. Check the **Recipients can edit** check box.
   f. Click **Share** to send the sharing email to your instructor.
   g. Click **Close** to close the *Share* window.

12. Click the **SkyDrive** link at the top to return to your *SkyDrive* folders. The file is automatically saved.

13. Click your name in the upper right corner and select **Sign Out**.

Independent Project 7-6

For this project, you check a presentation for accessibility, add *Alt Text* and adjust reading order, save a slide as a picture, and create a PDF file. You create a *SkyDrive* folder and upload files.
[Student Learning Outcomes 7.1, 7.3, 7.5]

Note to Students and Instructor:
   Students: *For this project, you share a SkyDrive file with your instructor.*
   Instructor: *To complete this project, your students need your Microsoft email address.*

File Needed: ***Up-SellServices-07.pptx***
Completed Project File Names: ***[your initials] PowerPoint 7-6a.pptx**, **[your initials] PowerPoint 7-6b.jpg**, and **[your initials] PowerPoint 7-6c.pdf***

Skills Covered in This Project

- Check a presentation for accessibility.
- Add *Alt Text* to a presentation and adjust reading order.
- Save a slide as a picture.
- Create a PDF document from a presentation.
- Log in to *SkyDrive*.
- Create a *SkyDrive* folder.
- Upload a file to your *SkyDrive* folder.

1. Open the presentation **Up-SellServices-07** and save it as *[your initials] PowerPoint 7-6a*.

2. Check accessibility and add *Alt Text*.
   a. Click the **File** tab, click **Check for Issues**, and select **Check Accessibility**.
   b. In the *Accessibility Checker* pane, errors are listed first. Select **Content Placeholder 3 (Slide 2)** under *Missing Alt Text*. The picture is selected on the slide.
   c. Right-click the picture and choose **Format Picture**.
   d. Click the **Size & Properties** button and click **Alt Text** (Figure 7-120).

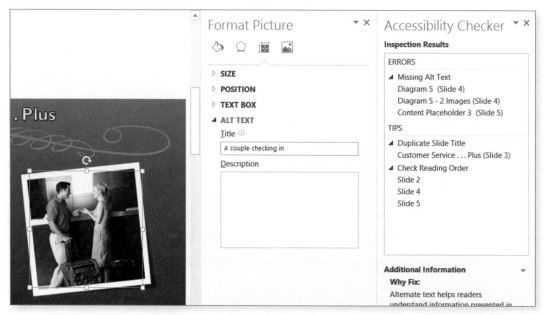

7-120 Add *Alt Text* to identify a picture

   e. Type the title and the description text as shown in the following table for items listed as errors in the *Accessibility Checker* pane. For the two images on slide 4, select them both before adding the *Alt Text*.

Item	Title Text	Description Text
Content Placeholder 3 (Slide 2)	A couple checking in	None
Diagram 5 (Slide 4)	How to build relationships	This diagram shows that guest satisfaction leads to repeat bookings.
Diagram 5 – 2 Images (Slide 4)	Vacations	Picture of vacationing family.
Content Placeholder 3 (Slide 5)	Front desk manager	Candace Parker

   f. Close the *Format Picture* pane.

3. In the *Accessibility Checker* pane, the first item under *Tips* indicates a duplicate title. In this case, the same title is used on slides 2 and 3. In this case, that use is acceptable.

4. In the *Accessibility Checker* pane, adjust the reading order for one of the three items.
   a. Select **Slide 2** under *Check Reading Order.*
   b. Open the **Selection Pane** and change the order: *Content Placeholder 2, Content Placeholder 3, and Title 1.*
   c. Close the *Accessibility Checker* and the *Selection* panes.
   d. Save the presentation.

5. Save a slide as a picture.
   a. Select **slide 1**.
   b. Click the **File** tab, choose **Export**, and select **Change File Type**.
   c. Select *JPEG File Interchange Format.*
   d. Click the **Save As** button to open the *Save As* dialog box.
   e. Change the file name to [your initials] PowerPoint 7-6b.
   f. Click **Save**. On the dialog box that opens, click **Just This One**.

6. Create a PDF file.
   a. Click the **File** tab, choose **Export**, and select **Create PDF/XPS Document**.
   b. Click **Create PDF/XPS**.
   c. Change the file name to [your initials] PowerPoint 7-6c.
   d. Deselect **Open file after publishing** and select **Minimum size (publishing online)**.
   e. Click the **Options** button to open the *Options* dialog box.
   f. For *Publish what,* select **Slides** and check **Frame slides**. Deselect **Document Properties** (Figure 7-121).
   g. Click **OK** to close the dialog box.
   h. Click **Publish**.

7-121 *Options* dialog box for saving a PDF file

7. Save and close the *[your initials] PowerPoint 7-6a* presentation.

8. Open an Internet browser window and log in to your *SkyDrive* account (www.skydrive.com).

9. Create a new folder and upload files to *SkyDrive.*
   a. Click **Files**.
   b. Click **Create** and select **Folder**.
   c. Name the folder Paradise Lakes Resort.

10. Upload files.
    a. Open the *Paradise Lakes Resort* folder.
    b. Click the **Upload** button and select the *[your initials] PowerPoint 7-6a*, *[your initials] PowerPoint 7-6b*, and *[your initials] PowerPoint 7-6c* files from your solution files. Click **Open**. The three files are added to the *Paradise Lakes Resort* folder.

11. Create a *SkyDrive* group.
    a. Click **Groups** on the left to open the *Groups* page.
    b. Type Paradise Lakes Resort in the *Group name* text box.
    c. Type your last name, first initial, and -PLR in the email area (for example, *GravesP-PLR*).
    d. Click **Create group** to *create your group*.

12. Send a group message.
    a. Select the **Paradise Lakes Resort** folder on the left.
    b. Click **Group actions** at the top and select **Send an email message**.
    c. The group email address automatically appears after *To.*
    d. Click **Add a Subject** and type [your initials] PowerPoint 7-6 files.
    e. Type a brief message in the body area.
    f. Click **Send**.

13. Click your name in the upper right and select **Sign Out**.

Improve It Project 7-7

For this project, you create a *SkyDrive* group and invite a member, upload a file, rename a file, and edit a presentation and add a comment using PowerPoint Web App.
[Student Learning Outcomes 7.5, 7.6, 7.7]

Note to Students and Instructor:
    Students*: For this project, you share a* SkyDrive *file with your instructor.*
    Instructor*: To complete this project, your students need your Microsoft email address.*

File Needed: ***CardiacCare-07.pptx***
Completed Project File Name: ***[your initials] PowerPoint 7-7.pptx***

Skills Covered in This Project

- Log in to *SkyDrive*.
- Create a *SkyDrive* group.
- Upload a file to a *SkyDrive* group.
- Rename a *SkyDrive* file.
- Edit a presentation in PowerPoint Web App.
- Add a comment to a slide in PowerPoint Web App.

---

1. Open an Internet browser and log in to your *SkyDrive* account (www.skydrive.com).
   a. Click **Files** to display the contents of your *SkyDrive* folder.
   b. Skip steps 2 and 3 if you have already created a *CMP Seminars* group.

2. Create a *SkyDrive* group.
   a. Click **Groups** to open the *Groups* page.
   b. Type CMP Seminars in the *Group name* text box.
   c. Type your last name, first initial, and -CMPseminars in the email area (for example, *GravesP-CMPseminars*) (Figure 7-122).
   d. Click **Create group** to create your group.

Groups
Groups make it easy to communicate and share stuff you keep on~~ ~~ club. Share files, photos, and calendar with the people in your gro~~ ~~ email - with Groups it's easy to stay connected.
Group name
CMP Seminars
Group email
GravesP-CMPseminars   @groups.live.com
Create group

7-122 Create a group in *SkyDrive*

3. Invite a member to your group.
   a. Confirm that the *CMP Seminars* group is selected in the *Groups* area on the left.
   b. Click the **Group actions** button at the top and select **Invite people**. An *Invite* window opens.
   c. Type your instructor's email address and click **Invite**.

4. Upload a file to your group.
   a. Click **Files** on the left and select *CMP Seminars*.
   b. Click the **Upload** button and select ***CardiacCare-07*** from your student files. Click **Open**.

    c. In the file list, check **CardiacCare-07**.

    d. Click the **Manage** button and select **Rename**. Name the file [your initials] PowerPoint 7-7.

5. Open a file in PowerPoint Web App.

    a. Click the *[your initials] PowerPoint 7-7* file to open it in PowerPoint Web App in read-only mode.

    b. Click the **Edit Presentation** button and select **Edit in PowerPoint Web App**.

6. Add text in the placeholders on three slides.

    Slide 2 Don't Let This Happen to You!

    Slide 4 Chest discomfort

           Discomfort in other areas of the upper body

           Shortness of breath

           Nausea or light-headedness

    Slide 5 85% of muscle damage takes place within the first hour

7. Apply the **Push** transition with **From Right** effect options to all slides (Figure 7-123).

8. Insert a comment on slide 6. In the comment box, type When this slide is displayed, we need to announce dates for our seminars on these topics.

9. View the presentation in *Slide Show* view (Figure 7-124).

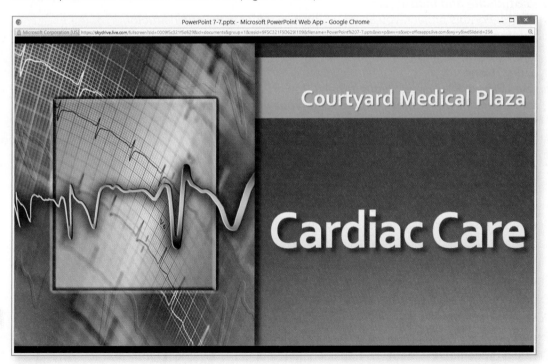

7-123 Apply a transition

7-124 *Slide Show* view in *Google Chrome*

10. Send an email message to your instructor.
    a. Click **Share** at the top to open the *Share* window.
    b. Select **Send email** on the left.
    c. Type your instructor's email address in the *To* area.
    d. Type a brief message in the body area.
    e. Check the **Recipients can edit** check box.
    f. Click **Share** to send the sharing email to your instructor.
    g. Click **Close** to close the *Share* window.

11. Click the **SkyDrive** link at the top to return to your *SkyDrive* folders. The file is automatically saved.

12. Click your name in the upper right and select **Sign Out**.

Challenge Project 7-8

Prepare a presentation for sharing by inspecting the document and checking accessibility. Export the presentation in several different formats. Create a *SkyDrive* folder, upload your files, and share them with your instructor.
[Student Learning Outcomes 7.1, 7.2, 7.3, 7.5]

Note to Students and Instructor:
Students: For this project, you share a SkyDrive folder with your instructor.
Instructor: To complete this project, your students need your Microsoft email address.

File Needed: None
Completed Project File Names: *[your initials] PowerPoint 7-8a.pptx, [your initials] PowerPoint 7-8b. jpg, [your initials] PowerPoint 7-8c.pdf, and [your initials] PowerPoint 7-8d.mp4*

Create a *SkyDrive* folder to store the files you create for this project. Modify your presentation according to the following guidelines:

- Select a presentation of your choice that you completed from a previous chapter.
- Inspect the presentation and remove personal or unneeded information.
- Check the presentation for accessibility and add *Alt Text* as needed. Adjust reading order if necessary.
- Mark the presentation as final.
- Save the presentation as *[your initials] PowerPoint 7-8a*.
- Export one slide from the presentation as a *.jpg* file and name it *[your initials] PowerPoint 7-8b*.
- Export all slides in the presentation as a PDF file and name it *[your initials] PowerPoint 7-8c*.
- Create a presentation video with transitions and animation. Name it *[your initials] PowerPoint 7-8d*.
- Create a *SkyDrive* folder and upload all files for this project. Share the files with your instructor.

Challenge Project 7-9

SkyDrive is an excellent place to store and organize your work. You can create a *SkyDrive* folder and subfolder to store files from all of your classes and share files or folders with your instructors. Remember, it is recommended that you do not store files with sensitive information in online locations. [Student Learning Outcomes 7.5, 7.6]

Note to Students and Instructor:
  Students: *For this project, you share a* SkyDrive *folder with your instructor.*
  Instructor: *To complete this project, your students need your Microsoft email address.*

File Needed: None
Completed Project File Name: New *SkyDrive* folder, subfolder, and files

Create a *SkyDrive* folder to store files for your classes. Modify your *SkyDrive* folder according to the following guidelines:

- Create a *SkyDrive* folder and name it after your school.
- Create subfolders for each of your classes and any other folders needed (e.g., "Financial Aid," "Clubs," "Internships," etc.).
- Upload files to each of the folders.
- Share the folder for this class with your instructor.

Challenge Project 7-10

SkyDrive and *SkyDrive* groups are wonderful tools to store, share, and edit documents when you are collaborating with others. For this project, you create a *SkyDrive* group for a club, organization, work team, or student group and invite members. [Student Learning Outcomes 7.5, 7.6, 7.7]

Note to Students and Instructor:
  Students: *For this project, you invite your instructor to become a member of a* SkyDrive *group.*
  Instructor: *To complete this project, your students need your Microsoft email address.*

File Needed: None
Completed Project File Name: New *SkyDrive* group, folders, and files

Create a new *SkyDrive* group for a club, organization, work team, or student group. Modify your *SkyDrive* group according to the following guidelines:

- Create a new *SkyDrive* group and invite members (be sure to include your instructor).
- Upload files for the group.
- Create folders in the group.
- Move or copy files as needed.
- Customize group options.
- Customize member roles in the group.
- Send a group email to members.

appendices

Common Office 2013 Keyboard Shortcuts

Action	Keyboard Shortcut
Save	Ctrl+S
Copy	Ctrl+C
Cut	Ctrl+X
Paste	Ctrl+V
Select all	Ctrl+A
Bold	Ctrl+B
Italic	Ctrl+I
Underline	Ctrl+U
Close *Start* page or *Backstage* view	Esc
Open *Help* dialog box	F1
Switch windows	Alt+Tab

PowerPoint 2013 Keyboard Shortcuts

Action	Keyboard Shortcut
File Management	
Open a new blank presentation	Ctrl+N
Open an existing presentation from the *Backstage* view	Ctrl+O
Open an existing presentation from the *Open* dialog box	Ctrl+F12
Open *Save As* dialog box	F12
Save	Ctrl+S
Editing	
Cut	Ctrl+X
Copy	Ctrl+C
Paste	Ctrl+V
Duplicate slides	Ctrl+D
Undo	Ctrl+Z
Redo	Ctrl+Y
Soft return, causes text to word-wrap to the next line	Shift+Enter
Select adjacent objects	Shift+click
Select nonadjacent objects	Ctrl+click
Keep height and width proportions when resizing	Shift+drag
Resize from the center of a shape and keep height and width proportions	Ctrl+Shift+drag

Action	Keyboard Shortcut
Place a copy of the computer screen on the *Clipboard*	Print Screen
Place a copy of the current window on the *Clipboard*	Alt+Print Screen
Slide Movement in Normal View	
Move to first slide	Home
Move to last slide	End
Move to next slide	Page Down or down arrow
Move to previous slide	Page Up or up arrow
Move from the slide title to the body placeholder	Ctrl+Enter
Slide Movement in Slide Show View	
Start a presentation slide show from the beginning	F5
Open *Presenter View* and start a slide show	Alt+F5
Advance to the next slide or start the next animation	N, spacebar, right arrow, down arrow, Enter, or Page Down
Go to the previous slide or start the previous animation	P, Backspace, left arrow, up arrow, or Page Up
Go to a particular slide	Slide number, Enter
Go to a particular slide by opening *All Slides* dialog box and selecting a slide title	Ctrl+S
Go to a hidden slide	H or slide number, Enter
Blanks the screen to black	B or period
Blanks the screen to white	W or comma
Stop or restart an automatic show	S or plus sign
Opens the *Insert Hyperlink* dialog box	Ctrl+K
Ink Markup in Slide Show View	
Change pointer to pen	Ctrl+P
Change pointer to arrow	Ctrl+A
Change pointer to eraser	Ctrl+E
Show or hide ink markup	Ctrl+M
Erase markings on the screen	E
Video Shortcuts in Slide Show View	
Stop playback	Alt+Q
Play or pause	Alt+P
Go to the next bookmark	Alt+End
Go to the previous bookmark	Alt+Home
Seek forward	Alt+Shift+Page Down
Seek backward	Alt+Shift+Page Up
Increase sound volume	Alt+Up
Lower sound volume	Alt+Down
Mute sound	Alt+U

glossary

3D Rotation Style effect option that includes parallel, perspective, and oblique options to create an illusion of depth.

A

Action Buttons Shapes that automatically have an action such as *Previous*, *Next*, *Beginning*, or *Home*; you can customize options to control what happens during a slide show if the shape is clicked (called *Mouse Click*) or if you point to the shape (called *Mouse Over*).

adjustment handle Yellow square on an object used to change shape dimensions.

Align Feature used to arrange objects evenly on the slide or in relationship to each other; horizontal alignment includes left, center, and right, and vertical alignment includes top, middle, and bottom.

Alt Text Text labels that identify a picture or graphic object; used with screen readers to accommodate individuals with visual impairments.

animation Movement of objects on a slide.

Animation Painter Tool that copies animation settings and applies them to another object in the same way the *Format Painter* copies format settings.

Animation Pane Pane that displays animation settings for multiple objects and multiple effects.

animation tag Small numbered box that appears on the slide next to an animated object when the *Animations* tab is active.

app Short for application; software program or Windows 8 application or accessory.

Area chart Chart type that shows data changes over time; emphasizes the total value of a trend.

Arrange All View option that displays tiled windows so you can see all open presentations at the same time.

Arrow Line style that provide arrowheads or other shapes for both ends of a line.

Arrow settings Line option that controls the size of the shape at both ends of an arrow.

Artistic Effects Picture effect that transforms a picture using various creative effects that resemble painting techniques such as *Pencil Sketch, Line Drawing, Watercolor Sponge, Glass, Plastic Wrap*, and many others.

audio A digital file inserted in a presentation that plays music or audio recordings such as sounds or a voice recording.

AutoCorrect Feature that recognizes and corrects commonly misspelled words and makes capitalization corrections.

AutoFormat Feature that replaces various punctuation marks as you type.

B

Background Removal Feature used to remove picture areas without affecting the original picture; the area removed appears transparent.

Banded Columns Table Styles option featuring columns that have alternating colors.

Banded Rows Table Styles option featuring rows that have alternating colors.

BAR chart Chart type that is similar to a column chart with bars shown horizontally.

Bevel Style effect option that applies light and dark areas to create a dimensional appearance so objects and text look raised or inset.

Bookmark Feature that designates a specific location in an audio or video file; a bookmark can start an animation effect.

border Line around text, paragraph, page, cell, table, or graphic object.

Brightness Picture correction option that darkens or lightens a picture by adding white or black.

Bring Forward Feature that adjusts the order of stacked objects by moving an object up one layer at a time.

Bring to Front Feature that adjusts the order of stacked objects by moving an object in front of all other objects.

build Animation technique that makes items gradually appear on a slide to focus attention; also called *progressive disclosure*.

C

Cap type Line option that controls the look of the ends of lines; usually applied to single lines or arrows.

Cascade View option that displays each presentation in a separate, layered window with its own *Ribbon*.

category Group of data values from each row in a spreadsheet.

cell Intersection of a column and a row.

Change Case Button used to change text case; such as from uppercase to lowercase.

Change Colors Gallery that lists different color combinations for *SmartArt* layouts based on theme colors.

Change Picture Command that replaces one picture with another while retaining the same size and effects.

chart Object that displays numeric data in the form of a graph to compare data values or display data trends.

Chart Area One of several chart background elements; background area where the entire chart is displayed in a frame.

Chart Styles Gallery that lists preset effects for chart elements.

Check Accessibility Tool that identifies potential issues that users with disabilities may have with your presentation when using a screen reader or other adaptive resources.

check box Box that allows you to choose one or more from a group of options.

Check Compatibility Tool that examines a presentation for compatibility issues between the current version of PowerPoint and versions before 2007.

Color Saturation Color option that controls the intensity of a color; colors that are vibrant are highly saturated and colors that are muted have a low saturation level.

Color Tone Color option that controls temperature values to make a picture's colors more cool or warm.

column Vertical grouping of cells in a table or spreadsheet; vertical area of text in a document or slide.

Column chart Chart type that shows a comparison of values or data changes over time.

Combo chart Chart type that is a combination of two chart types such as a column chart with a line chart.

Comments Collaboration feature that allows users to add notes on presentation slides without altering the design of slides.

Compare Collaboration feature that allows users to merge an original presentation with a revised presentation to consider reviewer feedback.

Compound type Line option that provides outlines with two or more lines that vary in thickness.

Compress Media Feature used to improve playback performance and to reduce presentation file size; different quality levels are available.

Compress Pictures Command that reduces presentation file size by reducing picture resolution.

connected services Third-party services users can add to Office application programs, such as Facebook, LinkedIn, and YouTube.

Connector Lines Tools that attach two or more shapes for custom diagrams; lines are available in different shapes.

constrain Keep lines straight, circles round, and rectangles square; press Shift or Ctrl when resizing.

context menu Menu of commands that appears when you right-click text or an object. Also called the shortcut menu.

context sensitive Describes menu options that change depending on what you have selected.

Contrast Picture correction option that adjusts the difference between the picture's lightest and darkest colors.

Convert Changes a *SmartArt* graphic to text or to shapes.

copy Duplicate text or other information.

Corrections Feature that improves picture appearance by adjusting *Sharpen*, *Soften*, *Contrast*, and *Brightness* options.

Crop Remove picture edges, change a picture to a shape from the *Shapes* gallery, or change to a specific aspect ratio size.

crosshair Large plus sign tool used to draw a shape.

Curve Line tool used to draw smooth curves; a line is formed each time you click and the line curves as you change direction.

Custom Path A type of *Motion Path* animation; you draw the path that an animated object follows.

Custom Slide Show Feature that creates a presentation within a presentation by creating a list of slides that can be arranged in any order.

cut Remove text or other information.

Cycle *SmartArt* graphic type used to illustrate a continuing sequence or concepts related to a central idea.

D

Dash type Line option that displays lines made with various combinations of dots and dashes.

Dashes Line styles that combine dots and dashes to make different patterns.

Data label Label that lists the value, category name, or series name of a component of a chart.

Data marker Symbol that represents a single point or value in a charted range of cell information; graphical representation of values shown as columns, bars, slices, or data points.

Data series Group of data values from each column in a spreadsheet.

Data table Chart element that shows the data that creates a chart in table format below a chart.

Delay Animation timing command used to make an animation begin at a specified time.

destination file File where an embedded or linked object is inserted.

destination program Office application where an embedded or linked object is inserted.

dialog box Window that opens and displays additional features.

Distribute Feature that creates even spacing between multiple slide objects.

Distribute Columns Table option that evenly distributes column width.

Distribute Rows Table option that evenly distributes row height.

document property Information about a file such as title, author name, subject, etc.

drop-down list List of options that displays when you click a button.

duplicate Create a copy of an object or a slide.

duration Length of time; dictates the speed of transitions and animations in a slide show.

E

edit mode Office Web Apps view where users can edit a file, add comments, and save a file.

Edit Points Editing feature used to change the curve of a line or shape; points are small black squares that control where lines curve or change direction.

Effect Option Command that controls the direction of slide transitions and animation movement.

embed Insert an object from another application; the source program is used from within PowerPoint for editing, but the object in PowerPoint can be changed independently and the source file is not affected.

embed code Instructions that enable linking to and displaying a video within PowerPoint; requires an Internet connection.

Emphasis Animation effect that calls attention to an object on the slide.

Encrypt with Password Tool that protects a presentation from being opened and edited; a password is required to open a presentation.

Entrance Animation effect that occurs when an object appears on the slide.

Exit Animation effect that occurs when an object leaves the slide.

explode Separate pie chart slices.

extract Create a regular folder from a zipped folder.

Eyedropper Tool used to match the exact color of an object.

F

Fade In Effect that causes an audio to gradually reach full volume or a video to gradually come into focus.

Fade Out Effect that causes an audio to gradually decrease volume or a video to gradually blur out.

File Explorer Window where you browse for, open, and manage files and folders (formerly called Windows Explorer).

file name extension A series of letters automatically added to a file name that identifies the type of file.

Find Feature that searches for specific text and/or formatting.

Flip Vertical/Flip Horizontal Drawing option used to make an object point in different directions or create a mirror image.

footer Displays content at the bottom of a document page or slide.

Format Painter Tool that duplicates formatting choices, such as font, font size, line spacing, indents, bullets, numbering, styles, etc., from one selection to another selection.

Freeform Line tool that is used to draw both straight and curved lines; when the end of the line you draw touches the beginning of the line, a shape is created with a solid fill color.

G

gallery Group of options on a tab.

Glow Style effect option that provides a colored area around an object that fades into the background color on the slide.

Gradient Option that blends two or more colors or light and dark variations of the current fill color in different directions.

grayscale Range of shades of black in a display or printout.

Gridlines Evenly spaced vertical and horizontal lines on a slide in *Normal* view that aid in object alignment; also the horizontal or vertical lines that appear in a chart area.

Group Command that connects multiple objects as one object. Also, area on a tab that contains related commands and options.

Guides One vertical and one horizontal line in the middle of the slide that you can move to check for consistent alignment; grids display in *Normal* view but not in *Slide Show* view.

H

Handout Printing option that displays several slides on each page in fixed positions based on the number of slides you select.

Handout Master Feature used to rearrange header and footer placeholders or to change fonts and add graphics for handouts.

header Displays content at the top of a document or object.

header row First row of a table.

Hide During Show Playback setting for audio or video that makes the playback icon invisible in *Reading* view or *Slide Show* view; used for automatic audio or video playback.

Hierarchy SmartArt graphic type used to illustrate a decision tree or top-to-bottom relationship such as an organization chart.

horizontal alignment Content positioning option that aligns material in relation to the left, center, right, or middle (justified) of the page or slide; can also refer to the position of objects in relation to each other.

Hyperlink Connection between two locations applied to text or objects; when you click a hyperlink, you move to a different slide, presentation, application, or web site.

I

ink annotations Markings that call attention to information you mark by writing or drawing on slides.

Inspect Document Tool that examines a presentation for hidden content, properties, or personal information that you may not want to share.

J

Join type Line option that controls the look of the connection point where two lines meet, such as the corner of a rectangle.

K

Keep Source Formatting Paste option that retains theme formatting from the source document in the material you are pasting.

Keep Text Only Paste option that inserts unformatted text.

keyboard shortcut Key or combination of keys that you press to apply a command.

kiosk presentation Self-running slide presentation that automatically loops.

L

launcher Button used to open a dialog box; shown on various groups.

Layout One of a series of predesigned slide templates that control the position of placeholder text.

Legend Descriptive text or key that describes a data series in a chart.

Line chart Chart type that shows data changes over time.

link Insert an object from another application that remains connected to the source document; the object opens in a separate window for editing in the source program and changes also appear in the PowerPoint object.

List *SmartArt* graphic type used to illustrate non-sequential or grouped information.

list indent The space between a bullet and the text that follows a bullet.

Lock Aspect Ratio Command used to maintain proportion when entering object height or width sizes.

Lock Drawing Mode Tool used to draw more than one of the same shape.

loop *Slide Show* effect that displays slides from beginning to end in a slide show and automatically repeats.

Loop until Stopped Playback setting for audio or video that repeats until you stop playback.

M

margin Blank space at the top, bottom, left, or right of a document; in a text box, the space between the outside of the box and the text within the box; in a table, the space between a cell border and the cell text.

Mark as Final Tool that makes a presentation a read-only file; protects a presentation from being accidentally altered.

Matrix *SmartArt* graphic type used to illustrate the relationship of four parts to the whole.

maximize Increase the size of the window of an open Office file so it fills the entire computer screen.

Merge Cells Command that combines two or more cells in a row or column.

Merge Shapes Command that combines two or more stacked shapes to create a single, new shape.

Microsoft account Free account that gives you access to an email account, *SkyDrive* online storage area, and Office Web Apps.

minimize Place an open Office file on the *Taskbar* so it is not displayed on the desktop.

monochromatic Color combinations containing only shades of one color.

Motion Path Type of animation that provides predefined paths for the direction of movement of an animated object.

multimedia Broad range of digital media that includes text, pictures, audio, and video combined with dynamic motion and interactivity; also called *rich media*.

N

New Window View option that opens a new window with a duplicate of the active presentation.

Normal view Default view option where you enter the content of slides and move between slides as you develop them.

Notes Page view View option that displays each slide on a page with space below the slide where you can type speaker notes.

O

Object linking and embedding (OLE) Technology developed by Microsoft for sharing objects between different Microsoft Office applications.

Office Web Apps Free online Microsoft Office software applications that allow users to create, save, and edit Office files; Office Web Apps are accessed from online *SkyDrive* accounts.

On Click Setting to begin animation or playback audio video files.

operating system Software that makes a computer function and controls the working environment.

Optimize Compatibility Feature used with media files to improve performance for a presentation that is displayed on different computers.

Outline view View option with an expanded pane to the left of the slide area that shows slide titles and bulleted text.

P

Package Presentation for CD Feature that saves a presentation and related files to a CD or a folder.

paste Place text or other objects that have been stored on the *Clipboard* in a new location.

Paste Options Options that control whether an object being inserted uses destination or source formatting; other options are available depending on the object.

Paste Special Feature used to insert objects as either embedded or linked objects.

Pattern Background color Color used with a foreground color to create a pattern.

Pattern Fill Option that applies a mixture of two colors to shapes in various dotted or crosshatch designs.

Pattern Foreground color Color used with a background color to create a pattern.

PDF (portable document format) File format used to convert a file into a static image.

Pen Tool used to write or draw on a slide during a slide show.

Photo Album Feature that creates a presentation from a group of pictures with one, two, or four pictures on a slide.

Picture Fill *Shape Fill* option that fills the *WordArt* or shape with a picture from a file or from the *Office.com Clip Art* collection.

Picture layout *SmartArt* graphic type used to show pictures as integral parts of many different diagrams.

Picture Paste option that pastes an object, even text, as a picture rather than editable text.

Pie chart Chart type that shows the values in a data series in proportional sizes that make up a whole pie.

pixel Abbreviated term for picture element; a single unit of information about color.

placeholder In PowerPoint, the area of a slide where you can add text, tables, charts, and pictures.

Play Across Slides Audio playback setting used to play audio throughout a presentation as slides advance.

Play Full Screen Video playback setting that expands a video to fill the screen.

Play in Background Audio playback setting used to play audio throughout a presentation as slides advance.

playback bar Area visible below an audio or video object that controls play, pause, move back, move forward, mute, and unmute; also displays elapsed time.

Plot Area One of several chart background elements; the rectangle between the vertical and horizontal axes that is behind the data markers.

Poster Frame Picture displayed as a preview image at the beginning of a video.

Presenter view View option that displays slides, speaker notes, a timer, and features helpful for a speaker; can be displayed on just one monitor or can be displayed on one monitor while the presentation is displayed at full-screen size on a second monitor or projector.

Process SmartArt graphic type used to illustrate sequential steps in a process or workflow.

program options Area in each Office application where you can make changes to the program settings.

Proofing Language Tool that allows you to choose a dictionary for a language so you can apply appropriate spell checking and grammar rules.

Pyramid SmartArt graphic type used to illustrate proportional or interconnected relationships.

Q

Quick Access toolbar Area located above the *Ribbon* with buttons you use to perform commonly used commands.

R

Radar chart Chart type that shows the combined values of several data series with values relative to a center point.

radio button Round button you click to choose one option from a list.

read-only mode Office Web Apps view where users can view a file.

Reading view View option that displays a slide show at full-screen or alternate window size determined by the viewer.

Recolor Changes picture colors to monotone color variations.

Record Audio Feature used to create an audio clip.

Recycle Bin Location where deleted files and folders are stored.

redo Repeat an action.

Reflection Style effect option that shows a mirror image below an object.

Regroup Command that connects ungrouped objects that were previously grouped.

Rehearse Timings Feature that helps you to judge the pace of the presentation.

Relationship SmartArt graphic type used to illustrate concepts that are connected such as contrasting, opposing, or converging.

remote control Device that enables a speaker to control a slide show when he or she steps away from the computer during a presentation.

Reorder Animation Animation timing command used to adjust animation sequence.

Replace Feature that enables you to change words that match your specifications.

Research Tool that finds dictionary definitions, synonyms, and language translation.

Reset Design Command that removes changes to a video by restoring it to its original design.

Reset Picture Command used to restore a picture's original characteristics and dimensions.

restore down Decrease the window size of an open Office file so it does not fill the entire computer screen.

Reviewing pane Area that displays reviewer comments and replies.

Rewind after Playing Playback setting for audio or video that makes playback start from the beginning.

RGB model Color model type typically used for computer displays; colors are made by blending values red, green, and blue.

Ribbon Bar that appears at the top of an Office application window and displays available commands.

rich media Broad range of digital media that includes text, pictures, audio, and video combined with dynamic motion and interactivity; also called *multimedia.*

Roles Settings in *SkyDrive* groups that control members' ability to view, edit, create, and delete folders and files in the group.

Rotate Drawing option used to make objects angle on the slide.

rotation handle Circular arrow on the top of an object used to make the object angle.

row Horizontal grouping of cells.

Ruler Feature that displays measurements above the slide and on the left with markers that indicate the current margin and indents.

S

Screen Clipping Feature that copies a portion of an application window and displays it on a slide.

Screenshot Feature that copies an entire application window and displays it on a slide.

ScreenTip Descriptive information about a button, drop-down list, launcher, or gallery selection; appears when you place your pointer on the item. Also text that displays when the user points to a hyperlink.

Scribble Line tool used to draw a continuous line; similar to writing.

Sections Organization feature used to divide a presentation using major topics; during a slide show, sections are not visible.

Send Backward Feature that adjusts the order of stacked objects by moving objects back one layer at a time.

Send to Back Feature that adjusts the order of stacked objects by moving an object behind all other objects.

Set Transparent Color Option that removes one color from a picture; used to remove solid backgrounds.

Shadow Style effect option that provides dimension by inserting a shadow behind or below an object.

Share Allow other users to access a *SkyDrive* folder or file.

Sharpen Picture correction option that makes picture details more evident.

sizing handles Squares that appear on the corners and sides of an object that resize the object.

SkyDrive Online (cloud) storage area that is a part of your Microsoft account where you can store and access documents from any computer with an Internet connection.

SkyDrive folder Windows folder that displays folders and files stored on a user's *SkyDrive* account; synchronizes folders and files stored in the *SkyDrive* folder with *SkyDrive* cloud storage.

SkyDrive groups Free Microsoft online service where users can be invited to become members; group members have access to folders and files stored in the *SkyDrive* group.

slide layout Slide development feature with built-in placeholders for text and other content such as tables, charts, or *SmartArt*.

Slide Master Feature that stores information about slide backgrounds, layouts, and fonts for each theme.

Slide Show view View option that displays slides in sequence at full-screen size for audience viewing.

Slide Sorter view View option that displays slides as thumbnails.

SmartArt graphics Diagrams used to illustrate concepts such as processes, cycles, or relationships.

SmartArt Styles Gallery that lists different effects for emphasizing shapes within a layout.

Soft Edges Style effect option that creates a feathered edge, which gradually blends into the background color.

Soften Picture correction option that creates a blending effect.

source file File where the original content of an embedded or linked object is stored.

source program Office application where an embedded or linked object was created.

speaker notes Reminders to help the speaker present; entered into the *Notes* pane and visible in *Notes* Pane view.

Split Cells Command that divides a single cell into two or more cells.

spreadsheet Data displayed in columns and rows.

Standard **slide sizing** Display option size that uses a 4:3 aspect ratio.

Start Animation timing command that controls when animation begins.

Stock chart Chart type that shows fluctuation of stock prices with high, low, and close values displayed over time.

Style **gallery** Collection of preset effects for text, shapes, pictures, or other objects.

Surface chart Chart type that shows the differences between two sets of data.

Switch View option that allows you to move between open presentations; only one presentation is displayed at a time.

T

tab Area on the *Ribbon* that lists groups of related commands and options.

tab stops Markers that indicate text indenting; spaced by default at every one-half inch.

table Information arranged in columns and rows.

table style Built-in formats for tables, which include a variety of borders, shading, alignment, and other options.

task pane Area to the left or right of an Office application window where you can customize settings.

Taskbar Horizontal area at the bottom of the Windows desktop where you can launch programs or open folders.

Template Controls theme characteristics for design consistency and provides sample content that can help to develop a new presentation; a PowerPoint template has a *.potx* file extension.

text box Area where you type text.

Text pane Area where you enter text for SmartArt shapes.

Texture Fill Shape Fill option that applies an image such as woven fabric or wood.

theme Collection of fonts, colors, and effects that you can apply to an entire document, workbook, or presentation.

theme colors Set of background and accent colors.

theme fonts Pair of fonts used for a presentation's headings and body text.

Thesaurus Resource tool that lists synonyms for a selected word.

thumbnail Small picture of an image or layout.

tick marks Symbols that identify the categories, values, or series on an axis.

Transform Style effect option used to change the shape of words.

transition Visual effect that occurs when one slide changes into another slide.

Translate Feature that converts words or short phrases into a different language.

Transparency Color setting that is adjusted by percentage to allow the background to show through objects.

Trigger Setting applied to a slide object so that when the object is clicked, the animation starts.

Trim Tool that removes playback time from the beginning or end of audio and video files.

U

undo Reverse an action.

Ungroup Command that separates grouped objects so you can modify them independently.

Use Destination Theme Paste option that applies the formatting of the destination presentation theme to the material you are pasting.

user name Name used when Microsoft Office is installed on a computer; by default, this is the author name for each presentation.

V

vertical alignment Content positioning option that aligns material in relation to the top, bottom, or middle of the page or slide; can also refer to the position of objects in relation to each other.

video A digital file inserted in your presentation that plays video; video combines both audio and visual components.

Volume Control that adjusts sound settings for audio and video for low, medium, high, or mute.

W

weight Thickness of an outline measured in points.

Widescreen **slide sizing** Display option size that uses a 16:9 aspect ratio; a 16:10 aspect ratio is also available.

Windows desktop Working area in Windows.

Windows *Start* **page** Opening area of Windows where you select and open programs or apps.

WordArt Graphic object that visually enhances text.

X

X-axis Axis displayed horizontally, usually on the bottom of a chart; also called the category axis.

XY chart Chart type that shows the relationships between several data series using two value axes.

Y

Y-axis Axis displayed vertically, usually on the left of a chart; also called the value axis.

Z

zipped (compressed) folder Folder that has a reduced file size and can be attached to an email.

Zoom Change file display size.

index

Symbols

- (hyphens), P6-361
+ (plus sign), zooming in during a slideshow, P3-166

Numbers

3-D category, P2-97
3-D Clustered Column, P2-123
3-D Column Chart, P2-107
3-D pie chart, P2-109, P2-110
3-D Pie type, P2-122
3D Rotation effect, P2-69
5-Point Star 13, as trigger, P5-287
16-point star, variations of, P4-205
24-Point Star, selecting, P4-215

A

accent colors, P2-71
Accept button, P6-392
Accept list arrow, P6-375
access, restricting to a presentation, P7-416
accessibility, checking, P7-417
Accessibility Checker pane, P7-411, P7-417, P7-418, P7-462
accessibility issues, solutions for, P7-412
Account area, on Backstage view, P7-426
action buttons
   creating, P5-291
   creating navigation controls with, P5-293
   inserting on Slide Master, P5-316–P5-317
   less noticeable on the slide, P6-368
   moving to the bottom of a slide, P5-293
   providing a way to move quickly back to a
      menu, P5-291
   setting, P5-291
Action Settings dialog box, P5-291, P5-293,
      P5-317
Add a Digital Signature, P7-416
Add a service drop-down list, P7-427
Add Animation button, P5-277, P5-281,
      P5-282, P5-283, P5-284, P5-286,
      P5-287, P5-288, P5-303, P5-313,
      P5-318, P5-319
   Appear Entrance effect, P5-289
   Custom Path, P5-289
   Fade, P5-319
   Fade Entrance effect, P5-313, P5-319,
      P5-321
   Fade Exit effect, P5-318, P5-320, P5-322
   Float In Entrance effect, P5-286
   Grow & Turn Entrance effect, P5-289
   selecting effects, P5-325
   Shrink and Turn Exit effect, P5-324
   Wheel Entrance effect, P5-324, P5-326
   Wipe Entrance effect, P5-318, P5-325
   Zoom Entrance effect, P5-324
Add Audio dialog box, P5-303

Add Bookmark button, P5-299, P5-308,
      P5-315, P5-321–P5-322
Add Comments button, P7-447
Add Gradient Stop button, P2-72, P3-144,
      P3-153
Add Motion Path dialog box, P5-284, P5-285,
      P5-288
Add Shape button, P2-99
Add Shape tab, P2-116
Adjust group, options, P5-304
adjustment handles, P2-67, P4-205
Adobe Acrobat, P7-420
Adobe Flash file, P5-295
Adobe Reader, P7-420, P7-421
Advance Slide options, in the Timing group,
      P1-35
Advance Streaming Format, P5-295
Advance to next slide button, P3-161
advanced animation, applying, P5-277–P5-286
Advanced Audio Coding audio, P5-295
Advanced Properties dialog box, P1-41
After Animation list arrow
   blue color, P5-324
   dark gold color, P5-318
   dark gray color, P5-286
   orange color, P5-313
   selecting a different color for text, P5-279
After Previous option, P5-282
After timing, P3-181
AIFF (Audio Interchange File Format) file,
      P5-295
.aiff extension, P5-295
Album Layout options, adjusted, P4-241
Align, Align to Slide, P4-217
Align button, P1-42, P4-208
   Align Bottom, P4-215, P4-249, P4-256
   Align Center, P4-250, P4-251, P4-253,
      P4-255, P4-258, P5-320
   Align Left, P4-215, P4-227, P4-250, P4-256
   Align Middle, P5-320
   Align Right, P4-253, P4-254
   Align Top, P4-227, P4-250, P4-253, P4-254
   in the Arrange group on the Home tab,
      P1-17
   in the Arrange group on the Picture Tools
      Format tab, P1-35
   Distribute Vertically, P4-251
   on the Drawing Tools Format tab, P1-17
Align buttons, P2-92
Align Left, selecting, P4-217
Align option, P5-304
Align Selected Objects option, P4-209
Align Text button, P3-154, P4-228, P4-254
Align Text list arrow, P4-203
Align to Slide option, P4-209
All at Once sequence option, P5-279
All Reference Books list box, P6-364, P6-369
All Slides, saving as a picture, P7-419
All slides dialog box, P3-166
Alt Text (Alternative text), adding, P7-412,
      P7-417, P7-461, P7-470

Alt+Ctrl+V, opening Paste Special dialog box,
      P6-353
Alt+Down video shortcut, P5-302
Alt+End video shortcut, P5-302
Alt+F5
   with one monitor, P3-180, P3-187
   using Presenter View, P3-161
Alt+Home video shortcut, P5-302
Alt+P video shortcut, P5-302
Alt+Print Screen, copying current window,
      P4-230
Alt+Q video shortcut, P5-302
Alt+Shift+Page Down video shortcut, P5-302
Alt+Shift+Page Up video shortcut, P5-302
Alt+U video shortcut, P5-302
Alt+Up video shortcut, P5-302
Animate as part of click sequence, P5-287
Animate text list arrow, options, P5-279
animated list, Effect Options, P5-278
animated objects, P5-281, P5-287
animated sequences, creating, P5-289
animated shapes, triggering, P5-321–P5-322
animation
   adding sound to, P5-302–P5-303
   adding to a selected object, P5-281
   applying, P3-147–P3-149, P3-155–P3-156,
      P3-189, P3-191, P3-195
   defined, P3-147
   ending before video ends, P5-300
   playing with video, P5-300
   settings, P5-309
   shortcuts, P5-279
   testing, P5-279
Animation Effect launcher, P5-313
animation effects, P3-178, P3-183–P3-184,
      P3-189, P3-191
   applying, P3-148, P5-319
   applying multiple, P5-318–P5-319, P5-324,
      P5-325
   applying two that display together, P5-288,
      P5-313
   arranged in categories, P3-147–P3-148
   for charts, P5-282–P5-283
Animation Effects dialog box, P5-280, P5-283
Animation gallery, P5-278, P5-282, P5-283,
      P5-284
animation list, expanding, P5-282
animation numbers, displaying, P3-148
animation order, rearranging, P5-287, P5-315
Animation Painter button, P5-281, P5-287,
      P5-288, P5-314, P5-319
Animation Pane, P5-309
   adjusting playback sequence, P5-298
   chevron icon, P5-282
   colored bar following each object name,
      P5-281
   expanded to show duration times, P5-319
   increasing the size of, P5-286
   making wider, P5-281
   for multiple objects and multiple effects,
      P5-279–P5-281

C

Can edit check box, P7-435
Cap type option, for lines, P2-70
Caps Lock key, accidental usage of, P6-360
captions, in Photo Album, P4-240
Cartoon style, applying, P2-122
Cascade option, P6-345
case, changing in placeholders, P1-18
case sensitivity, of passwords, P7-415
category, P2-102
CD, packaging a presentation to,
    P3-171–P3-172
cell alignment, P2-92
Cell Margins button, P2-92
Cell Text Layout dialog box, P2-92
cells
    merging and splitting in tables, P2-89
    moving to the next, P2-87
    resizing, P2-89
    selecting, P2-87, P2-88
    in tables, P2-85
Center alignment, changing cells to, P2-119
Center Vertically button, P2-121
"Chalk Sketch" picture, in grayscale, P5-320
Change Case button, P1-18, P4-228
Change Chart Type gallery, P2-105
Change Colors button, P2-100, P2-101,
    P2-106, P2-119, P3-183, P4-251,
    P4-255
Change Colors gallery, P2-98
Change File Type option, P1-14, P7-419,
    P7-424
Change Picture, P5-315
Change Picture command, P4-233
Change role button, P7-437
Change Shape, P2-68, P4-216
Change Source button, P6-351
Change Source dialog box, P6-351
changes, accepting or rejecting, P6-374,
    P6-375–P6-376, P6-378, P6-392
Character Spacing, changing, P2-83
Character Spacing button, P2-75
chart(s)
    creating, P2-101–P2-105
    enhancing, P2-105–P2-109
    inserting, P2-102–P2-103
Chart Animation tab, P5-283
Chart Area chart element, P2-103
chart background, changing, P2-107
Chart button, P2-122, P2-123
Chart Colors gallery, P2-106
chart elements, P2-103, P5-281
    animating, P5-282–P5-283, P5-287
    defined, P2-103
    formatting, P2-106–P2-107
Chart Elements button, P2-103, P2-108,
    P2-111, P2-122, P2-123
Chart Elements list arrow, P2-106
chart labels, changing, P2-108
chart series or category, adjusting timing for,
    P5-282
Chart Styles gallery, P2-105–P2-106
Chart Title chart element, P2-103
Chart Tools Design tab, P2-102
Chart Tools Format tab, P2-102, P2-107,
    P2-108
chart types, P2-101–P2-102, P2-105
Check Accessibility, P7-411–P7-412
Check Compatibility, P7-412–P7-413
Check for Issues button

Check Accessibility, P7-411, P7-417, P7-461
Check Compatibility, P7-413, P7-418,
    P7-458
Inspect Document, P7-410, P7-416
chevron icon, P5-280, P5-320
Choose a SmartArt Graphic dialog box, P2-95,
    P2-96, P2-99, P2-100, P2-122
Choose File to Merge with Current Presentation
    dialog box, P6-373, P6-377, P6-391
Choose Theme dialog box, P4-240
Choose Translation Language, P6-365
Classic Gardens and Landscapes (CGL), P2-66
Clear Table command, P2-91
Clear Timings on All Slides option, P3-173
Clear Timings options, P3-159
Click here to view the PDF of your document
    link, P7-446
Clipboard Launcher button, P4-236
Close Master View button, P1-28, P1-29,
    P1-46, P3-153, P4-221, P4-222, P4-223,
    P4-224, P4-225, P4-226, P4-229,
    P4-237, P4-245, P5-293, P5-317
"cloud" storage space, provided by Microsoft,
    P7-429
"cloud" technology, Office 2013 integrating,
    P7-409
clustered column chart, P2-105, P2-110, P2-111
Clustered Column layout, P2-110, P2-111
codec (compressor/decompressor), P5-294
collaboration
    in Office Web Apps, P7-447
    other options for, P7-448–P7-449
    sharing presentations, P7-409
Collapse All option, for sections, P6-355
color(s)
    applying different color options, P2-80
    changed on data series, P2-107
    changing at the same time in a SmartArt
        graphic, P2-98
    creating custom theme and backgrounds,
        P3-139–P3-147
    matching specific, P2-74
    psychology of, P3-142
    selecting custom, P2-72–P2-74
    shading and border, P2-91–P2-92
    symbolic meaning of, P3-142
    techniques for choosing in PowerPoint,
        P2-71
color backgrounds, on handouts, P4-226
color blending, controlling, P2-72
Color button, P2-80
color model, P2-73
Color option, P2-70, P5-304
Color Saturation options, P2-81
Color Tone options, P2-81
Colorful combinations, P2-106
Colors button, P1-28, P1-31, P1-46, P3-140,
    P3-153, P3-182, P3-186, P4-258
Colors dialog box, P2-72–P2-74, P3-182–
    P3-183, P3-186
    Custom tab, P2-73–P2-74
    opening, P3-141
    Standard tab, P2-73
Column chart type, P2-101
column width, P2-89, P2-90, P2-104
columns
    changing bulleted lists to, P6-384–P6-385
    inserting and deleting in tables, P2-88
    resizing, P2-89
    selecting, P2-86, P2-87, P2-88
    in tables, P2-85

Columns button, P4-204, P4-217, P4-251
Columns dialog box, P4-217
Combine option, P4-212, P4-213
Combo chart type, P2-102
Comment button, P7-448
comment icon, P6-371, P6-372, P7-448
comments
    adding and reviewing, P6-370–P6-376
    adding in SkyDrive, P7-466
    adding to presentations, P7-450
    editing and replying to, P6-372
    hiding, P6-371
    inserted, P6-399
    inserting, P6-371, P6-377, P6-388, P6-391
    in PowerPoint Web App, P7-447–P7-448
    reviewing, P6-374–P6-375
    reviewing and deleting, P6-374, P6-378,
        P6-391–P6-392
    time entered, P6-371
Comments button, in read-only mode, P7-447
Comments group, Next or Previous button in,
    P6-371
Comments pane, P6-373, P6-374, P6-388,
    P6-391, P6-391–P6-392, P7-469
    comment typed in, P6-371
    New button, P7-448
    opening, P6-371, P7-447
company logo, distorted by resizing, P4-212
Compare button, P6-373, P6-377, P6-391
Compare collaboration feature, P6-371, P6-372
Comparison layout, P1-15
comparison situations, animation working well
    for, P5-277
compatibility, with 97-2003 software, P7-458
Compatibility Checker dialog box, P7-418,
    P7-465
compatibility issues, between current version
    of PowerPoint and versions before 2007,
    P7-412
compatibility mode, opening in, P7-413
complex animations, working with, P5-286
Compound type option, for lines, P2-70
Compress Media button, Presentation Quality
    option, P5-310, P5-317, P5-323, P5-326
Compress Media dialog box, P5-305, P5-317
Compress Media option, showing total media
    file size, P5-305
Compress Pictures, P2-85
Compress Pictures dialog box, P2-82
compressing, pictures, P2-81–P2-82
compression, of media, P5-305
computer, placing during a presentation,
    P3-165
Computer & HD Displays option, P7-422
computer system, sound card and speakers for
    audio or video content, P5-294
Confirm Password dialog box, P7-415, P7-418,
    P7-458
connected services, P7-427
connecting lines, in a SmartArt graphic, P5-284
Connection sites, on a shape, P4-213
connector lines, applying, P4-217
constraining, shapes, P4-203
content
    adding from other sources, P6-343–P6-353
    selecting for presentations, P5-306
    using to create slides, P6-343–P6-344
Content with Caption layout, P1-15
context-specific paste options, P6-352
Continuous Cycle layout, P2-116
Continuous Picture List layout, P2-96